BUSINESS TO BUSINESS
MARKETING

BUSINESS TO BUSINESS
MARKETING

U C Mathur
Professor and Director MDP
Integrated Academy of Management and Technology
Ghaziabad, UP

An Imprint of

NEW AGE INTERNATIONAL (P) LIMITED, PUBLISHERS

New Delhi • Bangalore • Chennai • Cochin • Guwahati
Hyderabad • Kolkata • Lucknow • Mumbai
Visit us at **www.newagepublishers.com**

Published by New Age International (P) Ltd., Publishers
First Edition: 2008
Reprint: 2015

BRANCHES

- **Bangalore** 37/10, 8th Cross (Near Hanuman Temple), Azad Nagar, Chamarajpet Bangalore-560 018, Tel.: (080) 26756823, Telefax: 26756820 **E-mail: bangalore@newagepublishers.com**
- **Chennai** 26, Damodaran Street, T. Nagar, Chennai-600 017, Tel.: (044) 24353401 Telefax: 24351463, **E-mail: chennai@newagepublishers.com**
- **Cochin** CC-39/1016, Carrier Station Road, Ernakulam South, Cochin-682 016 Tel.: (0484) 2377303, Telefax: 4051303 **E-mail: cochin@newagepublishers.com**
- **Guwahati** Hemsen Complex, Mohd. Shah Road, Paltan Bazar, Near Starline Hotel Guwahati-781 008 Tel.: (0361) 2513881, Telefax: 2543669 **E-mail: guwahati@newagepublishers.com**
- **Hyderabad** 105, 1st Floor, Madhiray Kaveri Tower, 3-2-19, Azam Jahi Road, Near Kumar Theater Nimboliadda, Kachiguda, Hyderabad-500 027, Tel.: (040) 24652456 Telefax: 24652457 **E-mail: hyderabad@newagepublishers.com**
- **Kolkata** RDB Chambers (Formerly Lotus Cinema) 106A, 1st Floor, S N Banerjee Road Kolkata-700 014 Tel.: (033) 22273773, Telefax: 22275247 **E-mail: kolkata@newagepublishers.com**
- **Lucknow** 16-A, Jopling Road, Lucknow-226 001, Tel.: (0522) 2209578, 4045297 Telefax: 2204098, **E-mail:lucknow@newagepublishers.com**
- **Mumbai** 142C, Victor House, Ground Floor, N.M. Joshi Marg, Lower Parel Mumbai-400 013, Tel.: (022) 24927869, Telefax: 24915415 **E-mail: mumbai@newagepublishers.com**
- **New Delhi** 22, Golden House, Daryaganj, New Delhi-110 002 Tel.: (011) 23262368, 23262370, Telefax: 43551305 **E-mail: sales@newagepublishers.com**

ISBN: 978-81-224-2146-0

₹ 295.00

C-15-07-8597

Printed in India at Ajit Printing Press, New Delhi.
Typeset at In-house, New Delhi.

PUBLISHING GLOBALLY
NEW AGE INTERNATIONAL (P) LIMITED, PUBLISHERS
7/30 A, Daryaganj, New Delhi - 110002
Visit us at **www.newagepublishers.com**

Preface

Most persons in the country are buyers of consumer products, both the Fast Moving Consumer Durables and Consumer Durables. Besides, there is a large chunk of business of intermediary products that is the components, subassemblies and the raw materials needed by the manufacturers of FMCG and Consumer Durable products. However, the marketing of these products has been neglected to some extent as professional training has come about for B-to-B marketing only recently. This book is dedicated to the marketing of such products.

Indian market has matured for being able to absorb the latest technology products as also can supply some of such products in the Indian markets and for exports as well. Most significant example is that of computer software promoted in India, is the latest State of the Art product and it comes to India the same time it goes anywhere else. Software development has come to centre stage in country's business horizon. The development in software technology and the trained manpower strength in this area in the country are unsurpassed by most nations. In fact, Indian states like Karnataka, Andhra Pradesh are vying with each other for supremacy in software development. All this augurs well for Indian business and is a big plus for the country. Competition from multinational firms, more focused management, better-trained managers have become the norm rather than an exception. These new forces have had an impact on the most purposeful of all the management disciplines, marketing. A person can have the best of the manpower, technology, and finance but if he does not have marketing strengths he can just forget about any business today. It is not that these other functions of business are any less important; marketing can be considered as more equal among equals. Hence, the need for focused thrust in this key result area of Marketing Management, the B-to-B Marketing Management, is of paramount importance today.

It is said that change is the only constant thing in the world and it is true for marketing, as well. As the number of marketing firms increase (for a product) so do the diversities in pricing, distribution channels, advertising and promotion techniques, and one can never be sure that he knows whatever there is to know in the field of marketing. The product, technology, competition, distribution channels, ways of advertising and promotion are all in a state of continuous flux. Hence the "How To Know And Where To Find" becomes extremely important to the students and the practitioners of marketing management.

The focus of all these activities, the buyer, is at once thrilled to the core to witness an unprecedented growth of competitive products (see the number of colour TV sets in the market today) as also he is confused about a lot of things; which product to buy, what price is the right price or is he being cheated even by the known brands. Can a marketer take these situations as opportunities? If yes, then what are the parameters for him to look at, where can he get the best solutions to his typical situations? (It should be understood that each marketer's situation is always unique). Questions like these and many more need to be answered and this book makes an attempt at doing just that. Internet, information technology, cellular phones, satellite channels for television and fast travel has made the earth a smaller place today, but for the political fissures, which distance one nation from the other. The world has been divided by religions so far and yet the economic divide has been the most significant one from the twentieth century as it has produced a world of haves and have nots. Even then the developing nations like India offer one of the biggest markets for the marketers of the world. For this reason alone, the developed nations have to forget their political beliefs and look for markets where they can find them. Chinese political philosophy and system is totally at variance with the political system of the west and yet the USA is ignoring the political rough edges to tap the large Chinese market and vice versa.

When India was on the point of foreign exchange bankruptcy in 1991, the then government of the country with Mr. Manmohan Singh as the Finance Minister had gone to the World Bank and the IMF for obtaining loans. The West had already woken up to the huge market potential of India and the world finance bodies sought the opening of the markets of India, the second largest country on the basis of population and the largest democracy in the world, for the western firms before the loans could be considered. This resulted in the following major changes in the government's business policy-

1. De-licensing for manufacture of most products
2. Easy entry of foreign firms in the country with their investments and technology
3. Lowering of customs duty on imports
4. Decrease in the importance of the government firms, the Public Sector Undertakings.

The result of the changes can be seen eleven years down the line, in 2002 as follows—

1. Availability of multi brands for several products
2. Entry of Multinational firms
3. Increased choice of products for the customers
4. Heavy spending on advertising and promotion
5. Decline of stand- alone firms with indigenous technology (in fact Rahul Bajaj the doyen of Indian industry has been pleading for their cause with the government, which is in no mood to roll back any of the economic reforms; they want to move forward with more reforms now)
6. Excess production capacity generation by some firms in the hope of large market, where the actual sales figures belied the hopes. This could have been the result of incorrect market assessments by the firms. The firms are hoping that the demand will catch up with supplies and they would be better placed in the market then. Automobile firms are typical examples of over capacity in manufacturing.

India faces other challenges like, the political turmoil with the terrorism at its peak, corruption in high places, financial scams, increase in rich poor divide, social revolution with the advent of foreign TV Channels. As it has resulted in increasing the complexity in marketing of products, firms are keenly looking for **The Marketing Person** who can wield a magic wand and continuously bring profitable business to the firm, which brings me to the purpose of writing the book. While books on marketing management are available in India, this one covers the latest methods of business analysis, marketing theory, policies; implementation processes in lucid, easy to understand language. With ten case studies, big and small, it should prove to be a veritable boon to the students, teachers and practitioners of the marketing discipline.

The new opportunities for the buyers have created threats as well as challenges for the sellers. With on-line banking, on-line buying and selling outlets like bank branches, Bazee.com shopping malls may become redundant in foreseeable future. Present multi- storied super markets with central air conditioning and top brands, restaurants under one roof, which enchant the shoppers and window shoppers alike may even go in to oblivion, although today it is a little difficult to even imagine. Even a decade ago who would have believed that banking could be possible sitting at home through the Internet and the none could have thought of gradual erosion of the government owned Postal Department by the courier services.

Today's B-to-B customer is knowledgeable and wants more information from the sellers. Information technology is empowering the buyer with not only information but also comparisons within product groups, and customer wants products, which provide Value For Money to him. Earlier, the seller decided what he could make, with the available finance, technology, raw materials and manpower. And in those days of no or low levels of competition, in the seller's market, the firms did succeed. Today the change is just 180 degrees as the firms must look at what exactly the market wants and that too before the competitor does it to be a success.

Each chapter starts with the Aims and Outcomes expected out of the study of the chapter. At the end of the chapter a number of Questions for discussion have been provided for better understanding and for summarising the study of the chapter. Wherever possible the book uses interactive techniques by engaging the students and the teaching faculty into discussion to augment the learning experience.

The book contains a unique learning process and a valuable experience with the help of a **Marketing Game** that starts with the first chapter end and runs through the book. The Game has been created and crafted after long experimentation in classroom teaching and is class-tested in some of the better business schools of the country. It is hoped the students will make full use of the Game for making learning an interesting experience that will also bring the students as close to the corporate world as possibly they can get in a class room situation.

Firms are realizing the complexities of the markets and the futility of proliferating their products in the entire gamut of the market. Niche markets have, therefore, become the norm, as, within the selected niche, firms can better appreciate the needs of the customers, what would satisfy them and finally what would delight them. Advertising, promotion and other forms of communications like market oriented public relation have to be dovetailed to the niche market to be really effective in the plethora of such activities taking place all the time.

Pricing is no more a function of costing; it is more that of competition, brand image, and product positioning. Distribution channels have undergone major changes and the firms cannot just keep adhering to their age-old beliefs in this regard. The entire perspective of the firm's functioning needs a fresh approach and marketing must synergize with other functions of the firm in order to succeed. Most marketing failures are due to the mismatches between different areas. Firms, for instance, may have to reorganize their entire structure, not just the marketing department to come closer to the customer. Hence, for knowing the market, not just by gut feeling, as was happening in the1980s, firms need accurate information through market research carried out on regular basis. The firm's business philosophy, plans and policies, structures are in the state of continuous change. The product designs are no longer the function of engineers alone as the market researchers have a say in the new product development. Price fixation ceases to be function of cost to make, as it is now dependent on competition, product's brand image and value to the customer. For business communication, advertising and promotion several new avenues are now available to choose from, to the marketers. Several new and innovative distribution channels have sprung up and the marketers have to keep looking for newer additions. Innovative supply chain management keeping the suppliers as also the buyers as business partners, as against treating them as necessary evils is a must for firms if they have to remain on the forefront in the market. The idea of Just in Time supplies, which brings down the current assets, lowering the costs considerably would become possible only then.

Perhaps the most important and significant knowledge and skill area in B-to-B marketing is "Prospecting for New Customers". Directly associated with it is the "Personal Sales Calls Planning". These two have been given major coverage with innovative and highly successful methodology that would prove to be veritable boon to the students & will take them to great heights in the corporate worlds B-to-B marketing.

The author wishes to place on record his gratitude for the publishers New Age International for their support provided during the period it took to write the book.

U.C.Mathur
Delhi-110092

Contents

Preface (*v*)

1. **MARKETING BUSINESS-TO- BUSINESS—INTRODUCTION** 1
Aims and Outcomes of the Chapter • Purchase Negotiations in Tender and Non-tender Business • Industrial Marketing Research • Competition in Industrial Buying • Marketing and Economy • Marketing and Society • The Creative Art • Start of the B-to-B Marketing Game.

2. **MARKETING DEFINED** 33
Aims and Outcomes of the Chapter • Defining Marketing • Marketing Thought • Sales Contract • Sales Process • Market Evolution • Changing Business Scenario in the Twenty-first Century • Business Scenario in India • Market Environment • Present Scene in India • Business Myopia • Market and Manufacture • Patents and Patent Laws • Marketing Mix • Marketing Mix Factors • Rural Marketing • Marketing Game • Business General Environment.

3. **MARKETING MANAGEMENT—CONCEPTS** 81
Aims and Outcomes of the Chapter • Relationship Marketing • Competition • Market Environment • Profit and Profiteering • Cross Functional Structure • Organizational Culture • Structural Support to the Customers • Indirect Financial Support • Markets—the Customers • Case Study • Planning for Success • Gaining and Retaining Customers • Corporate Vision • Marketing Organization Structure • Chief Executive Officer • Market Based Marketing Organization • Core Process Based Organization • Flatter Organizations Structures • Networking Teams • Virtual Organizations • Technology and Innovation—Competitive Advantage • Innovation Decisions • Technology Plans • New Product Development • Marketing Game • New Entrants.

4. **ORGANIZATIONAL BUYING BEHAVIOUR** 119
Aims and Outcomes of the Chapter • Behaviour—Positivism and Interpretivism • Feeling and Emotions • Marketing Game.

5. **COMPETITION TYPES** 129
Aims and Outcomes of the Chapter • Competitive Advantage • Competitor's Strengths • Improving Market Share • Competitive Action • The Complete Marketing Plan • Marketing Myopia • Rolling Plan • Plans and Policies • Marketing Strategy • Selling Strategy.

6. **SALES FORCE MANAGEMENT** 151
Aims and Outcomes of the Chapter • Sales Forecasts • Planning Sales Calls • Locating New Customers • Detailed Call Planning • Sales Presentation • Planning Presentations for Specific Calls • Handling Objections • Handling Objections Details • Price Objection • Defining Sales Obstacles • Countering the Obstacles • Understanding People and Dealing with Them Effectively • Analysing a Talk for its Movers • Analysing Product for Sale Movers • Analysing a Faulty Situation for Correction-machine operation • The 4 Column Situation and Correction Analysis • Examples of Poor Quality and Loss Movers • Prospects Basic Needs and Desires • The Question Mover • The Personal Prestige Mover • Personal Prestige Can be Built by Action • The Contact Mover • Call Closing • Timing • Departure • Post Call Analysis • Customer Value • Salesperson—the Strategist • Purchase Order the Final Destination.

7. **BUSINESS-TO-BUSINESS MARKETING–INTERNATIONAL** 257
Aims and Outcomes of the Chapter • Global Outsourcing and Manufacturing • Information Outsourcing • International Environment for Business • Market Economy of the World • Mixed Economies • Countries Classifications • Macroeconomics Factors • Economic Growth • Inflation • Distribution Patterns—Industrial Goods • Customer Reach • International Markets of the Twenty-first Century • Market Information—As Competitive Advantage • Management Game.

8. **B-TO-B MARKETING SPECIFICS** 287
Aims and Outcomes of the Chapter • Customer Orientation • Over Selling • Different Approach to B-to-B Marketing • B-to-B Advertising • B-to-B Pricing • B-to-B Payment Terms • Buyers Purchase Viewpoint • Market Demand • Business Scenario in India • What Is Our Business? • Patents and Patent Laws • Knowledge is Business • Master-List of the Customers and Prospects • Modes of Payment • Public Relations • The PR Base • PR Too Depends on Endorcements

to an Extent! • Firms And Society • Crises Management • Media Planning • Marketing Game • Balance Score Card.

9. **MARKETING RESEARCH** 359
Aims and Outcomes of the Chapter • Introduction to Market Research • Marketing Research Objectives • Marketing Research Methods • Sample Selection • Data Processing and Analysis • Advertising Research and Dagmar • Advertising Research • Marketing Game.

10. **DISTRIBUTION OF GOODS** 389
Aims and Outcomes of the Chapter • Distribution Patterns for Consumer and Industrial Goods • Customer Convenience Buying • Multiple Product Manufacturers • Distribution Patterns for Industrial Goods • Marketing Logistics • Marketing Game.

11. **ADVERTISING PROMOTION, PR** 403
Aims and Outcomes of the Chapter • Advertising Defined • Personal Selling • Tasks for Advertising in the 21st Century • Advertising Mix Factors • Advertising Agency • The Media • Objectives of Advertising • Advertising Agency & Its Working • Advertiser and The Agency Selection • Advertising Agency Selection Process • Advertising Research and Dagmar • Media Planning and Product Positioning • Advertising Budget • Advertising And Creativity • The Indian Scene • The Design Theory • Art Direction—Elements of Design • The Advertising Challenge.

12. **STRATEGIES FOR B-B MANAGEMENT** 459
Aims and Outcomes of the Chapter • Product Related Analysis • Strategic Marketing Planning Process • Customer's Analysis • Market Analysis • Segmentation and Positioning • Business-to-Business or Industrial Segmentation • Product Positioning • Managing Across The Product Life Cycle (PLC) • Introductory Stage • Costs, Volumes and Experience Curve • Market Share Strategy • Product Life Cycle—Growth Stage Strategy • Position as a Follower in the Market • Strategies for Late Growth Stage in PLC • Strategies for the Maturity Stage of Product Life Cycle • Market Strategies in Decline Stage of Product Life Cycle • Portfolio Management Analysis • Boston Consultancy Group • GE Model • Customer, Competition and the Firm • Customer vs Client • Relationship Marketing • Markets of the Twenty-first Century • The Virtual Marts • The Marketing Plan.

13. **INTERNATIONAL MARKETING** 509
Aims and Outcomes of the Chapter • Free Trade Zones • Market Globalization • Cultural Aspects of Global Business • International Market Research • Marketing Channels • Marketing Game.

14. STRATEGIC AUDIT 535

Aims and Outcomes of the Chapter • Marketing • Organizational Behaviour • Management Team • Marketing Game.

15. CASE STUDIES 549

Understanding Case Studies : Case Study No.1: Faith Tyre Company • Case Study No.2: Aryan Lubricants • Case Study No. 3: Jags Electronics • Case Study No. 4: Pawan Sugar Mills • Case Study No. 5: Computers Ltd. (CL) • Case Study No. 6: Price Waterhouse-PW • Case Study No. 7: B to B Giant—Hindustan Graphite Electrodes • Case Study No. 8: International B-to-B Giant –Microsoft Inc. USA • Case Study No. 9: Infosys Technologies Ltd. • Case Study No. 10: Exhibitions India P. Ltd.

INDEX 583

CHAPTER 1

Marketing Business-to-Business—Introduction

Aims and Outcomes of the Chapter

The subject is introduced to the students in simple easy language and style to familiarise them with the basics of the subject and arouse curiosity for further learning by extensive study of the other chapters. It would make the students come to grips with the volatile business environment and let them discover what works and what does not, what are the ways of strategic formulation for B-to-B marketing. As we try to understand the business market, we should know how much it is different from the consumer market, what are its salient features, the buying decision process and the decision makers in the business. It is important to know the people who influence buying decisions. At times the government buys and it falls in somewhat different category.

Business buying is, "a process, by which the business defines its need for a product or service, finds out the various vendors supplying the product, scrutinizes each vendor carefully and then decides which is the best-suited one. The next step is the action step, of placing the order."

Business buying is distinguished from consumers as there are normally **fewer buyers, large volume buyers** and they tend to have a **long-term commitment** with the vendors/suppliers. The marketers therefore need to cultivate the buyers and build business relationships with them.

Business or Industrial Buying has the Following Main Features

- The demand of raw materials and components depends on the production plans of their buyers, and hence it is indirect or derived demand. If the car sales go down the sale of tyres will be affected too. Cement demand is connected to the construction activity in the country.

- As the buyers price their final product taking the prices of all the different components which go in to making of the product, the demand remains firm with little or no change with the changes in prices. Of course, buying from a particular firm may fluctuate if only it increases the price and other competitors do not.
- Increase in consumer goods demand skyrockets the demand of components and raw materials and capital goods.
- Major purchase decisions in a firm are group or team activities. The USER initiates the purchase action by sending his requisition to the PURCHASE MANAGER. (PM) PM then gets it vetted by the TECHNICAL MANAGER to get complete product specifications. Afterwards the tender is floated or the price bid called for from selected vendors. The FINANCE MANAGER then looks at the price bid. Finally the comparative pricing along with technical specification compliance by each of the bidders is studied and final purchase recommendations are made, to be approved by the CEO. The process is given below:

Fig. 1.1. Purchase Process

The people involved in the decision making process have one goal of buying the right product at competitive prices. However due to the nature of their activities it manifests differently as can be seen from the following:

User wants the product he has used earlier, or as he wants if it is a research project.

Purchase Manager wants to buy the traditional product to avoid inventory problems.

Technical Manager wants the State of the Art product.

Finance Manager wants Value for Money product.

The CEO wants only the best product.

While the product remains the same, its attributes and benefits can be put across to the various persons to satisfy their own needs as stated above. The decision process takes the shape of a triangle known as the decision triangle:

F— it is area of ignorance and sellers have to provide a lot of information to the buyer

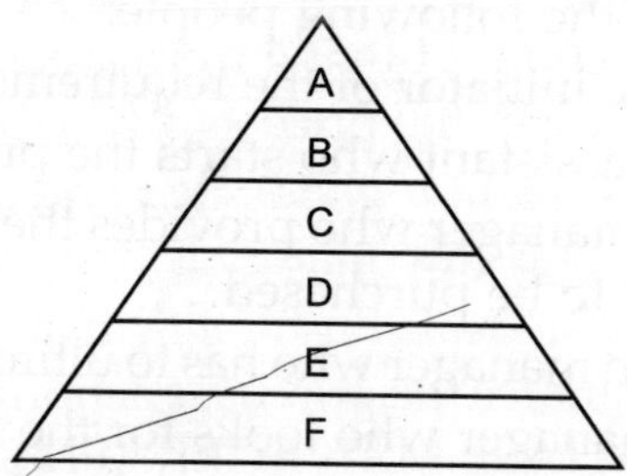

Fig. 1.2. Purchase Decision Triangle

E— it is the first level of doubts from the buyer, which must be clarified by the seller effectively.

D— it is the second level of hostility because of competitors hold on the customers. The sellers must give added benefits to counter the competitive stronghold.

C— in the third level the attack is direct, "Your product is too expensive or it is not good enough." At this point testimonials from important local and overseas customers must be shown to the customers. Additional guaranty can be offered if need be.

B— the customer usually likes to dither at this stage, "I have to ask my partners. I do not have the required authority" as can be seen mostly the customer is bluffing and incentive of prompt payment discount or order today to get extra credit facility can be given.

A— at this point the seller should offer an either/or option. "You want us to insure or you will take care of it." The answer to this question, "ok you do it" or "now" we will take care of it" means that now you can ask the buyer to sign the purchaser order.

Once the purchase order is in your hands DO NOT LINGER IN THE CUSTOMERS OFFICE. THANK HIM AND COME OUT FAST. At times the customer may just want to have another look at the order and say, "OK, the order is yours but leave it with me for the next two days when I will show it to my brother." The order could be shown to your competitor and the next day he may walk away with your order! This practical suggestion is the result of experience of a number of sellers and should not be ignored.

One important link in the decision process is the role of influencers and veto-ers. Influencers are the people who wield an extra-hierarchical authority, which is often unwritten and only understood. The veto-ers are the top most brass, like the firms Chairman who can veto the decisions of even the CEO. Thus, it can be seen that the decision process is channelled through the following people:

1. The user or the initiator of the requirement.
2. The purchase assistant who starts the purchase action.
3. The technical manager who provides the detailed specifications of the product to be purchased.
4. The production manager who has to ultimately approve its usage
5. The finance manager who looks for the investment angle.
6. The stores manager who has to arrange for the inventory and its control.
7. The influencers who help in decision-making process and can almost force a decision on the CEO.
8. The decider or the CEO whose ultimate responsibility is to see the profitable growth of the firm.
9. The veto-er who holds the final word, most likely he should be chairman of the firm.
10. Stoppers who are unofficial competitors agents and who try to keep the firm at bay by giving wrong information and misleading them while trying to pose as the best friend. The firm can be on guard against such people by trying to locate and isolate them.

In most firms for major purchases there is a Purchase committee, which is empowered to either, decide on the purchase or is only empowered to give its recommendation to the CEO. The sellers therefore must cultivate the firm's entire purchase team and communicate with the team members in the language best appreciated by each individual. For example the sellers can take the following communication route-

- To the user — Sir, the new product is so user friendly that you will find it twice as easy to use it than the present product.
- To the purchase person — Sir, once you buy the product, its reliability of supply and its quality will minimize your inventory worries.
- To the finance person — Sir, we give value for money and with lowest rejection rate in the industry you can be sure of production continuity.
- To the technical person — Sir, the state of the art product will let you be into the latest user friendly technology and your technical team would love to use the product for further innovating your own final product, much to the delight of your customers.

- To the influencers—Sir, you would be delighted if the firm was to buy our product as it will certainly enhance your own image in the firm.
- To the decider—Sir, we know of your desire to buy only the top of the line product and hence you will surely decide in favour of our product.
- To the vetoer—Sir, buying the product while vetoing others will raise the prestige of your firm and its brand equity.

In order to communicate to each of the above it is useful to get the counterparts of the purchase committee to talk to its members as follows:

Purchase manager with Sales Manager.

Production or Technical Manager with R&D Manager.

Finance Manager with Finance Manager.

CEO with CEO.

IN ALL SUCH MEETINGS THE MARKETING EXECUTIVE WORKS AS A LIAISON OR CO-ORDINATING PERSON FOR THE MEETINGS

Purchase Negotiations in Tender and Non-tender Business

Big volume buyers usually call the three to four short-listed vendors for final negotiations on price and terms of business. These negotiations are similar in both tender and non-tender business. The main consideration of the buyer is to get the best out of the deal by playing one vendor against the other. The dialogue goes something like this—

Buyer, "your prices are too high as compared to M/s. X your main competitor".

Seller, "I am sure you will compare our quality of the product and our service too".

Buyer, "yes, but price difference is so big that I can not justify purchasing from you".

Seller, "can you give me an idea of the price they have quoted?"

Buyer, "it is nearly twenty percent cheaper than your price".

In such cases, especially if the location is away from sellers headquarter; it is advisable for the seller, to keep the following information for carrying out successful negotiations:

- Comparative statement of previous quoted prices and negotiated prices for same product and with same competitors.

- Product costing with elements of fixed and variable costs.
- Floor prices, that are lowest prices up to which the seller has the firm's authority to go down to.
- Authority to modify terms of business like, payment terms, guaranty period, warranty terms faster delivery periods if these become necessary to clinch the order.

While the sanctity of the tender business is its transparency, most buyers would flaunt it for the sake of getting the best deal.

Industrial sales or B tom B sales can be long drawn out processes as the money value of orders is large, and the buyers want the best deal. Hence, several sales calls, visits by technical, financial experts, quality management team members, and turnkey project engineers become essential.

Industrial buying is mostly directly from the manufacturers but, in case of raw materials and components the sellers use the services of distribution channels, especially when there are several buyers strewn all over the country-side. In this case also the manufacturer has to provide technical support to the channel members. Buyers prefer to buy from those vendors who in some way are their customers too. The tyre company's fleet of cars is bought from the car manufacturer who buys tyres from them. Leasing and hire purchase is an option increasingly being used by buyers and the seller who offers the best option tends to get the deal. Several large firms hire out cars to be given to their employees rather than buying them as it saves capital expense.

Government tender business in India-there are two types of tenders, running contracts and rate contracts.

In running contracts, the DGS&D (Director General of Supply and Disposals) floats the tender and on receipt of offers negotiates with firms a rate and quantity and quality of the product along with other terms of business for a period of time and the offices of the government can then place direct orders on the vendor on those prices and terms; for this purpose the government office has to register itself with the DGS&D as a Direct Demanding Office.

The rate contract is for a product purchase at a fixed rate for the period of contract only.

Umbrella buying or turnkey solutions- business buyers prefer to buy a large range of products from one source and hence number of sellers tie up for providing turnkey solutions which can become cost effective as also take away the headache of dealing with several vendors.

In taking buying decisions the buyers are greatly influenced by WHO SAYS SO! In case industry leaders give a good reference for the turnkey operations the selling becomes easy.

In business purchasing long-term contracts with accepted vendors reduce buying problems to a large extent as vendors take special care of such customers by offering new products, first handling complaints quickly, giving prompt replacements of defective or even suspected defective goods. Most buyers however, keep at least one more vendor as marginal supplier to avoid getting into a problem of putting all the eggs in one basket.

Let us examine factors, which contribute to industrial purchases. - The **Macro-Economic** factors like demand and supply of money, the product demand and its life cycle position, rate of technological obsolescence, competition and governmental stability factors. The Organizational factors like purchase policy of reordering levels, policy of JUST IN TIME ORDERS, Vendor assessment procedures, centralized or decentralized purchasing and seasonality of business. Strikes, natural calamities also affect the buying process. In international buying cultural factors play an important role.

Industrial Buying Process- Let us now discuss the entire gamut of Industrial Buying Process. The following can be considered as industrial products:

- Capital goods, plant and machinery
- Turn key projects
- Raw materials
- Components
- Sub-assemblies

The method of marketing the capital goods and turn key projects have some commonality, while the other three come under one product group. Let us discuss the process of the capital goods sale and turn key projects or total systems. The number of buyers is small and the suppliers are mostly well known. The buyers approach the sellers who put up the bid, giving technical details as called for, assurance of quality, at times even the list of their sub-vendors and price information. Besides the following information is given in the quotations:

- Assembly and sub-assembly process, individual assembly and system guaranty and warranty.
- Facility and provision for training of buyer's technical personnel.
- Actual guaranty cards photocopies of bought out components.
- List of recommended spare parts with their prices.

- Price escalation clause.
- Installation and commissioning time period and costs and help, including man power needed by the seller from the buyer during installation and commission.
- Payment terms along with delivery schedule.
- Post guaranty period, cost of servicing and service contracts prices.
- Sellers seek the authority from the buyer to subcontract part of the job, like installation and commissioning.
- Sellers seek approval from buyer to receive payment on part supply of equipment.
- If there are variations in product specifications, these are brought out by the sellers and specifically approved by the buyer. In case such approval is not given then the sellers have to reconsider the entire bid.

The capital goods or turnkey projects are normally not manufactured by one firm. The firm, which makes the large part, takes the role of the lead bidder and others support the lead bidder with their quotes to the leaders.

In some major tenders the sellers are asked to submit two separate bids for the same tender, one containing technical compliance report of the tender specifications and the other gives the price and other commercial terms of the tender.

The buyer in such cases opens the technical compliance bid first and short-lists only those bidders who have full compliance of the tender specifications. Other bids are rejected.

Next, the technically compliant bidders commercial bids are opened and again the firms are shortlisted on the basis of acceptability of the price delivery terms and payment modes. From the shortlist the purchase and technical experts give the final recommendation to the Firm's CEO, regarding which bidder should be awarded the order. If two or more firms are close in the bids then the buyer calls them for negotiations.

For turnkey projects in India the government has started another method of awarding the business called BOT—Build, Operate and Transfer. In such jobs the seller builds the project, runs it for a selected period (and gains profit out of it) and then transfers it to the government. Bridges, highways are some examples of BOT projects.

Turnkey jobs or systems selling calls for a large variety of products and expertise in marketing finance technology and coordination between a large number of suppliers. For the customer the main advantage is that he has to deal with only one vendor.

The marketing person should be looking into the following aspects in the buyer's organization in industrial sales:

- The decision making process
- The hierarchy of decisions, including recommendations
- The authority to purchase at different levels
- Culture of innovation or status quo
- Purchasing from head quarters only
- Decentralized buying
- Internet's influence in the purchase department
- Product grouping like ABC Analysis
- Immediacy of demand, are they regularly asking for emergency supplies or it is only once in a while
- Long term business contract
- Short term contract
- On the spot buying
- Seasonality of their business and of their purchasing
- Single vendor preference or multiple vendors
- Do they provide advance payment if needed, or mobilisation fund as advance
- Payment reputation, are they prompt or do they delay payments
- Associated business and other assets and liabilities
- Firms reputation among vendors

In the last half of the twentieth century, the orientation of the firms had shifted from just purchase to material management. Today it has further changed to Supply Management or Supply Chain Management. The theory of Just in Time or JIT supplies is a corollary of supply chain management. Vendor long-term relationship ALMOST LIKE PARTNERSHIP, vendor development ensures continuity of good quality product supply whenever needed. These help the venders too as they are sure of getting the orders or better still they already always have a rolling supply order, which keeps getting replenished on its getting over with all ordered supplies made by the vendor.

However, the common practice even today is having multiple supply sources to ensure supplies even during any crisis, one vendor may face. Buyers tend to put a lot of products in the generic group where any vendor is good enough to supply and they have only shortest term purchase planning. The vendors would therefore do well to understand the mindset of the buyer and then decide about marketing strategies for the buyer.

Industrial Buyers have the following Considerations while Placing Orders:

- Inventory status, maximum minimum stock plans for each item to be purchased
- Reordering levels which depend on the difficulty of procuring the product due to its lack of suppliers, it being from far off places or overseas
- ABC Analysis of the products to be bought
- Production plans taking in to account the seasonality of the demand of the buyers' final product.
- Storage space
- Just in Time plan of procurement
- Past experience of product rejections

INDUSTRIAL MARKETING RESEARCH

In the first half of the twentieth century industrial marketing research was done by simple things like counting the number of chimneys or looking at the new industrial licenses issued by the government. Today, the industrial scene is much more complex as no license is required for setting up industries. However, information is available through secondary research as a number of magazines and journals are printed giving industrial information. State government has started industrial parks, which house a number of industries. There are clusters of industries in various parts of the country where the government provides tax concessions. Besides there are market research agencies, which are continuously involved in doing research, which can be purchased.

Industrial Purchase Decisions Can be Triggered by a Number of Reasons as Follows:

- Market research informs the need of a new innovative product for which capital-manufacturing equipment is required
- Old equipment needs to be replaced with state of art equipment
- Change in technology of manufacture
- Raw material or components purchased are sub-standard.
- Fresh vendor assessment

Once the need has been established it is necessary to correctly define the product, its detailed specifications, expected prices and possible vendors.

Looking for possible suppliers can start with existing vendors of similar products, Product finder journals, trade magazines and even competitors. In case of raw material and components trade journals, existing suppliers and competitors can be good source of information. Once the vendor list is finalized a limited tender or a request for quotation is made in writing where detailed specifications of the product and expected delivery time are given.

Final vender selection needs careful scanning of the following besides the scrutiny of its technical and commercial bid:

- Past record of the vendor
- List of its customers
- Testimonials from customers about the quality of product and service
- Visit to a manufacturing unit where the product may be in use in coordination with the vendor, with possibility of discussions with the users there.
- Vendors financial status
- Vendors flexibility of supplies

The next logical step is making a detailed purchase order giving product to be purchased with specifications price payment terms and delivery period with guaranty/warranty terms and other service facilities need to be specified.

Once the product is received and used its feedback from the user is essential for the purpose of re-buys from the same vendor.

Competition In Industrial Buying

Competition comes if the buyer starts vertical integration i.e., it starts to manufacture what it was buying from the firm. Vertical integration is of two types as follows:

- Forward vertical integration in which the vender can start to manufacture the product it was selling, for example the cloth maker starts to make readymade garments, or the television picture tube maker starts making television sets. In such case there is loss of a customer.
- Backward vertical integration in which the buyer starts to make the component he was buying for going in to his manufacture. For example, the cloth maker starts making yarn and television maker starts making the television picture tube. In such cases also a customer is lost.

MARKETING AND ECONOMY

A lot of laymen wonder about marketing and its subtleties. Let us discuss a few cases on this issue to understand it a little better. The marketing plans discussed below have been chosen as representative of different classes. These will provide an insight to the readers into the world of Marketing—

- Product launch—cell phones
- Maintain market share—Pepsi
- Create retail business—Chain of retail stores–1- Shopping Malls
- Provide salespersons with business opportunities- FMCG Products HLL
- Public interest advertising—pollution control on Delhi roads

Product launch—A few years ago, Airtel introduced an unknown product (at that time—cellular phones) to the Delhi public. There were banners across several main roads announcing **" there is something new in the air—Airtel".** A lot of speculation went on among the elite of the town and most persons were intrigued by the advertisement. People felt , may be it is a new TV channel. Others opined that it is a new airline. The debate went on till it was resolved with the launch of Airtel cell phone service in Delhi. It became the new status symbol for the Delhi public who has been status seekers for a long while due to pattern of population, which includes the bureaucrats, industrialists, and top persons from media, doctors, lawyers and diplomats. Later, when competition caught up with them Airtel started expanding their product, refining the services provided and making attractive price packages to stay ahead of competitors.

Airtel took the following points in to account:

- Tremendous opportunities Airtel provides to the modern business to communicate as and when the need arises. Pagers, the cruder version gave only text on a limited screen and it was not two-way communication.
- A proven technology in Europe, the GSM, which ensured up gradation of technology as it was happening any where in the world.
- Geographic coverage of large cities like Delhi, Mumbai. With roaming facility today you can be anywhere in the world and with the same cell phone you can be communicating with your friends, business associates around the world.

- Internet on cell phone, facility to send and receive text messages and conferencing facility has made the cell phone a veritable boon to the business executive of today.

Market share- Pepsi realized that unless they keep the product visibility on a permanent pedestal and keep the product on the top of the mind recall, their severest competitors, coke will steal their share in no time. With this realization, the now famous Pepsi- Coke Advertising wars started. Both the firms leave no opportunity to upstage the other. India is a land of celebrations round the year, may be it is religious festival or social people are out on the streets with perhaps unmatched gusto.

Regional considerations like Ganpati Mahotsav in Maharashtra, Durga pooja in Bengal, Pongal in the south, Baisakhi in Punjab are celebration times and the cold drink makes sure to be a part of the gala. You have to open the TV during celebration times and you will be virtually bombarded by the advertising campaigns of the cold drinks.

Retail chains are taking over the retail business from individual retailers as with bulk buying they can provide lower prices, have better merchandizing, use marketing and retailing expertise and provide real value for money to their customers. They face the following problems, which they try to answer through their marketing campaigns.

- Small individual retailers are more aware of the needs, mindsets and buying behaviour and patterns of the local customers.
- Home delivery, credit sale are better managed by small retailer.
- With lower per product inventory, loss on account of a product not selling is less.
- Faster inventory turn round means better profits.

Retail Store Chains have the following advantages:

- Uniformly good quality of products.
- Large variety of products.
- Multiple brands of the same product giving the buyer the right to choose.
- Hygienic conditions in the sales rooms.
- Play areas for the children accompanying the buyers for ease in buying.
- In house restaurant to refresh the shoppers.

Since the store are spread in different parts of the town, the chain uses local media like local cinema, press, handbills and billboards to catch the buyer's TOP OF THE MIND RECALL.

Providing salespersons with sales opportunities is done through a variety of advertising campaigns. The most effective ones are from

FMCG firms. Retail traffic increases for a new product indirect proportion to its awareness and **TOP OF THE MIND RECALL**. For example, if just a few,(say two or three in a day,) buyers ask for a new brand, the salesman will sell them any reputed brand which is in stock, instead. However, if twenty / thirty people ask for the product the retailer will be forced to stock the product else he will lose customers to competitive stores. We can see advertising develops sales pull, as against inventories, which provide sales push through inventory pressure.

In case of Industrial product/ business to business sales, advertising helps in making the buyer know about the product and mainly pre-sell the firm. In other words it helps in image building of the firm. In turn the sales persons of the firm get an easy access to the purchase persons of the firm. It helps the salesman to get a foot in the door.

Advertising helps in building public awareness towards social issues. We have all seen Advertisements, which propagate cleanliness, pollution control, small family norms, anti-dowry, child marriages. Such advertisements help in building consciousness among the public towards the cause and this in turn proves effective in eradicating the problem.

Besides, advertising, which is a marketing mix factor, helps in the following areas as well in the economic sphere:

- Advertising removes the pressures of governmental/ political or business control of the media, both print and electronic. In other words, since the media is not dependent financially on the government, political bigwigs and the Industrialists it can be bold in its editorial content and hence can play its rightful role as the watchdog of the institutions like bureaucracy, judiciary, legislature and business.
- Advertising helps build a fine tuned management system, which delivers what it promises through its advertisements. It helps in streamlining processes and procedures for both management and workers for optimizing results.
- Brand equity helps in improving product quality differentiating it from other similar products, which in turn benefits the buyers who get the right product at the right price.
- Advertising tends to reduce distribution costs in certain products, which are sold on their brand name only, without any need for further salesmanship. Personal selling becomes a lot easier as the buyer is already aware of the product and needs only to reinforce his positive ideas about the product.
- And finally, advertising has emerged as a major source of information about the product, its price, availability, and other

terms of business associated with the product like leasing options, detailed specifications.

- Advertising helps in R&D efforts, as the firms are sure that with the help of advertising they will be able to launch new products developed by their R&D.
- Building Brand Equity or improving firms image helps firms in pricing the products higher than the competition, as buyers get a mental picture of the quality of the product, which once established through usage of the product dictates repeat buys of the same product.

Advertising gives them vital information free which helps them in correct decision making most of the times.

Advertisement helps in providing entry barriers for new brands entry, as most customers become brand loyal with little place for a new comer. However, this statement holds less meaning as in certain products like FMCGs brand shift is most common as can be seen from the new brands introduced in the market. Hence entry barrier theory is most a theory only with not much relevance to reality.

As far as prices are concerned, advertising help build sales, increases revenues and therefore can in fact be instrumental in price reduction if the firm wants to do it. since, price cuts become equated to product quality, firms remain apprehensive in taking this measure, as they might just lose their market.

Advertising works as a sentinel of public conscience too. With the advent of color TV advertising is affecting the viewers much more than ever before. IT CAN BE A LOT MORE PERSUASIVE NOW! Buyers do have increasing choices, but the responsibility of proper and correct information lies squarely with the advertisers.

Marketing And Society

Marketing, it is alleged, makes people buy extra things, which they may never need. However, we can logically see that people normally make a budget of how much they want to spend on any particular product. The purchase decision is taken after a lot of investigations regarding alternates available, their quality, after sales service, price and depending on products value to the buyer the process becomes time consuming and cumbersome. However, advertising gives the buyers information which is verifiable and which helps in purchase decisions. We can infer that advertising helps in improving the product quality, buyers' value for their money and as a consequence helps develop buyers tastes for good standard products.

Health care products, feminine hygiene products marketing efforts improve the general awareness of buyers about health consciousness. Hence, quality of such products, which may be vital to the very well being of human beings, is of paramount importance. Advertisements, at a point are the only things buyers see before they even think of buying it. Therefore the relative importance of advertisements emerges from its dynamic effect on at times, gullible public.

On a different plane, products with bad advertising can take away even the good points of a product. The quality of advertisement often determines the product quality in buyers mind. Even mediocre products like Texla TV survived the onslaught of international brands as they had, as a policy placed their TV on an upscale market. Remains of their market share are still visible while several brands, which were better known, have bitten the dust.

There are products, which have been banned from being advertised like, liquors, cigarettes, and contraband goods, drugs. At times there are lacunae in the law, which debars advertising in one particular media and is allowed to be advertised in other media. Such imbalances create chaos in buyer's minds and uniformity on international forum should be taken in this regard.

Society is at times, inundated by advertising blitz, which become counter productive. The readers reject magazines full of advertising and little else. Same way, on TV and Radio if any advertisement is repeated too many times than even a good advertisement loses appeal and turns objectionable. While becoming eyesores to viewers, such advertisements show the shallowness of creative depth of the agency concerned.

Advertising Agencies have often been accused of exploiting the female form to enhance the advertising appeal. Whether the product is car tire, health food, lathe machine or even a screwdriver, it is considered useful to show a pretty girl unconnected to the product, in its advertisement. Despite protests from the socially forward people, such usage is on the increase. The motto seems to be GIVE THE VIEWERS WHAT THEY WANTS TO SEE. Censorship is conspicuous by its absence. Advertising Associations have been trying to set up a self-censorship body within the advertising network without any real success. Now, the changing societal norms, its permissiveness are reflected in the advertisements. The question therefore is, what leads to the present situation, the uncensored advertisements or the permissive society. It is definitely the need of the day to look at the present advertising scene from this point of view at the earliest.

Advertising creates value systems as people buy advertised products, which establishes a particular life style for the users of the products. Such products are, at times, purchased only to become a member of that particular elite set. This tendency is more visible in younger set and newly rich crowd. On the other hand advertisements help buyers realize their life style through the information provided in the advertisements. A person living near the sea may want to buy a boat. Seeing the advertisement of speedboat he may go for it as it is the Status Symbol of the elite. Product positioning, choice of media for the target market segment are all based on getting the right person to see or have the Opportunity To See The Advertisement. Hence it can be surmised that advertisement plays a useful role in moulding the upward mobile population in to the right groove.

Society revolves round certain norms like WHAT ARE THE DESIRABLE TANGIBLE PRODUCTS FOR ANY SET OF PEOPLE. Going beyond the product list meant for their set (however unwritten) people get tempted to buy things they can hardly afford. The element of materialism is born out of this desire. It was once said that all good things in life are for free. Now in the twenty-first century, drinking water is being purchased (mineral water), Air conditioners are purchased to provide the cool air we breathe. Even simple products like salt, sugar, and flour are branded to provide mental satisfaction and quality to the product, which were hitherto being sold as generic products. Marketing has therefore provided the consumers with options to buy from, but according to Anti-Materialistic Group, buy they must.

Advertising, when takes the role of puffery, then it becomes misleading and hence harmful to buyers. Puffery means exaggerations about the benefits of the product, which give a wrong picture to the buyers. The temptation to use superlatives to describe an ordinary product is possibly so overwhelming that we see many advertisements using puffery to attract the customers. It should be remembered that such advertisements are like the bucket with a hole and they do not carry any water in them.

When you meet the real rich people, you find that they are not given to materialism. Many Indian affluent persons can be seen wearing the traditional Dhoti Kurta with their modern day versions wear jeans and tee shirts.

Leisure time activities like trekking, jogging, camping, mountain climbing and other out door sports and health improving products like health foods, diet products personal gyms take a big advertising space and it helps in furthering the awareness of such activities and products, rendering valuable service to the society. Marketing mix factor, Advertising can now be redefined in twelve "A"s, as follows:

Advertising deals with providing correct information to the target market segment/s

Availability of products is confirmed

Awareness of the product benefits is highlighted

Assessment of product utility for the consumer

Adherent of the product- make people loyal to a brand

Attitude change—if the buyers have negative attitude towards your product it can be molded in its favour.

Acceptance of the product by the buyers through usage and trial.

Affordability gives the value for money picture to justify high prices

Accessibility—advertisements tell the buyers how and where they can buy the product

Aesthetics help in bringing out the best creativity to attract attention

Adventure adds to the dynamics of advertising campaigns and calls for innovative spirit in the creative team

Advertising lets the press remain free from outside controls, as it earns enough from the advertisements. It means an independent editorial policy can be maintained adding credibility to the press. It remains a moot debatable point whether advertisements can control press with huge revenues available to press through advertisements.

Advertising makes consumers use more of the product:

- Kodak says, "TAKE MORE PICTURES"
- Hero Honda motor bike advertisement says, "FILL IT, SHUT IT AND FORGET IT"
- BUY TWO SOAP CAKES AND GET ONE FREE

Increasing business can also be done to make customer aware of different uses of a product. Baking soda can be used to freshen refrigerators by removing odors from its contents. Advertising this aspect improved sales of baking soda to a large extent while it provided customers with a service unheard of by them. Orange juice was used only as a breakfast drink. Advertising it as a daylong freshener helped in increasing its sales considerably.

The third alternative for increasing sales is to add new customers for the product. An airline started advertising in the 50s and 60s of the last century that if your employee is traveling by train you are losing precious time, which converted in money, was a big lose to the firm. While the airlines may not find the approach as successful, small car sellers are asking the motorcycle users to change to more comfortable and weatherproof small car. It can be seen that such advertisements try to look like providing a social service too.

Advertising should help firms achieve Economies Of Scale In Manufacturing, Bulk Purchase Cost Effectiveness so that they can offer better benefits , bonuses to the employees who are part of the society.

How does it work? - The Advertising Campaign

In order to accurately assess the customer perception of the service provided by Airtel in Madhya Pradesh, they are doing constant information gathering to ensure not only customers acceptance of the service but for reinforcing the effectiveness of their advertising campaign.

With virtual monopoly of Maruti in small car segment, Hyundai was hard pressed to ensure refocusing the buyers mindset towards their Santro. They used the super star of the Indian screen, Shah Rukh Khan also, the teen idol to position their car in the right slot which paid them dividends in the form of market share in excess of their own expectations and also more than market share of Matiz, the Daewoo car, although, Daewoo have a distinct advantage of a longer presence in India with their large car Ceilo.

Thums up the cola drink, faces challenge from both Coke and Pepsi. To gain market share they are repositioning the product as an adult product taking in to account that both Coke and Pepsi have been targeting the youth market. "are you ready for the growing up challenge" is what another super star Salman Khan asks the audience in the advertisements.

Life Insurance Corporation of India was never in to big time advertising. Only after the setting up of a commission to look into privatization of insurance sector they started advertising campaign in a big way. They also up graded their product, made it more users friendly and improved their response time. All of which came about with big advertising splashes to keep the customers informed and motivated to buy their product.

Advertising planning process can be put graphically as follows:

Round the world advertising reaches millions of people in their homes, workplace and shops where they buy. Based on the product and Advertising budget media selection takes place for optimized results with the target segment. Today's marketing managers want to reach out to the customers at places selected by the customers to facilitate sale of their product, rather purchase of the product by the customers. Hence customer orientation of firms is complete and firms have to match up their efforts in production finance Human resources to reap the benefits of customer first concept.

Change as is said, is the only constant in the world. Hence even advertising is also evolving all the time. The advertising evolution is likely to become advertising revolution in the wake of Internet and e-Commerce. The media blitz of the twentieth century has surpassed all imaginable concepts and so have the creativity standards. Technology has been at the helm of these changes as will be described in coming chapters.

Practice is what makes one perfect. Hence, the students need to constantly practice what they are learning going through the book. Several case studies will make the practice sessions easy and enjoyable for the students.

A lot of local advertising goes on, including Cooperative Advertising, Trade Advertising, Point Of Purchase Advertising, and Business Advertising and Direct Mail Advertising. While low budgeted their needs are different including media selection These are in effect part of the entire exercise of advertising, but need special emphasis due to their special nature.

Advertising can be classified as generic and specific. In generic advertising effort is made to generate business for entire product range including all the brands, while specific advertising is done to promote sales of a particular brand only.

Examples of generic advertising are as follows:

- Drink more milk
- Eat more eggs
- Buy diamonds to please your wife (sponsored by de beers)

In social cause advertising it could be

- Exercise your right to vote
- Keep your city clean
- Plant one tree each year
- Each one teach one
- Anti- dowry campaigns
- Get your vehicle checked for polluting emissions
- Do not change lanes driving on this street.
- Pay your taxes in time and do not evade taxes

For specific products advertising brings in business due to advertising pull. Attractive advertisements become TOP OF THE MIND RECALL WHICH GETS TRANSLATED IN TO SALES.

Marketing function in a typical firm and its relations with other areas are as follows:

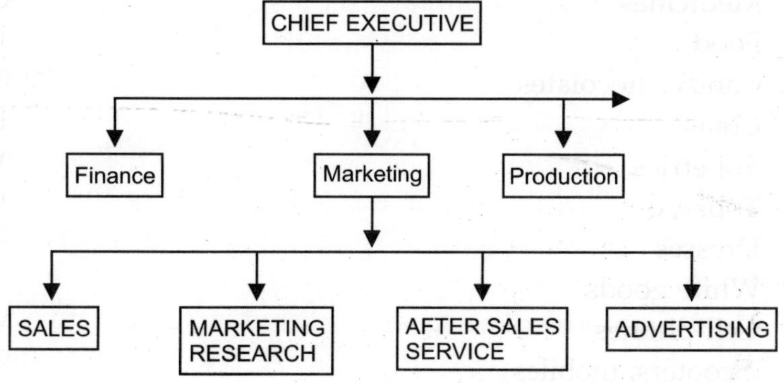

Fig. 1.3. Marketing Organisation

The following major organizations are concerned with advertising:

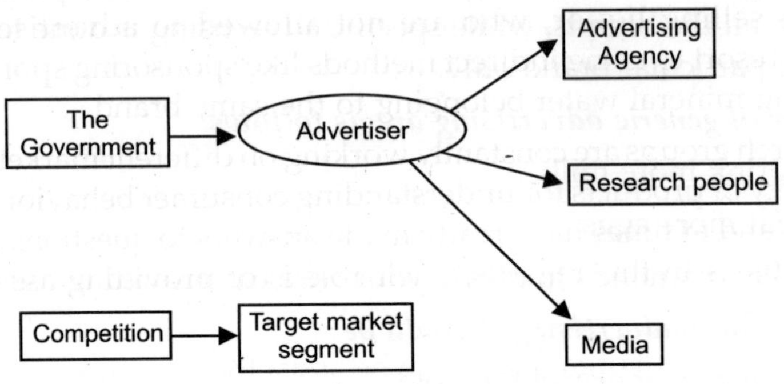

Fig. 1.4. Advertising System

The government lays down laws concerning advertising. In most countries, liquor, drugs are banned for advertising. In its own right government is also an advertiser.

Advertiser is on the hub of all Advertising activities as he is the one directly connected with the results of advertising. Business firms have to advertise goods to improve their brand image, which in turn helps them in increasing sales in a competitive situation. Besides public service organizations advertise to educate people for improving the quality of life for the citizens of the country. Following 16 industries are the top advertisers in any country:

1. Airlines
2. Appliances, TV, Radio
3. Cars
4. Medicines
5. Food,
6. Candy chocolates
7. Colas
8. Toiletries
9. Tobacco
10. Dresses
11. White goods
12. Cell-phones
13. Scooters, mobiles
14. Films
15. Watches
16. Service industry, like hotels

Government as advertiser has not been counted in the list. They are big advertisers for purchasing selling and recruitments.

Firms selling liquor, who are not allowed to advertise in most countries resort to using indirect methods like sponsoring sports events, advertising mineral water belonging to the same brand.

Research groups are constantly working on different market segment for a variety of products for understanding consumer behavior, life style mindsets, and at times have ready made answers to questions posed by the advertisers in this regards. Their role is of providing assistance to the agencies.

Role of different organizations who assist the advertisers can be seen in the block diagram given below:

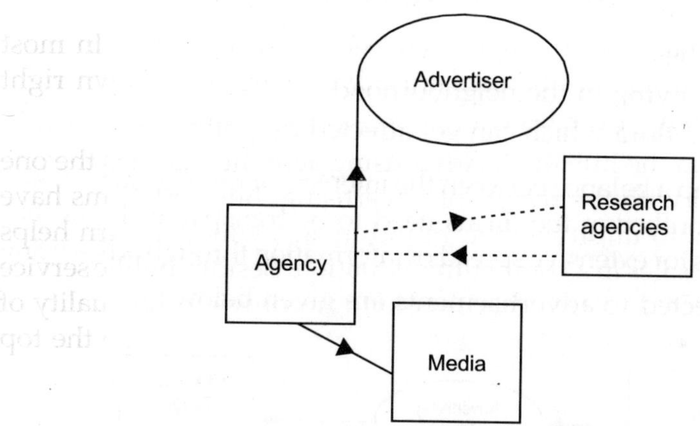

Fig. 1.5. Advertising Plan

DOTTED LINE DENOTES THE RESEARCH REPORT GIVEN TO THE AGENCY BY THE RESEARCH AGENCY

As can be seen, the agency plays the role of coordination between advertisers and the media. Research agencies are doing continuous research for understanding the effectiveness of different media as also the mindsets of target market segment.

Advertising has become an important discipline and plenty of literature is available on different aspects of advertising. There are books, magazines, reports, and videos dealing with the subject, some of them dating back to the turn of the twentieth century. Advertising has been seen from the following viewpoints:

- Psychological
- Social

- Philosophical
- Economic
- Management

The management perspective of marketing confirms the supremacy of market share and brand equity in each of the businesses. However, from the last decade of twentieth century, firms are becoming more and more aware of their responsibilities towards their stakeholders. The firm survives because of and for the stakeholders, which are listed below-

- Personnel-workers, management
- Buyers
- Suppliers
- Financial institutions
- Government
- Trade bodies
- Residents living in the neighborhood
- Fauna and flora which can get affected by polluting industries

In order to keep a balance between the interests of these groups, which at times can be conflicting too, firms need to be transparent in all their dealings. This calls for extensive spread of information through advertising.

Factors connected to advertisements are given below:

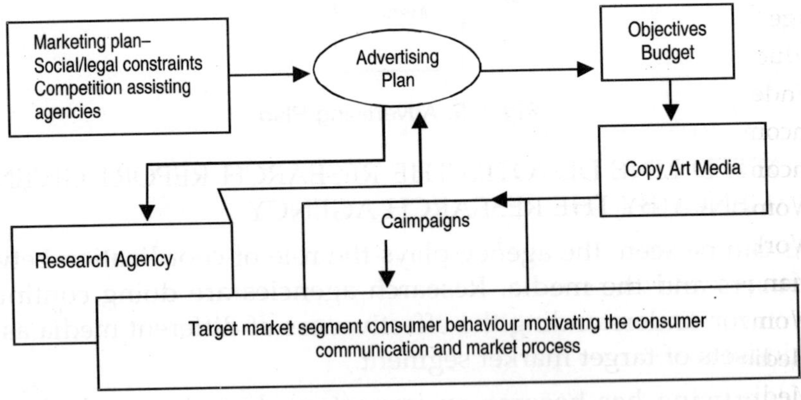

Fig. 1.6. Advertising Operations

The above given chart is self-explanatory. Marketing plans are made taking in view the social legal constraints, competition and agencies like advertising agency, distribution networks. From these plans advertising plans emerge. After defining the objectives and budget, creative team works to produce the artwork, which after client's acceptance goes to the media as per agreed schedule. The media is selected on the basis of segment being catered to.

In segmenting the market focus can be kept on concentration of customers in a defined geographic area or more than one group is selected and communication designed to suit the segments. At times going to a smaller segment helps as no competitor may be catering to the segment. In large segments competition is usually severe with price wars rendering it less attractive.

Smaller segments are useful in product launches when the seller is not too sure of market reaction to the product. Small firms, specialty product firms normally take the route of smaller segments.

Firms opting for large segments need to focus on each sub-segment for planning advertising campaign because mindsets, language and motivation may differ significantly for each sub-group. Firms even plan different products to catch the fancy of separate sub-segment. Maruti has its 800 version for the middle class segment while its Esteem covers the richer segment. Maruti segmentation goes beyond middle and rich class as they have Gypsy for the adventuress, van as multiuse vehicle.

Should women work in the offices brought mixed responses as follows:

Table 1.1. Response Table

Demographics	*Yes%*	*No%*
Age under 35	78	22
Age 35 and above	54	46
Education graduate	63	37
Undergraduate	60	40
Income 10,000 pm or less	80	20
Income 10,001 and above	45	55
Women are for home	55	45
Work place bad for women	60	40
Man is the house boss	80	20
Women's lib is good	40	60
Media liked by men TV	38	62
Media liked by women TV	55	45
MAGAZINES (MEN) INDIA TODAY	20	80
MAGAZINE (WOMEN) INDIA TODAY	5	95

Depending on the product you have to advertise the segment and the media can be chosen. Please note that the above table is only a hypothetical example. Such studies can be made by researchers and information obtained on it or similar aspects of market segment and media selection.

In India women work force has been on the rise. Population shifts from rural to urban areas is a major factor. Increasing population of teenage children and senior citizens is creating unparalleled business opportunities for some types of products.

While mass media rules the advertising communication, to find the most suitable communication plan for a particular segment, segment de-massification is being done. You pick up one or two representatives of the segment and then find out everything about that person for testing the **Created Communication** for the segment.

Once the segment is clearly defined the creative task begins.

The Creative Art

The creative artist has to know how the target audience will view and accept the art of the advertisement. Talking to children has to be in their language only. What really effects and stimulates the viewers must be clearly understood. How people acquire preconceived notions about products, which also puts distorted images of even a well-conceived advertisement, must be well known. This would avoid wrong messages from going to the market.

Consumers need to know about their needs and the products, which will best satisfy them in most cost effective manner. Do the customers ask their friends, relatives, or experts before making purchase decision. How the mindset is formed and where does the psychology come. Advertiser has to be a psychologist to give the right input, stimulus for the purpose. Uses of prominent persons as endorsers help in this direction but you have to know the correct person for endorsing the product.

To convert negative feelings for your product in to positive thoughts, needs an all round approach consisting of endorsements by the right people, proper merchandizing of the product and POINT OF PURCHASE advertising.

Next, the advertising creativity has to find the ACTUAL BENEFITS sought by the customers. Scanning competitive products and their advertisements will give an insight in to what significant benefits have been left out by the competition and this will help creative people to chart proper route taking these benefits in to account. The best analysis of competition is done by learning their four Ps, Product, Price, Placement and Promotion. The following table gives you an idea of what needs to be done-

Table 1.2. Benefit Table

A	B	C1-A	C1-B	C2-A	C2-B

A- Attributes of your product
B- Benefits which the customers will derive from the product
C1-A - Attributes of first competitor
C1-B - Benefits of first competitive products
C2-A - Attributes of second competitor
C2-B -Benefits of second competitors' products

Most advertising agencies use this method without sometimes making such a table.

(As an example, while the attribute of a shirt could be its silk cloth, the benefit, which the wearer would derive, would be an expression of his life style, as also, smooth flow of the shirt on the wearer's body.)

It must be remembered that the benefits derived as per firms own ideas may not be the same as the customers ideas. It is best to undertake advertising research to get the right picture to produce result-oriented art.

Analysis of the market for a particular product has to start from proper market segmentation, buyers profile, competitive strengths and weaknesses. Population shifts social-cultural changes, life style changes, and income distribution pattern helps in understanding the market dynamics better.

The task of market analysis becomes acute when the number of competitors is high and each one of them has distinct advantages in some area or the other. Taking cars in to account we can draw such a graph showing comfort and price as given below:

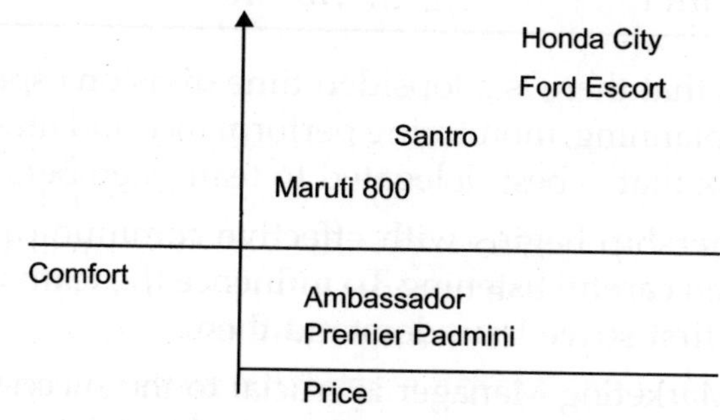

Fig. 1.7. Benefit Story Matrix

Ideally, advertising budget or expense on advertising should match or be a little less than the extra profits the advertising generates.

S=f (A), Where S is the sales figure, A is the advertising expense.

This equation presumes that, the only factor of sales is advertising, which as we know is not correct. Going with the presumption for the time being, gross margin of profit minus the advertising expense gives the net profit.

The manager must admit that politics in a firm is inevitable and should define the rules of politics like playing principled politics. It can be done by openness, honesty and transparency in operations.

Some forms of influence are so unobtrusive that they are not even considered as forms of power. These implicit forms of persuasion are perhaps the most effective ways for manager to influence his team and through the team members achieve the objectives.

One aspect of the manager's activities has a great impact on the outcome of the team effort is his time management. With proper time allocation much can be achieved without exerting undue pressure on him or on the team members. Given below is the statement, which shows in a general manner, how the managers want to spend their time and how they are spending it at the present. It should be an eye opener for them and for future managers for taking right corrective action while there is still TIME for them.

Table 1.3. Time Management

Manager's action	*Preferred time allocation(%)*	*Actual time spent(%)*
Marketing strategy development	30	10
Monitoring performance	20	40
Team leadership	30	15
Time for channel members	10	30
Team development	10	5

It can be seen that there is a lopsided time division especially in the areas of strategic planning, monitoring performance and time for channel members, the task that is best delegated to team members.

Effective leadership begins with effective communications, which in turn depends on careful listening To influence the team members the manager should first strive to understand them.

Selection of Marketing Manager is crucial to the success of the firm. In several disciplines even juniors can be asked to take over manager's position but it is not possible in the area of marketing. Some managers are good at working with an existing team for ongoing tasks. They may, not however, be able to take over as successful leaders of teams in changing business environments, as it exists today. Marketing Manager's position is pivotal, as the success of the firm in attaining its objectives is in direct proportion to the manager's ability to carry out his functions effectively.

A successful manager needs to have the leadership qualities as against ability to control the team. He should have a good understanding of human nature, an analytical mind, to be able to view the environment in the right perspective and take correct decisions. His leadership should provide impetus, enthusiasm and motivation to his team. As a role model his own actions should be exemplary, good for emulation. He should not be living in his ivory tower; he should be easily accessible to his team members. Managers need to be building bridges between his team and the rest of the firm. He must be the best Public Relations (with special emphasis on relationship with the channel members) person in the firm.

Managers must avoid getting into routine activities, which take away a lot of precious time, which they can put to good use in planning and human resource development. Another important activity for the manager is maintaining good relations with the competitors. In several cases even bitter competitors can cooperate like for new product development, import and exports and concept selling.

Finally, managers must be expert trainers in the area of providing service **to the customers, as it is only this area, which can never be copied and can create the desired** Sustainable Competitive Advantage **for the firm**

Questions for discussion—

1. How the industrial marketing differs from consumer marketing. Discuss giving examples?
2. What role negotiations play in industrial marketing?
3. How does vertical integration affect industrial business?

START OF THE B-TO-B MARKETING GAME

The start of the Game—

The students on their own or with the help of the faculty form teams for playing the game for which instructions are given at the end of each chapter. The tasks may not directly relate to the preceding chapter but they are connected with the subject being learnt.

The students are expected to create an ideal structure using group dynamics for which time will be allowed to conduct research that is practical and expresses your understanding of the international marketing environment and related business issues. Pick your topic quickly and work in groups of 4 to 6 students each. Some time should be spent in library research and some time in primary research. Organise and manage your time efficiently. Part of being a manager is self management and time management. Keep a good routine and don't waste time.

You have the freedom to organise amongst yourselves. Assign one person as the group leader who will be responsible that everyone reports to him/her. Meet and divide tasks among the group. Make sure that there is enough time for writing and editing the report. This usually takes more time than expected. The project should be relevant to today's marketing scenario. Some suggestions are given below:

A. Pick up an industrial product. Plan a proper marketing research to evaluate its market demand and to assess the buyer 's behaviour in the country.

Company studies These topics involve field interviews and correspondence combined with documentary sources. Students have to make full use of the libraries, of the institute as well as others like the US Library or the British Council library.

1. A b-to-b marketing audit. Design a marketing audit that a company can use to determine where it is in the stages of development of the corporation and what it should do with the information. Chapter on audit deals with the subject in great detail and the students should read it before starting the audit.
2. Reports analysing the marketing strategies of companies.
3. Product management. Under what circumstances have companies integrated their domestic and foreign industrial product planning and management? What factors have led to this integration? What are the explicit and hidden costs and benefits?
4. Marketing Data Analysis. Analysis of published data with implications for management.
5. Market performance analysis. Economic and social data combined with Company sales, earnings, and expenditure data and judgmental measures of competition could be used to measure and evaluate market performance in different countries.

Topic Reports

1. Marketing Research . by using Secondary sources and personal interviews. If you do this type of report, make sure that your report has practical recommendations for marketing managers.

2. Pricing policies. Examine the pricing method used by a company or group of companies and make recommendations for improvements. Explain why you recommended these changes.
3. Pricing strategy in the multinational corporation for inflationary markets.
4. How Indian programmers can solve software problems in the United Sates while the Americans are sleeping.(the question of time lag) A proposal to an American software company (e.g. Microsoft) to engage software professionals in Bangalore to find time-sensitive solutions at a competitive rate, making use of the difference in time zones and pay scales.
5. Using the Internet to scan and search for international business opportunities. This can be a company study or a report. Ideally students can do their research on the Internet, interviewing company representatives who have used the Internet to expand internationally.
6. Creating equidistance in viewing the customer. Suggest a strategy where international competitors can be as close to the customer whether the customer is located 5 km away or 10,000 km away.
7. An original research project that fulfils the requirement of international marketing and involves both primary and secondary research and is doable in two weeks.

As soon as the project is agreed by the group, a proposal should be written and an approval must be taken from the faculty who will question the students and make sure that the project can be achieved.

Task for the students—define the data needed by a B-to-B Firm for taking marketing decisions and also discuss how the firm should go about collecting and using it?

AIMS A

Marketing

con

the

Stu

fram

the

Mar

price,

The soc

satisfac

welfare

organiz

compar

long ter

Mar

century

seen be

and the

Satisfac

to, in th

second

growth

the ver

Profit

profits

of the fir

CHAPTER 2

Marketing Defined

AIMS AND OUTCOMES OF THE CHAPTER

Marketing has assumed great importance due to the onslaught of competitive forces and the students need to familiarise themselves with the different multifarious vignettes of this all important discipline. Students will get to know the various aspects of marketing, its basic framework and equip them with the basic knowledge that will help them in learning the subtleties of the subject.

Marketing is a system of interrelated activities designed to develop, price, promote and distribute goods and services to a group of customers. The societal concept of marketing is a philosophy that defines the satisfaction and delight of consumers on a long-term basis, besides welfare of public using a holistic marketing approach for reaching the organizational goals. The marketing managers must maximize the company's profitability as its products are sold. They should plan for long term customer satisfaction using the marketing plans.

Marketing as a discipline has come of age in the twenty first century. With immense challenges, there are also opportunities never seen before. As marketers, people are involved with people's needs and their satisfaction. To take a step forward the theory of Customer Satisfaction, we talk of **Customer Delight**. A firm's task therefore comes to, in the first instance, having products required by the people and secondly, marketing the products for profit, because with profit comes growth. Without growth stagnation sets in, which eventually erodes the very foundation of the firm rendering it ineffective and unprofitable. Profit making as against profiteering is a legitimate objective as only profits provide for the benefits, which should accrue, to the stakeholders of the firm.

Today's market place can be defined as having complex and chaotic competitive environment. It is therefore essential for the students and the practitioners of marketing as a discipline to fathom the complexities, to be able to analyze the same and have the right perspective before marketing strategies can be planned. The twenty-first century has thrown open the following new challenges in the area of marketing:

- Information technology and Internet
- Customer Relationship Management
- Globalization of markets
- Emergence of brand equity as a marketing tool

Looking at the international business scenario, we find that nations are at different levels of economic standards. Coupled to it is the rapid globalization of markets and market economy pervading the world markets. The marketers would, therefore find exciting challenges available to them in the world markets, as there would be sweeping divergence of needs waiting to be met along with several world players vying for the same business. The new business paradigm has substituted the old theory of management based on production, increase in productivity as in the old regime all that was manufactured sold and gave profits to the seller. Following are some of the main constituents of the new paradigm:

1. Product improvements based on new technologies, at times at reduced cost of manufacturing
2. Higher allocable surpluses, people having larger buying power
3. Availability of larger variety of goods at competitive prices
4. More knowledgeable customers, with increased advertising exposure
5. Improved methods of product placement to bring them within easy reach of the customers
6. Superior and new media availability for better access with the segmented markets
7. Better techniques available for marketing research to keep marketers better informed about the market needs. More product demand based information data banks available

Companies must understand that their competitors also know the major challenge before marketers come from the above stated situation. Hence there is the need to excel and out perform the competition. Therefore, instead of becoming a slave of the multifaced information the marketers should use it for proper planning of marketing strategies on a continual basis.

Based on the above, the new marketing strategies should become customer oriented as is reflected in the following-

Importance of marketing as a functional area of the company must be underscored, as it can never be overemphasized. Imagine a company having the best of the technology, manpower, finances but no marketing at all. Can anyone imagine such a company surviving in today's competitive environment?

Therefore the latest marketing mantra can be stated as follows:

Change product-to-product and service

Change customer satisfaction to customer delight

Change product quality to product's perceived value by the customer

The existing industrial and business world comprises certain functional areas including the following:

1. Marketing
2. Finance and accounting
3. Human resource
4. Production

Besides there are certain societal and physical factors that have an impact on a company's business like the following:

1. Political and legal environment of the country
2. Macroeconomics environment
3. Geographic effects
4. Moral values, ethics and beliefs of the populace

The companies face competition that can be defined as competitors having major price advantage, product innovation or better technology. There can be variations in the impact of competition brand-wise, product-wise or area-wise

As companies plan to enter international markets they can have the following objectives with them:

1. Expansion of sales volumes
2. Acquisition of resources
3. Diversification
4. Minimizing the risk from competition

Companies can go to the international markets taking the following routes:

1. Importing and exporting
2. Licensing and franchising
3. Turnkey operations

4. Joint ventures
5. Wholly owned subsidiaries
6. Tourism and transportation
7. Management contracts
8. Direct and portfolio management

With more and more markets opening up in the world trade joining the market driven economy companies are axing global competition and hence they must plan to go international to increase their markets and offset the effects of international players in the home markets.

Large firms of today in India (and elsewhere too) like Tata Steels came about because of the entrepreneurial spirit of Founding Fathers who started as dealers in steel scrap. Nanda's of Escorts started as transporters but it was the dynamic vision of the management, which carved out a giant business enterprise. Companies grow as they earn profits and in India the period prior to the 1991 was perhaps the golden age for Indian business, with low level of competition for firms to keep achieving progress. Now with increased competition with several international players, Multi National Companies, (MNCs) in the arena it would be the better-managed firm, which would be the winner. Marketing as a discipline is emerging to assist the firms in this arduous task before them in the twenty first century.

The days of passivity or boardroom policy making are over, never to come back. The dynamics of the market has assumed the role of decision maker and the firms would do well to keep a constant vigil on the same. A view of the market seen from the Marketing Managers room could be warped and it is the real market place, which holds the answers to the myriads of problems and questions faced by the firms.

Firms have been taking the structured route to making marketing plans which are all to the good. However, now is the time as never before, to take the unorthodox innovative stands and for creating newer premises towards the achievement of firms goals of profitability and growth.

Changes in competitive environment with new players emerging each day, and in changing socio-culture ethos, the plans and policies of yesterday may not work today and tomorrow and yet firms have to decide about the same now. Will the new policy and plans be more effective in the scenario shifts taking place? An attempt is being made to answer these and related questions in this chapter and in the book.

Marketers pride themselves as creators of demand, promoters of goods and of bridging the demand supply gap. Their role is becoming increasingly difficult by the day, because of the rapid changes taking place in the market. Hence, the importance of marketing as a discipline has grown many fold in the last few years.

Marketing goes through the following phases:

1. *Opportunity based marketing:* It deals with the generation of idea by the entrepreneur who believes that a particular product will sell in a given market. He goes about manufacturing the product and then selling it. Most giants of businesses round the world started in this fashion.
2. *Structured formula based marketing:* As companies achieve success they plan to move ahead by increasing their product range, marketing areas through well planned exercises. At this time competition makes its appearance and companies have to start aggressive selling techniques, advertising and promotion plans to combat the same.
3. *Customer centred marketing:* In the last century companies got stuck in their own quagmire of market ignorance. Today, companies investing in market knowledge, ready to be on the customer's side on a continuous basis to get a feel of what the customer really wants are more likely to survive the increasing onslaught of competitive forces.

Marketing wants to get answers to questions like the best ways of planning strategies for creating markets, promoting and supplying goods to the customers. They want answers to the five W and one H question given below:

- Who are our customers?
- What product they want to buy?
- Where they want to buy it?
- Why they want to buy?
- What price they are willing to pay for it?
- How they want to buy-cash or credit?

Seeing the importance of marketing function, while most companies have Marketing Managers, the function remains under the direct supervision of the CEO of the company. The CEO needs to keep the hierarchy in the marketing department on the flatter side to assist in faster decision-making. The days of armchair marketing management are over and success comes only to those who are with their customer for maximum time. This way they will understand the real buyer's whims and fancies besides his approach to brand understanding and brand attitudes. This does not reduce the need for marketing research on continuous basis. Besides the CEO needs to select only the strongly committed and excessively active marketing team members if he is looking for unqualified success. The idea is to develop great relations with the customers. Therefore the study of Customers Relationship Management has assumed importance in today's marketing. Some companies build ownership clubs where the customers meet. This is true in the car industry. Another tool used by marketers is the Market Focus tool, where the entire marketing strength is focused on a selected market segment. This focus builds synergy between the sellers and buyers as it leads to thinking commonality. Limited distribution geographic area coupled with intense advertising and promotion as against the larger coverage, would bring in more loyal customers. However, the main sales plank should always remain the company's product quality and the entire organization must be committed to upholding it. The next two exercises needed are brand building and image building of the company.

The company has to understand the level of satisfaction or delight the customers derive from its product as also the value they attach to it. Value can be seen as a combination of the product benefits, its price and the service provided by the company. Value is considered as the ratio between the benefits and the price the customer pays for the product. Customers get both physical and emotional benefits from the product like the Mercedes car gives ease of travel plus an idea of comfort and status. Companies can increase the value by increasing the possible benefits; along with reducing the selling price.

The marketers can perceive the type of demand that exists in the market for their products, starting from a situation of no demand to latent demand, besides there can be irregular demand, seasonal demand, full demand and overfull demand. Once the marketer becomes aware of the kind of demand that exists, he can plan marketing strategies accordingly.

Marketers sell the Products, which can be classified as follows:

A. Consumer goods including
   a. Consumer Durables like cars, refrigerators, air conditioners,
   b. Fast Moving Consumer Goods (FMCGs), like soaps, shampoos, petrol

B. Industrial goods including
   a. Capital Goods, like cotton mill, steel rolling mill,
   b. Raw Materials and Components, like TV Picture tubes, plastic, wood, cotton

c. Consumables, like power, water, gas

C. Services, like hotels, hospitals, travel agencies

Besides other product in the market are ideas, events, properties, people, organizations, and information.

From the above it can be seen that there are different kinds of markets as given below:

1. Consumer market
2. Business market
3. Services market
4. Global market

Today the **Service Industry** has become a major thrust area and needs special marketing techniques. Hotels, Airlines, Hospitals, Electricity Supply, Telecom as products have their own set of demands and are catered to in different styles. However, the main focus remains on the most important person in the game of marketing – the **Customer**. It may be worth mentioning here that most products have service component and most services have a product component too.

Product supply chain determines the speed with which a product can reach the ultimate customer. While the longer the chain bigger the add-on sales commission, it would help the customers in getting the product where they want it.

Companies need to be thoroughly aware of the **competition** they are facing in their market. It could be of their Brand, when competitors offer similar product at competitive prices and are catering to the same group of customers. Industry competition is seen as all the firms offering same products. Then there is competition of form like the railways face from bus service. Generic competition covers all the products vying for the rupee being spent by the customers on any product purchase.

In the past, say first half of twentieth century, the importance of different disciplines of management was equal as shown below in figure [2.1]

Marketing	Finance
Personner	Production

Fig. 2.1. Management Functions

Later on, in the seventies came the concept that marketing is most important of the disciplines and the shift in importance can be shown as in figure 2.2.

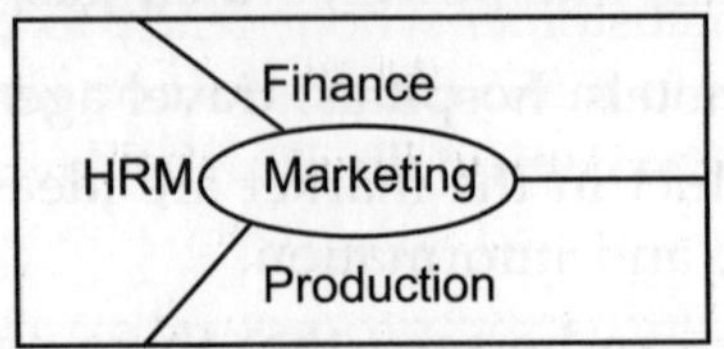

Fig. 2.2. Management Functions

As given above, personnel, finance and production started revolving around marketing. The picture changed again and in the last decade of twentieth century, the focus shifted from marketing, to Customer as shown in figure 2.3.

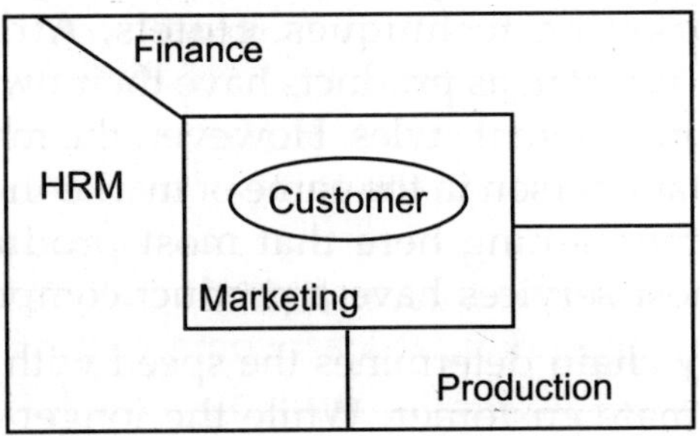

Fig. 2.3. New Focus on Management Functions

There are types of markets as per the products listed above, the consumer markets, industrial markets and service markets. Now with globalization a reality, in India the global markets for these products have opened up and need careful study.

Defining Marketing

Marketing is defined in the following ways by eminent marketing personalities:

1. From Philip Kotler—Marketing is a social process by which individuals and groups obtain what they need and want through creating offering and freely exchanging products and services of value with others.
2. Peter Drucker another Management Guru defines marketing as follows:

   There will always, one can assume, be need for some selling. But the aim of marketing is to make selling superfluous. The aim of marketing is to know and understand the customer so well that the product or service fits him and sells itself. Ideally, marketing should result in a customer who is ready to buy. All that should be needed then is to make the product or service available.

3. The American Marketing Association defines marketing as follows:

Marketing Management is the process of planning and executing the conception, pricing, promotion, and distribution of ideas, goods and services to create exchanges that satisfy individual and organizational goals.

All these definitions have some merit in them and yet the last one from American Marketing Association is the most relevant today.

MARKETING THOUGHT

The basics of marketing can be fully evaluated by understanding the following:

The area in which the product is to be sold relates to the buyers. The FMCGs are products for mass consumption and are sold through marketing channels. It implies that for the product there is a demand and if not the entire population, at least some part of it needs it and would buy it if it is made available to them, with easy access. Hence there is a need to define the market.

Market defined—market for a product can be defined as the geographic area in which most of the buyers reside. As the products use changes with age, income, cultural background, religion, the market definition takes a broader perspective. As each group of customers need a large number of products. There are a number of brands available for each product, sales outlets with multiple products; sometimes even bundled together. This has transformed the market in the last century.

Besides the physical market, we all know about a virtual market, which has emerged as shopping is being done by logging on to the Internet too.

The business sequence can be shown as follow in figure 2.4

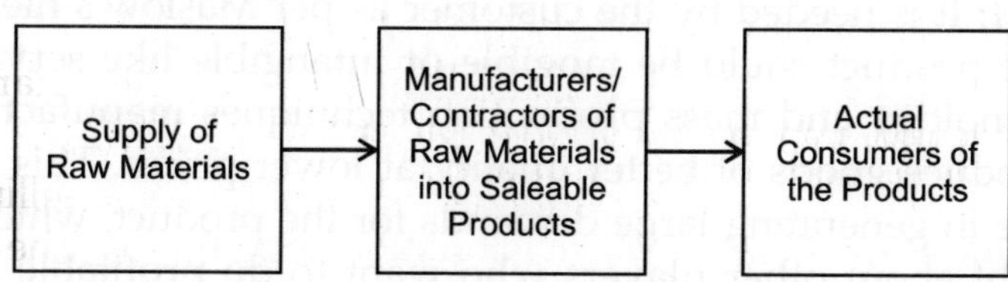

Fig. 2.4. The Business Sequence

Hence, the manufacturers are customers of the raw material suppliers, as the consumers are the customers of manufactured products.

The manufacturer has to buy or arrange the following:

- Human resources
- Technology or information
- Capital goods
- Finances
- Ancillaries like power, water
- Raw materials

These are therefore, the products, which are bought and sold. Buying and selling are legal transactions, which are governed by the sales contracts as given below:

Sales Contract

A sales contract has the following characteristics:

- At least two parties
- A product/service one of the parties wants to sell and the others want to buy
- There is a price or consideration to be paid in exchange of the product/service
- The exchange of product/service with its price takes place with total consent and willingness of all parties concerned
- Each party believes that the transaction has been fair to them.
- The product/service to be sold must be a legal/legitimate product for the contract to be valid and legally binding on the concerned parties

Consequent to the above, a gift given by one party to the other is not sale and transaction of dubious product like drugs is not legally valid.

Now let us discuss the concept of four Ps as relevant to marketing.

The 4 Ps are- Product, Price, Placement and Promotion, these relate to the customer directly as follows:

Product: It is needed by the customer as per Maslow's hierarchy of needs. The product could be tangible or intangible like service. With better technology and mass production techniques manufacturers are able to produce goods of better quality at lower prices. This has been responsible in generating large demands for the product, which in turn has brought about other players who want to do profitable business. Thus competition comes in, which divides the total business and profits.

Competition is good and useful especially for the customers as it gives them the choice of brands and reasonable prices.

In order to be one up on competition marketers have to ensure the suitability of the product for the customers, its quality, performance and aesthetics. Product planning therefore should never start only with availability of technology and finance, but with knowledge of the market regarding market needs.

Price: It is the worth of the product in customer's mind. If the customer finds price high than he is not likely to buy it. The customer judges the production its satisfaction value as follows-

Satisfaction Value: Price/usefulness of the product.

Placement: Provides customers Convenience of shopping without problems.

Promotion: It is the communication, which makes customer aware of the availability, price and distribution channels of the product.

If we consider the historical concept of period before the advent of markets, people were fulfilling their needs by exchanging the products they possessed, bartering them. Later on with multi-product and multiple sellers the concept of money and markets came about, which changed the way of doing business completely in the market place. In India even today there are Melas or weekly Hats or Bazaars, which cater to the needs of people, living in the vicinity.

Severe competition has helped markets to develop. Sellers are considering the needs of buyers and trying to fulfill them in manners most suited to the customers. A business is set up for making profits and profit and growth remain its most basic goals. In order to generate profits, which in turn would be responsible for organizational growth, firms take to satisfying the customer. The next stage is providing delight to the customer. Most marketers describe customer as the king. The business exists because of the customer and it is not the other way round.

In good old days of the first half of the twentieth century, the competition was mild and most products were sold and profits came from volume business. There was always a scarcity of products. it was only in the last quarter of the century, that firms started feeling the onslaught of competition.

Today, with competition becoming severe for almost all the products the marketers have realized that profits will come only by satisfying customer needs and with customer satisfaction.

We have discussed the Maslow's hierarchy of needs. Let us now see what types of needs are there—

- Needs expressed by the customers—I want electronic washing machine
- Needs as real or genuine needs—a low cost affordable washing machine
- Implied needs—prompt after sales service
- Needs for making customers happy—free washing powder for a month

This gives the seller an opportunity to satisfy the different needs to ensure that the customers stay with them.

Beyond the customer's needs:

The adventurous and innovative minds have been developing products without knowing customer's demands or even bothering about sales prospects of the product. But for the human ingenuity, even the wheel would not have been invented leave aside later products which kept on revolutionizing the human existence, like, the locomotives, internal combustion engine, aircraft, electricity, telephone with its new version of cell-phone. The list is almost endless, but today, we cannot imagine our lives without these products.

Once a new concept product is invented, productionized and is ready for market, the task of marketing starts, as starting from concept selling, the product demand creation and supply has to be organized.

Profitability: With increasing competition profits in most product sales have eroded. Marketers have, therefore changed the age-old orientation by putting the customer first in the hierarchy of their business, the CEO, DOES NOT HOLD THE POSITION OF SUPERIORITY ANY MORE. Likewise, the front line managers who are actively soliciting business from the customers and who are directly in the know of their needs are the decision makers affecting the business and not the CEO.

This market turnaround has taken place worldwide due to following emerging factors in the world of business:

- Competition takes away much of the business
- Customers are not loyal to their products
- Competitors are using promotional tactics to win over the customers
- Products may have reached stage of maturity
- Advertising and selling costs are increasing

It is therefore important that marketers trust the front line managers to decide about the way they handle the customers. They are the eyes and ears of the firm and are in the best position to take the most appropriate decisions.

Let us understand the major business processes to integrate the same with marketing.

There are three CORE PROCESSES in business, namely, Product Development Process, Demand Management Process and Order Fulfillment Process. They can be defined as follows-

Product Development Process: Focusses on

1. Product idea generation mostly by the entrepreneur,
2. Confirmation of the need of the product in the market of the idea (product) by market research,
3. R&D for development of technology or purchase of technology.

Once the product is ready for the market after going through this process, it becomes the responsibility of the Production Department, which has to productionize it.

Demand Management Process: Includes,

1. Continuous market surveys to keep a hand on the market pulse, which helps firms remain proactive to customer needs and market dynamics,
2. Pricing and related aspects of discounts, leasing options, distribution network, personal selling, advertising, promotion and credit and it's control.

Order Fulfillment Process: Starts with—

1. Vendor development, purchasing, inbound logistics to conversion/production/manufacturing followed by outbound logistics.

It can be noticed that the **Demand Management Process** deals with the marketing aspects of business. It is definitely a Core Process as it builds up the firm's cash base, brings in profits and becomes responsible for its growth.

In the period post liberalization i.e. 1991, marketing is not only for providing value for money but also a sustained interest in continuous usage of the product by what marketers today call the Customer's Delight. Naturally the marketer cannot provide customer's delight to the entire population and hence he has to locate his niche/segment market. Once the market has been identified as THE market segment, marketer has to produce product to suit that segment. For example the market segment for Mercedes car in India would be the affluent class, while for Maruti 800 it would be urban middle class.

At this point it is good to understand the sale process, which ULTIMATELY is the aim of marketing as given below:

SALES PROCESS

There are usually two parties in a sale, the seller and the buyer. There has to be a product and the consideration against which the seller is going to transfer the product's ownership to the buyer that is its price. The process can be depicted as follows in figure 2.5-

Fig. 2.5. The Sales Process I

When there is a seller offering a product, which is accepted, to be bought by a buyer against payment it amounts to a sales contract and it is valid in the court of law. Hence it is important for both sellers and buyers to understand the entire system of sales-purchase. And that system, in today's world of severe competitive product offerings takes the shape of MARKETING, as against pure selling of good old days.

In a larger context, with several players offering the same product, as also there are several buyers, the market place can be depicted as given below in figure 2.6.

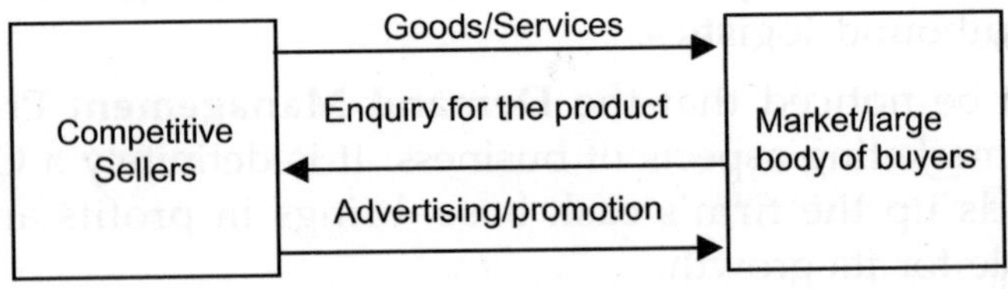

Fig. 2.6. The Sales Process II

Competitive sellers advertising and promote their products. On viewing the same, the large body of customer enquires about the product. Next, the customer buys the product in exchange of money, which he pays to the seller.

Market consists of firm's product buyers, competitive product buyers and present non-buyers, who could be potential buyers tomorrow. Potential buyers may have a latent demand, which can manifest once the right type of communication reaches them as shown in figure 2.7 below:

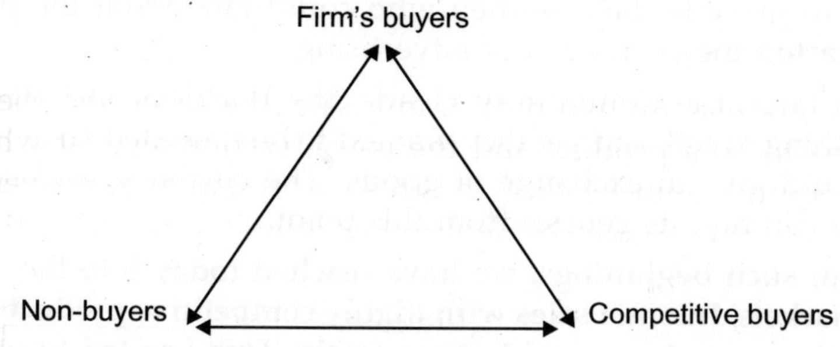

Fig. 2.7. Potential Buyer

Buyer motivation depends on the satisfaction or benefits, which can be derived from the product. As can be seen there are tangible benefits or benefits which help in making some area in a persons life easier for the buyer or benefit could be such, which provide mental or psychic satisfaction to the buyer.

Competition cannot be and should not be wished away as they play a vital role in the marketing process that of keeping firms on their toes. Competition also provides the customers with choices of products available in the market to make them aware of the real worth of firm's product. Competition comes from firms with same products or similar products. Some extension of competition takes place when a TV Manufacturer feels that refrigerator manufacturers also provide him competition and so do holiday tour operators, who vie for the buyers rupees.

Before going into the next steps in marketing of today, let us look at the evolution of marketing as we see it.

Market Evolution

In the beginning of the time, people lived in caves, hunted for food and searched for edible roots, fruits. The division of work or of labor started with more proficient hunters going for the beasts while others kept the search for vegetable foods. Next, minerals were found. The women were engaged in preparing food for eating and shaping the animal hides for wearing and using minerals as cosmetics. We can consider the women as manufacturers of that time.

Later, people found that they had a little surplus of a few items of food or clothing while they needed some others. This leads to persons going with their ware to neighboring areas to barter their products with those of the areas they were visiting. These persons were the first salesmen. As the commerce increased, it became necessary for some people to precede the salesmen who could talk about the products. Thus started the profession of advertising.

Still later, the Community Heads, the Warriors and others who had nothing to sell, and yet they wanted to buy, needed an item, which they could give in exchange of goods. The currency, and monetary systems can find its genesis from this point.

From such beginnings, we have reached today into the world of supermarkets, Internet sales with highly competitive products coming out in the market on a continuous basis. This has led to organized market research into the needs of the customers, Research and Development for developing such products, besides other innovative products which find market eventually, like the cell phone, diverse and complex product distribution systems. The government of the country with it's monitory systems, money supply organizations and greater awareness of products and their needs among the customers, has made the market place complex as also rewarding.

Initially, however, Sales Management was, under the purview of the Producers of goods, the Manufacturers who went out with their produce to sell to the market place. With increase in number of producers, the supply became smore than the demand for most products, resulting in the specialized discipline of Salesmanship. With increase in competition, it was soon found that only glib talk of a salesman was not enough. Paying public wanted value for money. An era of quality consciousness, better packaging, branding started emerging.

The sequence of market development can thus be shown as given below in figure 2.8.

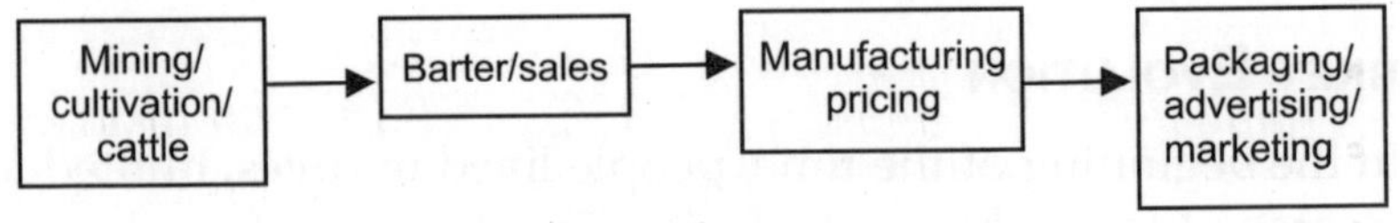

Fig. 2.8. Market Development

Later periods saw the burgeoning Distribution Channels, rise of Middleman, the Agency System, Credit Sales, and Hire-Purchase.

Over a period of time the concept of just Selling got converted into the Grand Marketing Phenomenon.

Tracing back the evolution of commerce, we find that after the age of barter, beginning from last decade of nineteenth century, sales became an important discipline in business. During that time Industrial Revolution started in Europe followed by Mass Manufacturing Techniques –the Assembly Line Operation, which as per experts was propagated by Henry Ford of the Ford Motor Company. The result was increased production of Goods. Hence, for most products, the supply exceeded demand. It was natural, under the circumstances that the manufacturers had to resort to hard sell, or power selling techniques. Salesmanship became an extremely valued profession. Successful salesmen believed that salesmen are born and people cannot be trained to become good salesmen. And yet training for salesmanship started in right earnest in early twentieth century.

At that time, besides Salesman's profession, other areas of work opened up like that of Brokers, Sales Agents, Distributors and the Service People. Detailed discussion on the subject is available elsewhere in the book on chapter on distribution.

BROKERS – a broker rarely handles the goods. He helps manufacturers to sell the products and for getting the orders for sale-concluding the sales contract, he gets Commission or brokerage from the manufacturer on the basis of the value of the contract. The manufacturer supplies the goods to the buyer, invoices the goods and collects the money. In some cases the broker could be involved in getting the payments on behalf of the manufacturer depending on the agreement between the broker and the manufacturer.

Agents are the people, who act on behalf of some other person, like on behalf of the manufacturers. In trade there are several types of agents, like—

- Selling agents
- Commission agents
- Consignment agents
- Advertising agents
- Forwarding agents
- Buying agents
- Collection agents
- Credit enquiry agents

Detailed discussion about these also is available in the book in the chapter on distribution.

CHANGING BUSINESS SCENARIO IN THE TWENTY-FIRST CENTURY

- Opening of country's economy
- Global competition
- Better quality products
- A large variety of models of same products
- High- tech products
- New channels of distribution
- New channels/media for advertising
- Educated well informed customers, who are aware of their rights
- Complaint redress forums

In 1991, Government of India changed the rules of the business game as follows:

- Removal of license to manufacture for most products
- Foreign equity allowed in industries
- Lower rates of import duty
- Partial convertibility of rupee
- Lowering of importance of government/public sector business

The above resulted in several global players getting in to the country with massive investments. Later changes in governments, led to slowing down of economy and reforms and in many cases foreign firms found that the large investments have not borne the expected results e.g. Daewoo Motors. However with a large purchase group of some two hundred million people, the foreign firms believe that they can yet make a profit by just perseving in India.

Lowering import duty has helped in exports as export related manufacturers could get their raw materials imported without any problem. This has also helped foreign firms in getting their products for Indian market, giving Indian customer the choice of a variety of goods, of better quality and well-known international brands.

Partial convertibility of Rupee has helped exporters in more that one way, by allowing them unrestricted imports.

Public sector or government owned firms have lost their importance over the years and now the government has put quite a few of them for disinvestments. The fact that there is a ministry of Disinvestments in the Centre shows the importance the government of India places on these disinvestments.

Let us examine some of the areas the sales person of the twentieth century has to cover, either singly or as a team. The following points give an idea of the activities connected with the Sales Persons:

- Order taker- the role of order— taker for the sales person is age old conventional one. In the early twentieth century the salesman (there were hardly any sales girls at that time), were carrying their ware with them to show samples to the customers and to demonstrate if the product called for the same. In fact co-passengers, while travelling in a train, mistook an oil company salesman for a masseur as he was carrying small sample bottles of lubricating oil.
- Delivery Sales Person— for products of mass consumption like milk, fuel, the salesman carries the product in tankers and makes a sale by down loading the same at the customer's premises in his containers.
- Sales Promoter—the person does not take orders from the customers. He only makes the customer interested in the product with the help of demonstrations and discussions. Pharmaceutical firms have these types of Medical supervisors who meet with the doctors with product literature and samples and try to convince the doctor for prescribing the medicine.
- Technical Sales Person—he is usually an engineer who has proficiency in optimizing the usage of the product and he works with the customer's engineers as their technical support person.
- Demand Manager—the sales person is required to create demand by concept selling, demonstrations and product promotions.
- Solution Giver—has the answers to customer's problems. He works like an applications laboratory whose job is to tackle live problems and provide answers. He is a big aid to the order taker salesman.
- Overseas Salesman—who handles international business for the firm. His main job is to sell the Country first and bring INDIA'S BRAND EQUITY on the top, before he can sell his products.

Business Scenario in India

While the Industrial Revolution had started in Europe in the eighteenth century it did not touch India till the period after country's independence in 1947. After 1947, the first Prime Minister Pundit Jawaharlal Nehru and the Government of India made the country a socialist republic, with emphasis on government's role in business and industry. A large number of Public Sector Undertakings were formed with government funding and management. Private sector companies were considered as dishonest and therefore, there was a lot of government control with licenses and permits required by the businessmen. Without the approval of the government officers the private entrepreneur could not do any business. This led to rampant corruption and bribery as means of getting approvals speedily by the government offices. A new breed of Power Brokers emerged as go-betweens between business and the government. The only concession to private business was for the small-scale sector. Business suffered, as the Public Sector firms could not bring about the needed economic growth due to governmental interference and lack of accountability of the managers. And private sector was already handicapped.

There were a few exceptions though, like the Bajaj group, the Reliance group, who forged ahead despite the hurdles. The early big names of Tata, Birla, Modi, Singhania , Bangur, to name a few, kept the struggle going.

It was only in 1991, that the government found itself on the back foot with regard to its Foreign Exchange reserves, which had reached an all time low. On the request of the government of India, the World Bank and IMF agreed to provide loans on the condition that India opens it's business boundaries to international players. This resulted in the economic reforms stated above.

Market Environment

Introduction—Marketers find business opportunities to succeed, make profits and grow. These opportunities appear outside of the firm, in the market place for which constant vigil is required. Marketer cannot just afford to wait for changes in market place to take place. He has to be closely associated with the changes; at times he can be instrumental, to an extent in making the changes. Even if he cannot mould the changes to his benefit, he should certainly monitor the same to get the maximum mileage from the changes.

In the twenty-first century the following can be highlighted as predominant changes or happenings in India:

- Market globalization and its effect on Indian economy
- Market recession
- Larger number of women in urban workforce including in positions of strength.
- Large production capacities, mostly idle

- Emergence of IT sector and its decline
- Growth of Management Schools
- Strong satellite television base with hundreds of channels giving jobs to millions of Indians.
- Invasion of Chinese products in various fields.
- Political problems including internal and external threats to country's suzerainty.
- Religious fundamentalism
- Privatization of government owned firms
- Genetic engineering and its effect of farm produce
- Rampant misuse of public funds

Market Globalization: In 1991, the then government of India decided to open the country's economy to the outside world, which resulted in several Multi-national firms starting their operations in India. While it brought severe competition for the Indian firms, in its wake it opened up a variety of products, competitive prices, superior quality, for the Indian customer. The removal of import restrictions on products, technology and finance it was expected that Indian economy would start booming. However, due to global recession, cash flow limitations it did not happen. With adequate measures and the political will of government, the business and economy should be looking up again by the year 2003. India has yet to fully enjoy the fruits of liberalized, privatized and globalized Indian economy

Market Recession: When the production or the availability of goods exceeds its demand, the industry faces recession. Added to the large production bases set up by the MNC Companies, the tragedy of 11th September 2001, in America and that of 12th December 2001 in India has further made the market apprehensive causing to down size the demand of goods and services further. Tourism industry has been the worst sufferer as traveling to sensitive areas is no longer popular. Reduction in interest rates, ease of getting loans is the means of rejuvenating the market.

Women Managers: With pursuit of higher living standards, one income does not cope with the demand. Women at different levels in almost each area of work are a common phenomenon. The result is need of time saving consumer durables like washing machines, vacuum cleaners, instant foods, and microwave ovens. It also involves setting up of crèches for the children or **may be return to the joint family system where the grand parents can look after the small children.**

Idle Production Capacities: An assessment of the sales promotional plans for virtually all the products in the consumer range tells that the excess capacity generated by the industry is responsible for the recession in the market as also, labor layoffs resulting in labor unrest. Export markets need to be targeted to come out of the problem.

IT Sector's Emergence: From the 1995, IT industry got a major boost because of improvement in landline telephony improvements. Internet, e-mail, e-commerce are the things of today and tomorrow. With information becoming available on fingertips, decision making corporate process has vastly speeded up. IT and computer education took giant strides in the last five years but today at least temporarily it has lost its glory. LAN, WAN and Internet connectivity has been helped by larger storage capacities in the computer today as also greatly increased speeds. No field of the government or private enterprise is untouched by IT today.

Growth of Management Schools: With the type of corporate growth envisaged in the early part of 1990s, the need for trained managers was deeply felt and several small or big Management Schools were opened. With sudden increase in numbers, the quality of students and that of the faculty both suffered. As the business did not take off, the MBAs coming out of these schools are getting frustrate with lack of job potential which causes them to take up any job and such under employed managers can do much harm to the firm they are serving and themselves too.

Television Explosion: From 1982, the colour TV came to India, followed by terrestrial links and satellite channels. This has resulted in creation of countless jobs in both software and hard ware areas. More than 100 channels need news software feeds, social serials, sitcoms, news and thrillers. Number of actors, producers, and directors to the light man, spot boys are all needed. Further, television has become arguably the most popular advertising media, due to its instant audio-visual effect on the audience. Television offers the opportunity to actually demonstrate the use of the product and its benefits.

Foreign Goods Especially Chinese: Opening of economy has created competition for all sectors of Indian business, including small-scale sector. Chinese have taken the opportunity to fully exploit the market in India. Small glass figurines, fancy tidbits, pirated software are available at affordable prices. Chinese entry in to WTO may have positive effect on the Chinese exporters and we get Chinese products, which are in consonance with world trade practices. Our small scale and other marketers should take a cue from the Chinese and start exporting to china to compensate for the loss in market share in India because of the Chinese invasion in the market.

Political Turmoil within the Country and in the World: The happenings on the World Trade Tower in the USA, attack on Indian parliament, Afghanistan, happenings in Gujarat, besides other places in the country and the world have had an adverse effect on the business in the country. A stable government and peace in the region are fundamental to the health of business and commerce in any country.

Religious Fundamentalism: India is a secular country, which gives equal importance to every religion. The Gujarat turmoil, its repercussions in the rest of the country have done a lot of damage for business in the country.

Privatization of Government Firms: From the time India became independent, the government had been giving greater importance to the government owned firms as compared to the private firms. Due to lack of accountability, and inefficiency the government firms have been losing almost from the beginning, barring a few exceptions. Now the government has started giving some of the firms in to private hands to improve their own finance by getting the sale price and also giving these firms a chance to recover from the losses and add to the Gross Domestic Product of the country.

Genetic Engineering and Farm Produce: Genetic engineering has helped in the green revolution happening once again in the country. With self-sufficiency in food grains India can hope to export them as well and can now really concentrate on total economic development.

Rampant Misuse of Public Funds: Bribery and corruption has become a way of life in the country. It will be the major task of the youth to ensure that these are put to end at the earliest. A major reason of erosion of welfare funds is that they do not reach the real and genuine needy persons and others in the middle take a big piece of cake.

Looking at the Indian life, its economics and politics, a lot many areas affecting business can be isolated. More importantly, the above-mentioned factors are ever changing and marketers must keep a close vigil on them to accurately assess the opportunities and threats offered by them. Given below is a method of doing just that.

Business General Environment: The following need to be studied, assessed, screened and monitored in the context of the country for correct planning of marketing strategies.

- *Demographic Factors:* these are brought out in the census of the country, factors like, population dispersion in towns, villages, income levels for families, sex ratios, religious numbers. Shifts of population from villages to towns, from small towns to metro towns provide business opportunities, which no marketer can afford to miss. For a start low cost housing, clothings, transportation eateries are needed.
- *Social Factors:* like increase of working women in towns at all levels of income. It has given rise to a big boost in demand for time saving equipments like, washing machines, vacuum cleaners, microwave ovens, precooked foods. As women are coming out of homes, better dresses, cosmetics, health gyms are required. With double family income leisure time activities products, holiday outings, travels are looking up.
- *Cultural Factors:* India is a land of rich cultural heritage. Its culture is rich and diverse. Marketers and advertisers take full advantage of knowing the buying season in different parts of the country. During Deepavali, Hindus buy new clothes, household articles and exchange gifts. Muslims do it on Eid, Christians on Christmas. The cultural ethos provides innumerable themes for promoting sales. India is a vast country, with twenty languages spoken, several religions and varied cultures and sub-cultures. For example, in Punjab, there is the Punjabi culture and with in there is the Sikh sub culture. Karnataka has the Kannad culture and then the Coorg Subculture.
- *Political Factors:* It was the political will of the then government, which led to LPG, (Liberalization, Privatization and Globalization.), in 1991. The influx of foreign capital, setting up manufacturing bases, joint ventures all sprung up from then onwards. Changes in Cash Reserve Ratio, taxation rates, duties are the political factors which have a major impact on business.
- *Legal Factors:* Supreme Courts directives have made car manufactures change the emission standards to Euro II. Diesel buses are on their way out in Delhi for the same reason. Ignoring the law of the lands can be detrimental to the interests of the firms operating in the country.
- *Macroeconomics Factors:* The interest rates, taxes and duties, balance of payment situation with the countries the firm wants to do business with, foreign currency rate fluctuations have major impacts on business and they must be well understood by the firm.

- *Technology Factors:* In the past decade, information technology, telecom, biotechnology, genetic engineering have revolutionized the business scene in the world as also Indian business scene.
- *Global Factors:* From the last decade, breaking of the Berlin wall with reunification of Germanys, breaking up of the USSR, and more recent attack on the World Trade Tower in the New York, on the Indian parliament liberation of Afghanistan have affected business worldwide and most countries are trying to recover the lost ground. On the brighter side the development in the area of medicine, agriculture and farming cloning of the sheep have helped in the giant strides the world is taking towards a better future for its children. Following are the major elements in globalized economy:
  - i. World becoming smaller due to faster movement through supersonic jets, faster world communications through Internet.
  - ii. Strong trade zones like European Union, NAFTA, ASEAN
  - iii. Market economy in Russia
  - iv. Multinational, Transnational firms
  - v. International strategic alliances
  - vi. Global brands in foods like Kellogg's and cars

Indian business irrespective of its size cannot remain unaffected by the onslaught of globalization. Small firms, which were protected by government laws, are now facing severe competition from well-known international brands, and unless they have been able to sign up with a reputed international technology they are getting left out in the race. Surviving in the market jungle today can be defined by the criticality of the firm's marketing strength only.

Competitive Business environment can be studied with the help of Michael Porter's 5 Force Model.

Present Scene in India

Now the present scene in India can be described as follows:

- A good number of MNC's have started operating in the country.
- Some Indian business have got foreign technology and finance
- Market growth has slowed down world wide and more so in India
- Stock market has been giving shocks with fluctuations and scams
- Terrorists have further down- swept the market, especially in areas like Kashmir

- Advertising and almost continuous promotion has become omnipresent
- Job market has slowed down both in India and elsewhere.
- IT Industry has had a set back
- Lot of firms are busy in down sizing/ right sizing their operations

What the future holds is difficult to predict. One thing, which can be said with certainty, is that while specialists will give way to generalists, to handle cross functional areas, like marketing and purchasing, innovation and quality of their products will play a vital role in the success of any firm.

India is a vast country with lots of diversities. Punjab and Andhra are known as the granaries of India. Farm labour during harvesting season, migrates to Punjab from Bihar. Bihar is a rich state in minerals including iron and coal. It boasts of large steel plants and yet it has remained largely under developed. Youths have taken to guns and there are a lot of Mafia gangs operating in Bihar. West Bengal and Kerala have had Marxist influence. West Bengal has suffered from labor unrest resulting in migration of industries from there, which was, at a time the industrial capital of the country. Kerala has the highest literacy rate in the country. Uttar Pradesh, Bihar and Madhya Pradesh were three largest states and now they have been bifurcated. Hopefully, this will help them in becoming better managed. Mumbai has emerged as the commercial capital and Bangalore as the IT capital of the country. Bangalore is a cosmopolitan city with good climate through out the year.

India has large disparities as far as personal incomes are concerned. More than seventy percent of population lives in villages, with farming as their source of income. With increase in population the land size per family gets smaller ever so often, resulting in migration from villages to towns. Metros like Delhi and Mumbai population increase has taken its toll on the civic services, which keep crumbling. With better health facilities, average age has increased and now India has a large population of senior citizens. Teen population has also increased with improved health care.

India has seen social evolution of women who are now taking active part in various activities. They can be seen in offices, politics, and defense services, practically in each sphere of human endeavour.

A good businessperson needs to keep a close watch over these happenings to trace business opportunities, as newer products are needed now with innovative ideas, better distribution and customer communication. Working women need time saving devices like, vacuum cleaners, washing machines, pressure cookers, precooked foods.

Indian business suffers from lack of awareness among international community about the quality of its products. A few black sheep who got orders from overseas by sending good samples and later on, down grading product quality, have tarnished country's image, which needs to be redeemed. Concentrated efforts by the government and industry are required for changing the India Brand image overseas. We have many pluses like low cost labor, raw materials and a large trained work force. Today, Industry, Commerce and the Government are busy in trying to correct things and their effort needs to be strengthened and speeded up. Indian Embassies abroad play a vital role in projecting the right image of the country, its products and services in the countries they operate. They can also provide inputs to Indian business about product demand patterns overseas.

To take an example, Japanese embassy in India is doing a great job in helping Japanese business in locating business opportunities for Japanese firms. Besides, Japanese organization Jethro is providing the information on Indian industry. Japan also has a number of business liaison offices, which assist Japanese business in getting a foothold in India. All these have resulted in better Japanese business activities in India.

International business today needs continuous information on the following aspects for different countries, where Indian firms want to do business:

- Business environment of the country
- Product demand projection
- Competitive forces

This calls for continuous Marketing Research, and Indian business must organize it as required. Besides, the Government of India needs to reassess its efforts in building India Brand Equity, for which proper planning and funding are important. These efforts will surely bring fruits and result in better International Business from India. A few years ago the Government had started such a program and now it needs to be reactivated with greater zeal.

Besides the traditional exports from India of core products, exports and joint ventures for other products need to be planned. India has a large heritage of ethnic goods, labour oriented products, which need to be nurtured with care. India is also rich in culture, has a large number of religious places, and other places of tourist interests. Tourist industry is still in its infancy if we compare ourselves with the total international tourism. India needs better infrastructure in terms of hotels, transportation, communication and entertainment to attract tourists from the world over.

Unfortunately, India's image has been badly tarnished with the numerous scams, which have surfaced in the recent past. To an outsider, India appears to be ridden with corruption, infested with cheats and its people are supposed to be lacking character. It is time that the people got their act together and kept the country's interest uppermost and not their own.

Ethics in business is a must if we are to emerge as a world lead player in business and commerce as well. Our firms have been blamed for transgression in to Intellectual property rights area with availability of pirated products has become a reality. As regards advertising is concerned there exists a body, the Advertising Standards Council of India that monitors transgression by advertisment and the council can ban any advertisement, which is considered as obscene or incorrect.

Business Myopia

Business needs to define its purpose, its goals and objectives to become successful. Usually business is started with a visionary's zeal. The entrepreneur feels the market demand of a product and plans to meet the demand. However, misdirected enthusiasm can only bring grief to the entrepreneur.

Therefore, the need for a business definition and the purpose of business cannot be overemphasized.

What is Our Business?

At every stage we have to understand our business, where we stand and where we want to be. How are we doing in key areas of our business? The following need to be analyzed for making an assessment about the business:

- Profit and loss
- Resource allocation parameters
- Product/s leadership position
- Profit centers
- Organizational structure

In business we convert resources and technological and market knowledge into increased economic value and thereby have a satisfied customer. It is this knowledge which keeps firms afloat and lack of it make them sink. From this premise emerges the age-old saying that the CUSTOMER IS OUR BUSINESS.

Manufacturer's perception of business is his product range, the market demand, competition and his market share. He sees it as an extension of his manufacturing and selling base. After all what he is making, he is selling to the customers who are in the market for the same product. Today, the manufacturer wants his customer to be satisfied by his product. It is accepted that the customers do not buy a product. They buy the satisfaction they derive out of the product. Customers however, view the business as market places with several sellers and thousands of products, some of which may provide them with a degree of satisfaction. They do not even know the number of sellers of a particular product unless they are going to buy the same, at which time they start looking for alternate suppliers of a product. Sellers are aware of the plus points of their firm, its products and seldom look in to or even try to understand their handicaps and minus points. It is always a good idea to crosscheck their own assessment of their good and bad points and areas.

With this view only the businessmen have gone from the concept of selling to that of marketing, which encompasses activities like marketing research, competitive strategies, new market planning and innovative business communications including advertising and publicity. What we have to understand is, are we only doing lip service to these words and are we only involved in the game of selling, which would lead the firm to disaster.

Existing situation is more close to the following:

1. Customer is hardly buying the product, which the seller thinks he is selling. He is buying the satisfaction the product is providing to him. Therefore, if another product provides better satisfaction or a different type of satisfaction he will buy that product. For example, instead of buying a washing machine the customer may use the money for a trip to a hill station.
2. Hence products in direct competition are not the only one's to watch for.
3. Manufacturers and sellers have an idea of what the customer wants. The sellers soon discover how wrong they can be in their idea as the product is launched in the market. TV sellers keep talking about the large number of features, most of which are never used by the buyers, who would prefer just a reliable, east to operate TV.

4. Sellers keep stressing on a particular quality of their product, little realizing that it could be of little use to the buyers. Detergent sellers have been busy in discussions in kitty parties about whose sari is the whitest. Most times, these women are not even cleaning the garments themselves and seldom wear white dresses. To move the customers in to buying decision for the firm's product, it is useful to know what the customer considers as the useful quality. Rational behaviour from the customer is another mistake sellers make. We all as customers buy products we rarely use or buy on impulse to please some one. A lot of study has gone in to Consumer Behaviour to establish some rationality in a psychic activity. Sellers have to know the cause of irrational behaviour and adopt their strategy to suit it. Any attempt to change it would be an exercise in futility.
5. Each seller has to focus on his product. However it must be understood that it is one of the million products out in the market. Customer is a non-caring forgetful person and brands and persons associated with the products are of least importance to him. Large firms close down bringing a lot of problems to their stakeholders. The customer however is least bothered about it. This is the harsh reality, which the firms seldom accept.
6. Most firms assume that they know who their customers are. Understanding the market it should be assumed that firms are usually unaware of it and should get to know the same. Do you think the payer is the buyer or the person who decides the purchase is the customer? There can be firms whose customer group defies a definition. Take the case of a steel plant. Anyone wanting steel is the customer; he may be building houses, cars or even utensils.
7. Could be a builder, a designer, an architect, and a manufacturer among others. Capital equipment manufacturers may find it difficult to define their customers.

It is therefore important to find out where the market exists. One should seek answers to questions like:

- Who wants the product?
- When does he want it?
- Where does he want it?
- What price he is willing to pay for it?

- What is the purpose for which he is buying the product?
- What does the product do for him in his life?
- What are the factors influencing the purchase?
- Who is the competitor?
- What are the competitor's plans?

For each firm, there are the following categories of customers:

- The buyers
- The non-buyers who buy competitive products
- The non-buyers who do not buy the product at all
- The non-buyers who buy the product only rarely
- The vacillators who keep shifting purchase between the firm and competition

It may be a good idea to find out how the customer is spending his discretionary income, the income (also called the disposable income), which he is left with after he has made all necessary payments. How the customer spends money and time? How are the customers trying to get satisfaction from the money they are spending? These insights will offer a clearer idea of consumer's behaviour than any other type of research.

Do we know what our customers and non-customers are buying from our competition and with what satisfaction levels? Are they in competition with our products and services directly and are the satisfaction levels remaining constant or changing both for our products and those of competition? Answers to these questions will provide the required strategies for future action in terms of products and services.

As we get the answers we come to the crunch, do our present and future products likely to provide better satisfaction levels to the customers than those from the competition?

It may be a good idea to play the devil's advocate at this point. Let us ask the question, can our customers do without buying our products? Will it be economic consideration, political will or market changes which will decide on the subject? Can low priced products give way to high performance products irrespective of higher price? Do we have the capacity to meet with such and similar situations? How does the customer work out the value and economics as compared to his satisfaction levels with different products? We have to really know our customers and prospective customers who are buying from competitors today.

It can thus be assumed that it is the knowledge about various elements of business, which is critical to the success of the firm. The knowledge needed is in the following areas:

- Own products, their plus and minus points
- Competitor's products, their plus and minus points
- Niche market, and its business potential
- Relevant customer group, the buyers, users and the purchase decision makers
- Market dynamics

The knowledge needs to be used for, first understanding the market and then planning strategies for achieving leadership position in the market. The knowledge should lead to excellence in operations of the firm else; leadership position will remain a pipe dream only. Profits, on a continued basis result from application of the specialized knowledge by the firm. Excellence in core areas like technology, marketing, finance, government liaison or human resource management is typical of all top-notch firms. The firm need not be large in size, but some core competencies will lead it to a high profit area. What the firm does well and what it does poorly are known facts to the firm and if it wishes it can make the weak areas as strong as others, with determination and will power.

Let us discuss some of the knowledge areas, which help in achieving success:

- Knowledge of own business can be easily understood as the areas of excellence within the firm. Some firms excel in marketing, others in new product development, and yet some pride themselves in the quality of their products and their operations. Knowledge of firm's core competence is important.
- Knowledge of customer needs, both specified or known and unspecified, becomes essential for business development.
- Knowledge of "the state of art technology" relevant to the firm
- Knowledge of competition, their products, markets, technology, core competence and business methods is a must to counter competition.

It must be understood that knowledge is true only for a short period of time and it must be updated for it to remain valid and useful. Let us discuss the different aspects of business as follows:

MARKET AND MANUFACTURE

In the beginning, the producers or manufacturers were small, they sold their wares in local areas, and once the demand for the product got established, the buyers used to throng around the manufacturers to pick up the product as given in figure 2.9

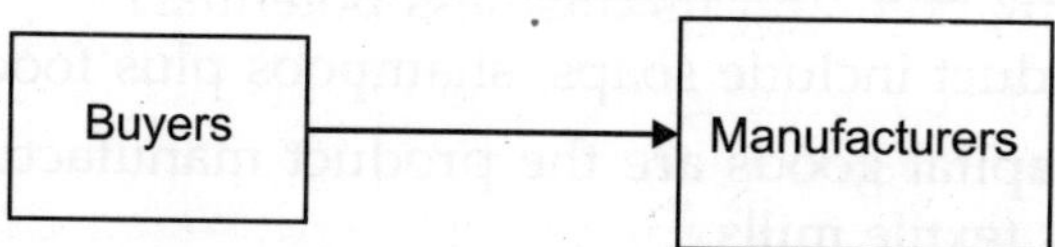

Fig. 2.9. Manufacture Driven Economy

In India till the first half of twentieth century, it was totally sellers market; whatever the manufacturer produced was easily sold. The emphasis was on production and quality was not of much importance. The main reason for the situation was lack of competition and near monopoly situation for almost all the products.

Later on as the competition started seeping in to most business it became imperative that Sales people coordinate with manufacturing team, to give them the idea of demand and the volumes or numbers of product which can be sold, to enable them in production planning. The stress so far stayed on manufacturing. A good firm was which had always a few more orders than the quantity, which could be produced in the given time. This put pressure on manufacturing to produce more goods, further putting the Quality on the back burner.

As manufacturing need raw materials they are buyers of the same plus they buy certain components made by others. Hence, now the picture looks as given below:

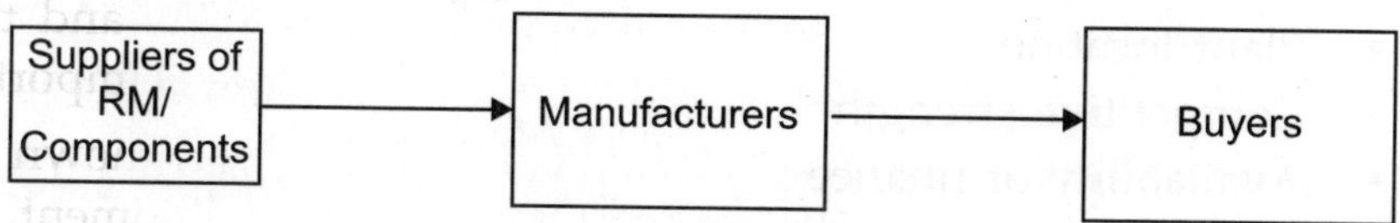

Fig. 2.10. Emphasis on Manufacture

Later still people started just BUYING /SELLING and became vendrs or middleman.

It was from 1991, that India opened its door to foreign players and competition became a major force to reckon with by the businessmen of India.

As for each of the product there is a distinct customer group, they need different types of selling efforts. The common factors remain as given below:

- Knowledge of market segment
- Knowledge of competition
- Business environment
- Product life cycle

Consumer durables could be as varied as cars, air conditioners, vacuum cleaners, and washing machines to computers.

FMCGs product include soaps, shampoos plus food items.

Industrial capital goods are the product manufacturing machines like sugar mills, textile mills.

Raw materials are iron, steel, rubber, wood and others.

Industrial consumables include, water, power, gasses, which consumed in the manufacturing process.

Service includes the hotel industry, airlines, hospitals, insurance

Manufacturing units are established for making those products, which can be sold by the selling department, and therefore manufacturing and sales need to work in close coordination. In actual practice, some manufacturers are essentially assemblers of components, which they purchase. Others have continuous operating process like the chemical plants.

Sales organization is designed to sell the products made by the manufacturing unit. However, it is found that once the sales set up is in place, they can sell a lot more product, which have common customers. Bata sells shoes and besides they also sell shoe polish, brushes, laces and socks as these products complement the sale of shoes.

Manufacturing plans of firms differ quite a lot. These depend on the market situation as also on the following points:

- Plant location
- Competitive strength
- Availability of finance
- Access to raw materials
- Access to the distribution channels

When a new entrepreneur wants to set up a competitive plant, these factors provide entry barriers to him and he has to find solutions to get the best results in these areas.

The success of any venture depends on the marketability of its products. Hence, it is of utmost importance that before selecting the product for manufacture and sale, thorough Marketing Research is conducted.

Imagine a firm, which has the best of technology, location of the factory, financial resources, manpower but no market/ sales. You can imagine the fate of such a firm. Sooner than later, there will be big lock on its doors and it will go in to liquidation.

Production in a one-man shop is ideal as it is **Hand Crafted** and made exactly to customer requirements. It is like tailor made suit. In such a case, the production is limited to the capacity of one person. Handicraft, expensive jewelry, and designer clothes belong to this category of products.

In order to reach a large number of customers, **Mass Production Techniques** are used, like the Assembly line production. This was introduced by Henry Ford in his car-manufacturing factory and has since become the well-tested technique for large-scale manufacture.

The latest trend however is of fast changing customer needs. It is therefore necessary to have as much flexibility built in the manufacturing process as possible to take care of changing trends and demands of the customers. This is more important in areas where the rate of obsolescence is high and cost of replacing the product with other not so high.

Branded and Generic Products: Most marketers want to sell branded products. Even commonplace items like wheat flour; salt and sugar have become branded products now, as branding enables the buyers to be selective in buying a particular brand only as compared to other brands. It helps sellers in highlighting the virtues of the products to catch more business. However, over a period of time even brands become generic names, as Bata is synonymous with shoes, Mobil oil with engine oil, Dalda with vanaspati ghee. Heavy advertising effort establishes the brand therefore can backfire too, if the brand gets to be accepted as a generic name rather than the brand of a firm. Care needs to be taken in this regard for avoiding such a situation.

PATENTS AND PATENT LAWS

If the manufacturer is making a product for which he has a Registered Patent under the country's Patent laws, than he can feel secure that other competing firms will not be able to use the same design in their manufacturing process and the firm can enjoy monopoly situation at least till the expiry of the Patent. However, firms should take care of getting the Patents renewed much before the expiry date to avoid any embarrassment on account of getting caught by competition that comes with a copied product. Such copies are usually a shade better and lower in cost because the firm has not spent any money in developing the same except spending on copying costs, which is also known as Reverse Engineering.

Brands: Any firm, which becomes a Market leader normally, has at least one Lead Brand. The firm tries to sell its other products under the umbrella of that brand. Sometimes, firms use the popular brand to sell other products, either bundled with it or way of promotion of lesser-known product in coordination with the main brand. Computer sellers are known for selling bundled products when they can sell slow moving products along with fast moving ones. Brand image or brand equity is perhaps one of the two most important aspects of any business the other being market share.

Once a firm has established one of its brands as a leader it diversifies to include complementary products. This helps in increasing turn over, as also profits of the firm. However, if the new products clash with the existing ones, or their quality can be suspect in the beginning, such products could do harm to the established product. It is therefore necessary to consider remaining supplier of only Specialized Products about which the firm is sure on quality and which enjoy a good brand image. Firms can also provide Quality service for these Special products, which will lead them in to better and increasing Brand image/equity and profitable sales. Thus there is always a dilemma of having specialized product or generic mass-produced ones. Today, firms are trying to customize mass produced products to gain customer goodwill. For example, you can get a Maruti car from the manufacturer with customized seats.

However, nothing can take the place of good service given by the seller for the product to the customer for increasing business and thereby increasing profits. Availability of reliable service and genuine spare parts can surely increase business as these ensure longer usage of the product, which make them cost effective to the buyers.

Today in most consumer products, which are not health related, there are three quality categories—

1. Top quality, for the rich and discerning buyers, sold through Super markets and boutiques.
2. Second Quality for the middle income buyers sold through utility stores and bargain counters.
3. Third Quality for the working class buyers sold through bargain stores and small shops.

In case of health related and food products, there are Government regulations, which control the quality standards of the products.

As can be seen, manufacturing function is meant to create a product, which can be used by the buyers. It therefore, becomes a conversion process, as there are a number of sub-products or components and raw materials, which go in to the manufacture of any product. Home cooking is a good example of food manufacture. The cook buys meat, vegetables, cooking oil, condiments and stoves and then he goes through a process to convert the ingredients in to edible food. It is difficult to imagine any one person who can grow his own vegetables, keep his poultry and manufacture stove for cooking. Cooking therefore is a conversion process.

As there are many other manufacturers in each area, it is important that manufacturer keeps his cost of manufacture as low as possible without compromising on his quality standards.

Quality Standards- firms, through market surveys find out the correct specification of the product they plan to make. These specifications are then converted to manufacturing standards and firms have to keep meeting these specifications for each unit produced by them. For exporting to Europe and other places, the foreign buyers now want that Indian firms follow ISO 9000 STANDARDS. These standards help firms in maintaining their procedures and specifications and assist in tracing causes of deviations if there are any these standards are meant to keep a check on the manufacturing process.

For product standardization each country has its own body, mostly Government owned which defines standards for various products. While mostly it is not mandatory for firms to conform to these specifications, nevertheless it helps in product marketing to an extent to have products with these specifications.

Market Share: In order to improve market share, firms have to fight competitive forces. This can be down by different means; some of them are as follows:

- Differentiation— as customers are always looking for products, which are different from other similar products, sellers try to give a little modification in the product or service, distribution to make a marked change from the run of the mill operations. These differences should be cost effective, noticeable and acceptable to the customers.
- Cost leadership—product manufacturing cost have a major bearing on how well it can be sold in the market. If all

competitive products are equally acceptable to the customers, the firm with lower cost will gain advantage over competitors. Cost leadership is obtained by either achieving economies of scale of manufacture when the firm is able to reduce unit **fixed cost**. For reducing **variable cost** firms have to look for experience curve.

- Quick response to market demand and needs can also provide definite competitive advantage to firms as it helps them to catch the customers with a product they are waiting for.
- Advertising/Sales Promotion.

With increased competition, differentiation does not last long, because, competing firms catch up and COPY products are soon available in the market. These copy products are made a little better than original. Hence firms, which plan product differentiation, have to continuously keep upgrading their products. Otherwise, ME-TOO products can take a good share of market share.

Customers need to know about the firm's products. Therefore communication with them is of utmost importance. This communication takes place in the following ways:

1. Personal meetings/seminars
2. Advertising/sales promotion

Since these areas of marketing are of importance they are dealt with in separate chapters.

Marketing Mix

Marketing has become an important activity in the life of human beings. It transcends nations, regions, cultural diversities and languages. People are engaged in business for profit and growth. It is therefore necessary to know and understand how best these can be achieved.

Marketing Mix Factors

In each of the product cases, there are some common and some different factors for profitable. These are called the **Marketing Mix Factors**, which can be compared with the ingredients like herbs, oil, condiments, vegetables, meat a chef has, using which he can cook a delicious meal. Similarly the Marketing Manager can plan profitable sales using the following factors, known as Marketing Mix Factors given below:

1. Marketing research
2. Product

3. Packaging
4. Brand
5. Trade mark
6. Label
7. Price
8. Transportation
9. Distribution
10. Sales promotion
11. Advertising
12. Retail sales and merchandizing
13. Personal selling
14. Credit and its control
15. Training of sales personnel

Product: There are the following types of products in the market for which different firms look for markets:

1. Consumer durables
2. Fast moving consumer goods—FMCGs
3. Industrial capital goods
4. Industrial raw materials and components
5. Industrial consumables
6. Service
7. Events
8. People
9. Places
10. Properties
11. Firms
12. Information
13. Research outputs

Packaging: An attractive package definitely catches the customer's eyes and it becomes an important factor especially for FMCG Products' sales. It also helps in brand and product recall when the customer goes to the market to make a purchase. Packaging helps in shelf displays and shops can utilize the shelf space optimally with the right king of packaging. It is also used in advertising of the product, thus creating a TOP OF THE MIND RECALL for the product.

Brand: It is the most visible form of advertising, as the product gets noticed in the shops counters, show-windows and shelves. Buyers can be prompted to buy once they have seen the products brand. An easily pronounced brand creates a positive memory of the product in customer's mind. Repeated advertising is used to strengthen the brand name. The value of the brand or its equity determines its usage and sales. Brand names are chosen from the following, normally:

1. Manufacturer's family name-Godrej, Tata, Birla
2. Town's name-Champagne
3. Product use name
4. Fancy name-which the manufacturer likes
5. Name which is easy to pronounce

Trade Mark: Sometimes the brand name and the trademarks are the same. Trademarks are legal signs by which the products are identified. Two competing products cannot have the same trademark. Any infringement of the trademark act can be sued in the court of law.

Label: The trademark, or the brand name is usually placed on the package, which is called the label. Label gives, besides the brand name, the product specifications, method of use, ingredients, expiry date, date and batch of manufacture. It is mandatory by the government to give some information like the expiry date for products like food and medicines.

Price: It is perhaps the most important of the factors as it defines the buying decisions for most products. Price changes bring about changes in quantity, which is sold as higher price may limit buyers and lower price encourage them to buy the product. Most products have price elasticity of sales. However, some products do sell in certain markets irrespective of price variations, which may occur, like the high value Mercedes car. While offering price to the customers, sellers give the price in one of the following manners:

1. Price includes excise duty and applicable sales tax.
2. Price excludes sales tax but includes excise duty
3. Price excludes both sales tax and excise duty
4. Furthermore, the applicability of price at which location, like ex-Factory, FOR, FOB, C&F, CIF

Transportation: Movement of goods from the manufacturers plant to the distribution system is important as, timeliness availability of goods can make sales easy. Competitive situation calls for speed and economy in movement of goods.

Distribution: Ideally, if the manufacturers can reach their customers directly without the middlemen, a lot of saving can be made as then no middlemen commission need to be paid. However, in reality, it is seldom possible and that is the reason that a large range of distribution channels is required. Some of the popular chains of distribution are given below in figure 2.11.

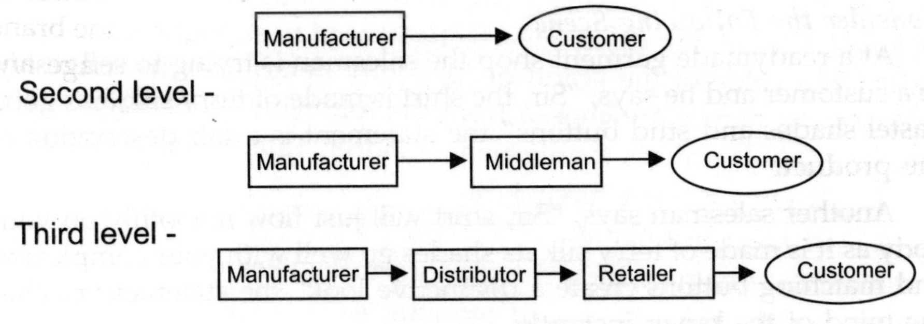

Fig. 2.11. Supply Chains

Detailed discussion on distribution, which include having firm's own shops and franchise operations is given in a separate chapter.

Sales Promotion: Sellers resort to promoting their products by offering incentives to the buyers, which makes the purchase attractive. These days we are seeing everyday that "buy two and get one free" several sellers are offering different type of incentives in a big way. These promotional offers are for both the customers and dealers or retailers. As the customers including retailers are offered an instant benefit, they are gently forced in to buying the product.

Advertising: The sellers are also trying to get customers attention on the product through non-personal communication by advertising through suitable media. In the last ten years newer media have emerged and with computer aided design facilities advertising has become more forceful and its used has spread widely. Advertising provides the customers the right to choose a product which best fulfills their needs. It is also used to combat severe competition.

Retail Sales and Merchandizing: Retail shops bring consumer products close to the customers and they fulfill a major need. In each shop there are a number of products and several brands of each product. How these are displayed and which brand gets the best place on the shelf are important areas of merchandizing, which help firms in increasing sales and gaining market share.

Personal Selling and Salesmanship: With the best of displays and products it is not very likely that the firm will get the eye of the customer. It is the persuasiveness of the seller or his salesman, which makes a difference. The salesman has to learn to talk the language that the customer understands best. The salesman should be able to drive home the benefits and the satisfaction the customer is going to derive out of the Rupee he is spending in purchasing the product.

Consider the Following Scene

At a readymade garment shop the salesman is trying to sell a shirt to a customer and he says, "Sir, the shirt is made of terry silk, has good pastel shades and stud buttons" the statement is a fair description of the product.

Another salesman says, "Sir, shirt will just flow smoothly on your body as it is made of terry silk its shades go well with your complexion and matching buttons create a distinctive look" the statement catches the mind of the buyer instantly.

Credit and Its Control: A credit buyer normally buys a little more because he is not paying for the product just then. It is human psychology that immunes the buyer of the thought that finally he has to make the payment and perhaps with interest. Credit can therefore be used judiciously as a sales tool with ample safeguards against fraudulent buyers.

Training of Sales Persons: As new products are introduced by the firm, new markets emerge with increase in competition, the firm has to innovate, place new methods and structures and systems. The sales people must be therefore continuously trained in to the latest so that they keep their work optimized always.

Marketing gurus have been talking of the four Ps of marketing, that is, Product, Price, Placement and Promotion. In other words **Products** should signify the benefit accruing to the customer, **Price** the cost of the benefit, **Placement** the ease of buying and **Promotion** the knowledge base provided for the benefit of customer through advertisement and promotion.

Let us take a practical view of marketing as it exists today in Indian context. You walk in any firm's marketing office and you will find these activities going on there—

- Sales, receiving enquiry letters, sending quotation letters
- Complaint receipts and redresses
- Advertising and promotional plans
- Field sales management

For these tasks the following basic Marketing Organization is needed as given below in figure 2.12.

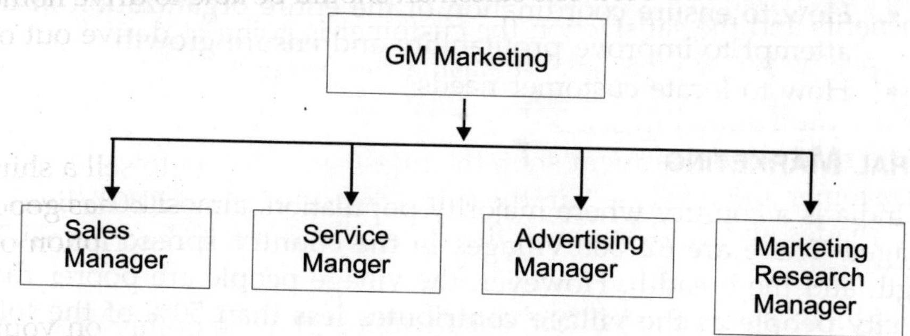

Fig. 2.12. Marketing Organization

As can be seen Marketing Research is not a part of marketing team in many cases and the firm's hire outside agencies to get Marketing Research done as and when need arises.

Sales Managers normally look after sales of a given geographic area and they do so with the help of regional managers, area managers and executives. The job entails locating customers, appointing dealers, setting up the distribution network following up for orders, coordinating with production unit for supplies and ensuring payments for sales made.

Service Manager looks after the After sales service of the product, including the guarantee service and after the guarantee period is over, the paid service ensure that customers get the optimum usage of the products.

Advertising Manager arranges proper advertising of products, the firm for image building and plans to advertise promotional plans made by the marketing team.

Marketing Research Managers are part of some large firms and their tasks are continuous market surveys for keeping their hands on the pulse of the market. Marketing Managers have to find answers to some questions on continuous basis like the one's given below:

- Right market segment for the product and also peripheral segments.
- Price sensitivity of the market
- How to improve profitability
- How to increase brand equity
- How to measure the effectiveness of advertising and promotion.
- How to broad base our distribution channel and keep them all profit making

- How to ensure coordination of the entire organization in the attempt to improve profitability and ensure growth
- How to locate customer needs

Rural Marketing

India is a country where majority population, almost 80% lives in villages. There are 627000 villages in the country spread across its length and the breadth. However, the village people are poorer than the city people as the village contributes less than 50% of the total country's income. However, now the situation is gradually changing for the better.

There are 25 official languages and some four hundred dialects spoken in the country. Most world religions have their adherents here.

In the first half of the twentieth century, people were using neem or babul tree's twig for cleaning their teeth. Today, they are using tooth powder or toothpaste. Instead of groundnuts the children are asking for chocolate candies. Face cream or lotions have replaced Besan as a face cleanser.

Appreciating the size of the rural market, major companies, including, Hindustan Lever, P&G have made special strategies for targeting rural markets. Business environment in rural India is given below-

Demographic: The population has been steadily increasing in the villages, making per capita land holdings ever so small, reducing their income in the same proportion. This has resulted in migration from villages to towns either on temporary basis during off seasons for agriculture or on a more permanent basis as people come to cities looking for employment.

Social: There are women in the agriculture fields, in panchayats, child marriages are still prevalent in certain parts of the country, like Rajasthan. In certain states villagers have taken to arms and crime due to lack of employment, perhaps. Education levels differ from state to state, as Kerala boasts of highest percentage of educated persons.

Cultural: Villagers celebrate festivals with a lot of gusto, especially the harvest time, religious festivals, marriages and childbirths.

Political: The green revolution was the result of the government's policy of research on agriculture. Milk cooperatives came about for the milk farmers with the pioneering efforts of the Amul organization. The government has been providing subsidies on farm inputs, tax holidays for farm profits, purchase of farm produce on a minimum price fixed by the government and has of late given a lot of concessions on agro packaging and processing industry.

Legal: Government has enacted law against child marriages and dowry. However, it would need a concerted effort from the village folk themselves before the evil can be eradicated.

Macroeconomics: A lot of effort has gone into setting up of rural banks, farm insurance schemes. Rural electrification, roads have been given priority in the governments planning process. Cottage industries and handicrafts have been given the desire impetus by the government.

Technology: Today most villages of the country have the radio coverage and the TV spread is increasing by the day. Next, telephones, Internet would become ubiquitous in the villages soon. Tractors, harvesters, seeders, pesticides, fertilizers, quality seeds, scientific guidance on farming by the agriculture research institutes is enabling the farmers to get better yield from their farms.

Global: WTO has clearly defined the methods of agriculture exports from India and the government is finding it hard to counter the extra subsidies given by the affluent nations that make their produce more competitive. Our leadership is busy in countering it through diplomacy in the WTO. Some countries have patented some of Indian products, like Basmati rice, turmeric, as their own much to the country's regret.

Rural Products: Most products required in cities are also needed in the rural markets with a few exceptions as given below:

1. FMCG products like cosmetics, food items like cooking oil, kerosene, and medicines
2. Consumer durables like refrigerators, stoves, motor cycles
3. Farm products like tractors, harvesters, seeders, seeds, fertilizers, pesticides, and diesel, water supply for household use including drinking purposes and for watering the farms
4. Services like, health clinics, water supply, electricity, eateries, inns
5. Housing

Pricing in rural markets is tricky because the companies spend more on transporting the products as compared to transporting to the cities. However, the paying power in rural areas is much less. Companies can therefore plan to have low cost packaging with a bit of attractive glitter while keeping the product unchanged in most cases. The companies can work out the rural customers MTBP, Mean Time Between Purchase. They will find that the rural customer will stretch the purchase time much longer. This would be true for most FMCG products. Food items however would be needed as per household requirements.

Product distribution in rural markets takes the following route:

Products are kept for sale at the grocers' shops, diesel/kerosene dealers, and tractor repair shops. Besides, companies sell through mobile vans that cover the villages mostly on the days of their weekly markets. These vans carry advertising materials, audiovisual equipments for showing movies besides company's advertisements and the products for sale, samples like shampoo sachets for test marketing of the products.

Product promotion in rural markets is done through the vans. Besides, radio has a wide coverage as it covers the entire country geographically, is used. Additionally, television reach has increased of late and with better electricity availability it has become a good option, more especially because of its universal appeal. Pamphlets, loudspeaker announcements during weekly markets, mostly on roaming rickshaws, banner on elephants and camels are used in many areas.

Villages need schools, as the literacy levels are still poor. Technical and computer education are becoming increasingly important even in villages. There is a great need for libraries, bookstores and newspapers, magazines in local languages.

Income levels in the rural India can be described as follows:

High in certain areas for rich land owning farmers

Low for farmers with small lands

Very low for farm hands and migratory farmers

Village industries, cottage and small scale, handlooms, milk farming, sheep rearing need governmental support or infusion of cooperatives in these areas. The Amul examples must be replicated in other parts of the country. The village Bania, who has been the proverbial loan shark, is fast disappearing as a tribe and yet the rural banking needs much more thrust. A number of banks have started branches in villages and yet they are affected by non-availability of collaterals for giving loans to farmers. Farm insurance would go a long way in settling this problem it is hoped. Bad crops further obstructs the interest payments leading to bad debts that retards the progress for which the banks have been setup.

Customers have needs, which are obvious, like the need for food, clothing, and shelter. Some of these needs are explicitly mentioned like the need of a house. However, what is real is the need of the house in a locality close to office, school and shopping plaza. Besides, the un-stated need could be of a big house.

Firms face the challenges of new competition, both local and global, new technologies as they cater to consumers in business-to-business area and individuals. In order to ascertain the product needed by the consumers, market research is undertaken, which offers information about the product, price, placement, i.e., distribution system needed and the methods of communicating to the consumers about the product, i.e., advertising and promotion, the famous 4 Ps of marketing.

In order to prepare the right 4 Ps, firms define their market segment in which the product would be best accepted. The firms try to understand the exact needs of the segment in order to be able to meet the same. In order to build loyal customers firms are trying relationship marketing, to ensure that consumers feel obligated to buy the same product again and again. Quantity discounts, free gifts are some of the means to build relationships with the consumers. Since the competition is doing exactly the same, it is the firm with better strategy, which wins. Changes from the earlier concepts of production orientation, to product orientation and later on to market orientation has helped firms in fine tuning their marketing strategies to suit the consumers from their chosen market segment. The concept of providing socially acceptable products, which do not affect the biodiversity, which are not ecologically degrading the area, is gaining ground rapidly.

Relationship marketing is the latest and yet most powerful trend in marketing today. Firms cannot provide satisfaction to their customers unless they know them well, customers' needs, and desires.

Rural India has emerged as a big potential market and companies have to recognize its value. Companies have to look at the 4Ps of marketing, product, price, promotion and placement from the village customers' point of view, to succeed in the rural markets.

Question for Discussion

1. Discuss the marketing mix factors; how these are used by firms to gain competitive advantage?
2. How do relationships help in marketing products?
3. Are segments useful to firms in marketing their products? If yes, how?
4. How should the companies plan their entry in the rural markets? How would they have to modify the 4Ps to be successful in rural areas of the country?

Marketing Game

As by now the teams have been formed and company selected and they have decided about the product the company wants to do b-to-b marketing the following needs to be done by the team:

Scan the general business environment factors-demographic, social, cultural, political, legal, macroeconomics, technology and global, that would have an impact on business of the company.

CHAPTER 3

Marketing Management—Concepts

AIMS AND OUTCOMES OF THE CHAPTER

Once the students have learnt the 4 marketing Ps, the time is ripe to understand market segmentation and product positioning. The chapter takes the students into the marketing concepts essential for getting expertise on the subject.

To understand marketing it is useful to discuss some basic concepts as follows:

1. *Market Segmentation:* Market Segmentation is required because products can be used or be needed by only a part of the entire population. The concept of segmentation focuses on the particular group or class of customer who would be definitely interested in the product. A history textbook will be of interest to the students and teachers of history. Spices used in cooking will be needed by cooks, both in homes and in hotels. Can a customer group afford to buy a product, although it may be requiring the same? For example, can low-income people buy an expensive watch worth four thousand rupees? The population can therefore be divided in to income groups, rich, poor and mid-income groups. Depending on the product to be sold, further narrow classification can be done.
2. *Targeting Markets:* Markets have evolved from purely physical locations where buying selling is taking place to Super markets where a lot of products from diverse manufacturers are sold under one roof. Then there are need-based markets like health care products market, sports goods market. Markets can be for different age groups, religion followers and people market, where jobs are offered to jobseekers. Marketers have to decide which market they want to sell their products, and they become the targets for the firm.

3. *Customers and Prospective Customers:* Customers and Prospective Customers are the people or organizations that either need the product or could be brain washed in to buying the product. As they have a number of sources from whom they can buy, the sellers need to have really efficient persuasion or brain washing technique. At times, buyers are also users, but it is not always so. One family member buys toiletries, which are used by the rest of the family. The decision to buy one particular brand could be the buyers, or it could be of the user member of the family; in India servants do a lot of buying for the family they work for and they are guided by the dictates of the family members mostly.
4. *What the Customers Need:* Starting from physical needs of food, clothing, shelter, healthcare and education they have needs of recreation, sports, entertainment and other leisure time activities. Sellers stimulate these needs by educating the customers through advertisements and personal selling. Some basic products like food is demanded by the buyers. However, as the choice of branded food keeps increasing, for a product as common as salt several brands are available, sellers keep focusing the attention of buyers by communicating to them about their brands. Demand creation is done for totally new innovative products like cell phones, which was done through concept selling the product usage even before the product was offered in the market. It must be accepted that some where in the mind set of target customers the latent need existed for the cell phones. At times however, with demand growth and increased competition, improved or more innovative products have to be introduced in the market, which helps in retaining or improving the firm's market share. Firms with better Research and Development facilities fare better in competitive situations. Attractive products or good-looking packages help in selling as *they catch the customer's eye better*. Besides, social and peer pressure gives buyers the required motivation for buying a product, even if they do not really need it. Credit cards or other credit sales makes people/customers buy more than their need or more than they can actually afford and hence several social scientists consider pressure selling as a incurable malaise of the modern day.
5. *Product or Service:* Satisfies the customers needs or provides the benefit sought by the customer. Branded products have an

identity of their own and their sales can be quantified accurately. Firms look for enhancing the value of their brand through its quality, advertising and personal sales.

6. *Product Benefits and its Value to the Customers:* it is an important area for sellers as better the value for money for the customer, in his view the better the chances of his buying the product.

Value to the customer can be defined as follows:

Value = product benefits and its emotional value to the buyer as compared to its cost to the customer, including time and effort costs.

Sales contracts – for sales to be made on a legally valid and binding manner the following conditions must be met-

i. There are at least two parties to the contract, both have something for the other; one may have a product and the other money to buy the product
ii. Each party can offer its product/money and also accept the offer
iii. Each party accepts the other as a reasonable party and the contract as genuine and reasonable
iv. The product or service on offer is not contraband for sale like drugs

Hence, it can be seen that when one party gives a gift to another party it can not be considered as sale as ther e is no payment involved in the transfer of goods from one party to the other.

The ideal sought by the sellers is that the buyers become their friends and to do so they sell quality products, offer good service and attractive terms of business, which, over a period of time make their customers their friends with long-term relationship.

Relationship Marketing

Customer Relationship Management (CRM) System is designed specifically to address the unique challenges facing the industry. The focus and experience working with the people, processes and technologies within the industry has allowed the customers to successfully implement and achieve their CRM objectives.

CRM-Definition

CRM is a customer-centric business strategy that requires alignment among people, processes and technologies to achieve growth and profitability.

It has become the key words in today's marketing language with much greater effort and money going in to it.

Marketers having to cover a large geographic area need to have sales outlets at numerous places in their target market place. They need a distribution channel, which goes up to the retail stores where the customers go to buy their products. New channels like the Internet, and tele shopping have come up to enable customers have interactions with the sellers without them having to taking time off for shopping. Sellers need to communicate to the buyers all the time about their products, their benefits, prices that is done through personal selling at the retail outlets and through advertisements. The interactive channels of Internet and tele shopping help customers gather information about the product as also in buying the same.

Competition

As there are several sellers of the same product, the customers have those many choices. It is the competition, which keeps firms on their toes, as they have to constantly endeavour to provide a good product at a reasonable price from which the customers can derive benefits they want and which makes them happy, delighted. Competition can be of several types as given below:

i. Similar product competition—where competitive products offer same or similar benefits to the customer on same type of prices. In India, automobile sector has, Maruti Zen, Santro, Matiz and Indica in same competition bracket.

ii. Same industry competition—where the firms making same products. For cars, all the car manufacturers, irrespective of the size, price become competitors.

iii. Usage competition—takes in to consideration products providing similar usage are considered as competition. For cars, motor cycles, scooters, busses become competition

iv. Competition for customer's money—car sellers can consider sellers of Consumer products, vacation travel as competition.

Market Environment

Competition is a significant factor, which creates business environment for the firm. Besides, its suppliers, buyers, new competitors planning to enter the field and substitute product sellers make environment in which the firm operates.

The general environment factors, which affect marketing are, demographic, socio-cultural, political-legal, country's economics, technology and global business.

Marketing Mix Factors are the factors, which assist the marketing team in achieving the targets. They are discussed in detail elsewhere in the book.

From the early days of the twentieth century, the sellers and buyers concepts have undergone major changes as given below:

Table 3.1. Buyer Concepts

Period	*Concept*
1935–1955	Production
1956–1965	Product
1966–1991	Selling
1992–to present	Marketing/customer

Production concept stage sellers in India believed that whatever is produced in large numbers and sold widely will be bought by the customers.

During Product stage the focus shifted to the quality of the products as people became more quality conscious than before.

During Selling period, competition started raising its head and sellers had to resort to aggressive selling techniques. Advertising became a useful tool in the game of marketing.

Marketing concept focused on the customers needs, combating competition through better advertising and promotion plans. From that period the customer became the king, pursued by competitive sellers. Business being conducted by firms is meant for earning profits and for growing. This is possible by proper selection of customer groups through market segmentation, understanding the needs of the customers and dovetailing the products to meet the needs, selection of the right distribution channel and well directed communication to the customers through advertising. Profits thus generated help the firms to grow further for increased market share and profits. The decision making process in the customer based concepts starts with the customers and also concludes with business relationship with the customers. The IDEAL SYSTEM would be when the entire organization, including, other functions than Marketing like Finance, Production, Human Resource Development and Purchasing all view the business from the customer's point of view. Only then the firm's Customer Orientation becomes complete. Customers have their needs, which the firm wants to satisfy with its products. Customer's needs could be seen as given below:

- *The Known Needs:* Needs clearly perceived by the customer, like the need for house.
- *The Unknown Needs:* Need for a low cost house in the vicinity of office and school complex.
- *The Unspecified Needs:* Like the need for easy power, water and phone connections in the house.
- *The Need for Customer's Delight:* Like free membership of nearby club coming with the house.
- *The Need for Social Approval:* The need for peer group and friend's circle approving and appreciating the house.

To be really effective the efforts need to have a continuous approach, as can be seen below:

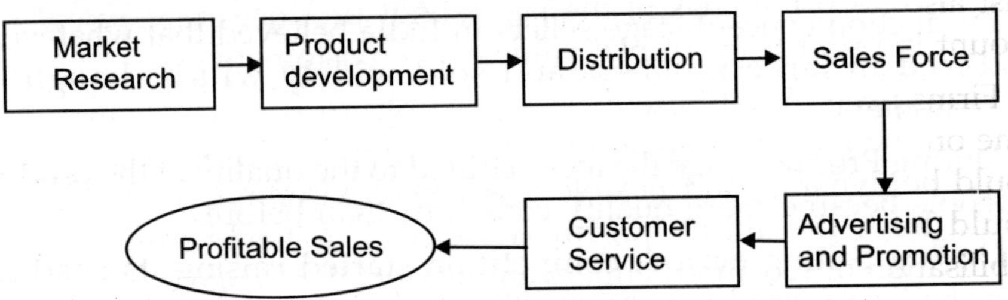

Fig. 3.1. Selling Plan

The integrated plan for marketing results in profits and growth for the firm. For other departments or functional areas like Purchase, the Purchase Manager should visualize the ultimate customer's benefit by purchasing the raw materials of the right specifications with no compromise on quality. This would minimize the rejection at the initial inspection stage, improve productivity and reduce losses. The HR Manager should keep the customer in mind while recruiting the marketing personnel or even training his own team of HR People to enable them better understand the needs of marketing in terms of training and motivation.

Profit and Profiteering

Profits come from sale of goods at price higher than the cost of manufacture. However, if the price is kept high, especially in the monopoly markets it is called profiteering and it is unethical, illegal in most cases. In today's world full of competitors, the price keeps getting depressed because of competitive forces. The firm has to provide value for money and customer's delight to be able to claim a good price with reasonable profit. It is the firm's ability to deliver the goods at a reasonable price, which ultimately benefits the firm with profits. However, if the customers do not derive the expected benefits from the product, the sale and profits would be only short lived. Competition is always round the corner watching the firm's activities like a hawk and proactive actions for customers benefits are required for really sustained profitability. Price plays a significant role in determining firm's profits, and yet price is most of the time linked with product quality or customer's perception of the product quality. The idea of increasing sales by lowering price could become counterproductive at times.

Firms need to assess the needs and demands of target market segment and provide the product to satisfy the same with more value addition and cost effective marketing than their competitors. Firms must also keep the laws of the land about product usage safety in to account in order to be of real value to the customers.

Firms need to optimise their plans, policies and actions in order to come on the top and remain there. The firms' organizational structure should be dynamic and flexible to accept environmental changes and should have the ability to, fine-tune itself for achieving its goals. Mobilisation of recourses, timely and correct deployment of resources, process control all add up to benefits to the stakeholders of the firms, like it's buyers, suppliers, employees, and the government. Doing good to the buyers should not be at the expense of suppliers. The firm should have highly motivated work force who will generate top quality product and services for the ultimate delight of the buyers, repeat orders, better profits and dividends for the stock holders.

It is said that the successful people do not do things right, they do the right things. Efficiency in people can be defined as doing things right and effectiveness as doing the right things. Hence, if a firm is doing the right things rightly, it is both efficient and effective.

Firms need to have core competencies in most of the functional areas of business like resource generation, marketing, purchasing, manufacturing, human resource management, product development and government relations. The best technicians can become the best service managers with motivation and training. With flat organizations, multi-tasking and cross-functional teams are the order of the day, as without these goals cannot be achieved.

The usual functional structures of the firms are giving way to cross-functional structures as follow:

Table 3.2. Functional Structure

		CEO			
Marketing	**Production**	**Human Resource**	**Finance**	**R&D**	**Legal**

Cross Functional Structure

Table 3.3. Cross Functional Structure

	Resources	
	Product development	
Suppliers ⟵	**Demand management**	**⟶ Buyers**
	Order fulfilment	
	Controls	

As can be seen in cross-functional structures, Product Development involves R&D, Purchase of technology, market assessment or market research for the product. Demand management includes setting up distribution systems; sales force management and order fulfilment relates to manufacture, inventory management or even out-sourcing the production activities. Such cross-functional activities help in bridging the connectivity of functional areas and hence prove their worth.

A firm needs the following resources for its operations:

- Financial
- Human
- Technological
- Infrastructure
- Information
- Capital/ manufacturing goods

With the rate of obsolescence shortening the PLC, it may be prudent not to invest in capital goods and instead of buying equipment; they can be leased or rented. Outsourcing of subassemblies manufacture can be another option. Most shoe suppliers from the USA have outsourced their product from the Far East.

Organizational Culture

It is one of the important areas, which create excellence in the firms, which lead to achievements of the goals. Organizational culture can be described as, "The way we do things here". It is what an organization will do and will not do. Culture of a corporate entity can be felt, seen, but it is difficult to define the culture. There is culture of brisk polite activity, culture of sluggishness, of customer orientation and of employee orientation. Firms with a laid back culture find it difficult to shed it and become more active and dynamic. However, it is possible to change the culture of a firm. it is a long process, needs patience, perseverance and continuous effort.

Informal groups, teams play an important role in modifying a firm's culture. It starts with infusing stories of success in the informal groups, which would have its effect over a period of time. The firm's goals and objectives, its vision and mission statements must be known, understood, accepted by the entire team of the firm. All the workers and management must be committed to them. It is the unity of purpose, which joins firm in to one holistic organization, and helps build its cultural base.

Congruence of culture becomes extremely essential in case of mergers and acquisitions as any major cultural clash could jeopardize the success of the new organization. The best of financial resource, technology and human resource cannot ensure success unless there is a cultural meeting of minds as well.

With ever changing environment of business most firms are busy in trying to dovetail their operations to suit the environment. The firms, which remain proactive, which have long-range policies and plans and people committed to them are most likely to become achievers.

The firm needs to have a customer-oriented approach to its operations, should be focusing on making and keeping its employees motivated and committed, should have a quality plan for continuous improvement, should understand its responsibility towards its stockholders. The firm leadership should be having a farsighted approach for creating a future for it.

Marketing strategies of planning a proactive stance in the market come from a value system where excellence is encouraged, despite emphasis on teamwork. Leadership qualities in person at any level or hierarchy are given due recognition. The best employees are committed to customer satisfaction and customer delight at all times.

Supply Chain Management

The firm, which can optimize the operations of its supply chain, gets in- built competitive advantage. Supply chain for a readymade gents suits manufacturer can be seen below:

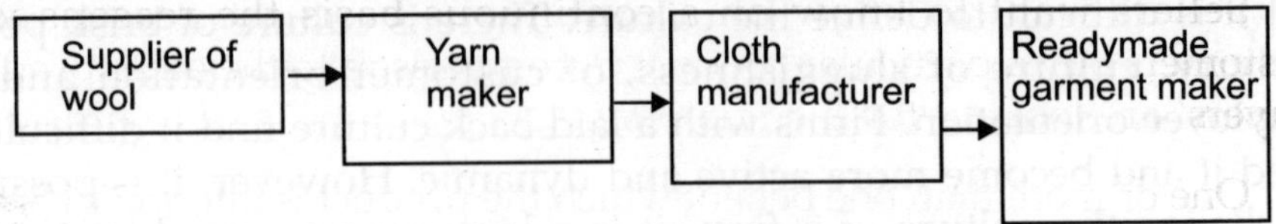

Fig. 3.2. Supply Chain

If the supply chain can be managed that each buyer gets products when needed and of uniform quality they can all optimize their operations. Concept of JUST IN TIME can be introduced effectively only when the entire chain is ready for it.

STRUCTURAL SUPPORT TO THE CUSTOMERS

In France, the telephone company was providing Minitel a computer terminal which could access through the French telecom network a large number of services like ordering air tickets, buying items of daily needs, cinema tickets and a whole lot more. Such equipment makes the customer loyal for a long time.

INDIRECT FINANCIAL SUPPORT

"Our mo-bike gives twenty percentage better mileage than the competitive bike. Hence if you run your bike for two thousand kilometres per month you gain up to rupees ten thousand in a year." The sales person should be ready with actual calculations to prove the point. In industrial selling- B-to-B business it is at times easy to demonstrate. The customer starts questioning the competitors about the savings they can provide. "Use our lubricating oils and your equipment wear and tear will reduce by ten percent." Even better is saying that your maintenance time will reduce and you will be able to produce ten percent more because of this factor.

MARKETS—THE CUSTOMERS

A number of new innovative products were introduced in the second half of the twentieth century, like the television, speed cars, SST Jets and in India several products got a countrywide spread like telephones, railways and air travel. Therefore concept selling was a regular feature in the market place. Today, for most products there are a number of suppliers and marketers have to be fighting competition. Only in a few new products like, mobile phones concept or the idea of using the product had to be accepted by the target market segment and hence concept selling had to be resorted to.

Sellers want to know on a continuous basis the reasons why customers buy a particular product in comparison to the other product. Buyers' are looking for the following:

One or more than one benefit which the product is offering to buyer. How these benefits comparing with those offered by the competitors. As against the benefits what does it cost to obtain the product, use it and finally sell it as junk? Buyers balance the cost and benefit and decide to buy the product or not. Even in low cost item instant decisions these activities take place albeit quickly in buyers mind. A major deciding factor is the product usage, which is guarantied by the sellers through written guaranty as also availability of service personnel, spares at the right place, time and at the right price.

Brand image plays a major role in buying decision, besides product benefits in relation to its price, salesman's behaviour and thoroughness of the service needed and provided for optimizing product usage by the customer. Product price, time and effort it takes to organize the purchase and customer's mindset are the factors, which are weighed against the benefits the product offers.

In case of industry purchase there are other extraneous factors, which decide the purchase as given below:

- Purchase Manager's personal likes and dislike of product, brand or seller's people
- Management policy of buying only lowest priced product (its use may turn out to be the most expensive in the long run)
- Management long-term relationship with a seller.
- Understand dealings between seller and buyer
- Proximity of service facility of a product
- Product endorsement by close friends, associates
- Buyer's innovative nature

Marketers learn fast that better benefits and value for money offered to the customer always wins the race.

Case Study

ABC Cooperative Sugar Mill was coming up in the western India. The order for plant and machinery was placed on a firm in Maharashtra. Tenders were floated for transportation of the plant and machinery from Maharashtra to west India. The lowest tender got the order.

Now imagine each piece of large equipment being hauled by two long wooden rails fitted with steel wheels of six-inch diameter pulled by two oxen covering about a thousand kilometres. There were at least eight derailments and ninety percent equipment reached in damaged condition. It is difficult to calculate the resultant losses. Such buying decisions need careful study of the actual delivery, and not just the one promised by the seller. Hence the sellers must give not only value for money but a proper usable product too.

There is a saying, "you can use the earthen pot for cooking only once". If the product does not satisfy the customer there is no repeat sale to the same customer. Besides, one dissatisfied customer can influence several others in not buying the product through *Word of Mouth Publicity.*

It is important to keep a track on customers buying pattern. There are usually three types of customers.

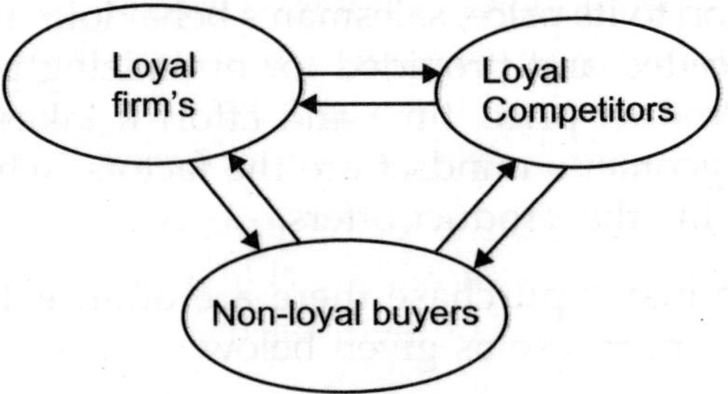

Fig. 3.3. Type of Buyers

Firms want that customers from the other two groups should shift to their loyal block. There are basically three methods of increasing the firm's market share as follows:

1. Take competitors customers
2. Get new customers
3. Convert non-loyal customers as loyal customers

As the firm is trying to steal customers from competitors, so are the competitors trying to do. A lost buyer, the one who has gone to the competitor, can provide valuable information about the lacunae of the firm; where does the problem lie? Is it in the product itself, has the competitor come out with a better product; or is it due to the firm's terms of business like price, or is it the firm's service? Gaining a lost customer is more difficult task than gaining new customer. Firms need to have senior people listening to the negative aspects of their business from these customers. Most firms have a **Complaint Cell**. Some have **Suggestion Plans** also where the customers can offer suggestions to the firm for improving their operation. Listening to and removing complaints giving serious consideration to the customer's suggestions not only help in keeping the customers loyal, these are the useful ways of augmenting customer relationship.

Firms adopt **Customer Surveys** to understand customers' attitudes towards the firms and their products. Service industry, like hotel, airlines, private telecom firms resort to these surveys. Some firms have a continuous system of having these surveys, for keeping their systems and skills honed all the time. The surveys give **Loyalty Indicators** for the firms customers and the firms can device strategies on their basis to upgrade the same.

Customer forms the market and a lost customer is market lost. If it is better technology than can the firm offer sops like discounts prior to improving and may be bettering their own technology. Is it price, or some competitor's promotional scheme? Firms must know to be able to react for regaining the customer. Otherwise they can plan to hit competitors where it will hurt them and the firm will regain its market share. This quid-pro-quo is also known as **Cross Parry.**

The best approach is that of being proactive to the market needs and demands and the firms should be able to fulfil these in their own innovative style, before the competition tries to catch up with them. The secret is to remain on one ladder higher than competition all the time. This calls for a high degree of management skills, sense of urgency and proper timing.

Planning for Success

In the last century success came from the firms own plans for profit and growth. If the firm was able to declare dividends to the stockholders, it was enough. Today unless the firm is ready to take full care of all its stakeholders success may remain illusive.

Stakeholders can be categorized in two types—

1. Internal stakeholders – the management and the employees
2. External stakeholders – suppliers of the firm, buyers, and distribution channel members, financers, bankers, the government and the community.

While the management tends to look after itself, are they taking good care of the employees too? Similarly, if the suppliers do not get a fair deal from the firm they will not be loyal and it could cause problems for the firm. Buyer group is naturally important for the firm, as after the initial purchase if the firm wants them to keep buying their products, the firm must build relationships with them. Distribution channel members are in fact the first buyers and they must be always on the right side of the firm. Finance is the bloodline of any firm and therefore financers need to be nurtured, not just by abiding by the written agreements, but also by the firms behaviour pattern. Bankers provide working capital; they should be treated as financers. The government of the land feeds on the taxes the firm pays. Firms must obey the laws of the land. The community provides the firm with employees and as good corporate citizen the firm must look after the welfare of the community. The firm should not pollute the environment by sending noxious fumes, polluted liquids and noise.

In order to be competitive (by gaining competitive advantage), the firms should optimize their cumulative skills, managerial, technical and financial. Gone are the days when achieving excellence in different functional areas, like marketing, finance, production and human resource management firms could thrive in competitive markets. It is important to have multi tasking forces, cross functional teams in order to not just survive, but excel in the competitive world. The stress should be on gaining superiority over competition rather than maintaining status quo. In today's market you either go up or go down. There is no place for remaining where the firm has been (in fact because of competitive forces, if the firm tries to increase its position it may end up from where it started.)

High performers work on cross-functional skills, unlike what was happening in the past when excellence in functional areas could see the firms reach the top.

Outsourcing has become an important tool in the manager's armoury. Manpower, technology, infrastructure like transportation and handling of materials, power, marketing research could well be outsourced with less cost and better results. Lower costs, more managerial free time can be utilized for strategic planning of the firm.

It all boils down to providing the customers value for money and mental and material satisfaction in their buying transaction with the firm. And this has to be done in better ways than what the competition is doing. Then only the firm gains **Competitive Advantage.** Hence, the firm has to start working towards Core Processes rather than working with functional areas.

Core processes can be described as follows:

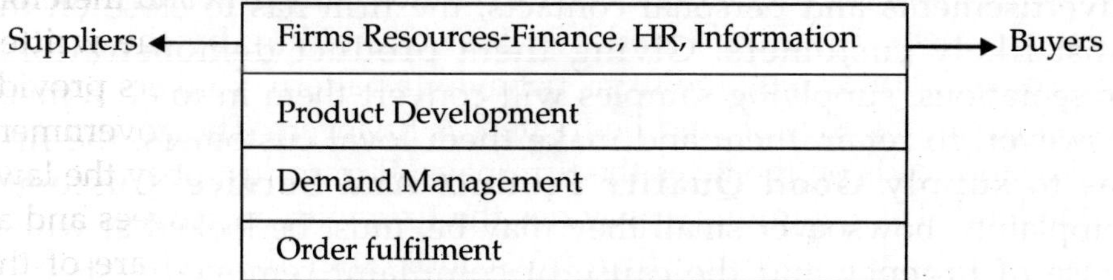

Fig. 3.4. Core Processes

As can be seen the resources of the firm are outside of the firm. Once the firm decides on entering a business, it has to acquire the same. Next, it has to identify the product it wants to market. It starts with idea generation, study of the market (Market Research), obtaining technology by purchase, reverse engineering or through Research and Development. Once the product has been selected it is test marketed. It is followed by creating demand through advertisements and promotional plans, marketing channels, retail outlets. The last step is delivery of the product against the order and getting paid for it. The sales cycle gets completed and from this point it gets repeated for further orders. For the system to succeed the management needs to have controls to ensure that the firm's laid down plans and policies are adhered to and it remains on track for profit and growth. The important aspect is retaining old and getting new customers. Mainly, the quality of product and the firm's service are responsible for it.

Market And Its Culture-as per Maslow, people have some basic needs like, physiological, need for safety, sociological, need for recognition and for self-actualization.

To satisfy the needs people need products and in this way we are all customers at one time or the other. Our actions are guided by, among other things our culture too. Likewise, firms to have their culture and while it can easily change its plans and policies; it is not easy to change its culture. Culture is a way of life, shared experiences, stories, beliefs, and ethical standards. In India there is a big culture linked market for ethnic products, products connected to religious activities.

Summary – if people are customers and customers are markets, where do we start looking for them, how do we retain them? The secrets are, get more customers, make them happy and satisfied, loyal, and while doing, so go for more.

Firms need to select their business area, mostly geographic or of industry clusters. Since, these contain customers and also non-customers, market segmentation is required at this stage. Next, through advertisements and personal contacts, the firm has to close on the most likely customers. Giving them product demonstrations, presentations, supplying samples will convert them in to customers. However, to retain them and make them loyal customers, the firm has to supply **Good Quality Product And Service**. Customer complaints, howsoever small they may be, must be looked at with a sense of urgency and the cause of complaint removed fastest. **A satisfied customer may help the firm get ten more customers, while one dissatisfied customer will definitely ensure the firm not getting hundred customers through word of mouth publicity**.

Today, the firms want not just to satisfy the customer, but also to delight the customer. A delighted customer is a loyal one, usually buys the complete range of products offered by the firm, gives positive word of mouth publicity to his friends about the products and mostly ignores competitive promotional plans. **Selling after sales**, involves, periodic contacts with the customers with new developments in product ranges, new promotional plans, reaching out with Newsletters. In other words building relationships with the customers-Relationship Marketing. Even for FMCGs, sellers are trying hard to make the customer a client by offering gifts, which are found in product containers. (Client has one to one relationship with the seller, like the doctor's clients or the lawyer's clients)

Following is the list of what is sold and bought in the market:

- Products
- Service
- Manpower
- Technology
- Property
- Ideas
- Organizations
- Information

Products can be divided into the following categories:

- Fast Moving Consumer Goods
- Consumer Durables
- Industrial capital goods
- Industrial raw materials and components
- Industrial consumables
- Services

An element of service is always included in all the products. Customers have become discerning and they demand the top quality product and its associated service. In order to upgrade this aspect of the business the firm's management has to adopt Total Quality Management (TQM).

In Total Quality Management firms endeavor to keep upgrading the quality of their products and services continuously in a planned manner. Firm's long run profitability depends on its customer's total satisfaction, which in turn comes from adopting TQM. Firms get better customer satisfaction and resultant favorable response, which improves the profit picture for the firm.

Let us understand what is QUALITY of a product or service.

Product Quality – can be defined as product meeting its specifications, which have been finalized by Marketing Research conducted to ascertain market needs. A quality product is the one, which while in use, satisfies or delights the customer.

American Society for Quality Control defines Quality as follows:

Quality is the totality of features and characteristics of a product or service that bear on its ability to satisfy stated or implied needs. Maruti and Honda City both meet with their own respective quality standards and customers consider these products as of good quality. However, with far better performance Mercedes car is known as a better or higher quality product.

With training in quality management and worker empowerment the worker in the factory and the field salesman can keep improving the quality of their product/service delivery and this is the essence of TQM.

Gaining and Retaining Customers

Introduction—firms, which plan for short-term gain or profit, tend to lose in the long run. Careful planning and sustained efforts to work the plans only can make firms successful. There are four stages to the planning process—

1. Environment analysis
2. Strategic planning
3. Plan implementation
4. Built in control systems

Environment Analysis—firms operate in the business environment of the area/country in which they operate. Business environment consists of the General business environment and the Competitive business environment.

General environment factors are given below:

- Demographic—population density, growth, migration from villages to towns, income dispersion, language spoken, religion form the demographic environment of the business area the firm wants to cater to. For example, in India lot of villagers keep shifting to towns. Sellers can look for opportunities in the migration.
- Social environment—increase in women workforce provides a major challenge of home convenience products like vacuum cleaners, washing machines, and ovens, ready to cook food.
- Cultural environment—India has a rich cultural heritage. In state of the country has festivals of their own and then there are national festivals. Sellers find festival time in India a veritable boon for the business, as traditionally lot of new products are purchased during festivals, like, Eid, Deepavali.
- Political environment—laws on pollution, emission norms for vehicles. Political Will is required for sustaining liberalized economy and the role of foreign player in the country. Firms need to understand political environment to be able to take full advantage of the same.
- Legal system of the country lays down the standards of business and commerce. Consumer protection laws are meant to ensure that no seller can take any individual for a ride, by over charging, selling wrong product.
- Macroeconomic environment covers the prevailing interest rates, balance of payment between countries, monitory reserves and surpluses, exchange rates.
- Global environment—world economy and world politics are getting intermingled as national political interests get subsumed in the economic interests. With more countries including china opting for open economy, competition is forging ahead in countries including India.

Michael Porter's Five Force Model shown below- best describes Competitive Environment.

	Threat of New Entrants	
Bargaining power of suppliers	**Rivalry amongst existing players**	Bargaining power of buyers
	Threat of substitute products	

Fig. 3.5. Five Force Model

As is well known, existing players provide the greatest challenge to the firm. Proactive firms try to create entry barriers to dissuade new firms from entering the business. Patented products, unique technology, strong hold on channel members, tight control of suppliers and product use delight of the buyers prove to be good barriers.

If the rail fare goes high, people could find it better to fly. Firms must know the substitute products, their marketing strategies, to be always ahead of them.

If there are a large number of suppliers, then, firms can pick and choose and keep their bargaining power. However when they care for only a handful of suppliers and they have many buyers, it is useful to have long range relationships, contracts with them.

In the same way, if there are only a few buyers and the firm has number of competitors, the buyers will have the bargaining power. It is best to provide value additions and superior service to the customers. Brand equity provides the market edge to the firm.

Let us reiterate the obvious, "**Markets or customers are people with cash, the marketing team of a firm tries to lure them in to buying the products in preference to competitive product. The product comes from manufacturing (own or outsourced), and the raw material, manpower, technology, information about the market are the backbone of the final marketing operations**".

It is also true that the firm with no specific aim goes astray. Therefore the management must provide a Vision to the organization, get it accepted by the entire workforce to make it a **Way Of Life** in the organization.

Corporate Vision

It is an idea, theory or commitment for doing good to known and unknown persons, the customers. In public life and in politics too only the visionaries have achieved great successes. Mahatma Gandhi had a vision of an independent India, with villages as the core of developmental activities. Pundit Nehru's vision was of an India with socialistic pattern of society.

In business Rahul Bajaj's vision can be described as " providing a low cost two wheeler of international quality to the middle and lower middle class of the country." There is no mention of setting up of factories, marketing and making profit in the vision statement. Vision is inspirational in nature, can be written down or even unwritten; it should be accepted by the firm's team and they should be committed to it.

Strategic Mission

Strategic mission of an organization defines its business, gives it its character, its reason for existence, boundaries within which it would operate, what it would do and what it would not do. It also provides behavior norms for its members. Mission statement is firms image before its stakeholders. It tells what are the areas the firm wants to enter and with what product ranges. It forms the main stream and binding force for the different activities of the firm.

Goal

They are mission statements concretized which give the firm its economic and non-economic areas of operation. They provide the firm's team with a clear guideline about actions needed to be taken.

Objectives

They are the end results for which the firm puts their resources and skills. They are time bound, talk of trade offs and serve as base for resolving conflicts in the firm.

Firm's Business—the firm has to decide the range of activities in which it will operate as follow:

- Industries—will the firm work in consumer durable area, FMCG, or industrial products. In consumer durables will it be cars, mo-bikes or white goods like refrigerators. Or will it work in a combination of durables?
- Products—the range and usage category. Will it be a single hotel or a hotel chain; five star or any other category?
- Skills and competencies—technical know-how purchase or Research and Development, assimilation of technology, technology upgrades for gaining and maintaining competitive advantage.
- Geographic and income group market segmentation—are the products elitists, for common people and will the firm sell only in local market or in the entire country. Will it go global?

Cost Center or Profit Center approach—large businesses, which become unwieldy for management, are made in to Cost or Profit centers where each center must look after its interests as a separate unit and show its profit. Many loss making areas of firms take a piggy ride on profit making areas with no justification at all.

From the mid seventies of the twentieth century major changes have taken place in the marketing process worldwide and its effect has reached India too in the last decade of that century.

Pre 1970 process can be described as given below:

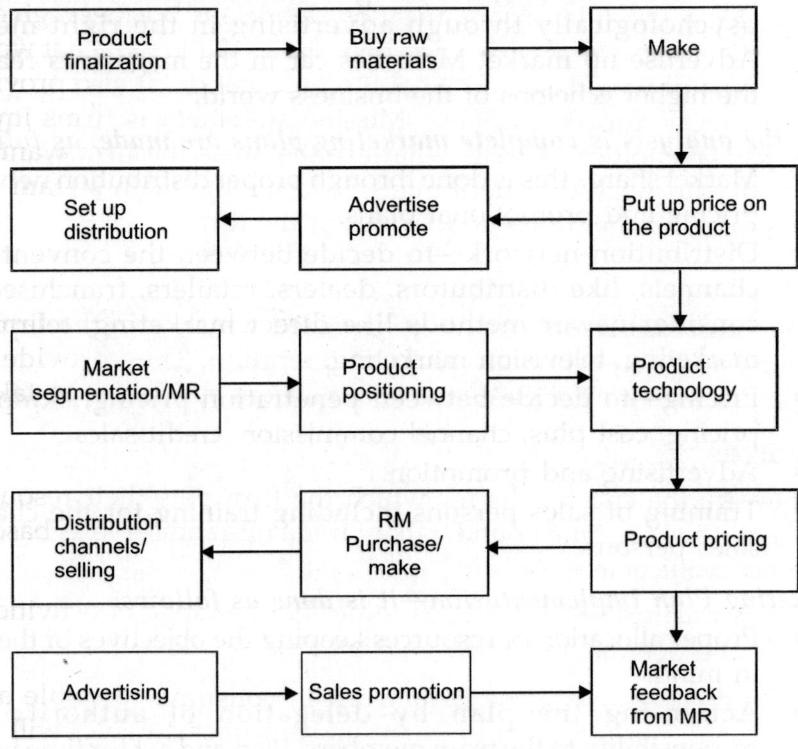

Fig. 3.6. Business Process

It can be seen that there is greater emphasis while planning marketing strategies is now on market information, competitive actions and changes in business environments.

Plans for the Marketing Department of a firm consists of the following three areas—

- Market situation analysis—it consists of understanding the General and Competitive business environment, opportunities and threats that the firm faces. Marketing Research gives the business potential in the given market segment, new competition being planned. Consumer behavior and trends of growth or decline in the market.
- Market Segment—for each product, there is a market segment from which the customers are most likely to buy the product. Market Research gives a clear idea of the segment/s, which would be the most likely buyers of the product.

- Product Positioning—firms try to place the product, both physically through the right distribution channel and psychologically through advertising in the right media,. Advertise up market Mercedes car in the magazines read by the higher echelons of the business world.

After the analysis is complete marketing plans are made, as follows:

- Market share –this is done through proper distribution network, pricing and promotional plans.
- Distribution network—to decide between the conventional channels, like distributors, dealers, retailers, franchisees or consider newer methods like direct marketing, telephone marketing, television marketing.
- Pricing—to decide between penetration pricing, skimming pricing, cost plus, channel commission, credit sales.
- Advertising and promotion.
- Training of sales persons including training for the channel sales persons.

Marketing Plan Implementation—it is done as follows:

- Proper allocation of resources keeping the objectives of the firm in mind.
- Action-ing the plan by delegation of authority and responsibility to the team members. Plan and act for time bound results.
- Benchmarking and controlling the results through a feed-back system.

Marketing Organization Structure

Business in India has been undergoing changes much faster now than ever before. Business environment, both general and competitive is changing rapidly. Hence, an organization structure, which does not match up to the needs of the changes, loses the market in no time. It is therefore imperative for firms to keep themselves abreast of the changes to enable them to modify themselves according to the circumstances and market situation. Flatter organization where decision-making is spread across the tiers is taking roots at the present. In marketing, no manager can even survive by remaining away from the market place. The days of ivory tower existence are over.

In the first half of the twentieth century, with no or low competition, the stress used to be on manufacturing and sales. The idea of marketing as we understand today was not even remotely known, at least in India. Hence the organization for selling of 1950s can be seen below:

Organization Structure Based On Sales-

CHIEF EXECUTIVE OFFICER

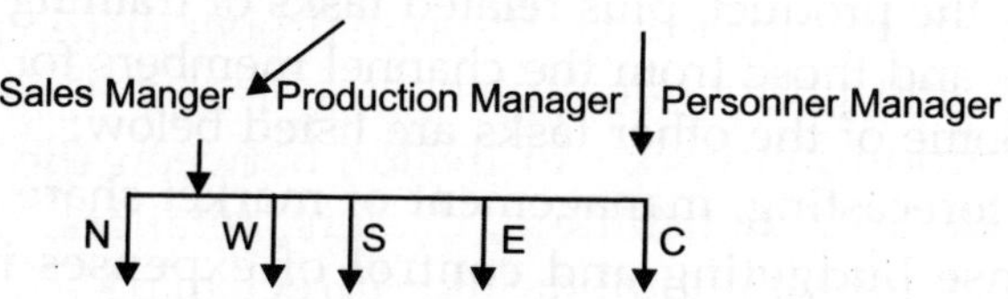

Fig. 3.7. Organisation Chart

Regional managers—north, west, south, east and central India.

The Sales Manager with his regional managers and a team of salesmen with each regional manager was engaged in selling the firms products. Any market research or advertising was got done by outside agencies.

As the firm's business expanded and competition became a reality, the designation of Sales Manager got converted in to that of Marketing Manager, who assumed integrated responsibility of the different functions of marketing. Thus the marketing department was born with organization structure as given below:

Marketing Department Based Organization Structure:

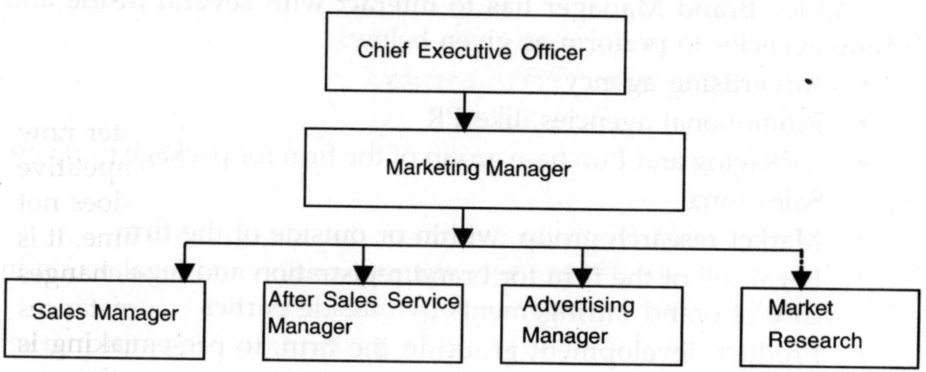

Fig. 3.8. Marketing Organisation Chart

Later on, **Product or Brand Managers** were introduced depending on the product group and severity of competition.

Product or Brand Managers are responsible for the products or brands they are handling. In Hindustan Levers, there could be a

Manager for soaps and shampoos, another one for cooking oils. Or they can have a brand manager just for Lux toilet soap. The task for these managers is to plan total marketing strategy for their brands, like, selection of the product (after market surveys), pricing the product, organizing the distribution network, planning advertising and sales promotion for the product, plus related tasks of training the salesmen, both the firms and those from the channel members for achieving the best results. Some of the other tasks are listed below:

- Sales forecasting, management of market share of the firm.
- Expense budgeting and control of expenses in the area in his control.
- Obtaining feedback from distribution channel members and users about the product and starting product improvement action.
- Continuous market watch for competitive activities.
- Assessment of needs for new products akin to the products being handled.
- Improvement in retail trade through follow ups, better merchandizing support, including shop layouts, window dressing, color schemes, interior decorations.
- Proposing improvement in packaging of the product, including planning variety of sizes, shapes of the packages.

When the Brand/Product Managers do their job well, the job of Marketing Manager becomes easy.

Product/Brand Manager has to interact with several inside and outside agencies to perform as given below:

- Advertising agency
- Promotional agencies, like PR
- Packaging and Purchase group of the firm for package purchase
- Sales force
- Market research group, within or outside of the firm
- Legal cell of the firm for brand registration and legal action in case of brand infringements by outside parties
- Product development group in the firm, to pre-empt market demand changes
- Finance Manager of the firm for getting financial allocations for advertising, promotion changed packaging, training of personnel.

Product management suffers from lack of coordination with other functional areas, like quality management, purchasing, and processing and human resource management. To enable the product manager's function to their full capacity and utility, their role must be clearly defined. Any ambiguity, or transgression in to other roles would cause not only hardship to the product managers but also hinder smooth operation of the department and therefore of the firm.

Understanding the problem areas and building a conflict resolving mechanism in to the system can help sort out the friction between the functional managers and product managers. Besides, the objectives laid down for the product manager should be measurable and once the managers understand the result orientation they would themselves avoid conflicts, which in any case only impede their work and therefore hamper results.

Market Based Marketing Organization

For Products, which are purchased by a distinct variety of customers, the marketing organization needs to take the special requirements of the customer groups. Let us take an example—

PC s are sold to the following category of customers:

- As home PCs
- For business and industry
- As part of manufacturing process

For each category, special type of selling efforts and technical expertise is needed. The marketing department can therefore be organized as follows:

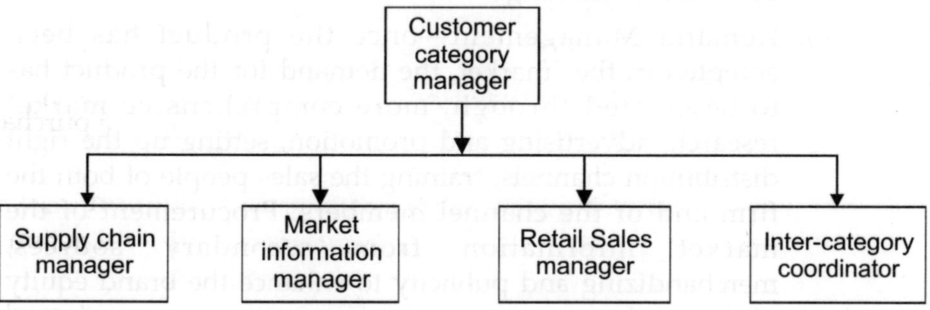

Fig. 3.9. Market Based Organisation

Core Process Based Organization

Functional structures have been found lacking, as they do not provide for inter-functional coordination, which results in each functional head becoming a feudal lord with little or no empathy for other functions. Lack of coordination can be removed by two methods as given below:

1. Creating teams with one member from each functional area, e.g., one from Marketing, one from Operations or Production, one from Human Resource Management and one from Finance.

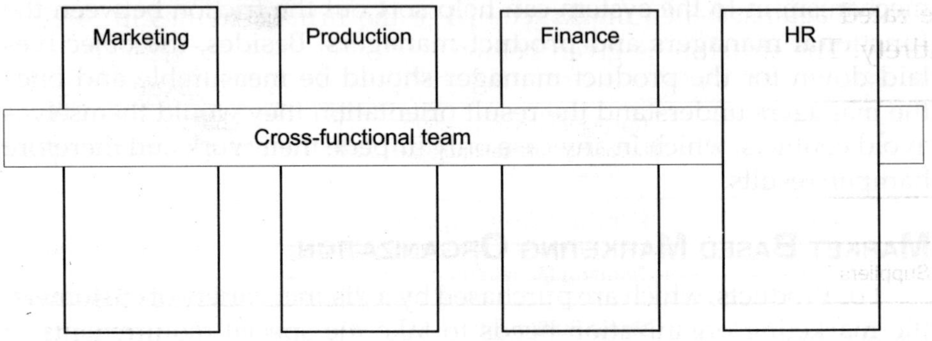

Fig. 3.10. Cross Functional Team

2. Cross functional structure- there are the following three areas of activity in any firm, and the structure takes in to account the best way of operating through these activities—
   i. Product development—activities connected to new product idea development, manufacturing technology- purchase of technology or indigenous development through R&D, market research to find its market, pilot production, leading up to test marketing.
   ii. Demand Management—once the product has been accepted in the market, the demand for the product has to be created through, more comprehensive market research, advertising and promotion, setting up the right distribution channels, training the sales people of both the firm and of the channel members. Procurement of the market information from secondary sources, merchandizing and publicity to enhance the brand equity of the products.
   iii. Order fulfilment—these activities start once the order is received and start with materials management including inventories and the latest innovation of JUST IN TIME supplies from the vendors to ensure that the current assets remain at the lowest possible levels and money is not blocked in inventories, more than really essential;

conversion of raw material into finished saleable product, finished goods inventory and outward logistics of dispatches to the customers.

These cross functional activities, along with resource management-the financial, human, technology and information resource, infrastructure and finally the management controls, where the activities are rated against bench marks, complete the firms activities in there entirety. The structure is given below:

	Resources-finance, HR, Infrastructure, technology, information	
	Product Development	
Suppliers ←	**Demand Management**	→ Buyers
	Order Fulfilment	
	Controls-benchmarking results	

Fig. 3.11. Cross Functional Chart

Flatter Organizations Structures

The need for faster decision making and coming closer to the customer has led to flatter organization structures. The first contact with the customer knows him and his problems best and hence within the firm's guidelines, he should be taking the decisions with regards to his customers. This has led to the CEOs coming closer to the men on the first level when they can motivate them and give moral support when necessary. In Information Technology area, these have become popular, as there are only three tiers in the firm's hierarchy as given below:

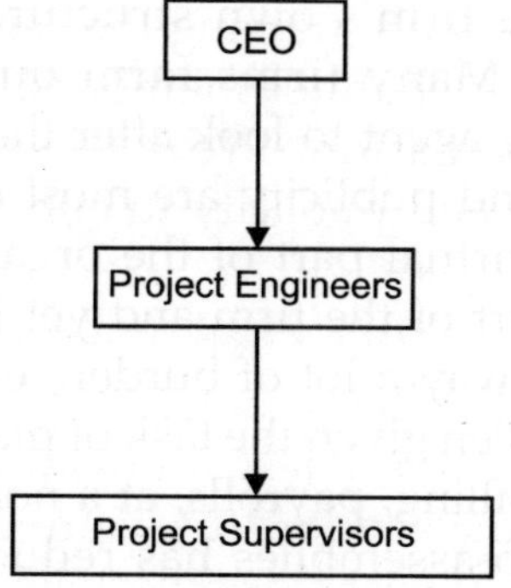

Fig. 3.12. Flat Organisation Chart

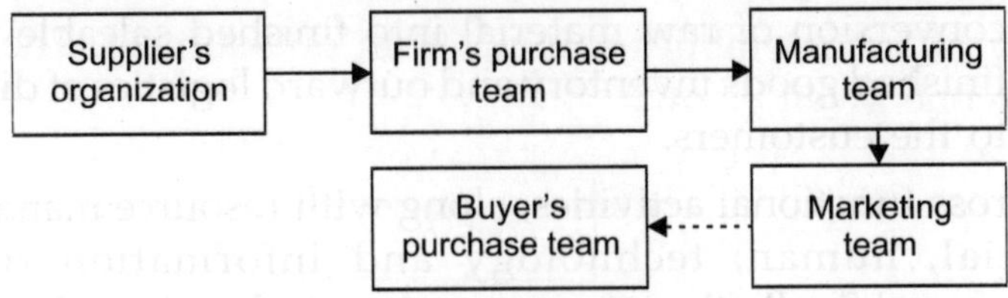

Fig. 3.13. B to B Process

Other small/medium size organizations are considering having flat structure, which gives them decision speeds, shortening the response time with inside and outside customers, adding one rung in the competitive advantage ladder.

Networking Teams

An extension of flat structures is networking teams, where the functions are divided in to teams, which are homogenous in nature, work for a common goal and extend their arms to other teams for coordination. These are inter-firm and intra-firm teams. A few examples are given below:

Marketing team could be subdivided as sales, advertising after sales service and marketing research teams. The concept of networking is new in India but is likely to catch up due to its flexibility, ease and speed of decision-making.

Virtual Organizations

The concept of virtual organizational structure is not new to India. As stated earlier, even in the first half of the twentieth century, sales departments of firms did not have a separate market research cell. When the need arose, outside agencies were given the task of conducting the research. Virtual organizational structures are those which do not form the firm's own structure, but which are there available to the firm. Many firms farm out selling functions by appointing a sole selling agent to look after the same. Others farm out research. Advertising and publicity are most common areas given to outside agencies. The virtual part of the organization is non-existent on the organization chart of the firm and yet it exists, it performs the given tasks and takes away a lot of burden, expense and worry from the firm. One firm has even given the task of maintaining their accounts and finance including billing, payrolls, at a nominal expense. Farming out manufacture of sub-assemblies has reduced the manpower to a great extent in many firms, all they need to do is keep a strict vigil on the quality of subassemblies coming from outsourcing. The structure would like one given below:

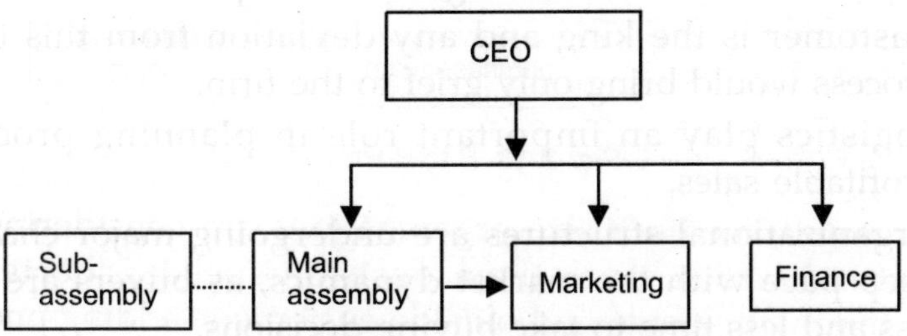

Fig. 3.14. Virtual Organisation Chart

As can be seen the sub-assembly has been framed out and it figures in the organization chart only in dotted lines.

With the advent of globalization liberalization and privatization of Indian economy, a large influx of international firms has started their operations in India and more are likely to enter the Indian market. Managers have to therefore upgrade their concepts and systems. Some of the ideas are given below for them:

- Satisfying customers with a long-term commitment for supply of good quality goods with innovative features and life long service support for the products, with availability of spare parts and service engineers.
- Offering a complete range of products under one brand umbrella of consistently good quality for enhancing customer loyalty.
- Customization of even mass-produced products for catering to discerning buyers. Maruti car can be purchased with customer's own interior specifications like seats, ceiling and stereo system. De-massification of message in advertising is meant to speak the language of a single representative of the market segment.
- Relationship marketing helps in keeping customers loyal for a long period of time. Newsletters, special events regular personal contacts help in building relationships for increased and sustained profits.
- Data files for constant contacts at several levels, personal and through advertisements, direct mails are useful to combat competitive forces.
- Partnership with suppliers and dealers help in firm's effort by keeping products of top quality on the top of the retailer's

displays. Greater the involvement of the firms personnel from each area and of every level, better the chances of continuous improvement in sustained growth and profits.

- Customer is the king and any deviation from this thought process would bring only grief to the firm.
- Logistics play an important role in planning process for profitable sales.
- Organizational structures are undergoing major changes to keep pace with the market dynamics, as buyers are having less and less time to take buying decisions.

Technology and Innovation—Competitive Advantage

Innovation, research and development have been the fruits of human endeavour, which have come about on their own and have not been dependent on any desire or need of the market / customers. Right from the time the wheel was invented it was not supported or called for by a market demand. There is no upper limit of human ingenuity except what comes in the human mind. Steam engine, aeroplane, radio transmission, telephone and now the cell phone, atomic energy, satellite channels, space travel computers are a few examples of basic research, which have done wonders for human life as also drastically changed the way we live, think and act. Alexander Graham Bell was trying to develop a device to help his deaf aunt to enable her to listen. The device he built has transformed the entire communication system, bringing peoples of the world closer despite the distances today, working on the base already available researchers are busy in applied or industrial research in their attempt to make the life a little more easy, comfortable and convenient; making life more full. With the economic divide in the world where there are rich nations who can indulge in developing fancy cars, speed boats, super sonic jets, the poor nations are trying to develop low cost items of daily needs, food, clothing shelter, medical care and education.

Usually the fundamental research is left to the confines of the academics like the universities, industrial or product development and research is the prerogative of business and industrial houses and some stand alone research organizations, which sell their research findings to business houses. Before the product developed by research can be manufactured it has to undergo the following steps:

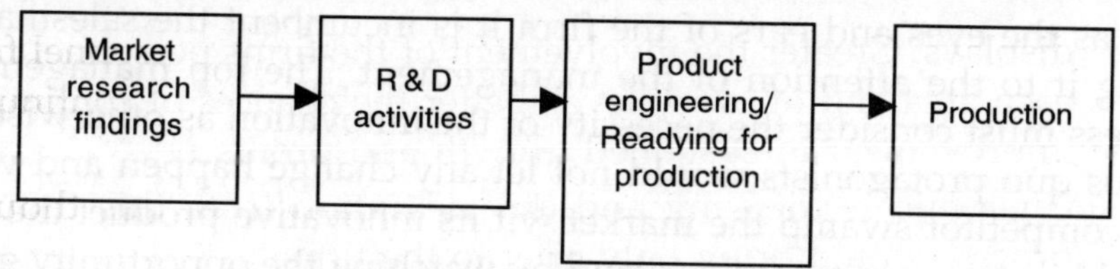

Fig. 3.15. Product Development Process

A product launched today, with just a hunch that it will sell and make profits for the firm can become a dicey. Hence, most firm would invest huge amounts in production only after they have scanned the market demand competitive products and product life cycle. R&D activities start when the firm is reasonably sure that the product will not fail in the market. An R&D design and drawings usually need the engineering process where the production engineers and systems group make production designs when the product gets ready for being sent to the production unit.

New products, innovations do not easily find favor with the management; the marketing team is the only one in the know of the salability of the product and all others including production team, purchasing find the new product a hindrance in their activities, a retarding factor. The problem is overcome by remaining transparent with the teams even during market research period through the engineering phase.

As the new brands and products come appearing in the market the existing firms must plan to differentiate their products at a reasonable costs to remain in the market. The changing customer demands, tastes have created an urgency factor for such differentiated products. It has also reduced the life cycle of most products. Many well-established firms can get derail if they do not have the new product or differentiated product in their product portfolio. The levels of hierarchy make the decision making a major problem, as it is difficult to have everyone to agree to one proposal. The firms, which can afford to put money in research, believe in maintaining status quo, and the smaller firms strive hard to innovate through research and come out a winner. In such cases stand alone research units with no affiliation with any business house, with confidence of proving their product can sell their designs to the firms looking for the same, big and small.

Innovation Decisions

The first contact the firm has with the buyers is through the sales team. It is the salesman who gets to know about the changing trends and as the eyes and ears of the firm it is incumbent the salesman to bring it to the attention of the management. The top management, no less must consider the necessity of the innovation as otherwise the status quo protagonists would not let any change happen and when the competitor swamp the market wit its innovative product the firm would just remain a passive stand by watching the opportunity going a begging in front of them.

The major success to the firm comes from the new products and not from copying others. In most cases copied products betray the seller's lack of knowledge about the product and hence are only short-lived products.

For Sustainable Competitive Advantage three basic methods need to be discussed viz. *a.* differentiation, *b.* cost leadership *c.* quick response. The firm can effectively use its R&D for achieving competitive advantage using all the three methods as given below-

- Product differentiation can best be achieved by adding value to the product for the benefit of the customer. First came the cell phones, which became an instant rage with the customers. Then started a race for giving SMALLER, LIGHTER cell phones. Next the value addition race began, with Internet connectivity, digital built-in camera in the cell phones. Memory bank, SMS facility, hands free usage, are already there and yet the customer is looking for yet some more features. Old cell phones are discarded for the sake of new and this customer desire keeps spurring the research engineers in to putting bigger wonders in the small cell phone.
- Cost leadership is possible with improved technology, simpler methods of production and with increase in product demand created by the product differentiation, which allows the firm to achieve the economies of scale.
- Quick response to market needs (at times known and sometimes unknown needs, like that of cell phones before they were invented and introduced in the market, a no one was even aware of some product call cell phone.). Market demand, once it becomes known must excite the marketing personnel as opportunities for having a profitably selling product. In the task of bringing the new product to the market they have to heavily depend on the research engineers. A vibrant R&D Lab, which is constantly interacting with the marketing people, could gear up to develop the new product in as short a time as feasible. The first comers can become market leaders.

Retaining the leadership position depends on the firm's strategic plan considering the stage of product life cycle the product falls in as also the competitive activities.

Technology Plans

Innovations and technology upgrades have been the biggest forces in the market place, which have displaced several lead players with relative new comers, while sending the techno-backwards in to oblivion. Some firms may be indulging in industrial spying to gather competitive research information, others follow a more conservative route of tying up with independent research institutes, following up with technical journals, attending seminars on the subject and by listening to knowledgeable people including through gossip.

For introducing totally World New Products in the market, a product about which no customer has even an inkling market research is a fruitless exercise. Test marketing in the most suited segment, discussions with the customers about their response to the product's use and the benefits accrued to the customer, are more useful methods for new products. If the product is a high-tech one it is a good idea to have a technical expert ,when the sales person is talking to the customer taking his product feedback. A psychologist can be present under the guise of a salesman (as the customer may not like to talk to a psychologist at all), to monitor the customer's body language and his unsaid reactions.

The firm must analyze its own capability and capacity for product development and innovation. Besides these factors the most important factor is the firms top management's mindset towards the new product development and innovation. Lot of senior managers feel that since their products are selling well there is absolutely no need to spend in new developments, little they realize that they are sitting on a ticking time bomb, as somewhere a competitor is planning to displace their product with a new product.

New Product Development

Firms can have options of developing new products themselves, or buying out technology developed by someone else. For own development the firm must watch out for the following areas:

- Do they have the infrastructure for product development?
- Can they allocate the required resources, financial and human needed for the purpose?

- Does the management accept that all research would not bear fruit and is still ready to invest?
- Would the firm give autonomy to the development team?
- Has the firm a history of development successes or of failures?

An average expenditure on R&D by different category of firms is given below, which is by no means indicative of what a firm should be spending:

Table. 3.4. R & D Expenditure

Product group	*Expenditure on R&D as per cent of sales*
Medicines and drugs	11.5
Computers and computer communications	10
Automobiles	3.5
Electrical and electronics	3.5
Telecom	3.1
Service industry	1.0
Food	0.7

The all industry average in the USA comes to nearly 4 percent of sales turn over. This does not reflect all the research that is going on in the private and the government laboratories. Hence, technology transfer has become a big business in the entire world. Small firms especially are not in a position of having their own research department. Large firms are normally more for retaining status quo and therefore their research activities are more of showpieces only to impress the investing public, the buyers and venders as also the government. New products take time to get established in the market and hence most firms like to keep both old and new technology products together in the market till the old product is rejected by the buyers totally. This decision to bring in new technology and when to discard the old one has to be taken by considering the market forces into account. Every new technology product would behave differently in the market place and would have separate life cycle and predictions to precise which must be backed by continuous research. R &D is being carried out on, besides new product development, on new processes for manufacturing, in order to reduce production time and costs. The new processes could help the firm in bringing out new products at a faster pace.

When a new product idea is conceived in a firm, it appears as a new business opportunity and the R&D takes over from that point onwards till the design is ready for production. Product specifications are built and after trial production. The firm freezes these and production is launched. Till this point the firm is only in the spending mode. Only after this point, when the firm places the product in the market and it starts getting satisfied customers in greater numbers that the firm gets in to the profit zone and it remains there. Later on the product obsolescence takes over and it has to be phase out from the firm's portfolio. This period is shortening today, as new innovative products are rapidly converging on the market placed, with catchy designs, packages, advertising and promotional plans.

The technology can be obtained ideally from the firm's own R&D Lab. Alternately, firms can tap independent research agencies, engaged in research for selling the technology developed by them. Cooperation in competition is also possible, especially when the R&D costs are touching the skies. Joint venture agreements, license production provides access to technology from the other firms.

Besides the firms can have access to technology through two firms cooperating in development of technology. Funding the researchers needing the money for product development on the condition that the firm would obtain the technology at no extra cost. Different firms use different methods for the purpose.

One of the most important aspects of getting into new technology is the firm's ability and it's resourcefulness in being able to correctly imbibe the technology without any hiccups, and exploit the same to the optimum level. If the technology absorption were not properly done, the firms buying and selling the technology would keep blaming each other without any consequence. Therefore before going in for new technology, the firm should prepare itself for the same by recruiting the right persons needed to augment the existing team, getting the required equipments and the test instruments.

The firms should not think of new technology if it is a patented one, or it does not add to the competitive advantage of the firm. However, if the technology available is better and low in cost the firm should not hesitate in going for it. If the production is not a part of the firm and it is only into buying and selling, there is no reason for it to buy technology. If the technology is easily available it may be the right thing to buy it instead of developing it. Difficult technology should be developed by the firm as then the firm can totally customize it, patent it and make it really exclusive for enabling the firm in enjoying the competitive advantage for a long time.

The top management must be involved in the decision to introduce new technology to make it a success. The decision to go for new technology should be based on scanning the different technologies available or being researched, but only after the firm has ascertained about the market for the new technology product. If the product is new to the world, then the results of test marketing and in-depth interviews wit the customers would provide the right guidelines for full-fledged introduction of the product in the market. In house R&D can provide the firm with the desired flexibility to introduce the product at the most appropriate time. The firm must provide proper resources, finance and manpower and a practical time frame for research engineers for team to succeed. Most of the time the top management is just breathing down the neck of the engineers, causing them to do shoddy work and delays in project completion. The management must develop a culture conducive for innovative work, without being critical of failures, as even the best of the engineers do not succeed all the time. However , industrial research must develop an instinct of honouring time and of producing time bound results , even when the time period for completion of the project has been established by them only.

Questions for discussion

1. Do you believe there is any connection between Supply Chain and Cash flow? If yes, describe in detail.
2. Who are the internal and external customers in the supply chain? Describe their role in creating an efficient supply chain.
3. Please discuss if the organizational structure can have any bearing on its success as a marketing firm. If yes, what are the options available today for making the structures more customer-friendly?

MARKETING GAME

The team should scan the competitive business environment for the chosen product in the selected country using Porters five force model.

While understanding Competitive environment, it is useful to use Michael Porters five-force model. In good old days competition meant only the players in the field. The five-force model makes a comprehensive statement on what constitutes competition and is given below:

Table 3.5. Five Force Model

	New Entrants Threat	
Suppliers bargaining power	**Present competitors**	Buyer bargaining power
	Substitutes	

New Entrants

They pose a disguised threat as their entry time and manner is not known till the very last moment. Each business area has some entry barriers and exit barriers. If entry barrier is high and exit barrier low then it is the best place to be, because new firms will not enter and low performing firms will quit instead of trying to undersell and make every one lose profits. Entry barriers are one or more from the following list:

- Government regulations like licenses
- High project costs
- Technology difficult to obtain
- Market in maturity or decline stage
- Paucity of needed raw materials
- Non-availability of channel members

More players in the field mean excess production capacity; lower profit margins for the players.

Substitute Products

They need to be watched carefully as with innovation, new technology they can pose a major threat. Home interior walls can be covered by lime wash (choona), emulsion paints, wallpaper or wood panels. Each has its own pricing formula, plus and minus points.

Suppliers

Suppliers to the firm play a key role in product costs. If the buyers are few and suppliers several, then buyers will enjoy the power to bargain. In case there are only a handful of suppliers and several buyers, suppliers hold advantage.

Buyers

Buyers of the firm are always the most important part in the game of marketing. With large number of buyers and few suppliers, the buyers can be at the supplier's mercy.

The teams need to analyse competition in their chosen market, are they strong, large in number and aggressive, or the firm can lead the pack of competitors.

How to locate the competitors is a vital question for the firm. Pepsi knows that Coke is its biggest competitor, and yet they cannot neglect minor competitors. In the area of TVs in India, Sony, Samsung, Philips, are the known competitors and yet there are several small assemblers in each major centre and they account for nearly twenty-five per cent of total sale of TVs. Same thing is true for many industries including the computer industry. For this purpose the firm should arrange regular feedback from its marketing or field sales force, so that the real picture of competition, its business terms, and prices can be known. Otherwise the firm is fighting a battle with ghosts.

CHAPTER 4

Organizational Buying Behaviour

Aims and Outcomes of The Chapter

Organisational buyers behave differently then the consumers. The chapter deals with these differences to enable students appreciate the difference and plan their marketing communications in a suitable manner.

Organizations or firms involved in manufacturing goods purchase, Raw Materials and Components needed in the manufacturing process. They also buy consumables like electricity, water and gasses, which are consumed, in the manufacturing process. Such purchases by the firms are having the following characteristics:

1. Fewer buyers but Large quantity buyers
2. Close Supplier and Buyer relationship
3. Geographic concentration of buyers
4. Derived demand
5. Inelastic demand/ Fluctuating demand
6. Professional purchasing
7. Several buying influences

Firms produce large volumes of products and hence need large quantity of materials. An individual will buy a TV picture tube only as a replacement only if his TV set's picture tube has become defective. A TV set manufacturer will be buying picture tubes in thousands for putting them in the TV sets. Yet as compared to individual buyers, TV set manufacturers will be far less in number.

In most cases industries are established near the source of one or two major raw materials needed for manufacture. Hence, most industries are concentrated in that area. Gujarat has lot of cotton, which accounts for large number of textile mills in that region.

The demand of raw materials is derived from the plan of manufacture of products, which use the material. The tyre sale is dependent on the number of cars manufactured in a particular period.

For such intermediary products the demand remains inelastic over long periods of time with only marginal changes. However, it could also be grammatically changed in case the buyers find different usages of the product when the demand will increase. If the product becomes obsolete, the demand could just disappear, as happens often in fashion garments.

Purchase in such cases becomes a professional discipline. Depending on the value in money terms and also in availability terms, the importance is given to purchase decisions.

Buying situations can be classified as follows:

1. First buy is when a new firm makes the purchases or an old firm tries out a new product.
2. Re-buy takes place when a satisfied buyer buys the product again. This happens when besides the product other factors like firms after sales service, the buyer accepts behaviour of its sales people.
3. Modified re-buy is made when the manufacturer accepts customer's suggestions and product is suitably modified to suit the firm.
4. New task purchase depends on the launch of new products and is planned accordingly.

System for buying in the organizations consists of the following persons:

Initiators are the people who place the requirement of the product before the firm's authorities. In most firms they would be either R& D persons or purchase executives

Users are the people who define the product with specifications and would ultimately use it. They would be R&D Engineers, production engineers

Influencers are the people who influence the purchase decision, which brand; model to buy, from which dealer. These could be R&D Managers, consultants.

Deciders are the authorized people who can decide spending of money for making the purchase. They are of the rank of General Managers,

Approvers are the people with power of approving the purchase like Chief Executive Officers and Managing Directors.

Gatekeepers are those who filter information and see to it that only relevant information reaches the decision makers about the product. These could be receptionists, purchasing agents.

Consumer behavior in organizational buying therefore becomes complex, with a number of persons involved in the decision-making. Therefore unlike in consumer products the role of advertisement in organizational buying is limited to , an image building of the firm and providing detailed information to the buyers about the products.

Environment factors are also major influencers in organizational buying as follows:

Table 4.1. Environmental Factors

Environmental factors	*Organizational factors*	*Interpersonal factors*	*Individual*	*Business buyer*
Level of demand	Objectives	Interests	Age	-do-
Economic outlook	Policies	Authority	Income education for job position	-do-
Interest rate	Policies	Authority	-do-	-do-
Risk of technical changes	Procedures	Status	Personality	-do-
Political and regulatory developments	-do-	-do-	Attitude for risks	-do-
Competitive developments	Organizational structure	Empathy	-do-	-do-
Social	Systems	Persuasiveness	Culture	-do-

Environment factors like market demand of the product influences the quantity of purchase as also purchase frequency.

Economic outlook of the country gives the information on the money supply situation, interest rates for leasing and it has influence on purchase decisions.

If the firms know that a **new technically superior** product is going to be available in the near future, they would not risk large purchased of materials.

Political environment deals with the political will which allows or restricts trading, like the anti-dumping laws of the USA.

If the market is swaying towards **a better competitive product,** the firm may make only cautious purchases.

If **the sociological changes force** the market towards decline then also purchases get reduced. With the availability of packed wheat flour no one is buying wheat and getting it ground in a mill.

Organizational policy changes, changes in hierarchy levels, promotions, procedural changes and systems could alter the purchase pattern of the firm.

Factors connected to individual members of a firm like inter-personnel relations, people's authority, personal interests, empathy with suppliers and persuasiveness of marketers are important for purchase decisions.

Organizational buying decisions are taken by purchase committee consisting of –

1. *CEO, who only wants **the best in the line** product.*
2. *R&D Manager, who wants the **State of the art** product.*
3. *Financial Manager, who wants **value for money**, economical products.*
4. *Purchase Manager, who wants the usual product, to avoid **inventories** hassles.*
5. *Production Manager, who wants no change in assembly process unless new product helps in major **cost reduction.***

- Each one is a customer in his own right and his needs must be satisfied. It calls for communication excellence to put same points in different words to conform to their perception of need as follows-
- To the CEO, " Our product is top of the line as can be seen from our specifications, which incidentally, exceed the specifications given by competition and you can see the testimonials from our national and international customers which speak for themselves".
- To the R&D Manager, " you have heard of the latest proven technology in microprocessors based on fiber optics, you can open the equipment and see it for yourself that we are giving you the State of the Art Product".
- To the Finance Manager, " our product pricing is based on volume business and that is why we can give you the price of our product with latest technology comparable to the price offered by competition for their older generation product."

- To the Purchase Manager, " we believe that by the time our product reaches you, your old inventory would be almost exhausted and it would be easy for you to standardize on our State of the Art Product, which we are sure would make you even more respected member of your firm".
- To the Production Manger, " you would be able to reduce manufacturing time after the training, we will provide to you people, thus reducing the cost of manufacture considerably. Besides, with reduction in quality problem, the firm will get a better Brand image and After Sales Service team would become practically redundant".

It would be necessary to test the product before making the claims as mentioned above.

B-to-B sellers also must understand the consumer behavior because the decision chain in such purchases includes persons only.

Consumer behavior and firms responses find that firms do take care of how the consumer will behave.

1. ITC Agro introduced their branded Atta, HEALTH WORLD first in the south India, as their study showed that south Indians are more quality conscious then north Indians in the matter of a product like Atta, in spite of the fact that the Atta consumption in the north is nine times more than in the south. Once the brand gets established in the south, they will move to the north as well with region specific brands and tastes to suit different palates.
2. Dwarka Men's wear offering cool cotton trousers and shirts, choose the month of March 2000 to launch the product just before the onset of summer. They have successfully marketed their product in the West Asia Europe markets.
3. Targeting their cell phones for the youth of the country, Ericsson have introduced FM Radio in the phones which come in a range of bright colours to capture the fancy of the youth.

Behaviour—Positivism and Interpretivism

Positivism—prediction of buyer's action- Quantitative-consumer rationale, weigh alternatives. With market study, it can be predicted that x percent customers would buy the product.

Interpretivism—understanding consumer practices—qualitative-reality is subjective, each usage experience is unique, and research findings can be subjective. It cannot be generalized, as it is not easy to predict how many first buyers would go for repurchase of the product.

Attitudes play an important role in purchase actions and it is necessary to understand as to how they are formed—

- Direct experience from using the product, "the soap is too hard"
- Influence of family and friends, "Son, buy only Honda motorcycle, it is the best value for money"
- Direct marketing, Eureka Forbes salesman in your house, "see for yourself how easy it is to use the vacuum cleaner Sir"
- Exposure to advertisements, wife to husband, "see the mixer grinder ad on the TV and you would agree it is the best value for money"
- Personality factor, "I can not buy a motor cycle, only a car would do for me"

***Attitudes** – four functions*

- Utilitarian function—brand utility
- Ego-defensive function—product enhances self concept
- Value expressive function—consumer values, life style are reflected
- Knowledge function—fulfilling need to know

Also, there can be a combination of several of these functions.

The task before buyers is one of resolving conflicting attitudes as given below:

Tasty v/s healthy food, pizza or fruits

Quality v/s price, Wipro PC or the assembled one

Sturdy v/s elegant, jeans or silk

The decisions are taken on purchases on the following considerations-

The Family

Economics

Emotional support

Life style

Family socialization- manners, values, goals

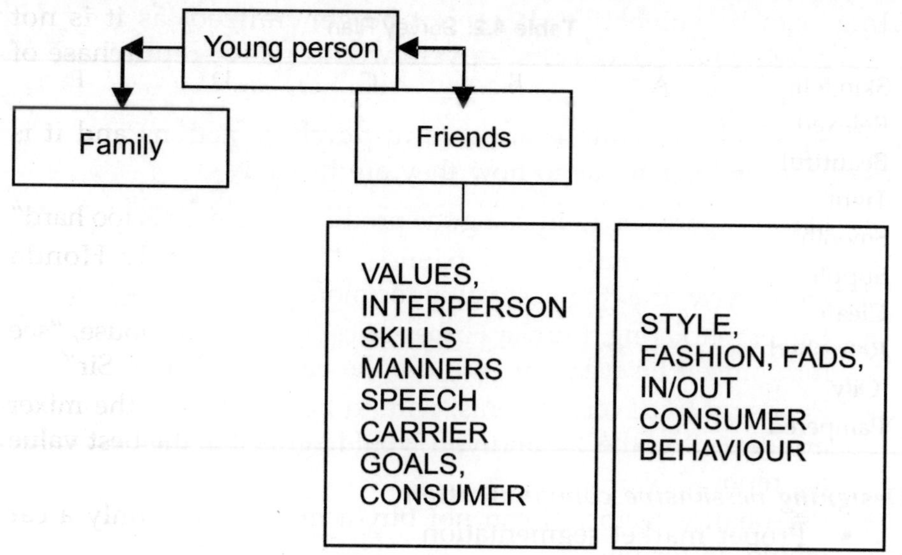

Fig. 4.1. Decision Plan

Family Consumer Roles

Husband/Wife

Children

Teens

Family life cycle, where lifestyle keeps changing as can be seen from the following:

- Bachelor—mostly carefree
- Honeymooners—need affordable luxuries
- Parents-young children—need baby products
- Parents-teenage children—need teen fad products, like FM Radio
- Parents with children away from home, health care products
- Dissolution—old age homes

Feeling and Emotions

These can be measured on a scale. Let us try out a skin cream and get reactions of women after they have used the cream on a scale as follows—

A-Like it very much—**B**-like it—**C**-nothing special—**D**-do not like—**E**-do not like it at all.

The survey can be done on the following parameters:

Table 4.2. Survey Plan

Skin felt	A	B	C	D	E
Relaxed					
Beautiful					
Tight					
Smooth					
Supple					
Clean					
Refreshed					
Oily					
Pampered					

Designing persuasive communication

- Proper market segmentation
- If product transcendent segmentation—umbrella messaging for all audience
- Good PR
- Media plan—consumer profile to match with media audience profile
- Each media is effective for some products, audiences and advertising objectives
- WWW
- Overlapping audience

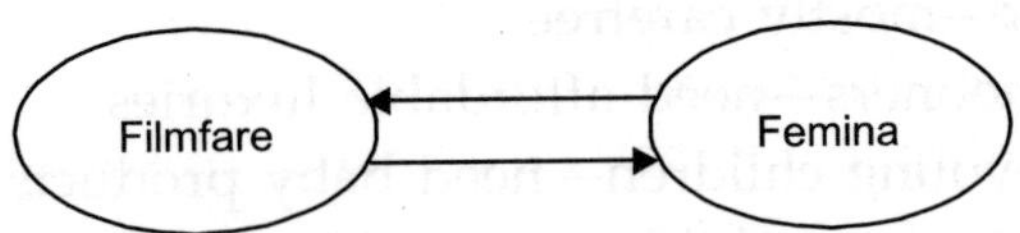

Fig. 4.2. Overlap Readership

Some customers read Filmfare other read Femina and yet other read both.

In advertising copy, it is important to think of the following:

- Copy appeal
- Copy length
- Endorsements
- Visuals
- Time limit offers
- Free trial offers
- Pricing

Example

You are the Marketing and Advertising manager of Advance Stereo Systems with five competitors, Philips, Videocon, BPL, AIWA and Sony. Your market share is 3%. You have to increase it to 5% in one year. Discuss the following questions about market and its behaviour-

1. What cultural, social personal and psychological factors influence the buyers most? What sort of research should be undertaken to know the buyer's attitude and behaviour?
2. What factors should advance focus on their marketing plan?
3. What kind of marketing activities should plan in advance to coincide with each stage of consumer buying process?

Plan your target market in Delhi, and look at the marketing mix factors for giving your recommendations to advance MD.

Purchase Decisions Plan

1. Problem recognition—when the need tends to become acute.
2. Information search—personal-family, friends, neighbours, acquaintances, Commercial-Advertising, Salesmen, dealers, packaging, displays, Public Source—Consumer Rating Organizations, Experiential-handling, examining, using the product.
3. Evaluation of alternatives with weightage given on parameters decided by you, cameras—size-weight, auto-focus, zoom, speed, price, hotels- location, cleanliness, atmosphere and price.

Purchase Decision—There can be a situation where after deciding to buy, you delay or even cancel the purchase. Sometimes if people close to you have a negative attitude towards the product you may not buy it. Secondly, there may be a change in situation.

Post purchase decisions—

The product could satisfy you.

If you are not satisfied then you could try to reverse the purchase action. Or sell of the product.

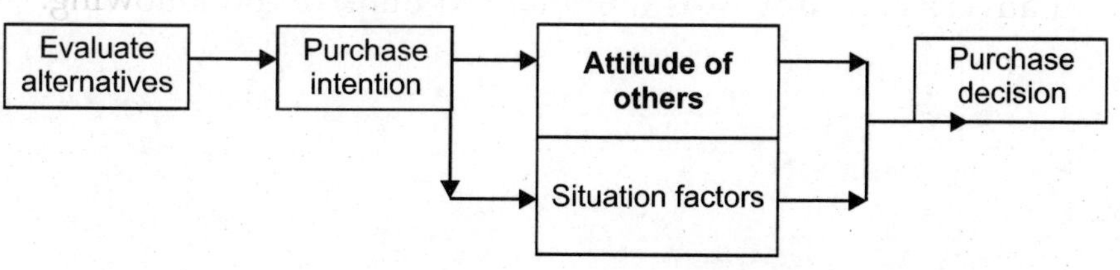

Fig. 4.3. Purchase Decision

Buying decisions are taken from emotional basis. Only seldom they are taken on rational reasoning. For consumer buyer it is important to understand the hierarchy of needs. Next, companies have to segment the markets in appropriate manner to get a proper product demand fit. In industrial buying mostly the buying decisions are taken jointly in a group and it is wise for the company to understand the group purchase dynamics.

Questions for Discussion

1. Discuss the reasons why it is important for sellers to understand buyer behaviour. How does it differ from industrial buying behaviour?
2. Does market segmentation help in understanding consumer behaviour?

Marketing Game

Study the Microsoft case and prepare answers to the following discussion questions:

1. What is Microsoft's approach to international business? Are they operating as an international, multinational, or global enterprise? What is the customer buying?
2. Evaluate Microsoft's marketing approach to the U. S. market. What changes, if any, would you make in the strategy for the U.S. market?
3. Evaluate the Microsoft's management and staffing for the American market. What changes, if any, would you make?
4. What significance, if any, does Microsoft's experience in the U.S. have for its approach to the rest of the world?

CHAPTER 5

Competition Types

Aims and Outcomes of the Chapter

One of the most important jobs of the marketing person is knowing his competitors well, how do they behave in the market place, what are their marketing strategies. The chapter takes the students in the realm of competition to arm them with wisdom of remaining proactive in the market place rather than reacting to competitive moves.

There are several types of competitors in the market as listed below:

- *Monopoly:* When there is only one supplier of a product in the given geographic area. In Indian Railways, Power and some defence supplies are enjoying monopoly status so far. In such cases there is a tendency of putting skimming prices, give less value for money. Only in case there is social commitment that price and service can be in line with the rest of the market.
- *Oligopoly:* When the supplies are made by a small number of major firms. Firms making core raw materials like iron, steel, oil belong to this category.
- *Differentiated Competition:* It is a phenomenon essentially of the Indian market. Industry is divided in to large scale organized players and small scale assemblers, sellers of pirated goods
- *Fragmented Market:* There are several suppliers of the product in the market with similar products and hence pure and perfect competition rules the market.

Competitive Advantage

Firms get their competitive advantage from the following sources:

1. *Differentiation:* Which can be made in either the product or any of the other marketing mix factors like price, promotion and placement.

2. *Cost Differential:* with the help of Economies of scale and Experience curve, firms can achieve lower costs and strategize their pricing to suit the market conditions for gaining market leadership.
3. *Response to Market:* understanding market needs and satisfying them at the appropriate time gives the firms an edge over competition.
4. *Market Focus:* can be achieved by getting in to a niche market and putting the marketing resources like advertising, promotion, personal selling in **that market.**
5. *Service:* differential in service is most difficult to copy, unlike product differential. Many ME TOO products come in the market no sooner a successful product is launched in the market. Services are the people based and hence despite any training given remains unique to the individual service provider.
6. *Vertical Integration:* when the firm takes to manufacturing upstream products like raw materials and components and also does its own retailing in the downstream area, it gains cost effectiveness due to better availability, low or no transaction cost and acceptable quality and better inventory management, it saves on costs too, besides in superior production planning.

Understanding competition- firms with same products, markets are the first level competitors. In order to compete with them the firm must know their strengths and weaknesses, core competencies, plans and policies and their keenness as a competitor.

Marketing research can be used to get competitive knowledge regarding customers' awareness of selected competitors, their perception of competitors product quality and perceived benefits by them, besides areas of product availability and the quality of their technical and sales teams. These can be tabulated as given below:

Table 5.1. Market Research Findings

	Competitor 1	*Competitor 2*	*Competitor 3*
Awareness of the customer	A	B	B
Product quality and benefits perception	A	B	B
Availability of product	B	A	C
Quality of technical support	C	C	D
Quality of sales team	B	B	B

A –Excellent B- Good C- Average D-Poor

Besides, the company has to learn the market share competitors enjoy individually, the top of the mind brand recall of competitive products and customers' attitude towards competition and their products.

COMPETITOR'S STRENGTHS

It could be in the following areas:

1. Product differentiation
2. Prices and discounts
3. Distribution channels
4. Cost of capital and ability to borrow funds at low interest rates
5. Loyal customers
6. Purchase
7. Man power—committed and loyal
8. Research for new product technology as per market demand
9. Government contacts
10. High brand equity and firm's image
11. Resource allocation

Competitors plans—to stay one-step ahead, competitors keep modifying their plans, as reactions to environment changes or as pro-active approach to anticipated competitive moves. In either case the firm needs to continuously monitor competitive plans and changes as they keep occurring. It will give the firm an insight into what the competitors are hoping to achieve by way of market share, geographic coverage and profits including cash flow situation of the competitors. Besides the mindset of competitive management, it is also the size of their organization. A small manufacturer who is able to sell his product in local area will not attempt to upset his market by any drastic strategic change unless he is setting up additional facilities for manufacture larger volumes. A cash rich competitor can indulge in selling at a loss to stave off new competitors from entering the market. Usually competitor's financial results of the last three years can give a good indication to their strengths and competencies. Competitors can be classified as per their strengths and mindsets of their management as follows:

1. *Market Leader:* With highest share of the market they spend a lot on retaining their position of leadership. As the market starts declining they try to reassess their options and strategies. They can hardly fight price wars.

2. *Major Competitor:* With dominant share they can spend on price war and take leadership position if they so desire. They are price leaders in the market; others follow their pricing policy of increasing or decreasing prices.
3. *Minor Competitor:* They need additional resource and management efforts before they can take on the leadership position.
4. *Unsatisfactory Competitors:* They have major management problems and are directionless. They need a bold innovative manager who can turn the organization around. Such competitors should be monitored for their potential as major treats.
5. *Problem Competitors:* Are mostly on their way out and with sensible planning the firm can convert their customers in to its own.

An assessment of competitors offers a major leverage in planning marketing strategies for the firm. Firms can plan resource allocation, management stress and results benchmarking from competitive knowledge.

Competitive cultural ethos plays an important role in their strategic planning of the market. Following gives an insight of different cultures prevalent in the firms:

- Dynamic culture where firms never lose sight of their goals and objectives, are always on the move in pursuit of these goals. They relentlessly strive to increase their market share and brand equity. Coke and Pepsi are two such firms and they ensure that the other does not get even an inch of their ground at any cost. Firms dealing with these competitors should remain as second or third player and wait for the time in future when the dominant player makes a mistake and slips down the ladder. Alternately, the firm could bring a totally new concept product and invest heavily in marketing it to get the better of dynamic competitor.
- Mystery competitor—the competitor who keeps his cards close to his chest till they are out in the market. New products, new package are brought about to startle competition. Firms need to assess the viability of these competitive moves before taking any competitive action.
- Follower competitor—tries to match others. Such competitors should never be taken lightly as while copying they do try to improve on the original and avoid making the mistakes the innovators have made. Patenting designs and technology could save firms from such loss of business and embarrassments.

- **Continuous Market Information** from the field force of firm's sales persons and channel members is the key to having an updated competitive information bank. Firm's field force should therefore be the EYES AND EARS of the firm. The information should be analyzed and competitive firms categorized as weak and strong competitor. Management must use the information as a proactive player and avoid **sudden market share jerks.**
- **Customers' assessment of competitors** is the most effective way of categorizing competition. A survey to find the assessment should be done on a regular basis. A sample of information to be acquired on a scale of 1 to 5 is given below:

Table 5.2. Assessment of Competitors

Competitor/ Attribute	*Product benefits*	*Service rating*	*Channel network coverage/ quality*	*Price/Value for money*
Competitor A				
Competitor B				
Competitor C				
Competitor D				

Besides, competitors market segment, their niche markets need to be known. It will help the firm in positioning its products for optimum results.

Improving Market Share

Notwithstanding severe competition, firms must plan to increase their market share. Firms need to look at the following methods for the purpose:

- Increase customer base by selling to more number of customers through market penetrating prices. Customers can be added from new geographic areas, which have not been exploited by the firm so far.
- Increase the way, the products can be used. Maruti has made their Omni van as a multipurpose vehicle. It can be used as a school bus, delivery van besides it can be used as a large family car.
- Increases usage of the product. *Brush your teeth twice a day/ daily shampoo of hair.*

In order to ensure that the competition does not take away the firm's market share it must make its customer's brand loyal on a long-term basis. Relationship marketing helps in this venture, where the firm is not just waiting to counter the competitive action but is proactively associating the customer to feel and believe that the firm is there only for him/her. When the competition has started its campaign to capture extra market share the firm has to decide on the following variables:

- Product price-is it giving value for money as associated by the brand or does it need any revision?
- Has the competition hit the firm at its lowest strong market? Is it worthwhile to fight competition there or should the firm look for that particular competitor's weak market and hit him there. (Cross Parry)
- Brand Equity needs to be improved by advertising, focused on the target market segment.
- Sales Promotion should be used to facilitate the customer's make up their minds in favour of your product and for making purchases. Countering competitive promotional activities requires close watch of the market movements of goods.

Generic Product as competitors- other than the main competitors of the firm selling same or similar products, there are other products too vying for the customer's rupee. The following examples will amplify the point:

- Motorcycle competing with car. Both are means of transportation. With several payment options as leasing, deferred payments at low interest rates, it is becoming easy for Indian customers to buy a car, although he may just be afford a motorcycle.
- White goods like refrigerators compete with TVs, washing machines as also with a week's holiday at a hill station.
- A new house could be competing with a foreign trip, or a luxury car.
- New cars compete with used cars. To cash on this market, firms like Maruti have started an organization which buys and sells used cars.
- Firms offer low rates on exchange-if the customers return their old product to the seller they get a discount on the new product price.

COMPETITIVE ACTION

If the firm cannot beat the competitor, it should join in the game with similar/diverse strategies. The ideal way, however, is to build the brand equity to such an extent that competition cannot even come near the firm's product sales. May be changed in market segment or getting in to niche market could be the answer. At a point when the firm is on a losing roll, it could plan to divest from that product area. If the trend towards competitive upsurge is of temporary nature, it may be a good idea to just hang on to product, by getting in to penetrating pricing.

Cross Parry—targeting competition in their weak area and doing it simultaneously for several competitors is nerve wrecking but effective way of beating competition. It creates the desired confusion among the competitors, may be they do not know what and who is hitting whom and how. It would need of continuous monitoring and a great degree of management commitment for the action.

Check List

Firms' need to monitor competitors' strategies and plans on a continuous basis. For this purpose they can be guided by a Check List, which ensures nothing is left out. The Check List covers the essential elements of a marketing plan and using it as base. Firms can modify it suitably to meet individual requirements. Some points in the list may not be relevant to some firms and they can be omitted. The numbering of points is not in any particular order and can be revised as per firm's convenience. Following are the areas for which the Check List can be used.

- Marketing Plan—comprehensive marketing plan can be developed by using the desired points from the checklist.
- Information gathering during market research phase can be simplified for data collection. Information on market forces, competition and the firm itself is required.
- Pre-testing and final evaluation of the plan can be built in the process.

Marketing Plan Checklist

Information summary on each competitive firm—

1. Activities
2. Management
3. Performance

4. USP of its products and service
5. Market life cycle—attractiveness growth maturity or decline stage

Financial Summary of the firm—

1. Firms capital resource
2. Future capital needs
3. Debt equity ratio
4. Cash flow
5. Finance deployment areas like salaries, purchasing, advertisements

Note—make the summary easy to understand, investment friendly and exciting otherwise the emerging marketing plan will also be drab and will not produce the desired results.

Competitors Plan For Markets—

1. Business in which they are involved
2. Products/services on offer
3. Market segment
4. Geographic coverage
5. Business history—formation date, products offered and dropped
6. Manufacturing or only trading
7. Annual sales total and product-wise
8. Annual profit total and product-wise
9. Return on equity for the last two years
10. Existing problems, cash crunch, labour or any other
11. Salvage plans if any

Industry Situation

i. Current volumes of business
ii. Growth trends for the next two years
iii. Competitors and their product-wise share of the market
iv. New entrants and competitors who have just left the market
v. Trends affecting business
    a. Economic
    b. Social
    c. Technological
    d. Government regulations
    e. Demographic

Product Analysis

a. Description of each product in detail
b. Product features and the customer benefits associated with each feature
c. Negative elements of each product
d. Patents covering the products and intellectual property rights
e. Higher market share reasons like early entry in the market
f. Possibility of covering the entire product range, related products, accessories

Market Research Analysis

1. Who are the major buyers
2. Where are they located
3. What motivates them to buy the product
4. When do they buy it
5. Is there seasonality in product demand
6. Market share of competitive firms and shifts in market share over the last one year
7. What motivates the customer (rank the following as per your priority)
    a. Price
    b. Quality
    c. Service
    d. Personal contacts
    e. Political pressures
    f. Incentives overt or covert

Prepare Master List of the Customers

1. Reasons why each customer has purchased the product
2. Customers lost with reasons thereof. Customer resistance
3. Action/s taken to overcome resistance from the customers

Market Size and Growth Potential

1. Size of the market in units and rupee value
2. Channel members market evaluation
3. Market potential for the next three years
    a. Industry trends
    b. New innovative product
    c. New technological developments
    d. Changing customer needs
    e. New government regulation or levy on the product

Competitors Terms of Business

1. Prices
2. Performance guaranties
3. Quality of service
4. Payment terms
5. Delivery periods
6. Package size/ bulk packaging pricing
7. Product variants if any

Competitive Management

1. Reaction time to competitive actions
2. Marketing strengths, efforts to increase market share
3. Finance and ability to generate funds
4. Operations, timely deliveries, purchase through optimum use of funds
5. Profits or lack of profits
6. Reactive or pro-active policies
7. Have they lost market share, if yes then to whom (their vulnerability in this regard)

Market Share and Sales

For Major customers with sizable demand

i. Type and quantities for which they can make yearly purchase commitments
ii. Last three years purchase of these customers, competitor-wise
iii. Last three year purchase from the firm
iv. Correlation with the following-
   a. Customers assessment of competition
   b. Customers product acceptance
   c. Production capacities and their utilization of each competitor
   d. Market projections based on competitive strengths and weaknesses or on industry growth
   e. Effect of Brand Equity, assessment of goodwill of competitors as reliable suppliers of quality products, which give value for money.

Intelligence on competitive activities can be gathered from several sources as given below:

a. Sales force
b. Channel members

c. Suppliers
d. MR Firms
e. Trade associations
f. Business associates of competitors
g. Observing the competitive actions
h. Published data
i. Internet

Customers get in to repurchase mode only when they find that the value they have gained from the product out weighs its price. This is one area that the companies must understand for their own products as compared to competitive products at times a low one time purchase price could lead to much larger expense for product usage as can be seen from the following:

Table 5.3. Customers & Competitors

All in Rupees	*Competitive brand 1*	*Competitive brand 2*	*Competitive brand 3*
Price	500	480	475
Transport to home	10	15	25
Maintenance costs	10	25	25
Usage costs	12	25	30
Disposal costs	20	15	25
Total cost	552	560	580

Marketing research can give the customers' perception of the benefits to be derived from the product attributes on a preference table where they give their choices in order of merit. Once the information becomes available, strategies can be formulated for meeting competitive moves as given below-

a. Defending its position—the company need to build strong brand equity of the product likely to face stiff competition
b. Build defensive network—to safeguard some of companies lesser known brand
c. Pre-emptive action—by remaining proactive and attacking the competitors before they even think about it.
d. Cross parry—it requires companies to hit the competition in their most vulnerable market

Profit Impact of Market Strategy—PIMS—it tells that profitability has a direct relationship with company's market share.

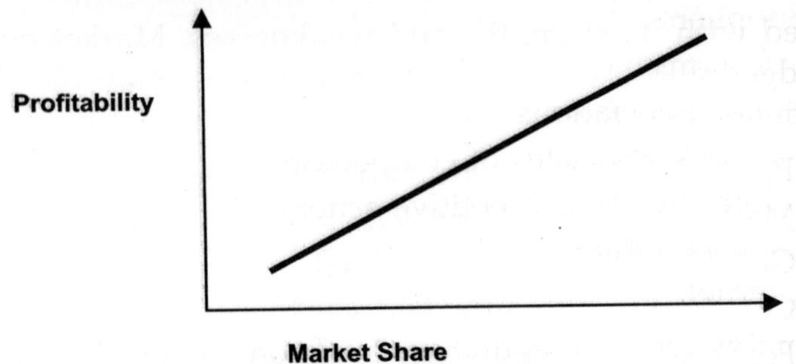

Fig. 5.1. Profit Picture

While in most cases it can be said that with larger market share profitability goes up. However, in a growing market, when competitors come to know about the growing profit curve, they too place their product in the same market segment, resulting in loss of market share for the company. However, if the company's strategy were of maintaining the market share then it would have to make large investments in marketing of the product by way of larger advertising and promotion, bigger commission to the trade partners and extra efforts in training of sales personnel, both the companies and those of the trade partners. These extra expenses will eat up the extra profits of additional sales and the graph would look like one given below-

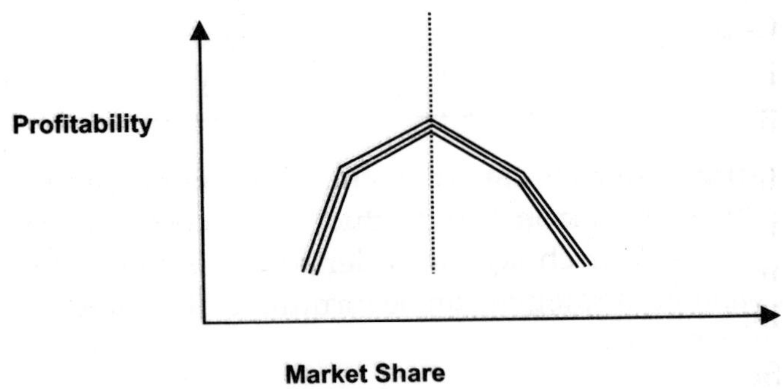

Fig. 5.2. Profit & Market Share

As can be seen from the graph, profitability goes down with increase in market share and hence the companies' should look for optimization of market share and profitability matrix in their favor.

The Complete Marketing Plan

Introduction- it is presumed that with the help of marketing research and test marketing the product has been finalized, as also its market segment and geographic coverage. Competition has been identified with its strengths and weaknesses. Market potential has been judged and business-monitoring organization has been set up for continuous feedback. In short the following has been done-

a. Product finalized with its detailed specifications
b. Market segments identified
c. Geographic coverage finalized
d. Competitive strengths and weaknesses known
e. Feedback mechanism put in to operation

The next step is to identify in an unbiased manner the firms own strengths and weaknesses, by doing a SWOT Analysis. Monitoring business environments, both general and competitive is non-stop activity.

Product Plan- does the product need any modifications to cater different market segments? For example, the same wheat flour could be sold in low cost package for one segment and in usable packs for the other, with a price differential. Coke is another example, which sells both in bottles and in cans. Cars can be sold with ACs, stereos or no- nonsense cars without any frills at a lower price.

To lower the cost for repeat buyers, Bourn vita, Horlicks and some cooking oils sell in low cost refill packs too.

Products have been broadly categorized as follows:

- Consumer Products—
  i. FMCG
  ii. Consumer Durables
- Industrial Products—
  i. Capital goods
  ii. Raw materials and components
  iii. Consumables
- Service

The management has to decide the products in detail, it wants to market. This also should answer the question, "What is the firm's business?" Inaccurate judgments could lead to marketing myopia.

Marketing Myopia

Myopia or short sightedness in marketing comes from a narrow vision of the firms business. Several movie studios in Hollywood had to close down, as they could not withstand the impact of Television, because they felt that they are in motion picture business. If they had rephrased their business as that of family entertainment they would have started their own TV channels. Some studios, which did that not only survived but also thrived, are examples of the fact. Firms therefore must define their business clearly taking the larger market spectrum in to account.

Customer targets—these are virtually the Sales targets redefined to cover the market segment both geographic and psychographics. The targets are then broken down sales area-wise. In practice the management gives the field a target, which is inflated by about ten percent. This is to drive or push the team in to action and with a sense of urgency.

Targeting customers is looking at the distribution channels, as they are the first line customers for consumer products. In case of industrial products the actual users could be the target customers.

Sales target planning—following needs to be considered for deciding sales targets:

a. Target period-yearly, six monthly, quarterly or monthly. These can then be broken down in to smaller time dimensions.
b. For FMCGs targets are quarterly or monthly
c. For consumer durables they are quarterly targets
d. For industrial products they are quarterly or six monthly targets
e. Seasonality of sales is taken in to account like warm clothes' sale during winter months.
f. Historical sales during same period of the last year or last few years.
g. Anticipated market growth
h. Current market share of the firm and plans for changes in market share

With the concept of Profit Centres the targets are made for each profit centre separately. The profit centre team with its leader has to accept the targets and devise plans of achieving the same. The key to target setting is that," **Targets should be achievable but only with a big stretch of efforts.** "The firm gets the best effort of the team from this approach and it puts a sense of urgency in to the team effort. On the contrary if the targets are too high, the team starts getting disheartened and if they are too low the team makes no or little effort and loses its enthusiasm. Team motivation and dynamism is vital to the success of the firm and no management plan is complete without ways of keeping the team fully enthused. Teams need to ensure that each member of the team fully contributes to its success, and weak links should be retrained, counseled or removed if everything else fails. Targets do take it to account the business environment changes and the profit plans of the firm.

Rolling Plan

For new products when no historical data about sales is available, firms have to depend on market research information. In such cases the sales targets need to be frequently updated in case of major deviations from the market research projections. The best method is the Rolling Plan, where the plan or target is made each month for a three months period, which allows firms to make corrections continuously. On January 1st, the plan for sales is made for January, February and March. On 1st February it is made for February, March and April. Rolling Plan also helps in meeting competitive challenges as they can be changed midstream too.

For industrial products purchase timetables of the industry, seasonality of demand and competitive manufacture should be given due importance. Sugar mills buy most products of their use during their cane crushing season except the products they need for maintenance during their off season.

Sales target must consider the position of the product in Product Life Cycle PLC and firms position that of market leadership or of follower. If the firm is a follower and is it first or second or nth follower. Management has to take a decision if it wants to change its position considering the PLC as well.

Plans and Policies

Once the sales targets have been firmed up, it is time to lay down policies, which would assist in achieving the same. Firms must be able to realize their potential in getting **Sustainable Competitive Advantage (SCA).** Following policies are useful for the purpose-

- As most firms operate in perfect competition, it is necessary to differentiate in a manner to enable the customers appreciate the firm and its products. Firms need to appear different than competition and it can be done as given below-
- Product—before the introduction of Kinetic Honda, scooters looked much the same. Kinetic came as a scooter, which gave a very distinguished look to scooters. Dove soap, which is not soap, is another example of product differentiation. At times the package, trademark or logo can make a difference.

- Service—is perhaps the most important area of differentiation, as it cannot be copied by competition in comparison to ME TOO products, which come up in the market after one product becomes a success. Promptness of service with a smile, product delivery, usage training, maintenance and availability of spares can make the firm stand out from its competition. Ease of getting the product, speed of delivery, installation and customer training in its usage are aspects of service, which can provide the firm its SCA.
- Distribution channels—geographic coverage, availability of ready stocks, merchandizing and displays and innovative ways of distribution can make the firm unique in the minds of the customers. Retail sales training and retail service are two areas, which help firms in achieving the Sustainable Competitive Advantage.
- Brand equity—it is perhaps the most distinguishing feature of the firm and therefore firms must keep continuous efforts by way of Advertising Public Relations and Publicity to improve on its brand equity. It provides a built-in competitive advantage and firms spend a lot of time and money trying to built and improve their brand equity.
- Quality—irregular quality standards, difference in batch quality can do lot of harm to the firms SCA. Firms, which exceed the quality norms by a good margin, gain major **SCA** over, firms, which just meet the standards. They can ask for and they do get higher prices as well. Quality can be considered as the product meeting with its specifications given by the manufacturers. Can the quality be sustained over period of the products life? Is it applicable quality both when the product is static as when it is in dynamic state? Can the product be repaired? If yes, then what are the parameters of availability of spares, trained technicians for repair work?
- Warranty—SCA can be from extended warranty periods given for the products, which in turn gets converted to the peace of mind for the customer.
- Personnel of a firm, mainly from the sales department as also dealer's salespersons, should be trained in to providing sustained quality service for gaining SCA.

Marketing Strategy

In the initial product offering the firm may consider two levels of market segmentation, the first one being where heavy start up selling and advertising efforts will be concentrated. On the second level the buyers who follow the early birds will be targeted.

The next level of strategy would be on Customer Contact. Personal contacts in the consumer products are through the sales persons of the retailers and hence they need to be trained in proper product selling techniques. For industrial products, the contacts could be by the firm's sales persons or distributor's salespersons, depending on the type of products being sold.

Products should be differentiated in accordance with their Unique Selling Preposition, be it product quality, price delivery warranty or service which goes with the product.

Products, which have seasonality in their sales like warm clothes, air conditioners, the marketing strategy should involve plans for out of season sales.

Price should be planned with careful consideration of Product Life Cycle, competitors pricing and firm's marketing objectives. For increasing market share, penetrating price could be kept while for increasing profits skimming prices could be considered. The following need careful consideration-

- Is price lower than competitors? Is the firm losing profits due to normal reason?
- Is pricing strategy carefully thought out?
- Do the prices cover both goods and services?
- Will the pricing strategy secure and increase product acceptance in the desired market segment?
- Maintain and increase the firm's market share as per marketing objectives?
- Provide profits?
- Can the higher price over competition be attributed to product's innovative nature, quality, warranty or service?

Price increase or decrease, influence on profitability are as a result of effect on sales. However the effect of price on sale is not always obvious. For example, price decrease often results in increase in profits. A good example is the decrease in long distance telephone rates, which have resulted in greater usage, and consequential increase in profits. Government regulations, changes in taxation rates are also responsible for changes in prices but as these affect the competitors also their impact can be on changes in total demand pattern but not on individual firms, unless some firm loses the opportunity of price changes to win customer goodwill.

A decrease in price by the firm will be normally matched by the competitors nullifying any advantage to the firm especially in the long run. It may result in price wars detrimental to all the competitive firms. However, price collaboration or cartel formation is illegal in India and most other countries.

Prices of product offered through the distribution channels can be subject to modifications by the channel members with or without the knowledge or approval of the firm. This helps the channel members in increasing their profitability. It however may result in damage to firm's fair name, and brand equity.

Price-Quality strategy—

Price and quality of a product do get associated with each other as given below:

Table 5.4. Price Quality Parity

	High price	*Medium price*	*Low price*
High quality	Premium goods	Loyal customers	Intensive growth
Medium quality	Overpriced product	Middle of the market	Bargain goods
Low quality	Fast profit	Shoddy goods	Discount goods

Consideration of the phase of PLC of the product must be considered. In growth stage, volumes of business and competitive action should be taken in to account. High or skimming prices can give short term gains and low prices can lead to change in quality concept about the product in customer's mind.

Selling Strategy

It is a vital task of the marketing department of a firm to plan out strategy for selling the products. Firm's salespersons, distribution channels, and their sales force are to be considered for the plan. Additions to the sales staff, channel network and area's coverage needs to be considered. Selection procedure for the additional staff, distribution channel members, their remunerations, salaries, commissions, discounts and margin share-out between the different channel members like, retailers, distributors should be finalized. Turnover discounts, cash sale discounts need special consideration.

Service and Warranty Policy need careful planning. Depending on products these could be either vital or inconsequential for purchase decisions. In consumer durable products, capital goods service and warranty play a major role in purchase decisions. (Maruti cars claim to have the widest service network in the country and this claim has become the firm's USP.)

Handling Of Complaints—it needs special consideration as even in the best quality products, problems can arise. It is the promptness, courtesy and expertise with which the complaint is handled makes the difference in repurchase decisions or in dropping the vendor altogether.

Advertising, Sales Promotion and Public Relations

Even for the top quality product, communications with the customer is vital. Plans for these communications are made as follows-

- Advertising plans including creativity, market segmentation, media, and timing of the campaign.
- Sales promotion is done to counter customer resistance for the purchase of the product offered by the firm. Planning sales promotion is done taking the market share objectives of the firm, product life cycle and it can be done both for the channel members as also for the customers.
- Publicity is organized as a vital communication link where the customers get the product information through editorial or expert comments, as it is not paid for by the firm without the possible bias in favour of the firm in advertising communication. The sponsors do not have control over the message.
- Advertising includes all paid non-personal messages to the consumers. The selection of media, budget, timing and contents of the messages are significant and important areas for the firm.
- Sales Promotion includes coupons, contests, money back guaranties, free samples, gift items and play a major role in purchase decisions of the buyers. With severity of competition, increasing sales promotion, has become a way of life for most firms.

The company that is customer oriented is better placed to identify business opportunities and help plan marketing strategies even in the face of severe competition. Considering its core competencies, strengths and weaknesses, the company can decide its market segment, needs of newer types of products and related services in the market. While competitors teach the success mantra no company can remain in business in fear of competition. Understanding the strengths and weaknesses of competitors and study of customers are essential for successful planning of marketing strategies. As competition is serving the same market segment the company must understand the competition from industry and market analysis. Competitive knowledge can be gained in a variety of ways and no effort should be spared for getting the same. The company should plan different types of strategies, like being aggressive or leave the market leadership as it entails heavy expenditure on marketing mix factors like advertising, sales channels and promotion.

Questions for Discussion

1. Competition is essential for a company. Discuss and elaborate, this statement.
2. Understanding competitive strengths is required for planning marketing strategies. Discuss.
3. How does Michael Porter's force model help in understanding competitive strengths?

Management game

Plan out the Critical Success Factors associated with the company.

Critical Success Factors

These are the factors, which govern the success of the firm. They are derived from the following:

i. Industry factors, whether it is growing, if ye s at what rate,
ii. Its position in the Market Life Cycle,
iii business general environment factors,
iv. Technology updates
v. Competition

For a car service **centre** the following would be the critical success factors:

- Population of vehicles in the area
- Growth rate of vehicle population
- Is the product just being introduced?
- Demography of the area

- Quality of service being provided
- Service equipments at the service centre.
- Number of trained servicemen
- Location of the service centre, easy ingress and egress
- Parking facility
- Service timings, twenty-four hours or less

Similarly Critical Success Factors of the company being analyzed can be determined.

CHAPTER 6

Sales Force Management

AIMS AND OUTCOMES OF THE CHAPTER

Sales management designs the sales force by defining the company's objectives, strategy, structure and compensation. Sales force is a vital component of marketing communication, as it is required to provide the unique link between the customer and the company. Once the sales objectives have been defined management has to see its implementation and control. Sales force management involves recruiting training, motivating and evaluating the sales team.

In the context of exchange of goods for cash two terms are used, marketing and Sales. Marketing is the overall umbrella, which covers product definition, product marketing research, pricing, distribution, promotion and sales. A sale is when the actual transaction takes place and money is exchanged for goods. Hence it assumes a great deal of importance in the game of marketing.

Many firms, considering the importance of both marketing and selling have separate Marketing Manager and Sales Manager for the two functions.

Sales Managers have the following roles to perform in the firm:

1. Defining sales policy of the firm
2. Marketing research
3. Pricing and terms of business
4. Distribution
5. Advertising, publicity and promotion
6. Selection, training and motivation of the salesmen
7. Sales territory allocation
8. Sales target for each territory

9. Sales forecasting
10. Expense budget for the department and for each salesman
11. Selling cost control
12. Reporting and control system

The Sales Policy of a firm starts with selection of product/s for sale, pricing of products, geographic coverage, distribution arrangements, distribution logistics, advertising, promotion and publicity plans. The policy is decided after the final approval of firms CEO, who considers the financial aspects of the policy before approving it.

Since marketing research, pricing, distribution, advertising and promotion have been covered in the book chapters, these are not being repeated here.

Selection, Training and Motivation of Salesmen: In the early part of the twentieth century, Salesmen were considered as gifted individuals, born with persuasive skills. Later on it has been proved that if the right type of candidate is selected he can be trained to become a Top class salesman. Firms therefore look for the right kind of recruit for the job who can be trained in the firm's culture and way of working. Getting the right people is difficult task as the breed of good salesman material is a rare commodity. Firm's Human Resource Managers, therefore use all possible methods to locate the right people. The increase in Business Management schools have made their life a little easier as the schools provide skilled persons with basic grounding in management.

Firms look for the following qualities in their salesmen:

- An aptitude for hard work
- Technical knowledge as required for selling the product
- Positive outlook
- Good communication skills, both oral and written
- Extrovert personality
- Helpful nature
- Requisite experience, if it is not a management trainee position

Human Resource Managers get the persons in one of the following ways:

- Promotions from inside the firm
- Competitors personnel
- Casual applications received by them
- Business schools campus interviews
- Advertisements in the press
- With the help of recruiting agencies

For technical products the inside promotions can be useful as they know about the product and can start becoming productive in less time. However, the inside person should have the basic selling attitude. For example, if he is not keen on travelling he cannot succeed in a selling career. Competitors' staff knows the business and can become useful, provided they are not the one's being off-loaded by the competitor because of their inefficiency.

Good firms usually have a databank of applications received by them, which have been sent by people, unsolicited, as they are interested in taking up a job with the firm. Such applications must be screened to find out if they contain any suitable candidates who can be called for a personal interview.

For Sales Trainee positions, the business schools are a good source and most good firms are regularly going there for campus interviews.

Press advertisements are a bit expensive, but they get the best rewards as, people who meet the exact specific requirements only apply and from them the right person/s can be selected.

In most towns a number of recruiting agencies have come up. They are good sources of candidates as they do all the spadework like going through the bio-data sheets, short-listing the right candidates who can be interviewed by the firm for final selection. These have been doing a good job as far as recruitment of senior persons are concerned.

The first task of the Sales Manager is to clearly write down the exact requirements, as specifications, like, "We need sales trainees, either sex, between twenty and twenty five years of age. Science graduates with management education will be preferred." A mention of the product/s they will sell and an idea of the remuneration they will get is necessary to get the right candidates for interview.

Training of salesmen- here are three main methods of providing training to the new entrants in the sales organization of a firm:

1. Class room training where the trainee is told about the plans, policies, methods of working, hierarchy levels, reporting levels, forms used in report writing. Besides, they are given extensive product knowledge, they are told about products benefits for the customers, its USP, and its comparative value with respect to competitive products.
2. On the job training when they work as understudy of one senior experienced salesman, watch him negotiate the sales deals and generally plan his work on a day-to-day basis.

3. Training on the job is like learning how to swim once the person is thrown inside the pool. For people with initiative and drive this is the best method. It allows the trainee to learn at his own speed unencumbered with some senior who may have become cynical because of his length of service and perhaps no promotion.
4. Besides the training given at the start, salesmen should keep receiving Refresher Courses to ensure that they are updated on to the firms' plans, new products and changes in the business environment. Such courses can be planned in-house or at a Training Institute, which offers such programs for the corporate executives in different disciplines in management.

Motivating the Salesmen: Salesmen are high-strong individuals with wide vision, initiative, drive, resourcefulness who have the ability to go out to face the customers. The customers come in a variety of temperaments moods, views and the salesmen have to fine-tune their own behaviour pattern according to the customers'. Salesmen believe in hard work, are result oriented and seldom broach and interference in their work, not even from their superiors in the firm. They believe that they are the Stars of the firm and should be treated as such. However, like all individuals, salesmen too need appreciation of their work and that becomes the biggest motivating factor for them. A healthy rivalry amongst the salesmen of a firm is another motivating factor. Firms plan sales contests within the sales team with awards for the best performers. To ensure that the contests are effective and bring the desired result, they should be planned on the following lines:

- Each salesman should be given a target to achieve clearly in writing.
- The contest should be on a time bound basis
- Weightage should be given to the strength of the competitors in each salesman's area.
- If there are several products, targets should be each one of them and not just for the one's where the sale is lagging from previous periods.
- The basis of targets should be historical sales of products in each area, plus any major change, which may have taken place, like development of new industrial centres.
- Judgment of contest winners should be done without any bias to prove fair play by the management.
- Winners should be given awards, acclaimed in the firm's newsletter and if the performance keeps improving, then they

can be promoted. (Promoting salesmen can be at times counter-productive because a good field man may not prove to be a good officer. In fact several salesmen in the USA even refuse desk, better paid jobs, because they do not want to miss the independence and the thrill of field work.)

Selection of salesmen/saleswomen—the usual method of selection is through the candidates' bio-data and interview. The Sales Manager is guided by the following factors while selecting his sales team.

1. Product to be sold, its technology, usage
2. Size of the firm
3. Distribution channels
4. Level of the customers to be met, e.g., Purchase Assistants, Technical Managers, or Managing Directors
5. Selling aptitude
6. Knowledge of the trade
7. Knowledge of the market, channels
8. Knowledge of local language
9. Knowledge of a foreign language, if the salesman has to be posted out of the country.
10. Product knowledge
11. Health, as travelling takes a big toll on the salesmen's health.
12. Duties of salesmen, Showroom or field work

Aptitude for selling obviously is important, which includes, ability to make friends easily, hard work, remaining focused even with plenty of travelling, negotiating skills and a genuine desire to help others, especially the customers, within the ambit of work or even outside of it. The salesmen can acquire most of the other characteristics but the aptitude must be within the person.

It is unfortunate that for actual selection of sales persons only the age old methods are still in vogue, The Human Resource person sees the applications, which at times are in the shape of a questionnaire given by the firm and filled by the candidates. To assist the Sales Manager, the HRD people have the first interview of the candidates, which at times assumes the role of interrogation which cover varied aspects of the candidate's life from childhood onwards, social activities, leisure time activities. Several executives can take the interview of a candidate collectively or individually. At times a written test is given, which is screened by psychologists, to find out the candidates reactions in times of stress. In some firms these are needed and in others may be only means of eliminating some candidates from selection, on the basis of personal bias.

Appointment of Sales persons—since the duties of salesmen are mostly in the field, without any direct supervision it is important that the terms of service in the organization are clearly set out, including, duties, responsibilities, authorities.

The authorities given to the salesmen assume great importance as the salesmen bind the firm in contracts involving large amounts of moneys. Terms of business inclusive of prices, payment terms, and delivery periods can be effective sales tools, and yet used incorrectly they can bring huge losses to the firm besides damage to the firm's reputation. Quotations given by the salesmen in the field need to be within the given parameters, and the authority to change the terms, e.g. price should be well defined and given in writing to avoid bad blood later on. (For big, major deals the Sales Manager is usually handily available to the salesman for advise or even assist in closing the negotiations, if the salesman feels the need.)

Credit as a sales tool is well accepted in business and yet unless creditworthiness is fully assessed care needs to be taken. Firms should have a credit rating form, which includes details about the customer's ability and willingness to pay dues well in time. Cash rich firms should NOT be taken as good paymasters as ability and willingness are two different things as far as credit is concerned.

Guarantees—Offer of guarantee to the customer constitutes focus of quality by the seller. Guarantee cost money and extending the guarantee period can prove to be expensive to the seller. Most new salesmen are not aware of the hidden costs involved in offering extended guarantees. Salesmen tend to quote, almost always incorrectly, the competition as having given increased guarantee to some obscure customer, to get a little leverage from the management in their selling effort. Proper investigations by the Sales Manager would reveal the truth in such cases and final decision can be taken only after such investigations have been made. Offer of extended guarantee is usually taken by the Sales Manager for the entire business, unless it is some tender business, especially government tender, where spot decisions are needed to be taken. In such cases, the salesman should be given the authority to make the changes in guarantee offered, if required. Similarly, at times special concessions are offered to get bulk orders, which would need the same type of care on the part of the salesman and the Sales Manager.

One area, in which most salesmen want authority is in settling of customers' claims. When the product sold is defective, stale, and unsaleable or not up to the sample shown or specifications given then the customer is entitled to get compensation for the same. In such cases the salesman should be authorized to give credit towards the claim, to ensure that customer goodwill is maintained. However, if the claim is quite large then the salesman should involve the Sales Manager in the decision making process and should inform the customer of the importance the firm gives to the customer, that the Sales Manager is looking in to the compensation against the claim. Such disputes are common when the customer is a channel member. The reputation of making genuine claims should be taken in to account while settling claims of the channel members.

Some unscrupulous salesmen are known to obtain customer's goodwill by allowing bigger credit than justified to make personal reputation rather than giving the right amount of credit. They even give a sob story of the firm's officers, who, they claim are not knowledgeable enough and that is why they have negated the salesman's recommendation regarding the claim. One wrong settlement of claim in favour of the customer could open floodgates, at times fuelled by competitors, that customers from other geographic areas could be making a bee line for getting their fake claims settled because of the bad precedence of one case.

Sales Territory Allocation: It is the job of the sales manager to ensure that the salesmen in his department are usefully employed, given equitable workload and can produce the best results. For this purpose, sales managers have to distribute the entire geographic area of business in salesmen's territories, which become the sole responsibility of individual salesman with regard to the sales activities in the areas. As the product range differs widely so do methods of territory allocation as can be seen from the following-

Consumer products—as the customer groups are wide spread geographically, the territories are divided as given below:

Equitable sales potential—(While dividing north India Rajasthan may have lower potential and hence it could be added to the Haryana state)

i. Concentration of business (If Delhi state has large potential it could be considered as an independent territory)
ii. Ease of territory coverage, which will help in reducing the back tracking for the salesman

iii. Product range specific areas on the basis of demographic divide—for product for low income groups territory could be the jhuggi-jhonpadi clusters, the slum areas in a town

Industrial products-as the customers are usually located in a cluster, several textile mills in one district—Ahemdabad, the territories are allocated on the basis of potential, of business in each cluster and the degree of difficulty in getting the business, competitors hold on the customer and the need for providing technical service to the customers.

Sales Targets: Based on the availability of product to the sales manager in one year, through the firm's own production or through outside procurements, the sales manager plans to sell the entire quantity of products. He fixes his own target for the year, which is then divided in to targets for each of the sales territories. The common method of target fixation is given below:

- Territory's total business potential
- Strength of the sales team
- Competitive strength
- Environment's effect on business in the territory.
- Target should be reachable but with a stretch

Given below is a format used for allocation of sales targets:

Table 6.1. Sales Target Allocation

Sales Manager's Target Period 2005–2006

Territory A	*Territory B*	*Territory C*	*Territory D*
PCs			
Modem			
Printers			
UPS			

The target is divided for each territory as follows:

Territory A

PCs	*Modem*	*Printers*	*UPS*
Sales Executive A			
Sales Executive B			
Sales Executive C			
Sales Executive D			

Each sales executive fixes the target of his dealers based on past performance, market potential, which is discussed with the dealer before finalization. One method of keeping record, dealer-wise as also monitoring dealer sales is given below, which shows product sales for each dealer on monthly basis and compares the sale with sales of the same month in the year/s gone by. This lets the salesman to locate the weak areas (products) in case of each dealer and helps the salesman in finding solutions for the decline in sales. This can be worked on progressive basis, which would indicate to the salesman the dealer's performance on a cumulative pattern for the year.

The statistics can be generated with the help of computers by feeding the sales invoices into it.

Table 6.2. Sales Statistics

Dealer's name

Products	*Sale Jan 2002*	*Sale Jan-May 2002*	*Sale Jan 2001*	*Sale Jan-May 2001*
PCs	547	2740	475	2500
Modem	34	150	42	173
Printer	65	351	45	254
UPS	120	450	140	520

As can be seen the dealer has done well in PCs and printers as compared to last year while they are worse off in modems and UPS. The salesman must find out the reasons for the ups and downs and ensure that the ups remain that way and the downs come up. In this manner the salesman would be able to evaluate the stress needed for each product and each dealer. Other areas of interest would be the growth pattern of the market, competitive share holding, effect on sale of the firm and competition of respective advertising and sales promotion of the competing firms. The increase in market share comes from either totally new customer who has not bought before at all and from taking competitors customers and each firm is trying for the same. The exception to the rule is when the firm decides to opt for only niche market leading to final divestment when the product is at decline stage of the PLC. The salesmen need to organize their work and time in a manner that desired results are ensured. For the purpose they need to plan the work for which they need the following inputs-

- Territory map giving locations of the main distributors, dealers, retailers, direct customers. This helps in tour planning when the salesmen can avoid backtracking by planning going in loops to cover the entire territory without having to resort to going back and forth.

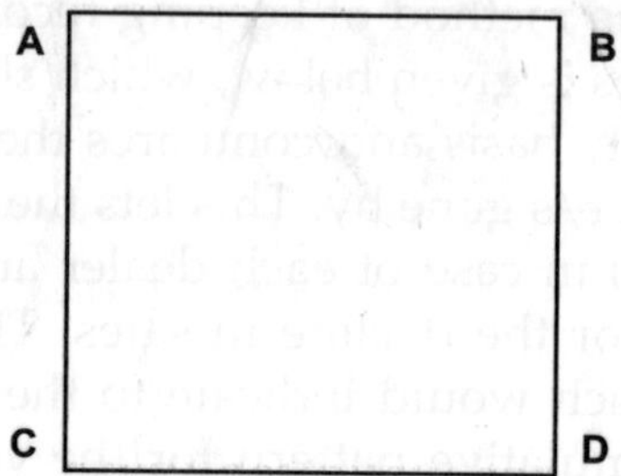

Fig. 6.1. Tour Plan

Starting from point A, the salesman can go to B then to C and D. If he goes from A to D and then comes back to A before going to B then he is wasting time and travelling expense. Structured tours help the customers and many firms believe that if the customers, including the channel members know that the firm's salesman will visit on the tenth of each month then they prepare themselves for the meeting as the agenda can be gone through in quick time and the desired result achieved. It also gives the impression of professionalism of the firm to the customers.

In case of industrial products, the target fixation takes in to account new customers (industries) emerging in the area, general and competitive environment and demand pattern of the final product of the customers. Business to Business sales requires the following extra ingredients for successfully meeting the targets:

- Complete knowledge of the customer's requirements, problems which need to be solved
- Level of technology involved in marketing the product. This would decide if a technical salesman should be making the call.
- Product knowledge and the benefits it offers to the customer in terms of safety of operations, economy, ease of usage and storage

The itinerary for both B to B salesman should be made on the following format (specimen only, subject to change as per individual firms needs):

Table 6.3. Tour Plan

Salesman ____________ *Area* ____________ *Month* ____________

Date	*Place*	*Customer*	*Person/s to be met*	*Purpose of the visit*	*Brief outcome/ follow up needed in time frame*

The full report of each visit should be on a format specimen given below:

1. Customer, firm's name, address, phone, fax, email.
2. Persons met with designation and vested authority.
3. Files, documents, literature, testimonials taken and discussed with the customer.
4. Objectives of the visit. It is useful to have one major and a few minor objectives, which should be in line with the major objective. In case the major objective is not achieved in a particular visit the salesman can try to achieve at least one of the minor objectives. Major objective of sales call is usually to get the purchase order. Minor objective could be to invite the customer for a product demonstration.
5. A brief account of the discussion held and the customer's viewpoint on the benefit story given for the product.
6. Result of the visit. Follow up action required, giving the names of the people who would take the action along with the time schedule for the same.
7. In case of retailers/dealers of the raw materials or components being sold to industry report format can be made as given below:

Table 6.4. Sales Statistics

Dealer ____________ *Date* ____________

Product	*Stock with the dealer*	*Last months sale*	*Average monthly/ seasonal sale*	*Purchase order received/enclosed*
PCs	12	7	12	25
Modem	7	8	5	10
Printers	8	5	8	10
UPS	4	8	10	25

As can be seen the dealer is running low on UPS stocks and the order execution should be carried out quickly to avoid loss of business. In some products extra stocks create a sales push on to the dealer, who has to reduce the inventory and blocked money and space and therefore he tries his best to sell the maximum quantities. A column can be made for giving the details of advance money received from the dealer towards the order.

Sales Forecasts

Different firms have separate defined periods for which they prepare a sales forecast. The forecast help the firm in the following activities-

- Building production quantities
- Controlling inventory levels
- Planning distribution network changes, if required
- Pricing decisions
- Recruitment, training of salesmen
- Increase in geographic coverage of sales
- Providing technical support to the sales team.
- Providing after sales service, guaranty and warranty services

Sales forecasts are made on the sales territory basis and then they are consolidated to get to the all India figure. In the first half of the twentieth century, sales forecast was made for periods ranging from one to seven years. It was possible to give long ranging forecast because the business and competitive environment were not changing much. In case of seven years forecast, it was assumed that the deviation level of each forward year could increase by five percent. In other words the first year the variation accepted between the actual sales seen after the year and the forecast could be within the range of plus, minus five percent. Next year it could go to ten percent and in the seventh year the variation could be as high as thirty-five per cent.

Today, the forecasting is being done for one year, which is reviewed quarterly to dovetail the production to the best fit for the market being catered to. In case of large value products the production is undertaken on the basis of orders received only to avoid inventory pileups. The forecast chart looks as given below:

Table 6.5. Historical Sales

Territory ________________ *Salesman* ________________

Products	2000	2001	2002	2003	2004	2005	2006
PCs	124	136	140	165	175	190	240
Modem	23	21	29	38	45	65	90
Printer	10	15	25	35	60	75	123
UPS	12	16	25	35	60	70	85
Lap tops	7	12	15	25	45	70	95

Sales forecast for the entire country is the sum total of the forecasts of all the territories plus the plans for exports made by the sales manager. Forecasting export trade is done on the following basis-

- Country wise sales plans
- Service facilities needed in each country
- Competitive products
- General and competitive business environments of the countries
- Political stability of the country
- Relationship with the foreign government

Planning Sales Calls

It should be assumed that the customer is a busy person and when he gives an appointment for a sales call, it is important that the salesman makes the best use of the time given, and hence the need for careful planning for each such call.

Planning sales calls should be done using the following steps-

- Study the customer's file; remember the name (with correct pronunciation), designation, level and authority of the person to be met. Review of any complaint from the customer, whether it has been attended to, satisfactorily so far or not. Is there any pending matter from the last call, which must be resolved before the call is made, or else the salesman may not be even welcome at the customer's premises. For example if the salesman had promised replacement of defective product and it has not taken place so far, the sales call would end up in bitter criticism from the customer and undue justification from the salesman. No concrete result can come from such a situation
- Plan the sales call objectives, both major and minor ones. It is better to write them down at least in first few calls.
- Carry the following in the briefcase to be used at the customers place
    1. Visiting cards
    2. Customer's file
    3. Product Literature, especially of new products being introduced
    4. Testimonials from other customers
    5. Firms letterheads
    6. Price lists
    7. Terms of business

8. Pen, pencils, erasers, carbon paper, stapler with staples
9. Products benefits for the customer along with benefits offered by competition (make sure your benefits always outscore the competitive benefits) the benefits should be written in sequence of their priority for the customer and it may be wise to alter the sequence for different levels of customers hierarchy. For example, the CEO will be interested only in the State of Art product, while the Finance Manager will look for Value For Money Product.
10. Sample of product, if required and if possible for demonstration purposes

The salesman should be smartly dressed and not gaudily and well groomed. In most cases it is essential to take prior appointment from the customer. It is useful to reach customer's office a few minutes early (while waiting the salesman can compose himself, revise the file papers, plan his opening sentences, use the toilet to feel fresh, comb his hair.)

In case of meeting a new customer, or one who has been mostly buying from competition dialogue plan, which has been found useful as at several steps the salesman is likely to find objections to his benefit story is given below. Of course the salesman must keep his wits about him to modify it as the sales call progresses.

The main objective of sales calls is getting the Purchase order from the customer. Salesmen usually plan a canned talk to persuade the customer to place the order on the salesman's firm. However, the salesman mostly, encounters resistance from the buyer due to the following reasons, one or all:

- The buyer is friendly to the competitors sales person
- Competitive product gives better value for money in the eyes of the buyer
- Competition provides better after sales service as per the buyer
- The users in the customer's side do not want a change, to avoid problems of duplicated inventories and confusion from unskilled/ illiterate workers about a new product
- The competition is providing some unspecified incentive, overtly or covertly to the buyer

Following are the steps needed in guiding the buyer in deciding in favour of placing the order on the firm. It is called the **Decision Triangle** (when more then one buying decision person is involved then the triangle could take the shape of **Decision Pyramid**.)

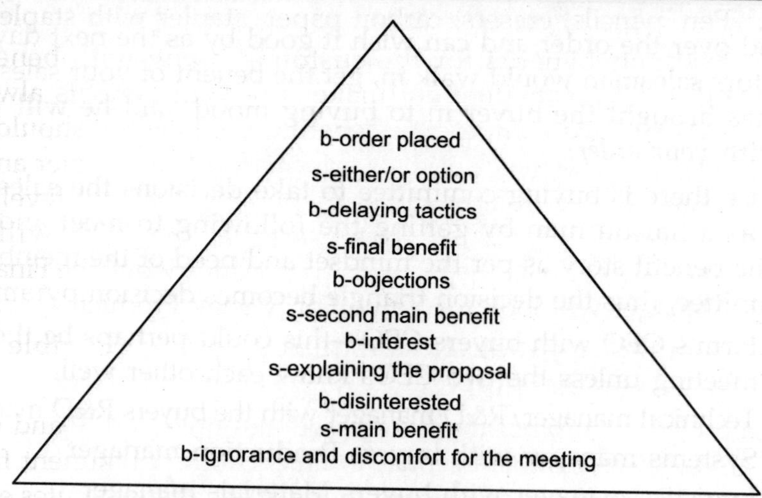

Fig. 6.2. Decision Process

As can be seen in the beginning of the interview the salesman is at a disadvantage as the customer is ignorant of his proposal. At this juncture it is best to give the most important benefit, which would attract the attention of the buyer. If the benefit could be translated in to savings in rupees, it will click well with the CEOs, Finance Managers, time saving will go well with production managers. Even after the main benefit, the salesman need not feel complacent as the competitive strengths are still working to defuse their effort. At this stage the salesman must explain the proposal and if the buyer wants he can call other members of decision-making team to join him. It will save time for both seller and the buyer. Otherwise, similar dialogue will have to be carried out with other members separately. After some interest is generated the salesman would do well to seize the opportunity by adding the other benefits till the buyer reaches the stage of purchase decision. At times there is a last hurdle, which is basically a delaying tactic on the part of the buyer, like I have to consult my father (who may not be even involved in the business at all). This can be surmounted by offering an option to the buyer, "would you want us to provide the transit insurance or you would cover it yourself?" if the customer says, "we will take the insurance cover ourselves" your deal is finalized. Once the salesman gets the purchase order, he must make sure to thank the buyer and leave his office without delay. It has been known that if the salesman stays long enough he may lose the order, "could you just give me that order back for a minute I want it to be checked once more by our auditors" you hand over the order and can wish it good by as the next day the competitors salesman would walk in, get the benefit of your sales talk which has brought the buyer in to buying mood, and he will walk away with *your order*.

In case there is buying committee to take decisions the salesman can act as a liaison man by getting the following to meet and put across the benefit story as per the mindset and need of the member of the committee, thus the decision triangle becomes decision pyramid—

- Firm's CEO with buyers CEO—this could perhaps be the last meeting unless the two CEOs know each other well.
- Technical manager/R&D manager with the buyers R&D manager
- Systems manager with buyers Production manager
- Logistics manager with buyers Materials manager
- Finance manager with buyers Finance manager

These meetings could be on one-to-one basis or altogether.

Locating New Customers

Marketers have to keep locating new customers. This exercise can be termed as Prospecting. In prospecting the sales person has to identify and qualify new customers as this is one of the most important way of creatively getting new business. The next step is to set up an objective for calls on the customers as well as on prospects. The sales person must know how to gather essential information about the prospect before making call plans. Next the call tactics need to be formulated.

The salesperson needs to have the right attitude before the call and this attitude can be developed. The sales person should ensure that he gets the prospect interested in his preposition quickly enough. It is always useful to verify the efficacy of the call plans.

The salesperson must be fully aware of the features of the product or the service he has to sell. He must be able to distinguish between the features and the derived benefits from the features of the product. This will help him in putting together an effective presentation while maintaining the prospect's interest and believability in the presentation. Most prospects will offer objections to change in their buying patterns (as they are perhaps buying from competition). The sales person must be able to distinguish between valid and superficial objections. The most important plan of sales calls is the way calls should be closed with the prospect's purchase orders in hand.

Finally sales persons need to know how to arrange a post call analysis to learn the gains of the plans as well as its shortcomings.

Prospecting

Prospecting can be divided into four parts, the advantages of having a skilled salesperson in the technique prospecting, learning the methods and sources for identifying and locating the worthwhile prospects, qualifying the prospects- by understanding the more desirable prospects from the less desirable one's, the relationship between prospecting and creative selling.

Every salesperson has to find new customer-the prospects. Customers are the existing buyers while prospects are likely buyers. Prospects can be considered as potential buyers of the company's products. Prospecting can be defined as "identifying and qualifying potential customers or prospects" salespersons need to learn the prospecting of potential customers to enable them to replace lost customers due to organisational changes, relocation, competitive activities. A skilled salesperson will be able to prioritise calls on prospects more likely to become customers, making the sale's calls more productive. Such salesperson will be able to broad base his customer list and increase the total number of his customers. He will reduce the number of unproductive calls in the process.

Prospect Identification

In several product groups, it is easy to identify the prospects, like the cotton supplier will know the textile mills as his prospects, the airlines would identify the travel agents as the prospects. However, for products with a large number of possible customers like insurance, office supplies it is more difficult to locate the prospects. In such cases companies develop ingenious techniques for identifying the prospects. One insurance company's sales manual has a list of 140 different sources of prospects of life insurance. Published data, lists, telephone directories are good source of potential customers. Today's telemarketers use these lists for calling on the prospects to know their interest in the product being sold. Salespersons use referrals extensively for locating prospects. Company's existing customers are known to recommend another possible buyer to the salesperson. This can happen on the buyer's own volition or on salesperson's request. At times even prospects can give referrals of other prospects and the salesperson can use the Endless Chain of prospecting potential customers. Besides, influential business leaders, community leaders can become source of prospecting for customers. These influential persons are found at the centre stage of power. Even bankers, lawyers, educators can be used as such sources.

One major area that brings about prospects is the enquiries, (that could have been generated because of companies advertising efforts or sales promotion,) that the company receives from prospects. These enquiries are passed on to the salespersons as business leads.

Salespersons should always be on the alert for locating new customers-the companies prospects. It is a good idea to develop a data bank that is kept updated for the prospects by adding the prospects from all the possible sources.

Once the salesperson has got the name of the prospect his task actually starts. The salesperson must find out in the prospects organisation the right person who should be met for business. Ideally the entire purchase decision hierarchy should be understood along with other particulars like phone, address, email address. A study confirms that 60 % of sales calls are made on wrong persons and are therefore ineffective. Sales calls are expensive as a lot of time is spent on planning and executing the calls. It is necessary that the time and effort are wisely invested. Salespersons should therefore, start with making calls on the best prospects, those whose chances of getting converted into customers are the best.

Qualifying the Customer

Qualifying helps the salesperson in selecting the best prospects on whom to call. The following three questions are used for qualifying the prospects:

1. Does the prospect meet with the company's policies?
2. Does the product fulfil a need of the prospect?
3. What is the current and future value of the prospect to the company?

In the case of company policy the salesperson should understand the prospects requirements on the following terms of business and the company's standards on the same:

1. Pricing and discounts
2. Credit as a sales tool
3. Cash discounts
4. Delivery needs
5. Order size
6. Servicing requirements

Prospects with odd or abnormal requirements that the company cannot comply with is not a good prospect as against the prospect who requires only the standard terms of business. Such prospects are likely to offer long term business association to the company. The other, even more important question is, do company's product and service, including delivery periods, fill the prospects needs? Prospects with urgent needs that can be met by the company have the best chance of becoming company's customers. However, in majority of cases the prospects do not see any need for the company's products in immediate future or even in the distant future. At such times it is the job of the salesperson to find out a way in which the company's product can satisfy some need of the prospect. It must be understood clearly that even if the prospect does not see any need of the company's product but the salesperson does see a need then the prospect is worth working on. A company modernising its plant will have need of a bigger, more powerful air conditioning system even if the company does not realise at the moment. It would be prudent for the salesperson to introduce his company's latest energy saving powerful air conditioning system when the buyer is in the right frame of mind to listen.

A napkin salesperson read in a magazine that one industrial laboratory had many delicate instruments that needed soft lint free cloth to wipe off dust from the instruments. While the purchase person of the laboratory may never have thought of buying napkins for the purpose, the alert salesperson saw the need and now that and similar several other laboratories are using the napkins.

Therefore, the salesperson should not get worried even if the prospect shows no interest in the product, and try to locate even hidden needs of which even the prospect is not aware.

The next level is to find out the present and future value of the prospect to the company. It stands to reason that the best efforts should be made on prospects with the greatest value to the company. The prospects capacity is one yardstick for measuring the value. The biggest buyer gets to be the best prospect. Big value frequent orders from the prospect make him most valuable. However, even a small buyer with future growth possibilities can never be ignored. Besides, the prospects reputation is a major factor in considering its value. A small buyer who is a community leader and much respected should be rated high on value even against the bigger volume buyers who may be poorly regarded in the business circles.

Summarising, the good prospect can be defined as the one that meets the business policy and terms of business of the company, has a definite need of the company's products and has a high present or future value for the company, or if the prospect enjoys leadership position in the industry or in the community.

So far a variety of techniques of prospecting have been studied. It is obvious that the prospecting techniques will differ greatly among the salespersons depending on the kind of selling job they are performing, the product. Prospecting for customers requires creative ability on the part of the salesperson. Salespersons creativity is perhaps the only limiting factor for developing prospecting plans for future customers. At the same time the creative salesperson can determine newer ways of product usage by the potential customers.

DETAILED CALL PLANNING

Note—In the following paragraphs the words used—Customer and Prospect are interchangeable.

Salespersons need to learn in detail the various aspects of call planning before a call is made on a customer or a prospect. Sales calls are costly and time consuming both for the salesperson and the buyer; it is essential that the calls are planned in advance and thoroughly. Some salespersons feel that playing by the ear will take them through a successful sales call. However, experience shows that such calls usually end in disaster. Planning needs to be first perceived in the mind only. Planning process takes the salesperson through what will be done in future well in advance. The sales calls are important assignments and the risk of lack of preparedness must be avoided at all cost. A successful call could generate business worth millions of rupees as the reverse is equally true. Call planning needs to be done in the following three steps-

1. Establish the call objective
2. Gather the essential information
3. Select appropriate strategies or tactics

Establishing the Call Objectives

The call objective is what the salesperson hopes to achieve when he meets the customer or the prospect face to face. The objective must be set before the call is made. Finally the objective that any salesperson has is to obtain an order from the customer or the prospect. The objective may quantify the order value for the call. However, more often than not, it takes several calls before an order can be obtained. Therefore each call may have a different objective, while the major objective of obtaining the order is always at the back of the salesperson's mind. The immediate objective could be to find out changes in buying patterns with the change of purchase team of the customer. Other objective is to persuade the customer or prospect to see a product demonstration. One objective could be to obtain permission to supply samples for trial purposes. There can be a variety of objectives of sales calls and the calls can be considered as fruitful if the objective for the call has been met. In any case since the final objective is getting the order, the other minor objectives should bring the main objective a little closer to the company. The objectives of preliminary calls should be used like the steps of an escalator that lead to the final destination, the order. The number of steps, or calls leading to the order would depend on the type of selling as also it will vary from customer to customer. Setting up objectives help the salesperson in keeping calls on track of achieving the main objective. For example if the salesperson wants to introduce a new type of denim cloth to the manufacturer of ready made garments, the following route can be taken:

1. First objective—to get the agreement of the buyer about need of the denim.
2. Second objective—demonstrate the new denim to key individuals
3. Convince the buyer that the price and other terms of business are right and get the order.

As can be seen the intermediate objectives were in line with the major objective of getting the order. The objectives must follow a sequence in ascending order like an escalator, as it will help the salesperson in getting the order rather quickly.

Gathering the Essential Information

Once the objective has been defined the next step is gathering essential information about the customer or the prospect. During the prospecting stage the salesperson has obtained some information. However, the more information he has the better chances of his success from the sales calls. While information gathering is time consuming it is important to collect the essential information.

The salesperson has to determine what constitutes the essential information on the prospect. It is the objective of the call that defines the information need of the salesperson. It is useful to prepare a check-list of information needs in order to avoid overlooking any necessary information item. Given below is a dedicated checklist, which should be altered by the salesperson to suit individual requirements:

Business Information Check List

1. Name
2. Address
3. Telephone numbers, Fax
4. Annual sales volume in rupees and units
5. Ownership
6. Management philosophy
7. Organisational structure
8. Key decision makers
9. Reputation
10. Competition details
11. Credit rating
12. Number of employees
13. Current problems faced by the company
14. Products/services sold
15. Markets targeted –segments
16. Key customers
17. Plans and policies on purchasing
18. Budget policy
19. Frequency of purchase
20. Seasonal factors
21. Key suppliers
22. Attitude towards price, quality, product innovations
23. Raw material used
24. Components made/bought
25. Manufacturing process
26. Administrative process
27. Machine and equipment used
28. Schedule of maintenance.
29. Volume potential for sales by the salesperson in rupees and in numbers
30. Previous experience with the salesperson's company
31. Salesperson's competition

The check List of Personal Information

1. Name with correct spelling and pronunciation
2. Address
3. Age with date of birth

4. Position—title, responsibility, authority, line of communication, basis of evaluation by superiors
5. Length of time with the company
6. Business background
7. Education
8. Business or professional affiliations
9. Social affiliations
10. Marital status, family background and number of children
11. Other interests—outside of the job
12. Personal aspirations
13. Personal peculiarities
14. Best time to visit

While several of the items listed may not be considered as essential it is a good idea to go through the checklist to ensure nothing of vital importance is left out.

Salesperson need to know the sources from where they can gather the information. Information on existing customers is usually available with the salesperson's company. Besides, customers or prospects who give the business leads are another source of information. Trade partners, the channel members, trade publications. Business calls should be used to gain information that help in adding onto the already available information. Prospects annual reports, balance sheets reveal important details on their financial standing, plans and new product launches. Prospects product literature, advertisements offer information that can be of use to the salesperson. The salesperson should use all possible means to get the information and keep it updated all the time.

Strategies and Tactics

Salespersons must plan their strategies for the sales calls to attain their call objectives. The calls normally follow the following pattern:

1. Approach
2. Presentation
3. Objections
4. Closing the call

Due to the importane of sales calls, call planning must become an essential part of the salesperson's activities and it should become a work habit with the salesperson. Planning being a mental activity should be carried out at a place where there are no distractions.

Salesperson should concentrate on the three elements of call planning, establishing the objective, gathering the essential information and selecting the appropriate tactics. The planning can be done mentally. However, it is recommended that for important call the plan must be written down. Given below is a standard form for planning sales calls:

Call Planner

Company
Address
Phone, fax
Name of the customer/ prospect
Call objective

Essential information on the company-on the individual

Tactics to use

a. Approach
b. Presentation
c. Objections
d. Closing

Approach

Once the call planning is complete, the salesperson starts the necessary arrangements to make the presentation before the customer or the prospect. This process is called approach that includes the purpose of approach and its definition. Besides the techniques of getting to see the prospect or the customer has to be learnt. The approach can be defined as the activity of the salesperson that begins with making arrangements to see the customer or the prospect and ends with the start of the presentation. The approach has three basic purposes:

1. To get to see the prospect or the customer
2. To put him in the right frame of mind for the presentation
3. To confirm the call plan

The first activity is to make an appointment for visiting the customer or the prospect. These appointments are made on telephone or through letters depending on time available between call and the appointment. In certain cases where the salesperson has become familiar with the customer and knows his routine, he may not make an appointment. For major business deals appointments must be considered as essential. The timing of the call should be to the customer or prospects convenience. If no appointment has been made then the time the customer is usually free or the time he has kept for such meetings must be kept in mind. Many business deals have been lost due to wrong timing of the sales call.

For the meeting the salesperson must be decently dressed, polite in demeanour. He will, in all probability meet with the receptionist, or the secretary of the person he has to meet and the first impressions on these buffers must be perfect. These buffers usually screen the salesperson before he is allowed to meet the main person. Decent dress, courteous behaviour would do wonders in such cases. In case an appointment has not been taken these buffers can blackball the salesperson. In such cases the best way to gain the appointment is to use the reference of some important person known to the customer or the prospect. Visiting cards, brochures or other mailed material to the prospect can also be used to gain the appointment. At times when the visiting card is given to the buffer the salesperson can write a small note on it to improve his chances for the meeting. These buffers or intermediaries play an important role in the salesperson getting the appointment. These are the virtual gatekeepers and it is best to keep them on the salesperson own side. The fact that the competitors are also doing the same thing should spur the salesperson into making friends of the buffers. Sending greeting cards to them, thank you notes and small gifts during festive periods will be of great help.

Most of the time the salesperson has to wait to meet the right person. The waiting time should be properly utilised by revising the presentation plans. The salesperson can try to obtain the essential information during the waiting time. The buffer may become a good source of such information. If none of these is possible the salesperson should keep some trade publications or other reading material to fully utilise the waiting time.

Presentation Ready

When the salesperson comes face to face with the customer, the first few minutes make the vital impact on whatever happens afterwards. The presentation success would largely depend on the frame of mind of the customer or the prospect. Following possibilities would prove the point:

1. The prospect has been extremely busy and is meeting the salesperson just out of courtesy.
2. The prospects company is passing through a minor crisis situation.

3. The prospect has to rush out to meet some VIP.
4. The prospect has to meet a deadline and he is already late.

The salesperson needs to keep a positive outlook in all such times and he can gradually convert the negative frame of mind into positive approach of the prospect. The salesperson should ensure that prospect does not consider himself obligated under some duress into meeting him. The prospect should be ready and willing to meet and this happens when the salesperson is ready to help, and remains positive during the meeting. The sincerity and helpful nature are the prerequisites of success in the meeting. A negative behaviour from the salesperson would surely evoke similar response from the prospect. At times the history of earlier calls comes as a barrier of positive outlook of the salesperson and brings in a feeling of inadequacy. Conversely a successful earlier call could make the salesperson over confident and aggressive. Salesperson's own business results can seriously affect his behaviour during the meeting. The maturity of the salesperson is in throwing off or ignoring these factors that tend to influence his behaviour.

The salesperson has to take each call as a fresh experience. The vital matter is of attitude the salesperson must have, and that should be positive and helpful towards the prospect. The attitude will help the salesperson in getting the prospect into transitional mode where the buyer's mind is gently moved from whatever he had been doing prior to the salesperson's meeting to an enthusiastic willingness to hear the presentation. The salesperson needs to build a good rapport with the prospect. Rapport is defined as a "harmonious relationship". The rapport can be built by even small things like knowing the title, and the correct pronunciation of his name. Small talk, like talk about his hobbies, sports or other non business subjects in which the prospect is genuinely interested will contribute to the rapport building exercise. However, the small talk bit must be kept small since the prospect would not want to waste his valuable time. The salesperson should also make the best usage of the meeting time. Once the rapport has been established the harmonious relationship with the prospect.

Salesperson has to bridge the gap between the social conversation and the specific business of the call. A variety of techniques are used for bridging the gap is given below:

1. At times a question is asked for the purpose. "If I can show you how to reduce maintenance cost by 5%, would it be of interest to you?" is such a question.

2. The other method could be of offering assistance, "I would like to check you air conditioning system for the coming summer. Of course there will be no charge".
3. Announcing a significant fact can be used to bridge the gap like, you will be happy to learn that since last December the Electricity supply company is saving rupees fifty lacs.
4. Each year with the use of computerised billing system supplied by us.
5. Sometimes the product like a miniature cell phone needs to be shown for bridging the gap.

The salesperson should always avoid such trite questions," how is business" or "how do things look". Such questions are likely to get a negative response leading to the entire presentation becoming negative from the prospect viewpoint. The other failed technique is, "I was in the neighbourhood and thought I would drop in". Summarising after the rapport has been built the salesperson needs to have a technique of bridging the gap between the social conversation and serious business talk.

Call Plan Verification

Call planning involves the three steps, establishing the objective, gathering essential information and selecting the right tactics. The salesperson believes that his objectives are attainable, information sufficient and tactics appropriate. However, it is a good idea to verify the plan if the opportunity for doing so presents itself. The verification becomes easy if the prospect is given full rein to talk fully and openly. Salesperson needs to ask a well worded question after the gap has been bridged between the small talk and serious business talk leading to the presentation. Questions like, "your new plant installation plan?" Or "your maintenance plan for the machinery"—would let the prospect hold the fort and he would enjoy talking about his ideas. The salesperson could ask, " which part of the machinery is difficult to maintain?" or " which is the most time consuming manual operation that you want transferred to a computer?" the purpose of these questions is to have the prospect talk about his needs. The talks should be carried on till the call plan has been verified by the salesperson. The questions should be broad based to allow a general response. The salesperson should keep showing his interest by interjecting with, "this is interesting, tell me more". Attentive listening will help the salesperson in his verification process of the call plan. If the salesperson feels he can modify the plan as he goes along. He can decide if the original objective is still attainable or should he modify it to an extent. He would also realise if he has sufficient essential information or he should let the prospect keep talking. He can also understand if his tactics will work or do they need to be altered too. Can he use the tactics in handling the objections and in closing the presentation? The verification is the last step before the salesperson begins the presentation. As he is verifying his information base, the salesperson should help the prospect in redefining his needs from being generic to the needs of salesperson products through persuasive communication.

Sales Presentation

The salesperson has by now understood that unless he has a defined objective, has obtained the essential information and planned the right tactics he should not even attempt the call on the prospect. The start of the call is when the salesperson, through his persuasive communication gets the prospect change his generic needs to specific needs of the salespersons products. Let us discuss the persuasive communication in some detail.

The salesperson's products have some inherent unique qualities that can be defined as Product Features. Features need not be restricted to product physical qualities alone. They could well be part of company policy, product availability, and related service. Countrywide advertising campaign would be part of company marketing policy. When the salesperson helps the distributor in managing the inventory the service offered is unique and personal. Each company has to provide proper training to its salesperson in understanding its product's unique qualities including the service and the marketing policy. Salespersons must keep themselves abreast on these counts.

The salesperson must understand that the customers buy a product only for the benefits it offers to them. Benefits can be defined as the satisfaction the product provides to the buyers. The prospects are going to buy a product only if it provides the needed benefit to them. Youngsters do not buy motor cycles; they buy the thrill they provide on high speeds. Women do not buy cosmetics; they buy the benefit of becoming alluring by using the same. However, different people are looking for different types of benefits from a product.

The salesperson therefore needs to list down the benefits different persons are looking from their product. Such a list needs to be continuously updated for each group of customers as the customer group keeps changing; market segment keeps changing with time. In early 1960s the transistor radio was the craze with the elite of the society and today they would feel ashamed if found near a transistor set. The benefits could include reduced cost of labour, reduced maintenance cost, better quality control and increased worker safety. For retail traders the benefits could be better protection from competitive actions, increased stock turnover, higher margins, less customer returns and complaints. A description of the product features would appear like a technical manual only. Likewise if the salesperson talks only about the benefits it would sound like parrot repeating what he has been taught. Persuasive communication should combine the two, with salesperson talking about the benefits along with the features from where the benefits are derived. Automatic transmission is a feature of some cars while convenience is the benefit to the car driver. Hence, if the salesperson tells the customer that with automatic transmission of our cars, you would find driving convenient and pleasurable, he is tying a feature with a benefit. For excelling in this type of communication the salesperson should prepare a Feature-Benefit worksheet, as given below:

Table 6.6. Feature – Benefit Worksheet

For –product-customer

Feature 1	Benefit 1	Benefit 2	Benefit 3	Benefit 4
Feature 2	Benefit 1	Benefit 2	Benefit 3	Benefit 4
Feature 3	Benefit 1	Benefit 2	Benefit 3	Benefit 4
Feature 4	Benefit 1	Benefit 2	Benefit 3	Benefit 4

Maslow's Hierarchy of needs gives a clear definition of different types of human needs and the salesperson would do well in relating the benefits to the needs, like physiological needs, need for safety, social acceptance need, need for recognition and respect and finally need for self actualisation, when the customer has attained the heights he had planned to achieve. It is assumed in the above worksheet that each feature will have multiple benefits.

Table 6.7. Feature – Benefit Worksheet for a Car

Features	*Benefits*
Big seats	Comfort and lifestyle
Leg room, head clearance	Comfort and lifestyle
Large Boot	Family luxury car
Power steering	Lifestyle
Plush finish	Self actualised owner
Countrywide service facility	Peace of mind – comfort
Easy payment plan	Economical
Exchange facility	Easy on budget, economical
Test drive possible	Reconfirmation of quality, lifestyle
Service pickup and delivery	Comfort
50 years experience	Peace of mind, lifestyle

Before the salesperson starts his presentation, he should have developed the feature benefit worksheet. The features should be first listed and then the benefits added on to the worksheet. In case of a car, the benefits can be listed as given below:

1. Comfort
2. Economy
3. Prestige enhancing lifestyle
4. Convenience
5. Safety

The salesperson should develop the Benefit Story using the possible benefits and writing down a paragraph for each benefit that will help him during the presentation , as given below-

Benefit Paragraph
Comfort

It is a comfortable car. The body is welded. The ride is so smooth you can pour tea or coffee from the jug and it will not spill. The large seats will take a well fed family of six and the leg room ensures comfortable seating for the long legged teenagers.

The large boot is much bigger than several cars with big boots. You can really load it up without damage to your luggage or to the car.

It is a comfortable car for you, your family and your luggage.

Benefit Paragraph
Economy

The car costs less to run. The engine is newly designed for maximum efficiency. It is made out of aluminium to save weight. As a result you get up to 20 kilometres per litre. It is a real miser with petrol.

You can see the engine is uncluttered. It results in time saving for quick adjustments.

The body is welded, which means no rattle repairs. Its rustproof too, it will stand up to all weather.

The aluminium silencer will last twice as long as the ordinary one. The finish stays shiny so you save on waxing the car.

If you have a car to trade in, we will give a fair trade –in allowance, through our used car department.

You just cannot beat the economy of this model.

Benefit Paragraph
Prestige Enhancer-Lifestyle Product

It is a modern car. The new engine—101 horsepower will let you climb hills as though they were not there. Cruising speed in this model will leave you with plenty to spare for passing on motor ways. You will not find a welded body like this even in the best imports of sports cars and the design and the gleaming finish makes it unusually attractive. Of course you get power steering, power breaks and automatic transmission to give the ride you will enjoy.

Benefit Paragraph
Convenience

The car makes driving easier and its uncluttered engine makes maintenance simpler too. It is, as can be seen " long and can be parked in places smaller than ever before for other cars. The car provides spare space in the garage".

The boot will easily hold enough luggage for the long trips planned in the new car. The finish is a cinch to keep glistening clean; only a cold water wash does it quickly.

For ease of driving, parking and safety, the car has power steering, power brakes and automatic transmission.

For periodic maintenance checkups and adjustments, there is complete modern service department at your disposal. If you like you can call me and will personally make arrangements for your service appointments. Should you need servicing in out of town locations in the country we have provided with a list of our numerous authorised service stations in the country along with a route maps so that you can never miss them. We have an easy payment plan so that you can keep your savings in the bank.

I would like to take you out on a test drive to show you how easy the car is to drive, first hand.

Benefit Paragraph
Safety

It is a solid car. These are real doors and the engine is placed up front for balance and greater control. You see the engine is V form and it gives a lower bonnet for battery visibility. The welded body gives you a substantial and strong car that takes all kinds of road punishments. Seat belts in rear seats are big safety plus of the car. You can rely on us to stand by the car. I have been selling cars for this dealer for the last fifteen years and hope to be here for another fifteen years.

As can be seen from the benefit paragraphs that all the benefits from different features on comfort have been listed at one place. Similarly the other list of benefits is used to form sentences in the proper sequence for highlighting the benefits. Once the benefit story has been developed the next step is to find techniques for Maintaining Interest of the prospect.

Maintaining Interest

Salesperson's presentations are in many ways like telling a story. An interesting story is easy to listen while the same is not true for a boring story. Therefore, the next element of persuasive communication is maintaining the interest of the prospect. There are a number of techniques of maintaining the prospects interest as given below:

Customising or Individualising the Benefits

This means that the salesperson directs everything he says towards the needs of the prospect he is facing. This is important because each prospect wants to know how the product will satisfy his specific needs. Such individualisation of benefits will ensure that prospect's interest is maintained. It must be understood that two prospects buying identical product may be motivated by different benefits. Car buyers may have different motivations as one may buy a car for its economy and the other for its convenience. Individualising the needs and benefits means selecting those benefits that would satisfy the need of a particular prospect. Hence the salesperson would have to scan the benefit paragraphs that are ideally suited to the prospects requirements. In other words the salesperson must develop a storehouse of all possible features/benefit stories to be able to build instant rapport and continued interest in the presentation by the prospect. The right selection of the benefit paragraph could mean success of the presentation and in obtaining the objective of the call.

Using Descriptive Language

The other method of maintaining the prospects interest is using descriptive language. For example the car salesperson while using the comfort paragraph, does not just say that the car ride will be smooth, he says, "the ride will be so smooth you can pour coffee" the vivid language helps in maintaining the prospects interest. In the economy paragraph, the salesperson says "the car is real miser on petrol" he is using the descriptive language to hold interest of the prospect. A good salesperson is ready with descriptive language that he has developed with practice and he uses it to good advantage to keep the interest of the prospect.

Participation

The salesperson can keep the interest of the prospect alive if he, instead of relating his benefit story even when the prospect is getting bored with it. Participation means getting him involved in the act. This can be done in the following ways-

Ask the prospect a question, which will ensure his active participation in the presentation. The salesperson can ask, "Do you recall the trouble you had during your last trip in your car?"

Have the prospect do some calculating or figuring out, which would involve him in the presentation. The prospect can be asked to calculate the kilo metres per litre the car will give by giving him some documented figures.

For communicating persuasively the salesperson has to ensure that the prospect remains interested in the presentation, which he can do by individualising the benefits for prospects needs, keep his language descriptive, and ensure prospect's participation.

Believability

The fifth element of persuasive communication is its believability. Unless the prospect believes in the salesperson the call can never be successful. One basic technique used by salesperson for ensuring the believability factor with the prospect is the use of testimonials. Testimonials are stories of satisfied customers that are most helpful for new products or when you are calling on a prospect. A testimonial issued by a reputed and respected company or person in the same field, help in convincing the prospect of the desirability of the product. Salespersons with thorough knowledge of product features and the benefits sought by the prospect can also make a believable presentation. His knowledge should be so extensive and exhaustive that he is able to politely answer all the questions asked by the prospect and give his benefit story convincingly. In the event the salesperson does not know the answer to a question it is best to admit it and confirm that in a day or two he will give the answer, instead of bluffing his way. Any wrong statement made is going to have a snowballing effect and the chances are that the prospect will soon become disillusioned with the salesperson and his presentation. The third technique for creating believability in the prospect results from the demeanour of the salesperson. It is easier to believe a sincere person. The salesperson should try to take the role of a personal counsellor to the prospect. He needs to under claim and over achieve the key points of his presentation. This way he will achieve the believability factor from the prospect.

Summarising there are three methods of achieving believability of the prospect, use of testimonials, having a thorough knowledge of product features and benefits and the salesperson's sincerity towards the prospect.

Demonstration

At times words are just not enough for achieving though call objective as the words appeal only to the prospect's sense of hearing. The other four senses are therefore neglected. We come to the sixth element of persuasive communication-demonstration. Demonstration means appealing to prospect's other sense to make the verbal presentation more persuasive. Demonstration in selling is basic. It is better for the buyer to enjoy chocolate slab rather than some one telling him how good it tastes. The housewife would rather feel the sari fabric than have a TV commercial describe how it feels.

Selling to the channel member, the retailer, if the salesperson does not describer the new advertising campaign but actually shows him the print copy.

A computer buyer would like to have hands on experience on the new model rather than only descriptive eulogy on the same. Buyers of air conditioning plant would be happy to visit an existing installation of the salespersons company and see for themselves the efficacy of the plant.

Salesperson has to decide what needs to be demonstrated and what need not be demonstrated. This requires a careful study of the Benefit Paragraphs. Statements that can be strengthened through an appeal to the other four senses should be carefully considered. Demonstrations make the features and benefits more believable. With some originality, zest and excitement can be added with the demonstration making the presentation more interesting.

Sellers of stainless steel products offer a key chain to the buyer as a proof of its rust proofing feature to increase the believability of the presentation.

Pictures of beautifully constructed villas can add the believability factor for the real estate salesperson.

With the huge dispersion of TV network in the country demonstration has become easy. Functions of an air compressor, farm equipment, dumpers, can be easily demonstrated on TV. In rural markets the advertising vans help in demonstrating the products with the use of audio-visual equipment.

Demonstration that can involve the prospect's active participation will help in maintaining his interest. You must have noticed the detergent advertisements where the group of housewives are asked to join in the actual process of using the detergent. It is a good idea to indirectly demonstrate the service facilities the company has, by showing their pictures and a map where dotted locations of the facilities have been marked.

Demonstrations make features and benefits more understandable and believable. If they are original they make presentation more interesting. If the demonstration requires the use of physical materials like, OHP, LCD Projector, charts the salesperson must ensure that the materials and the equipment are good working order and that the salesperson has personally used it several times. If the salesperson was to fumble through the demonstration the prospect will lose confidence. Therefore, all the equipment must be thoroughly checked before each call. Smooth demonstration would increase the believability of the presentation.

Planning Presentations for Specific Calls

Salesperson should list down the key elements of the presentation, the product features, benefits to stress, the technique of maintaining interest and achieving believability. Appeals to the other four senses that the salesperson plans to use must also be noted. The features and the benefits must be individualised for the prospect on each call. The demonstration planned must also be tailor-made for each prospect. The lap top computer salesperson gave a hands on demonstration to the users of the prospects company, talked about the economies in usage with the prospect's Finance Director and gave the benefit story highlighting the latest features to the CEO. A good presentation converts the need to desire through persuasive communication. Individualised demonstration makes the presentation more effective.

Handling Objections

As the salesperson makes his presentation towards achieving his call objectives, the prospect is likely to make statements detrimental to the achievement of objectives. These statements can be defined as objections. The salesperson must realise that these are normal parts of every sales call and should not be discouraged by them. In fact they may reveal new information that will help you to adjust your tactics. Realistically, therefore, objections should be considered as not deterrents in achievement of objectives but they may serve to help you in readjusting your sales tactics.

The following five steps need to be considered for handling objections:

The first step is listening to the prospect. The salesperson must train himself in the art of listening carefully to the objections raised by the prospects. Salespersons have a tendency to talk rather than to listen. A quiet and patient listener may find the prospect himself talking out of the objection. The prospect must be encouraged to speak uninterruptedly and the salesperson may get to know some additional information that he reveals, which could be of help to the salesperson. The prospect's manner of expressing the objection may confirm his personal negative feelings. The salesperson should not just listen to the words being spoken but also note the manner in which they are expressed. This way he will understand if the prospect has negative feelings as well as he may get some new information.

The second step is classifying the objections. Objections can be classified as valid or invalid. Let us consider the invalid objections. An objection is considered as invalid when there is a concealed reason for it. Actually the prospect covers up how he feels by saying something else and hence should not be taken literally. A reluctance to make purchase decision could be the concealed or underlying reason behind the stated invalid objection. If the prospect says, "I cannot afford it just now, see me in a month" there may be an invalid objection as the prospect cannot say he is unable to decide at the present time. The other concealed reason for an invalid objection could be an aversion to change on the part of the prospect. "Regarding your product I will have to talk to my partner" the prospect may be concealing his reason for buying your product since he has been buying from his present supplier for the past seven years. A prospect may raise an invalid objection if the salesperson has said something or done something to antagonise him. Hard selling on the part of salesperson may offend some prospect. A flippant or derogatory made unwittingly by the salesperson on some favourite project of the prospect could antagonise the prospect.

An invalid objection is only a subtle front for a concealed, underlying reason for the prospect's objection. As the invalid objections are now understood, let us study the valid objections. A valid objection can be taken literally, as the prospect means exactly what he says. For example if the prospect does not understand a technical point made by the salesperson he may raise a valid objection. "The new product is made of 16 gauge steel rather than 18 gauge" if the prospect does not know that the lower the gauge the thicker the steel, he may say, "I do not want something that is flimsy in construction". A valid objection may also be raised if the salesperson fails to stress the feature or the benefit of primary interest to the prospect. In case the buyer is especially interested in the construction of the product and the salesperson keeps emphasising on low price, he is stressing the wrong benefit.

Valid objections occur most frequently during the presentation.

HANDLING OBJECTIONS DETAILS

After the first part is over, that of listening and understanding valid and invalid objection, the next step is disarming. As you meet an objection you are faced with a disagreement. It is best to show consideration for the other person's viewpoint as follows:

1. One popular and effective method is, "yes but" method and it is meant to show consideration to the other person's point of view.
2. Other way of showing consideration is "that is an interesting observation"
3. Or "I am glad you brought it up"
4. And yet again, " yes I know how you feel, but"

As you show consideration for the prospect's viewpoint, you are in fact avoiding confrontation and arguments. Disarming prevents objections from developing into arguments between the prospect and the salesperson.

Once the salesperson has understood the techniques of listening, classifying and disarming it is time to understand the subject of answering the prospect's objections. Let us take the invalid objections first. For invalid objections the salespersons can use a number of answers like giving a token answer. For example, if the prospect says, "I am too busy right now" the salesperson can say disarmingly, "yes sir, everybody is busy these days but let me tell you...."

The other way of handling invalid objection is to ignore it completely by pausing and then continuing. The salesperson can divert the prospects attention away from the objection by bringing up some other interesting fact instead of handling the invalid objection directly. If the classification of the objection as invalid is correct it will nor recur. If the prospect says, "business is terrible", disarmingly the salesperson can reply, "things are pretty tough, but a few moments ago we agreed that our new machine would...."

While answering valid objections it was agreed that they need to be taken on their face value. One other technique is, "denial" that may be used to answer valid objections. The best time to use denial is when the objections are based on misunderstanding or misinterpretation of the salesperson's facts. Suppose the prospect says, "I am not interested in the sweaters as they are made of reconditioned wool" knowing that the label clearly shows that the product is 100% virgin wool, disarming the salesperson can say, "yes sir, I am glad you brought it up; the quality of wool is most important, but all our sweaters are made of 100% virgin wool. Let me show you how we clearly mark the fact on our label".

Another example is, when the prospect says "I am not buying now, times are too uncertain" the answer given disarmingly can be, "yes sir, but, among the certainties is a steady rise in cost of living and prices generally. You should protect yourself to a reasonable degree".

Next, the valid objections can be handled using the YIELD technique. It is used most frequently to overcome objections based on an existing advantage offered by the competition. The success of yield technique depends on the salesperson's ability to offset the existing benefit offered by the competition. For example if a doctor says, "your capsules are larger than those supplied by your competitor." The salesperson's response should be, "yes doctor, our capsule is larger but, it is especially designed for ease of swallowing".

In case you are uncertain if the objection is valid or not, the best way out is ask, "why?" The why question will give the salesperson the necessary information to decide whether to classify the objection as valid or as invalid. For example if the prospect say, "I want to look into some other offers". The salesperson can say, disarmingly, "yes, but why would you want to look into other deals now?" the answer should help the salesperson determine if the objection is valid or not.

So far the discussion on answering objections has been on, listening, classifying, disarming and yielding. The last manner of answering the objections is that of continuing the presentation. After answering the prospects objection, you should continue with the presentation. Otherwise, the prospect will feel he has to raise another objection. The direction of the presentation will depend on what the salesperson has learned from the objection. Suppose the prospect revealed a particular concern about his company's service, the salesperson should stress on those special features of his company's service that were left out in the answers to the objection.

Summarising, the salesperson well versed with the storehouse of benefit paragraphs will be able to adept his presentation in response to the reactions of the prospect. The salesperson must continue his presentation as he reinforces the answers to the objection. It will prevent the objection from recurring later in the call.

PRICE OBJECTION

After understanding the five ways of dealing with valid objections, let us consider a special case of valid objection, the price objection. The price objection is being handle separately because it is the one that plagues the salesperson most and is most difficult to handle. The price objections are of two types, "I cannot afford it" or, "I can get it for less".

The first type of price objection, "I cannot afford it" can be said as, "your price is too high", or "I cannot spend that much" or yet another, "I am looking for a cheaper product".

The salesperson's response in such cases can be, staring with denial, "yes sir, money is important, but, in the long run your savings will far outweigh this additional expenditure".

Normally the price objection is raised when the prospects knows that he can get the same product for a different price. If the salesperson knows his product has as higher price than the competitive product it is best to use the yield technique. Disarmingly the salesperson can say, "Yes our price is Rs.150 and competitive price is Rs.125, but, the difference of Rs.25 eliminated by the one year free service contract we are offering that the competition does not. You will agree that one year fee service is definitely more than Rs.25. It is best to talk about the small difference and justify it rather than talk about the main price amount".

DEFINING SALES OBSTACLES

Following are the major obstacles that a salesperson faces during making a sale:

Habit: The customer is in the habit of using competitive product or service and finds it difficult to change.

Fear: The customer fears the unknown and has unwarranted feeling of impending trouble of risk or of loss that confuses his thinking and causes him to evade opportunities that help him to maximise his capabilities.

Price: The customer fails to see the benefits that outweigh their money value.

Complaint: the customer voices or feels dissatisfaction on the company's product or service.

Detail: The customer believes that the trouble that he has to take in buying the product is not worth the effort.

Lack of Information: Sales progress gets impeded when the salesperson has not informed the customer either due to his own lack of knowledge on the same or when the customer lacks the technical skills to understand the sales talk. At times the customer could be lacking in imagination to visualise the benefits of the product or even when the salesperson's expressions are unclear and confusing.

Competition: The customer believes that the competitive benefits would be more suited to him.

It must be understood that at times companies face competition from dissimilar things like a housewife may choose a new cooking range over a new washing machine.

Friendship-Competition: The customer likes or respects competitive sales or other personnel or when the customer or the prospect believes that the competitive product will produce equal or greater amount of benefits to him.

Difficult Personality: The prospect lacks emotional control and he allows the difference of opinion to degenerate or he indulges in temper, rudeness or other unwarranted behaviour that retards progress towards sales.

Time: Customer feels that the company's product does not merit the time to be spent on its purchase, or if the sales call is made too late and yet any further postponement would cause failure of the talks or if the deliver requirements of the customer are urgent and cannot be met.

Release: The prospect wants a release from further discussion of the subject.

Divided Release: The prospect wants release as he sincerely or insincerely says he has to discuss the matter with someone not present.

Negative Mood or Manner: Salesperson's talk is creating through his frame of mind, manner of speaking and acting unfavourable reaction in the prospects mind causing dislike and lack of respect.

Poor Judgement: When the salesperson does not care for the following:

- Prevailing conditions.
- Comparing and separating right ways of doing things from wrong ways.
- Planning the sales call- when to call, what to say and what to do.

- Deciding how to use the product benefits in the talk from the customers' viewpoint.
- Noting the effect on the customer on what is said or done.
- Keeping control of emotions.
- Using knowledge of human nature and practical selling methods secured through study, analysis and experience.

Countering the Obstacles

Benefit: Describe any good result the customer will get from putting a good quality of the product to use.

Good Quality: Describe clearly the inherent trait or characteristic of the product or proposition or specific parts that make it possible to produce benefits when put to use.

Poor Quality: Clearly but tactfully describe traits and characteristics of an alternate product (competitive), that make it produce losses when put to use.

Loss: Describe the losses poor quality will bring ever so subtly.

Proposition: Inform the prospect the salesperson's name, company's name, brand, price, terms of business, delivery time.

Prestige: Clearly describe the reputation and achievements of his company, its personnel, its products, services, and the customers, endorsers who lend their support.

Personal Prestige: Inform the prospect of the salesperson's accomplishments, experience and good reputation that creates a feeling of respect and confidence in the prospect.

Pride: Inform the prospect of the respect he enjoys with the salesperson by stating his achievements, his company's accomplishments, or by asking his advice on some matter that he can comment on.

Assurance: Use any combination of words to qualify the above stated counters with tactful directness or that has power to calm or reassure the prospect.

Story: Give an account of an event that indirectly informs the prospect of reasons, emotions or both that help him in deciding in the salesperson's favour.

Good Turn: Salesperson should perform or offer to perform any good turn that has power to build liking and respect and which places the prospect under no obligation.

Contact: Classify the business or personal friendship between the salesperson and the prospect and mention friends, hobbies, other outside activities that establish common interests.

Explanation: make the meaning of technical terms used by classifying words and use similes, demonstrations, charts, presentations, photographs to clarify details of an operation.

Mood and Manner: salesperson's frame of mind, manner of speaking and actions should help create liking and respect for him in the prospect's mind.

Question: salesperson should ask questions indirectly as autosuggestion to reconfirm the sales story has become effective. The question could also be to elicit information in the form of investigation question.

Progress Signal: The salesperson should look out for signals from prospect in the form of comment or action to confirm that the salesperson has fully answered Prospect Viewpoint Questions adequately to keep things moving.

Good Judgement: classifies mindset operation where the ways of doing and saying things is done by Multiple Analysis for producing maximum benefits

Command: Any command used directly or with other counters that effectively produce desired result from the prospect.

First Benefit: is the first result produced when a Good Quality is put to use.

Major Interest Benefit: expresses a result that is one of the prospect's objective.

Favourable Condition: Is when the prospect's industry , company, group, or personal life from where he draws benefits or will benefit in future, and that is brought to his attention to prepare him to visualise that he has an opportunity to Benefit still further through the salesperson's Proposition. The favourable conditions also appeals to Pride elements and gives him still greater power to help him see and appreciate his Opportunity.

Unfavourable Conditions: Any situation that creates losses for the prospect, for which the prospect, the salesperson or his company are Not responsible and which brought to his attention discretely would help him see the Need for the Benefits of the salesperson's proposition.

Spar: Salesperson can use Spar as a special action for Mood and Manner, Assurance, and question , to meet the Obstacles in a serene and considerate manner so that the Objector's mind is reopened to reason.

The Twenty-first Century Challenge

With the multitudes of competitive companies, national, international and multinational in the fray, the salespersons are facing probably the greatest challenge ever encountered by any salesperson before. They are required to call on to the full, all their personal resources to meet the challenge. Some salespersons with years of experience have acquired a name for themselves in the market. Now they are required to compete with highly respected and internationally known brands by retaining the existing business and adding new channel members to cater to some hitherto virtually unknown markets.

The challenge is great and yet there are ways and means of countering it and coming out a winner. The salesperson with fortified skills, and with coordinated advertising campaigns is amply confident of meeting the challenges.

Challenges always brings opportunities and by effectively meeting the new competitive environment, the salesperson can develop self – pride as the salespersons grow in stature in the eyes of the management, channel members and the customers. The main objectives of learning about the twenty-first century challenges are the following:

1. To empower the salespersons to meet the challenges with new skills, as their job becomes more rewarding and satisfying with new ideas and methods for achieving profitable results that will give you pride.
2. To improve the confidence level of the channel members in the company as the salespersons with skills and ability would provide help the channel members in solving difficult problems.
3. To help the salespersons in effectively meeting the competition and with success their stature and value in the eyes of the company and the customers will increase. Salespersons should develop better personal resources for achieving the kind of sales and profits results that will enhance their prestige and importance in their company and with the channel members.

Analysing present knowledge plans the students should attempt to understand the following:

1. Describe what they consider the basic goals or objectives of a salesperson's job.

2. Describe the Critical Success Factors for any company from the customer's, channel member's and the company's viewpoint.
3. Describe the type of relationship they should have with the channel members in the present highly competitive age.
4. Pick up a well known product and list down all possible benefit that would accrue to the customer by its use.
5. Describe what is considered as important for fighting competition.

UNDERSTANDING PEOPLE AND DEALING WITH THEM EFFECTIVELY

Given below is Sales Analysis Chart:

As effective sellers the entire approach to sales has to be customer oriented to be of any use. Hence the first analysis is from the customer or the prospects viewpoint as follows:

1. Attention—do I like and respect the salesperson—
2. Interest—what can his proposition do for me?
3. Desire—can he support his claim?
4. Decision—is it the best thing to-do now?
5. Sale or Action—I will buy or act

Given below are the Emotion Movers that persuade the buyer into favourable action:

1. Mood and Manner
2. Personal Prestige
3. Good Turn
4. Contact
5. Assurance
6. Question
7. Command

Reason Movers

1. Benefit
2. Good Quality
3. Poor Quality (negative for competition)
4. Loss
5. Proposition
6. Prestige
7. Explanation
8. Story
9. Good Judgement

The Sale Calls Face the Following Obstacles:

1. Habit
2. Fear
3. Price
4. Complaint
5. Detail
6. Lack Of Information
7. Competition
8. Friendship Competition
9. Difficult Personality
10. Time
11. Release
12. Divided Release
13. Negative Mood And Manner
14. Poor Judgement

As is noticed there are favourable and unfavourable conditions when the salesperson has to use or perceive the following-

- Use test question
- Perceive Signal

Obstacles can be handled by using Spar or practice or solution efforts.

Scene 1

A benefit mover describes clearly good result that a prospect will get from putting to use a good quality.

Material BenefitsExamples

1. Save thirty thousand rupees
2. Reduce switching costs by 10%
3. Bring in more customers at lunch time
4. Enable you to finish your work in half the time
5. Improve the strength of the foundation

Physical Benefits Examples

1. Måke you more comfortable
2. Save you that heavy lifting
3. Prevent foot, leg , back pain
4. You can work in a more upright position
5. Keep the dust out of your nose lungs

Mental Benefits Examples-

1. You get more satisfaction out of your work
2. It will take a load out of your mind
3. Dealing with the company will be pleasant
4. The children will be perfectly safe
5. It may please the big boss

The benefit movers are having certain powers and some limitations too as given below:

Powers

The benefit movers enable the salesperson to predict for his prospect listener, the **interesting** and **desirable** results of doing what he has proposed. It appeals to the listener's basic motive for taking action in favour of the company. It answers the Prospects Viewpoint Question, " What good will your plan do?" and therefore noblest salesperson to talk from the prospect's viewpoint and best interest.

Limitations

The benefit movers lacks the power to support itself. It cannot answer the Prospect Viewpoint Question, "Can you support your claim" and therefore , unsupported , cannot give the prospect reason to believe benefit predictions or claims.

Scene 2

Good Quality Movers examples

A good quality mover describes the inherent trait or characteristic of a proposition or a specific part that makes it possible to produce Benefits when put to use.

Good Quality in Products

- Fine workmanship
- Improved design
- Mounted on live rubber
- Top grain cowhide
- Spring steel coils
- Three ply construction

Good Quality in Service

- Our servicemen are well trained and experienced
- Company is sound in finance
- We have carefully planned direct mail campaign

- We take hourly meter readings
- We apply heat evenly
- Our methodology is well tested in the field
- It is the practical way

Good Quality in Persons

- Honest and steady
- Skilled and experienced
- Intelligent
- Alert and enterprising
- Good natured
- Full of common sense
- Tactful
- Physically strong

The Powers and Limitations of the Good Quality Mover

Powers

The good quality mover enables salesperson to tell his prospect what makes possible the beneficial results of using the product he is offering. It has power to support the benefit claim and get them believed.

Limitations

The Good Quality Mover lacks the power to create interest and desire since it cannot describe the basic reason for buying , which is to obtain the Benefit.

Analysing a Talk for its Movers

The student needs to identify the benefit or the good quality mover as the analysis is made.

Example 1

A bank equipment salesperson sees in a bank that the bus carrying bank money was being bumped against the walls, scratching and marring the walls. He got an idea and he expressed himself as follows in his talk with the bank personnel-

Salesperson—you could easily protect your walls and decorations by placing a continuous rubber bumper at the bottom of each bus. That would eliminate the scratches and the mars the buses make and save a lot of repair and maintenance costs.

Prospect- what are the bumpers like?

The talk has started revolving around the salesperson's objective.

Example 2

An engineer wants his prospect to appreciate the Benefits that can be gained by the use of a automatic oil pump.

Engineer- machine shutdowns will be reduced to a minimum because this positive gear oil pump will automatically keep every bearing coated with oil.

Example 3

Salesperson –you always wanted to guard your workers health , I have just the practical way to protect their lungs. Got the time to hear about it?

Prospect- I will make time. What is it?

Benefits are possible because of the Good Qualities of the product.

Example 4

The shirt will be comfortable and long wearing because it is carefully tailored using terry silk material. It stays fresh, resists soiling all day long.

Analysing Product for Sale Movers

Salesperson needs to understand the sequencing of his thought process as he builds the benefit, good quality movers story. The analysis studies different kinds of reasons, as given below-

Product—Chest of drawers-extension arms

Table 6.8. Benefit Story

Benefits	*Good Quality*
1. File drawer can be rolled in and out of the cabinet rapidly with least effort	Sturdy, steel extension arms using giant size ball bearings
2. Saves operators energy	
3. Reduce errors due to fatigue	
4. Gets the desired correspondence quicker	
5. Time and expense saved	

Analysis of a proposition having both product and service parts

Table 6.9. Benefit Analysis

	Benefits	Good Qualities
Market Analysis		
Copy writing	1. First benefit-make a study of problems for which advertising is required 2. Write the copy then perfect it 3. Create copy that will get read 4. Bring inquiries	5. Trained and skilled copy writers, directed by experience and able supervisors
Art work Printing Papers		

ANALYSING A FAULTY SITUATION FOR CORRECTION- MACHINE OPERATION

Table 6.10. Correcting Faults

The situation		The correct plan	
Benefits	*Right way*	*Wrong way*	*Losses*
1. Machine operator wrists sag slightly at times	2. Cuffs and and wrists touch that causes space bars machine to space at wrong time.	3. By holding wrists in arched position	4. Keeps wrists from touching the bar 5. Machine will space perfectly

The Correction Talk

Salesperson—(in a pleasant manner) the easy way to make the machine space perfectly is by holding the wrists higher than usual that keeps cuffs and wrists from even the lightest touch of the space bar. You get perfect results.

THE 4 COLUMN SITUATION AND CORRECTION ANALYSIS

Wrong actions—

1. Kitchen utensils stored where they cause the cook to take extra steps, not justified.
2. Lawn mowing done in a shaggy way.
3. Child strews things in a room which; looks dirty.

Select situation and analyse using the Analysis Sequence.

Write short talk on correction of the situation, using the presentation sequence stating only the benefits which the right way of doing things will provide.

The thinking sequence starts with the wrong way and related losses and next come the right way and the benefits.

However, the Presentation Sequence starts by presenting the Benefits of the Right Way. The salesperson can mention the Wrong and the Losses only after pointing out the Right Way Benefits.

EXAMPLES OF POOR QUALITY AND LOSS MOVERS

Poor quality movers clearly but tactfully describe the inherent traits and characteristics of a proposition , a situation or alternate product and plans that make it probable that it will produce looses when put to use. It is recommended for highlighting the competitive products.

Loss Mover clearly but tactfully describes an undesirable result of putting poor quality product to use.

Examples

1. Steel corners of the truck carrying money will mar metal work and plaster walls that will cause considerable repair expense.
2. Engineers have found that reinforcement of steel bars less than 0.25 inch thick are too light and will fail to support even a slight overload.
3. Untested methods might prove unworkable.
4. Men lacking in experience can cause roads accidents.

Power and Limitations of Poor Quality and Loss Movers

Powers

Help listeners to make wise choice when used after the Benefit and Good Quality Movers.

Limitations

When used alone, they often sound threatening , one-sided and arouse opposition.

Conclusion

Benefit and good quality movers are compared with poor quality and loss movers to help prospect reach the right decision.

Salesperson –in cold climate kota stone will stand up well because its square edges will hold mortar better during summer when the snow would melt. Slate has slanting tin edges which often fail to hold mortar when snow is melting and the sun is hot. Kota stone is cheaper to remain and hold appearance longer I would recommend it.

(Students should analyse the sentence by segregating the benefits, good quality, loss and bad quality)

The material salesperson should arrange the 4 column analysis of sale movers as given below:

Table 6.11. Multiple Analysis I

Kota stone	***Kota stone***	***Slate***	***Slate***
Good qualities	*Benefits*	*Poor quality*	*losses*
1. Kota stone has thick, strong slabs, with square	2. Will hold mortar well in freezing and melting weather. Retain looks and appearance for years and is cheaper to maintain	3. Slate has razor edge thin slanting	4. Mortar will split awat from edges during edges melting season, requiring expensive repairs

Multiple Analysis of Products

The analysis covers the benefits and losses of different products, including competitive products as it helps in making a comparative study on the product having more benefits and less losses in comparison to the competitive product

Table 6.12. Multiple Analysis II

Kota stone		
Benefit	***Qualities***	***Losses***
Hold mortar will under canditions or hot water. Retain good appearance for year at low upkeep cost. Save on extra labour cost in a few years	Large sawn slabs having square edges one inch thick	More labour required to handle and to set. Costs to intall more in labour
Slate		
Benefit	***Qualities***	***Losses***
Provides delicate beauty in pattern and colour. Easier and faster to hadle and save about Rs. 10000 on labour of installing	Has a variety of colours and scalloped edged shapes. Edges thin and sharp	Mortar splits away from edges during snow melting season, beauty is marred, repair expense estimate at Rs. 5000 annually over ten year period

Analysis can be made in such a manner that only the benefits are highlighted as the losses are listed down by underplaying them. This gives the salesperson better idea on how to manage prospect's questions on competitive product. The best course ultimately is to lay stress on his own product Good Qualities and benefits that accrue through its use rather than decry competition where the chances of going wrong with incorrect statements are present .

Multiple Analysis of a Situation

The salesperson should make an effort to find the true interest of competitors with more benefits and least losses will be found.

Table 6.13. Benefit/Loss Story

Galvanised Conduit

Benefit	*Problem*	*Losses*
1. Intitial cost less to consumer, it will help the dealer procure the order and a quick sure profit profit made by the dealer	2. Can the galvanised conduit be sold for use where acid fumes are presernt	3. Acid will get through the conduit. Corrosion, stoppages will accrue. Dealers reputation will be damaged

Benefit	*Problem*	*Losses*
1. Consumer will find it will stand acid for years, will save more than its cost by avoiding a single breakdown 2. More profit for the dealer 3. Effort to sell the right product will get respect of the buyer	2. Will there be stress on buyer to buy zinc conduit with sealed surface?	3. Purchase will cost 40% more 4. Buyer may place order on someone else as his opposition may increase

In order to understand the above stated analyses the following dialogue gives real life situations that will take the students as close to corporate world as possible.

Reasoning process in a Multi-comparison form

Salesperson—(approaches his dealer, greets him pleasantly, shows appreciation for a new vehicle the dealer has purchased. Takes care of routine business and says calmly)—I talked to my office and was told that you and one of your contractors were working on a major wiring job with the Singh Corporation (pauses, waits for reply).

Dealer (says sadly)—yes, Ramesh, you know , the contractor and he tells me that a young assistant to the Works Manager is deaf to everything but low price.

Salesperson(slowly and thoughtfully)—I see, well, he can make sure, quick profit that way.

Dealer—I guess that the young fellow is really tough. He is trying for a shrewd bargain. Just a wise guy.

Salesperson—yes, I see, how much does the company need protection? How corrosive is the acid?

Dealer—plenty. That is what worries me.

Salesperson—I can see how you feel. But as a guess, how soon the corrosion might develop into power failures and production stoppages, if these stocks are used?

Dealer—well, it will take some time, may be months. But a price-chiseller usually gets what he pays for. And some contractors go for low bids and quote these stocks.

Salesperson—it is a tough situation. I see that. There is a big profit if zinc conduits are used by all of us. But what will happen if the stocks are used when wire failure starts? Will this young fellow convince his boss that the contractor and we are to be blamed and we will get a black eye with the local business.

Dealer—it could hurt the contractor. But people ought to know that a dealer only fills a contractor's orders.

Salesperson—they should know that. Do you think it would put the contractor right with the customers, Works Manager if he went to him and helped him to see the years of protection he will get by using zinc conduits?

Dealer—well-maybe. Making a big issue of protecting each days production might even make a big change in the young fellow's thinking and make it unnecessary to go up. But as you know these contractors often make low bids and do not fight for zinc conduits enough. But if he had your kind of backing he would feel strong. So how about going to the customer with him? I think I can fix a meeting just now.

Salesperson—it is a deal. I will try to make the young fellow or his boss see how much more good the zinc conduit will do. Make sure that the contractor understands that in order to avoid loss, we insist on zinc conduits.

Dealer—right boss (picks the phone)

Prospects Basic Needs and Desires

Most people have certain common basic needs and desires as given below:

Security—people need protection from loss of what they have, protection to health, income, skills, mental powers , their company assets that are connected to their security and survival and of others whose welfare they have at heart.

Progress—people want to improve their personal and their team or group conditions, want to learn more, to do things better, besides they want the following:

- To earn more
- To live better
- To give better things and opportunities to their families
- To do work that increases in importance and responsibility
- To help their company so that in turn they get more opportunities

Respect—people want the respect of customers, peers, employees, bosses, families and neighbours.

Satisfaction and Enjoyment from Work and Life—people want a sense of achievement, peace of mind, happy associations, a sense of belonging, a feeling that their work is important and beneficial, besides they want the happiness of doing more than just for money.

Responsibilities and Objectives of the Prospects Job

Once the salesperson appreciates and understands the type of responsibilities the prospects have he would be in a better position to tailor-make his sales presentation. A few of the responsibilities and job objectives are given below as examples:

Table 6.14. Job Responsibilities - A

President	*Production Manager*	*Materials Manager*
Keep company financially sound for survival, security and development	Keep production levels high, costs low enough to beat competition	Keep company adequately supplied and able to operate efficiently
Long term planning	Constantly improve production facilities	Avoid wastage of company funds
Build skilled competent management team for profitable successful operation	Constantly improve people skills, knowledge	Constantly improve the knowledge, skills, performance and morale of department personnel
Build company's Brand Equity	Improve health standards, reduce accident rate	Keep company's prestige high with sellers and secure helpful ideas and cooperation from them
Encourage and guide morale building	Maintain and improve human relations.	
Human Relations	Keep morale high and be respected	
Get along with others and be respected	Get along with others both vertically and horizontally, while getting the things right	Get along with company's other departments, hold respect of their people and get department's helpful service fully understood and used
Get satisfaction and pleasure out of work	Get satisfaction and pleasure out of work	Get satisfaction and pleasure out of work

Given below is similar statement for the supervisors and the workers

Table 6.15. Job Responsibilities - B

Supervisor	*Worker*
Get along with management and the workers	Be respected as a person by management and fellow workers
Get work done on schedule	Feel that the work done is important to company and customer
Help maintain and improve quality	Steady work and good pay
Keep costs low enough to compete and serve customer's best interest	Good bosses
Successfully interpret workers problems and attitudes to management	Chance to get ahead
Successfully interpret company problems and policies to workers	Good working conditions
Hold respect of workers and others in supervision and management	Job satisfaction, peace of mind and happiness
Handle complaints effectively and diplomatically and avoid possible grievances	
Be successful in persuading others to accept and cooperate with proposed ideas, plans	
Get satisfaction, pleasure and reward out of work and life	

Salespersons having learnt the value of customer analysis needs to fit the benefits to prospects job objectives as given below:

Example 1

The salesperson is talking to a road building contractor whose company security often depends upon making a profit in closely bid jobs. Hence that becomes his job objective and a major interest area.

Salesperson (for Road Grader is talking to road contractor whom he knows well)—to help our road contractor customers make a profit, our company makes a constant study of problems. The study goes right back to our designers. Take a tough problem of making a profit on closely bid jobs. One thing done, to help cut costs, w to equip the controls of our new road grader with an improved hydraulic dumper. It eases pressure surges and eliminates the shock of starting and stopping the cutting blade. An operator can now place the blade faster and make more accurate cuts and yet do 20% more work per hour.

Example 2

The salesperson talks to the Supervisor of the above stated road contracting company. He has learnt that this prospect has had trouble in keeping good operators because of many rural road jobs.

Road Grader Salesperson—to help keep good persons on the job when they are long way from home, our designers have equipped the controls of the new model with improved hydraulic dumper. It eases pressure surges and eliminates shocks of staring and stopping the blade. With LESS effort, the operator can place the blade faster, make more accurate cuts, and do 20 percent more work. The workmen love the machine and they actually stay on the job longer.

The talk continues—

Fit the Movers to Prospects Job Objectives

The table given below summarises the way it is done

Table 6.16. Good Quality/Benefit Matrix

Part	*Benefits*	*Good Qualities*
1. Damper	1. Eases pressure surges 2. Cutting blade starting stopping shocks eliminate 3. Blade placement by operator faster 4. Cut more accurate 5. 20 per cent more work with less effort 6. Cut operating costs 7. Make a profit on closely bid jobs	8. New model controls have an improved hydraulic damper

The Bridge of Understanding

The FIRST BENEFIT expresses the first helpful thing a Good Quality will do for ANY user.

A MAJOR INTEREST BENEFIT expresses a final result that is one of the prospect's objectives

Table 6.17(a). Benefit Story

Operating cost cut	Up to 20% more work with less effort	Keep the depth of cut more accurate	Operator can place blade faster	Shock of starting and stopping cutting eliminated	Eases pressure surges

Table 6.17(b). Bridge of Understanding

Major Interest Benefit		*Good Quality*
Make a profit on closely bid jobs	Road Grader	New model controls have an improved hydraulic damper

The Mood and Manner Mover

A person's frame of mind and manner of speaking and acting that help to create liking and respect is a Mood and Manner Mover.

When a listener/prospect sees a salesperson exhibit such Mod and Manner as the following, his emotions are favourable influenced:

1. Consideration and respect
2. Business like intent
3. Friendliness
4. Enthusiasm
5. Confidence
6. Tactfulness
7. Emotional control
8. Patience

Besides the above, when a listener /prospect sees a salesperson exhibit such Moods and Manners as follows his emotions are favourably influenced:

1. Earnestness
2. Seriousness
3. Due concern
4. Sympathy
5. Thoughtfulness
6. Alertness
7. Self-respect
8. Resolution

The inviting appearance of a shop, displays, product, brochure, person on the counter that create a favourable impression and helps to create liking and respect are also classified under Mood and Manner Movers.

Negative Mood and Manner

On the other hand there are Negative Mood and Manner that work as Obstacles as given below:

A salesperson's frame of mind and manner of speaking and acting that impresses a listener/prospect unfavourably and that create dislike and lack of respect form Negative Mood and Manner Obstacle.

When a salesperson shows the following to the prospect through looks and actions his(prospects) emotions are affected unfavourably:

1. Selfishness
2. Arrogance
3. Impatience
4. Slyness
5. Overconfidence
6. Brittle temper
7. Insincerity
8. Superiority
9. Dislike

When a prospect sees a salesperson whose looks and actions indicate the following the prospect's emotions are affected unfavourably.

When the appearance of a shop, display, brochure is uninviting and creates an atmosphere that puts the prospect in a negative mood the Negative Mood and Manner is active.

Is Negative Mood and Manner an Obstacle?

Do the Negative Moods and Manners , shown in these examples , place a negative influence over all that is said and therefore weaken or ruin their reasoning power?

Example 1

Supervisor- do you want to stay out of trouble with the inspectors? If so, watch these edges better. You are getting careless.

Example 2

Salesperson—listen , pack the Glass RIGHT HEREAFTER that is the only way to save us from this kind of trouble.

EMOTION MOVES USED TO PRESENT REASON MOVERS.

Example 1

An ASSURANCE MOVER is any combination used to present other Movers with tactful directness, or that has power to calm or reassure the prospect.

The Question Mover

A question used by the salesperson to present other Movers indirectly is a SUGGESTION QUESTION

A COMMAND MOVER is any command used by itself or in conjunction with some other Movers that effectively produce a desired action from the prospect

A STORY MOVER is an account of an occurrence that indirectly informs the prospect of Reason Movers, Emotion Movers or both.

AN ASSURANCE MOVER , USED TO PRESENT BENEFIT IDEAS POSITIVELY

Example

Machinery Salesperson— yes, Mr. Gupta, your men will have even more protection than they have now.

THE QUESTION MOVER, USED TO PRESENT BENEFITS RESPECTFULLY AND OPEN THE DOOR TO MORE POSITIVE TACTICS

Example

· Salesperson to experienced retailer—what would you think of this idea for getting faster turnover on storage cabinets? (shows window display plans).

Retailer Prospect—why do you have household items rather than office items in two of these cabinets?

Salesperson—I think it will catch the eye of many of the women who pass the shop and bring some of them in to buy cabinets or some other items.

(TALK CONTINUES)

THE COMMAND MOVER , USED TO PRESENT REASON MOVERS

Example

Salesperson—(to retailer)—take the lower profit, faster turnover plan!

THE STORY MOVER, USED TO PRESNT REASON MOVERS INDIRECTLY

Example

Salesperson- over in Kolkata last week I saw how Hindustan Motors is making their big reduction in rejects. First of all, they are practically eliminating paint fading by—.(story continues)

Food for Thought

It is interesting to understand that conclusions that are made are the product of a person's own mind and they become the basis on which he plans and acts. See how well you agree with the following:

1. The basic motive in taking any action is to Benefit. A prospect can become INTERESTED only when he sees Benefits available.
2. A prospect is a person or group that can be Benefited to a desirable degree and who has the money or credit or is able to take the action proposed.
3. Effective planning of a sale begins with the finding of Benefits that will be interest to EACH prospect, Benefits for himself and others whose interest he has at heart.
4. The Benefit Mover has the power to create interest by answering the Prospect-Viewpoint question, " What GOOD will your plan do?"
5. The Benefit, Good Quality, Poor Quality and Loss Movers have power to develop interest into desire to take action since they answer the Prospect-Viewpoint question, "Can you support your(Benefit) claim?"

Three forms in which the prospects reason , when they make it clear that their purpose is to Benefit are as given below-

1. The Benefit and God Quality Form
2. The Comparison Form
3. The Conclusion Form

Any form of reasoning can be in Assurance style, Question style, Command or Story style, or in a mixture of these styles. The Assurance and Command styles are Direct, the Question and Story styles are Indirect.

Styles of presenting Reason Movers appeal mainly to the emotions and have power to open the listening mind to the reception of speaker's reasoning.

The Mood and Manner Mover is an essential par of all presentation styles. It is the Emotion Mover that goes to work first in creating "liking and respect" and in answering the Prospect-viewpoint question, " Do I like and respect you".

Tact is practiced by avoiding the expression of Negative Impulse Judgements.

The recognition of Forms of Reasoning and Styles of Presenting Reason Movers will provide a guide for practicing TO-THE-POINT reasoning of Reason Movers. Such practice provides a background to present ideas effectively without conscious effort.

It is not expected that facing his prospect the salesperson will pause and say to himself, "Now I will use the Conclusion Form and present my ideas in Assurance Style" anymore than he will pause and think, "Now I will use a noun, a verb and an adverb".

The Personal Prestige Mover

A Personal Prestige Mover clearly describes the good reputation or achievement of the salesperson's company, its personnel, its products, its services or customers, endorsers who lend prestige. It provides the prospect with evidence that Benefit claims can be believed.

Example 1

Purchase Manager to the Purchase Committee—the most experienced and reliable person in the paper business is Raghav Gupta.

Example 2

Prospect—on phone—Mr. Mathur told me of the clerical time and expense you have saved him. I would be happy if you come over to see me.

The examples show that good reputation built previously is active. In th next example the speaker tries to build his Prestige.

Example 1

Salesperson—during the two years I was at the factory, a problem in electronic controls crept up and we could solve it in no time.

Example 2

Manager to worker—sure, I know this machine, Verma. I operated it for four years.

Personal Prestige Can be Built by Action

Example

Salesperson dismantles part of the machine he is selling and then puts it together.

Limitation

The power of the Personal Prestige Mover gets weak if the listener gets the impression that the speaker is trying to brag or is talking mainly to build his own confidence.

The Appeal to Pride Mover

An Appeal to Pride Mover confirms the salesperson's respect for the prospect by stating the achievements of the prospect , his company or by asking for advice.

Example 1

Salesperson to his dealer- as I came in, I heard some persons saying some nice things about the excellent job done on your display windows. You are making quite a success with you, is it not ?

Example 2

Salesperson to another non-competitive salesperson—we are working on the colour scheme of our carton. Since you have done pioneering job in this area we would welcome any advice you would kindly give.

Example 3

Salesperson—our engineers thought that a reduction in maintenance costs would be one of the main things an engineer of your special experience would demand.

Example 4

Service Engineer—the engineers in our Head Office will understand how you feel. They know you have always been fair-minded; so I am sure I can have this corrected in a day or two.

Example 5

Service Manager—our Delhi Manager wrote to me about how well you planned the increase in sales of your engines in the North India.

Example 6

Salesperson—I really like the hardwood shop floors, they look nice and long lasting.

Misuse of Compliments

Example 1

Salesperson—you have a really well appointed office. It looks great.

The prospect has heard such a remark often over the past six years and further, he knows his office is nice but nothing unusual. On the day of the compliment it was rather dirty.

Example 2

Salesperson—you have made one of the best displays in the windows that I have seen. However, the way the special products are displayed really look shabby from the street.

If you soft paddle your criticism with a compliment the listener will always expect criticism whenever you offer a compliment.

Example 3

Salesperson of Bank Equipment to Bank teller—you sure can count money fast.

Teller—I ought to, I have been doing it for twenty years.

A prospect may not get any pleasure or satisfaction from a compliment on a task he performs as routine. On the other hand, a compliment put in a Question Style like, "in counting these brand new notes how do you keep a few from sticking together?" can Appeal to Pride Power.

The Good Turn Mover

A Good Turn Mover is a favour or free service performed or offered by the salesperson that has the power to build liking and respect and that places the prospect under no obligation.

Example 1

Salesperson—you can have my copy of the Planning Commission's Report on the Five year plan.

Example 2

Salesperson to the prospect—your supplier is in Rampur, is it not. I am going there tomorrow on business. Suppose I drop in at the supplier's place and see if I speed up things a little.

Example 3

Salesperson to prospect—I just heard you are planning to go to Jaipur next Monday. I too have plans of going there by car. You are most welcome to come with me and I will drop you in Jaipur wherever you want.

Example 4

Salesperson for Retail prospect—I have time on hand, if you want I can count the stock just arrived for you.

Example 5

An experienced engineer solved his prospect's problem unconnected to his own business. In this way he did a Good Turn and later , the prospect said to another person in his company, "that fellow really knows his business" (Personal Prestige is earned through doing a Good Turn.)

THE CONTACT MOVER

A Contact Mover is defined as classifying the business or personal friendship developed between a salesperson and a customer or the mention of common friends, hobbies, and other outside interest activities that help establish common interests.

When a prospect likes and treats a salesperson with more consideration because he is impressed by his Mood and Manner a Contact has begun. When a prospect is favourably impressed on finding that the salesperson is having a common friend or a person he respects, a degree of Contact is formed. When a prospect and the salesperson love to talk about r practice the same hobby a Contact is active. The strongest type of Contact comes about when the customer appreciates the benefits that the salesperson has enabled him to enjoy.

Examples of Contact Mover in Action

Example 1

Salesperson—I am Ramesh from Colgate company. Your friend Mr. Kapil suggested I drop in and introduce myself.

Prospect—oh yes, Kapil phoned me about you.

Example 2

Salesperson—I may have a solution to your leaks problem. Can I call you tomorrow, I want half an hour of your time.

Prospect—how about nine thirty?

Common Uses of the Command, Question and Assurance Movers.

The student must understand that the Command, Question and Assurance Movers are not used only to PRESENT Reason Movers. The following examples

Example 1 Command Mover—command used for routine directions

Salesperson to associate—look at the second paragraph, son.

Example 2 Ccommand used to calm the customer

Salesperson on phone—do not worry it will do your job.

Mrs. Raj—it will do the cleaning easily.

Example 1 Question Mover used to elicit needed information

Salesperson—at your Rampur plant how many barrels of oil you use daily?

Example 2 Assurance Mover used to be calm.

Salesperson—I know how you feel. I understand that you can rely on the delivery date.

Assurance used to calm help PREPARE the prospect to listen to reason.

ASSURANCE MOVER used to instil trust and confidence and to help PREPARE prospect to open his mind to reason.

Example 3

Salesperson—there are four models Mr. Roy. All are built differently. The one that will do your work best is model 3 (follow with the Benefit Mover).

The first two Assurances used in the example have power to build confidence in the prospect and they therefore help PREPARE him to open his mind to the reception of Benefit ideas.

The purpose of Emotion Movers is to place the listener in a mood that will open his psyche to reason. The effective use of Emotion Movers, which is so much part of effective personality , is made possible by Sales Analysis. Such analysis often enables a salesperson to make specific improvements in his use of Emotion Movers. The foundation of instinctive or conscious utilisation of such Movers is the conviction that the listener can be Benefited to a degree that will OUTWEIGH the cost.

Getting the Sales Talks Started

Example 1

Salesperson—I am Ramesh of Shiv Papers and since I am new to the area I came in to introduce myself.

Prospect—glad you did. Have a chair.

Salesperson—thank you. For the past five years I have worked out of Jaipur. By the way before I left Mr. Gopal said to say hello for him.

Prospect—Gopal? I saw him at the Mumbai convention last month. Good man.

Salesperson—yes, that he is. During the past three years he has taught me a lot about producing low cost frozen food boxes.

Secretary— sorry for interrupting Mr. Verma is here to see you.

Prospect—all right. Ask him to come in.

Salesperson—rising—thanks for letting me call on you without appointment. I am sure and glad to have met you.

Prospect—yes, call me up in a week or so. I want to hear about the low cost boxes experience.

Example 2

Salesperson is making a repeat call on a customer who has benefited a lot from the salesperson's company in the past. Personal Prestige and Contact are therefore established, plus a reasonable degree of liking and respect. On his last call he created Interest in a plan he proposed, was stopped by a problem and now he starts in a friendly and pleasant manner.

Salesperson—how are you Mr. Verma?

Prospect—fine. Thanks. Have a seat. I will be right back. (leaves and comes back shortly)- been to movies lately?

Salesperson—have not had a chance. I was called back to the Head Office. And while I was there I think we found the solution to your colour draining problem.

Prospect—is that so?

Salesperson—(continues his story)

Example 3-INQUIRY

Prospect—(enters the office and asks)- is your salesperson named Sinha in?

Salesperson(who is in)—how do you do sir?

Prospect—my name is P K Agarwal of the Planet Publishing House. I have seen your desk top publishing unit with BB and Company in working status. I thought I would come in and see the new model 55 you advertise.

Salesperson—good. Come with me Mr. Agarwal and I WILL SHOW you the model. It is in the demonstration room down the hall. (PAUSE) I appreciate your coming, to see us and I am glad I happened to be here too. (PAUSE)—Do you have a problem something like what they had at the BB?

Prospect—no, we send out about ten thousand notices per month and they are printed as you can see. Raja of BB Company thinks your process might save us considerable money and I want to find that out.

Salesperson—(decides that the sale has MOVED into Desire zone for him and as he demonstrates the model he will carry on from the using rupees savings as his Major-Interest Benefit—says)—I think we will find that Mr. Raja is right.

Types of Calls and Objectives of the Calls

The COMPLETELY CREATIVE CALL exists when the prospect has no intention of buying and when MOTION has to be created from the start.

Various Objectives of the COMPLETELY CREATIVE CALL are given below:

1. To get acquainted , build Personal Prestige, make a Contact and secure essential information for future use
2. To get permission to make a survey or a demonstration or to get the prospect to try or test a product
3. To start and move the Sale to Interest, Desire or Decision

Partly Created Sales

The Inquiry—when the prospect has been moved to Interest or Desire to buy by means of advertising, satisfied customers, articles in magazines, and make an INQUIRY, one type of Partly Created Sales exists.

Objectives in dealing with an inquiry—to build Liking and Respect for self, to find out how far the Sale has progressed, to pick the Sale up at whatever point it has reached and MOVE it forward as far as possible by use of Emotion and Reason Movers.

The Favourable-Attention Call—when on his first Call the Salesperson finds that his company or product or plan is already known and respected to the extent that favourable Attention is easily secured, or when someone has built Personal Prestige for him or when a user has created Interest for him.

The problem for the salesperson is to capitalise upon the help secured and to use Emotion and Reason Movers to develop the Sale further.

The Follow-up Call exists when the salesperson has gained ATTENTION on a previous call or created Interest and develop it into desire to buy.

The objective is to maintain favourable ATTENTION by means of Emotion Movers and to MOVE the Sale forward by use of Emotion and Reason Movers.

The Service Call exists when the purpose of the visit is to Give service or find out if service is needed or to clear up misunderstandings or errors.

The main purpose of these classifications of the types of calls is to make it clear that wherever progress has already been made, it is not necessary to start back from the beginning but to use Movers to take it from there and carry on from the progress point that exists.

The Prestige Movers

When the good reputation of a company , its personnel, product or service or its customers and endorsers provide the prospect with evidence that Benefit claim can be believed, the Prestige Mover is active

Examples of Prestige Movers in Action

User Prestige

1. The Delhi plant of Smart ACs have been using the system for the past ten years.
2. The Parliament house, the President's house and the PM's house have all been renovated by our company.
3. Jayant Enterprises have been using our accounting software for the last six years.

Company and Personnel Prestige

1. The new monitoring software is one of the greatest achievements of our Research Laboratories.
2. Each one of our GMs have received national commendation for their efforts.
3. Our company has been the pioneer in seamless tubing, a fact that makes us proud.
4. We are responsible of at least 70% of production of artificial rubber in the country.
5. We are the largest and oldest company in the business and also the most respected one.
6. We hold the record of 100% zero defect production.

Product or Service Prestige

1. More of these painting machines are employed in the automobile industry than any other.
2. It was the first cooker in the market and has remained the marker leader ever since.
3. The TV manufacturers of the country have taken our standards as their norms.
4. Yes, this road paving machine is used in every state of the country.

Prestige of Process, Plan , Idea, Policy

1. The plan has been recognised by the Government recognised Railway Reconstruction Authority.
2. The formula has worked in managing the mines in Bihar.

3. Our MD has approved of the idea to merge the two production units.

Problems in the Use of the Prestige Mover

Example A

Systems salesperson (After introducing himself , and having been invited to have a chair, thanks the prospect and says easily)—

From your recent magazine article I learnt of your interest in reducing the cost of operating records as well as machines. Since a practical and economically operated system for inventory control record has been developed by our company I hoped you would like to see it. I have come with an invitation for you to visit our factory to give you a demonstration. Could you give me about ten minutes now

Prospect—smiles—let us hear it

Example B

Systems Salesperson (After introducing himself and having been invited to have a seat, thanks the prospect and says proudly)—

My company is the oldest and largest in the field. We serve the Brass Group of companies. As an example of the advantage there is, in dealing with us , here is the inventory control system we produce for that group

The Story Mover

A Story Mover is an account of an occurrence that indirectly informs the prospect of the Reason Movers, Emotion Movers or both.

Example 1

A salesperson whose products are industrial motors had, three weeks before , been told by a customer that cutting operating costs was his major problem. Now he returns and on his Follow-up Call , is told by a secretary that the prospect is about to leave for a trip through one of the company plants. Here is how he uses Emotion and Benefit Movers to answer the first two Prospect-view questions and thereafter uses the STORY to provide Evidence that his claim can be believed.

Salesperson—how are you Mr. Singh.

Prospect-very good , thanks.

Salesperson—do you remember that last month you had told me cost cutting was a major problem.

Prospect—it still is. I am about to leave for the plant and that is one thing on my mind.

Salesperson—good. I think I have an idea that can save them about 20% on finishing bases.

Prospect—that so? What is it?

Salesperson—by using a 10 hp motor instead of a smaller one and by using carbide cutters a smooth finish can be made with ONE fast cut. The reason I am sure of this is that I have seen it done at the Banguluru plant of HMT. As they stated, chips fall like gravel . Deep and smooth cuts are made and their cost reduction has come to more than 25%.

Prospect—but what about the chatter?

Salesperson—I am glad you thought of that. They control it by—(talk continues).

Example 2

Salesperson—(to customer who has just taken delivery of 10 drums of transformer oil)- I dropped in to thank you for your lube oil order and to make sure you have received in tact. Your stores Manager tells me that he is planning to move it into the closed store area this afternoon which is good news as this will ensure that the oil is protected from moisture and hold its dielectric strength. The reason I am concerned is that two years ago a customer in Mumbai insisted upon taking delivery of 50 drums of the same oil , while they did not have storage room for the same. When I checked, it had not been stored yet but they promised to get it under cover. However, it stayed out side through out the monsoon. When they wanted to use it they found that its dielectric strength was affected so much by the moisture that it had to be condemned and they lost the entire investment.

The stories are given in some detail to show the various Reason Movers they contain.

Examples of some stories that have been used.

Story that contains Appeal to Pride, Personal Prestige, Contact Movers. Used to build Liking and Respect.

Story that Presents Benefit and other Movers indirectly. Used to answer Prospect's Viewpoint questions.

Story of a company achievement in developing products, services or plans that increased Benefits to users. Used to support Benefit claims.

Stories telling endorsements won from doctors, scientists, associations used to support Benefit claims.

Story that presents Poor Quality and Loss Movers indirectly, following the direct use of Benefit and Good Quality Movers.

Research

Some examples of the use of Prestige Movers to research the need of company's products.

Example 1

Salesperson—I heard about your big increase in sales in Gujarat, your dealers must be full of praise of your products and their lasting quality

Prospect—we are proud of our record there, and all through the area for that matter.

Salesperson—the reason I came today to see you was on the problem of increasing the lifer of your cutting tools—

Example 2

Salesperson—the last time I had called on you I was told about how you started out small and built this big business empire. The most interesting thing was how you made all the rich people of the town your customers.

It made me think that with such a fine trade, you are in a special positing to make a nice profit on high quality storage cabinets—

Favourable Condition.

A Favourable Condition is a situation in a prospect's industry, company, group or personal life that he is already benefiting or will benefit and that, when brought to his attention helps prepare him to see he has an Opportunity to Benefit still further through the salesperson's proposition.

When the efforts of the Prospect or his company have created the Favourable Condition it has appeal to Pride elements and stilt greater power to help him see and appreciate his Opportunity.

Appeal to Pride on Favourable Conditions

Example 1

Salesperson to Distributor-you have built a fine team of salespersons, Ram. You can trust them to solve problems for your prospects and customers on your regular line. Hence, it seems to me you are set to male some nice extra profit by taking on small motors—(talk continues)

Example 2

Research Officer to Management—the survey shows that the area has grown steadily for the last twenty years. It gives indication of continuous growth. Its per capita income is above the country's average.

Its farms are highly productive and its manufacture diversified. While details are ready to be given, the general view is that it is a safe, profitable location for a storage depot.

Example 3

Salesperson—how large is the payroll estimated for your new plant?

Prospect—around Rs. 100 lacs.

Salesperson—so much! Well you must be bringing some top mechanical engineers too?

Prospect—yes, several, in fact.

Salesperson—what an opportunity for a housing complex, like this for instance shows some layouts of such complexes his company has built in the past.

Unfavourable Conditions.

An Unfavourable Condition is any situation creating losses for the prospect, for which the prospect, the salesperson or their companies are NOT RERSPONSIBLE, and which brought to the attention of the prospect , tactfully will help him see his NEED for the Benefits of the salesperson's proposition.

Part of the talk illustrating use of Unfavourable Conditions.

Sales Engineer—as long as the coal is loaded in open cars in monsoon time, it will be full of moisture. When this coal is pulverised it packs like putty and causes sparkles in the furnace, that quickly lowers the efficiency of the furnace.

The one way to solve the problem of getting full efficiency from such fuel is, of course , to have a pulverize equipped with a properly designed hot plate.

Salesperson now shows illustrations and tells how the hot plate in his product dries coal and makes it as efficient as coal from the mine in proper condition.

The Difference Between Unfavourable Conditions and Poor Quality and Loss Movers.

The usefulness of separating Poor Quality and Loss Movers from Unfavourable Conditions for the prospect is that it reminds that Unfavourable Condition idea can usually be mentioned BEFORE Benefits without arousing resentment while Poor Quality and Loss Movers are effective when used AFTER Benefit and Good Quality Movers.

Example 1—use of Unfavourable Conditions

Salesperson—is the monsoon giving your bus drivers the same schedule—troubles I hear so much about?

Prospect—it sure is. We are having our troubles.

Salesperson—to help solve the schedule problems our engineers are doing a lot of careful research on wheel bearing protection.

Last winter, for example BEST in Mumbai made tests which, their records show make it possible to practically eliminate bearing failures—(develops the story).

Example 2—use of Poor Quality ad Loss Mover

Salesperson—I know you are having a lot of wheel bearing failures, due to the grease you are using and—

Prospect—where did YOU get the idea we are having a LOT of failures?—(relations can get strained).

Unfavourable AND Favourable Conditions used to prepare Prospect to Appreciate his Need and Opportunity to Benefit.

Example 1

Salesperson—(has built personal prestige and contact)- how is the new raise in shipping rates going to affect your Kerala market?

Prospect—well, the southern competition will have the advantage in price. That is the picture.

Salesperson—what about this idea? With the dealers, there, getting such good prices and demand for your product, could you HOLD up your sales and profits if I could get you a big supply of rare raw materials at old prices?

Prospect—how big a supply are you thinking of?

The Proposition Mover

The name of the company and its salesperson, the product, service or plan and the price, terms of business, delivery are classified as the Proposition Movers.

Example 1

The Capital Cabinet Manufacturing Company will furnish two models cabinets at Rs. 35,000 each FOR Delhi net. The payment terms are 30 days from despatch and shipment will be made within six weeks of receipt of the order.

Example 2

These direct mail folders will cost Rs. 25 each for a minimum order of 10,000 numbers.

Example 3

The Singh Corporation offers this Annual Maintenance Contract for your Air Conditioners.

Example 4

I am Mitra from the Krone Crane company.

Forms of Closing the Sale.

The Benefit Sum-up and Close (Assurance Form).

Salesperson—to sum up, Mr. Roy, this cable will give you complete protection from breakdown. Your workmen will be protected from accidents due to the cutting of the cover. You will always be glad you chose it.

The Benefit Sum up and Close (Question Form)

Salesperson—now, are there any questions I can answer about protection from breakdowns, or protection from accidents or time saving? Would you want it all sent to this mining area?

The Split—Decision Form of Close

1. How would you want it to be sent, by truck or by train?
2. Which colour would you prefer, white or blue?
3. Would you prefer a May delivery better than June?

The Question Form of Close

1. What is your idea on your quantity requirement?
2. How soon would you want it installed?

The Assurance Form of Close

1. You will do well to take this office Mr. Gupta
2. Ramesh, I will order fast if I were you.

The Command Form of Close

1. Order the purchase now, do not delay.
2. Do what is recommended Mr. Seth.

Combination Closes

1. Do that Ram. You will be glad you did.
2. You will need it for monsoon will you not? If so, order should be laced now.

The Explanation Mover

Works used to make clear the meaning of a technical term or details of an operation, are Explanation Movers. Demonstrations, photographs, blue prints, when use to make details clear are too known as Explanation Movers.

Example 1

The system should work well for us. The schedule is well planned. In this area the metres are ready on Tuesday. The billing machine operators prepare the ills on Thursday and they are sent to the customers on Friday.

Example 2

It will reduce the amount of power required because it works on sound gravity principle shown here.

Example 3

Salesperson—(about a poisonous matter sold as powder) you will find the material safe to handle and easy to measure as it is compressed into uniform tablets, looking like mini moth balls.

Example 4

Salesperson—you place the sheets of paper on paper on the transfer surface like this—and pull the lever—

Example 5

To get perfect results you place the paper sheets accurately on the transfer plate like this—. Next you pull down the lever like this, slowly and evenly.

Example 6

This is the delicious pure custard we advertised in India Today. Ease taste it.

The usefulness of a technical equipment is made easy and clear by demonstration and trial run.

Progress Signals and the Progress Test Questions

Progress Signals are comments and actions of a prospect that indicate that Prospect Viewpoint Questions have been or are being answered adequately enough to keep them moving.

A question asked by the salesperson to test the progress being made in a talk is a Progress Test Question.

Example 1

Salesperson—your workers will be fully protected from shock-accidents since the tough tellurium cover has been placed on the cable. It ill protect the men even if they hit it with a pick axe.

Prospect—will it not cut?

Salesperson—it not only does not cut that way, it stays whole even if one of your switch engine accidentally runs over it. Does it surprise you?

Prospect-well it is a welcome surprise.

Salesperson-over at the Mayurbhanj mines the workers have not only been protected from such accidents, but has not been a production breakdown, due to cable cutting in two years.

Example 2

Salesperson—how does that look to you Mr. Prospect?

Example 3

Salesperson—have I made that clear to you Mr. Prospect?

Prospect—yes I understand

Salesperson—(continues his talk).

Example 4

Salesperson—would it be safe to say that the time of at least two workers could be saved?

Prospect—well, I would say so.

Salesperson—in that case the system would pay for itself in just one year as its total cost is—minimum.

Example 5

Salesperson—(after covering certain Benefit and several important Good Quality Movers)—that is sound construction, is it not Mr. Jai?

Prospect—good. Well thought out.

Types of Progress Signals

1. Prospect listens carefully
2. Prospect nods and says " very interesting"
3. Prospect says, " I understand. That is clear.
4. Prospect asks, "sounds good but I do not quite see how the oil can do that? (wants more information on Good Quality)

Test Question Types

(sometimes they can be combined with other Movers)

1. Is that clear Mr. Ghosh?
2. Did I make it clear why the noise gets reduced by anchoring the motor like this?
3. Is the saving desirable?
4. Are you happy with the safety part of the investment?

Timely Placement of the Test Question

Success of The Test Question depends on keeping it in line with the Prospect View-point question being answered and by not asking the question that goes beyond the information given to the prospect.

Examples

Salesperson—is there a problem of that type in your industry?

Salesperson selling financial deals regarding security features of an investment—that is the most important thing for you is it not?

Salesperson—have we offered a satisfactory solution to your quality improvement problem.?

Prospect—yes I think you have.

Salesperson—good. The next problem then is, can operating costs be reduced to a decent level——(talks carry on).

Limitations of The Test Question.

The listener cannot answer in a manner that indicates progress if the question relates to something on which he has not yet been educated.

The question that ties back into a difference of opinion in a way that is embarrassing to the prospect is a non use of the test. For example, "do you see how wrong you have been?"

Obstacle Descriptors

Habit: The Habit Obstacle is active when a person has been performing a task in a particular way for a long time and just by the force of habit would not like to change even if there is a much better way of performing the task. Such people become immune to change of ideas and create a strong resistance to the progress of sale.

Fear: The Fear Obstacle is operating when a person has a justified fear of impending problems, of risk and consequent loss that overtakes his rational thinking. It causes him to by-pass the opportunity and keep performing below his potential with the help of new ideas.

Price: The Price Obstacle is active when the prospect does not realise the Benefits offered would outweigh their money value.

Complaint: The Complaint Obstacle is active when the prospect shows his dissatisfaction through words or actions.

Detail: The Detail Obstacle is operating when the prospect is of the opinion that the proposed plan is not worth the effort it will require to obtain and put it to use.

Lack of Information: The Lack of Information Obstacle is operating when the progress of sales gets hampered when the salesperson has not yet fully informed the prospect or he lacks the information. At times the prospect may not have the technical knowledge to understand the proposal. Prospect may not be able to get the full significance of the benefits that will be enjoyed. It can also happen if the salesperson's talk is unclear or confusing to the prospect.

Competition: The Competition Obstacle is active when the prospect compares the Benefits or Good Qualities of the plan with another competitive plan and believe the later offers better benefits than the proposed plan.

(At times competition can be in dissimilar things like microwave oven and washing machine).

Friendship: The Friendship-Competition Obstacle works when a competitive salesperson or his company personnel has the liking and respect of the prospect and when the prospect believes that competitive product would produce similar or even better Benefits.

Difficult Personality: The Difficult Personality Obstacle is active when a prospect lacks emotional control when he allows a difference of opinion to deteriorate into a personal attack or when he bursts out in anger, in rudeness, in deceit or other uncalled for behaviour which retards the progress.

Time: The Time Obstacle is active when the prospect thinks that the product or the plan under consideration is not worth the time it will need or it is late for making any changes. On the positive side the Time Obstacle can be used to convey to the prospect that any delay in decision will endanger success.

Release: The Release Obstacle is operative when the prospect wants to be released from further consideration of the plan.

The Divided Release: The Divided Release Obstacle is active when the prospect sincerely or insincerely seeks to end the interview by saying that he will take up the matter with a person not present.

Negative Mood and Manner: The Negative Mood and Manner Obstacle is active when a salesperson's frame of mind and manner of speaking and acting impresses the prospect unfavourably and creates dislike and lack of confidence.

Poor Judgment: The Poor Judgment Obstacle is created by the salesperson's lack of consideration in looking at the ground realities, in separating the right ways of doing things from wrong, in planning the sales call, in deciding how to use the Benefit Story from the prospect's Viewpoint. At times the salesperson can show disregard for the prospects reactions as the talks progress. The worst happens when the salesperson loses control of his emotions and forgets his knowledge of human nature and the practical selling techniques of study, analysis, planning and experience.

Examples of Obstacles

Prospect—your proposal is likely to upset our work. We would not be interested.

Prospect—it is too much money. There is no point in talking about it.

Financer—if we have to choose between air compressor you offer and the new furniture; one thing is sure our budget cannot stand both.

Prospect—if you had called even a week ago we would have been glad to have you in the deal.

Prospect—we would need to keep our office force working overtime for weeks to install such a system.

Prospect—frankly we buy all our supplies from X Tone Company. Swami of that company is very well liked around here.

Prospect—how do you people expect to be believed with your kind of delivery performance?

The Spar

The Spar is a special use of Emotion Movers, frequently Mood and Manners, Assurance and Question, to meet Obstacles in a calming and considerate manner so the objector's mind is reopened to reason. Conditions are also used a Spar at times.

The Spar in Action

Example 1

Prospect-what are you trying to get away with. This new machine looks hard to operate to me.

Salesperson—it does? Well, I guess it would look that way to anybody—yet you will be running it like feather touch only as an expert in just two hours. I mean it.

Prospect-right—that suits me!

Example 2

Lady Prospect—do not try to talk to me into that. My husband would become mad if I bought the sofa of that colour.

Salesperson—he would? Well I can understand that—would this colour please him?

Example 3

Prospect—Ram, we have been using riveted joints in our castings for years and our customers have been perfectly satisfied.

Salesperson—that is right Sir. It was the cost cutting angle I have been thinking of—(continues)

Note—the Spar may take just a second or two or it might be quite long

How the Movers in the Spar have been expressed

Assurance

1. I know how you feel—
2. I understand—
3. That is how it struck me at first—
4. I am glad you told me—

Question

1. Is that so?
2. It has?
3. You did?

Mood and Manner

1. Calmly
2. Sincerely
3. Earnestly
4. Politely
5. Sympathetically
6. Surprised

Meeting the Obstacles

Obstacle

Prospect—why we have to keep records for twenty years. Our work is quite satisfactory. Is it not?

Example 1—The SPAR

We know your work has been satisfactory. You have been doing great job. The idea now is to make your job more satisfactory to YOU, to lighten your rush hour burden. And with the modern visible record system , you will find it easy to keep posting up to the last minute.

Example 2—The Dominating Method

Calm down. Listen to me. This is being done for your own good, to make it easier for you to keep your work and you better appreciate it.

Check List for Situations

Does the company have a need for my Proposition? Can the money be secured? Have I got a Prospect?

Are things being done, used or planned by this company that are causing or will cause loss?

Are the laws, economic environment, operating conditions or acts of others causing Unfavourable Conditions that create a NEED for my product, service or plan?

Do Favourable Conditions exist that provide the Prospect with an opportunity to Benefit through my Proposition?

What Major Benefits can I use to answer the second Prospect-viewpoint question and create Interest?

How can I best expand and support my Major Benefit claims?- shall I rely on Benefit, Good Quality, Prestige and Story Movers or Poor Quality and Loss Movers essential to understanding and appreciation of the Benefits?

Of all the possible Obstacles which are most likely to be active?

How can I use Major Benefits to avoid or weaken such Obstacles? Am I prepared to Spar effectively and make a good and sound Solution —Effort if Obstacles are voiced?

What company official should I see? What do I know about him? Is Personal Prestige or Contact active? How can I use Emotion Movers to build or maintain Liking and Respect? What Style shall I use to present my Major Benefit?

After studying the situation can I say that I have Faith in my plan? Do I FEEL that I can help the prospect reach worthwhile objectives and do I look forward to seeing him?

If satisfactory answers to all the above questions cannot be found before the sales call, tactful use of the Investigative Question will be needed during the call.

Prospects Situation.

Started Day-Night Medical Shop.

24-hour operation by medical shop in the heart of the City Centre

Yes.

Do you gain late and early hours business.

Yes.

City laws permit Twenty four hour operation by medical shops.

Extra sales and profits.

Earlier there was fear, lack of information and the force of habit inhibiting the prospect.

Extra profit outweighs extra expenses.

Sales talk outline.

Twenty-four hours operation.

Night service also friendly earnest and sincere.

Business build plans to be worked out.

Build friendship.

Good operation, good staff, better service to customers.

Good location.

Extra sales, extra profits over extra expense.

Night person hiring who can take care of details-send direct mail, post records in the computer, keep the shop clean.

Prospect-worth a trial, certainly!

Note benefit of the night person doing detailing work proved to be desirable to the prospect.

Call Closing

Call closing can be defined as a direct attempt on the part of the salesperson to attain the objective of the call. Let us, therefore discuss the techniques the salesperson can use to obtain his call objective. At this point you may be wondering if the salesperson knows his objective, makes a good approach, gives an effective presentation, and handles objections skilfully, it should be sufficient to attain the call objectives. The problem arises because most persons are reluctant to take decisions especially if they involve spending money. Salesperson's good approach, effective presentation, skilful handling of objections normally moves the prospect to the verge of agreement with the objective. However, the reluctance may still remain. Closing techniques are, therefore, direct attempts by the salesperson to nudge the fully persuaded prospect to make a favourable decision.

The first closing technique can be called assumptive. The assumptive technique is used when the salesperson senses that the buyer is almost at the point of making a decision in favour of the objective and has met with little resistance. When the salesperson is using the assumptive technique he does nothing more than act as though a favourable decision has been made with respect to the call objective. A machine tool salesperson, whose call objective was to arrange for the buyer to visit nearby plant in order to see the machine in operation, uses the assumptive technique. Sensing the favourable decision, he says, "let me use your phone to tell them we will be over there this afternoon" the salesperson has assumed that the favourable decision has been taken.

Another closing technique is of giving choice to the prospect. The technique is used when the salesperson senses that the buyer is close to agreement with his call objective but there still remains some resistance. The choice technique is a direct way of asking the prospect to make a favourable decision. In using the technique the salesperson gives the prospect a choice between two buying alternatives. The prospect does not have to select between order or no order, he has a choice between something and another thing. A shirt salesperson saying, "Would you buy the green shirt" leaves the option of saying no and walking out. Once the salesperson knows that the prospect is nearly ready to decide in favour of his objective, he could say, "which one should I pack, the green or the light blue one?" the moment the prospect says the blue one, you have achieved your objective. In B-to-B sales, the question that can be asked just before the final decision could be, "you would like us to arrange for transit insurance or would you like to organise it?"

In another situation where installation and commissioning of a plant is involved, the salesperson can nudge the prospect into decision by saying, "should I send my installation team next week or would you prefer earlier."

Suppose the salesperson is selling room air conditioners and for nudging the prospect into action says, "so it is the two ton one you will buy" he may get an answer , "NO". After sensing that the decision is near in his favour he should say, "1.5 ton or 2 ton, which is the one", and the chances are he will get the order for one of them.

The choice technique should be used when the salesperson has sensed that the decision in his favour is almost reached to help the prospect feel happier as he gets the last word and psychologically mastery over the salesperson. Anyway, you have achieved the call objective.

The third closing technique is the Summary technique. This technique is used in conjunction with the choice technique after several features and benefits have been emphasised. The salesperson should summarise using those features and benefits that have stimulated the greatest desire in prospects mind. In this technique the salesperson uses the summary as he reviews the features and benefits putting them in a capsule form. Your interest in economy and convenience will be fully realised by our low rate contract, our quality maintenance service and our low cost spare parts. The summary technique is best used along with the choice technique.

The fourth closing technique is named the Special Feature Technique. The features of a product have been defined earlier as unique qualities of the product. Sometimes, one of the features of the product may be used as closing technique to bring about favourable decision. If a product is in limited supply, it becomes its special feature. "These imported hoses do not come for the next six months. Shall I book hundred for you?" Prospects take favourable decision because they do not want to lose out on anything.

The favourable feature technique should be used only when the salesperson is sure of his facts and should be used with utmost care. Dishonest or short-sighted approach is absolutely not recommended.

TIMING

As the salesperson learns about the closing techniques where a nudge is required to gain the call objective, it is a good idea to learn how to sense the right time when the prospect has been persuaded enough and his desire to buy has reached the peak. The timing gives the salesperson the clue when to use the closing technique. If the salesperson delays too long before using the closing technique, the prospect may make a favourable decision on his own. This may be all right except too much time has gone into the presentation. If the closing technique is used prematurely he may cause an objection to be raised. When the prospect is not fully convinced he needs a nudge to help him take a favourable decision. Therefore, proper timing will help the salesperson to attain his call objective quickly as well as to avoid objections. Prospects indicate through various means that their interest and desire are at a peak and they are ready for a favourable decision. The salesperson must be alert to the cues or the signs that tell that the right time to use the closing technique has come.

Sometimes the cues are obvious like the prospect asking, how soon can he get the samples? The salesperson should know that this is the right time to use the closing technique. The salesperson should reply, "In two days, shall I deliver it to you or have them mailed?" The salesperson is using the choice technique of call closing.

Another example of obvious clue is when the prospect says, "Can the survey be done after working hours?" The salesperson's reply should be, "certainly, I will have our engineer in at 5 pm tomorrow" once the clues are seen the salesperson should move quickly to close the call.

However, the clues normally are not so obvious. The salesperson should be alert to recognise the subtle clues like a smile of agreement or a nod other mention of a specific feature or benefit. Understanding the subtle clue the salesperson should use the losing technique. Prospect may start examining the sales aid and start some figure work, examine his stock he is on the verge of a favourable decision and the time is ripe for using the closing technique.

Summarising, the salesperson should be alert to understand the obvious and also the subtle clues given by the prospect and that is the time for the use of closing technique.

DEPARTURE

The next step of the call is the departure and there are a few rules for an effective departure. At the end of the call, either the salesperson has attained his objective or he has not achieved it. In either case he must make an effective departure.

In case the objective has been achieved the salesperson should reassure the prospect that he has made a wise decision. Most people want such a reassurance. "Your decision to renew your service contract with us was an intelligent one that will mean continuous economies for your organisation" once the reassurance has been given it is best to leave quickly. Lingering on is not business like. Thank for the order and leave quickly is a golden rule. If a good rapport has been built a referral can be obtained before leaving.

However, if the objective has not been achieved remember the minor objective that keeps the door open and at least achieve it. The minor objectives should all be in line with the major call objectives, like, "when do you think it would be appropriate for me to contact you again". Or "we are organising a seminar/an exhibition and I would like to personally invite you for the same." As he gains the minor objective his feeling of disappointment will vanish and he will be ready for the next call in a positive frame of mind. The minor objective may ultimately lead the salesperson in achieving the major objective sooner than the salesperson can imagine. It is difficult to realise that the customer would get disillusioned with his existing supplier and that would be time he will think of you if you have left a good favourable impression on him.

The salesperson should appreciate that while the main objective has not been attained, the minor objective has been achieved, as well as more information has been gathered about the prospect's company as well as about the prospect himself, that will be useful in future calls.

Post Call Analysis

After completing the call it is necessary to analyse the call just completed. The analysis starts with comparing the result of the call with the established call objective. The comparison will help the salesperson plan his next call on this prospect. If the sales objective of the call has been achieved the salesperson can consider the manner in which to plan the next call to escalate the prospect up towards some long range goal. If the objective was not attained the salesperson should critically review to determine the cause of failure, starting from the formulation of the call objective, was it too ambitious, too broad or, perhaps too specific. The salesperson should take a look at the essential information gathered before making the call. Were there gaps in the information, and how serious were they?

Next he should analyse the tactics used. Were the techniques used either in approach, presentation, handling of objections or closing inadequate? Were they the cause of his failure to attain the objective of the call?

Summarising the salesperson should review the three steps the salesperson had taken in planning the call as follows:

1. Establish the call objective
2. Gather the essential information
3. Select appropriate tactics

Only after such a critical review should the salesperson plan his next call on the same prospect.

Post call analysis serves a primary purpose of providing a sound basis for planning the next call on the prospect. Post call analysis can serve a secondary, broader purpose of helping the salesperson in his personal development. In other words, post call analysis should point out some of the strengths and weaknesses in the salesperson's overall performance which should go beyond this one call. The salesperson must accept the primary responsibility for the call failure and use the post call analysis for improving on his call planning. For example did the post call review reveal a growing deficiency in some aspects of product knowledge, or weakness in a special skill such as group presentation? Did the call analysis, instead prove the existence of some new fund strengths in handling people or in thinking creatively?

Summarising, post call analysis and personal development go hand in hand. The salesperson who uses each call experience for the purpose of personal improvement will move more rapidly toward a higher level of effective sales performance.

Sales Expense Budget-marketing manager has the following expense categories in his department:

- Salaries—these are normally standard and not subject to change except once a year when increments and promotions are announced.
- Travelling expense—to keep a watch on travelling expense, the firm should plan structured tours of the salesmen wherever possible. Exigencies can be taken care of on ad-hoc basis.
- Research expense—can be kept under control by keeping the research files updated by doing small surveys and also using secondary research when availabnle.
- Communications—telephone, fax, letters–junctions use of the facilities would help reduce costs.
- Office rentals—these are fixed expenses and not much can be done unless some drastic steps are required like closing down some of the offices, when the firm may have decided to divest from some product.
- Stationery expense—this is another hidden expense which if controlled can bring noticeable results.
- Goods transport/logistics/depots/firms own shops—the chapter on logistics covers the expense control possible in the area.
- Commission to channel members—the commission to channel members depends mostly on competitive factors and the strengths of the members. Dealers are for ever complaining of the bigger disconunt offered by the competition, which in fact could possibly be only a method of getting bigger discounts from the firm.
- Advertising and promotion—use of adverstising and promotion in these days of severe competition is absolutely essential for keeping the market share. To make these tools effective, pre–testing should be undertaken in all cases. At times, publicity, which is free, not paid for help build the firms image and sales much more than paid advertising as there is an aura of truth attached to publicity due to its editorial nature.

Yearly expense budget is made and reviewed on a quarterly basis to ensure that the poeple in the department are well within the allocated budget. Any deviations are also monitored, accounted for and justified. Corrective action where needed is taken.

Firm's profitability comes from the gross profit reduced by expenses. To increase profit, attempts are made to increase gross profit by increasing sales and by reducing expenses. Marketing Manager must keep a close watch on the expenses; else even with increase in sale there would be lower profits. In most firms due to competition based profit squeeze, attempts are made on a continuous basis to deep expenses under control and budgeting is a method of achieving the same.

Sales Cost Control: As the costs of marketing comes from each of the salesman, the budget can be sub-divided into budget for each sales territory and the manager can keep proper control while approving the expense vouchers of the salesmen. Any deviation from the budget must have prior approval of the manager.

Reporting and Control System: In today 's world of email and Internet, it is easy; for the salesman to post even daily reports ot the manager. However, structured reporting helps as it becomes universal and not people specific. Besides travel itinerary, the salesman should send the following reports to the manager on a bound basis to enable the manager take corrective steps where needed and to provide the desired timely assistance to the salesman—

- Sales forecast and actual orders received, dispatches made on a customer wise product wise basis as per the suggested format given below:

Table 6.18. Sales Forecast

Customer—(Dealer) or Direct-customer ______ Period 2002-2003

Product	*Sales objective*	*Orders received*	*Orders dispatched*	*Shortfall in orders/dispatches*
PCs	250	210	205	40/45
Modems	120	120	110	0/10
Printers	60	35	30	25/30
UPS	100	80	60	20/40

Besides, a consolidated territory picture can be sent on the same base. Another report, which is important, is the age analysis of outstanding dues in each territory. And salesmen's plan on a time bound manner of liquidating the same, as can be seen from below:

Table 6.19. Outstanding Amount Analysis

The following format can be used:

Customer	*Overdue amount*	*15 days old*	*30 days old*	*60 days old*	*120 days old*	*>120 days old*
ABC Ltd.	320,5000	20,0000	100,0000	1050000	500000	500000
XYZ Ltd.	2500000	2000000	500000	Nil	Nil	Nil

The form can be extended by one more column where the salesman can write the dates when the outstanding would be cleared.

Questions for discussion:

1. What are purely the sales functions?
2. What are the methods employed for selecting and retaining salesmen?
3. How the tours should be planned to make them effective?
4. What are methods the salesmen should use in preparing their sales calls?
5. How should the marketing manager keep control of the salesmen's activities?

Business leaders have realized the importance of understanding the technological developments in the area of manufacturing technology and technology of product itself. Internationally they find opportunities emerging in a spectrum of nations that are ready to join the world market economy. The real effects of globalisation need to be seen in the context of opening of markets in hitherto closed countries, which were trying to safeguard the interests of their own industries. India was among these nations till 1991.

The other area that has emerged in recent years is the number and types of products that are available for sale. A partial list of the products is given below:

1. FMCG Products
2. Consumer durables
3. Industrial capital goods
4. Industrial consumables
5. Industrial raw materials and components
6. Services
7. Events
8. Ideas
9. Research outputs
10. Manpower
11. Property
12. Places
13. Information
14. Ideas
15. Organisations

Companies have found that unless they can build a meaningful relationship with their customers there is every possibility that the customers would go for competitive products. Companies have to build relationships not only with their user customers but also with the channel members, suppliers and even financers. These long-term relationships bind the company with these important groups of people for long-term loyalty on both sides.

Next companies need to learn the art and science of creating and managing demand of their products. Decisions on the marketing mix factors have assumed great importance with competition ever ready to look for loop holes in the companies planning process. Companies have to carefully formulate their product specifications, package design, pricing, channels of distribution, after sales service besides advertising and promotion. These need to be totally and directly in line with the customers' known and even unknown expectations. Product benefits for different customers have to be identified and refined to become close to the language spoken and understood by the selected customers. Companies have to carve out market segments for this purpose. Companies' plan marketing research for knowing the real needs of the customers, the way they buy the products, from mega marts, neighbourhood shops or from virtual electronic market place.

Companies have to find out on a continuous basis the changing environment of business and competition to remain proactive and ahead of competition. Michael Porter's five-force model is a good starting point for analysing competitive environment. Considering the competitive strength companies can ill afford to remain oriented to production, as was the case in the first half of the last century. Today, market has to be main or the only focus for the companies while planning their marketing strategies. However, companies have to keep the interests of stakeholders in their decision-making and work towards a double bottom line that includes the welfare of stakeholders besides that of shareholders alone.

Customer Value

Customer buys products for the benefits he derives from the same. These benefits are the perceived values as per the customer's notions. The perceived value can be defined as the difference between the total customer assigned value and the total customer cost for buying the product. Sellers have to understand the perceived value by the customer and if it is low then the product is in the wrong market segment or is not being properly marketed. It is said that nobody buys a product.

People buy the satisfaction or the benefits the products provide to them. The seller may make tall claim about the value or product performance that will provide customer satisfaction or even customer delight. However, what really matters is the customer's belief regarding the product satisfaction levels with him. Providing customer satisfaction and customers delight has become the most important mission for the company and if the company can use it as its driving force it is bound to succeed despite tough competition.

Companies survive and thrive only if they make their customers loyal to them and add on to other customers, either from the non-buyers group or from among the customers presently buying from competition. The companies need to continuously innovate, research for new products for which the demand may be obvious or even dormant. Besides proper management of key areas as materials management with just in time inventory controls and training of the marketing personnel, both of the company and from the channel members would go a long way in optimized value chain management for the increased value addition for the customer. The supply line starts from suppliers of raw materials through the assembly process to the movement of finished goods to the customers' premises. Customers could be the channel members or the final users in case of B-to-B business. Companies with better supply chain management get sustainable competitive advantage, as they are able to deliver the products at the right time needed by the customers. Companies realize that it is much cheaper, (about 70%) to retain customers than to get new customers. Financial benefits like loans, training in proper usage of the product, publicizing company's social assistance programmes like, free education for village children, adopting villages for overall development and even planting trees for providing green coverage in towns. These activities create goodwill for the company amongst the citizens, who are also the company's customers.

Product and service quality plays an important role in forming customers' attitudes in favour of the products. Consistency in quality, meeting the quality standards lay down by the government for the products (especially true for medicines and food products) and usage ease are the main factors considered by the customers regarding formation of attitudes towards the product. Initially, prospective customers try to get the opinion of their elders, peers and knowledgeable people about the product. Once they buy and use it their own experience forms their attitudes towards the product. TQM, Total Quality Management is therefore the essential ingredient in the success story as it is followed by TCM, Total Customer Management. Product quality is just one area of quality to be looked in to in TQM. Others are quality of service being provided to the customer, quality of knowledge about customers, and their behaviour, buying habits. Marketing research too requires top quality work for obtaining the correct information about the product demand, customers likes and dislikes and their buying patterns. For providing quality service companies have to train their sales team along with the sales teams of the channel members.

SALESPERSON—THE STRATEGIST

Salespersons are known as the eyes and ears of the company. They are most reliable and timely source of information on market dynamics, business general and competitive environment. They are also the vital link the company has with its customers. They are the personal communicators to the customers, prospective customers and company's most effective PR persons.

Companies decide about the sales teams taking into account the sales objectives, the geographic area that needs to be covered, the distribution of sales territory amongst the team members and their compensation packets. Companies need sales persons who are committed and motivated to sell its products, who believe in its products, policies, and its culture and business philosophies. With increasing competitions, new players keep trying to attract the best salespersons. Companies must keep a close vigil on the loyalty factor of the sales team. For this reason alone, companies do well to keep them happy by providing them with adequate incentives, both monetary and non monetary like improved perks, paid holidays for good work done by them.

Sales team has the following tasks cut out for them:

1. Researching for customers, knowing their buying habits, likes and dislikes
2. Planning sales calls on the customers and the prospects for effective results-improving profitable sales
3. Informing the customers about company's plans for product launches, pricing strategies and options.
4. Personal selling-this the most important part both for Business-to Business sales and sales to the channel members.
5. Providing or organizing service to the customers for optimizing use of the products sold.

6. Maintaining relationships with the customers through non-sales contacts
7. Gathering market information and communicating the same to the company.

Companies organize their sales teams in the following manner:

1. Dividing their sales area into territories that can be managed by a single sales person that are easy to cover, have enough business potential not to frustrate the sales person.
2. Recruiting the sales person considering their education, experience, personal background, ability and keenness to learn the companies' way of doing business and those who are happy with their initial package.
3. Training the sales persons into knowledge about company's products, sales policies, competition and the way they have to go about doing their business with on the job training (usually given by sending the recruit with experienced member of the team.), making them understand the communication plans for giving the correct benefit story to the customers about the products. Besides they need to be trained in relationship building both with external and internal customers and for being a good PR person for the company.
4. Monitoring and supervising the sales team for ensuring they achieve their targets of sales, expense budgets and profitability
5. Motivating the sales persons through incentives, praise for jobs done well, for achieving targets.
6. Making proper evaluation of the efforts made by the sales persons individually and in teams to encourage team efforts.

Sales results come with a clear understanding of the salespersons about the customer's behaviour patterns, buying habits, buying motivations and buying periods. Besides, they should be fully knowledgeable in the art of salesmanship, the art of persuasion where the customer is led through steps from his area of ignorance or even dislike of company's products to liking, and leading to purchase action. Later, they have to ensure proper usage of the products by the customers so that they derive the promised benefits from the products. This would lead to customer to re-buy, retention and his loyalty towards the products and the firm.

Given below is a specimen of an Application Form required to be filled by a prospective dealer or distributor of B-to-B Sellers.

Application Form

1. Name of the firm with address, phone, fax details
2. Type of the firm, ownership, partnership, private limited or public limited
3. Name and address phone numbers of owners/top managers, decision makers
4. Type of present business-manufacturing, marketing, distribution of goods, dealership, any other (to be specified)
5. Products being handled with names of suppliers of the products
6. Geographic Areas covered –number of dealers/retailers in their system, selling the products
7. Strength of their personnel, their sales staff with qualifications, technical and general.
8. Technical expertise
9. Service facilities available with locations of the service facilities
10. Firms credit rating
11. Bank references
12. Capital assets with the firm unencumbered by hypothecation
13. Immovable unencumbered personal assets
14. References of their other suppliers
15. References of their customers and dealers
16. Marketing organization
17. Reputation in the market through references of well known persons
18. Quality of sales and service personnel
19. Competitive products sold/ handled with yearly throughout
20. Last three years balancesheets

The selection board of the firm constituting the Marketing and Sales managers, Finance manager and the CEO, then rates the application forms. The selected distributors/dealers sign an agreement with the firm; a specimen of the same is given below. before signing the agreement, legal experts should vet it.

Specimen of Agreement to be signed by the firm with the distributor on requisite stamp paper.

This agreement signed on the ______day of the ______(month) in the year __________, between M/S. ABC with their registered office at ______________________(address) hereinafter called the Seller by their authorized signatory (name of the signatory) and M/S. XYZ with their registered office at _________________________________(address) hereinafter called the Buyer by their authorized signatory (name of the signatory), where by both parties agree to fulfil their commitments as stated in the agreement. The Seller has its products to sell, details given in the annexure 1, and the Buyer is interested in buying the products for resale the both have agreed to put their signatures to the agreement for the purpose. Given below are the respective obligations the parties have to undertake—

Sellers undertake to supply the buyers their products for resale in the designated areas as per annexure 2 of the agreement. The buyer will be paid a commission at the rate of five per cent of the retail price of the seller or any discounted price, whichever is lower. The commission will be paid on a quarterly basis only for the previous quarter. Seller will train the buyer's ten salesmen free of cost in the selling of the products. They will also train ten technicians in service of the product. Seller will fix sales targets for the buyers after consultations with the buyer and buyer will then arrange for meeting the target. Seller will arrange for advertisement and promotional plans as required and the buyer will participate in these as well.

Buyers undertake to observe the rates and other terms of business as given by the sellers. They also undertake to sell the products in the designated market and generally promote the product. They undertake not to sell the products in areas other than the one given to them.

The agreement will hold good for an initial period of one year and any extension of time will be made by mutual agreement in writing. Either party can terminate the agreement by giving three months notice to the other, without assigning any reason for the same.

Any dispute arising out of the agreement will be sorted out by mutual discussion or third party arbitration. Courts in Delhi will only have jurisdiction on the agreement.

The agreement signed on _____________day of __________2006 at Delhi

Signature of the sellers authorized signatory.

Signature of the buyers authorized signatory.

Signatures of the witnesses of the two parties.

Questions for Discussion

1. What are purely the sales functions?
2. What are the methods employed for selecting and retaining salesmen?

3. How the tours should be planned to make them effective?
4. What are methods the salesmen should use in preparing their sales calls?
5. How should the marketing manager keep control of the salesmen's activities?

Purchase Order the Final Destination

The entire organization, which a firm builds, is, ultimately for one single purpose, which is to obtain the purchase order, make supplies against the order and obtain payment. The cycle keeps repeating for the benefit of the firm. It must be understood that unless the benefit is mutual, of the seller and the buyer, the sale will either not be made or it will be a freak sale, not to be repeated. In case of industrial or business –to-business sales, the interaction is between the manufacturing firm and the user firm of the product. In case of FMCG products it is between the manufacturer and the distribution channel member. In both the cases the seller wants to obtain the purchase order. How this is done, its procedure is discussed in this chapter. The following are the steps taken for the purpose:

- The buyer floats an enquiry, which could be written or even verbal, which is received by the seller either as verbal request, a letter or through press advertisements.
- The manufacturer/seller scrutinizes the enquiry to match the requirement with what he can offer.
- If the seller finds a good match, he sends a quotation letter, which is also known as an offer (or a tender bid, in case of enquiry is generated through a tender notice).
- The buyer scrutinizes the offer to see if the product matches with his requirement, sees the price quoted, and compares the offer with offers submitted by other sellers.
- The buyer decides to place the purchase order on one firm and then a written order is placed. In case the buyer does not agree to any clause of the offer, he discusses the same and both parties negotiate the terms; if they arrive at consensus then the order can be placed, which becomes a legally binding sales contract, binding on both seller and the buyer.

Enquiry letter—the buyer, who needs a product, generates the enquiry asking the potential suppliers to send their quotations for examination and scrutiny. The buyer, who can find the sellers of the product, directs his enquiry to them only, which is known as limited enquiry. In case the buyer does not know the sellers of the product or if there are several sellers, he either arranges a market survey to find that out the main one's or releases an advertisement in the press, which is hopefully read by the sellers.

The entire tender business is carried out in the following manner, which helps in obtaining the quotations from the right parties:

- Enquiry letter is sent to the known limited suppliers, based on previous experience of purchasing the same products. This is known as floatation of limited tender.
- Invitation to tender letter is placed as an advertisement in selected newspapers to enable the likely and keen buyers to obtain the tender documents from the buyers, mostly at a cost, which de-motivates the casual seller from making a bid for the tender and thus helps the buyer from unnecessary extra scrutiny of their tenders.

Following is a specimen of an enquiry letter:

ABC Ltd. **Phone 221412**
X Industrial Area RAMPUR, UP Fax 221413
Ref. No. PUR/COMPRESSOR **Date 8th June 2002**

XYZ Compressors Ltd.
Ferry Road
Goa

Dear Sirs,

We require 400 TECUMSEH BRAND compressors for air-conditioners being manufactured by us per month from January 2003. We request you to kindly send your detailed quotations giving, terms of business and technical details of your product. Our specifications for the compressors are given in the enclosure. We expect your reply by the 30th June 2002 positively.

Yours very truly,

For ABC Ltd.
Jag Mohan
Purchase Manager
Encl; -As above

In response to the above enquiry letter a quotation letter is sent as per the following specimen:

XYZ COMPRESSORS Ltd.
Ferry Road, Goa
Ref. No. Comp/00245
Date 15th June 2002
ABC Ltd.
X Industrial Area
Rampur, UP

Kind Attention – Mr. Jag Mohan—Purchase Manager

Dear Sirs,

Kindly refer to your Enquiry Letter Number PUR/COMPRESSOR dated 8th June 2002 regarding your requirement of our compressors to be installed within your air conditioners. We take pleasure in giving below our prices and terms of business, which we hope you will find to your satisfaction:

Tecumseh brand compressors –technical literature is enclosed, which you will notice matches with your specifications completely. Should you require any additional information we shall be too happy to provide the same

Prices as on date are given below; the prices are inclusive of excise duty as applicable on date. Actual excise duty will be charged as applicable on the date of dispatch. Sales tax is extra @ 4% ad-valorem on our getting the form C from you. Otherwise sales tax will be charged @ 10% ad velorem.

Compressor 0.5 ton capacity	Rs. 2500
0.75 ton capacity	Rs. 3000
1.0 ton capacity	Rs. 4000
1.5 ton capacity	Rs. 5500
2.0 ton capacity	Rs. 7000

The prices, are subject to change without notice after sixty days from the date of the quotation, are ex-factory, with the compressors in transport worthy packages.

Delivery period, we confirm that we will be able to supply you the compressors at the rate of 400 per month from January 2003, provided we get your purchase order in our office before 1st October 2002. The delivery period is subject to the force ma-jeure clause given below.

Payment terms—you will open a revolving Letter of credit in our favor for full value of one month's supplies, which will be automatically replenished after each dispatch. The supplies will be made by goods train and normally you should get the same within seven days of dispatch. In the unlikely event of non-receipt of payment please note that the supplies would be stopped till the full payment is received. On overdue payments, beyond fifteen days, you would be charged interest at the rate of 15% per annum.

Guaranty—the compressors are guarantied for a period of one year. In case of manufacturing defective found and accepted by our engineers, we would provide free replacement of the defective compressor, provided it has been used as per our standard specifications and the parameters given therein. You will send the defective compressor, declared defective by engineer approved by us (we will nominate some engineers in each of your market area as defined by you) to our factory at our expense and the new compressor will be sent at once to you, also at our expense. For providing prompt replacement to your valued customers, we suggest that you keep in stock a few service compressors. Please note that you should not try to repair the compressors or get anyone to repair them, otherwise the guaranty will become null and void. The compressors cannot be repaired at all.

Force Majeure—while care will be taken to adhere to the delivery required by you, in case of any act of God, like floods, earthquake, fire or strike of infrastructure component as also our workers, we will be absolved of our commitment of supplies. Once the problem gets settled we will resume supplies as soon as possible.

Validity of the quotation—the quotation will remain valid for a period of two months from the date of this offer and the prices are subject to change without notice after this period.

We are confident that you will find our quotation as per your requirements and we await your valued order for prompt action at our end.

Thanking you in anticipation of your order and assuring of our best attention at all times, we remain,

Yours very truly

For XYZ Ltd.
Sham Nath
Marketing Manager

ABC Ltd. after going through the offer will send a letter, perhaps as given below:

ABC Ltd. **Phone 221412**

X Industrial Area **Fax 221413**

Ref. No. PUR/COMPRESSOR RAMPUR, UP Date 28th June 2002

XYZ Compressors Ltd.
Ferry Road
Goa

Attention—Mr. Sham Nath, Marketing Manager

Dear Sir,

We thank you for your quotation letter No.Comp-00245, dated 15th June 2002. We have the following comments to make:

- Payment terms—please note that we do not open LCs for domestic purchasing. However you are welcome to send the documents through bank. We will provide the details in our purchase order if we decide to place it to you. While we will ensure prompt payment of your bills we will not accept payment of any interest, as this is not an industry norm.
- Delivery period—please note that as there is seasonality of demand in our business, we will give you only a week's notice in any change in schedule. We confirm that our yearly off take from you will not vary beyond ten percent from the figure given, unless we are forced to reschedule our production due to force majeure. In that case our requirements will be revised and you will be informed about it as soon as possible. **In normal circumstances delivery will remain the essence of our order. Please note we will charge 0.5% as liquidated damages in case of default on supplies without any valid reason.**
- Price—since we are buying large quantities of compressors, we expect a downward revision of prices of at least thirty per cent.
- Validity period—please extend the validity of the offer at least by a month to enable us to consider your reply to this letter, which we expect to receive within a fortnight.
- Please send a list of your existing customers to us for our reference.

Yours very truly,

For ABC Ltd.
Jag Mohan
Purchase Manager

XYZ Ltd. will reply to the above is given below:

XYZ COMPRESSORS Ltd.

Ferry Road

Goa

Ref. No. Comp/00245

Date 8th July 2002

ABC Ltd.

X Industrial Area

Rampur, UP

Kind Attention—Mr. Jag Mohan, Purchase Manager

Dear Sirs,

We are grateful for your letter of 28th June 2002. Our point—wise reply to your queries is given below:

- Payment terms—while we will be more comfortable if an LC is opened for the supplies, as is being done by our other customers, for the time being we accept your payment plan. However, payment delayed beyond 120 days will incur interest at the rate mentioned in our quotation.
- Delivery period—we accept your comments. However, please remove the liquidated damages clause, as this is definitely not an industry norm.
- Prices—ad a special case, to show our goodwill to your firm, we offer you a 10% quantity discount, which will not remain operative if you buy less than ninety percent of compressors ordered.
- Validity of our offer is extended for thirty days from the date of this letter.
- A list of customers, with their addresses and phone numbers is given for your reference. Should you so desire we can take you to one of our customers and you can ascertain directly from him about our products and us.

Thanking you in anticipation of your order and assuring of our best attention at all times, we remain,

Yours very truly

For XYZ Ltd.

Sham Nath

Marketing Manager

ABCLtd's response to the letter is given below.

ABC Ltd. **Phone 221412**

X Industrial Area **Fax 221413**

Ref. No. PUR/COMPRESSOR RAMPUR, UP Date 18th July 2002

XYZ Compressors Ltd.

Ferry Road

Goa

Attention—Mr. Sham Nath, Marketing Manager

Dear Sir,

We are thankful to you for your prompt reply to our letter. We are agreeable to your terms stated in the letter of 8th July 2002 and hence place our order from the compressors on you. Should the need be felt in future we will consider your offer of visiting one of your customers. Our purchase order is enclosed in duplicate. Please return one copy duly signed in token of accepting the order.

We hope to have a satisfying and fruitful association with you

Thanking you,

Yours very truly,

For ABC Ltd.

Jag Mohan

Purchase Manager

ABC Ltd. **Phone 221412**

X Industrial Area **Fax 221413**

RAMPUR, UP Date 18th July 2002

Purchase Order

We take pleasure in placing our purchase order for compressors to your firm, which is non transferable without our written approval. The supplies are to be made from January 2003, till December 2003, in equal monthly instaslments—

Compressor 0.5 ton capacity	10pm @ Rs. 2250
0.75 ton capacity	10pm @Rs. 2500
1.0 ton capacity	50pm @Rs. 3500
1.5 ton capacity	300pm @Rs. 4950
2.0 ton capacity	30pm @Rs. 6300

Payments will be made with documents through bank. Our bankers are:
Punjab National Bank
Mill road Rampur, UP.
We accept your force majeure clause along with ours.
We accept your guaranty for the compressors
Other terms and conditions are as per our letters with you, (copy enclosed)
Signed by authorized signatory

The specimen given is just specimen only. Each product and each deal needs different types of letters and the students must understand this factor.

Once a firm makes an offer and it is accepted by the other in full, it becomes a legally binding contract on both firms and any deviation from the contract can be challenged in the court of law. To ensure that the contract is legally enforceable the following need to be understood:

- Parties have general agreement to the contract, to create legal relationship
- Parties must be competent to contract
- The consideration or exchange of goods and money must be lawful
- The goods must be legally saleable

Once a contract is made between two firms, it is the general intent and common behaviour towards each other, which rule the business. The contract comes in to play only if one party does something totally contrary to the spirit of the contract, virtually cheating the other party, when the matter is sent to the courts for penalising the culprit.

In a sales contract there have to be

1. At least two parties i.e., the buyer and the seller.
2. There must be a product to be sold and consideration or money to be given in exchange of the same.
3. The consideration must be reasonable for the contract to be valid. (You cannot contract to sell a brand new Mercedes for Rs. Ten thousand only)
4. The persons signing the contract must have legal authority of their firms, like a power of attorney or ownership rights.
5. The product must be a legal one and not contraband like drugs.
6. The contract must be clear to both parties without any ambiguity in its meaning.
7. Contracts must be in writing

Bilateral contracts are when there are only two parties to the contract. However in case of an offer made public in the press many parties could be purchasing the product and in such cases it becomes a multi-lateral contract.

Questions for Discussion and Activity

Please write down an enquiry letter for intention to purchase TV picture tubes for your TV Manufacturing unit in Noida. Then make a reply for the same as marketing manager of BPL Picture tube plant in Ghaziabad. The entire correspondence should end in signing a sales contract by the two parties.

Marketing Game

Plan out the Critical Success Factors associated with the company.

Critical Success Factors

These are the factors, which govern the success of the firm. They are derived from the following:

i. Industry factors, whether it is growing, if yes at what rate,
ii. Its position in the Market Life Cycle,
iii. business general environment factors,
iv. Technology updates
v. Competition

For a car service centre the following would be the critical success factors:

- Population of vehicles in the area
- Growth rate of vehicle population
- Is the product just being introduced?
- Demography of the area
- Quality of service being provided
- Service equipments at the service centre.
- Number of trained servicemen
- Location of the service centre, easy ingress and egress
- Parking facility
- Service timings, twenty-four hours or less

Similarly Critical Success Factors of the company being analyzed can be determined.

CHAPTER 7

Business-to-Business Marketing—International

AIMS AND OUTCOMES OF THE CHAPTER

With global marketing phenomenon taking roots in the countries marketing needs an international focus to succeed. The chapter takes the students in the area of global business marketing with especial emphasis on Business Out-processing Operation.

GLOBAL OUTSOURCING AND MANUFACTURING

Companies have been outsourcing their raw materials and components for a long time now, since the second quarter of the twentieth century due to the following reasons:

1. Low cost of labour
2. Low infrastructure cost
3. Availability of technology
4. Availability of raw materials
5. Proximity to the markets

Certain countries of the east and south, which that are either underdeveloped or are developing have low cost labour that helps in low cost manufacturing. This becomes a big incentive for the western business giants to get the labour intensive work down in such locations. The theory of Absolute Advantage of nations as the main driver for international business was propounded by the 17th century philosopher Adam Smith and to a large extent it still holds good.

Addidas and Nike, of the USA found that as their own labour cost was high as compared to some eastern nations they started outsourcing the manufacture of shoes to these countries. As a rough comparison the costs of rich and poor countries manufacturing is given below:

S.No.	Poor Countries	Rich Countries
1. Labour cost per shoe pair	$ 5	$50
2. Infrastructure per shoe	$ 2	$20
3. Transport per shoe	$ 1	$5

The shoe companies of the west discovered the absolute advantage of outsourcing shoe manufacturing to the poor countries. The manufacturing can, however shift from one country to another when the costs start increasing in the first country. Korea and Taiwan are two examples of countries where labour costs have risen substantially in the last fifty years.

INFORMATION OUTSOURCING

Rich countries have found that keeping, managing and disseminating information for their customers and other stakeholders has become expensive and it is a lot cheaper to set up centres in third world countries like India for this purpose. Initially the software development in the US was organized on the basis of manpower exports to that country from India. Today the trend is of getting the software developed in India for export to the US. A large number of Call Centres have come up around Delhi where the customers from the US interact with the centres to get information about the status of their account with the company. The information is available in the centre and if required it can be computed there itself.

Companies have several options, like getting components from other countries and assembling them in the home country for local consumption and for exports. Besides, the company can arrange components in a host country, assemble the product there, import into home country and other countries as well, as given below:

1. Outsourcing material, assembly in home country, host country/countries or both.
2. Manufacture of components, assembly in home country, host country/countries or both.
3. Product sales in home country, host country/countries or both.

Most companies prefer to use home country raw materials and components as it helps in avoiding problems of distances, political problems, currency fluctuation problems, tariff variations, and the problems arising out of dealing with different languages. However, companies keep looking at global sourcing to reduce costs and for improving the product quality. Finally outsourcing should provide the company with cost reduction, quality improvements, increased access to international state of the art technology and improvement in reliability and delivery process.

According to Ford motor company they have an extensive global network for obtaining components needed in the two manufacturing facilities they have in Europe. For example, some of the components they get from the UK are, clutch, ignition, oil pump, speedometer, battery, steering wheel, fuel tank, glass and locks. Other locations they outsource the components are as follows:

1. Austria—tyres, radiator and heater hoses
2. Belgium—tyres, tubes, seat pads, brakes and trims
3. Italy—cylinder head, carburettor, glass, lamps, and defrost grill
4. Canada—glass and radio
5. Japan—starter, alternator, roller and cone bearings, windscreen washer pumps
6. Norway—exhaust ranges and tyres
7. Sweden—hose clamps, cylinder bolts, exhaust pipes, pressings and hardware
8. Denmark—fan belt
9. Switzerland—under chassis coating, speedometer, and gears
10. Holland—tyres, paints and hardware
11. United States—EGR valves, wheel nuts, hydraulic tappet and glass
12. Germany—locks, pistons, front disc, distributor, weather-strips, rocker arm, speedometer, fuel tank, cylinder bolt, cylinder head gasket, front wheel knuckles, rear wheel spindle, transmission cases, clutch cases, steering column, battery and glass
13. France—alternator, cylinder head, master cylinder, brakes, under chassis coating, weather strips, clutch release bearings, steering shaft and joints, seat pads and frames, transmission cases, clutch cases, tyres, suspension bushes, ventilation units, heater hose clamps, sealers and hardware.

As can be seen, the company has, for certain critical components arranged for more than one source of supply, while their production bases are just two in Europe, in Halewood UK and in Saarlouis Germany.

The companies add foreign supplier to the domestic ones, for ensuring reliability of supplies. In some cases, the technical expertise may be available only overseas along with capacity to supply the components as per the company's requirements. Outsourcing overseas could allow the company to get better quality components, besides it could help in fighting competition from home suppliers base from where other manufacturers are also obtaining the components. It helps in opening up the international markets to the company. Moreover, if competition is outsourcing their components, the company should find out the economic viability of doing so and then plan its own offshore sourcing.

The companies have to take a stand on making the products or buying it for sales. At times some components could be made and some others could be bought out. Companies could go for vertical integration and get into manufacturing of the downstream components. The other option is to just buy them from outside suppliers. Outsourcing should be resorted to where the supplier has the advantage of economies of scale, better technology, have lower manufacturing cost structure or incentives for higher levels of production. Components that are critical should be outsourced with great care as it would bind the company to the source that could play truant by not supplying on time and pressurizing the company for better prices, cash payments. The quality management of the suppliers need careful scrutiny and at times may need imparting training to suppliers' engineers in proper testing methods and the value of TQM. When the suppliers can provide quality products, constantly upgraded technological innovations, economies of scales translated into price reductions the company can look for long term relationship with such suppliers. At times when such a supplier has been found, the company would be tempted to vertically integrate the supplier in its own ambit. Else, the company can opt for long term agreements, cooperation in technology up gradation, finance, manpower planning, management expertise for maintaining close contacts where the supplier feels almost one wit the company. In such a scenario, the company can even change the components, their specifications and yet get the same at a low price, enabling the company to plan new models at competitive prices. The value chain can in a way become an arm of the company.

Companies have several options before them as they plan their purchase function. They can go in for totally local purchase when the controls are easier, time for obtaining supplies shorter and price negotiations can be conducted with relative ease, as the supplier is aware of the business ethos of the country. The companies can plan small supply sizes with lower cash requirements. And the latest "Just in Time" inventory management becomes more possible.

Next, the companies can selectively locate international component manufacturers, with the necessary qualifications to become suppliers.

It could start as a one off purchase deal and ultimately become a regular supply commitment from both the suppliers' side and the company. Finally companies can plan global outsourcing strategies to obtain the benefits available in different part of the world, like that of some country having better technology, other having low cost labour and yet another having easy availability of the required raw materials.

Companies use number of ways for getting overseas supplies, like involving the home office purchase department to do the job. They could use foreign subsidiaries or business units for selecting the suppliers most suited for their operations. Some companies that have international offices use them for organizing outsourcing in the countries they operate. The most advanced companies using international outsourcing in an integrated manner for worldwide operations. These centralized operations are most useful when the money value of purchase is high; the components are of strategic importance, including the value of quality and if they have high technology inputs. The companies can plan to obtain up to 70% of their requirements from one source. The supply agreements can be also on long-term basis which may be up to five years. The purchase actions could be centralized from home office for keeping direct control on the vital purchases.

International Environment for Business

Introduction—in dealing with different countries it is essential to understand their business environments before embarking on overseas business. There are cultural differences among nations as well as differences in economic levels, besides the political and legal differences.

There are great differences between political and legal systems between countries and MNCs have to formulate and implement their strategies taking these differences in to account.

The role of the political system is to be the cohesive force in the society. The two opposing systems on the political horizons are democracy with people participation in the running of the government and totalitarianism where a group of people or even one-person wields the political power. In democracy citizens enjoy widespread freedom, especially in the areas of political rights and civil liberties Managers have to deal with several forms of government approach to business and stability of the governments in different countries they must have the foresight to influence and respond to government action and any stimuli provided by it. Managers must also learn the ethically correct behaviour and operations for each country they operate in, at times law may not provide the guidelines in this regard.

There are several types of economies in the world, with many differences between them. These differences affect management decisions in significant manner. In market economy countries individuals have the power to allocate control and distribute through their actions the economic resources. Incidentally in planned economies the government does it. However, in the twenty first century most countries are headed towards market driven economy and are succeeding in reaching there in varying degrees and these imbalances provide the challenge to the international business manager of today. Key factors that influencer the MNC decision making process are the country's economic growth, privatization, inflation, balance of payment between countries and external debt.

Countries with the high growth rates in their economy are able to exploit these human and natural resources most efficiently. On the other hand the developing nations like India provide large market potential (more especially since the west nation market are saturated with products and are having mostly replacement market). These countries are showing strong economic growth, investing in them would help in further developing the market, notwithstanding the risk factor involved due to political instability in some countries.

Let us discuss the economic differences and the ways of dealing with them.

Economic Business Environment

India became independent in 1947 and the then government of India with Mr. Jawahar Lal Nehru as the first Prime Minister of India, decided that the country would have the socialistic pattern of society, with major economic developments to be in the hands of the government. The birth of the Public Sector Undertakings took place with a number of firms like, Bharat Heavy Electricals, Hindustan Machine Tools, Hindustan Steels coming in to existence. Private sector was considered, as having only unscrupulous people who wanted to cheat the government and the public. This resulted in the Permit License Raj, where the government bureaucracy started doling out favours in return of monetary gains. The Public Sector suffered from lack of accountability and undue interference from the political bosses. The bribery and corruption became so big that it is today the hydra like monster rising its head higher and higher each day.

However, the realization came in 1991, that the country can not live in isolation and it had to open up its economy. Internationally two major changes had taken place. First was the destruction of USSR, which resulted in dismantling of communism from a major world area. At the same time the other major communist power China started going the capitalistic way in no mean measure. The only semblance of communism remains today only in Cuba. Till mid 20th century, there were two major economic ideologies, the American market based economy and the state controlled economy of the communist regimes. And then there was the third type, the mixed economy, which was practiced in India among a few other nations. Mixed economy was meant to give equal imspetus to the government and private enterprise. With this ideology, a new corporate sector was born, the Joint sector, where both the private and the government were financiers of the project. This was started to get the government approvals quickly and then run the organization on the lines of a private venture. However, the conflicting decisions by both the owners and tight government audit never allowed it to flourish as an economic force in the country.

Hence, it can be seen that the business organization matrix would look as given below in Table 7.1

Table 7.1. Business Organisation Matrix

	Private ownership	*Mixed/joint ownership*	*Public or government ownership*
Market control	Market driven private ownership	Market driven joint ownership	Market driven government ownership
Mixed	Mixed control/ private ownership	Mixed control/ joint ownership	Mixed control/ government ownership
Government control	Government control/ private ownership	Government control/ joint ownership	Government control/ government ownership

The government ownership of firms gave them tremendous leverage in getting business from the government, including a substantial price preference. In other words, a government owned firm would get an order for supplies from the government even if its prices are substantially higher. This leads to extensive non accountability factor as the price could be loaded with factors of inefficiency as also takes care of any underhand dealings, which tended to increase the price. It should not be construed that such inefficiencies did not figure in the private ownership firms. Yet their numbers were few and the accountability factor mostly took care of the inefficient and corrupt elements in the private sector.

Since, now we are truly in the age of market economy in practically the entire world, let us take a look at what exactly is market economy.

Market Economy of the World

Today in the twenty-first century, most countries are part of market driven economy. It is product quality, price, brand equity and availability of products, which play a major role in market dynamics. These factors have been given the celebrated name of four Ps. The product demand is also dependent on the market segment's business environment, like, demographic, social, cultural, political and legal factors. Competitive factors too play a major role in establishing business shares among the various players.

The factories churn out products, with the help of employees, raw materials and consumables and the employees are in a way buyers of the products. Employees work for wages and use the wages for making the purchases. (The products may be from one factory and buyers from another factory or any other discipline.)

Market Economy brings the customer in to main focus as he gets competitive products to choose from, competitive prices and firms vie with each other in product positioning and placement besides in communicating to the customers through multitude of advertising formats. The firms too are free to opt for certain markets, segments and channels of distribution. Thus the interplay between buyers and sellers depends on the supply and demand situation and on the strengths of the firms. The strength comes from product quality, service to the customer and generation of brand equity.

Market economy can be best understood by comparing it with the closed economies of the communist world, where the manufacture is restricted by the government and so is the supply. We all have heard of the days of rationing in the Soviet Union. (In fact even in India there was rationing of essential products till the first half of the last century.)

Market economy can come to a country only if the restrictions on production, rules to regulate the supply and purchase including imports of raw materials are not removed by the government and industry freed to take its own decisions in these matters on the basis of market needs. A look at the pre 1991 era is sufficient to understand the stranglehold the government had on the markets during the period prior to the reforms, as follows:

- For manufacturing any product firms needed a manufacturing license from the government's ministry of industries.
- For foreign equity participation and technology transfer even more stringent approvals were required from ministry of industries and the RBI.
- For import of raw materials a lot of approvals were required from the industry ministry and the Reserve Bank of India.
- The custom duty on most products was high up to even 300% ad-velorem.
- Interest rates for borrowing was high.

Since 1991,with major changes in the industrial policy the government of India has tried to bring the country's economy in the market control. Yet a few more reforms are needed like full convertibility of money for the purpose.

For free economy the control of the government on business should be non-existent. The government's task should be the safe guard the interests of all its citizens. They should be free to choose their vocation, be it buying selling manufacturing, buying selling property and pursue it, as they desire without interference from the government as long as they do not do any legal transgressions.

In the communist regime the entire production planning, raw materials procurement, doling out rationed quantities was centralized with the government. Seeing the growth and development of west, most countries of the erstwhile soviet group have opted out of the central planning and now they are looking at joining the market driven economy.

Mixed Economies

In India, the mixed economy was created with the joint sector ventures, where the private and government were both partners. While such firms tried to get the best of both, i.e., easy government approvals and speedier decision-making process associated with the private sector. In the end, mostly they lost out on both counts as the government felt that their only responsibility is to control the activity of the firm, and the private partner felt that the government is interfering a lot.

Even in purely private firms there is an element of outside control in the form of directors on their board from the financial institutions and the banks that have financed the firm. Besides, there is the compulsory statutory audit by outside auditors. Despite these controls, the last few years have seen a large number of scams through either the equity market or through fake loan companies. It is in this context that the government of India is looking for checks and balances and has assigned the task to Securities and Exchange Control Board-SEBI.

The world over it can be seen that while in China there is greater degree of governmental control, Japan has lesser, where market forces determine the market dynamics. Some countries like Hungry, Taiwan are partly under free market with only some governmental interference, countries like Russia, Mexico are mostly not free. Likewise Cuba would be considered totally not free from governmental interference.

Products like Power supply and telecommunication have remained in the government set up inmost countries and today in India these products face competition from the private firms. This has created an era of competition, much to the benefit of the consumers and it has resulted in the streamlining process in the government firms in order to make them more efficient. Manufacturing and supply of defence equipment is usually the last of the product groups to come to the private sector, while in India, paradoxically, the defence services did not think twice while purchasing their products from foreign private firms.

The discussion on how much of governmental interference is good for the country's economic growth goes on eternally in most countries.

Developed countries like Germany, Sweden and France have low level of government ownership. They are highly taxed in the private sector and the money thus collected is used in welfare measures. In France government ownership of business sector is greater as compared to the other two, like the telecom companies keep shuttling there between private and government ownership. Japanese system is based on government's influence on the private sector firms. Japan has been channelling the investment flow in the direction of their choice through setting targets and giving monitory incentives. Their Ministry of International Trade and Industry guides the firms through strategic planning for investment and production with minimal controls.

The other dimension of economic environment deals with the fact whether the country is a developed one, developing or underdeveloped. UN and its subsidiaries have several plans for helping the poor nations and Indian firms must take advantage of the largesse offered to such nations by helping them come up in the economic order. It has been proven beyond doubt that countries, which opt for market economy, tend to grow economically faster than that have, which do not. China and India are typical examples of accelerated growth in these countries after they opened up to market based economy.

Politics plays a major role in the life of any country. Countries like the USA, Japan believe that in a democratic free market set up customers are free thinking individuals who know what is best for them and they decide the fate of firms in the market place. There are no sops or financial crutches available to non- performers. It is therefore easy to understand that only the genuine firm, which believes in its product and is ready to provide customer satisfaction, is going to survive.

Countries which have been having totalitarianism as their political philosophy believe that firms should not be let loose to cheat the gullible customers and the restraints are provided by the governmental controls and interference in the shape of checkers, inspectors and auditors. Even France during its Socialists rule had taken over several of the country's private firms under its hold.

There are in fact no truly free economies as even in the US there are economic boundaries like the import quota system for textile imports from developing nations like India. Even the WTO is controlled by the dollar power, which restricts trade from developing countries through uncalled for restrictions and stringent product specifications. The other impediment towards free economic one world, are the trade pacts and trade zones.

It can be safely concluded that each country has its unique system of private and government ownership and control, depending on their system of governance, the status in the development process and their political situation. Therefore it becomes imperative for firms entering foreign countries to understand the type of economic conditions prevail in the overseas markets they plan to enter.

For the benefit of new entrepreneurs it is necessary to put countries in economic zones. The competitiveness of countries in the international market depends on the following factors-

- Production and productivity
- Demand and its management

Production factors are based on the following:

- Capital resource
- Human resource
- Information resource
- Infrastructure
- Physical resource
- Management

Firms have to set up resourceing systems for the above in different countries, which would define the firms production and its productivity.

Demand and its management would include home country's demand and its growth and international demand. The best way to ascertain the demands is through marketing research.

Countries Classifications

Countries are classified on the following basis:

- GNP-Gross National Product
- GDP- Gross Domestic Product
- Per Capita Income
- Quality Of Life Or Life Style
- Purchasing Power
- Macroeconomics Factors

Gross National Product—is in essence the sum-total of country's economic activity and can be defined as "the value of goods and services produced during the year from the country's resources", the actual manufacture could take place in the country or even outside.

GNP is the sum of domestic production plus the moneys received by residents from overseas on account of labour or capital investments by way of dividends reduced by the outflow of money made to non residents.

Gross Domestic Product or GDP takes into account the entire domestic production irrespective of the fact that the production is from Indian resources or foreign. It describes the economic activities with in the borders of the country.

World Bank has, however accepted the GNP as true representative of a country's wealth, for working on banks analysis for development plans in the country. Based on 1994 figures the classification of countries on the basis of Per Capita Income is given below:

Table 7.2. Country Classification

Low income	$725	or	less
Lower-middle income	$726	-	$2895
Upper-middle income	$2896	-	$8956
Middle income	$726	-	$8956
High income	$8957	or	more

The low and middle-income countries are known as developing countries, while high-income countries are the developed ones. The classifications have since been changed to include **Countries with Economies in Transition,** CEIT, like China, Russia and Cuba.

Per Capita Income

World Bank has categorized countries on the basis of Per Capita Income GNP as given below (only selected countries have been included in the list. It will be noticed that with the exception of Australia and New Zealand, the rich countries are located in the northern- hemisphere.

Table 7.3. Economic Divide of Countries

Rich countries per capita GNP $8957 or more	*Upper middle per capita GNP between $2896-8955*	*Lower Middle per capita GNP between $726-2895*	*Low income per capita GNP $725 or less*
Australia	Argentina	Bolivia	Afghanistan
Austria	Brazil	Bulgaria	Bangladesh
Belgium	Chile	Croatia	China
Canada	Greece	Cuba	Egypt
Denmark	Hungary	Indonesia	Ghana
France	Korea Republic	Iran	India
Germany	Malaysia	Iraq	Kenya
Netherlands	Mauritius	Jordan	Mongolia
New Zealand	Mexico	Korea Dem. Rep	Myanmar
Spain	Oman	Lebanon	Nigeria
Sweden	Saudi Arabia	Morocco	Nepal
UAE	South Africa	Philippines	Pakistan
UK	Uruguay	Poland	Sri Lanka
USA		Russia	Zimbabwe

While the rich nations are only 20% of all the nations, they generate almost 80% of the world GNP. Countries in low income about 30%, bring in only about 5% of the world GNP.

Purchasing Power—World Bank believes that while GNP is a good indicator of country's wealth, it does not tell about the benefits accruing to the developmental work. Purchasing Power Parity tells about the purchase value of local currency in home country, against one-dollar purchase value in the USA. Purchasing power of local currency is compared to that of a dollar.

Life Style—it is measured by taking in to account the following:

- Life expectancy
- Education levels
- Healthcare programs
- Income and allocable surplus as purchasing power
- Welfare of women

As per 1996 surveys, the top 5 countries, which emerge as winners in these criteria, are the following:

1. Canada
2. USA
3. Japan
4. Holland
5. Norway

In a list of 174 countries, India ranks 135th, China 108th and Russia 57th.

In many countries while the wealth generation takes place, the rich are becoming richer and the poor remain as they were. Despite this most people in the world are satisfied with their lot and believe that they are living in a world, which is better than the world of their parents grew up. However, they also believe that their children will be living in a world, which would be worse than today's world. India's philosophy of contentment under any circumstances has left many citizens so occupied with their miserable existence that they know nothing better.

Pakistan, on the other hand has a lot of petro-dollars coming via the gulf, which has given their middle class a better standard of living than their counterparts in India. However the war hysteria in Pakistan does not allow the extra wealth to be of good to the country as they use it for keep honing the war machinery.

With the opening up of the country's markets to the world the customers now have a choice of different brands and the urban markets are replete with durable goods of international standards.

Macroeconomics Factors

Developing countries like India have their GDP distributed on the following lines:

1. Agriculture—30%

2. Industry—30%
3. Manufacturing—25%
4. Service—15%

For a developed country like UK, the distribution is as given below:

1. Agriculture—2%
2. Industry—32%
3. Manufacturing—22%
4. Service—66%

The nations from affluent group are more service oriented. Most of their requirements are met with imports as with high labour costs they can not produce goods economically as compared to less developed nations. Hence the stress goes to service industry, which caters to the recreation needs of the population. This is directly related to the quality of life in these countries.

The communist theory was equal distribution of whatever wealth is existing, while market economy looks at increasing the wealth and believes in its distribution as per individual efforts in producing the wealth, which would indirectly make every one richer than their existing status.

Economic Growth

The business and economic activity in any country depends on a stable government, low inflation rate and high growth rate. India is aiming at 6 to 7 percent growth each year. Similarly other developing nations can plan growth rates and by 2020,60% of the world GNP could be from the today's developing counties. The rich nations want to invest in high growth countries like China, Malaysia, Mexico and the poor nations like India, Pakistan miss the FDI (Foreign Direct Investment). With the new industrial policy India has started getting FDI, yet more of it definitely required. It is hoped that with stable government and increase in reforms for inviting FDI, there would be substantial improvement in FDI. Today, India gets about 10% of the FDI as compared to what China gets.

Inflation

Inflation is the measure of country's cost of living, interest rates, exchange rates and it involves the political and economic system of the country. It is the consumer price index variation over a period of time. Inflation can cause increase in interest rates to offer real interest on interest-able assets, as also for slowing the economic development rate to fight inflation.

Distribution Patterns—Industrial Goods

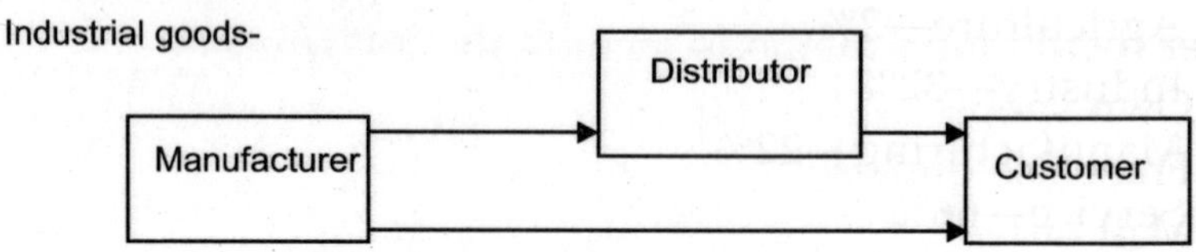

Fig. 7.1. Distribution Plan

As can be seen, in industrial goods, the sale is made either directly to the customer or through a distributor. Capital goods sale is usually made directly to the customer, because of the following reasons-

- Technicalities have to be explained to the customer, which are best done by the manufacturer.
- Mostly large sums of money are involved and customer wants best price without middleman's commission.
- Installation and commissioning of the equipment is involved, best done by the manufacturer's engineers
- After sales service is complicated

In case of sale of raw materials and components the manufacturers sell through a distributor network the size of which is finalized taking the geographic area, which needs to be covered by the manufacturer.

For the sake of comparison, the following is the distribution pattern for Consumer goods

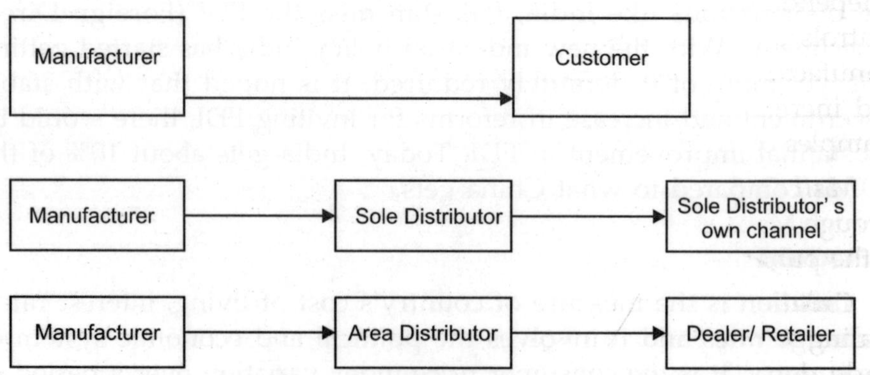

Fig. 7.2. Distribution Pattern

Very small firms, who have limited market, like bakeries may resort to direct selling to their customers. **Very large firms** have sole distributors with their own network of dealers and retailers. We will discuss the merits and demerits of each of the methods of distribution and some other methods as well.

Other distribution methods include the following-

- Own shops
- Franchise outlets
- Mail order
- Catalogue sales
- Web marketing
- Agency operations
- Stockists
- Consignment agents

Own Shop: Many manufacturers like Bata, Usha and Singer have their own i.e. company owned sales outlets (shops) these shops ensure that the products are available to the customer in good quantity, of right quality, at the right price. Besides, as the shops products of the firm only the control on sale can be more effective as compared to the sales being made through dealers and retailers who handle competitive products as well. The above mentioned firms realized the great assets they had in their own shops and as the firms had only a limited range of products, the shops, mostly in prime locations were not being fully utilized. These firms, therefore added complementary products and made their shops as sales outlets for complete range of products in their particular fields.

Franchise Outlets: The manufacturers give legal rights to an independent business entity to run franchisers business (under some controls by franchiser, like quality control). The franchisees help the manufacturers to add to their business, have bigger geographic coverage and increase their market share. MacDonald's, Pizza Hut are two examples of manufacturers who have used franchise system effectively.

Mail Order: Some products like Readers Digest magazine are sold through Mail Order. Customers are requested to send their orders directly to the publishers, who send the product directly to the customers.

Catalogue Sales: are a variant of mail order, as here the firms dealing with a number of products get colourful attractive catalogues made describing the products. These catalogues are then sold or distributed to a large number of prospective customers, who select products from the catalogue and place order on the firm. The firms have to ensure that the quality of the product sold is the same as mentioned in the catalogue; otherwise, the negative publicity with bad product sold will spoil the firm's business.

Web Marketing: The spread of computers and Internet has opened the doors for marketing or selling on the Internet. Pick up any channel on the net and you will find a number of advertisements. The customers can place orders on the net itself and give their credit card number. The sellers will surely dispatch the product against the order. Since there are no expenses on shops, effective reduction in prices can be made. The only danger of these types of sales is that the customer does not get to see the product before they get the same.

Agency Operation: Agents are independent businessmen who help manufacturers in selling their products. The agents obtain orders from the customers, which they forward to the manufacturers. On the conclusion of the transaction, the agent gets Agency Commission for his efforts in getting the orders. Agents can be both for buying and selling products. They have long-term agreements with the manufacturers and they operate within the terms and conditions of the contract. Their task includes negotiating the sales contract with the buyers on behalf of the manufacturers for which they have the authority. They build long-term relationships with the buyers who benefit as they get consistently good products at uniform prices.

Stockists: Manufacturers some times appoint stockists who are businessmen with storage space. The stockist's job is to keep stocks on behalf of the manufacturer and dispatch the same to distributors and retailers on receiving instructions from the manufacturer. For the use of their storage space and their efforts in making dispatches they get a commission from the manufacturers. Normally they are not involved in actual selling effort of the firm.

Consignment Agents: These businessmen are required to keep stocks of manufacturers merchandise on their behalf and as and when they are able to sell the products they send their money received to the manufacturer. For their efforts they are paid a commission on sales. These types of agents are especially needed when a product is introduced in the market and the channel members are not sure of its saleability.

Unlike in the first half of the twentieth century, when the manufacturer as per his convenience decided the channel, now the channel selection depends mainly on market survey report, which tells the manufacturer, **how** the customer wants to buy the product. Main criteria can be summed up as follows:

- Customer reach for the channel
- Customer convenience of buying
- Service facility needed by the product and its availability with the channel
- Number of products available from one manufacturer for the channel

Customer Reach

Sales orientation of the first half of twentieth century was mainly on manufacture. Once the product is in the market it was sold. Competition was almost absent in most products. In some products there was total monopoly and the manufacturer could set his terms of sale. In majority of products however, there were a few manufacturers. In other words there was oligopoly and the manufacturers could join hands and control market prices. Later on in order to avoid the situation of cartel formation the Government of India set up Monopolies And Restrictive Trade Practices Commission (MRTPC).

Today in the beginning of the twenty-first century, manufacturers are facing severe competition in practically all the products and the manufacturer who can place his product within easy reach of the buyer definitely gains advantage over other competitors.

Taking this view Eureka Forbes has started personalized selling of their products, which include Consumer durables like Vacuum Cleaners, Water Purifiers. The sales are made by firm's salespersons visiting the homes and offices of prospective customers with sample of the product, when they can give live demonstration to convince the customers and obtain an order.

Many retailers have resorted to home delivery systems, including for consumer durables. The customer can buy a product by telephone order or through Internet purchase and the product is delivered to his home. Such purchases are paid for by either cash or through credit cards. This is catching the industrial market also. However, it depends on the trust the buyers have on the sellers.

International Markets of the Twenty-first Century

When a firm enters the market, it has some commitments to its customers, and those are based on the utility, need and performance of its product. With shrinking business world, even political distances can be shortened as no nation can remain as an island. Therefore, in order to not just survive, but also to thrive in the market place, the firms must have a global vision of the market, even if it is selling only locally, as otherwise foreign firms are going to cut in to their business sharply. Hence the nature of commitment of the firms has to widen just not to cope with international competition but also in order to beat them in their own countries as well. The steps required are the following:

- In-depth or intensive marketing within the country
- Extension of geographic boundaries of the markets
- Penetrating pricing strategy
- Strong merchandizing effort
- Advertising, promotion strategy
- New product plans
- New products to be sold in new markets
- Vertical integration of manufacturing base

Intensive marketing—Depending of product surpluses firms have to take a view, which would encourage them in to going in for aggressive selling to their present customers. Gillette is a case in point. When they started with their use and throw Presto razors, they were giving individual razors. Later on they came out with a pack of five razors, taking away the customers choice of product—switch midstream. Built-in gifts schemes, leasing options, deferred payment plans all tend to intensify the thrust of marketing on the customer.

Geographic extensions—customers in India are now much more discerning about the quality of product they purchase and hence products from India are matching international standards. It is therefore in fitness of business that if Indian firms face competition from foreign firms they must find countries where they have a competitive advantage because of low cost manpower, latest technology products.

Penetrating pricing—our products have a built in cost advantage over their foreign counterparts. Yet in export markets the competition could be from other developing countries. Products can be sold on marginal costing, provided there is a good base of sales in India.

Merchandizing is the icing in the cake, the showmanship of products. In order to cater to the sophisticated customers the firms must pay great attention on merchandizing aspect of retailing.

Advertising and promotion are the buzzwords in today's business and need special thrust on a continuous basis.

New products come from either customer needs or new product development, technology innovation.

Marketing research is essential for scanning world markets for new products and these researches pay dividends by optimizing marketing efforts in the right countries and through right channels of distribution.

Vertical diversification helps in reducing transfer costs as when the firm gets its raw materials, from it's own source.

Well-established firms find themselves becoming top heavy over a period of time, especially in the growth stages of life cycle. Downsizing or right sizing as it is called today is the order of the day for such firms. The steps required for right sizing are given below-

- A quick audit of the firm's activities to segregate the superfluous ones. Fixing an objective of right sizing exercise.
- Closure of all superfluous activities (those activities, which do not generate any value for the customers.)
- Outsourcing activities, which can be given to outside persons/firms.
- Reducing manpower across the board, in every department at all levels.
- Giving more important assignments and better pay to remaining people.
- Consolidating the gains of reduced activities.
- Bench marking results with the objective with which the firm had started the task.
- If the right sizing does not succeed, it may be a good idea to divest from the product areas completely.

Firms have realized that they cannot operate in isolation. Coordination between two firms can help both in some even when they may be competing with each other as can be seen from the following examples-

- A cash rich firm joins hands with a technology rich firm. Both gain in terms of market share and profits.
- Promotion plans can be jointly worked out. The industry bodies do it regularly when they fight against any government legislation.
- Logistics support can be provided, which will reduce the costs substantially for both the firms. If two neighbouring firm can use one common road, power and telephone line it could mean a lot of saving.
- Price collaborations are popular in hospitality industry like hotels, airlines which all provide similar benefits to customers, like upgrades, free tickets for mileage used or free stay for nights used and paid for.

Because of the fast changing market scenario, and business environment, it is best to take the following steps for creating strategies for markets:

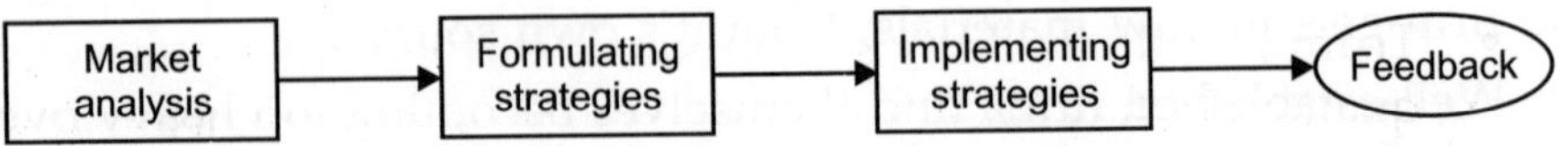

As the firm goes in to implementation stage, it should not forget that even then changes are taking place in the market environments. Feedback therefore becomes a powerful tool of ensuring satisfactory management of marketing strategies.

Market Analysis: It starts with Michael Porter's Five Force model and goes on to understand the general environment factors described in the book at several places. However, continuous monitoring of the environment is essential as the competition keeps growing each day.

Planning the Strategy: Starts with allocation of resources, money, human, information and infrastructure in the right area of marketing. It must be budgeted as to how much will be spent on advertising, after sales service, marketing research, developing the new areas, travelling, dealer commission, promotional plans in view of the sales targets finalized by the marketing department. Each sales team needs certain inputs like travelling, communications, live demonstrations (if required by the product), to meet its commitment on sales objectives and these must be provided. New business horizons, like new geographic coverage, new product launches call for separate budgets. Care needs to be taken in manpower planning and deployment to ensure that the people working together work as a team, are congruent in operations, complement each other and are well balanced both in numbers and in experience. Market Information System, MIS, should be kept updated with inputs from the market, sales invoices, and dispatches. Authority to take decisions, along with accountability must be expressed perhaps in writing so that each member of the team knows his tasks, what he can do and what he cannot. Importance of scientific planning for the market has been brought to focus by the myriads of non-achievers who start with a bang and end with a whimper in no time.

Since competing firms have similar goals and objectives the firm, which implements the strategy wins with better profits and improved brand equity.

Implementation of the strategy requires the following steps to be taken by the firm:

- Team members to remain totally motivated, committed to their tasks.
- Team should be fully in the know of their quantitative and qualitative targets.
- Qualitative targets like improvement in brand image, training of team members should be taken as seriously as the quantitative targets.
- Individual members of the team perform their tasks as also assist other members whenever necessary.
- Team leader should act more as a coordinator than a monitor. His actions should inspire the team.
- Assessment of achievement must be made first by each member and then for the team jointly by the team at regular intervals without waiting for the year to end.
- Success story of any member must be circulated within the team to inspire others and also to learn from the methods used to achieve the success. Failure should also be discussed, not to push people down but to learn from any mistakes the losing team may have made.

Feedback: The last mentioned point goes as feedback to the management for use in other areas the firm may be operating. The feedback helps in reframing the strategies and therefore timely feedback is extremely important for the continued success of the firm.

Controls: management must have inbuilt control systems to ensure that one unscrupulous person cannot hijack the entire organization by deviating from the targets of the firm to promote his own targets. At times even sincere persons lose track in the route of day-to-day operations. Punishment or correction needs to be introduced at some stage before things go really wrong. The results should be compared with the targets already accepted by the team, in the following manner:

- With the targets.
- If the team has exceeded the targets then with industry growth. The company must also know exactly the reasons of good performance so that it can be continued and replicated in other area as well.
- With historical figures.
- With new targets if new competitor/s have emerged during the period under review.

- With customer feedback about quality of goods and services offered by the team.
- With the R&D group if improvements have been called for in the product.

New challenges in the twenty first century for the marketers

Global politics and economics are the most pronounced factors affecting today's business. Open markets one one hand and economic zones on the other, anti dumping laws and quota systems for imports by some nations, hostilities in many parts of the world, war like situations and the faster communication, faster movements, have thrown the challenges. For marketers these have opened several new routes as also closed some old ones as given below:

- Quality standards at par internationally, ISO 9000 Series
- Low labour costs
- A large technical workforce
- English as a known language
- IT, software expertise
- Presence of several multinational companies already in the country.
- Spread of Internet in the country
- Emergence of e-signatures leading to e-commerce

The firms which can gear themselves up to the challenges have a bright future both nationally and in the international markets.

The Virtual Marts—Internet or Web has the potential of becoming a force to reckon with as a marketing tool. As the PC population increases both in homes and in the offices surfing the net will become more popular. Bazee.com in India has started its business where sellers, both individual and firms can place their products for sale. Websites auctioning products, including airline tickets have emerged. These are only tips of the proverbial iceberg and much more can be expected in the area of web marketing.

These virtual shops with little overheads can give the well established super markets, the only negatives at present are their credibility among the Indian buyers as also the real life buying experience where the Indian housewife excels, doing window shopping bargaining and generally having a great time out of the house. Unless the lady feels the silk of the sari, she is not confident of buying it. It is perhaps time or some innovative, ingenious technique which could help the lady in overcoming these fears.

Hence, the marketer's route to success is as follows:

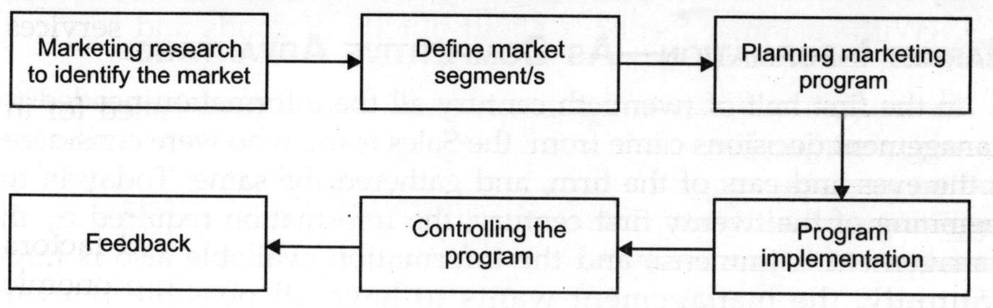

Fig. 7.3. Market Plan

Firms need to make a rolling marketing plan, which may be made for a year, but is reviewed every month and corrected if deviations are found in the business environment factors, both general and competitive.

The marketing plan should contain the following:

- Executive summary giving the highlights of the plans, especially the control points.
- General and competitive environment factors, new products from competition, market growth forecasts and summary of the findings of marketing research.
- Comparative statement of strengths and weaknesses of the firm vis-à-vis competitors, with emphasis on the customer benefits derived from the usage of products from the firms, both its own and competitors.
- Profitable sales plan for the entire product available for sale, either by manufacture or by purchase, taking the 4 Ps and the people into account.
- Fixing individual quantitative and qualitative targets, qualitative targets could be in the nature of continuous training programs, market feedbacks.
- Profit picture derived out of sales revenue and marketing expense budgets.

The word strategy is more commonly used in planning by the defence forces. In the same parlance, marketing in severe competitive markets is like facing a war like situation where the competitor is ready to gobble up firms not ready to face them. It becomes a do or die situation and hence all the possible loopholes need to be plugged, which becomes easy by using a systematic planning and control approach.

Tasks for the students- locate the changes taking place in the business environment and discuss how firms can take full advantage of the same, despite severe competition in the market place.

Market Information—As Competitive Advantage

In the first half of twentieth century all the information needed for management decisions came from the Sales team, who were considered as the eyes and ears of the firm, and gathered the same. Today in the beginning of the twenty first century, the Information required by the management is immense and the information available also is huge. Naturally, the management wants to have all possible relevant information before taking decisions. International Marketing Research is one tool for gathering data, sifting it and isolating the relevant information. Information Technology has progressed so fast that it has in many cases taken over the primary responsibility of business decisions.

Competitive Advantage: The firm, which has obtained accurate and timely information, gains the Competitive Advantage over other competing firms. Indian business and economy today is on the threshold of information revolution. Information converted in to knowledge provides the firm with the power, which it can use to overcome obstacles in its way and dominate the market. Therefore information or knowledge is an asset in its own right.

Information can be defined as, "organized, structured data relevant to the firm and hence having meaning and utility for the firm" thus the value of the information can be quantified to remove the abstract ideas attached to it. The decision depending on the information has a value to the firm. Focusing on this aspect it should be easy for the firm to assign a value to the data. In this context market research is undertaken by firms at a price. Firms try to locate previous similar situations and data connected with them, from secondary sources. They go to the customers and ask direct questions to gather data, which can be converted in to information and knowledge for decision-making.

The information helps in decision making with both in upstream operations, in transactions with the suppliers and downstream in transactions with the buyers. Beyond buying and selling the information about the suppliers and the buyers stays in the data bank including transaction details and actual situation negotiations leading to the transaction, which is frequently updated.

The stored information can in many cases prove to be a money-spinner if properly utilized as follows:

- Higher profits from sales, because of the ability to sell more units per sale, have bigger sale volumes, charge higher prices due to information on the customer and also due to customization of product and service and outbound logistics.

- Lower material cost, through information on the suppliers, organization of Just in Time supplies, bulk ordering for lower price, economic inventory levels and inbound logistics.
- Marketing of the information itself to other firms (may not be in direct competition with the firm).

It may not be easy to quantify the net gains of information as given above but with time it is quite possible to develop a mathematical model, which would calculate the extra gains. In order that the information remains profitable it has to remain updated and therefore the Information Mission should create an infrastructure for Information Continuum information helps firms in better transaction management and yet it remains in the background of quotations, delivery periods and payments. Information on customer real needs, buying habits, personality types provide a backdrop for the dealings with the customers. In this context it becomes imperative that the information is authentic and in real time. It helps in value addition to the customers and therefore brings extra profits to the sellers as follows:

Customized product for the target market segment comes through knowledge of the segment. The sellers get better market share, can ask for higher prices and still keep the customers satisfied and delighted. The firm can reduce the selling cost, cost of advertisements and distribution by making the product more purchasable.

Looking at the BCG Matrix the market position of products is located on the level of market growth and firms market share. Since the upheavals in the market place are taking place much faster now than ever before, there is the need to have the most recent information. With more use the information gives better results. Being useful in a time frame only there is an element of urgency, both in obtaining the information and in using the same. The firm, which does it better and faster, is usually the winner. The timeframe between a product moving from question mark quadrant to Star and from Star to Cash Cow is shortening due to information about new customer needs and new product developments, both being interrelated. By the same theory products land up faster in the Dog quadrant now. The Product Life Cycle is shortening because of the Information Revolution.

Table 7.4. BCG Matrix

HIGH	STAR	QUESTION MARK
MARKET GROWTH		
LOW	CASH COW	COW DOG
FIRM'S MARKET SHARE	HIGH	LOW

With real time availability of information about customers preferences, major, minor modifications, customization of product becomes inevitable, causing the shortening the life cycle of the products. Management therefore must give great consideration to the higher rate of obsolescence of product while taking the basic investment decisions on manufacturing goods. More firms may opt for outsourcing the product or at least the subassemblies to reduce the capital costs. It has also spurred the R&D efforts of the firms, which are required to keep the firm abreast with the latest market needs.

A major change occurring as a result is the definition of the industry; it is now defined in terms of market or customer needs and not in terms of product specifications and its benefits to the customer. Competition from firms other than conventional competitors is going to be a direct threat as information rich competitors can always redefine its products to suit the customer more than the firm's product. (Readymade cooked food cans compete with raw materials like pulses, flour, vegetables, meat, fish and poultry.)

It is therefore better to define customer and market needs, buying characteristics, consumer behaviour of the target market segment and match these with the product characteristics and benefits occurring to the customers from the product rather than going about it in the reverse order of first selecting the product characteristics and benefits and than trying to match these with the customer and market demands. The difference may appear trivial. But in today's context it is vital for the success of the firm.

Information base has changed the distribution system in some products. Where time is of vital importance, like airline bookings, computer communications have taken over the booking counters. In case of physical goods too, online sales, auctions may remove the need of supermarkets, drug stores and over the counter sales. One can imagine the non-necessity of distribution channels, huge market complexes, and increase in profit margins by virtue of non-payment of commission to the channel members. The benefits could be passed on to the customers or kept by the firm for diversification and growth.

Distribution Channels: The role of distribution channels has been of sellers of products only. The sooner they assume additional role of information provider about the authentic market demands, consumer behaviour patterns and buying habits the faster the channel members will find themselves back in to the thick of the firm's business. Multi-brand dealers will ultimately have to choose their favourite brand, to which they would provide with real time information and may drop representing the other firms.

Advertising and Promotion: A knowledge of customer's mindset, his aspirations values and desires would enable the sellers to communicate with him bettering an appropriate language, provide the right incentives during promotions and get better results. Advertising agencies are on the look out for such information and they pay well to the research agencies to acquire the information.

MIS: Computers have made the information banks a reality and real time information update is happening today. The IT Revolution is changing the market place, buyers attitudes in time saving Internet purchases, and much more is happening every day in this area. Cell phones, mobile Internet, business transactions on cell phones SMS are slowly but surely ruffling the business feathers, and firms would ignore these paradigm shifts at their own risk.

Question for Discussion

Discuss the ways IT Revolution can be harnessed to help the business to the advantage of the firm.

MANAGEMENT GAME

The students should learn the Mackenzie's 7S Model and use it in the Game as given below:

The best way to look at the imperative of improving performance is through the Mackenzie's 7S Model, which is given below:

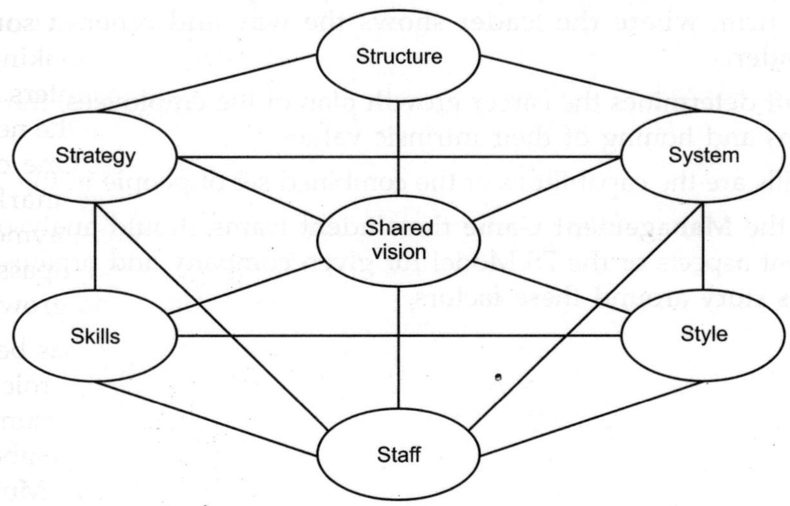

Fig. 7.4. 7S Model

The model has Shared Vision at the centre, and the other remarkable thing about it is that each of the Ss is interconnected with no hierarchy about them.

Shared Vision or the Super Ordinate Goals are of higher order, which go beyond profit, ROI, growth and similar economic or financial measures. They are certain guiding concepts – a set of values and aspirations often unwritten, that go beyond conventional formal statements of quantified corporate goals and objectives.

Mahatma Gandhi's vision was of India with its heart in the villages, as he believed that unless the villages prosper India couldn't become prosperous.

JRD Tata's vision for India was that of an industrially developed nation.

Dabur's vision is the Ayurvedic resurrection in India.

7S Model

Strategy is a set of actions, plans and policies aimed at obtaining sustainable competitive advantage for the firm.

Structures show the firms reporting line up, the organization chart, functional divisions and their integration.

System gives the flow chart of operations, the processes; quality control system, manufacturing process, information system.

Style shows the working philosophy, the time management, and behaviour with seniors, juniors and the peer group by the personnel of the firm, where the leader shows the way and others emulate the leader.

Staff determines the career growth plan of the employees, training patterns and honing of their intrinsic values.

Skills are the capabilities of the combined set of people in the firm.

In the **Management Game** the student teams should analyse the different aspects of the 7S Model for given company and organise its success story around these factors.

CHAPTER 8

Business-to-Business Marketing Specifics

AIMS AND OUTCOMES OF THE CHAPTER

B-to-B marketing has several variants as well as approaches to combat competition. The way business marketing is conducted, its various manifestations are discussed in the chapter to equip the students with skills, knowledge and gives a practical exposure on the subject.

Marketing discipline in the twenty-first century focusses on the customer, instead of manufacturing, which was the companies' major strengths in the last century, at least in its first half. Competition has given the buyers several options for making purchases. Customer satisfaction has become the driving force for the companies. With opening up of markets and economy India has opened its doors to foreign players in practically every field of human activity and business. Companies that can innovate products and service, maintain their quality and remain customer oriented are more likely to succeed than others. It is the cutting edge of technology, new distribution patterns, latest communication techniques that would govern the fortunes of the companies.

Industrial sellers have to understand clearly the customers needs and only then can they organize a perfect fit for the same using their products, as it is or its modified version, provided the demand of the modified product is sufficient to justify the effort of the modification. Product demand and demand projections are of vital importance in product decisions. At times, the new version may sell much more because there may be latent demand for it that surfaces once it is introduced in the market, as can be seen from the following:

1. Existing product-competitive product/s-comparative assessment
2. Best fit as per customer requirement
3. Assessment of modification needs, if any

4. Redesign the product-test it with the customers' requirements
5. Give samples for trials with the customers
6. Get customer's feedback and act on it
7. Get a long-range business perspective for the product

Companies have to keep analyzing the market dynamics to get a good understanding of their market share and then decide if they are comfortable with it or want to increase it. Increasing market share would involve increased expenses on marketing, including advertising, personal selling and added commission to the middlemen. At times it may be a wise choice to lie low on market share as the company makes better profits at least on temporary basis. Market volumes could increase when the total market goes up. Profits could increase with lower marketing costs too.

In industrial business, market persons have to keep their eyes and ears open to locate business opportunities as and when they show up. Missed opportunities can prove to be costly lapses for the company.

In the first half of the twentieth century, industrial sellers used to look for new chimneys on the industrial belts, as they would indicate new business opportunities for them. Marketing research was conducted by the travelling salesmen who were trained to locate chimneys, besides new industrial estates. For specific product groups companies would organize secondary research usually from the government records, DAVP publications, industrial product user companies balance sheets.

Once the company had located a business opportunity it had to understand if its core competencies match with the customer's requirements. Companies also needed to know the value of the customer to the company, on a time frame, like short term, medium and long-term basis, as it would provide it with a yardstick for making marketing plans for the customer.

Industrial selling is of two types as given below:

1. Product sales
2. Selling of solutions

As companies are planning relationship building with the customers, it is better to sell solutions rather than more products.

Example

In the first half of the last century, the oil companies were selling lubricating oils to the industry. One oil company became a pioneer in selling solutions, rather than oils. It would not only train the customers' engineers in proper lubrication methods but also work out an oiling programme that would bring about the top most efficiency in the oiled machines and reduce oil consumption by proper time scheduling. As the oil company gave these savings in rupees to the customer the business was of the oil company for decades.

In B-to-B business at times extra investments are required. The company must organize a value analysis of the business before committing the supplies to the customer. The analysis would enable the company realize the real worth of the business as compared to the expense involved. At times the newly generated business could help the company in opening up businesses in same industry group with no extra effort or resource allocation as a spin off.

A good marketer would look for improvement opportunities in his customer's organization, when he visits even on routine calls. For example a salesperson found that the security of his customer's premises was not good enough. He immediately advised his colleague of his security division with a request that he should visit the customer at once. As the opportunity is located, the company should locate and identify the core competencies within the company that would be useful in handling the customer for sales. Any deficiency in the competency should be augmented if the company really believes that the business is worth the expense.

Competitors and Their Advantage

After this SWOT analysis should be undertaken with regard to the competitors. Such analyses would disclose the competitive advantage associated with the company and its competitors. Company should understand any spin offs possible as a result of the business coming from the customer. It is essential that when company invests in improving its competencies it has to get the best from the changed strengths of the company. Before the investment is actually made it would be prudent to project the P&L statement in the new circumstances. Therefore it can be summarized that a company's marketing tasks starts with locating improvement opportunities and goes on a given below:

1. Improvement opportunities seen at the customer's premises.
2. Creation of opportunities based on intrinsic company's strengths and customers' known or even unknown needs.
3. Modification of applicable core competencies if required.

4. Locating other areas of business that could benefit from the modifications.
5. Deriving a new P&L statement on its basis.
6. Funds allocation for carrying out the modification, if they are justified.

Success gained with the customers must be recorded and testimonial obtained from the customer. These testimonials play a vital role in B-to-B marketing, a "who says so" becomes the best sales pitch. Several advertisements carrying such testimonials can be seen in the press. However, any equipment that can save expenditure for the customer, like energy saving devices, theft protection, labour saving, that can be immediately converted into rupees saved have great sales appeal. Besides, products falling in the following categories too sell by customers' testimonials:

1. Products improving productivity
2. Products saving manufacturing time
3. Products saving inventory space
4. Products from Just in Time suppliers
5. Products that add prestige value to the purchaser in the company
6. Products that are lower in cost than competitive products and yet do the job equally well.

Suppliers to the water and power supply systems are well aware that the need for these products is growing rapidly in the country and there is no need for creation of demand for products associated with these areas. However, for most products the general awareness is limited and hence, there is need for exploring industries where the product could be used in the following manner:

From the stage of no demand companies have to take these steps-

1. To creation of demand through product information, benefit story associated with the product, (the benefits customers would derive from the use of the product).
2. Demonstrate the benefits to the customers along with the value product purchase would create for the firm (like lowering production cost and time, ease of inventory management and the prestige that comes from the purchase of the product for the buyer and his company).
3. Modify or create new products based on the demand or the latent demand in the industrial market.

4. Plan strategy for marketing including pricing, service and distribution channels best suited for the customers.

Customers are always trying to find out possible options before they make the purchase decision. The company would do well if it can offer some alternatives from his own product range. Products could be meant for cost reduction in the customer's production process, save manufacturing time, reduce manufacturing steps.

It must be understood clearly that the customers do not exist for the company. The company has to exist for the customers. The markets, where the customers exist are eternal, the product demand keeps changing as does the rest of the marketing mix factors, but it exists nevertheless. It is for the company to take best advantage the market offers by being on its right side, by offering products closest to the customer's needs; (the limiting factor could be technology or materials availability) one way is to differentiate the product by adding value to it as per the customers needs.

For example, a shampoo can be made to put sheen on the hair in addition to cleaning, the back seat of a car can be made to tilt backwards. This would to convert it to become a bed for long distance travel.

B-to-B marketing advantage

It comes from the following areas:

1. Customer satisfaction
2. Customer relationship management
3. Providing options to the customers
4. Add value to the product
5. Prompt supplies or Just in Time supplies if required

Companies have come to realize that unless they can gain customers' confidence through, product quality and product's perceivable benefits, better than competitor's, customer service support, they have little chance of gaining customer loyalty.

Customer Orientation

It is imperative that not just the marketing team, but the entire organization becomes customer oriented. Organizational structure should be cantered towards meeting the customer's requirements. Organizational culture should provide synergic empathy with the customers. These are important areas that have been neglected so far by most companies. The following examples would further clarify the methods of becoming customer oriented for different company disciplines.

HR and administration—to ensure that persons recruited in various disciplines of the company are fully aware of the focus the company keeps on the customers. Its administration team should protect and show courtesy to the visitors to the company including the customers.

Finance should help the marketing team in suggesting the best payment options, including leasing, deferred payment and advise the customers through the marketing team the pros and cons of each method. Correct billing, proper records of customer transactions and detailed account of outstanding dues would further help the company in maintaining good relationship with customers, without causing embarrassment to them. For example when the customer has delayed payment, harsh words could alienate him away from the company and he may land up in competitors camp. Instead a polite but firm letter could help solve the tangle.

Over Selling

In the B-to-B marketing salespersons tend to oversell the company. They promise options, product specifications and terms of business that cannot be sustained by the company.

1. Salesperson tells the customer, "We can offer diesel model of the car in the next two weeks", when the company has no plan to make the diesel model.
2. Customer gets the option of mobile phone with camera and blue tooth when the company can give only with camera.
3. Customer is told he need not pay a down payment for the product and give only in instalments, when the company rules do not permit such credit at all.
4. A customer buying an air conditioning plant is given commissioning date of the plant when the company knows fully well that it would not be possible to adhere to that date.

It is always prudent to offer less and deliver more; this way the customer would feel delighted and look forward to doing further business with the company. Wrong information can at the best give temporary advantage to the company, as when the truth comes out it would have lost a customer. At times salespersons promise a tight delivery schedule to put pressure on to the manufacturing unit. However, it is best if these pressure tactics are used only for internal use and not for the customers.

Other problem of overselling comes when the company brings out a new improved product and the salesperson has so strongly sold the old product that the company would find it difficult to compete with the own obsolete product. Heavy advertising, personal selling and customer testimonials serve as selling tools in such cases.

With rapid technological advances taking place in practically all, the different business areas the PLC has been reducing dramatically in the twenty-first century. New product do not have a proven track record that makes it more difficult for the companies to put them in customers' mindset, displacing their own products or competitive products.

Companies need to realize that while business terms like credit, installment payments, accessories available are good selling points, the most important customer consideration is the product specification and what benefits they can obtain from the same. Once the customer accepts that the product does to job as the customer expects it to do, other terms are the icing on the cake only. Consequently if the product does not perform as required then the rest of the terms of business are of no value at all.

Different Approach to B-to-B Marketing

Consumer marketing and industrial marketing differ in several ways. Industrial buyer looks for benefits that accrue from the product usage where as consumer buyers want good "value for money". Industrial buyers are interested in the following benefits from the product:

1. Low overall purchase cost
2. Ease of storage
3. Easy inventory management
4. Ease of product usage
5. Training by the seller in product usage
6. Longer shelf life of the product
7. Just in Time supplies by the seller, if required to keep current assets low and improve cash flow

Industrial selling market segmentation is based on the industries that would use the product and their location. However, consumer segments are mainly based on demographics and psychographics of the consumers.

Industrial customers stake in the purchase is high as his entire production could depend on it. Purchase managers are the persons put on the mat for wrong or high cost purchases. Industrial sellers, therefore have a major responsibility to ensure that the product they sell is best for use by the buyers, adds to the prestige of the buyer as a mature and responsible buyer. In case of "Project or turn key operations" the buyers place their entire trust on the suppliers/turnkey operators. Industrial purchase is made to increase productivity, get better manufacturing technology, expand production base, improve profitability and for growth. Consumers buy products for their personal use for adding to their comforts and making a lifestyle statement.

Industrial buyers look for the economics of purchase through the change in the Internal Rate of Return of expense incurred in making the purchase. Besides, business needs of updating, expansion, improving productivity and ease of maintaining the manufacturing units are the other reasons for making purchases. Purchase committees comprising the following—take purchase decisions, especially of high cost purchases:

1. Purchase Manager acts as the convener of the committee.
2. Finance Manager to look after the cost to the company with comparisons of different bids .
3. Technical Manager to evaluate the technical aspects of the bids
4. R&D Manager for looking at the technology to ascertain if it is the latest, "State of the Art" one.
5. Production Manager to understand the way the product can be used and to ensure it matches with the existing systems. If there is no match then he should be comfortable that the seller would provide him or her the training needed for proper usage of the product.
6. The sellers have to convince these people through personal presentations, dialogues and testimonials from other important customers those using the product. The process is, therefore, slow, drawn out and laborious. However, once the company receives the order it adds a lot to the revenue of the company.
7. In most cases the buyers analyse the offers received from the different suppliers in two stages, one, the technical aspects. Any offer that does not meet with the technical requirements of the buyers can be removed from the further analysis. Next, the buyers analyse the commercial part of the bid that gives the prices and terms of business. As the remaining all bidders meet the technical requirements, of the company that has given the lowest price and best terms, gets the order.
8. Buyers place a lot of stress on the maintainability or the ease of maintenance, the support the supplier can provide to them in this respect.

9. Sellers need to understand the psyche of the buyers' team involved in the buying decision and cater to each individually as well as collectively to support those psychological needs. Each person needs to be given adequate personal attention and presales service.
10. Sellers must realize that each customer in the industrial business is unique and no mass selling technique would work for them.

B-to-B Advertising

B-to-B advertising is important mainly for creating awareness about the company, improving its corporate brand image and for providing products technical specifications. Companies can opt for technical journals pertaining to the buyers business as media, besides, at times newspapers, and TV can also be used. TV has the advantage that product usage can be demonstrated on it. Companies can organize product presentations for one or a few customers that operate in the same area. While personal selling plays a major role in B-to-B marketing, advertising cannot be ruled out at all. Companies may find their customers in clusters, lie the textile mills in Ahmedabad, steel plants in Bihar, and sugar mills in west UP, and Maharashtra and therefore advertising needs to be used for company's image building and building brand equity. TV advertising that addresses the top executives can use the time slot along with the news and use FM Radio that these people listen to during driving to and from their offices.

B-to-B Pricing

Pricing strategy is of the foremost importance because in the competitive business buyers prefer the low cost supplier, everything else being common. However, the buyers must be made aware of certain hidden costs that do not get reflected in the quotations some companies submit. These hidden costs could be as given below:

1. Cost of certain spare parts essential to the product
2. Cost of accessories required
3. Cost of transportation
4. Cost of installation and commissioning of the equipment purchased
5. Cost of training of the buyers personnel into proper usage of the product
6. Cost of user manuals and other documents

In most cases companies must work out pricing formula individually for each bid they make because each case is different. Some of the reasons of the differences are given below:

1. Customer's location and its distance from the sellers place to work out the actual transport costs to the customer.
2. Cost of mobilisation of resources, including manpower at the customer's site.
3. Cost of pipelines, ducting, power needs, water supply required and local labour force costs.
4. Cost of taxes to be paid in the customer's location (for example, CST if the customer's premises are in different state than the seller's location).

Besides, the company must know the usual price quoted by competition and work up their own competitive advantage for each of the bids they make, along with competitive pricing. Companies should be aware that in most bids, there are negotiations held by the buyer with each bidder and hence, they should keep room for manoeuvring during negotiations.

Companies can take advantage of the latest technology they may have obtained that would give them competitive advantage without price reductions.

The bids must contain special mention of the increase in profitability and productivity as a result of the purchase of product by the buyers. The customers are looking for low cost solutions for improving their efficiency, enhancing returns, having easy operations that would result in increase in business. It should have a low payout period too. And these areas should be stated in the bids in prominent places.

The company can, however, charge a skimming price under the following circumstances:

1. If the product is unique and useful to the customer
2. If the company has a dominant brand equity
3. If the buyer has bought it earlier with full satisfaction
4. If it becomes part of a major system in the buyer's manufacturing unit.

B-to-B Payment Terms

Industrial customers tend to prefer buying products, especially the capital equipment on credit and the company offering longer credit period is usually preferred, if other terms are similar between competitors. Credit period is often the area where companies negotiate to get the best terms. Long credit means investment by the seller and therefore is expensive. Yet, companies can reduce their risk as well as financial involvement by making a bank offer credit a in case of leasing where the title of goods remain in joint custody that of the buyer and the bank. Bill discounting is another method where bills are drawn on the buyer and paid by the bank before the due date when the customer pays the amount to the bank. Of course the bank charges is interest for this facility. The bank credit is offered on hypothecation of the equipment purchased by the amount loaned by the bank. The buyer looks at the investments from the viewpoint of gaining business growth and higher rate of returns. The importance of industrial purchase comes from the money involved in the transactions and a wrong purchase can land the buyer in serious trouble, as the cost of replacement is high, selling price of used equipment low. The buyer also has to pay double the transaction cost including taxation, profits. The buyer may lose production time due to shut down of the production plant due to the incorrect purchase of high value. This could cause catastrophe of immense magnitude for the buyer.

B-to-B marketing calls for greater degree of company's commitment towards the customer. FMCG sellers just sell their products to the buyers and the replacement cost of products that do not satisfy the customer is low. At best toothpaste can be discarded by the buyer who loses thirty to forty rupees only. However in case of capital goods, the replacement cost could be into region of lacs of rupees. Most capital goods are sold on the basis of sale of total package consisting of the following:

1. Equipment
2. Necessary accessories
3. Recommended spare parts
4. Installation and commissioning with the required piping, ducting
5. Training of buyers personnel in proper use and maintenance of the equipment
6. Field trials wherever required
7. Guarantee and warranty service of the equipment.

It can be safely confirmed that once a company gets a purchase order of turnkey project unless he is totally committed to the project he can never deliver the project to the entire satisfaction of the buyer. The turkey operations are long-term business cooperation between buyers and the sellers. It should offer a good profit margin to the seller and a good amount of peace of mind and satisfaction to the buyers. Project business is also time sensitive and the seller has to ensure timely delivery of the project. Sellers have to ensure availability of repair and maintenance facility during the life of the products used in the turnkey project, availability of spare parts.

B-to-B buyers usually purchase the following type of products:

1. Turnkey project
2. Individual equipments
3. Spare parts
4. Accessories
5. Components and sub-assemblies
6. Products in semi knocked down—SKD condition
7. Products in completely knocked down—CKD condition

The most critical of these is the turnkey operations. Equipment sale is more based on the required specifications, maintainability of the equipment and its price, besides the facility for servicing it by the seller.

Spare parts, sub-assemblies and accessories are normally required by the buyer on a time-based plan. These give higher margin of profits than even the equipments, because these are essential for the continuous use of the equipment and are available only from the seller. However, the seller should not think of profiteering as too high a profit margin could lead to disenchantment with the seller and the buyer may just snap ties with him.

Component suppliers have the option of selling directly to the buyers or go through the distribution route. The low cost components like nuts and bolts are sold through the distribution channels, while car engines, seats could be sold directly to the buyers. Such sales are known as sales to OEMs—the Original Equipment Manufacturers. Certain components like tyres, tubes are sold both in the reseller market through channel members and directly to the OEMs of cars.

SKD and CKD products are usually sold internally in one company that may have separate business units for manufacturing different phases of the product and company may just have a transaction or transfer cost to gauge profit accruing to different units.

Buyers Purchase Viewpoint

Buyers need to go in for new products, capital equipments, when their old equipment becomes obsolete or a new technology emerges that will give the company boost in productivity, improvement in product quality, lowering the rejection rates. When new strong competitor enters the market (as happened in India after 1991 when the government opened the doors for international players to enter the country with their products). At such times it is not only imperative for the company to modernize its equipment but it becomes a matter for its very survival in the market.

Companies want to grow in the market and for this reason they go for additional, preferably more modern equipment to increase their production and productivity. They decide on the equipments to be purchased on the following criteria:

1. Operational ease
2. Reduction in production cycle time and costs
3. For obtaining competitive advantage
4. For being able to use suppliers service facilities
5. Products that have low payback periods
6. Products used by other major companies, as it adds prestige to the buying process

B-to-B buyers purchase decisions are taken through their hierarchy as given below:

1. Low value orders are decided by the Purchase Officers
2. Purchase or Materials Managers decides slightly higher value orders
3. Real high value orders are looked at by an evaluation committee that advises the purchase committee

The Purchase Committee consists of the following members of the buyer's team—

1. Managing Director—who chairs the committee
2. Technical Manager who looks at the technical aspects of the bids
3. Finance Manager who scrutinizes the financial implications of the bids
4. R&D Manager who decides if the product is latest "State of the Art" product or not
5. Production Manager who looks at the product from the point of its match with the rest of the existing equipment and its ease of use
6. Purchase Manager or the Materials Manager who is usually the convener of the committee

A good Marketing Manager would get persons from his own company to sell the product, one to one to each of these persons from the buyer's team. For instance, he would do the selling job with the purchase manager, and let others interact as given below:

Table 8.1. Negotiating Teams

Sellers Team	*Buyers Team*
M.D.	M.D.
Technical Manager	Technical Manager
Finance Manager	Finance Manager
R&D Manager	R&D Manager
Production Manager	Technical and Systems Managers
Purchase Manager	Marketing Manager

In each of the above, the seller's team member has to convince his counterpart about the benefits of the product as per the mindset of the person. Therefore, the decision taken by the B-to-B buyer is based on several layers of persons in the purchase committee and the technical experts of the buyer's team. Once such rapport is built between the seller and the buyer it brings about customer's loyalty, that goes to the extent of the customer recommending the company to other customers of the same products and customer giving testimonials to the seller that could be used to get business from other customers. Finally, a good product well accepted by the customer, service to the customer beyond his expectations, exceeding satisfaction levels and breaking into the arena of providing customers delight would in turn build a lasting relationship between the buyer and the seller. When the seller provides good service, the buyer becomes emotionally attached and sentimental about the company. This attachment does not break easily unless of course, the seller's personnel do something silly to alienate the buyer. Simple courtesy does not cost anything and yet it can build bridges, strengthen relationships and make the customer play in the hands of the seller. The sellers should make the buyers feel that the sellers are their unobtrusive appendages, almost in their backyard, ready to help out in any situation through thick and thin at any hour of day or night. Such loyalty from the sellers would invoke similar loyalty from the buyers as well. It is rightly said, "What goes around, comes around". Conversely, if the seller shows indifference or disdain towards the buyer at any point overtly or even covertly, it would surely mean disaster in the relationship between the two and the seller can then just forget about doing any business with the customer completely. If the seller has delighted the customer once, or on a day, it means practically nothing because competition is always aggressively pursuing the customer who can be persuaded by the competition to change sides. There is no let up possible in continuous relationship building exercise and actions for the customers' well being by the seller as possible. And that would only keep the seller proactively involved in the right way with the buyers.

MARKET DEMAND

Demands of B-to-B business are generated in the most unpredictable manner and hence demand analysis by the sellers is a difficult task. The sellers have to keep their eyes and ears open all the time, besides they have to keep assessing the demand looking at the following areas:

1. Customer's plans of expansion, renovation and modernisation
2. Historical business numbers
3. Business or demand trends as predicted by the industry pundits, magazines and journals.
4. New government rules, regulations and policies
5. New substitute products in the market
6. Demand of the customer's product that uses the company's product

B-to-B demand is a derived demand based on the demand for the final product being made by the customer. For example the sale of tyres to OEMs, the car manufacturers depend on the demand for cars. The demand of cars depends on the levels of various indices, like the GNP, GDP and Per Capita Income. Besides the CRR-Cash Reserve Ratio that has a bearing on the market money supply position, and the borrowing rate of interest would guide the demand for cars. The interesting thing about the business is that while the demand is based on the vagaries of the industries growth, the selling has to be done to the individual members of the buying teams.

B-to-B demand being derived from the demand of final product depends on the macroeconomic factors, the GDP, GNP Per Capita Income and interest rates for borrowing and microeconomic factors like disposable income with the buyers of the final product. The demand can also be influenced by inflation rates, investment climate and global "supply and demand" paradigm.

It is therefore important to find out where the market exists. One should seek answers to questions like—

- Who wants the product
- When does he want it
- Where does he want it

- What price he is willing to pay for it
- What is the purpose for which he is buying the product
- What does the product do for him in his life
- What are the factors influencing the purchase
- Who is the competitor
- What are his plans.

For each firm, there are the following categories of customers:

- The buyers
- The non-buyers who buy competitive products
- The non-buyers who do not buy the product at all
- The non-buyers who buy the product only rarely
- The vacillators who keep shifting purchase between the firm and competition.

How does the customer work out the value and economies as compared to his satisfaction levels with different products? We have to really know our customers and prospective customers who are buying from competitors today.

It can thus be assumed that it is the knowledge about various elements of business, which is critical to the success of the firm. The knowledge needed is in the following areas:

- Own products, their plus and minus points
- Competitor's products, their plus and minus points
- Niche market, and its business potential
- Relevant customer group, the buyers, users and the purchase decision makers
- Market dynamics.

The knowledge needs to be used for, first understanding the market and then planning strategies for achieving leadership position in the market. The knowledge should lead to excellence in operations of the firm else; leadership position will remain a pipe dream only. Profits, on a continued basis result from application of the specialized knowledge by the members of the firm. Excellence in core areas like technology, marketing, finance, government liaison or human resource management is typical of all top-notch firms. The firm need not be large in size, but some core competencies will lead it to a high profit area. What the firm does well and what it does poorly are known facts to the firm and if it wishes it can make the weak areas as strong as others, with determination and will power.

Let us discuss some of the knowledge areas, which help in achieving success—

- Knowledge of own business can be easily understood as the areas of excellence within the firm. Some firms excel in marketing, others in new product development, and yet some pride themselves in the quality of their products and their operations. Knowledge of firm's core competence is important
- Knowledge of customer needs, both specified or known and unspecified, becomes essential for business development.
- Knowledge of "the state of art technology" relevant to the firm.
- Knowledge of competition, their products, markets, technology, core competence and business methods is a must to counter competition.

It must be understood that knowledge is true only for a short period of time and it must be updated for it to remain valid and useful.

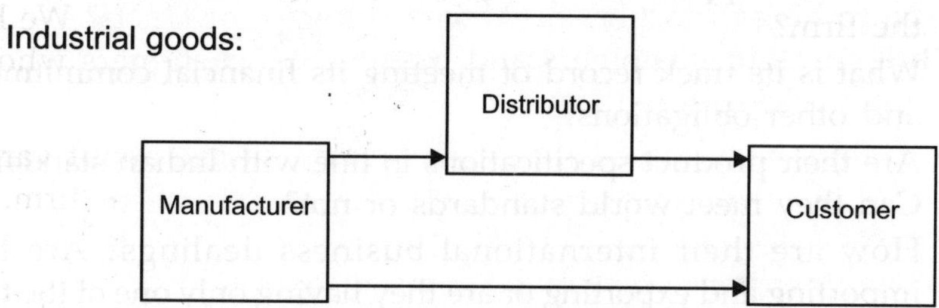

Fig. 8.1. B to B Channel

As can be seen, in industrial goods, the sale is made either directly to the customer or through a distributor. Capital goods sale is usually made directly to the customer, because of the following reasons:

- Technicalities have to be explained to the customer, which are best done by the manufacturer.
- Mostly large sums of money are involved and customer wants best price without middleman's commission.
- Installation and commissioning of the equipment is involved, best done by the manufacturer's engineers.
- After sales service is complicated.

In case of sale of Raw Materials and components the manufacturers sell through a distributor network the size of which is finalized taking the geographic area, which needs to be covered by the manufacturer.

Competitive Analysis

Next let us look at the analysis to be done for the competitors. The firm must know, who are its competitors. There are direct and indirect competitors for most of the firms. The study of competitors is most useful if it is done with the customer-based approach. Once the firm has identified its direct competitors in the first instant, it is useful to evaluate **each of the competitors** on the following parameters—

- What are their business goals and objectives?
- What is the commitment level of the managers and stakeholders of the firms in competition?
- How do the managers of the firm view its growth prospects? Have they at any time considered its closure? What are the barriers to its exiting from the business?
- What is its cost structure, financial structure, cash flow position, assets and liabilities.
- How its suppliers, financiers and distribution system view the firm?
- What is its track record of meeting its financial commitments and other obligations?
- Are their product specifications in line with Indian standards? Can they meet world standards or not?
- How are their international business dealings? Are they importing and exporting or are they having only one of the two?
- Where have they positioned their product, is it up-market or for the masses? Is the product pricing in line with their product positioning?
- Are their advertising and promotional efforts congruent with their product positioning?
- How is the firm's Public Relations effort rated?
- How is the firm's Brand Equity rated?
- What are the firm's core competencies?
- What are the firm's strengths and weaknesses?
- What are the firms unmet needs as far as the customers are concerned? Unmet needs are because of, (a) customers dissatisfaction of the product, (b) customers problems. There are unmet needs of which the customer is aware and there are some of which the customers may not be even aware. Competitors take advantage by advertising their own met needs and firms unmet needs of the customers.

It is useful to do a SWOT Analysis at this stage for each of the competitors.

To sum up the following is the table for different types of analyses:

Table 8.2. Business Analysis

Market Analysis	*Firm's Analysis*	*Competitive Analysis*	*Competitive Analysis*
1. Size of the market	1. Level of customer satisfaction	1. Sales performance	9. Capacity /its utilization
2. Growth prospects	2. Brand loyalty	2. Market share	10. Product-wise market share
3. Profitability	3. Product quality	3. Brand equity status	11. Segmentwise sales
4. Cost structure	4. Service quality	4. Objectives/ goals	12. Channels/ sales force
5. Channels	5. Brand association	5. Marketing strategies	13. Advertising/ promotion
6. Trends	6. Relative costs	6. Organizational culture	14. Reaction time
7. Key Success Factors	7. New product activities	7. Cost structure	15. Experience barriers curve/exit
	8. Managers capabilities and performance	8. Strenghts and weaknesses	16. Value chain

Once the systems are put in place these activities mentioned in the table become automatic and they do not take much time, while they do provide the vital information for making strategic marketing decisions.

For example, the capabilities of a firm could include its financial strength; marketing base and its constraints could be lack of motivation in the personnel. The analysis should take the Core Competencies in to account.

Competitors analysis requires the prudent use of secondary and primary information to determine current and likely strategies. Customers can be employed to classify uses and benefits of products and to rank the competitors.

Let us see the **Assets and Skills** grid for competitors. These can be divided in to two parts as follows:

1. Primary—product development, product quality, product manufacturing cost, product differentiation, customer satisfaction and market share.
2. Secondary—flexi-production, financial muscle, sales force, distribution network, brand image/equity, advertising and promotion, quality of service and growth of the market for the product.

Business-to-Business or Industrial Segmentation

Industries buy raw materials and components from suppliers. The suppliers segment their customers as follows:

- Company size—the larger the company the more product it is likely to buy, be better paymaster (as it has to keep its name as a good company). Sometimes medium size companies prove to be good as they are trying to grow and their reputation is vital for them.
- Innovative companies—they have the lead user concept, want to be the first users of the product. Small companies have the advantage of being flexible in their production and other plans

Let us examine some of the areas the sales person of the twentieth century has to cover, either singly or as a team. The following give an idea of the activities connected with the Sales Persons:

- Order taker—the role of order taker for the sales person is age old conventional. In the early twentieth century the salesman (there were hardly any sales girls at that time), were carrying their ware with them to show samples to the customers and to demonstrate if the product called for the same. In fact co-passengers, while travelling in a train, mistook an oil company salesman for a masseur as he was carrying small sample bottles of lubricating oil.
- Delivery Sales Person—for products of mass consumption like milk, fuel the salesman carries the product in tankers and makes a sale by down loading the same at the customer's premises in his containers.
- Sales Promoter—the person does not take orders from the customers. He only makes the customer interested in the product with the help of demonstrations and discussions. Pharmaceutical firms have these types of Medical supervisors who meet with the doctors with product literature and samples and tries to convince the doctor to prescribe the medicine.

- Technical Sales Person—he is usually an engineer who has proficiency in optimizing the usage of the product and he works with the customers' engineers as their technical support person.
- Demand Manager—the sales person is required to create demand by concept selling, demonstrations and product promotions.
- Solution Giver—has the answers to customer's problems. He works like an applications laboratory whose job is to tackle live problems and provide answers. He is a big aid to the order taker salesman.
- Overseas Salesman—who handles international business for the firm. His main job is to sell the Country first and bring India's Brand Equity on the top, before he can sell his products.

Business Scenario in India

While the Industrial Revolution had started in Europe in the eighteenth century it did not touch India till the period after country's independence in 1947, when the first Prime Minister Pandit Jawaharlal Nehru and the Government of India made the country a socialist republic, with emphasis on government's role in business and industry. A large number of Public Sector Undertakings were formed with government funding and management. Private sector companies were considered as dishonest and therefore there was a lot of government control with license and permit Raj. Without the approval of the government officers the private entrepreneur could not do any business. This led to rampant corruption and bribery as a means of getting things done speedily in the government offices. A new breed of Power Brokers emerged as go-betweens between business and the government. The only concession to private business was for the small-scale sector. Business suffered as the Public Sector firms could not bring about the needed economic growth and private sector was handicapped.

There were a few exceptions though, like the Bajaj group, the Reliance group, who forged ahead despite the hurdles. The early big names of Tata, Birla, Modi, Singhania, Bangur, to name a few, kept the struggle going.

It was only in 1991, that the government found itself on the back foot with regard to its Foreign Exchange reserves, which had reached an all time low. On the request of the Government of India, the World Bank and IMF agreed to provide loans on the condition that India opens it's business boundaries to international players. This resulted in the economic reforms stated above.

Now the present scene in India can be described as follows:

1. A good number of MNC's have started operating in the country.
2. Some Indian business have got foreign technology and finance.
3. Market growth has slowed down world wide and more so in India.
4. Stock market has been giving shocks with fluctuations and scams
5. Terrorism from across the border have further down swept the market.
6. Advertising and almost continuous promotion has become omnipresent.
7. Job market has slowed down both in India and elsewhere.
8. IT Industry has had a set back and is slowly recovering from it.
9. Lot of firms are busy in down sizing/right sizing their operations to remain out of the red.

What the future holds is difficult to predict. One thing, which can be said with certainty, is that while specialist managers will give way to generalists, innovation and quality will play a vital role in the success of any firm.

India is a vast country with lots of diversities. Punjab and Andhra are known as the granaries of India. Farm labour during harvesting season migrates to Punjab from Bihar. Bihar is a rich state in minerals including iron and coal. It boasts of large steel plants and yet it has remained largely under developed. Youths have taken to guns and there are a lot of Mafia gangs operating in Bihar. West Bengal and Kerala have had Marxist influence. West Bengal has suffered from labour unrest resulting in migration of industries from there, which was, at a time the industrial capital of the country. Kerala has the highest literacy rate in the country. Uttar Pradesh, Bihar and Madhya Pradesh were three largest states and now they have been bifurcated. Hopefully, this will help them in becoming better managed. Mumbai has emerged as the commercial capital and Bangalore as the IT capital of the country. Hyderabad is vying for the honour with Bangalore. Bangalore is a cosmopolitan city with good climate through out the year.

India has large disparities as far as personal incomes are concerned. More than seventy percent of population lives in villages, with farming as their source of income. With increase in population the land size per family gets smaller ever so often, resulting in lowering of per capita income and resultant migration from villages to towns. Metros like Delhi and Mumbai population increase has taken its toll on the civic services, which keep crumbling. With better health facilities, average age has increased and now India has a large population of senior citizens. Teen population has also increased with improved health care.

India has seen social evolution of women who are now taking active part in various activities. They can be seen in offices, politics, and defence services, practically in each sphere of human endeavour.

A good businessperson needs to keep a close watch over these happenings to trace business opportunities, as newer products are needed now with innovative ideas, better distribution and customer communication.

Indian business suffers from lack of awareness among international community about the quality of its products. A few black sheep who got orders from overseas by sending good samples and later on down grading product quality have tarnished country's image, which needs to be redeemed. Concentrated efforts by the government and industry are required for changing the India Brand image. We have many pluses like low cost labour, availability of raw materials and minerals and a large trained work force. Today Industry, Commerce and the Government are busy in trying to correct things and their effort needs to be strengthened and speeded up. Indian Embassies abroad play a vital role in projecting the right image of the country, its products and services in the countries they operate. They can also provide inputs to Indian business about product demand patterns overseas.

To take an example, Japanese embassy in India is doing a great job in helping Japanese business in locating business opportunities for Japanese firms. Besides, Japanese organization Jethro is providing the information on Indian industry. Japan also has a number of business liaison offices, which assist Japanese business in getting a foothold in India.

International business today needs continuous information on the following aspects for different countries:

- Changing Business environment of the country
- Product demand projection
- Competitive forces

This calls for continuous Marketing Research, and Indian business tries to organize it as required. Besides, the Government of India needs to reassess its efforts in building Brand India.

What Is Our Business?

At every stage we have to understand our business, where we stand and where we want to be? How are we doing in key areas of our business? The following need to be analyzed for making an assessment about the business:

- Profit and loss
- Resource allocation
- Product/s leadership position
- Profit centres
- Organisational structure

In business we convert resources and technological and market knowledge into increased economic value and thereby have a satisfied customer. It is knowledge which keeps firms afloat and lack of it make them sink. From this premise emerges the age-old saying that the **Customer is our Business.**

Manufacturer's perception of business is his product range, the market demand, competition and his market share. He sees it as an extension of his manufacturing and selling base. After all what he is making he is selling to the customers who are in the market for he same product. Today, the manufacturer wants his customer to be satisfied by his product. It is accepted that the customers do not buy a product. They buy the satisfaction they derive out of the product.

Customers however, view the business as market places with several players and thousands of products, some of which may provide them with a degree of satisfaction. They do not even know the number of sellers of a particular product unless they are going to buy the same, at which time they start looking for alternate suppliers of a product. Sellers are aware of the plus points of their firm, its products and seldom look in to or even try to understand their handicaps and minus points. It is always a good idea to crosscheck their own assessment of their good and bad points and areas.

With this view only the businessmen have gone from the concept of selling to that of marketing, which encompasses activities like marketing research, competitive strategies, new market planning and innovative business communications including advertising and publicity. What we have to understand is, are we only doing lip service to these words or are we only involved in the game of selling?

Existing situation is more close to the following:

1. Customer is hardly buying the product, which the seller thinks he is selling. He is buying the satisfaction the product is providing to him. Therefore, if another product provides better

satisfaction or a different type of satisfaction he will buy that product. For example, instead of buying a washing machine the customer may use the money for a trip to a hill station.

2. Hence products in direct competition are not the only one's to watch for.
3. Manufacturers and sellers have an idea of what the customer wants. The sellers soon discover how wrong they can be in their idea as the product is launched in the market.
4. Sellers keep harping on a particular quality of their product, little realizing that it could be of little use to the buyers. Detergent sellers have been showing discussions in kitty parties about whose sari is the whitest. Most times, women are not even cleaning the garments themselves and seldom wear white dresses. To move the customers in to buying decision for the firm's product, it is useful to know what the customer considers as the useful quality. Rational behaviour from the customer is another mistake sellers make. We all as customers buy products we rarely use or buy on impulse to please some one. A lot of study has gone in to Consumer Behaviour to establish some rationality in a psychic activity. Sellers have to know the cause of irrational behaviour and adopt their strategy to suit it. Any attempt to change it would be an exercise in futility.
5. Each seller has to focus on his product. However it must be understood that it is one of the million products out in the market. Customer is a non-caring forgetful person and brands and persons associated with the products are of least importance to him. Large firms close down bringing a lot of problems to their stakeholders. The customer however is least bothered about it. This is the harsh reality, which the firms seldom accept.
6. Most firms assume that they know who their customers are. Understanding the market it should be assumed that firms are usually unaware of it and should get to know. Do you think the payer is the buyer or the person who decides is the customer? There can be firms whose customer group defines a definition. Take the case of a steel plant. Anyone wanting steel is the customer; he
7. Could be a builder, a designer, an architect, and a manufacturer among others. Capital equipment manufacturers may find it difficult to define their customers.

Patents and Patent Laws

If the manufacturer is making a product for which he has a Registered Patent under the country's Patent laws, than he can feel secure that other competing firms will not be able to use the same design in their manufacturing process and the firm can enjoy monopoly situation at least till the expiry of the Patent. However, firms should take care of getting the Patents renewed much before the expiry date to avoid any embarrassment on account of getting caught by competition that comes with a copied product. Such copies are usually a shade better and lower in cost because the firm has not spent any money in developing the same except spending on copying costs, which is also known as Reverse Engineering.

Brands: Any firm, which becomes a Market leader normally, has at least one Lead Brand. The firm tries to sell its other products under the umbrella of that brand. Sometimes, firms use the popular brand to sell other products, either bundled with it or way of promotion of lesser-known product in coordination with the main brand. Computer sellers are known for selling bundled products when they can sell slow moving products along with fast moving ones. Brand image or brand equity is perhaps one of the two most important aspects of any business the other being market share.

Once a firm has established one of its brands as a leader it diversifies to include complementary products. This helps in increasing turn over, as also profits of the firm. However, if the new products clash with the existing ones, or their quality can be suspect in the beginning, such products could do harm to the established product. It is therefore necessary to consider remaining supplier of only Specialized Products about which the firm is sure on quality and which enjoy a good brand image. Firms can also provide Quality service for these Special products, which will lead them in to better and increasing Brand image/equity and profitable sales. Thus there is always a dilemma of having specialized product or generic mass-produced ones. Today, firms are trying to customize mass produced products to gain customer goodwill. For example, you can get a Maruti car from the manufacturer with customized seats.

However, nothing can take the place of good service given by the seller for the product to the customer for increasing business and thereby increasing profits. Availability of reliable service and genuine spare parts can surely increase business as these ensure longer usage of the product, which make them cost effective to the buyers.

Quality Standards—firms, through market surveys find out the correct specification of the product they plan to make. These specifications are then converted to manufacturing standards and firms have to keep meeting these specifications for each unit produced by them. For exporting to Europe and other places, the foreign buyers now want that Indian firms follow ISO 9000 Standards. These standards help firms in maintaining their specifications and assist in tracing causes of deviations if there are any these standards are meant to keep a check on the manufacturing process.

For Product standardization each country has its own body, mostly Government owned which defines standards for various products. While mostly it is not mandatory for firms to conform to these specifications, nevertheless it helps in product marketing to an extent to have products with these specifications.

Knowledge is Business

Today's customer is knowledgeable in a lot of things pertaining to his business, more especially the products he wants to buy. Consequently, the seller must also be fully in the know of the entire business scenario that affects his business, including the following areas:

1. They must have a detailed understanding of their customers, including the decision makers, the business initiators, the advisors, evaluators and gatekeepers who keep the unwanted suppliers out of the race through their clout.
2. They must know fully well their product, its USPs, its benefits for the customers, its ease of usage and its testimonials from other customers.
3. They must be fully aware of the general and competitive business environment in which they are operating.
4. They must be fully aware of the major and minor competitors, their strengths ad weaknesses.

In the consumer market the customer or the buyer has to be studied to understand his buying behaviour, his likes and dislikes. The customers can be segmented to give a buyers spectrum for the purpose of communicating with them in the way, the language they understand in each colour of the spectrum. In B-to-B business there are a number of persons involved in the decision process, the sellers must know the buying behaviour, the mindset of each individual member of the buying team. The B-to-B customer in India is a young entrepreneur, a professional industrialist or family owned businessperson. Each of these have their own peculiar characteristics and purchase behaviour.

Master-List of the Customers and Prospects

Data Bank

The information given is essential for the success of any B-to-B marketing company and therefore it must be gathered with care, precision and must be kept updated all the time. It should be job of the field sales force to ensure the data is always correct and is having latest information.

Customer's Corporate Data

Name, address, phone, fax and e-mail

Key personnel with their designations and direct phone and mobile numbers

Address of the R&D facility if it is located elsewhere

Key personnel of the R&D with their designations and phone AND mobile details

Addresses of the Strategic Business Units with phone fax email

Key personnel of the SBUs. With their direct phone and mobile numbers

Address of branch offices with phone, fax and email

Key personnel of the branch offices with their direct phone and mobile numbers

Name and addresses of their bankers

Personal information about the key personnel stated above

Name with designation, home address, phone and mobile

Qualifications

Experience in the trade and with the company

Powers and authority

Role in purchases made by the company

(Is the person the initiator, buyer, user, decider, influencer, gatekeeper or vetoer)

Personal Traits and Characteristics

Friendly, aloof, extrovert, introvert,

Hobbies

Scrupulously honest

Accepts party invitations

Accepts gifts on festive occasions

Accepts bribe (this should not mean that the seller would offer him the bribe)

Accepts favours while maintaining that these would not affect his purchase decisions.

Family Details

Married with children

Married without children

Number of years married (optional)

Family hobbies, entertainment activities, holiday's ventures

Psychographics-Life Style

High profile

Extravagant

Moderate

Just with basics, within known means

Club membership and usage

Extra-curricular activities

Personal goals and ambitions

The data stated above is by no means exhaustive. It is only indicative ąnd would largely depend on individual company's (sellers) needs and also on how much of it can be accurately collected. The aim of the company should be gathered as much data as possible as it would come handy one time or the other.

The data would reflect on key persons buying attitudes, beliefs and focus. The psychologists among the sellers team should be able to decipher from the data what benefits should be targeted on which person so that the sales talk can be made precise and dovetailed for the individuals.

Personality types—Friendly, aloof, extrovert, introvert

People can be slotted into different personality types. Some persons may appear frivolous on the surface but it could just be façade for the serious types. Some persons are normally cheerful; while others are most of the time sullen or morose. The reasons for their attitude could be based on their family life and that is why it is a good idea to know about the family background of the persons concerned. Some persons open up only after a while, but when they do they can become quite friendly. Sellers have to draw the line between being friendly and in indulging in bribery.

Several persons show a haughty attitude towards the salespersons, making them believe that they are upright and cannot be bought for business favours. However, chances are that these persons could be already bought by the competition. However, their demeanour changes drastically once they realize that their game of friendship with another supplier is up. At such times he would first squirm and then try devious ways to show that if required they would open up to you too. The word, "impossible" to denote your chances of getting their business, changes to I M Possible. In such cases the purchase decisions are biased and based on the sellers intimacy with one or more than one person from the decision committee. Companies have to take major decisions in such situations, if they want to follow the bribery route (this should be eschewed totally as it would certainly lead to catastrophic results in the long run, as such things do not remain secret for long) it is better to accept short term frustrations rather than go for long term debacle with the customer by becoming blacklisted by the buyers.

B-to-B buyers are looking for cost effective products. They should be made aware of the total cost of the purchase that include the following:

1. Cost of the search for the product or for turnkey suppliers.
2. Cost of the product and services.
3. Hidden costs of transportation, travelling of sellers' engineers for installation and commission of the equipment.
4. Cost of spares needed in the first year of operation of the equipment, if not quoted in advance.
5. Cost of documentation, service manuals, equipment layouts, wiring diagrams.
6. Cost of low MTBF, Mean Time Between Failures; this could be result of bad assembly, components mismatch or even wrong wiring during assembly that short circuits the equipment.

Cost cutting measures could become profit-cutting methods that could lead to catastrophic results of closure of the company. However, good suppliers can supply products at competitive rates on turnkey basis as well, by giving the customers benefits of better technology that gives lower cost of production and the benefits of large-scale manufacturing.

A good buyer uses his technical skills to decide the product with the best technology, service and turnkey capabilities and then starts price negotiations with those suppliers that meet with the technological requirements of needs of the equipment.

A major problem in India is that of receipt of payment for the supplies made. Companies can use different kinds of baits with the buyers including prompt payment discounts, lower price for advance payments, either full or at least part payment. Companies can offer longer free service periods depending on their confidence on the quality of their product and service, if this would result in speedy payments. Credit is a useful sales tool. However, if misused it could create lots of problems between the buyers and sellers. B-to-B sellers should be in a position to ask for bank guaranty from their buyers in case sale is made on credit. The sellers could also get the buyer to hypothecate the equipment being sold to the buyers.

Modes of Payment

"Customer is the king, is supreme" and his word is the law for the sellers. Understanding this maxim, the seller should also learn to be polite and yet firm in extending credit to the customers. Companies are planning Customer Relationship Management, bringing in customer delight instead of just satisfaction and yet the use of credit as a sales tool is wrought with dangerous portents, because, even the most sincere buyers can take the seller for a ride by delaying payment by giving one excuse or the other. Open-ended credit is the most risky form of payment that the seller can offer to the buyer. This can be one only when the seller has already got valued assets hypothecated in their name from the customer. The seller must look the problem logically; if there is no payment then there is no sale and the seller has just gifted the product to the buyer. There is no such thing like gifting products in business. In B-to-B marketing, payments can be made in any of the following methods:

Advance payment in cash or bank draft

Part payment in advance, the balance on shipment of goods

Part payment in advance balance in two instalments, once on receipt of the goods and a small balance amount on commissioning of the equipment.

Entire payment through Letter of Credit to be opened by the buyers on the sellers for full amount of the invoice

Part payment in advance, balance in the form of "delayed payment" bank usance bills

Letters of credit are of several types as given below:

Allowing part shipment of goods-rolling LCs

Irrevocable LC without recourse

Irrevocable LC with recourse

Revocable LC without recourse

Revocable LC with recourse

Sales Promotion

Business environment, the world over has gone sea changes in the last decade, more so because of the political upheavals, like disintegration of USSR, opening up of China, turmoil in far-east economies. Let us understand the business environment, as it exists in India today:

1. Severe international competition
2. Large middle and upper middle consumer class
3. Changes in money supply and interest rates

These factors have led to an era of continuous sales promotion. It is therefore important to learn what is Sales promotion and how it can be made effective.

With number of products in each group increasing the customer is the main beneficiary. However, he is also a bit confused as each advertiser is telling the benefit story to him. The need to give that extra benefit to clinch the order leads to promotion.

Consumers need extra stimulus to buy the product. The dealers or retailers need that extra benefit to stock and push the product these promotional activities MUST be advertised to be of any value in increasing market share.

In sales promotion the marketers are giving some thing extra. This is in lieu of price reduction. Price reduction, unlike promotion gets to be an extended expense, while promotional expense can be withdrawn any time you feel you have achieved your objectives.

Sales promotion provides extra incentive, an offer of direct inducements that enhance the basic value of a product for a limited time to stimulate immediate distributor commitment, sales force effectiveness and consumer purchasing.

Coke and Pepsi advertise in order to promote sales as well to encourage retail trade to keep their products.

Customer Promotion

- Test our new product or re-buy. Added incentives make people give new products a try.
- Be loyal to us, we are there to look after you through our promotional plans.
- Buy more—Pepsi says, "yeh dil mange more"—the heart wants more.
- Buy our entire range—for this purpose sometimes products are bundled together.

- Promotion increases sales immediately. It helps in advertising and other marketing efforts like personal selling. Just as it is important to advertise the promotions so that the customer gets to know about it. Lack of advertising for the target market will render the promotion campaign unrewarding and the objectives will not be met.

Trade promotion helps in the following manner:

- Get better distributors
- Better shelf space at the retail stores
- Superior merchandizing
- Increase stocks and sales push
- Training the sales personnel of retailers
- Better product knowledge (as a spin off)
- Improvement in dealer responses in future

Sales promotion takes up to 70 of total marketing budget and hence it is a major factor, which needs constant nurturing. The main reasons for the shift towards promotion are as follows:

- Immediate results- with focus on meeting target sales promotion provides quick response technique.
- Measuring effectiveness- as the results are quick to achieve, promotional plans results can be seen early.
- Retailers have acquired a status they never had, as through computerized information base they know their customers, their buying powers and habits best. Therefore, promotion plans with retailers at the hub, can be most effective.
- Increased competition and plethora of products make you vie for customer's money. Advertising may not provide the motivation needed for making customers buy your products.
- Buyer's loyalty is limited and can be enhanced with active participation of retailers. Since your competitors are doing exactly the same, you have to be on the constant look out for better and more rewarding promotional plans both your customers and retailers.

There are various ways of product promotion

Buy one get one free,

Buy now pay later,

Take a free sample with each purchase of our other product you just purchased.

Many firms offer discount coupons as incentive to buy at a lower price. When the customer goes to redeem the coupon a good salesman can sell a lot of the company products. At least the customer would have tried your product and may be, he will like it so much that he buys again.

Special low cost packs are offered as promotion to encourage trial. Similarly, some firms give money-back offers where in the unlikely event of the customer not liking the product he can get the money back. Experience shows that hardly anyone ever comes to return the product for cash, unless the product is defective.

Contests are also used as sales promotions. If your product package has a gift written on it you get it, Colgate offers, millions of rupees, besides other goodies like computers.

Hotels and airlines offer high usage, discounts, and frequent flyers free tickets as promotion plans.

Trade promotion plans offer the following to retailers:

- Display incentives for better merchandizing and shelf use
- Short term discounts for inventory control and sales push
- Turn over discounts are given for achieving sales targets
- Assistance in running sales contests among retailers sales persons
- Cooperative advertising with the retailers where Advertising expense is shared on mutually agreed basis.

Sales promotion is an offer of direct money saving to the customer without diluting products brand equity (as can happen in case of price reductions). Consumer sales promotion encourages new product sales, increase usage of existing products, helps sales of entire range of products and adds to selling efforts. Retail promotion helps in building inventories with the distribution network and indirectly acts as a sales push in the market as no one can keep large inventories for long.

Depending on product and trade practices firms send dealers on trips to foreign countries on achieving the targets. Some firms offer cars and other consumer goods as incentive to achieve the sales as planned. Promotion programmes are known to increase sales and market share, which lasts as long as competition does not retaliate. Hence it is wise to be closely observing competitive activities, and being pro-active rather than reacting to losing situations.

Ideally the sales graph for sales promotion should be as follows:

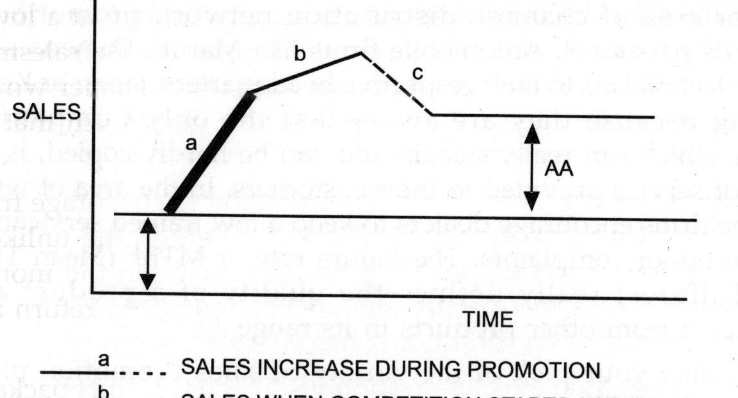

a ---- SALES INCREASE DURING PROMOTION

b ---- SALES WHEN COMPETITION STARTS ACTION

c ---- SALES DECREASE WITH INCREASED COMPETITIVE ACTION

AA ---- AA-RESIDUAL SALES AFTER THE PROMOTION IS OVER

Fig. 8.2. Sales Promotion

As can be seen the firm has gained quite a substantial amount of market share. (Additional sales AA) but do not forget this is the ideal situation. Competition is always there to counter the firm's moves and hence the need for continuity in promotion plans!

As can be seen Sales Promotion is a short time plan to increase sales. It can be used for the following reasons:

- Loss of sales due to production problems
- New product or variant launches
- To beat the competitors plans
- Increase in production capacity

Generally a combination approach is required, that of consumer promotion and dealers promotion plan. However, if there is only consumer promotion it increases the sales and profit of the dealer too and hence the channel members welcome it.

One major reason of failure of promotion plan is the dishonesty of dealers, who do not give the extra benefit to the consumer and pocket it themselves. Many of us have purchased a cake of soap, which was to be given as free gift with a bottle of shampoo, as written on the soap package. While most dealers and retailers play the game honestly as they know that ultimate advantage is going to be theirs because of increased sales and profits, firms should be careful in selecting dealers and retailers in the initial stage itself.

A major area of channel/distribution network promotion is training of its sales team.

A major area of channel/distribution network promotion is training of its personnel. Automobile firms like Maruti, Daewoo send their dealer technicians to their respective headquarters, Japan or Korea for training because they are aware that the only Competitive Advantage, which can really sustain and can be hardly copied, is the excellence of service provided to their customers. In the area of white goods, some firms encourage dealers to keep a few trained servicemen to attend to minor complaints. The failure rate or MTBF (Mean Time Between Failures) really defines the quality of a product and differentiates it from other products in its range.

Finally, take your pick of the variety of sales Promotion plans available or think of some new innovative promotion technique, whatever, but always remain pro-active to the market needs, situations and environment changes.

Price

Ideally, advertising budget or expense on advertising should match or be a little less than the extra profits the advertising generates.

S = f (A), Where S is the sales figure, A is the advertising expense.

This equation presumes that, the only factor of sales is advertising, which as we know is not correct. Going with the presumption for the time being, gross margin of profit minus the advertising expense gives the net profit—

Net Profit = Gross Profit – Advertising Expense

In case the advertising expense increases beyond the gross margin the firm runs in to losses

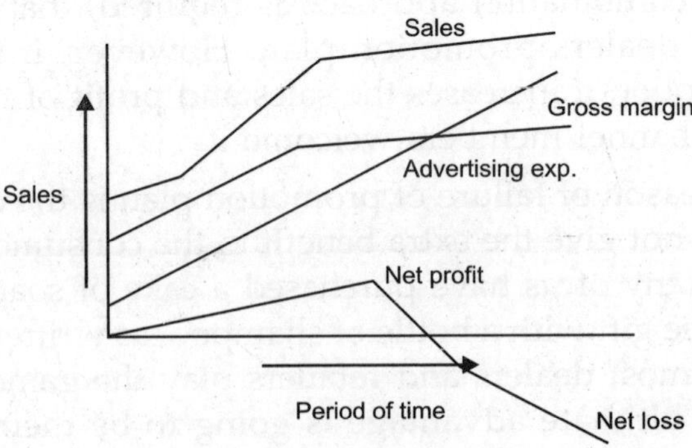

Fig. 8.3. P & L Study

The main disadvantage of this analysis is that it presumes that the sales comes only through advertising, while other factors like sales efforts, pricing promotion and after sales service play an important role in increasing sales.

Trends and Indications

Let us discuss some macro-economic indicators, which are only indicative (for correct figures the students will do well to find them out.).

Country's GNP has increased from 1980 till today by about seven times on current prices. Similarly the Per Capita GNP has also increased by six times in the same period.

Annual consumption of some of core products has also gone up as follows:

Table 8.3. Core Product Usage

PRODUCT	ANNUAL INCREASE IN %
FOOD AND BEVERAGE	12.5
CLOTHING AND FOOTWEAR	12.5
RENT FUEL AND POWER	11.8
TRANSPORT AND COMMUNICATION	25.5

USAGE OF CONSUMER DURABLES IN URBAN AND RURAL AREAS ARE AS FOLLOWS:

Table 8.4. Usage of Consumer Durability

Product	*Urban %*	*Rural %*
Cooking gas	52	5
Pressure cooker	45	17
Refrigerator	30	2
Radio	32	25
TV	70	22
Fans	80	35
Cycles	55	50
Two wheelers	25	6
Cars	5	1
Mixer grinder	45	5
Washing machines	25	Trace

Let us see how the FMCG products have gone in to urban and rural markets—

Table 8.5. FMCG Usage

FMCG Products	*Urban %*	*Rural %*
Toilet soap	99	90
Tooth paste	70	36
Tooth powder	35	30
Washing powder	95	90
Utensils cleaning agent	50	7

Next taking food items in to account the picture is as given below:

Table 8.6. Food Consumption

Products	*Urban %*	*Rural %*
Tea	90	75
Coffee	25	5
Cooking oils	98	98
Butter	22	5
Jam	17	1
Tomato sauce	40	10

Personal products usage in urban and rural markets—

Table 8.7. Personal Products

Products	*Urban %*	*Rural %*
Shampoo	30	10
Hair oil	90	85
Talc powder	50	28
Watches	65	25
Chocolates	22	3
Soft drinks	60	15
Sweets and toffees	30	12

Cosmetics usage in urban and rural areas:

Table 8.8. Cosmetics

Products	*Urban %*	*Rural %*
Nail polish	45	30
Lipstick	30	15
Eye make-up	12	6
Face make-up	7	1
Perfume	15	2

Shaving products usage in urban and rural markets:

Table 8.9. Shaving Products

Products	*Urban %*	*Rural %*
Shaving cream	45	10
After shave lotion	15	2

Personal consumption products usage in urban and rural markets:

Table 8.10. Personal Products

Products	*Urban %*	*Rural %*
Pan masala	8	7
Supari	14	14
Bidi	8	18
Cigarette	8	2

Household savings for urban and rural markets:

Subject	*Urban Saving %*	*Rural Saving %*
Bank savings account	30	9
Insurance	12	4
Others	35	12

Household income patterns-
Classification of income is as follows:

Income norm	*Income in Rs. Per Year Range*
Elite class	Above 1,000,000
High income	600,000 – 1,000,000
Upper middle class	240,000 – 599,999
Middle class	60,000 – 239,999
Lower middle class	24,000 – 59,000
Lower class	12,000 – 23,999

Income divide in urban and rural markets:

Income Norm	*Urban %*	*Rural %*
Elite class	1.1	0.3
High income	3	1
Upper middle class	5	3
Middle class	10	8
Lower middle class	35	13.7
Lower class	45.9	74

World Marketing Strength

The Information given herein under is based on 1995 report and should be taken as such:

Country	*Overall Rank*	*Infrastructure*
USA	1	2
Singapore	2	12
Japan	4	28
Germany	6	11
Canada	12	3
UK	18	16
China	34	45
India	39	43
South Africa	42	19
Mexico	44	33
Russia	48	48

It is based on world competitiveness report 1995

GENERAL DEMOGRAPHIC FACTORS OF INDIA—

CENSUS 1991—URBAN-25.7%, RURAL-74.3%

Religious dispersion

Table 8.11. Religious Dispersion

Religions	*% of Population Practicing*
Hindu	82
Muslim	13
Christians	2
Sikhs	2
Buddhists	1
Others	Trace

Languages spoken

Table 8.12. Language Spread

Language	*% Speaking*	*Language*	*%Speaking*
Hindi	40	Gujarati	5
Telugu	9	Kannada	4.1
Bengali	7.8	Malayalam	3.9
Marathi	7.5	Oriya	3.5
Tamil	6.8	Punjabi	2.8
Urdu	6.3	Others	2.3

Media Expanse

Given below are some estimates of media coverage of the population:

Table 8.13. Media Coverage

Television	87 %
Press	35%
Radio	45%
Cinema	40%

Television coverage is almost the same across male and female population, over the age groups between 12 –70 years, except that in case of rural India it tapers down to almost 50%.

Press coverage is also lower in the rural areas at about 22%

Radio reach is almost the same in urban and rural areas.

Cinema reach drops down to a mere 22% in rural India.

Till 1996, the top advertisers were as follows:

1. Cigarettes
2. Consumer electronics
3. Soft drinks
4. Traders
5. Soaps and detergents
6. Cosmetics
7. Food products
8. Cars and two wheelers
9. Tea and coffee
10. Tyres and tubes

Top ten advertisers:

1. Hindustan Lever Ltd.
2. ITC
3. Coke
4. Pepsi
5. Colgate
6. Mac Dowels
7. Nestles
8. Philips
9. Godfrey Philip
10. BPL

The daily newspapers in different languages:

Assamese	Dainik Assam, Dainik Janmabhoomi
Bengali	Anand Bazar Patrika, Aajkaal,
English	Assam Tribune, The Asian Age, Deccan Chronicle, Deccan Herald, Hindu, Hitwada, Hindustan Times, Indian Express, Pioneer, Statesman, Telegraph, The Tribune, The Times of India,
English-Financial	Financial Express, Economic Times, Business Standard
Gujarati	Gujarat Samachar, Mumbai Samachar, Jaihind,
Hindi	Aj, Amar Ujala, Daily Jagran, Dainik Tribune, Hindustan, Nai Dunia, Nav Bharat Times, Punjab Kesari, Ranchi Express, Rajasthan Patrika,
Kannada	Kannada Prabha, Prajavani, Samyukya Karnataka, Udayavani
Malayalam	Kerala Kaumudi, Malayalam Manorama, Mathribhumi
Marathi	Lokmat, Loksatta, Maharashtra Times, Gomantak, Sakal,
Oriya	Prajatantra, Samaj, Sambad
Tamil	Daily Thanthi, Dinaman, Dinakaran, Dinamalar,
Telugu	Andhra Patrika, Andhra Jyoti, Eenadu
Urdu	Hind Samachar and Inquilab

Important magazines in different languages:

Assamese	Assam Bani, Janmabhoomi, Prantik
Bengali	Anandalok, Desh
English	Business Today, Business India, Business World, Cosmopolitan, Femina, Filmfare, India Today, Readers Digest, Sports World, Society, The Week, Women's Era,
Gujarati	Abhiyan,
Hindi	Grihshobha, Manohar Kahaniyan, Sarita, Sarika, Maya
Kannada	Mayura, Taranga
Malayalam	Malayalam Manorama,
Marathi	Chitralekha, Lokprabha,
Oriya	Suchanta
Tamil	Ananda Viketan, Kalkandu
Telugu	Andhra Bhoomi, Andhra Prabha

TV Channels:

Sun TV	Tamil	Channel V	English, Hindi
Gemini	Telugu	Star Sports	English

ESPN Sports	English	Star	English, Hindi
M TV Music	English, Hindi	Star Movies	English
Sony	Hindi	Zee	Hindi
BBC World	English	Zee Cinema	Hindi
Discovery	English	Zee TV	Hindi/Regional
CNN	English	Sabe	Hindi
DD1	Hindi	Set Max	Hindi
DD Metro	Hindi	DD	Regional

Besides, a number of channels are added now and then.

Commercial advertising rates of the channels depend on the following factors:

- GEOGRAPHIC COVERAGE OF THE CHANNEL
- LANGUAGE USED
- TYPES OF PROGRAMMES
- TRP RATINGS OF THE INDIVIDUAL PROGRAMMES
- TELECAST TIME

DOORDARSHAN HAS DIVIDED ITS TIME AS FOLLOWS:

SAS—Super A Special-film based Programmes

SA—Super A Hindi English News, Serials

As—A Special Sunday Morning Serials

A—Late night films/serials

B—Afternoon/late night

People do not concentrate and the answers you get may be not as accurate as you take them to be.

People get varied perceptions about the advertisements as can be seen from the following statements:

- For a successful campaign the agency claims the total sales increase is due to their creative effort.
- In case of failure of a retail campaign, the retailer feels that the misadventure of marketing/advertising is thankfully over never to be tried again.
- In B-to-B business (industrial marketing), the sales team always takes the credit and yet acknowledges the fact that the advertising campaign helped them in getting the door opened.
- In elections the defeated candidate will blame the marketing/advertising campaign that it did not reflect his true image.

These may be partly true and in order to be impartial, one has to assume that only when advertising is playing a major role in the marketing, and other factors are either dormant or nonexistent can the evaluation be properly judged.

Working plan for assessing the marketing/advertising effort can be worked out in the following manner:

Divide the market into two equal segments. As you start running your usual campaign, continue it for a period say, two months. Next while you continue the campaign in both the segments in one segment (only), start a spot advertising campaign.

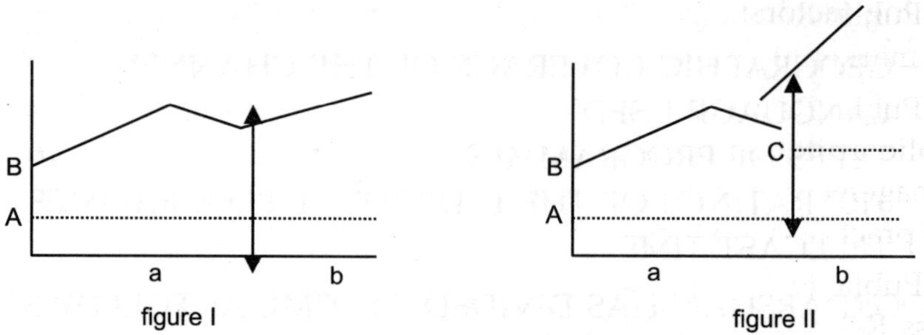

Fig. 8.4. Ad. Campaign Effects

On the horizontal line the time period is divided as *a* and *b*. A is the regular advertising campaign, B is the sale figure. In the second graph you see that after half period C a spot campaign has been started which has given rise to sales.

In figure I market sales before the TV spot campaign is Rs. 600,000
Sales during the spot campaign is Rs. 630,000.

Public Relations

Focus is on defining PR, common objectives of PR, the PR process, and the target public for PR the PR Message. PR can be and usually is an effective form of creating positive marketing climate for the firm and thus becomes part of marketing communication methods.

Introduction

What we see on TV as advertisements for eggs, milk and diamonds is not direct marketing/advertising as you hardly find any sponsor. Drink more milk, eat eggs everyday are meant to create awareness among the public and hence can be called PR Campaigns. Unfortunately, the task of PR is not appreciated by most of the persons and it tends to become a thankless one. In election campaigns, after the candidate has finished and gone his secretary remains to answer the questions regarding how the speech should be interpreted for improving the candidate's image. After the corporate Chairman has given an expose of the firm's plans, its elaboration and explanation is done by the PR Persons. Press releases are part of the PR job. In case of any catastrophe the PR has to explain how the firm is coping with it and the damage control measures it is going to take. The famous oil spill in the ocean had the oil company's PR People on their toes. It may bee added that in such crises situations even the CEO takes the role of PR.

Public Relations covers all the communications of the firm except the marketing/advertising and personal selling communications.

Public Relations can be defined as, "the process of understanding public attitudes on relevant issues, interpreting these attitudes for Management, and then working either to go the organizational polices and practices with those attitudes or to modify the attitudes themselves."

Publicity is only one aspect of PR Job, which covers the making of Press Releases given regarding the firms activities and plans. Besides PR is useful tool in creating positive ambient.

Cue for the sale of firm's products in the target market segment.

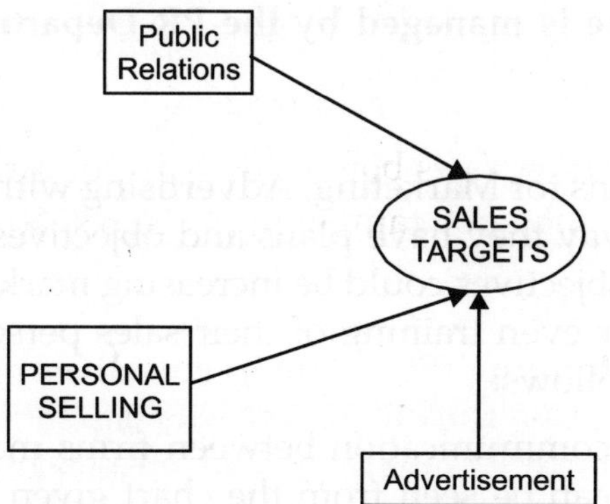

Fig. 8.5. Advertising Sales Targets

PUBLIC relations task in marketing activities is subtle. Nonetheless it is equally important, as through PR, the firm is able to build custom/customer base not as a hard sell exercise, but with gaining customer support. This is dine with great finesse and yet with bringing customers on the right side of the firm. ***You like us you buy from us.***

The main features of PR are as follows:

- When the firms arrange PR activities they do not have total control on the message being sent. It becomes the prerogative of the editors of the media and they can surely use their right. In personal selling or in marketing/advertising the firm talks all good things about the product. In case of PR the media men can express their likes and dislikes in their reports and not just what the firm wants them to do.
- PR is addressed to several different classes of people, the customers being one of them. The message goes to the firm's stakeholders, the buyers, the sellers, the investors, banks, the government, local bodies, trade associations and social activists like the environment protection groups. It pays to keep these people on the firm's right side.
- PR does not have any direct media cost as the PR Message goes in the form of medias editorial. No media space or time needs to be purchased for PR.
- PR besides assisting in improving sales also does a number of preplanned tasks like improving investors interest in the firm. Labor relations and activities connected with labor welfare get publicity through PR.
- **The most visible role of PR is seen during Annual General Meetings of the Shareholders of the firms. The entire programme is managed by the PR Department of the firms.**

The PR Base

Firms have plans for Marketing, Advertising with proper laid down objectives. Same way they have plans and objectives for PR Activities. While marketing objectives could be increasing market share, enlarging geographic base or even training of their sales persons, PR Objectives can be stated as follows:

- Two way communication between firms management and its public, as can be seen from the chart given below:

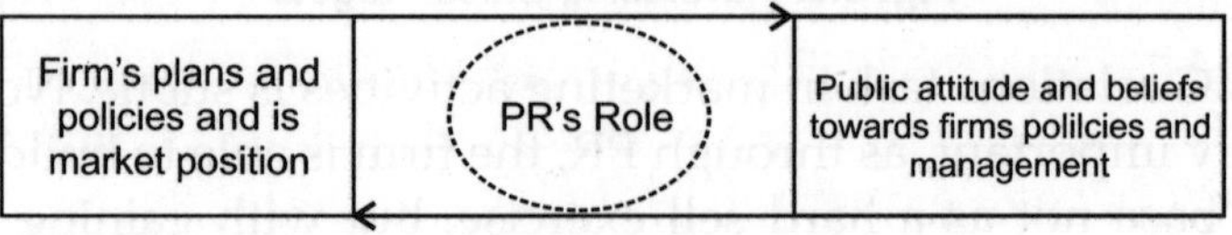

Fig. 8.6. Communicating with Public

PR Department, therefore is not just the custodian of firms information base, but it also plays a dynamic role in highlighting the public opinion about the firm as it tends to modify it in favor of the firm.

An example of the effect of PR activities or lack of them will clarify the point for the students.

It was in 1960s that the Bangalore based excellent public sector firm Hindustan Aeronautics Ltd. had been manufacturing small aircrafts used to spray insecticides in the vast expanse of agricultural land. Some of these aircrafts crash-landed due to some technical problem and such a good firm went in to disrepute. It took a lot of PR work to bring it back as a major technology driven firm in the Indian mindset.

As against this, about the same time an American firm operating in India came to know that its Aviation Turbo Fuel (ATF) has got a tiny trace of extra moisture than specified. The firm promptly downgraded the ATF as Kerosene oil and gave prominent PR advertisements in this regard thus taking a mileage from an otherwise sure disastrous situation for the firm. The high image of the firm in the publics mind carried the day for the firm.

For this purpose it becomes the foremost task of the PR Department of any firm to keep its eyes and ears close to the ground and plan pro-active interaction rather than trying to retrieve lost ground on any account.

- PR has to coordinate between public opinion and firms plans and policies. This would help even at the last minute for taking corrective action if needed. Most firms are aware of the strong sentiments of the public towards environment and pollution control. As the firms take measures in the direction of becoming non polluting industry they should also keep the public informed about their actions in this regard. Plans and policies are not enough as the public wants to know the action firms are taking. Firms need to address themselves with other socially relevant issues like GROW MORE TREES, ADOPTING FOR MAINTAINING GREEN AREAS OF THE TOWN. THE FIRMS ARE corporate citizens of the country and it is imperative that they behave as such. It is equally important to let the public know that you are a responsible corporate citizen and this is achieved through PR.

- As new competitive firms start operating they can, with a little effort develop a good public image. Even if your firms image has been good so far , where does it stand in competition today. The best way to answer the question is to have a survey conducted and after that take any corrective measures as required.

With the advent of several reputed TV Brands like AIWA, SONY, THOMSON and LG, firms like Videocon and BPL would have taken a bigger beating but for their good public image. Hence you can imagine that the task of PR is endless.

- As a marketing mix factor PR has to come up with the most significant factor of the firm, which is promoting sales of goods. This is done mainly through press releases, which tell about the firms achievements, plans and changes being brought about for increasing efficiency and customer satisfaction. These press releases play a vital role perhaps much grater than direct advertising as these items when published in the newspapers come under the editorial purview and hence get greater credibility than advertising. The only danger is of editorial pencil which may remove even the punch lines and make the whole thing drab.
- Firms gain good mileage through their brand equity. With high brand equity firms can charge higher prices and still sell in large quantities. It is the name sells in most cases. Name provides for guarantee of quality. For the people for whom price is of no consequence, brand is what they buy. Even price conscious people buy good brand product for vale for money and product life thus rendering them as economical to the buyers.
- Damage Control is a major responsibility of PR. This task is usually needed to be performed once in a long while it is of great importance as not handling it properly could lead to greater disaster. Natural calamities like floods, earthquakes cause problems for firms, but how the firms deal with the problems and what becomes the publics perception about it is of importance to the firms. Then there are man made problems like the Bhopal gas leak. Smaller hazards keep on plaguing the firms and only good PR can nullify the negative effect of these on the firms image and as a rub off on the firms sales and profits. IT IS THE REPUTATION OF THE FIRM ITS GOODWILL WHICH IS AT STAKE!

Marketing Research for the effect of communication sent by the firms to the public is important as the perceptions of the message sent could be different with the sender firm and the receiver. Understanding the nature of public acceptance will help PR Manager to tailor the next message according to the corrections required.

As we have seen PRs objective is different from that of advertising. PR has to project the public view of the firm in the first instant. PR Managers are in constant contact with the public, the opinion leaders, the government and the customers. These contacts provide with knowledge of the attitudes of people as the PR person has to be alert to catch even stray phrase of significance to the firm.

One problem which many firms feel that they are being perceived as laid back firms Philips had this image till eighties in the 20th century. With dynamically pursuing the task of changing the image their PR Department did bring about a turn around in the public mind.

When the readers read any article from the editors it has a different effect on them then seeing the advertisements.

Earlier the success of PR Campaign was measured by the column centimeter space it could get in the favored media. Bigger the space, better the PR. It does not however tell you the effect of the space gained has had on the public mindset The ultimate test, as in the case of advertising comes from the increase in sales figures and change for the better in the customers attitude towards your product. For understanding the attitude changes , adverting research type research is required to be done.

Unlike advertising research where the target segment is the group of customers likely to purchase your product, in case of PR, the public consists of investors, stockholders, customers and suppliers towards whom the PR Effort is directed.

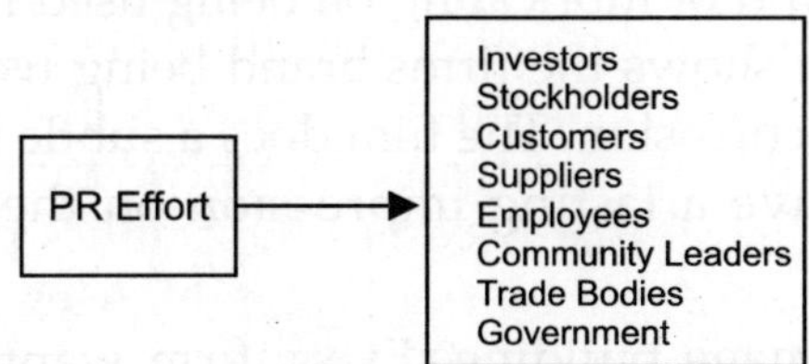

Fig. 8.7. PR Tasks

Public Relations Manager's job is to have a firm grip of the media available for transmitting the message to the public. Understanding media thus is an important aspect of his job. In this case, PR Manager approaches the media editors, correspondents with information about the firm, its activities and plans. This is useful information, which makes the media and the PR Interdependent.

These days a lot of advertising uses direct attack on competition, which if not refuted can create misinformation among the customers. Between two competitive toothpaste brands the difference of opinion came regarding the time one of them kept the mouth of the user fresh. Ten hours said one firm and soon the competitor said fifteen hours. A PR job would have sufficed by telling through editorial comments about the true nature of the toothpaste.

With plethora of Non Banking Financial Institutions, to gain advantage one such firm advertised the norms public should use to assess the firms. The advertisement had a reverse effect as many persons read it out of context and felt that that particular NBFC is not good. It took a lot of effort as also their PR Teams rapport with the press, which helped them in retrieving the situation and giving their side of the story as a press release.

PR Too Depends on Endorsements to An Extent!

If the firm says in the advertisement that their Matiz car is the best in its range, public may or may not accept the statement. The thinking becomes "any way it is their advertisement and who will ever say any thing bad about their product." However if Murad Ali Baig says the same thing or the editor of Motoring Times says it, the public is surely going to believe it.

Marketing efforts too get a boost with the help of MARKETING PR activities.

A technical short film shows how the car engine gets corroded because of friction between cylinder walls and the piston rings. Next it shows good brand of lubricating oil being used halves the corrosion. And then the film shows the firms brand being used totally removing any possibility of corrosion. The film does a subtle job of Marketing PR as the visuals leave a lasting impression on the viewers about the efficacy of the oil.

PR helps in image building. Every firm wants to be known as a good corporate citizen. When the public is shown a movie which highlights the efforts taken by the firm in removing pollutants from its effluents going in the river, it endorses the public opinion about the firm as a good corporate citizen. Such films help mold the opinion when negative opinions have already been formed. Following scenes will give other examples of PR, which incidentally create goodwill for the firm, which does get reflected in the sale of its products.

- The CEO of the firm presenting a cheque of Rs. 1,000,000 for the Gujarat relief fund to the Prime Minister of India.
- Marketing Director presenting specially designed cars for the handicapped persons at a discounted price.
- President of the firm sponsoring and inaugurating a sports event for the blind.
- Firm offering scholarships to the deserving children of its workers for higher studies.

Such events if not given right publicity would go unheard and unsung. It becomes the major task of the PR Department to ensure that the good deed does rub off on the cash register of the firm bringing in extra profitable sales.

It is said the, **a company is known by the men it keeps**. And how? Good, happy, hard working employees do provide a good general back drop in the public's mind. Firms go out of their way these days to keep their employees happy. Perquisites like good housing, medical aid for the family, sports activities, and children's education are a must for this purpose. PR's job is to focus the public attention on the theme of happy workmen. The firm automatically gets a boost as a good firm, as only a good employer can be good firm and who wants to do business with a firm which is not good. A good example of Personnel PR is the advertisement of Tata Steels, in which happy employees are shown involved in various activities are shown. In the end the advertisement says, **"We also make steel"**.

Firms And Society

Firms do have some dependence on the society in which they operate. They get employees, investments, and home sub-assemblers. Society too gets employment opportunities, better living standards. A factory in a backward area like Mankapur in UP State got a big boost when public sector firm ITI established it factory there with French collaboration. The entire country side was transformed in to a thriving industrial town from its earlier days of a sleepy laid back village. ITI HAD THE OPPORTUNITY OF building its image as a big benevolent corporate citizen. The fact that they did every thing to protect the environment of the area was surely a plus point.

Firms do good to the community and the society in which they operate. PR has to press home the advantage and get the right mileage which is firms due.

PR and the Government

In the era prior to 1992, when the government of India opened up country's economy, private business was overloaded with government liaison work. The government lowly paid staff doled out permits and licenses and it became the breeding ground for corrupt politicians and public servants. With the change brought about in 1992, firms are no longer facing the vice like grip. Yet, there are areas, which still need to be smoothened, and interaction with the government becomes a primary task of the PR Department of any firm.

Industry lobby, with industry trader associations like ASSOCHEM, CII, FICCI are liaising with the government to sort out their problems.

The Investing Public

Investments as equity, bonds are made in the firms you can trust. Hence the PR task for investors is the same ass for Marketing PR. Investment PR is a highly specialized job which entails a thorough knowledge of money market, interest rates prevailing in the market, firms financial position and needs. PR person has to market firm's financial status to encourage investing public in coming to the firm. Investment PR requires that information about the investors should be provided to the firm and about the firm to the investing public.

How to? What are the means available to the Investment PR persons to provide accurate and fast information to the investing public?

Press Releases

These are the most commonly used methods of disseminating information. The firm selects the information to be given, then it is written down in a language normally used in the press. You can use the reporters format or the one used by journalists. If it is given as a good news coverage then the chances of its being read by the public are high.

Press Conferences

When the firms have to say a great deal, like when they have to announce the annual financial report and balance sheet, firms have their Annual General Meetings (AGM) where press is invited. Unlike in press releases in press conferences the media people can ask questions to elicit replies reconfirm their thinking and be objective about the firm. Besides AGMs firms call press conferences at product launches, public issues.

CRISES MANAGEMENT

When the firms face situations like strike, natural calamity or strike the must inform the stakeholders including shareholders. Non-information leads to speculations and hence leads to mis-information with disastrous results. It is the ability of Crisis PR, which helps firm tide over the crisis with the least damage to its reputation and its sales.

Public Relations function deals with the public opinion and informs the firm about the same. It also tells the public about the results and plans and policies of the firm. It helps the firm in coordinating its activities to keep in tune with public likes and dislikes. It can help the firm in to moulding public opinion in its favour. PR is use to help in selling the products as also in managing crisis situations.

Questions for Discussion

1. Crisis management is the job of PR. Discuss.
2. Corporate PR and Marketing PR are different. How?

MEDIA PLANNING

The questions to be answered are the following:

- Whom are we trying to reach?
- Where are they located?
- The best time for them to see the advertisements.

To answer the first question we have to know the exact market segment. Since all the people could be prospective buyers, some are more inclined to buy. These marketers segregate through demographic, psychographics social class and life style categories. It is believed that people in one segment would behave in similar manner and would have same type of needs and preferences. Rich people with trendy life style will be reading magazines like Vogue, Cosmopolitan, while those not in that class will not be reading these magazines. This helps I focusing on the segment directly interested in your product.

In India 70% per cent people live in villages. The balance thirty percent in cities has a different mind set than that of the villagers. With several languages spoken in the country, there are newspapers, magazines for each language and they are the best media to reach the people of the area using a particular language. Products used by towns can be advertised in English as it is the language which most people understand.

Television as a media has a wide reach today and telecasting is available in several languages. If price is not a major deterrent then TV as a media is most effective.

In order to find the answer to the question "what to advertise and when?", it is best to see the creative advertisement. If the Ad is pictorial full of exquisite colours then glossy magazines are the right print media. If a lot of demonstration is to be shown, use TV.

Magazines have their definite readership and language flavour. What will go well in India Today will look out of place in a movie magazine.

Readership surveys of magazines tell us the following:

- Percentage of men and women readers.
- Percentage of age group in each case, for example what percentage of women readers in the age group of 25 to 34 read Femina's every issue.
- Percentage of income groups reading a magazine, for example what percentage of men in the income group of Rs. 25,000 pm read India Today's each issue.
- Percentage of education segment, for example, what percentage of graduates read each issue of Business India.

In the same way information is available with respect to marital status of the readers, number of children they have, what religion they practice.

Given below is the Advertising volume in the USA in the year 1980.

Table 8.14. US Ad. Spent

Media	*Million $*	*%*	*Media*	*Million $*	*%*
Newspaper total	15,615	28.5	TV Total	11,330	20.7
National	2335	4.3	Network	5105	9.3
Local	13,280	24.2	Spot	3260	6.0
Mags. total	3225	5.9	Local	2965	5.4
Weekly	1440	2.6	Radio total	3690	6.7
Women's	795	1.5	Network	185	0.3
Monthly	990	1.8	Local	2755	5.0
Farm publications	135	0.3	Direct mail	7655	14
Outdoor	610	1.1	National total	30,435	55.6
Business publications	1695	3.1	Local	24,316	44.6
Misc.	10,795	19.7	Grand total	54,750	100

Media Status

Newspapers – good for information, news, entertainment and local activities.

Reading public is adults mainly elderly, better educated and comfortably off.

Wide market coverage

Consumer Magazines—good for current social and cultural events, mostly local, glossy but quality not uniform in every magazine. Reading public is athletes, cooks, housewives, hobbyists and investing public. Circulation in large and medium size towns.

Specific Magazines—good for special needs, like women magazines, film based, health, cooking, business, sports and cultural/ social magazines. They are for the trendy public and they increase their awareness of the social and cultural environments.

Radio—is a media of the masses, highly varied in content, from news to classical music to art and film music. The media covers entire country and with FM it is becoming popular again amongst the youth as it provides clear voiced music of all variety. Especially popular in villages where colour TV is not yet available. Can be used as a media for the masses and for the youth with FM. Radio does not provide international exposure in a way TV does with satellite channels.

Television is most visible and covering large part of the country including the remote villages. Great impact due to audio-visual effect can use it to give LIVE demonstrations. Viewers are from the entire market including all segments, the whole family (timing may differ for parents and children). Advertising costs high. Uncertain about reaching the desired segment as TV remote is used to blank advertisements most of the time.

Outdoor advertising has high visibility in a limited way, for the people on the road. It distracts drivers and hence is being banned by some states including Delhi. Gives brand awareness and broad product view.

Direct Mail- selective and personal, becoming popular, the mailer controls the persons who will get to read the mail but has no control on their responses.

Cable TV—uses the superimposing technique, mostly not acceptable to the channel owners. Low cost and local advertising is possible. Viewers find it an irritant as they watch their favourite program.

Yellow Pages—mass media, with phone owners, limited usage.

New media on the cards—in France phone service has provided small computers Minitel to their subscribers, from which they can contact, banks, shops, travel services among other services. Computers, at home has software, which superimposes, advertisements with any matter you may be browsing on the Internet. You see the advertisements on the bottom of the computer screen in supermarkets, big screens show views of their sells area and products telling the viewers where in the mart they can find a particular product. This is an extension of the POINT OF PURCHASE (POP), which has remained in vogue for a time.

Introduction: In order to make the music albums popular, singers and others in the music world have started resorting to showing music videos with vibrant motion/colours and action which attracts the young mind. Music videos are short films which have specialized directors actors dancers and the crew.

Situation: Music videos are good entertainers ads. They also advertise the music albums. Discuss if you rate them as advertisements or as entertainment. If they are a bit of both, discuss their role as advertisement. Do the music videos follow the telecasting norms of decency in India? Do you think in this way, subtle advertising of music albums through music videos is side tracking the real advertising time?

Solutions: Divide the class in to groups of five persons, who will form an Advertising Agency. Each group will do the following:

- Give a name to their agency
- Allot portfolios among themselves as given below:
  - i. CEO
  - ii. Account Director
  - iii. Creative director
  - iv. Copywriter
  - v. Media planner

Next, jointly they meet a firm and take a brief for planning its advertising for the next year. (select a firm where one member has easy access to the top brass, in case it is not possible, ask your professor to give you a hypothetical firm's brief.)

- After getting the brief, find out the target market segment. Most likely, the client will give you ample information on this subject.
- Next, the media planner should suggest the right media for reaching the target segment. This is discussed and finalized after taking clients approval.
- Keeping the media in view, the creative persons should work out an advertising layout. CEO and others then test the layout through advertising research in the market segment and modify the layout if needed.

- Find out the current rates of media purchasing and finalize the budget. It should be in line with the budget idea given by the client.
- Prepare their individual portfolio of such TOTAL ADVERTISING PLAN and keep with them. These will come handy when the students go out for job interviews.

As a corollary, find out who are the members of other market segments who will be exposed to the advertisements and discuss if a demand which can not be met is being created by the advertisement. If yes, is it ethical? Especially for countries like India.

Now add one more member to the team, and he should play-act the role of advertising manager of the client's firm now, arrange a meeting of your team with the advertising manager and discuss the campaign with him. (if possible do it with the real advertiser's man) prepare for the meeting, anticipate the question he is going to ask and your answers to them. One member should be asked to minute the meeting.

At the end of the meeting, please analyze the entire episode with the help of your professor and locate the improvement opportunities in your presentation.

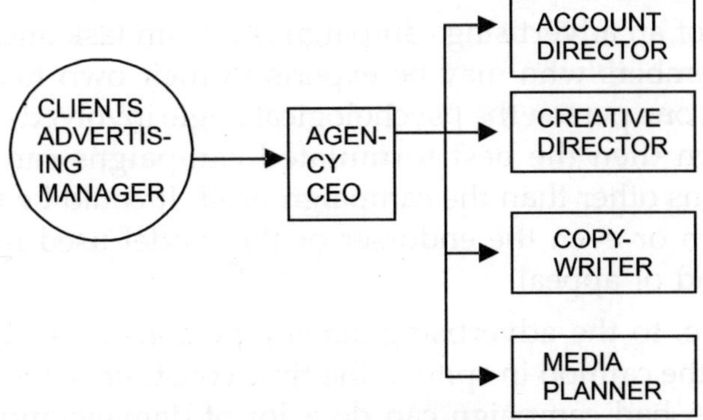

Fig. 8.8. Ad. Agency Operation

Once the team has been formed it can be used to do many such tasks. A well made campaign is a reward to the students it itself.

Bob Jones, the Advertising Pundit from the UK, says, *"Of course advertisers want accountability, but it must often be measured in a more modest and intangible way than we would like. I am afraid that we will have to accept that much advertising can repay fully over long periods of time and its payback is impossible to monitor with any degree of precision."*

We find that millions of rupees are spent on advertising every day. Firms spend up to 30% of their profit after-tax on advertising. What is the method in the paradoxical situation? We will try to analyze the same in this chapter.

Are the products made by us needed or used by any one? If yes then who are they, when and how they buy and what they are willing to pay for it? An advertising agency needs to understand answers to these questions in great degree of accuracy.

Successful campaigns are the result of this knowledge and how the agency uses it to a large degree. Besides they should know the market changes occurring on a continuous basis and be good at communicating. An excellent copy writer using good correct language may not be able to cause even a ripple if the copy is high flouting and going above the intelligence level of the target market. The mind sets of the people, the slang they use, and the imagery acceptable or valued by them will create the right impact. What matters most to the copy writer in a product may have little interest to his audience. The life style of advertising people, with good salaries may be totally at variance with the customer group. As film actors sometimes live in the slum areas to get a feel of the place and the mind sets of the dwellers there, it will be a good idea for the agency people to at least investigate the target market segment persons in depth with an open mind.

Making of an advertising campaign is a team task and that is were the team members who may be experts in their own field of activity must teach a one person the psychological angle involved of their target market. Even then the best formulated campaigns can go haywire due to reasons other than the campaign itself. It could be the timing of the campaign or even the endorser or the model used may not have the right kind of appeal.

Therefore, to the advertising agency persons it is suggested that they use all the caution in spite of the time constraints and the dreaded dead lines. A bad campaign can do a lot of damage and a good one can bring in additional revenues to off set any loss due to delay in the launch of the campaign. One only wishes that the clients understand this fundamental part of advertising!

The dilemma faced by the people in the advertising fold, both the clients people and those from the agency is that when there are a number of controllable and non-controllable variables in the marketing mix, it is the advertising which gets the axe for non achievement of marketing targets. The following graphic shows it clearly:

MARKETING GOALS ACHIEVEMENT CHANNELS:

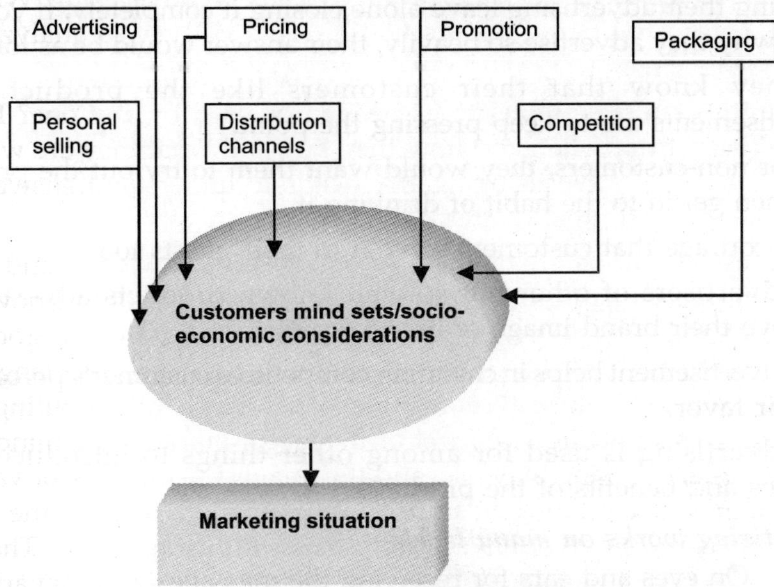

Fig. 8.9. Marketing Goals

Were the increased sales due to advertising or due to better discounts to the dealers, the Maruti car makers may be guessing!

Was the celebrity endorsement responsible or was it personal sales efforts by the sales team the AC makers may worry about.

Similarly in each situation where the sales targets have been exceeded or sales have fallen short of the targets, the dilemma will always be there.

Customer mind set and the socio-economic factors are non-discernable like a black box and what comes out of it is only indicator available. The efficacy of advertising can at best be seen in its absence. Just try to imagine a week with no advertisement on any media of Coke. It will have disastrous effect on its sales. In the first few days the hard-core Coke drinkers will not have any drink. Later on they may start drinking any other drink.

There are three types of customers:

- Hard core addicts- they will not take any other drink for at least a month.
- Moderately addicted to coke will change to other drinks in a weeks time.
- Not at all Coke addicts will change over to other drink on the first day itself.

It is therefore impossible for any of the colas to even think of reducing their advertising leave alone closing it completely. If you ask Coke why they advertise so heavily, their answer would be as follows-

They know that their customers like the product. The advertisements are to keep pressing the point.

For non-customers, they would want them to try out the product and then get in to the habit of drinking it.

Encourage that customers serve it to their guests too.

Advertisers of other not so well known products advertise to improve their brand image or brand equity.

Advertisement helps in changing competitive customer's perception in their favor.

Advertising is used for among other things to introduce new features and benefits of the products.

Advertising works on many levels—

- On eyes and ears for receiving the message
- On the mindset for understanding the message
- On the heart where feelings create the goodwill and proper response

Therefore while testing an advertisement the following questions need to be answered:

For the eyes and ears—

i. Did the advertisement reach?
ii. Did it catch the customers attention?
iii. Did it bring in the Top of the mind recall?
iv. Was it seen or heard or both?

For the mindset—

i. Was the advertisement understood in the way it was meant to be understood?
ii. Did the customer get the message?
iii. Were the message and brand read together?
iv. Was the message not clear?

For the heart—

i. Was the product accepted by the customer?
ii. Did it change the customers attitude about the brand in its favor?
iii. Did the feelings change after seeing the advertisement?
iv. Did the brand perception change?

v. Did it change the perception of competing brands against them?
vi. Did the purchase action take place?

At this point the customers can be asked about the difference the advertisement made, was it the music, a phrase or the slogan or the design, the artwork, and it will give you an insight about the success or nonsuccess of the advertisement.

Advertisers and the agency both keenly await the result of such a response. It is not worthwhile to stand on ego and keep imagining that I am the best creative person and can do no wrong. Remember that a lot of money is involved in the game of advertising and it may have little effect on you as the agency man but it could make or break a product and with it its firm.

Some reactions about the advertisements could read as follows-

- A loser in the elections, "if only my image was properly advertised".
- Advertising Agency after successful launch of product, "the sales graph is ample proof of our campaign was a big success".
- A retailer may lament after spending money on advertising with out increase in business, "it does not work for us, period".
- Industrial marketing manager may be sure of his team but still want advertising to get a foot in the door for his sales persons.

Advertising—Focus on Controversial Matters

Raymond advertises its suiting as for the COMPLETE MAN; it looks at the market segment of the rich and elite. Even sellers like Manikchand Gutka, claim that it is for the top people only. Lots of advertising can be seen in media everyday for the high bracket. First of all do the products deliver? Can they really match up with the expectations of that customer group?

Creative art focuses on the mindsets of the people. It is believed that every one tries to mold or get molded as per his or her environments and fellow beings. Thus people develop symmetry in their behavior pattern. If there is no precedence of behavior people develop one.

Advertising is, fluid, dynamic and it lacks a permanent structure. It also means that advertising creativity comes more from the creative person rather then from the customers. That is why in many cases the advertisement liked by the agency is severely criticized by the viewers. Each one sees what he wants to see, only a view of one of the sides or parameters of advertising.

The blind men's bluff is an appropriate example for the case. Six blind men feel the elephant's body and have their reactions as follows:

The first touches the side and says it is a wall
The second touches the feet and says it is a tree
The third touches the tusk and calls it a spear
The fourth feels the trunk and says it is a snake
The fifth touches its ear and calls it a fan
Finally the sixth touches the tail and calls it a rope.

If we were to ask people if the advertisement was interesting the answers will be:

- Industrial product Ad—not at all
- Radio jingle—sure
- Classified – hardly
- TV Commercial—of course yes
- Direct mail—some times

Advertising is therefore a part of the entire socio-cultural system:

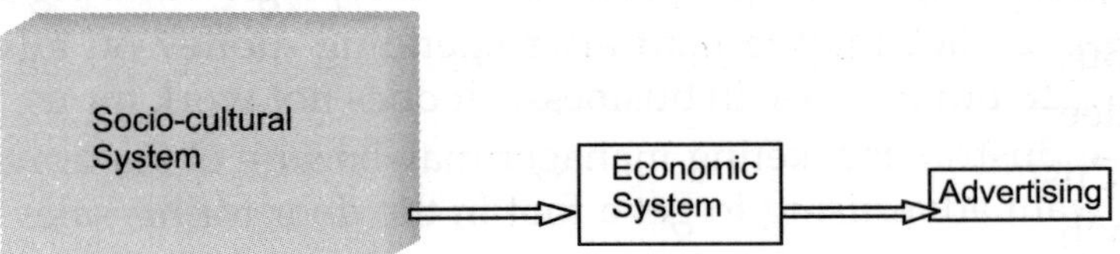

Fig. 8.10. Socio-cultural System & Advertising

Basically, persons are highly self-centered. They like to take care of their own interests. People are usually apathetic towards their surroundings unless they start interfering with their self-interest. Therefore as a corollary, to make them interested talk of things of their interest.

Free market is supposed to be product of the USA. In free markets the individual buyers decide what to buy and what not to buy. The manufacturers and sellers have to manufacture the same products. The process is the reverse of Raw materials, production and marketing:

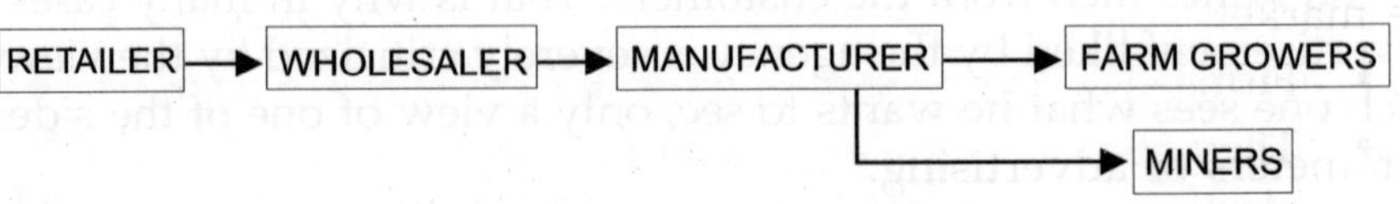

Fig. 8.11. Reverse Process

FREE MARKET ENCOURAGES COMPETITION, WHICH IS TO THE BENEFIT OF THE CONSUMER.

Competition among the sellers and suppliers forces the manufacturers to keep on innovating and differentiating their products. Prices on the other hand depend on competition and demand supply equation.

Selling Price = a f (competition + supply demand gap)
Where a is the cost of manufacture and f is function.

To complex matters we have the GNP, salaries wages rents interest rates, dividends which all define the market.

Free market believes that the customers are wise and sane people who decide on only merits of the products. Yet, there are skeptical who believe that the contrary is true and the customers need to be nurtured and educated. The government of the land comes to the rescue by formulating laws for the protection of the customers.

Free thinkers want the following to be happening in the market place:

- Buyers and Sellers should be free to carry on their trade as they deem fit within the law of the land.
- Customers should be accepted as a person with intelligence who can make right decisions.
- Competition provides the required checks and balances in the market place, which is beneficial to the entire community.

Free market including advertising is on the firing line for reasons given below:

- Suppliers can force buyers in to buying their products by alluring advertisements not always justified.
- Buyers may be given lop sided view by telling them only favorable things about the product.
- MNCs and large businesses dominate the market and can squeeze out small players who may be offering a good product through sheer money power.

Business Guru R. Nadar has the following remedy for the ills of free market:

- Firms should remain honest in their dealings
- They should stop corrupting the politicians with underhand election funds
- Be good to workers by providing healthy work environment

- Stop polluting the planet by disposing solid liquid and gaseous effluents in to the earths surface
- Start long range planning for the benefit of their stakeholders

Let us see how advertising can be dangerous to the society in the world—

- In the west teens have started using alcohol in an increasing manner, while the sports events show the healthy sports persons enjoying drinks in TEAM SPIRIT!
- Billions of dollars are spent in advertising of cigarettes—the main cause of a lot of terminal problems.
- AD Films for contraceptives have become pornographic and the entire family sees these together.
- Freedom to buy could lead to unnecessary purchases. People are supposed to become wiser after making a few mistakes. Could the mistakes prove too costly?
- Appeals to children who have no financial knowledge can become a big embarrassment if nothing else to the parents
- Children and women are fully exploited and at times for the sake of a few rupees they let themselves be exploited to the detriment of the society.
- At times the truth becomes a victim as it is twisted out of shape to give it the right colour accepted and appreciate by the customers.

As a first step towards rationalization a code of self-regulation has come in place in many countries. Advertising Agency Associations monitor the Ads and play the role of internal censure for the offensive Ads.

James Roman has commented on the Ads with children that the advertising has reached its nadir of marketing when they have allowed children to be manipulated and programmed to act as advertising surrogates promoting the latest industry virtues.

Others have proposed a ban on advertisements directed towards children who are young to understand the purpose of the Ads, mainly children below the age of eight years.

They have suggested ban on Ads for candies, which are harmful for the teeth especially of children of age group 8–11.

Ads for candies for older children should have reference of health problems eating candies could bring to them.

It has been said that there is no harmful effect on children because of these Ads except that at the grocers shops children pester the parents sometimes in to buying the products.

Finally, it has to be seen how truthful the Advertisements are. Is puffery the main theme or has it been totally avoided. See the following copy:

- The toothpaste gives round the clock protection against harmful germs. (are germs of some other kinds too)
- Use the masala and forget mothers cooking (how can masala cook the food?)
- Use the talcum powder and feel cool (is it a powder or an air conditioner?)
- Use the soap and become a beauty in ten days (is the soap also a cosmetologist?)

In your daily life you will find so many of these types of advertisements. Is it not possible at all to find out the real advantages and benefits and highlight them?

Information, which the customers are looking for, is given below. Some of these are mandatory from the government as well:

- On the package give, weight, size, volume, quantity, date of manufacture and date of expiry
- Possible harmful effects of the products
- Price inclusive of all taxes
- Country of manufacture

Information beyond the advertisements comes from topical articles from experts, like Murad Ali Beg writing about cars, Tarla Dalal writing about food. Such articles if they appear in one consumer magazine will do a lot of good to both buyers and to sellers.

Table 8.15. Advertising Plus & Minus Points

Advertising plus and minus points:

Plus Points	*Minus Points*
Economic growth, helps develop competition	Expenditure can be avoided, creates competition on items other than price like brand equity
New product market development, competition keeps firms on their toes	Creates entry barriers, for competition can equate business possibilities
Helps in marketing effort, increases market chances	Can raise costs and prices
Provides information to the customers, ensures quality of the product, increases demand	Wrong information to customers, puffery

Checking the balance sheet of advertising we can safely say that it is a valuable communication vehicle which provides the customers with a variety and choices for their purchase action. Firms take advantage of one brand doing well to group it with other products to make them equally popular in highly competitive areas, bunching of products to sell more is a known practice, especially in IT and computers.

Advertising—A Mass Communication System

Advertising implies mass communication as the advertiser is communicating with large number of people whom it is unlikely to meet or know. Advertiser does not know the circumstances when the message given by him is seen or heard by the people. Advertiser also does not get any feed back about the immediate response of the viewers after seeing the advertisement.

On the other side of the coin, the advertiser can reach a large number of people at a cost, which is low when compared to the money, and time he will spend if he has to meet all of them personally. And practically it is not even possible as by the time he has finished meeting all, the product about which the meeting is taking place may even become obsolete. In order to make the most of the advertising effort, advertisers have the facility to make the advertising interesting, attractive and eye catching. With TV as a media, and computer graphics the possibilities are immense.

It is an accepted fact that no two persons are alike. The brain chemistry differs which ensures that each one will behave differently given the same stimulus. Even the same person behaves in different manner with the same stimulus, depending on his mood, surroundings, state of health.

Behaviour depends on psychological factors and environmental factors.

Given below is graphic of advertising process:

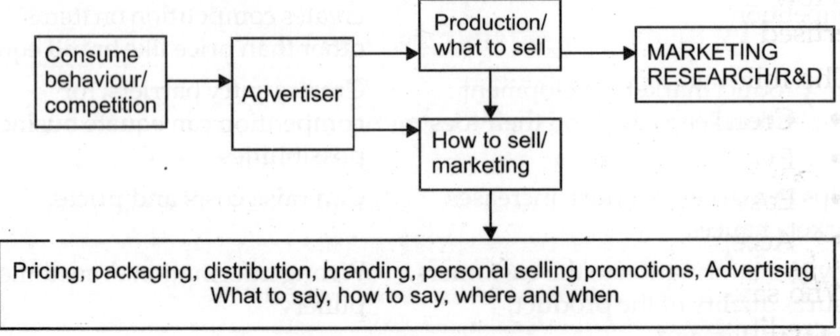

Fig. 8.12. Ad. Operations

Creativity comes from generating several ideas, and then through screening process gets the right idea.

Some years back, in a Cricket World Cup, Coke was declared as the official drink for the event. Naturally, the main competitors, Pepsi were having rough weather, till they got it right. When some body said, after all what is so official about the cold drink, the slogan game as a breath of fresh air, THERE IS NOTHING OFFICAL ABOUT IT *DRINK Pepsi!*

While making an Ad, care has to be taken to differentiate between providing awareness and creating emotional bonding with the product. For this purpose the following can be used:

Product benefit ranking

Adjectives to be used

Metaphors to be used

Success stories to be told

Endorsers to be selected

For commercials activities around the filming have to be activated

The use of USP (Unique Selling Preposition), or several USPs depending on plan of advertisement, and the media is a big help in creating an eye catching Ad—

- Advertisements must specify the benefits buyers will get from use of the product (if possible, depending on the product and more especially in industrial products, the benefit can be translated in Rupees per unit of time, and it will have great pulling power).
- The benefits should be different from what competition is offering.
- The benefit must be strong enough to become a driving force for the millions of viewers.

How the agencies try to see that the customers buy the products advertised by them, how do they persuade them.

The following points need to be considered in this respect:

- Creativity of the Advertisement
- Eye catching presentation
- Easy understanding of the matter
- Accepting of the proposal given in the advertisement.

Who says so is important in advertisements. The endorsers should have credibility with the customers. A professor of law or a leading lawyer best endorses a law book. However, if the lawyer is taken for a model who is saying good things about the book because the money he is getting from it the credibility goes down.

A pretty girl advertising a lipstick will be accepted as she would be considered as an expert, while she may be a poor model for detergents as customers may not believe that she has ever washed her clothes.

Once the viewers accept the source, they tend to put the advertisement in their memory and would recall it at the purchase time even though they may have forgotten the endorser.

The advertisement becomes eye catching if the firm has good brand equity. Similarly if the endorser is well respected then the advertisement gains the attractiveness.

For creating a positive attitude of the customers, the following methods are used:

- Expressing views in a way which is of interest of the viewers.
- Enhancing customers ego by praising him for taking the right decisions.
- Making statements, which can be verified by the viewers, through logical reasoning.
- Giving the benefits the customers will derive from the products. At times living the conclusion to be drawn to the viewers to arouse their curiosity. The cream makes skin smooth and glowing, have you tried it?
- Giving the competitive benefits with stress on the positive side of your product and not so positive of the competitors. The comparison highlights the product as the right choice. These days competitive advertisements have become the vogue. Care must be taken to give the right picture, the truth and nothing but the truth, because otherwise you may be dragged in to courts by the competitors.
- Emotions play a vital role in purchase made by people, although most will not agree to this statement. FOR A PRETTIER YOU! GET THE MAN OF YOUR CHOICE-USE XXYY COSMETICS
- DO YOU KNOW WHAT WILL HAPPEN WHEN YOU ARE NO MORE? SAVE FOR YOUR LOVED ONES, INSURE WITH US—LIC
- WHAT LIFE YOU WANT TO GIVE TO YOUR GRAND CHILDREN? VOTE FOR A POLLUTION FREE WORLD—GROW MORE TREES!
- TODAY YOUR FRIENDLY NEIGHBOUR MAY KILL YOU—an advertisement against drunken driving

Now that you have got your customers to buy your products how are you going to retain them? The onslaught of competitive forces is never ending.

Raising your brand equity through is one way of doing it. next, the risk associated with the change need to be stressed, "change your cars engine oil and lower the time of overhaul".

"The substitute toothpastes cause tooth decay , are you willing to risk it?" or, "you did try to change once and it lead to disaster. Please make sane decisions now".

Continuous sales promotional plans are other methods albeit they can be copied sooner than later. **The customers can be immunized against the virus of competitive product by putting your own product on its rightful pedestal.**

Another method is to keep stating what the competition is saying and then one by one refuting all their claims, logically.

You sell pure fruit juices. Competition claims that no fruit juice can have a shelf life to be able to sell in the entire country. Talk about it and then give proof of your several filling and juice extracting facilities round the country.

You have to sell the metro rail to the local public. So far, personal transport has been in use, as other public transport like the bus has been over crowded and public does not want to go near it. Talk about the cost saving, rising petrol costs, and reducing pollution levels, making roads safe for children.

In most advertising there are four factors, which need to be considered together—

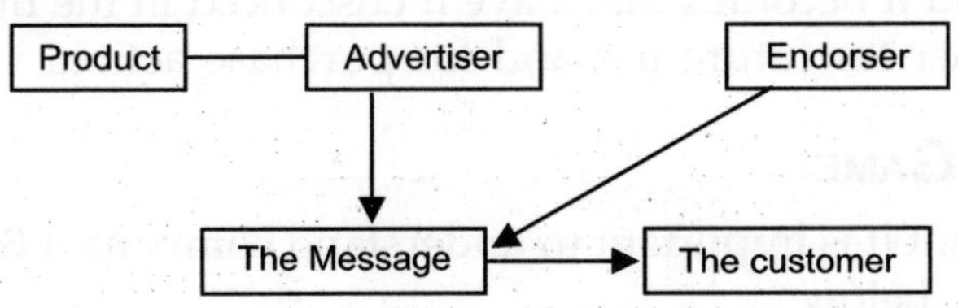

Fig. 8.13. Advertising Factors

Person belonging to a group with similar attitudes should make endorsement. Furthermore he should stand the customers self-scrutiny test. He should be imaging the self-testing of the customer. He or she should be likeable and attractive. If the product qualities are of nebulous in nature and cannot be verified easily then endorsements will be more useful. The customers should know endorsers as worthy of their acceptance. Endorser should take care to project his image as that of an outsider! He should talk like an expert, endorse the firms product only, and not competitors, should give a long time endorsement.

Messages should give information most sought out by the customers. The message should appear to the customer as unambiguous, acceptable and convincing. The concept of product benefits should match with what the customer is looking for.

One way is to point out what is missing in customer's life and then propose the product as fulfilment of what is missing, " having lived all my life in the terrible heat of Delhi, I have no whereto go." **Why, this summer go to Switzerland, at least for the climate, BUY OUR SILENT BEST COOL ACs.**

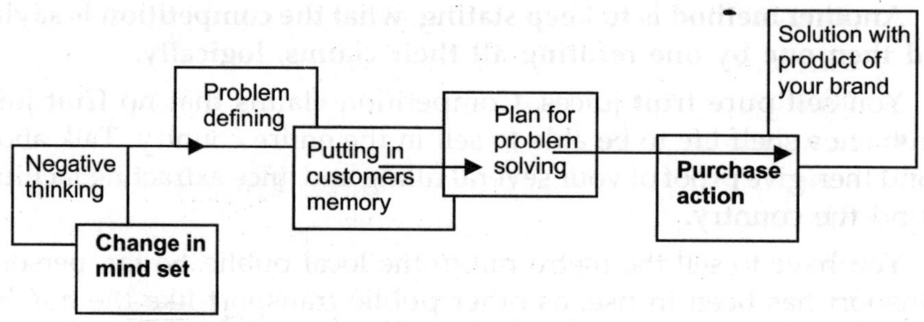

Fig. 8.14. Influencing the Customer

People start with negative thinking NO, IT IS JUST NOT POSSIBLE. This defined their problem and then they plan to solve the problem at this point the advertisement comes hand to suggest a solution and change the perspective of negative thought. With your brand implanted in buyers mind it becomes easy have it ensconced in the memory bank of the customer for future use and for purchase action.

Marketing Game

At this point it is important to understand company's Balance Score Card as given below:

Balance Score Card

To understand the holistic picture of a firm it is important to address four areas, which decide the possibility of successful result in a firm, which are given below:

1. Customer
2. Finance

3. Operations
4. Organization

Customer—the firm works for the customers, earns profits and grows because of them; the firm needs to know its market share and brand value. The firm's position is determined by its competitive advantage over competition. Firms gain Competitive Advantage by one or all of the following means:

- Achieving uniqueness over competition, in the product, price, placement, and promotion or in service; provide differentiation, which is liked and appreciated by the customer and which does not jack up the price to an extent not acceptable to the customer. (Providing gold wiring inside a TV Set in place of copper wiring is an extreme example of total opportunity loss with product differentiation and high pricing). Customers look for differentiated product as it gives them satisfaction and ego boosting by making them owner of a product none else possesses.
- Low cost of production, which is achieved by economies of scale of manufacture and by experience curve of the workers who improve the productivity over time and reduce production rejections. Lowering the cost should never be at the cost of product quality because it could become counterproductive and the firm may lose the entire market. With lower cost of production, the firm generates cash, which can be utilized in firm's growth or at times of severe price competition in hitting at the competition.
- Quick Response—the firm meeting the requirements of the customers first gains advantage over latter competitive firms.

Finance—it is mainly used to determine the profitability of the firm, its growth and the economic value it is adding to itself (Economic Value Added—EVA). EVA can be seen as the true indicator of firm's financial health, rather than the usual Return On Investment—ROI.

EVA can be arrived at in the following manner:

EVA = PAT—(INTEREST ON DEBT + COST OF EQUITY CAPITAL)

PAT is profit after tax and cost of equity is calculated by taking average risk adjusted rate of return, which equity or shareholder will get if he invests his money elsewhere. Firms can increase EVA by getting lower cost capital or by using less capital.

Operations—to analyze the firms operations, the core processes, the product development, demand management and order fulfilment processes must be looked into. How the firm can obtain competitive advantage from these processes.

Understanding the following areas of the firm is required for organizational analysis

- Leadership based on leading by example, motivating personnel rather than ordering them about
- Motivation and energy level of the workmen
- Firm's ability to accept change when required
- Learning mode of the firm.

CHAPTER 9

Marketing Research

Aims and Outcomes of the Chapter

Market scenario is both complex and chaotic due to major competitors now operating in the country, in most products, including industrial or B-to-B products and for this reason the managers cannot just depend on their experience or their gut feeling for taking marketing decisions. Marketing Research has therefore become an important tool used by the marketers to understand the marketing opportunities, marketing problems as well as for making marketing strategies. The students will earn the different ways of conducting the research for the company's benefit.

For the students of Marketing it is important to understand the theory and practical applications of Market Research. This material will provide the students an insight in to the vital aspect of Market Research (MR) in easy to understand language without the clutter of MR jargon. With a view to making reading interesting, several examples have been included. Also included are a number of Case Studies for getting in to real life situations.

MR is associated with primary research for most beginners. However as we know, MR starts with secondary research, which can be conducted by looking at an immense amount of data already available somewhere and we need to locate it. Secondary data can provide valuable information regarding market size historically and future growth patterns.

Qualitative Research is an integral part of MR. It helps in product development, design and modifications. It also can assist in locating the right market segment for the products, as qualitative research directs us towards the customer's mindsets, in the course of studying the subject and also in the real life corporate world.

Some amount of redundancy has been built in to the chapter for the sake of reminding students at appropriate places.

INTRODUCTION TO MARKET RESEARCH

Before the student starts learning Market Research, it may be useful to have a recap of Marketing Mix Factors. Marketing has become an all-pervasive discipline, in as much that no business, industry can remain untouched by marketing. In good old days, when there were only a handful of manufacturers of a product, competition was limited or just not there, marketing as we understand it today was a luxury only as it was not required. Manufacturers made the products and sold it in the market. The stress was on Sales. In India even up to sixties, in the twentieth century, manufacturers were confident of selling their products at a profit without the fear of some body under cutting them as there was enough business for all. Competition increased, especially after India liberalized its economy, and the floodgates of international players were opened. Now, the competition has become a vital force the business has to reckon with.

With increased competition, firms need to play their cards according to the competition and market condition. Hence, the need to systematically understand competition and Market conditions and of Market Research!

Let us take an example. When you want to buy an expensive thing like Motorcycle, how would you decide to go about it? Most likely you will take some of these steps—

- Check out on the different brands available by visiting motorcycle dealers.
- Compare the prices, specifications like HP, after sales service, and dealer's attitude towards customers.
- Ask your relations, friends, colleagues who own bikes about their experiences, views about different bikes.
- Look for the advertisements in different media like newspapers, magazines, TV to get as much information you can get about competitive bikes.
- See your budget and then take a decision based on the gathered facts.

Same way, as a seller it is important to know what product the buyer wants, where he wants it, what price he is ready to pay for the product, how would he like to pay for it, by credit card, cash, cheque, or by some hire-purchase arrangement? Getting the answers of these questions is the task before MR.

Let us examine what constitutes marketing in the twenty-first century. To start with let us again understand the Marketing-Mix factors as given below:

1. Market Research- (including market survey, and analysis) this factor, as will be seen is used for virtually all other Marketing Mix factors.
2. Product
3. Brand
4. Packaging
5. Trade Mark
6. Logo
7. Label
8. Price
9. Placement or simply, distribution
10. Promotion—or sales promotion
11. Advertising
12. Credit and it's control
13. Personal selling
14. Training of marketing personnel of the firm and retailers

Items 3 to 7 are directly related to the product

As already stated Market Research (MR) can be undertaken for any of the above stated factors. Besides, MR is conducted to get the total market potential, its possible growth and strengths and weaknesses of competition in respect to the marketing mix factors.

Starting with the **Product,** MR can be conducted to get information or trends in the following areas:

- Is there a demand for the product?
- If yes, in which market segment?
- What is the level of demand?
- Is there a demand in peripheral segments? If yes then what is its level?
- Is the product acceptable to the market as it is, or any modification would be necessary?
- Are the product package, brand, trademark, label and logo eye-catching enough?
- Is the package size acceptable?

(At this point, please pick up a FMCG product and get the market information about its acceptance with respect to any area from 3 to 7. You may ask only your close friends or relatives, say 4–5 in number.)

MR can be conducted to ascertain the market acceptability of **price** *vis-à-vis* competitive product and its price. It may be important to know the hidden costs of competition, like extra, for immediate delivery, and lower discount levels for the distribution channels. Most dealers of competitive products try to play one against the other by implying that your competitor is paying higher discounts while the case may be just the reverse.

In pricing it is of utmost importance to find out the **real** competitive price and also to know if the products under comparison are having similar if not the same specifications, or are we comparing apples with oranges?

Higher prices, as we know can be charged by firms for better product, immediate delivery, better brand name (higher BRAND equity). Yet, to be sure of the right price to be charged for your product it is best to conduct MR and be sure that you are making reasonable profits and not losing money by undercutting on price.

Placement or Distribution Channels: It is normally believed that for a given product, there is a set distribution channel. However, now with the advent of several new channels it may be worthwhile to make sure that you are using the most appropriate channel/s. Internet market, tele-shopping, and telemarketing are some of the newer ways of placing the product in the market. It depends on the product and the market segment you are going to cater which should decide the channel.

Advertising and Promotion: It is need to be planned carefully, as a lot of money is going into these heads. Naturally a wise marketer would like to consider the best way to promote and advertise his or her product. Due to the special significance of Advertising Research, it will be discussed at length later on.

Market Research can be compared to the army spy network, which gathers information about the enemy so that strategies can be made to defeat the enemy.

Advertising has been defined by the American Marketing Association as **"the gathering, recording and analyzing of all data about problems relating to the transfer and sale of goods and services from producer to consumer".**

MR ultimately builds a data bank or creates an Information System for the firm to remain pro-active in the market place and acquire and maintain its position. Since the market, competition and customer needs are ever changing in today's business, it is important to have a dynamic, continuous MR in the organization.

Here, we can differentiate MR and Market Information System—(MIS) as follows:

- MR is mainly for finding solutions while MIS is also needed to prevent problems from occurring.
- While both are continuous processes, MR is usually conducted on the basis of problem solution in the area of marketing.
- MR provides external information while MIS is mostly for internal data.

People sometimes confuse Market Research with Marketing Research. Let us see how marketing guru Richard D. Crips defines them—

Marketing research is the systematic, objective and exhaustive research, for the study of the facts relevant to any problem in the field of marketing.

Market research is restricted to the study of actual and potential buyers, their location, their actual and potential value of purchases and their motives and habits.

Let us examine the process involved in conducting MR—

Significant elements of MR process can be shown as follows:

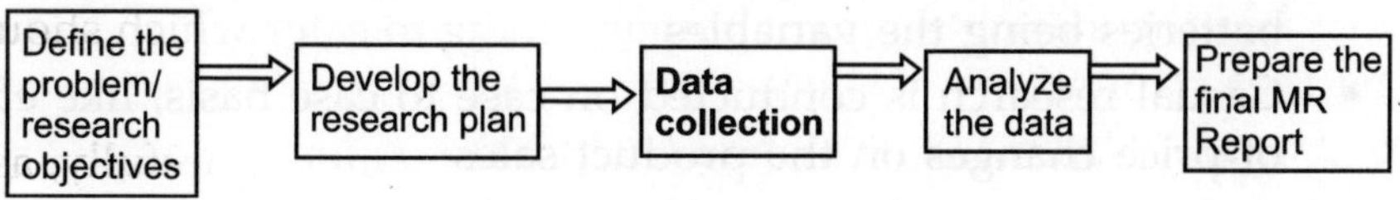

Fig. 9.1. MR Process

Marketing Research Objectives

From the viewpoint of Marketing Manager, the most useful role of MR is in the area of market demand and supply, in ever changing, mostly growing market and increasing competition.

It is important to define MR objectives as the starting point of MR. The accuracy of the objective definition would be the key factor in the accuracy of MR findings. Main objectives of MR are as follows:

- Demand projection for the product in a given area for an acceptable period like one year. This takes into account the historical demand of past years, market dynamics and changing business environment

- Competitive activities, product differentiation, entry barriers.
- Competitive market share
- Brand positions
- Competitive prices vis-à-vis brand equity
- Advertising and promotional strengths of competition.

The next range of MR objectives are in the area of **customers needs,** as given below:

- What product benefits customers are seeking
- Product usage with different customer groups, light or heavy usage
- Top of the mind recall
- Price and quality perceptions
- Purchase decision procedures, who are the persons involved in it
- Reasons for brand preferences.

Let us see the types of MR being conducted—

- Exploratory research is conducted to confirm thoughts and ideas. Since these are conducted in small areas, they are low in cost and they take less time.
- Statistical research deals with frequency of events like the purchase action. Such research provides inputs for analysis, as the variables for the research are pre-decided, as how often car batteries are changed in Maruti cars, time, and brand of batteries being the variables
- Casual research is conducted on case to case basis, like effect of price changes on the product sales

Primary MR or Market Survey is conducted by collecting data or information directly from the consumers. Before launching on a full scale survey which entails heavy expenditure, it is advisable to conduct a Sample survey where the survey is conducted in a limited area to test the methods used. Both Qualitative and Quantitative information can be gathered through market surveys.

The survey can be conduced in several ways as follows:

- *Observation Method:* If you want to know the number of vehicles polluting the atmosphere in Delhi, you could stand near congested crossing and observe the vehicles, which are polluting, for a month or so which would give you enough information as sample survey. More detailed information would take much more time, many more crossings and persons observing the polluting vehicles. Cameras and other signal gathering devices can be used like the smoke detectors, speed sensors for knowing the average speed of vehicles passing through a particular point.

- Personal interviews—in this method you with your team meet a number of users personally, ask them questions as per a predetermined questionnaire and get first hand information from them. The information collected is then used to extrapolate for the entire customer group to get the real answers. These surveys are time consuming and expensive, but more accurate. These Questionnaire methods will be discussed at length later on.
- Mail surveys are conducted by sending the questionnaire to a number of customers with request for filling them and returning to the surveyor. The method is not expensive, but it may not give accurate results, as the rate of getting replies from the customers is poor. Also the information which comes in may be skewed as people when replying to such questionnaires, tend to give inflated figure.
- Telephone surveys are conducted as a low cost easy method of gathering information. The problem in such surveys is the fact that people replying to telephone may not be the right persons.

Marketing Research Methods

There are two basic methods of doing Marketing Research:

1. Primary Research
2. Secondary Research

As normally secondary research is done first, we will discuss it first. Sources of secondary data are as follows:

- Firm's internal source, include, P/L Statements, inventory levels, sales visit reports, previous MR Reports.
- Incoming staff members who may be coming from competitive firms.
- Government publications and notifications, like from Directorate of audio visual publicity, Research organizations.
- Trade publications- each trade has its own journals which carry information about the historical business and projections. Magazines on Computers, IT, Electronics, Cinema, TV,

Agriculture, Science and Technology, Dress designing, Interior Decoration, practically every possible area of business are in the market.

- Competitors balance sheets.
- Publications of Industry Associations like FICCI, CII, ASSOCHEM.
- All India Management Association journal.
- Trade and Business newspapers and magazines like Financial Times, Business Today, Business India.
- Internet.
- Market Research Organizations, like ORG-Marg, who sell MR Reports at a price.
- Sales statistics of product's dealers.
- Publications of Reserve Bank of India, financial Institutions like, IFCI, IDBI, ICICI, UTI.
- Foreign Government Data, International publications- these help in the area of international business as also at the introductory stage of products as they can tell about the rate of product penetration in other countries as a bench mark for India. Of course other economic parameters, which may be differentiating the countries, will have to be kept in mind.

Secondary data as the name itself suggests, is the data for which some body else has done the job of collecting the information as Primary data.

At this stage it may be a good idea for the students to get some secondary Market Survey data, by gathering information from libraries, where old copies of newspapers, magazines and other publications are available. (You may also list down as many secondary sources as possible from where you can get the data). Please collect information about any one of the following:

- **Mid-size car price variation in the last three years.**
- **Washing powders, introduction of several new brands in the last three years.**
- **New distribution systems in the area of Consumer durables.**

To get an idea about the objectives let us take Surf Excel as the product. You can find out the following from your respondents (persons you are going to talk about the product):

1. Reasons why housewives prefer the product.
2. What types of housewives are likely to use the product?

3. In a given area how many would be using the product?
4. How many more would use it if cheaper package is used to sell to another segment at a lower rate?
5. Besides package and price what are other factors, which help the buyer to decide in favour of the product?

Once the objectives are well defined, it is important to go to get the source of data.

Focus group research is conducted by inviting some ten persons from the market segment of the product, to get to know from them their views about the product, its price, channels of distribution. The expert conductor of the meeting will ask them, "What do you think about the quality of Surf Excel"

With free and easy dialogue, and without the burden of family presence, persons come out and give their frank opinions.

Questionnaire method can be used for collecting information in the case of Surf Excel. It consists of relevant questions, which the respondents can easily answer. It is the most common and effective way of getting the answers as it means direct contact with the user and gets the replies to the problems baffling the marketer.

Questionnaire consists of questions, which are closed type, where options are provided and the respondent has to just give his choice from among the options.

The questions can be asked in the following manner:

- Yes/No type —did you personally select the product? -Yes/no
- Multiple choice—who helped you in the selection- brother/ sister/uncle/friend
- Answers are given on a five point scale:
  1. I like the Surf Excel very much
  2. I like it all right
  3. I barely like it
  4. I do not like it
  5. I do not like it at all.

The first part of the questionnaire consists of demographic information about the respondent. A sample is given below:

Name:

Address Phone/fax/e-mail

Age: below 25/25–40/41–60/60+

Income level/pm below Rs. 5000/5001–15,000/15,001–30,000/30,001–50,000/50,001–80,000/80,001 +

Family size—below 3/3–5/6–9

People find it easier to give a range for age, income rather than giving accurate figures, as it could be less embarrassing.

Questionnaires should be carefully developed, tested through a sample test, modified as required and then used for gathering information.

Questions can, at times, influence the answers. Hence to make them totally objective, they should be carefully prepared.

Close ended questions, like giving answer choices guide the respondent into the area with which the researcher is familiar.

Open-ended questions get the respondents to use their own words and individualistic replies come from such questions. Such questions are useful in exploratory type of MR. However, if time is an important factor, it is better to ask close questions, which can be answered in lesser time.

Open-ended question could be- "What is your opinion about Surf Excel as a detergent powder?"

Or, "what is the first name which comes to your mind when you think of detergents?"

Or, the interviewer shows the respondent, an extra clean used shirt and asks, "What does the shirt remind you of?"

Or, the interviewer shows the respondent a picture of Surf Excel and asks, "What can it do for you?"

Questions should be as simple as possible, direct to the point, with no possibility of any ambiguity.

The questions should follow a pattern, a logical sequence.

It is time that the students prepare a questionnaire for conducting MR for any one of the following products:

- **A car**
- **Cosmetics**
- **Readymade garments**

The student can select a brand and build the questionnaire around that brand.

Testing the questionnaire needs to be done next. For the purpose a small sample is adequate. It should be from the market segment for which the product is meant. If any question is found to be difficult, or objectionable it should be modified or removed. A mix of 20–25 respondents should be normally sufficient for the test purposes.

A sample questionnaire is given below:

Sir/Madam,

This is a survey of households with respect to small cars purchase. We request you to kindly help in filling the questionnaire giving your ideas, as we attach great value to your judgment in this regard. We thank you in anticipation of your cooperation.

1. Do you have a small car? yes/no.
2. If yes, please tell its model and make.
3. If no, then please go to the last question.
4. Buying the small car, what were you looking for?
5. What is your opinion on the features of small cars listed below:

Features	*A*	*B*	*C*	*D*	*E*
Design					
Availability of colors					
Horse power					
Speeds possible					
Seats and sitting comfort					
AC/Stereo					
Safety aspects					
Service facilities					
Luggage space					

(Since this is only a sample many questions have been left out)

A-EXTREMELY IMPORTANT, B—IMPORTANT, C—SOMEWHAT REQUIRED, D—MAY BE REQUIRED E NOT NEEDED AT ALL

6. How do you rate the price of your car, is it high, medium, low for the car? Did you get value for money?
7. Did you make outright purchase or took the hire purchase option? If you bought the car under H/P, which company offered the loan?
8. Who all helped you in deciding about the car? Rate the following as per their importance:

- Wife/husband
- Sons/daughters
- Other relatives
- Neighbours
- Colleagues

9. Did you see any advertisement of the car prior to purchase and if yes, did it help in decision-making?
10. Some statements are given below. Please give your opinion on the same.

Statement	YES/YES	YES/	YES
Small cars			
are family cars			
Status symbols			
Good for town run			
Roads not suitable			
for small cars			

1.1 About yourself please—
- Name-(optional)
- Age—below 25/26–35/36–50/51 and above
- Education level—undergraduate level/graduate/post graduate/doctorate
- Family income pm—less than 7000/7001–10,000/10,001–15,000/15,001–30,000/30,001–60,000/60,001 and above
- Purchase decision process—who all are involved in the family?

Thanks for your valuable time!

The students should make a questionnaire with the above sample only as a guideline.

Second sample of a questionnaire, for a furniture maker would be as follows:

Questionnaire

1. When did you last change your main furniture—
   i. Less than one year back
   ii. 1–3 years
   iii. more than three years
2. What type of furniture did you buy—
   i. Wooden

ii. Wrought iron
iii. SUNMICA top
iv. Combination

3. What style furniture did you buy:
   i. Continental type
   ii. Indian style
   iii. Ethnic
4. Which member of the family went with you to select the furniture- wife/husband, brother/sister/father/mother/others/friend/or did you go alone?
5. Why did you select this type of furniture?
6. Did you consult any Interior Decorator? If yes, then whom?
7. Who were consulted?

Consultation with-	Type of furniture	Style of furniture
Self Brothers/sisters,		
Wife/husband,		
Advertisements,		
Interior decorator,		
Dealer of furniture		

8. What were the essential features you sought in the furniture

Factors	Most Essential	Essential
Desirable		
Durability		
Finish		
Range of colours		
Matching sets		
Price		

9. Please give your particulars as follows:
   i. Name
   ii. Age (give a range as suggested earlier)
   iii. Income—(give a range)
   iv. Occupation

Thanks!

Now it is time to understand, what we are going to survey? Who are our target audience? Defining the market segment, the right geographic area, gives us the parameters, along which we have to organize the survey. We call it the Universe or the population, for the purpose of the MR. the universe, or the total population for Surf Excel would be the entire middle and high-income group of a town.

Organizing a Market Survey for the ENTIRE universe can, and usually is, a time consuming, expensive process. It may take so much time meeting and asking questions from a million people, that by the time the results appear the product itself may become obsolete. Therefore the Survey is done on the basis of a sample of the universe, which is made using well-established techniques.

Sample size

The larger number of people to be interviewed, the better or more reliable the result. However, in practice, it is better to cover a much smaller sample, may be one percent of the universe to get reasonably good results, in lesser time and money. It really depends on how the sample gets selected.

Sample Selection

There can be two ways of selecting a sample:

1. *Probability Sample*—it ensures that each of the members of the universe have equal chance or probability of being selected for the survey. It helps in understanding the levels errors on account of the sample selected. There are three ways of probability sampling-
   i. Simple random sample—every member has an equal opportunity of being in the survey.
   ii. Stratified random survey—the population/universe is divided into mutually exclusive groups such as, age, income and then random samples are taken from each group.
   iii. Cluster sample—the population is divided as per geographic divisions, like for example Delhi could be divided into, north, south, east, west and central zones and sample taken from each zone on random basis.
2. *Non-probability Sample*—as the cost and time involved in probability sample surveys is quite high, MR people use non-probability sample. This can be done in three ways:
   i. Convenience sample—the research person selects the persons most easily met for the MR.

ii. Judgement sample—researcher uses his judgement about the sample, which would provide the most accurate answers.

iii. Quota sample—the researcher meets with a set of persons in each category.

As an example, in sampling methods, if one person is not available then no one else takes his place except in quota sample method where the researcher has to find out another person in the same category and meet him.

At times even with proper sampling errors creep in to the collected data. The reasons of such errors are given below:

- A portion of population may have been omitted.
- People not included in the sample may differ widely from those interviewed.
- Substitute interviewees may not be right ones if you are not able to meet the person in the sample.
- The respondents find questionnaire difficult.
- Respondents may not have enough information on the subject or they may not like to reveal it for some reason.
- Some questions in the questionnaire may have a bias or slant towards one answer.
- Interviewer may not be fully qualified to take up the job of getting respondents opinion.

The researcher must take these in to account when analyzing the collected data.

When systematically the sample is drawn, it helps as, data collection becomes lower in cost, and it is easy to control.

Planning Samples

Let us plan a sample for EPABX of large size say which cater to 1000 lines. Who would be interested in the EPABX?

1. Industrial units, MNCs, large Indian firms, public sector companies.
2. Government departments and offices.
3. R&D Labs in private and government sector.
4. Banks, Indian and foreign, Financial institutions.
5. Universities and educational institutions like IITs and IIMS.

As a starting point let us get list of all the organizations in the population group with a turnover of Rs. 50 crores.

Pick up 100% of organizations with turnover of Rs. 500 crores.

Select 20 units from the organizations with turnover of more than Rs. 100 crores but less than Rs.500 crores.

Select 15 units with turnover of less than Rs. 100 crores.

Pick up all the government departments and their head offices.

Likewise select some units from each of the other categories.

To sum up the sampling technique for EPABX 1000— can be as follows:

- Defining the population
- Sampling unit would be the firms and offices having population needing about 800 phones.
- Sample size could be 400.

TASK FOR THE STUDENTS—Please develop a questionnaire for the organizations for the EPABX Survey.

As per Philip Kotler the marketing guru their are characteristics of a good Market Research as follows:

1. Scientific method—effective MR, is conducted on scientific lines, with formulation of hypothesis, theory, testing and results.
2. Creativity—a teenage clothing firm gave video cameras to several young persons, who were asked to film the discos restaurants where the teenagers went most of the time.
3. Multiple-methods—to increase credibility-marketing people use several methods together.
4. Value and cost of information—marketing persons have to find out the cost to value ratio of the MR. For example, if the MR is to find the extra sale on decreasing the price to some extent, and it is found that the cost of research outweighs the profit benefit, such MR should not be undertaken. For example, if the increase in sales is likely to bring extra profits of Rupees ten lacs, and the research is going to cost twelve lacs, it is not worthwhile to conduct the MR.
5. MR Managers must take a close look at the assumptions made by the marketing personnel, as they may be lop-sided.
6. MR should not use the survey, to sell the product.

Managers because of the following reasons, are sparsely using marketing Research:

- When marketing team has a problem with some options and Market Research does not pin point towards a solution it makes MR of not much use. Only with a **well-defined problem** can the MR provide the right answers.
- When MR personnel are not fully qualified to do the job, they will not be able to get the right answers.
- MR takes time to be complete in all respects to give valuable market insight. When time is not enough MR may not give correct results.
- Market research reports sometimes give only indications, trends and not concrete facts, which is not appreciated by the marketing team.

Students should plan Market Research objectives in view of the above and develop a questionnaire for the same.

Example

Given below is an imaginary discussion between the Managing Director and Marketing Manager of a Television manufacturing company, who are scanning the Indian TV market to enter the same after achieving big success in the western markets like Europe and the USA.

MM, " We have seen the growth of Indian's TV market. In the last three years it has been growing at a steady rate of five per cent, which is much better than the growth of negative two percent in the developed world. However, as you, a number of MNC's are in the field like, Thomson, Sony, AIWA, Samsung, LG, and a number of Japanese firms are well entrenched through selling kits for assembly in India, such as Toshiba. Now we have to plan our strategy for entering this growing yet difficult market. What are your ideas on the matter."

MD, " I believe there is still big room for players like us who believe in their product and customized service which no one can provide. you should be trying for at least seven per cent market share in the second year of our operation."

MM, " I would like to organize a market survey to know what the market wants and who would buy our rather higher priced products."

MD, "By all means get your market information updated, keep me informed and let us plan our marketing strategies based on your information."

Following is the brief the MM gave to the market research agency—Our information on Indian TV Market is as follows:

In 1986, the market was of 4 million TV sets in the country. More than 75% of these sets were b/w versions. Colour TV came to India as late as 1982. Only after the liberalization of economy, In 1991, the demand started to grow rapidly. By 2000 AD, 6 Million colour sets were being planned for sale. The growth of manufacturers has been rapid too.

The growth and competition has brought several changes in the product offerings. Multi-channel, remote operated, several firms are making Colour TVs. Innovations like flat square screens, Picture-in-picture, ambience light adjusters, virtually automatic TV Sets, with memory, data bank of information are in the market, some features may be yet trying to find their feet in the market, due to concepts being new and high costs.

You have to find out which of the features plus, Internet access TV, would find a reasonable demand in the market. We want to put the best features in our sets and get 7% market share in second year of our operation.

Please organize MR, and send your recommendations within a period of three month, covering North Indian markets.

The MR report says:

- TV Manufacturers, are coming out with latest innovations and they try to educate the buyers about the same. Most of the time the customers are unaware of the benefits the innovations provide and may have a little reluctance for purchasing such **difficult** to use products.
- The buyers commonly understand picture and sound quality.
- Price, warranty, after-sales service, play an important role in purchase decisions.
- Psychological aspects such as, looks, foreign collaboration, brand equity too have their value.

Since the price of TV Sets is quite high, TV purchase is a high involvement purchase. Opinions of other users, friends, neighbours, colleagues, and sometimes the TV dealers are sought. With some twenty brands and each brand having four to six models, the task of decision-making is rather onerous one.

The following features of colour TVs were tested of a scale of one to five in several areas in the northern India and the results obtained are given along side:

Table 9.1. Research Scores

Feature	*Mean Score*	*Position*
Picture quality	5	1
Sound quality	5	2
After sales service	4.9	3
Price	4.2	4
Brand equity	3.8	5
Appearance	3.3	6
Foreign collaboration	3	7
Picture in picture	3	8
Internet capable	3	9
Dealers location	2.8	10
Friends recommendations	2.8	11

As can be seen the customers place a good deal of importance on picture and sound quality, followed by after sales service and price. Distinct features do play a role in purchase decisions, but it seems that their relative importance is less due to the latent fear in the minds of buyers that they may be paying high price for features they may not be able to use due to their being too high tech. Hence, the conclusion can be drawn that while new features will bring more business as they would certainly differentiate the products, a lot of concept selling as also, training in the usage would be required, before the benefits can be cashed in.

Advertising for creating and enhancing brand equity is a must, as brand plays a major decisive role in purchase actions of the customers.

Areas like built-in stabilizers are not in consideration at all as most TV has the feature. Same way Remote-control feature has become common and hence it ceases to be a differentiating point.

Advertising too has become the done thing and at best, it is a negative factor. In other words, less or no advertising would mean poor quality marketing effort.

Market Research should be avoided if enough **time** can not be given for the research. Also, if **budget** does not permit thorough enquiry, or **information** possible is not going to be sufficient, MR can be avoided. If marketing people want to get the research done only for having their **decisions endorsed** it need not be undertaken.

On the contrary, marketing people can get valuable inputs from MR, like demand forecasting, product specifications, advertising and promotion plans endorsement, locating new markets, market segments, finalizing distribution channels for optimizing their effectiveness, MR can also help in making strategic plans for the firm.

The MR Process can be shown in graphic form as given below:

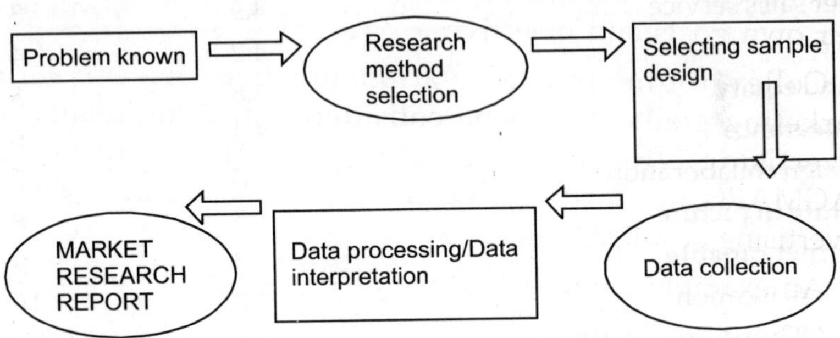

Fig. 9.2. MR Plan

For instance if management problem is of poor market image, or low brand equity, MR would find out " what is the exact brand equity of the firm with the target market segment".

If the management wants to know if the advertising budget is adequate or not, MR would try to find out, "the effectiveness of advertising".

And if the marketing team wants to know the customers of the product, the MR would find out "the target customers of the segment."

If sales are stuck in recession, MR would "find out the price elasticity of the product in the selected segment".

For new product development, MR would find out if new product needs to be developed. And if yes, with what specifications.

Data Processing and Analysis

In data analysis, it is important to understand that based on application the scale of measurement is made. For instance, when you apply, classification of sex, geographic area, or social class, when objects are either identical or different, **nominal scale** is used.

If ranking or preferences, class standing are the applications then objects could be smaller or larger, **Rank order scale is used.**

For altitude measurements, temperature scales, when intervals between adjoining ranks are equal, **interval** scale is used.

For sales, income, units made, **ratio** scale is used.

Advertising Research and DAGMAR

We have seen that in order to be focused on firm's overall goals, marketing department has to play a vital role as the revenue earnings of the firms are mainly from selling of products. Hence, once the firms goals have been formulated the marketing and advertising people set their own goals and objectives.

Colley found that a relationship between advertising and marketing goals should be considered and his theory says, that advertising efforts can bring results, which can be measured. DAGMAR's full form is, "Defining advertising goals for measured advertising results."

An example would make the theory simple to understand.

"There are 20 million scooter owners in India. Out of them only three million accept that four stroke scooter engine would be more power and fuel efficient. In two years time through Advertising this figure to be increased to seven million".

The Simple Job of Advertising is to:

1. Inform the customers about the firms products.
2. Focus on the benefits the customers would derive from using the product, in order to motivate them into buying the same.
3. To ensure that the firms customers stay true to the firm for repeat purchase, advertising is done to remind the customers.

The objectives of advertising have been discussed earlier. With the changing business environment, product life cycle shifts the objectives keep moving too. The DAGMAR theory needs constant updating and vigilance to be of real value.

Hence, DAGMAR becomes effective only when there is continuous Advertising Research is conducted as per requirement.

Advertising Research

Advertising research is being extensively used by, both advertisers and advertising agencies, to pre-test the campaign, evaluate the media's effectiveness, understanding the market segment best suited for the firm's products.

Most firms arrange for Market Research for obtaining market segments viewpoints and preferences about products in their category. These researches tell about product acceptance levels, brand awareness, Top of the mind recall as also modifications needed in the products. A significant part of market research is Advertising Research, which concentrates on the type of advertising campaign, would be most suitable for the product, the ideal time for the product launch, limitations of the product. Advertising research tries to correct any aberrations in the selected market segment for the product.

Advertising research tells the advertisers about the type of creativity, the language including slang and dialect would stimulate the segment.

Take the example of an Air compressor advertisement. It talked about the ozone layer depletion and need for having clean air. It also hinted at the specific design of the compressor without talking about its usage. Technical managers seeing the advertisement thought that it is some sort of air cleaner for the homes especially when they saw a pretty girl waving from the advertisement. After the research findings became clear another campaign was launched giving technical details with photographs of the compressor section by section, which attracted the attention of technical people who asked for more information about the product.

It will be difficult to find an advertisement of a perfume, which gives its chemical formula. Instead, the advertisement would be talking about love, and euphoria created by the perfume. The advertisement are the result of the research conducted which says that in personal care products people are interested in what it would do to them. It is said that no body buys a product. They buy the performance promised or given by the product.

Media research is conducted to establish the suitability of a particular medium. Some advertisements have a dotted line cutout telling the readers to cut it and post to the advertiser for additional information, free sample or a demonstration of the product. The number of prints of the media is compared to the cut-out responses to know about its readership and correctness of the media for the target segment.

Research on the advertising copy is done with the help of Primary research, when individual customers are contacted to get their reactions to the advertisement. It conforms the acceptance level of the campaign and can be used to determine the frequency of the insertions in the media.

Advertising research helps in making advertising campaigns more powerful thereby they become better able to perform the task of meeting advertising objectives.

Advertising costs are high. To make the best impact research ensures that advertisement is creatively acceptable, in the right media with correct frequency and for the chosen market segment.

The current Nescafe advertisement starts with a woman enjoying a mug full of the brew. The research had shown that women enjoy coffee during a lull in their work, be it household chores or office work. Later in the advertisement some men are also shown as it would be too risky to ignore a major customer group, in fact fifty percent of the population.

Advertising research results thus show the advertiser how to place correct advertisements at the correct places and at the most appropriate times-making them both effective and efficient.

How the **Research is conducted?** Let us understand in some detail:

- Testing research methods is done by having a **Preliminary research (PR)**. It calls for a small sample size and it only validates the reasons, objectives and creativity of the campaign.
- After PR, advertisers are interested in finding out the likes and dislikes of the customers, reasons for the same. Research is conducted by doing primary Survey, by **interviewing** customer groups. Such a research is similar to the market research, as information needed is akin to the one required in market research.
- Advertising research can also be conducted by **observation**. Researchers stand near shopping malls and observe the shoppers, their likes and dislikes, their behaviour pattern. Such a researcher has to note down his observations without prejudice, objectively, otherwise the deductions would be entirely lopsided. **It may be useful to note that watching/ observing customers in shops for collecting data without their knowledge may not be purely ethical. Also, asking questions may look like selling gimmicks rather then advertising or market research.**

To find out why people stay in a particular hotel the research would ask questions as follows:

- Do you stay here for its location ,its food, and ambience?
- Do you stay for the health club conference facility?
- Do you stay because it comes within your budget?
- Do you find service a favorable factor here?
- Is the staff cordial enough?
- Have the hotel helped you in any crisis situation?

- Does the hotel provide extra care and benefits to regular customers?
- How is communication system of the hotel?
- Does the room service give prompt service and does it have a good enough range of dishes?
- The next type of research can be termed as IDEA—RESEARCH where attempt is made to understand how some changes in an advertising campaign would affect the result as far as the advertising objectives are concerned. For example, would increase in advertising size improve its acceptance, or its frequency improves ***Top of the mind recall.***

Methodology

1. DEFINE RESEARCH OBJECTIVE, LIST OUT PROBLEMS FOR WHICH ANSWERS HAVE TO FOUND—Has the market acceptance increased for the new Maruti 800 car?, or does the new detergent help in catching the mood of the housewife better with its non-caustic chemical formula, easy on the hands? While framing the questions it is advisable to make them short and unambiguous, to ensure right response. For getting response on relative likes and dislikes it is correct to give just five options,

   (a) like the product greatly, will surely buy it

   (b) like it and may buy it

   (c) the product is just like others, may or may not buy it

   (d) do not like it and it is unlikely that I buy it

   (e) the product is bad and I will never buy it.

   Care should be taken on the following areas while planning the research:

- Time and money spent should be commensurate with the objective of the research. For example if the benefit to be obtained from the research amounts to Rupees two million, it would not be prudent to spend two and a half million on the research. In the same way if the research is going to take one year in fashion industry, the very purpose of the research would be defeated.
- Research results would, at best give indicators for decision-making not perfect answers.
- Going through the exact methods to be used by the field researchers in detail would make you more aware of the nitty-gritty and less vulnerable to problems, which can occur due to subjectivity of the researchers.

- Be specific what has to be done rather than leave it to the field people who may come up with unnecessary, redundant data. It may look good that you are in the know of several facts, but you should understand the cost and time implications. It is better to get just enough information.
- Research budget need careful analysis. It may be apt to spend some amount of money when the decision to be based on the research is for large sums of money and it includes avoidance or limiting risk for the firm. Naturally for simple problems, many times previous experience is the best guideline for decision making and no research need to be conducted.
- Getting the research done for your book rack or your shelf only is not a good idea. Unless you are sure that people who are going to use the research findings it may be only an exercise in futility. Remember that people generally do not want to change their ways just because of some research findings.
- Many times the firm may already have the data called for, or available with another source, e.g. some research organization like ORG-Marg.

Secondary research data is available from a variety of sources, including the firm's own records, Trade publications, and government publications and from Research firms like ORG-MARG.

Secondary data is valuable information and its analysis can give the right direction for marketing and advertising. Firstly it takes less time and effort. Plus it could prove to useful if it is not out dated.

Finding the Right Sample Size

Imagine sending teams to contact the entire population. Even a single metro town like Delhi has 1.4 million population. It would be exercise in futility, because, by the time the research report comes out the problem or the situation, which triggered the research, would have disappeared. Hence only a carefully chosen sample is used for being met for getting the data. The sample selection is done on the following lines:

- Probability sample—where each person from the population (also known as the universe) has known opportunity of being part of the sample, not necessarily equal chance.
- Simple random sample, is also probability sample except it is where each member has equal opportunity of being included. If there are 35,000 lady motorists in Delhi, and you want to have a sample of 350, pick up every 100th lady motorist.

- Stratified random sample would require to further sub-divide the lady motorist in age groups, 18 to 25, 26 to 40, 41 to 60 and above 60. then you choose equal number from each age group as your sample.
- Segregating the universe geographically could make cluster sample. Equal number of lady motorists from north, south, east, west and central Delhi would make the cluster sample.
- Non-probability sample is where each sub category is given a specific equal number. 100 graduates and 100 postgraduates would comprise the quota sample, as it is called.
- Judgement sample is when you decide the sample members on the basis of their value to the research.
- Convenience sample is when you go to the people you find convenient to contact.

  The non-probability sample leaves a margin of doubt whether the sample is truly representative of the universe.

  Selecting a sample by itself is important, as it helps in understanding the results of the research better.

RESEARCH DOES NOT PROVIDE RESULTS OR FACTS, IT ONLY GIVES TENDENCIES. SAMPLE SIZE DETERMINES THE ACCURACY LEVELS. AT TIMES IT IS IMPORTANT TO SACRIFICE ACCURACY FOR SPEED AND BUDGET

Advertising research can be carried out **before the launch** of the advertising campaign. It helps in media planning, copy testing along with test marketing the product to be advertised.

Advertising research carried out **during the campaign** focuses on Dealer audit, sales analysis and customers response based on contests or reply cutouts given with the advertisements for customers to fill in their comments and send back to the advertiser.

After the campaign gets over, as per DAGMAR, **research is done to assess the effectiveness of the campaign** on the parameter of the objective of the advertising campaign. At this time **Consumer Panel Surveys** are conducted for structured responses.

Consumer Panels are predetermined group of people mostly of one geographic and demographic segment like lady members of a Kitty party. These persons are in the know of their task of making assessments of the campaigns and inform the advertiser about their views.

Selecting research sample needs knowledge of market, the universe and quantitative techniques.

Gathering information or data collection can be done by in-depth interviews where the respondent (Interviewee, one member of the sample chosen), is asked questions from a well-structured questionnaire. The respondent can give his own views as well as lot of time is given for each question. The interviewer must be adept at organizing such interviews and later on in making a coherent and lucid report.

When the interview is conducted in a well accepted and known group called the Focus group, same type of in-depth incisive questions can be asked. The problem, which can arise, is the conflict within the group with diverse views.

The questions can be of two types, simple **straightforward types** where the answer can be yes or no. However, when it is important to understand the mindsets it is better to use **projective** questions which can be vague and which would evoke emotional, sentimental and creative answers.

What product you associate with Hrithik Roshan?

When you think of color think of whom?

Sixty years young, climbing the staircase?

Just do it. Which product it conveys?

These are just a few samples.

How do you rate the following hotels in Delhi:

- Maurya Sheraton
- Taj Mansingh
- The Oberoi
- Hyatt Regency
- Taj Palace

The way I look is important to me

- Strongly agree
- Agree
- Normal
- Disagree
- Strongly disagree

Surveys, observations and experiments with the help of questionnaires, checklists and plans help in completing the advertising surveys. Then comes the important aspect of analysis and report writing.

Research , as stated must be used or else the time and money is a total waste. Research results enable firms in reassessing their goals on the basis of new opportunities, in confirming the target segment and creating a useful message for the segment.

Advertising results can be measured by simple brand recall tests with the target segment. These can be aided or unaided recalls.

"Which is the best toothpaste in the market?"

"Which blue and red bottle drink gives most satisfaction ?"

Research confirms the strong views held by the firm. If there is major divergence then a re-look is required at the objectives , sample and methods adopted in the research. A very apt example of how the research could go wrong is given below-

A firm planned to start manufacture of Fax machines in India in 1980s. The task of finding out the demand and product acceptance levels was given to an outside research agency by the firm. The result was flattering in as much that 80% respondents were looking forward to buying a fax machine. When the note was sent to Department of Telecommunications Government of India, it came back saying that the telecom network was not efficient enough to make fax a success.(It was only in late eighties that Digital electronic exchanges, fiber optic cables made the telecom network good enough for fax to operate.)

The research should make you aware of consumer's behaviour towards competitive product.

> Advertising research is a part of marketing research, confined to development of advertising plan, creative work, market segment and the best possible media, which would cater to the segment. The research should increase the effectiveness and efficiency of the advertising campaign. Data collection is done from primary sources as also secondary, already available sources. In primary data collection it is important to select the sample correctly. The research steps are,
>
> A setting up goals for the research,
> B finding the sources of secondary information/data.
> C analyzing secondary data
> D planning sample for primary research
> E data collection
> F data analysis and report writing
>
> The advertising campaign is pre-tested and post tested to ensure that it works.

Guidelines for Making a Questionnaire

Ask basic questions about respondents name, address. While asking his age and income, give a range, age between 18–30, 31–45, 46–60, and 61 above.

- Income between Rupees 3000–7000, 8000–15,000, 16,000–30,000.
- Questions with possible two answers—Did you buy the watch yourself, yes or no ?
- Multiple choice questions—Who advised you to buy the watch, your father, uncle, sister or cousin ?
- Likert scale questions—The watch is considered best value for money—tick one you consider right—(a) strongly disagree, (b) disagree, (c) neutral, (d) agree, (e) strongly agree
- Differential scale—the hotel is

large ---------- small
Modern ---------- outmoded
Hotel staff ---------- experienced
inexperienced
Courteous ---------- disinterested

Questions on importance of the product can be put on extremely important, very important, important, and not very important, to not at all important.

Intentions to buy can be asked on a rating scale as sure to buy, perhaps, may not, will not and will never buy.

Open-ended questions like, "what do you think of our hotel? " Can be answered by the respondents in any way they like. Associations can tell you about the aided recalls, like

Welcome
Hotel
TravQuestions—

1. Sampling method is important in advertising research. Discuss some methods for planning the sample.
2. Besides questionnaires are there are other methods for gathering information. Discuss.
3. What type of methodology should be adopted for advertising research?
4. Describe some possible objectives of advertising research.

Marketing Game

Discuss the need for control points for marketing teams, how they can be formalized for different type of products, channels.

Company studies—These topics involve field interviews and correspondence combined with documentary sources.

1. A marketing audit. Design a marketing audit that a company can use to determine where it is in the stages of development of the l corporation and what it should do with the information.
2. Reports analyzing the marketing strategies of companies.
3. Product management. Under what circumstances have companies integrated their domestic and foreign product planning and management? What factors have led to this integration? What are the explicit and hidden costs and benefits?

CHAPTER 10

Distribution of Goods

AIMS AND OUTCOMES OF THE CHAPTER

Once the firm has completed Marketing Research and decided about the product/s they want to introduce in the market having selected the niche market, the firm needs to ensure that its customers and prospective customers are aware of the product and their usage, and the product is available to them at convenient shops. The first objective of communicating with customers is done through personal selling and advertising. The second is done through organizing proper distribution system. In this chapter we are discussing the distribution methods available for firms. The firms can choose the method best suited to their needs taking the product, its service requirements into account. The students learn the different methods of product distribution, including B-to-B product distribution besides management of lmogistics.

For the manufacturer of a product there are two basic distribution systems.

The first one is as given below:

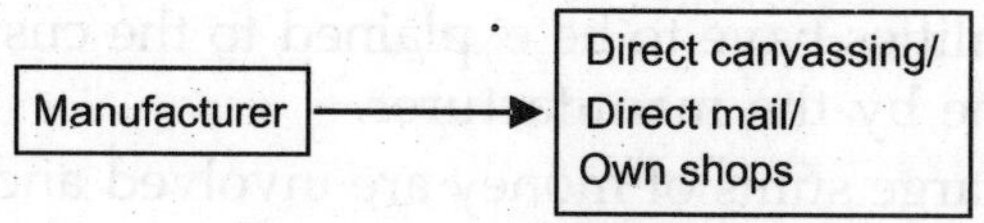

Fig. 10.1. Basic Channel

In the above method the manufacturer, sells by personal selling, through direct mail or from firm's own shops, (like Bata shops)

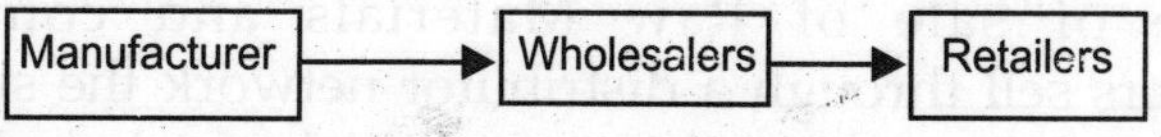

Fig. 10.2. Distribution Channel

In the second method there can be a number of intermediaries as given below:

In the indirect method the simple method starts from manufacturers who sell the product to wholesaler who in turn sells it to retailer for sale to the ultimate customer. At each step, some amount of money as profit is given which adds to the selling price of the product to the customer. In most cases the manufacturer follows the set pattern of product distribution as per trade practices, or how the competitors are distributing their products. However, blindly following competition is not the answer, as competitors may be having different scales of production or any other basic difference with the firm. Innovations in distribution methods are taking place and firms should take advantage of the new methods.

Let us examine the two broad categories of products and their presently accepted distribution patterns:

Distribution Patterns For Consumer And Industrial Goods

Industrial Goods:

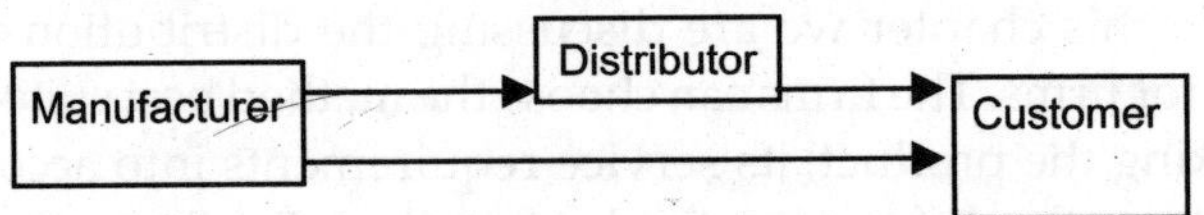

Fig. 10.3. Industrial Goods Channels

As can be seen, in industrial goods, the sale is made either directly to the customer or through a distributor. Capital goods sale is usually made directly to the customer, because of the following reasons:

- Technicalities have to be explained to the customer, which are best done by the manufacturer.
- Mostly large sums of money are involved and customer wants best price without middleman's commission.
- Installation and commissioning of the equipment is involved, best done by the manufacturer's engineers
- After sales service is complicated

In case of sale of Raw Materials and components the manufacturers sell through a distributor network the size of which is finalized taking the geographic area, which needs to be covered by the manufacturer.

Consumer Goods

These are usually sold through the distribution channels as follows:

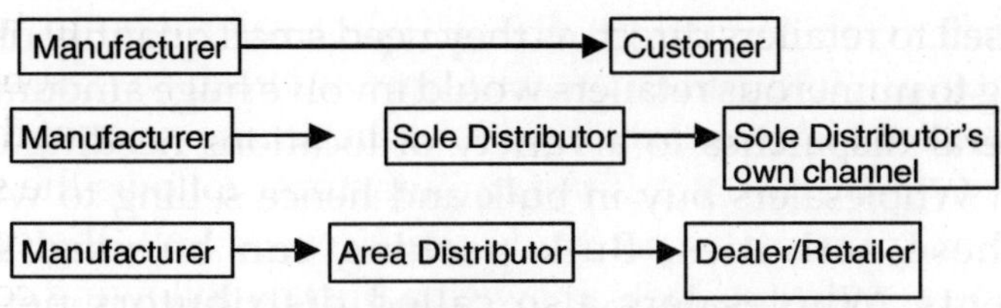

Fig. 10.4. Consumer Goods Channels

Customer Convenience Buying

In every residential locality Convenience stores or retail outlets have come up. These shops keep stocks of a variety of products of daily needs, which the residents buy. As the shops keep competitive products they sell the products as per the following plan:

- Brand as per customers demand
- Brand on the basis of sales commission they get from the firm. If the customer has no choice the shopkeeper will try to sell such a product where he gets maximum profit.
- In case the shop does not have the customer demanded brand it will try to convince the customer to buy the brand in stock.

No manufacturer can afford to avoid the retail shops, which cover the convenience criteria for the customers.

Sales with Service—several consumer durable products require service to be provided to the product on either periodic basis like automobiles or once in a while basis like Air-conditioners. Retailers who can provide such service should sell all such products, which need regular service. Maruti car dealers are selected only on the condition that they can provide proper service to the sold cars. In fact Maruti provides technical training to the engineers of their dealers. The dealers have to maintain stocks of spare parts and accessories, which enables them to provide timely proper service.

Multiple Product Manufacturers

When one manufacturer can supply a variety to products needed by one type of customers like, Hindustan Lever then they need to have distributors who can invest in inventories and prime location for their retail sales outlets.

We will discuss the value of wholesalers in the distribution system. Manufacturers need retailers most, as they are the link between the manufacturer and the consumer. However, manufacturers find it difficult to sell to retailers direct, as they need small quantity of products only. Selling to numerous retailers would involve huge amount of billing action, several dispatches to a variety of locations needing enormous manpower. Wholesalers buy in bulk and hence selling to wholesalers reduces these activities. Bulk packing can be used for large consignments. Wholesalers also called distributors perform the following functions for the manufacturer:

- Buy in bulk.
- Making "small customer size" packages.
- Buying variety of products and making matched sets as required by the customers, like soap and soap dish, tooth paste and tooth brush.
- Stocking products in large quantity ensuring that the dealer is never out of stock without having to invest in large inventory himself.
- Low cost transport to retailers can be provided as for small quantity they need not hire trucks. They can use tempos, three wheelers and hand trolleys.
- Provide information regarding competitive activities, new products in the market change in prices they can be virtual market surveyors for the firm.
- Provide credit, loans and leasing facility (either themselves or through a leasing agency) to the customers.
- Share in advertising and promotion arranged by the firm.

As many firms are resorting to direct selling to the retail trade and sometimes to the customers, wholesalers may become obsolete in the future.

Wholesalers have been performing important role in the business of the manufacturers, most important being that of making bulk purchases. It is for this reason that the wholesalers prefer to sell products of only one manufacturer. They may take up sale of other manufacturer if there is no competition involved. Furthermore, wholesalers take up products from other manufacturers if they complement their main product either as an accessory or original component. The exclusivity of product sale is legally not appropriate under the MRTP Act. Most firms however keep the exclusivity clause in the agreement as unwritten.

In order to survive in the distribution race, Wholesalers/ Distributors, have started to re-focus their strategies as under:

- Distributors/wholesalers divest themselves of small jobs and concentrate on the distribution as their main line of business. It provides the required focus to the task of distribution.
- Distributors/wholesalers take up product servicing as per standards laid by the manufacturers. They invest in service equipments, service consumables and stock of spares required for providing quality service to the customers.
- Distributors/wholesalers take up other customer oriented activities like providing leasing options to the customers, through their retailers.
- Distributors/wholesalers get their persons trained in servicing of product and in sales techniques. They impart this training to the sales and service people of retailers to enhance value addition to the products.
- Distributors/wholesalers help the manufacturers in meeting their sales targets.

Distribution Patterns for Industrial Goods

Industrial Goods

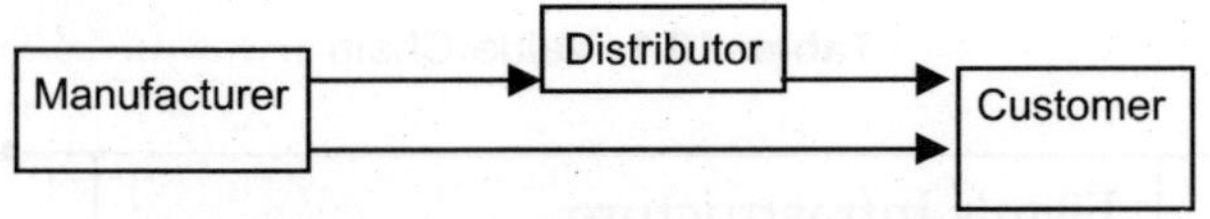

Fig. 10.5. Industrial Channel of Distribution

As can be seen, in industrial goods, the sale is made either directly to the customer or through a distributor. Capital goods sale is usually made directly to the customer, because of the following reasons:

- Technicalities have to be explained to the customer, which are best done by the manufacturer.
- Mostly large sums of money are involved and customer wants best price without middleman's commission.
- Installation and commissioning of the equipment is involved, best done by the manufacturer's engineers.
- After sales service is complicated.

In case of sale of Raw Materials and components the manufacturers sell through a distributor network the size of which is finalized taking the geographic area that needs to be covered by the manufacturer.

Marketing Logistics

After the goods have been manufactured they need to be placed at the most convenient locations, Retail Outlets, to make buying the goods easy for the buyers. The actual transportation, storage and inventory management are part of background or secondary activities. Yet one look at them would make you realize that these are extremely important activities. The firm may have the most suitable product for the customers, but if they cannot find the same easily the value of the product diminishes drastically. Logistics can be defined in this context as follows:

"Planning, operating and managing with the help of modern Information System, the movement of goods from manufacturers to the buyers, in shortest possible time and in the most economical manner."

Michael Porter, the Management Guru has drawn up a Value Chain given below, which summarizes these activities in a matrix. The value mentioned is the value the chain adds to the goods FOR THE CUSTOMERS!

The activities of any firm can be divided in to two groups:

1. Primary Activities
2. Secondary Activities

Michael Porter's Value Chain Analysis is given below:

Table. 10.1. Value Chain

Suppliers ◄—— ——► Customers

Firm's Infrastructure
Human Resource Management
Technology
Information System

In bound logistics	Operations/Production	Marketing	Service	Out bound logistics

As can be seen the Porter's Analysis helps in understanding the various functional areas of a firm. On the left hand there are Suppliers who provide the Raw Materials and Components, which are converted in to finished product through the operations or production process. On the right side are the customers, the ultimate destination of the finished products of the firm. And the value part of the Value Chain is the value the firms provide through the entire process to the customers.

It is important to understand that unless the firm is adding value to the customers through the conversion or production process the firm can never sustain itself in the market.

In this chapter we are dealing with mainly the outbound logistics.

The area of outbound logistics starts with the distribution system of the firm and can be divided as follows:

- Distribution network—Wholesalers and retailers
- The Customers
- Finished goods stores
- Demand forecasting and management
- Inventory management
- Final packaging
- Order processing
- Transportation
- Generation of information
- Billing, in some cases

Distribution network of any firm depends on the range of products, existing pattern in the trade; customer needs as also practicality of the network. While the distribution systems will be discussed in detail in subsequent chapter the following gives the distribution channels currently in vogue:

- Sole Distributor
- Area distributor
- Stockists
- Agents, Commission Agents
- Dealers
- Franchisees
- Own shops
- Retailers
- Tele-marketing
- Tele-shopping
- Internet shopping

Movement of goods from the manufacturers or sellers takes place on receipt of orders from the customers (the distribution channel members are customers for the seller). Next steps are as follows:

- Final packing of the product, if required
- Arranging for the transport carrier
- Making dispatch documents, delivery notes, packing lists

- Actual loading on the carrier
- Transit insurance, if required
- Inventory update

It is important to look at the customer instructions carefully and adhere to them meticulously. In case some instructions cannot be met with, these must be clarified and modified by communicating with the customers. Any oversight in the matter could cause major problems at the time of getting payments from the customers.

As can be seen from below, expenses on transport are substantial when the costing of the product is done (the figures are arbitrary only to give an idea).

Selling price of Rs. 100 is made up of the following costs:

Table. 10.2. Cost Analysis

Cost of money	16
Raw materials	24
Transportation up to the customer	28
Manufacturing or conversion	8
Overheads/profits	24

As can be seen, while most CEOs lay stress on cost reduction in manufacturing expenses, the real place is in transportation. For in land transport, the following vehicles are used:

- Railways—goods trains, passenger trains
- Trucks
- Air cargo service
- River boats

Within town areas, small tempos, hand or bullockcarts, cycle carts are used.

Example

One firm making TV Picture tubes had to send the tubes all round the country from a center in the west India. The normal mode was by trucks carrying the goods for long haulage of even a few thousand kilometers. With bad roads, battered trucks, inevitably ten percent of the cargo was damaged in transit due to accidents, or transshipments. TV picture tubes being fragile were easily damaged. While insurance firms were reimbursing for the physical loss of the product, the loss of production of TV Sets could not be compensated.

The answer was found by calling railway authorities. They suggested use of Container service, which also provided door-to-door service. The containers would come to the factory on special trucks, get loaded and then they would go on the trucks to the railway yard to get connected to a goods train meant for the destination needed. In one stroke, the problem of damages to the goods was solved. Additional benefit came by way of less expense on packing as the containers were of the right size to fit in the required number of tubes with no extra space for the tubes to have any moving space. Besides it also brought in saving in transport costs and with the same money the customers could buy more tubes.

Since the movement of goods involves mostly more than one organization it calls for coordinated efforts between the supplying firm, the receiving firm or individual and the carrier. The term, which encompasses the entire operation, is **logistics. The value of logistics can be increased by the following:**

- Integration of product movement, information system and cash flow
- Coordinated responsibility of both internal and external efforts
- Efficient and effective methods of logistics
- Strengths and cooperation of external customers

Transportation for outbound logistics calls for the following decisions:

- Transport company's choice
- Mode selection
- Freight considerations

Warehousing has the following areas of activities:

- Receiving, unloading the goods
- Inspection of the goods
- Receiving the orders
- Repacking, if needed
- Billing, if required
- Shipment or transportation
- Inventory records management

Decision-making depends on a good planned information system. The information process flow is as follows:

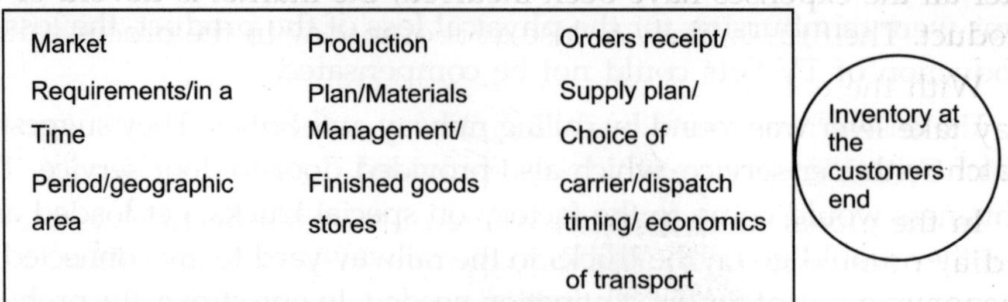

Fig. 10.6. Information Flow

Example

Look at the plight of a Sugar Mill. The mill runs usually on seasonal basis, as the sugar cane is cultivated during a short period only in a year. The most important Raw Material in a sugar mill is the sugar cane. Each sugar mill has a limited capacity to use the cane. At times the sugar farmers bring huge amount of cane which the mill can not use as also the space for cane storage gets filled up. In order to regulate the flow of cane, the mills have provided the farmers, with Walkie-talkie systems and they can bring in the trucks just at the right time when they do not have to wait for a long time in queues and the mill is also happy that they get the cane just at the right time when they need the same.

Tasks for the students—find out a suitable system of logistics, which would help the firm in overcoming the problem.

With computerized inventory management, faster communication systems, the firms can ensure that their customers have the product just when they need the same, reducing their inventory and cash blocking burden (more relevant in case of business purchasing).

One important method of gaining Competitive Advantage is QUICK RESPONSE, which the firms can provide to the market demands.

It is well known saying that, *it is the early bird, which gets the worm.* Same way in the market place the firm that can place its product before others gets the customers attention and becomes the market leader. With prudent decisions it can keep the leadership position for a long time as per its plans.

Logistics, including transportation can be used judiciously to provide the market with products at the most appropriate time. The Japanese have given the world an approach to the situation known as **Just in Time.** This adds to the competitive advantage to the firm's armoury.

Many firms spend a lot of money on New Product Launches. These are followed by major promotional plans. Imagine a situation when, after all the expenses have been incurred, the market is devoid of the product. The firm is likely to lose a lot of money in the process.

With the emergence of e-commerce, while the entire transaction may take less time, the actual receipt of goods by the customer must match with the speed to the possible extent

In the global market place, where most firms find themselves in India, outsourcing of finished goods is becoming a common phenomenon. It calls for a thorough knowledge of logistics, which the firm can plan internationally. International shipments, air cargos, ships and in some cases road transport are the usual means of transport and each one has its own set of advantages and problems Payment terms, banking regulations currency fluctuations and delivery date sanctity become important criteria for decision making.

Going back in time, till 1960s, the business scenario in India was quite different than what it is today. Competition was practically non-existent, there was great emphasis on government or Public sector, and lots of benefits were given to the small-scale sector. Core products like Telecom, defense, and power were exclusively meant for the government agencies. In fact it would not be an exaggeration to say that the private sector was looked at by the government with suspicion. The business was regulated and controlled through license and permits, which were doled out to the private sector ready to make heavy investments with great reluctance. With little or no competition the firms entrenched in business was making money even with indifferent product quality.

The Supply Chain of that period would look as given below:

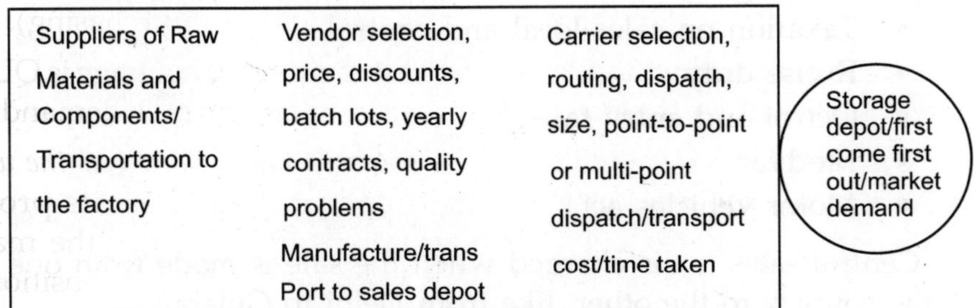

Fig. 10.7. Supply Chain

Products are pushed on to the channel members to build **push pressure**. Firms own Finished Goods Stores are stocked to serve the market demand. In case of consumer goods, the dispatches are made to the first line customers, the distributors. For small towns, the distributors are unable to take full truckloads. In such situations, point to multi-point supply is made to more than one destination, serving several distributors.

Firms finished storage depots have the following tasks to perform:

- Unloading goods from the trucks
- Stacking in the depot
- Inventory management
- Repacking or un-bulking if required
- Transport to the channel members
- Transit insurance, if required

Logistic costs have been calculated and they vary from 7% to 35% depending on the product and the market.

Logistic Movement has a bearing on the profitability of the firm as also on its cash flow. Hence the decisions on the following need special consideration:

- Factory site
- Geographic markets
- Sources of main Raw Materials and Components
- Factory own depots locations
- Transport facilities
- Inventory Management
- Packaging
- Material handling equipment

Besides, the government role is important in logistics planning due to the following reasons:

- Taxation on sales-local and central
- Excise duty
- Octroi and entry tax
- Modvat
- Motor vehicles act

Central sales tax is charged when the sale is made from one state of the country to the other, like from Delhi to Gujarat

Local sales tax is charged when the sale is made with in a state

Excise duty is charged on manufacture of the products

Octroi is charged when the product enters some municipal areas.

Modvat is modifies value added tax

The Motor Vehicle Act controls movement of trucks

Question for discussion

Distribution channels provide the bridge between the manufacturer and the customer. Can it become company's competitive advantage? Discuss.

MARKETING GAME

Discuss the need for control points for marketing teams, how they can be formalized for different type of products, channels.

Company studies those topics which involve field interviews and correspondence combined with documentary sources.

1. A marketing audit. Design a marketing audit that a company can use to determine where it is in the stages of development of the corporation and what it should do with the information.
2. Reports analyzing the marketing strategies of companies.
3. Product management. Under what circumstances have companies integrated their domestic and foreign product planning and management? What factors have led to this integration? What are the explicit and hidden costs and benefits?

CHAPTER 11

Advertising Promotion, PR

Aims and Outcomes of The Chapter

Advertising often grips people's minds, their psyche, in a way that a make-belief world, a virtual world, gets created. So, what exactly is Advertising? Who wants it, for whom is it created and how? These and several such questions we will answer in this chapter. How the advertiser can hit the bull's eye of consumer psyche every time! Besides the role of sales promotion and Public Relations in marketing is discussed comprehensively.

Advertising Management today has become an important area of business and that is why, even common man, laypersons are quite aware of the subject. However for a professional, it is essential that not only the subject is learnt thoroughly but even subtle nuances are understood so that the person becomes comfortable with it. With practice expertise can be gained to strengthen the skills. Advertising is a fast moving, glamorous discipline and yet without proper concepts it can become quite trivial.

Advertising Defined

Advertising texts have given a few definitions of Advertising. With the thrust of media variants, i.e. several new media being available, the definition can now be modified. First we take the most popular definition, which is as follows:

AMA (American Marketing Association), defines advertising as—

Any paid form of non-personal presentation and promotion of ideas, goods and services of an identified sponsor.

*The communication is non-personal, as nobody has personally conveyed it. What we witness in retail shops when the salesman talks to us to sell a product is that he is personally communicating with us and hence by the definition it is not Advertising.

*The presentation is for promoting the ideas, goods and services to create awareness and assist in selling the product.

*A known person or firm does advertising. This becomes essential to avoid wrong messages being advertised, or sometimes the message becoming useless, as the potential buyer would not know to whom to approach for buying the product, idea or service advertised if advertiser is unknown.

Advertising can be considered as the Soul of Marketing in today's world of complex and severe competition. Or it can be a substitute elder brother who helps in takings purchase decisions.

Advertisement for target audience—it is important that the people who are likely buyers see the advertisement message. Hence advertisers cater to different market segments with the help of separate media as also target-specific message. Advertisement for Toyota car would not have any takers in a slum cluster; advertisement for low cost clothing material would be of no use to the wealthy elite.

Consumer advertising deals with the actual buyers and users of the market segment and therefore uses a language and a medium best seen by the target segment.

Business advertising converging on target segment has to be in magazines seen by Purchase and technical persons of firms. For instance an advertisement for TV picture tubes would be best seen in magazines of TV trade.

Geographic area coverage of media assists in focusing on the target segment where the firm believes there is maximum business potential. A firm wanting to distribute its products on all India bases would have to look at national press, magazines with national circulation and readership, and national TV, including satellite and cable TV channels.

Similarly, firms wanting to do business internationally would select the right media; satellite TV, Internet or national press of the defined countries where the firms want to do business.

Hence, it can be surmised that Advertising plays multi-faceted roles in Business. Not only it informs the target segment of customers but persuades them too to buy the product or avail service offered by the Advertiser.

Since the communication is non-personal, the one drawback remains as no immediate and direct reaction or response is available to the sponsor of the advertising.

Personal Selling

In case of consumer goods, Personal Selling effort is 20% and advertising backup support is 80%.

In case of Industrial products personal selling is 80% and advertising support is 20%.

Table 11.1. Advertising *vs* Personal Selling

	Personal selling	*Advertising*
Consumer products	20%	80%
Industrial products	80%	20%

Tasks for Advertising in the 21st Century

Let us discuss the tasks before Advertising in the twenty-first century. In case of new innovating products, the target segment may not even be aware of the product hence and the first task of advertising is to bring about product awareness in the segment. The task steps are given below

From the level of unawareness to

1. Awareness—to
2. Knowledge about the existence of the product in the market—to
3. Desire of possession of the product—to
4. Conviction about its utility value and related benefits—to
5. Brand preference—to
6. Purchase action—to
7. Product's continuous evaluation—to
8. Repeat purchase decisions.

Imagine the time when cell phones had not invaded our country. The marketers had to resort to teaser Advertisements to arouse curiosity among target segment, which created awareness, and as the product was launched firms got good response.

It is worthwhile to mention that a BAD product cannot be sold and as a corollary should not be advertised.

Advertising Mix Factors

Advertising is one of the Marketing Mix Factors. Let us analyze Advertising Mix Factors. There are six sides to Advertising in totality. They are given below:

1. Advertiser
2. Advertising Agency
3. Media
4. PR Consultants
5. Ancillary Services
6. Freelance Services

Advertisers can be categorized as Profit Making Organizations and Non Profit Making Organizations. The first category consists of the following:

Government and government bodies including public sector companies. The government advertises for purchasing through tenders, selling surpluses, recruitment through Public Service Commissions.

Manufacturers advertise when they to sell direct to consumer like power, industrial raw materials. They advertise to buy from the market what raw materials components they need to manufacture their finished products.

1. Service Providers like travel agents, hotels, airlines, advertise to sell their services.
2. Importers advertise to sell their goods to the target segment.
3. Distributors, Retailers and other members of distribution channel advertise to sell their products. Since their area of operation is limited their advertising is also confined to the geographic area they serve.
4. Mail Order Suppliers advertise so that their catalogues are purchased by their target segment, which could result in their getting orders by mail. Burlington's and Readers Digest are examples of mail order suppliers.

The second category of advertisers are non-governmental organizations, like family planning groups, destitute children help groups, de-addiction centers.

Advertising Agency

The main role played by Advertising Agencies is that of Communication experts, who assist the Advertisers in obtaining optimized benefit for the money they spend in advertising by ensuring that the target segment gets at least an **OPPORTUNITY TO SEE (OTS)** the product advertisement. The advertisements given in properly selected media, which result in improved brand awareness and consequently improved sales and profits which are is the major tasks of advertising.

There are several types of Advertising Agencies operating in the market place to suit different needs of Advertisers. Many times one Advertiser uses one agency for one type of Advertisement and a separate one for other needs. Major types of Agencies are given below:

- Large full function agency
- Medium size full function agency
- Specialized technical agencies
- Hot Shops
- Agency of Records

Large full function agency comprises of the following departments:

- Account servicing department
- Account planning department
- Creative – art, copy, visualizer
- Media planning department
- Electronic media coordinator
- Research department
- Budgeting and billing department

In India, HTA, Lintas, are two of the most famous Advertising Agencies.

Medium size full function Agency may not have Research and account planning departments. Otherwise they are similar to large agencies and they graduate to large agencies as their billing and business increases.

Specialized Technical Agencies are agencies working for niche market i.e. Financial Firms, IT Companies, TV Companies. They normally keep experts in their area of specialization either on their role or on consultancy panel.

Hot Shops are small lean mean agencies, which operate on low overheads and do quality work by hiring experts on job basis.

AOR or Agency of Records is the agency with large business portfolio and surplus resources. Such agencies buy popular media space in bulk, use it at advantageous cost and sell it to smaller agencies in times of their need. For their investment they take 2%profit margin from the smaller agencies.

THE MEDIA

From the earlier days of hand painted posters, media has come up with Cable and Satellite TV Revolution. Joining the bandwagon is Internet and Computer designing of advertisements.

Broadly media are characterized as follows: -

Press

Electronic

Computer, Internet

Outdoor

Point of purchase

Direct Mail

Miscellaneous

Press relates to Newspaper dailies, English, Hindi and regional language papers, Magazines, in different languages, targeting various segments, cultural, religious, sports, fashion, films, wildlife the list is a long one. The advertiser has to look for the right paper, magazines which are read by the target segment to ensure OTS (Opportunity To See). Many top executives have virtually no time to watch Television and hence they get the news and other information from newspapers and business magazines. Marketers of products meant for this market segment should therefore use newspapers and magazines to reach the target segment effectively. Expensive cars, laptop computers, and expensive dress materials could fall in the category.

Electronic Media relates to Television, Radio, Videocassettes. Television as a media for advertising has made the biggest impact on almost all the segments of customers. Satellite and cable TV have invaded practically all homes. Viewer-ship of TV has increased manifold and terms like couch potato have been invented for people who are constantly viewing the TV. This fact has opened up advertising vistas for majority of the products. Advertiser has only to understand the programme one-segment views and then he can plan to place his advertisement during that particular programme. Similarly, FM channel of the radio has become popular in Metro towns with a large teenage following. Products meant for teens can be advertised on FM with great certainty of success. Tele-marketing and Tele-shopping are making strides as the latest media. Products are sold through telephones in one case while in the other; TV is used for demonstrating the working of the product and orders solicited.

Computer and Internet—the medium of communication of computers and the Internet are relatively new in India but they are making giant strides in advertising and marketing world.

HENCE, in present day context it is important to understand these to succeed. With on line e-Commerce, banking, and purchasing it is expected that people with buying power will be more hooked to computers then ever before. It is important to note that Information technology is the future of communications with computers and telecommunications joining hands to provide the safest, fastest and low cost reliable communication. Advertisers need to understand the medium and take full advantage of the same.

OUTDOOR—relates to Hoarding, billboards, neon signs, bus panels, kiosks, balloons and the like. Advertisers use these as reminder advertisements as well as product launch ads too.

Direct Mail—several marketers resort to sending technical literature by post to prospective customers, including Readers Digest, Burlington.

Point Of Purchase Advertising—it has been updated with technological advances. Retail shops were content earlier with posters, danglers and products innovative packaging. Today, multimedia has provided with interactive computer screens where the customers can get any information about the shop including availability of product, stocks prices. Many shops keep continuous TV Programmes with animation, cartoons and product-advertisements.

Tele shopping is becoming popular but gradually, as the Indian shopper wants to see and feel the touch of the product before buying it. Additionally, shopping expeditions become fun time outings for the family and it would be difficult to replace them by **television—on screen—shops.**

Tele-marketing uses the telephone line to tell the prospective customers about the services the marketer is providing and is, at times a good approach to elicit right response from the customer.

Miscellaneous Advertising Media

We have all seen big balloons in the sky carrying advertising messages, advertisements on bus panels, yellow pages, directories, rail and air tickets, even on matchboxes. We have also witnessed advertisements on camels and elephants especially designed for village fairs. Human imagination can only limit to the extent people will locate an existing unutilized medium or discover or invent one for the purpose.

India has witnessed lowering of prices of Newspapers from Rupees four to Rupees one and a half. This drastic reduction has been possible because of heavy advertising revenue the newspapers get. In order to get a good share of advertising, the press depends on its circulation figures- higher the circulation greater the advertising revenue. And yet, in view of heavy competition the newspapers face, they resort to selling and advertising their space too. Let us see how it is done—

- Rate cards—these are mailed or given to advertising agencies and advertisers to make them aware of advertising costs for advertising in the paper.
- Direct mail with copies of successful campaigns and Promotional folders.
- Maps of geographic areas covered with its demographic details.
- Availability of research material.
- Copies of special numbers and advance programme of special issues.
- For TV Channels—information about TV Programmes of interest like films chat shows.
- Outdoor—hoarding positions availability and number of vehicles passing through that place.

PR Consultants

As we compare advertising with newspaper's own coverage it becomes clear that editorial coverage invariably gets better credence to advertisement, since it appears as unbiased opinion of a third party, i.e. the newspaper editor. Hence, advertisers always wish to boost their image and they find Public Relation (PR) consultants have good contacts with the press and as a PR exercise they get features written about the firm and its products making invaluable and significant contribution towards image building programme of the firm as independent views unconnected to the firm have better credibility with the prospective customer then the advertising campaign of the firm.

Public Relations as function helps firms evaluate their standing, brand image and credibility in the market place. Since brand building and brand equity come through advertising and PR, it becomes imperative to integrate them at certain level.

Ancillary Services

Advertising Agencies have to take the help of several ancillary service providers, as it would be too expensive to have every one on the payroll. Major services, which are hired by agencies, are as follows-

- Independent producers of advertising short films for TV or cinema. Not even large Advertising agencies keep a Film making division. They all hire on contract independent specialist producers. These producers are then briefed by the agency persons regarding their client's requirements from then on, from selection of film script to location, models cameraman, lights among other film making items are arranged by the producer in consultation with the agency and the advertiser.

- Manufacturers of point of purchase advertising material, like, posters and danglers.
- Direct mail houses who take upon themselves to arrange the address data bank and the advertising material to be sent along with its frequency of dispatch.
- Manufacturers of containers, packing material and cartons who provide the advertiser with packages, which become part of advertisement.
- Printing presses, litho press, typesetters, who are required for print media advertisements.
- Electrical and electronic panel makers.
- Manufacturers of working models.
- Gift suppliers.
- Audio-visual equipment suppliers.
- Merchandisers.
- Desk top publishers.

Freelance service providers like, copywriters, and artists, visualizers, who are hired for specific jobs by small agencies like hot shops, and at times by small advertisers themselves, who cannot afford to hire an agency.

The challenge of creating a powerful advertisement, which can change the mindset of the market segment, has assumed great importance in the twenty first century. With advancements in technology of communication as also in product groups and constant up-gradations more and more money is going to be spent in years to come in advertising. As marketers and advertisers the firms should be ready with the necessary tools of the job.

Advertising is, as understood by now is part of the marketing game. To better plan advertising, firms will have to reinforce their marketing plans. Selection of markets for the product, distribution network, pricing and the timing of its launch would effect and determine the type of advertisement campaign should be created and what would be best media for the same. Therefore from marketing plans and budgets, advertising plans and budgets would evolve.

Advertising is therefore part of business strategy as can be seen below:

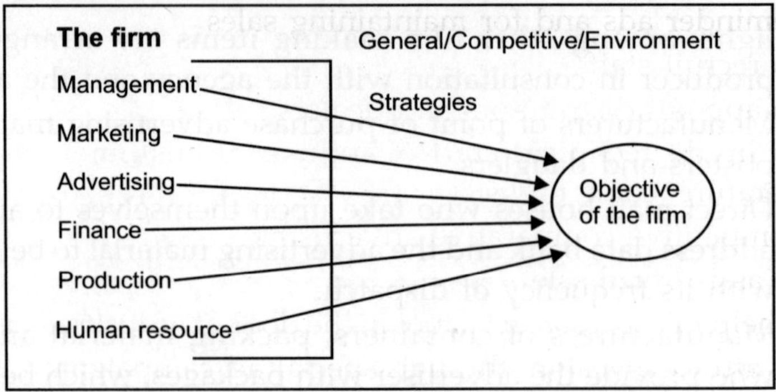

Fig. 11.1. Advertising as Business Strategy

Questions for Discussion

1. What are the marketing mix factors and how is integrated with them?
2. What are the six elements of advertising mix?

Objectives of Advertising

Given below are some of the objectives of advertising:

Sales as objective

Communication

Prompt direct action

Encourage customer to ask for information

Giving Message of need and its satisfaction

Products success stories to reinforce product/ brand loyalty

The benefit story

Attitude change

Reassurances

Besides, the purposes of advertising are as follows:

1. Launch of a new product
2. Modification in products
3. Changes in price
4. New packing—or, Promotional plans, e.g. **buy one get one free**
5. Distributor's and retailer's address
6. Educating the customers for proper usage of the product
7. To retrieve lost sales, e.g. due to strike in the factory

8. Reminder ads and for maintaining sales
9. To recruit staff
10. To appoint distributors and dealers
11. To invite technical staff of industrial customer to ask for literature, come to visit
12. Competitive comparative advertising
13. To assist retail sale
14. to help salesperson get a foot in the door of industrial customers
15. To attract investors through special ad campaigns
16. To export/go international (separate chapter is provided for this topic)
17. To announce financial results of the firm
18. To sell direct e.g. Readers Digest

Sales as Objective: Business today is for continuous improvement in the bottom line. Profit remains the prime motive and to achieve a reasonable return on investment firms have to struggle as competitors are equally focussed on the same subject. Advertising is a distinct aid to improving sales. Many advertising agencies refute that advertising should directly increase sales. However, the ultimate use of advertising must be to improve profitable sales.

Communication: Advertising is used as a means of communication as marketers want to provide information about their products to the target segment. Marketers also inform about new products in the pipeline, discount offers, new retail outlets and of late exchange offers.

A. the first step in business communication through advertising is of creating **awareness,** for product launches it becomes critical that target segment gets to know about the product
B. **Comprehension** should result in potential customer getting to know features of the product.
C. **Acceptance** of the product as a means of satisfying customers needs, whether they buy it or not.
D. **Belief that** it is this product only which the customer needs.
E. **Purchase** action is the next step, as the customer has fully understood the value he/she will derive from the product.
F. **Usage and repeat buy** results from satisfaction of customer and going beyond satisfaction the product delights the customer.

Thus the chain goes on, which starts with customer's awareness of the product.

Price Changes: Product prices convey to the buyers a lot more than just what they are paying for. Prices denote quality of the product besides authenticity of supply. In industrial products prices could be including packing, taxes duties and transport/ insurance costs. Unless marketers make a clean statement of the prices there can be lot of room for cheating the customers. Hence, good marketers invariably announce the price changes through advertising in the media right for the segment.

Prompt Direct Action: By today and get a 20% discount or the offer ends in just two days, are the gimmicks to prompt the customer in to action. These offers must be advertised for letting the segment know and take advantage of the offer.

Customers are encouraged to seek more information through teaser advertisement. When Bharti Telecom introduced Airtel their cellular phone service in Delhi the city roads were carrying banners saying "THERE IS SOME THING NEW IN THE AIR- AIRTEL" Several industrial product Ads give only basic specifications to generate curiosity and interest which prompts customer to ask for specification details.

Message of need and its satisfaction has become one of the most common objectives of advertising. In summer months the emphasis on thirst and cold drinks, the colas is well known and literally millions of Rupees are spent on such Ads. Advertising in College Billboards for books pinpoints the need for books and how this can be fulfilled.

Product success stories are advertised to reinforce customer's commitment of purchasing the product. Hero Honda have been advertising the fact that their scooter is the only one to have climbed the high mountain pass of Khardungla, confirming the high quality of the product, which in turn would make the customers delighted and prospective buyers consider strongly about purchasing the scooter. Customer's brand loyalty can not be taken for granted by any marketer. Such stories could improve the chances of having brand loyal customers.

Benefit story is usually the fundamental theme of most Ads. It could be promise of fairer skin (Creams), better health (Tonics), better mileage (fuel efficient car), the list is endless. Researchers tell that people do not buy products; **they buy the satisfaction or delight** they are likely to obtain from the product. Car is not just a car; it is a comfortable means of transportation. An example of the Benefit story is given below for Maruti Esteem car.

The benefit story can be made for any product as it sifts the features from the benefits, which can be gained from a product. These benefits ultimately converge on the basic needs of people as per Maslow's hierarchy of needs.

Table 11.2. Benefit Story

Car Features	*Benefits from the Feature*
Sleek sedan model	Projecting high life style
Comfortable seats, leg room	Physical comfort
Big luggage boot	Family car
High power engine	High life style/youth
Power windows	Comfort
Countrywide service	Peace of mind

Now if we recall the birthday Ad, where the husband is driving in his esteem with his wife and a child, he stops the car to buy some thing and the child brings out the cake from the dickey sitting in the backseat, the wife puts the Happy birthday tape and they surprise the husband on his return when he hears the song and sees the cake. Then the family drives away towards the horizon. The Ad tells that Esteem is a luxury family car.

Attitude Change: When the marketer finds that the competitor is firmly entrenched in the target segment, the advertising becomes more aggressive, as it is necessary to have a change of attitude in the customer group. Lot of comparative Ads are used for this purpose. The customers are informed in great detail about the shortcomings of competitive products as compared to their products. However this approach is wrought with difficulties, as it may not be possible to prove the point and then competitor can go to the court of law and claim heavy damages.

The toothpaste Ads of Colgate were too farfetched as the claims made by them were not easy to prove and hence they had to revise the Ads.

Reassurance: It becomes imperative for marketers to keep their customers on their side as competition is always trying to get them to their side. Reassuring Ads which keep confirming the quality of the product, its availability at reasonable price and in products with long life cycles are a must to keep the sales going.

Product Launches: every day a new product is being introduced in the market, sometimes with great fanfare and sometimes tamely. Medimix soap was introduced with minimum advertising. Only when its sales picked up that the makers started big AD Campaign, which has raised the awareness level and hopefully would get increased market share. Whirlpool started sales of their washing machines with much advertising and is reaping the bounty of good share of the market.

Product launch provides the biggest challenge to both advertiser and the advertising agency, since the success of the product depends greatly on its launch.

It is important to learn about **Product Life Cycle** at this stage. Each product goes through its life cycle, which starts with its introduction, then it comes to growth followed by maturity and finally terminating in decline stage.

1. Introduction stage—when a new product is introduced in the market, as, cell-phones were, in the beginning the first buyers purchase it. These people are society leaders, innovators and experimenters. Naturally, they have the financial power to back their purchases. Since the number of such buyers is small the sales graph moves slowly during this stage.
2. Growth stage—after the first buyers (early birds), the first followers buy the product, who wait to see the utility of the product through the experience of early birds. Since this category of buyers is larger than the first one the sales jump up and marketers must provide for increased supplies of the product in the market. (It can be assumed that in India most products are in growth stage as product demand keeps increasing as the, due to economic policies each year a small per cent of lower income group gets into the next slab of income with better purchasing power.)

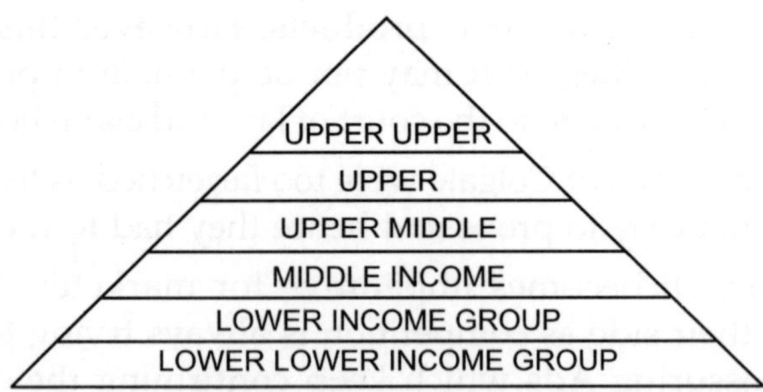

Fig. 11.2. Income Triangle

The top most part is of the elitist group with a small per cent of population in it, say 0.5%.

The second level is bigger than the first like 5%.

The third level could be 15%, while the fourth 20%. The lower income group could be 25% and lower-lower 30% of the population. Hence any shift of even one percent of lower- lower-to-lower and lower to middle could change the demographic pattern considerably.

Introduction stage of product needs major advertising effort for product launch, which could include concept selling, product introduction, price and distribution network announcements for the target segment customers.

In growth stage, the early marketers have the initial advantage. They can not relax because competition with ME TOO or even better products comes in the market.

In maturity stage as the market gets stagnant, sales is almost static, only replacement purchases take place. In such situations firms have to plan their strategies, whether they want to stay in the market with heavy advertisement or divest, quit.

In decline stage with severe competition many firms do quit, as can be seen in the VCR market. If the firm decides to stay it will have to create new markets uses of the product.

Product modifications call for informing the prospective customers about **"What is new and what it would do for the customer or what extra benefits are available in the new product"** the Computer and IT Industry is the most innovative one where everyday something new happens and marketers want to be the first one's to introduce the product. Product life cycle of such constantly developing products is short and the marketers have to reap the benefits of high sales in shortest possible time. Hence heavy doses of advertisements are fed to the customers.

Price changes—as is known price is normally the single most important feature of a product, which helps customers, decide about its purchase.

Price changes, discount offers, extended guaranties and warranties have become part of marketing strategy. However, unless the customer gets to know about the changes, he cannot take favorable decisions. Hence there is the need to advertise price changes.

In order to motivate customers into buying action price changes are made. If the announcement of price reduction is made well in advance, the competitors will get time to take preemptive measures, negating any benefit which could accrue by price reduction in terms of increased sales. Timeliness is of great importance when firms want to announce price reductions. Maruti reduced the price of their 800 cc car and made sudden announcement, which gave a big boost to its sales during ensuing period.

Package: When the firm's feel that some staleness has crept into their product and product modifications are not possible in the immediate future, they change the package, giving it a modern look, which in turn attracts the customers attention resulting in increased sales.

A look at the FMCG's would confirm that package change is a common phenomenon. And it does tend to increase sales, provided the customers are made fully aware of the new package, else, some customers may not buy the product considering it as a new untested product. This is done through advertising.

Promotional Plans: Firms face loss of market share and sometimes the market shrinks albeit temporarily. In such events, firms want to make purchasing of their products more attractive than that of competitor. This is done by means of promotional plans. Buy one get one free, buy a car get a stereo free, get a TV set and get a walkman free; these and similar offers help firms to bring extra share of the market.

In fact, such offers amount to price reduction to an extent. Yet, while price reductions have a tendency of being of a more permanent nature, promotions can be withdrawn as and when the firm thinks it has achieved its market share goal. Bringing back original price gives the firm back its profit margin. However, Maruti took nearly a year before they could restore the original price of its 800 cc model.

Products sell through the **distribution channels**; the importance of the channels cannot be minimized unless an alternative system of sale is found out. Firms have to inform the segment customers about the location where they can get the product. Therefore they advertise the names addresses and phone numbers of the sales outlets.

As the channel members also benefit from the advertisements firms like to have cooperative AD Campaigns where the middlemen, persons in the distribution network participate in Advertising expense.

Some products are highly technical in nature and wrong or improper use of the product could make it unserviceable. Even cars usage, mileage and functioning would improve if it is maintained properly. In sale of plant and machinery, capital goods such education of the customer is almost mandatory. Even in smaller products like domestic electric appliances, voltage and current specifications are part of **the education programme**, which is advertised to reach the target segment.

Sometimes firms lose business due to reasons beyond their control, like strike by workers or natural calamity. In such events, as customers needing the product have bought from competitors, it is important to advertise the fact that **the firm is back in business**. To further supplement their marketing efforts, firms can resort to some promotional plan and advertise it. This would be the best cover for the earlier mishap.

Most general advertising noticed is in **reminder category**. Pepsi and Coke Advertising blitz, which often takes the shape of business war, is an excellent example of reminder Ads.

Amul has been in business for a long time now. It is a well-established brand with good market share, innovative marketing and successful reminder advertising. By the way, Amul uses cartoon clips to good effect in these reminder Ads. Comic or cartoon clips can be used if the product justifies it.

Advertisements are given for **recruitment of staff** by firms. These could be part of newspapers classified category or these could be on special pages. These days most newspapers and business magazines have sections devoted to recruitment by firms.

Recruitment advertising too has an indirect effect as they subtly remind the customers of the firm's existence.

Advertisements are given to **appoint Distributors, dealers, agents, retailers franchisees and C&F Agents**. Marketers normally know the people who are in the same trade and they can opt from that list when planning to appoint a channel member. Advertising can give firms a wider selection. In case of new areas with geographic business expansion, advertisements can be a real boon.

Firms have to declare their **semi-annual and annual profit** and loss accounts and the balance sheet. These periodic results can help in consolidating the brand equity too.

For **Industrial Products Advertising** is meant to assist the sales persons in getting appointments with the customer personnel, like the proverbial foot in the door.

Besides, since normally big money is involved in purchase of industrial products customers need lot more information in the first instant even to arouse their curiosity. Hence industrial product advertising takes two different forms as follows:

1. Advertising details of the product
2. Image building advertising, which keeps the firm in constant focus of the buyer.

Firms planning to get investors to buy their shares resort to heavy advertising to create not just a ripple but a storm in the financial market so that small and big **investors queue up to buy their shares.** There are specialized advertising agencies like Saubhagya and Clea who have the expertise of such advertising.

With **global business** a fact of life firms would be neglecting international markets at their own risk and peril. Several Indian firms are already Multinational companies and more are to follow. In such a situation international advertising has assumed importance. Several MNC Advertising Agencies have set up offices in India and are providing advertising support for multinational businesses.

Main objectives of advertising are, to increase profitable sales, improve market share and the brand image. Brand image builds brand equity, which in turn brings brand loyalty.

PHILIP KOTLER on marketing "**The best advertising is done by satisfied customers.**"

Five Ms of Advertising (according to Kotler)—

1. Mission—to include Sales Goals and Advertising objectives
2. Money—for considering, stage in PLC Market share and consumer base, Competition and clutter, Advertising frequency Product substitutability
3. Message—generation, evaluation and selection, execution, and social responsibility of the message
4. Media—reach frequency and impact, major types specific chosen media, timing, and geographic media allocation
5. Measurement—impact on sales and awareness

Advertising Agency & Its Working

In the new millennium business scene can be described as having increased competition, better products, new media availability and constant threat of new entrants and substitute products.

Advertising agency have therefore becoming important and yet, back-ground partners of firms. As there are several different types of advertisers there are different types of advertising agencies to cater to their demand. With SPECIALIZED PRODUCT GROUPS coming in the market, like computers and peripherals, video products, telecom products, the need of specialized agency has been felt as never before. Sure enough such agencies are evolving or existing agencies are hiring persons who are technically qualified to understand the new business.

Let us see a typical organization chart of a full function Advertising Agency.

Table 11.3. Organization Chart of Advertising Agency

Chief Executive Officer

Client Group 1	*Client Group 2*	*Client Group 3*	*Client Group 4*
Account Management	Creative Services	Media Services	Research services
Account Manager/Executive	Art Director, Copywriter	Press	In House research
Account Planner	Visualizer	Electronic Media	Outside research agency

A functional head who has the experience and skills is positioned in each of the areas, Account Management, Creative, Media and Research. In some agencies they do not have a Research department and they hire the services of outside research organizations like ORG-Marg in India.

Full service Agencies are capable of providing entire range of advertising services to their clients.

Advertising agency work starts with a **Brief** from the client to their Account Executive.

The brief constitutes of the following points:

- Details of client's activities.
- Clients market share, brands and their equity
- Competitive brands and their value
- Marketing objectives
- Advertising objectives
- An idea of budget meant for advertising

The role of Advertising Agency in marketing efforts of a firm can be compared to that of a doctor who treats a patient and must be told everything necessary for his treatment and cure and same type of confidentiality is expected from the agency.

The **Account Executive (AE)**, works as a close link between the agency and its client. He represents the client at the agency and ensures that the agency works within the framework of clients brief and in the allotted time. The word DEADLINE is perhaps the most used word in any agency- as it has to meet the target date of releasing the ad campaign to the media after its acceptance by the client. The AE arranges the agency resources, creative, media budgetary to get the best campaign for the client. AE puts across agency's plans and the campaign to the client to get their approval. It is more of a sandwich kind of a role, yet it is very satisfying once the campaigns planned are executed and bring desired results.

The Creative Department is equally important in an Advertising Agency, which is as follows:

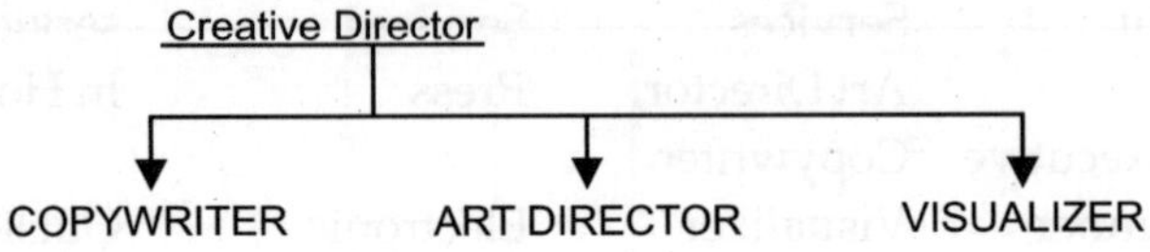

Fig. 11.3. Creative Deptt. of Advertising Agency

CREATIVE DIRECTOR is responsible for the entire creative work of the agency, including, copywriting, art designing work and planning sketches for TV Commercials. The Visualiser's job is to ensure that copy and art is placed at the right places and the total effect of advertisement is eye catching. Copywriter writes the Copy, the written word in any advertisement. The Art Director creates the visuals, the drawings, photos and sketches in the advertising campaign. Art Director also works as the Visualizer in most Advertising Agencies.

Motivating Factors

They also focus on the suitability of the chosen market segment/s. For this purpose either they have a research unit of their own or they hire outside agency for gathering information. Some agencies have Research Directors to head the department.

In certain agencies the trend is to have Account Planning Department which arranges for the Customers view point, gathered from market research to interact with creative and media for best results.

The Media Director heads Media Department where the media research is conducted to find which would be the right media for the campaign. They plan the media, frequency for advertising; it's cost and coverage. They are responsible for purchasing media space for print media and time for Production Department does the Print and Broadcast, Telecast production work, including hiring free lance TV Commercial makers.

Traffic Controller Department coordinates the work of different departments in the agency and ensures that no client work is side tracked or delayed.

Marketing Department of the agency arranges information on the market segment, what excites the customers, what are the electronic media, like Radio and TV.

AGENCY management is conducted on day-to-day basis, which, among other activities involve, money and men management.

Agency organization chart is given below:

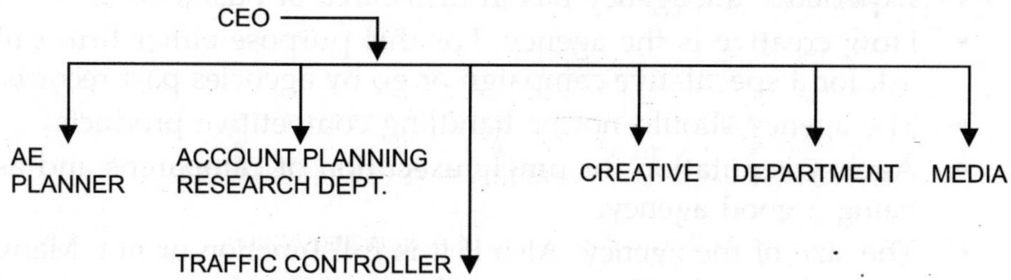

Fig. 11.4. Agency Organization Chart

Most of the full service agencies have similar structures; the designations may differ from agency to agency.

Full Service Agency is geared to provide complete ranges of services to its clients, to plan create and implement the advertising as per clients needs. In India, HTA, CLARION, LINTAS are some of the full service agencies. The agency proposes complete communication solutions to its client, the creative, the budget and the media.

Limited Service Agency—usually these agencies do not provide full service. They concentrate on creative aspects of advertising. They are well appreciated and used by clients looking for high quality creative work while depending on other sources for media planning and execution of the campaign. They are also known as creative boutiques or hot shops. Because of their lean organization they can be quite competitive.

Agency of Records is the large agency with financial muscle as they buy media in bulk and sell the space not needed by them at a profit of 2% to those agencies who are looking for media space at the peak season.

Specialized agencies operate to serve niche markets like financial advertising, resorted to before a firm plans to have a public issue of its shares. In India Clea and Sobhagya are two such agencies.

Agency profits and payments come from commissions they get from the media for selling space to their clients. The rate of commission has been 15%. Besides, agencies also get from their clients directly fees, markups and incentive based commissions.

For the media like outdoor, special boards, directories the agency puts a mark up on the price given by the media and gets paid for its efforts. In the case of incentive base, the client pays the agency on the basis of the results obtained by the advertising campaign.

Advertiser and The Agency Selection

The firms look into the following aspects of different agencies:

- Experience the agency has in firms area of business.
- How creative is the agency. For this purpose either firm can ask for a speculative campaign or go by agencies past records.
- The agency should not be handling competitive products.
- Agency reputation for timely execution of campaigns and as being a good agency.
- The size of the agency. Also if it is full function or not. Many times the local office may not have all the departments and agency sends its work to its head office, which can be time consuming. If fast work is a must such agencies even if they are well reputed can be avoided.
- Whether the agency has experience of international advertising or not.
- Ability of key persons.
- Compatibility with the firm's personnel.
- Cost consciousness of the agency. They are not throwing clients money away needlessly.

When an advertiser decides to appoint a new advertising agency he calls selected agencies to present their credentials and advertising concepts mainly in line with firms advertising needs.

Next step is asking the short-listed agencies to present a speculative campaign to the advertiser. Since the speculative plans are time consuming and cost money, many agencies refrain from making such a presentation.

Advertising agencies seldom advertise to get clients. Usually, prospective clients see their work and the clients approach the agencies. If any agency has to go openly after a client, it is done subtly through direct mails or informally at social gathering

The following gives an idea of how to select an advertising agency.

Advertising Agency Selection Process

The following is the method of selection used by the Advertisers for selecting an Advertising Agency:

Account contacts—the agency should understand clients business, both commercially and technically. If required the agency should hire proper technical staff for the purpose as any miss match in understanding the brief could at the least mean more time wasted with the agency and at worst, wrong advertising message going to the media and through it to the ultimate customers.

Agency maintains confidentiality and does NOT handle competitive products.

Agency meets deadlines always as a habit.

Agency staff turn over is within reason.

Agency gives great importance to its creative work which is usually good and unique, not just a distorted copy of some other advertisement Indian or foreign.

Agency keeps high quality standards as per the firms needs.

Agency has an eye on costs too.

Agency has good rapport with the media and PR Consultants.

Agency media plan is consistent with the target market segment for firms products.

Agency knows competitive media strategy

Agency knows the market and can confirm their claim from their research work.

Relationship between advertiser and the agency—

- Advertiser should know the working of the agency and its key personnel.
- Ideally, the Agency should be used as an extension of advertisers marketing department.
- Acceptance of the advertising budget and **mode of payment** must be clearly defined and understood by both advertiser and the agency.
- Agency should allow advertiser to visit the agency.
- Agency should simplify its paper work.
- Account executive should understand the structure of competition
- Agency should meet dead lines always.
- Agency should have specialized people to handle technical aspects of clients brief.
- Agency should inform clients about legal and ethical sides of advertising their products.

For best results, Advertisers do well by having an Advertising Manager in their Marketing Department. These managers have to liaise with the advertising agency and other service providers. They have to understand the four Ps of their firm and of competition too. They give the brief to the agency. They have to plan the advertising budget in association with the marketing manager. They are also required to arrange for press releases as publicity material.

Advertising Managers have to assess the efficacy of advertising campaigns by keeping a track of communications both verbal and written received on the basis of the advertising campaign.

Graphic Representation of the working of an Advertising Agency is given below:

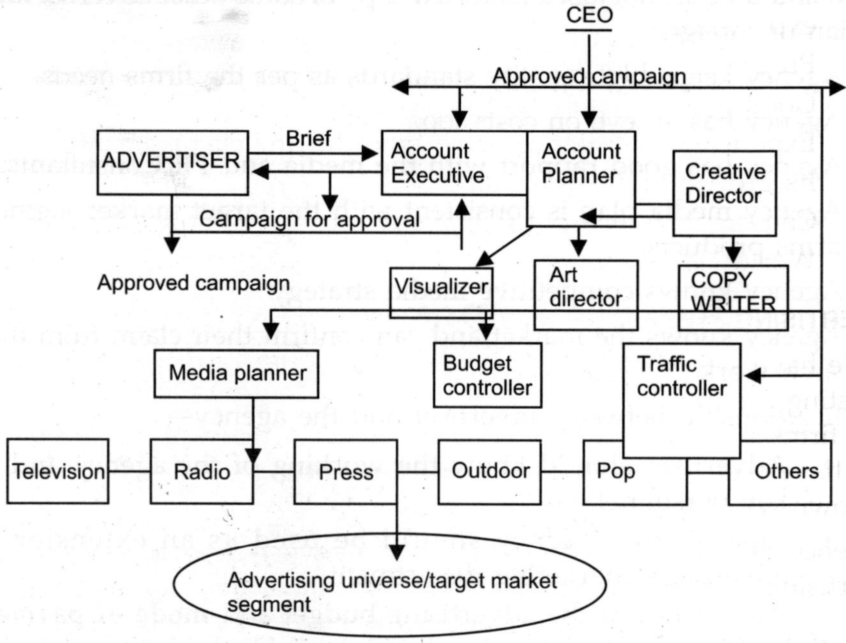

Fig. 11.5. Advertising Process

Some large business houses have their own in-house agencies. The advertiser in such cases has total control over the agency. The agency is tuned to the work culture of the firm and thus better appreciates the type of work required from the agency. They know the product and the plans and policies well and the brief requirements do become really brief. The agency becomes virtually part of the firms marketing team and this helps in better-coordinated efforts. The agency also is committed to providing the same, good service and undivided attention to even smaller members of the group.

In house agencies have the disadvantage of having outside group clients feeling neglected, in favour of house clients. Hence the in-house agency has to understand the trade offs required and/or dilution of outside commitments.

Agency Rating: Advertising Agencies are rated by the advertisers on the following parameters:

- Creativity, Originality and Liveliness
- Keenness in understanding the clients problems
- Management Team
- Understanding of the Market and its problems
- Caliber of personnel, their consumer orientation and their experience
- Progressive and flexible
- Good media department
- Experience in using research work for the clients benefit
- Its growth and expansion
- Can organize ***below the line*** advertising material
- Worldwide network

ADVERTISING RESEARCH AND DAGMAR

We have seen that in order to be focused on firms overall goals, marketing department has to play a vital role as the revenue earnings of the firms are mainly from selling of products. Hence, once the firm's goals have been formulated the marketing and advertising people set their own goals and objectives.

Hence, DAGMAR becomes effective only when there is continuous Advertising Research is conducted as per requirement.

Advertising Research

Advertising research is being extensively used by, both advertisers and advertising agencies, to pre-test the campaign, evaluate the media's effectiveness, understanding the market segment best suited for the firm's products.

Most firms arrange for Market Research for obtaining market segments viewpoints and preferences about products in their category. These researches tell about product acceptance levels.

Advertising research tells the advertisers about the type of creativity, the language including slang and dialect would stimulate the segment.

It will be difficult to find an advertisement of a perfume, which gives its chemical formula. Instead, the advertisement would be talking about love, and euphoria created by the perfume. The advertisement are the result of the research conducted which says that in personal care products people are interested in what it would do to them. It is said that no body buys a product. They buy the performance promised or given by the product.

Media research is conducted to establish the suitability of a particular medium. Some advertisements have a dotted line cutout telling the readers to cut it and post to the advertiser for additional information, free sample or a demonstration of the product. The number of prints of the media is compared to the cutout responses to know about its readership and correctness of the media for the target segment.

Research on the advertising copy is done with the help of Primary research, when individual customers are contacted to get their reactions to the advertisement. It conforms the acceptance level of the campaign and can be used to determine the frequency of the insertions in the media.

Advertising research helps in making advertising campaigns more powerful thereby they become better able to perform the task of meeting advertising objectives.

Advertising costs are high. To make the best impact research ensures that advertisement is creatively acceptable, in the right media with correct frequency and for the chosen market segment.

The current Nescafe advertisement starts with a woman enjoying a mug full of the brew. The research had shown that women enjoy coffee during a lull in their work, be it household chores or office work. Later in the advertisement some men are also shown as it would be too risky to ignore a major customer group, in fact fifty percent of the population.

Advertising research results thus shows the advertiser how to place correct advertisements at the correct places and at the most appropriate times-making them both effective and efficient.

- After PR, advertisers are interested in finding out the likes and dislikes of the customers, reasons for the same. Research is conducted by doing primary Survey, by **interviewing** customer groups. Such a research is similar to the market research, as information needed is akin to the one required in market research.
- Advertising research can also be conducted by **observation.** Researchers stand near shopping malls and observe the shoppers, their likes and dislikes, their behaviour pattern. Such a researcher has to note down his observations without

prejudice, objectively; otherwise the deductions would be entirely lopsided. **It may be useful to note that watching/ observing customers in shops for collecting data without their knowledge may not be purely ethical. Also, asking questions may look like selling gimmicks rather then advertising or market research.**

- The next type of research can be termed as IDEA- RESEARCH where attempt is made to understand how some changes in an advertising campaign would effect the result as far as the advertising objectives are concerned. For example, would increase in advertising size improve its acceptance, or its frequency improves ***Top of the mind recall.***

Care should be taken on the following areas while planning the research-

- Time and money spent should be commensurate with the objective of the research. For example if the benefit to be obtained from the research amounts to Rupees two million, it would not be prudent to spend two and a half million on the research. In the same way if the research is going to take one year in fashion industry, the very purpose of the research would be defeated.
- Research results would, at best give indicators for decision-making not perfect answers.
- Going through the exact methods to be used by the field researchers in detail would make you more aware of the nitty-gritty and less vulnerable to problems, which can occur due to subjectivity of the researchers.
- Be specific what has to be done rather than leave it to the field people who may come up with unnecessary, redundant data. It may look good that you are in the know of several facts, but you should understand the cost and time implications. It is better to get just enough information.
- Research budget need careful analysis. It may be apt to spend some amount of money when the decision to be based on the research is for large sums of money and it includes avoidance or limiting risk for the firm. Naturally for simple problems, many times previous experience is the best guideline for decision making and no research need to be conducted.
- Getting the research done for your bookrack or your shelf only is not a good idea. Unless you are sure that people who are going to use the research findings it may be only an exercise in

futility. Remember that people generally do not want to change their ways just because of some research findings.

- Many times the firm may already have the data called for, or available with another source, e.g.. Some research organization like ORG-Marg.

Secondary research data is available from a variety of sources, as it is the research already done by somebody earlier. Government publications, industry data, Magazines, Internet are some of the sources of secondary data.

Advertising research can be carried out **before the launch** of the advertising campaign. It helps in media planning, copy testing along with test marketing the product to be advertised.

Advertising research carried out **during the campaign** focuses on Dealer audit, sales analysis and customers response based on contests or reply cutouts given with the advertisements for customers to fill in their comments and send back to the advertiser.

After the campaign gets over, as per DAGMAR, **research is done to assess the effectiveness of the campaign** on the parameter of the objective of the advertising campaign. At this time **Consumer Panel Surveys** are conducted for structured responses.

Consumer panels are predetermined group of people mostly of one geographic and demographic segment like lady members of a Kitty party. These persons are in the know of their task of making assessments of the campaigns and inform the advertiser about their views.

Selecting research sample needs knowledge of market, the universe and quantitative techniques.

Gathering information or data collection can be done by in-depth interviews where the respondent (Interviewee, one member of the sample chosen), is asked questions from a well structured questionnaire. The respondent can give his own views as well as lot of time is given for each question. The interviewer must be adept at organizing such interviews and later on in making a coherent and lucid report.

When the interview is conducted in a well accepted and known group called the Focus group, same type of in-depth incisive questions can be asked. The problem, which can arise, is the conflict within the group with diverse views.

The questions can be of two types, simple **straightforward types** where the answer can be yes or no. However, when it is important to understand the mindsets it is better to use **projective** questions which can be vague and which would evoke emotional, sentimental and creative answers.

What product you associate with Shah Rukh Khan?

When you think of colour think of WHAT?

Sixty years young, climbing the staircase?

Just do it. Which product it conveys?

These are just a few samples.

How do you rate the following hotels in Delhi?

- Maurya Sheraton
- Taj Mansingh
- The Oberoi
- Hyatt Regency
- Taj Palace

The way I look is important to me

- Strongly agree
- Agree
- Normal
- Disagree
- Strongly disagree

Surveys, observations and experiments with the help of questionnaires, checklists and plans help in completing the advertising surveys. Then comes the important aspect of analysis and report writing.

Research, as stated must be used or else the time and money is a total waste. Research results enable firms in reassessing their goals on the basis of new opportunities, in confirming the target segment and creating a useful message for the segment.

Advertising results can be measured by simple brand recall tests with the target segment. These can be aided or unaided recalls.

"Which is the best toothpaste in the market?"

"Which blue and red bottle drink gives most satisfaction?"

Research confirms the strong views held by the firm. If there is major divergence then a re-look is required at the objectives, sample and methods adopted in the research. A very apt example of how the research could go wrong is given below:

A firm planned to start manufacture of Fax machines in India in 1980s, the task of finding out the demand and product acceptance levels was given to an outside research agency by the firm. The result was flattering in as much that 80% respondents were looking forward to buying a fax machine. When the note was sent to Department of Telecommunications Government of India, it came back saying that the telecom network was not efficient enough to make fax a success.(It was only in late eighties that Digital electronic exchanges, fiber optic cables made the telecom network good enough for fax to operate.)

Advertising research is a part of marketing research, confined to development of advertising plan, creative work, market segment and the best possible media, which would cater to the segment. The research should increase the effectiveness and efficiency of the advertising campaign. Data collection is done from primary sources as also secondary, already available sources. In primary data collection it is important to select the sample correctly. The research steps are,

A. setting up goals for the research,

B. finding the sources of secondary information/data.

C. analyzing secondary data

D. planning sample for primary research

E. data collection

F. data analysis and report writing

The advertising campaign is pre-tested and post tested to ensure that it works.

Research does not provide results or facts, it only gives tendencies. Sample size determines the accuracy levels. At times it is important to sacrifice accuracy for speed.

Guidelines for Making a Questionnaire –

Ask basic questions about respondents name, address. While asking his age and income, give a range, age between 18–30, 31–45, 46–60, and 61 above.

- Income between Rupees 3000–7000, 8000–15000, 16000–30000
- Questions with possible two answers: Did you buy the watch yourself, yes or no ?
- Multiple choice questions: Who advised you to buy the watch, your father, uncle, sister or cousin ?
- Likert scale questions: The watch is considered best value for money: tick one you consider right— (a) strongly disagree, (b) disagree, (c) neutral, (d) agree, (e) strongly agree.

- Differential scale: the hotel is

	large	______	small
	Modern	______	outmoded
Hotel staff	Experienced	______	inexperienced
	Courteous	______	disinterested

Questions on importance of the product can be put on extremely important, very important, important, not very important to not at all important.

Intentions to buy can be asked on a rating scale as sure to buy, perhaps, may not, will not and will never buy.

Open ended questions like, "what do you think of our hotel?" can be answered by the respondents in any way they like. Associations can tell you about the aided recalls, like

Welcome

Hotel

Travel

Media Planning and Product Positioning

We have seen that, from marketing plans we can develop advertising plans. As a step further, from the advertising plans the media plans will emerge. Advertising campaigns send messages to the prospective customers. It is therefore important that the message carrier, i.e. the media is chosen wisely. Besides, the timing and timeliness of the message gives it the required thrust and acceptance. Major advertising cost comes from the media costs. It becomes imperative that care is taken for proper and optimum use of the media. Hence the media planning has assumed a vital role in the exciting game of advertising.

Media Planning

The market place is brimming with a large variety of media. Therefore an intelligent approach to deciding the proper media is **media planning.**

Some of the well-known and often used media are given below:

Newspapers—they provide information about politics, sports, business and socio-cultural life of a community. A large percentage, about 80% educated people read newspapers. More educated and well-to do, read English language newspapers, other read Hindi or regional language papers. Newspapers are printed from most metro cities and due to heavy competition; the price of newspapers has been going down. The newspaper profits come from the advertisements printed in them. Newspaper owners have not only accepted their role as a vehicle of advertisements, they have geared themselves up for improved coverage, better print and paper and competitive advertisement rates. FMCG firms having wide distribution network use newspapers. They are good for providing information about products, firms and their local distribution network. The main shortcoming of newspaper as media is that the readership of newspapers among the youth is limited.

The newspapers are of several kinds as given below:

- National English language
- National Hindi
- National business
- Regional language
- Newspaper supplements
- Midday and eveningers
- Tabloids

Newspapers have their own advertising departments, which are engaged in selling advertising space. They pursue both the advertisers as well as the agencies to book the space. Special efforts are made during festive season and occasions like cricket test matches.

The newspaper sells space at a column centimeter rate. There are special rates for special positions in the newspaper like front page, solus position, when no other advertisement appears on the same page/ place. Advertisements for sports goods can be usefully advertised on the sports page of the newspaper. Newspapers are now accepting colour advertisements too. Teaser advertisements are carried out in split runs in newspapers, when a part of the advertisement is carried in one part of the newspaper and the rest in the next part. On their part newspapers carry out surveys about buying patterns, habits and seasonality of sale of selected products.

The main advantages of newspapers are as follows:

- Advertisers can focus on the geographic area they want to cover.
- Newspapers get their readers total attention.
- Size of the advertisement does not matter.
- Advertisements can be put in the newspapers quickly.
- It is easy to talk to the readers to know their views about the advertisement.

Magazines: Magazines come in different disciplines, like magazines for consumers, for film fans, for women and then there are technical magazines dedicated to science & technology, computers, and other engineering disciplines like chemical engineering, genetics, medical sciences.

Magazines can be categorized as follows:

- Political
- Social
- Professional for doctors, engineers
- Regional language
- Film
- Computer based
- Wild life
- Arts
- Theater
- Newspaper magazine supplements

Magazines carry the current events, new developments and plans of the concerned area. Their coverage is limited, their getup glossy but could be of indifferent quality. They are published from most major cities and in all possible languages of the land. The price of magazines depends on its coverage, gloss and can be very different for magazines even from the same town, publisher or discipline.

Magazines adorn the homes of the elite as also of the commoner. They put the buyers in a special group and boost their egos. The disadvantage of advertising in magazines can be the excessive clutter of Advertisements in most magazines. And yet, the elite and the busy business magnet have hardly any time for looking at any thing else except some business magazines.

The main advantages of magazines as media are given below:

- Easy to select magazine for the target segment.
- Readership surveys easy.
- Can plan advertising to equate with the magazines interests.
- Message stays with the reader for a long time (as long as the magazine is on the writing desk.
- Advertising quality can be good.

Radio: With the advent of television especially the colour variety, radio listening has lost much of its appeal at least in the areas where TV Coverage is good and TV signal strong. In Indian remote villages only radio reach is confirmed and the radio remains a good advertising media. From film music to news radio provides entertainment of the audio kind, which is useful for advertising products for **rural markets.** FM radio (Frequency Modulation) has emerged as a major technological development because of its excellent voice quality in a given range of geographic area. **Metro teenagers** are hooked on to FM Radios music programmes the media caters to entire country geographically. The media costs are comparatively low.

The major disadvantage of radio as media is advertising clutter seen heard on radio. Major advantages are given below:

- Easy to place the advertisement in local radio station.
- Easy to conduct listeners research.
- Can be connected to radio programmes.
- It is possible to increase or decrease the advertising frequency at reasonable notice.

Television is definitely the most sought after entertainment media, which can be quite intoxicating, in the sense that people get hooked on to TV programmes. During the first telecast of the epics Ramayana and Mahabharat most city people were glued to the television sets, canceling even their important appointments. For advertisers, with the popularity of the media, it also manifests itself to being used for demonstrations, which along with the advertisement message, reaffirms the customers views in favor of the product.

Television caters to the entire family, as during the day, each member of the family sits down to watch one or the other TV programme, albeit at separate times. During noon and afternoon when the husband goes to work, the housewife watches TV. Without meaning to be gender biased, the programmers place programs of women's interest at that time.

Andrew Sullivan writes in the New York Times Magazine, *"Meanwhile on TV., America's Fox Family Channel has introduced two separate channels for boys and girls, boyzChannel and girlzChannel, to attract advertisers and consumers more efficiently."* Fox executives told Wall Street Journal that this move reflects what TV researcher tells them about viewing habits: *In general terms,* girls *are more interested in entertainment that is more relationship-oriented,* while boys are *action-oriented.*

When the TV started for the first time in India in early sixty's, telecast was limited to two hours a day of black and white programmes. From those days to present times with continuous twenty-four hours programme and that too on more than forty channels TV has taken giant strides forward.

The popularity of TV programmes are such along with wide area coverage that advertisers are ready to pay huge amounts for telecasting their advertising films. With live demonstration of the product in use TV advertising has taken the role of personal selling to a large extent.

The only negative aspect of TV advertising is the high cost of advertising. With rising income levels, and the race for purchasing new products, the advertising expense is on the increase with no sign of its coming down. The positive points of the TV are given below:

- Ability to demonstrate the product as working model.
- Creativity can reach new heights.
- Advertising quality can be excellent.
- Can reach millions of viewers.
- It can be telecast as often as the budget permits.
- Audience research can be easily conducted.

Out Door Media: In the area where hoardings, billboards and kiosks are placed provide high exposure advertising. Car owners are most effected people from the outdoor signs, in as much that in DELHI, the government has put a ban on outdoor media to avoid distractions caused by the hoardings.

The cost of the media is commensurate with its limited usage. The media, where allowed by the government is most often used to promote the firm, its brand and one single most important (at a time) product of the firm.

The negative aspect of the media is its limited reach, lack of opportunity for giving detailed product information and in some cases government regulations, e.g. Delhi.

The plus points of outdoor media are given below:

- Advertiser can select geographic coverage
- Creativity possibilities are good.

Point of Purchase (POP): In retail business POP plays a major role in advertising. Following are the usual POP Materials used:

- Posters
- Danglers
- Sign boards
- Streamers
- In-store closed circuit TV, which continuously shows, product displays at various levels as in-store commercials.

- Merchandizing, which decorates the shop displays
- Shop main signboards
- Window displays

In most shops due to multiple brands on display, there is a clutter of POP, which takes away the main benefits of POP.

Plus points of POP are as follows:

- Consumer research is possible
- Impact is direct on the viewer
- Can be changed easily
- Advertising material creativity can be directed to the shops clientele's needs.

Direct Mail: Direct Mail is the letters to customers. The letters can be crafted with a personalized format and approach. They sometimes take the role as the chosen media, especially in high value personal products like digital diary, PC, and service industry offers like from the hotels, airlines. Care should be taken to ensure that the Direct Mail letter looks like a normal business communication otherwise there are chances that the letter is put in the waste paper basket. With plethora of mail received by executives, they read only the ones, which look business like and readable.

The target market segment can be reached quite accurately with specific mailing addresses being available to the marketers from trade and industry associations.

The cost of direct mail can be quite varied on the basis of quality of the material and size of the mailing list. Since direct mail is targeted to only the real consumer with no aberrations, they can be focused and personalized, making the readers feel important. Care should be taken to ensure that even from the envelope the mailer gives the impression of a personal letter. Else the direct mail has the possibility of being consigned to the readers waste paper basket. As most corporate buyers get hundreds of direct mailers daily, they have to select only just a few for their perusal. Hence, even with its close contact with the customer Direct mail remains a back seat media.

Direct Mail scores high on the following points:

- Selection of customer groups
- Geographic coverage
- Flexibility in creativity

- Size and frequency of the message can be as desired by the advertiser to suit the product
- Advertisements quality can be good.

Cable Television and Satellite Channels: While the cable TV has local factor, satellite channels offer fare from all over the world.

Cable TV is developing quite fast. It gives priority to local news and events. Good media for retail shops, stores and low volume business!

Satellite TV, with channels from all over the world, like CNN, BBC, STAR, ZEE, NATIONAL GEOGRAPHIC, ANIMAL KINGDOM besides our own **Doordarshan** channels. Each one has its own viewer ship, which provides flexibility and focus for the desired market segment to the advertiser. The channel is popular with the upper class with growing spread and with enthusiasts of sports, movies, events and talk shows.

Media cost of local cable TV is reasonable while satellite TV costs vary on the basis of individual programme TRPs (Television Rating Points, which are indicators of programme viewer ship and popularity.)

The advantages of the SATELLITE CHANNEL media are as follows:

- Advertisements can cross international boundaries
- Creativity gets major thrust
- National marketing networks can make full use of the media
- Viewership consists of even elitists members of the society

Cable TV has the following plus points for the advertisers:

- Low cost advertising
- Local brands can use the media to advantage
- Demonstrations of working of products easy
- Quality of telecast is suspect, at times.

Miscellaneous Media—starting from yellow Pages, to directories, encyclopedias, rail and air tickets, Bus panels, sky balloons, elephants and camels, the list is endless. Yellow pages to directories, encyclopedias, rail and air tickets, Bus panels, sky balloons, elephants and camels, the list is endless. Yellow pages in particular have got the fancy of the middle and upper class in urban India. Most prospective customers use the yellow pages. Its usefulness comes from the fact that people look at the yellow pages just before making purchase decisions. However, mostly yellow pages do not dynamically promote a particular product. These media are mostly supplementary media used for reinforcing the main thrust media. Movie halls have slide shows as also video advertising, which are effective limited to the audience who are in a way captive and thus forced in to seeing the advertisements.

A rough estimate of media usage is as follows:

- Print, including newspapers and magazines—30%
- Television—40%
- Radio—7%
- Pop (point of purchase), and outdoor—3%
- Direct Mail—14%
- Miscellaneous—6%

The first three, print, radio and television are called ***above the line media*** while others, ***below the line media.*** The distinguishing factor being how the agency gets paid for the use of the media. In case of *above the line media*, the media pays the advertisings agency a commission @ 15%. For below the line media, the agency bills the advertiser with a markup on the media bills, which again is usually 15%.

Each member of the media make claim of their usage, readership or viewer ship, to woo the advertising campaigns. While for the print media ABC, an independent body publishes the exact print copies giving its coverage and penetration in the segment, for TV, the TRPs tell the popularity of a particular TV channel and its individual programme.

There are other media available now as follow:

1. Videotapes with movies- the number of movies-on-tape hired each year is increasing each year. With advent of video disks they will too form a new media in India.
2. Advertisements on computer software discs.
3. Internet has emerged as a major advertising media worldwide because of the following reasons:
   - Coverage on the web is world wide
   - Availability of huge amount of information on the net
   - Entertainment sites like chat rooms
   - Creativity is boundless, with little or no censorship so far
   - Live demonstrations with audio and video clips makes it really interesting
   - Interactivity of the media—as it take the customer from information search to buying action- just a click away, (with the help of credit cards)

The possibilities of new media emerging are immense and the advertisers would be looking keenly for developments in the area.

Product Positioning

There are several cars in the Indian market. From the low cost Maruti 800 to Honda City, from Fiat Uno to BMW? What type of people these cars belong to? People buy cars not just for going from one place to the other; they also project their life style. The car marketers put their cars in the slot meant for them. BMWs are positioned for the top bracket of customers, while Maruti is in the middle-income group.

Chocolates, ice creams and cheese may be your favourite eats, and then you would have the brands preferred by you. The mental picture of a product and its brand in your mind is the result of the advertisements you watch and the product quality.

As marketers and advertisers how do you gain a particular position? It is the sum total of the quality, price and advertising effort which goes in to the product.

The marketer therefore attempts product positioning, but actually it is the market, which places a product in its position.

Microsoft has got their product Windows positioned at the top by sheer force of heavy advertisement and consistent quality.

Indian car market leaders Maruti (volume business-wise) would like the customers to believe that their cars are offering greater value for money. Followers like Fiat, Daewoo and Santro would have the customers acknowledge that their cars are as good or better then Maruti.

Positioning planning- the following steps need to be taken:

- Get the real picture of your product in comparison to the competitive products. It is better to do a SWOT analysis of the products in the market including yours without any bias.
- Select the market segment carefully.
- Understand the consumers need, the benefits he seeks to get from the product. It will help in making the advertisements in tune with the consumer thought process.
- Check the competitive position.
- State your products position.

Advertising Budget

As mentioned in the chapter on Advertising Agencies, the Agency gets a *brief* from the client or the advertiser. Among other information the brief contains the clients budget, which has been earmarked for spending on advertising. It therefore becomes the job of the agency to prepare the advertising campaign keeping in view the allocated budget.

Several times the agency, however finds that the budget is not exactly adequate for doing justice to the objective/s of the advertisement. If the difference is minor, the agency can persuade, in the interest of campaigns success, the client for upward revising the budget. In case of major differences it is necessary that the agency is prepared to defend the extra expenditure on advertising they want the client to incur.

Major expenditure in the campaign is required for the media. In case of below the line media, the agency adds a percentage on money spent, usually 15 % towards their cost coverage and profit.

The methods used in deciding the Advertising Budget are giving below:

- Launch of the product advertising
- Main competitors budgets
- Based on the firms objectives for advertising
- Historical Sales method
- Task based
- Arbitrary method
- Criterion of affordability
- Top drawer

Let us discuss these methods in detail.

Product launches—when firms bring out new products in the market, they have to achieve the following for a success launch of the product:

1. Product awareness among the target market segment
2. Knowledge of availability of the product
3. Understanding of main benefits provided by the product for the customers
4. Service availability for the product
5. Multiple usage of the product if relevant
6. Peripheral segments for the product

Simply, the product can never be purchased unless the customers are in the know of the same. For cottage industry, when production levels are low, **word of mouth publicity** helps in making the product known to prospective customers. Word of mouth publicity is an effective form of making people aware of the product and it happens without any apparent effort on the part of the marketer. And since it is not paid for, it does not fall in the category of advertising.

Product launches, therefore require concentrated advertising effort, increasing the budget manifold. However depending on the product, the market segment and the geographic area to be covered, the budget can be suitably made.

During the launch stage of the product, availability of the product for the segment has to be ensured. Also, if the customer wants to buy the product he must know where he can get it. Imagine a situation where a heavily advertised product is not available in the market. It will surely result in the customer buying competitive product and when the product does become available competition would have taken a march over the advertiser. Of course, if the product shortage is created as a strategy to generate demand, care should be taken to monitor and watch the situation closely.

Products are purchased for the benefits the offer to the customer. Any advertising has to cover these benefits. Writing the benefit story may take time and space and increase the advertising budget. Considering the importance of benefit story especially in the product launch stage spending the extra Rupee would be well worth it.

Most products need to be serviced to be able to give the benefits promised. Hence the customer must be told about the availability of service facility with the advertiser.

There is a bit of a risk factor in over or under budgeting the advertising campaign.

Most FMCG firms spend 7–10% of their sales revenue in advertising.

Procter & Gamble spends about 6%; while Unilever spends 7.5% advertising is considered as an investment by the firms.

Advertising Budgets are made after gathering lot of information like, competitive situation, market growth, product life cycle and test reports of advertising sample response. Marketing and advertising goals are then framed, which give geographic and demographic coverage of market. Advertising budget gives the money value of the advertising plan. The client approves the budget and only after that any advertising action like release of advertisements in the media takes place. Depending of the agency-client relationship sometimes the agency can book the space in advance. Later on the agency has to maintain control on advertising expenses in line with the approved budget. In case of media rates increase prior approval of the client is needed.

There are several methods used in selecting the advertising budget. The most commonly used are given below:

- *Sales Volume Percentage:* For example if previous years sales of the firm was Rupees 10 crore, 5% of it would put the advertising budget at Rupees 0.5 crore. The percentage is worked out on the basis of, firm's historical budget, industry norms or on the basis of prevailing market conditions. If the market has started upward trend then one percent extra amount could be put for advertising budget. Following the method without considering market conditions could create major problems. If the firm's market share has been going down, the management may decide to increase the advertising budget. However, if the product is in decline stage of life cycle, the firm could consider divestment. In such an event, only marginal advertising effort to help clear the stocks may be enough. On the contrary, even in the decline stage of product life cycle, if the firm finds competitive firms are getting out, they may go for taking the leadership position and pick up the demand left over by competing firms, before finally closing down.

- *Unit of Sale:* Consumer durable firms like carmakers use this method as a variant on sales percentage. While mostly it works out same as the percentage method, here the firm is putting an amount of advertising expense on the car as add on.
- *Competitive Parity Method:* Competitive information regarding their sales, distribution pattern and advertising must be carefully studied by the firm. It will provide the correlation between the competitive sales and advertising effort. Depending on the firms strategy of increasing market share, or steadying the share, decision can be made to have a bigger or smaller budget than competition. However, instead of reacting to competitive advertising results, firms would do well to be proactive in their approach to marketing by planning their own goals of marketing and then, the advertising budget would emerge from the same.
- *Meeting the Objectives Method:* Marketing and advertising people are tuned to the objectives they have made for them to achieve. Working backwards, taking each item of objective like, increasing geographic sales area, increasing market awareness by a certain percentage over the figure obtained from advertising research, they add up the amounts needed for each activity. The advertising team, both of the firm and the agency, best accepts this method.
- *Historical Method:* In this method last years advertising budget is adopted for the year with a view that practically no change

has taken place in the market and market growth is slow, which does not justify any addition to the budget. As an additional feature to this method, last year's budget could be multiplied by a factor to cover **media rates increases**.

- *Affordability Method:* Some firms believe that advertising is perhaps necessary, and yet not important enough. They make budgets for all the other expenses, like raw material purchase, salary and wages; power, rents and they consider the balance amount in the budget as advertising budget.
- *Total Group Budget:* In case of multiple unit organization a total amount is decided as advertising budget and each unit gets a share of according to the needs. This method helps the group to segregate some amount for corporate group advertising for building the image of the group.
- *Percentage of Anticipated Turn Over:* This method is useful in markets, which are dynamic, the product is in the steep of product life cycle, as it provides for potential business as well.
- *Elasticity Method:* Takes in to consideration seasonality of business as also its periodicity. It has been known that some products have better sales every two years, or every five years as the economy booms appear with certain periodicity. This method takes in to view the demand and supply situation and is more used in industrial products.
- *Ideal Campaign:* The firms is in a do or die situation and in order to survive they resort to the budget which can give them the ideal advertising campaign, resulting in, turn around of the firm.
- *Market Model or Operations Research:* Market research gives the comparative figures of sales as per advertising effort, and decision is made in accordance with the desired sales. An example is given below:
    1. For advertising budget of Rupees one lac, the sales would be worth Rupees 15 lac.
    2. For advertising budget of Rupees three lac, the sales would be worth Rupees 40 lac.
    3. For advertising budget of Rupees 5 lac, the sales would be worth Rupees 150 lac.
- *Per Capita Population Basis:* Takes the total population to be served and an amount is fixed for each member of the population. It is used in generic products, which are not differentiated and have large number of common buyers.

- *Flexi-plan:* The budget is not firmed up and is changed as per market demand. In today's world of increasingly severe competition, many firms resort to this technique of budgeting.

Finally, there is the **Composite method**, which takes into consideration several factors in formulating the advertising budget as follows:

- Firms past sales
- Future sales projections
- Production capacity
- Market environment
- Sales problems
- Efficiency level of sales personnel
- Seasonality of the market
- Regional considerations
- Changing media scenario and changing media impact on the target market segment
- Market trends and results of advertising and marketing research

Estimates of advertising expense in some industries as a percentage of their turn over is given below:

- Cold drinks 10%
- Cosmetics 11%
- Games and toys 14%
- Air courier service 15%

Advertising budget should be kept floating in increasing order as long as the incremental sales generate profit which off sets the extra money spent on advertising. It must be remembered that finding a direct relation between extra advertising and additional sales generated is at best a theoretical exercise, as there are numerous other reasons, other then extra advertising which also help in increasing sales, like improved distribution network, better availability, promotional plans.

Most widely used approach to advertising budget is ***percentage of sales,*** which could result in heavy advertising of well-known, established products.

The objective and task based budget helps in focusing on more appropriate advertising plans and these help in reaching the objectives to a large extent.

Budget finalization, is normally done by interaction between several members of the firm who put forth their views and justify them. Many times it is the owner of the firm who ultimately prevails over others rendering the exercise useless.

In the past, historical data was a good indicator of amount required for achieving the objectives. With increasing competition, it has become imperative that a close watch is kept on the market and competition.

Creative Strategy—Art and Copy

As can be imagined, with media as diverse as newspaper, magazines, TV, Internet and out door, the advertising agency has an interesting and tough job creating the advertising. Usually, the press advertising consists of art and copy.

For written advertising, art and copy are put on the paper. For TV and radio advertising moving pictures and sound is also required.

Advertising And Creativity

Usually, the advertising consists of art and copy.

For written advertising, art and copy are put on the paper. For TV and radio advertising moving pictures and sound is also required.

The diversity makes the creative jobs interestingly diverse. And therefore people involved are also mostly different.

In print media copy is usually can be created with unlimited imagination. Using words in different fonts sizes and designs, numbers, pictures, sketches, cartoons and placing these as per a design creates a large unlimited variety of copy. The size of the advertising matter or copy can be also as per the media. A long worded copy is used to fill the page and also to make information about the product available to the prospective customers. A short copy can be used for, making a teaser advertisement or to differentiate the advertisement from the usual ***run of the mill*** advertising.

The art work can be using pictures, photographs, cartoons, sketches, paintings, with possibilities of places these at any part of the advertisement, in any size or shape. Logos trademarks brands; firm's signatures are used in print advertisements. Sometimes; charts, tables and figures are used as well. Depending on the target market segment, stress can be on celebrity endorsers of the product, with their photographs in action. For products for children use of animals is considered as useful.

Use of colour, open spaces, borders enhances the impact.

For radio or purely audio advertising (it could include pre-recorded cassettes too), the listeners are going to listen and not read or see the advertising. It becomes important to select the spoken words with care. Besides the voice of speakers and singers should be suiting the lyrics and the product. The music, both accompaniments and background music are selected with care depending the situation. Special effects can create the needed ambience of the advertisement.

Television offers the maxim opportunity of creativity. Being an audio-visual media, it offers maximum attractiveness. As a low cost means of entertainment, a large number of persons get hooked on to the TV. In fact, the term couch potato has been coined for the persons who are addicted to the TV.

TV offers the greatest challenge to the creativity of the advertising agency. Not only it offers ability to demonstrate the product, it can keep sustained interest of the viewers. It naturally calls for specialized people who are experts in their fields and has generated numerous types of jobs, like the job of Ad-film producer, director, music people, and models. These would be discussed in some detail in this chapter.

Let us examine creativity from the viewpoint of the customer, whom we are trying to attract. Going by Maslow's hierarchy of needs on one side and the benefits provided by the product, the job of creative person is to match the main and important needs of segment customers with the appropriate benefits. For example, benefit of lower price in bath soap (from Rupees 60 to Rupees 50) would have little impact on the high-income segment. Perhaps, more important would be the skin care elements of the soap.

Pick up any soap advertisement of luxury expensive soap, you would find that the advertiser is talking about bringing beauty and soft skin to the users, and only pretty nubile models are chosen to endorse the soap.

The Indian Scene

A country rich in culture and cultural diversity with year round festivals calendar, the advertisers find the festival time well suited to promote some of the products. Deepavali time exchange of gifts is considered essential. Gift manufacturers make special efforts just before Deepavali to advertise their products. Festivities themselves provide various options for catching the attention of target segment, as has been amply proved by soft drink marketers. Deepavali, Eid, Ganesh Chaturthi are full of advertisements, one because on festivals people are on holidays and two, they are in the mood to spend. Firms give annual bonus during Deepavali which helps the buyers to be more flexible with money.

Use of Indian classical music, film and folk music enhances the appeal of radio and TV advertisements. Seven notes of music make the Indian music resplendent with myriads of subtle variations and certain market segment is definitely appreciative of the same. Indian theater dates back to centuries when Banbhatt, and Kalidas moved the populace with their dramatic artistry. Today, the theater movement has again come to the fore and with it the scriptwriters and other dramatis personae. The element of suspense and surprise, a sure winner in drama is also successfully in advertisements so also is humor.

Family planning and other social issues like literacy, health and education all use drama, street plays to advantage. As people enjoy the play the social message is put across to the captive audience. As the message is built-in the theme, the audience are not likely to walk out of the play.

Rural advertising uses street plays effectively to reach the message to the audience.

The task before the Copt-writer is to make the copy exciting, original, and easy-to-understand, logical in sequence with **movement and unified.**

The Design Theory

The design concepts as practiced in copy writing are as follows:

- Unity in headline of the advertisement, art, copy, logo and firms signatures
- Innovation—variety, as it is said is the essence of advertising
- Balance—the advertisement should look balanced
- Rhythm—It should have a natural flow, lucidity
- Harmony—it should be pleasing to the readers eyes
- Emphasis—it should provide stress at the right places
- Excitement—it should make people look up and notice
- It should be eye catching, as most advertisements are not even seen by the target audience
- Arousing curiosity—use of teaser advertising is a good example
- Repetitive—repetition helps in customer retention and top of the mind recall.
- Creating wonderment- awe-inspiring

Some examples of advertisements covering these aspects are given for ease of understanding.

It may be of interest at this stage to know how some advertisements get **killed**.

We see many advertisements on television and read in newspapers and magazines, which are over done, the repetition is too much rendering them unpalatable to the target audience. There has to be fine balance in the right amount of exposure and overkill.

Wrong timing can kill any advertisement like nothing else can. Advertising woolen clothes in summer can be a fruitless exercise.

Sometimes advertisements are placed in the media, even before the product is properly made available in the market and the distribution channels set up.

If retailing is not properly organized, salesmen not well trained then the advertising effort can become useless.

If the product is not properly priced, it may have poor effect on sales, the prime objective of advertising. Lower price may be construed as denoting a lower quality product and high price could make the product out-priced in the market in the present competitive age.

With suspected quality of the product, and without proper after-sales-service, no amount of advertising can help the product.

If the media is wrongly selected for the target segment it can derail any good advertisement.

Similarly, wrong segmentation of the market will cause heartburns to the advertiser.

Esoteric advertising or brash, too high flouting messages would not cut any ice with the target segment.

Creativity in advertising calls for an over view of the market, competitive situation and the firms strengths and weaknesses. In fact SWOT analysis is done which provides lot of ideas for creativity. The following areas need special attention:

- *The Objectives Laid Down for Advertising:* Advertising is an invaluable aid for informing and persuading the target segment in favor of the product.
- *The Target Market:* The copywriter must have a good knowledge of the segment the marketer is targeting. Many times the segment tells as to what it wants to read or see. The teenage and young adults targeted by cold drink makers, like Coke and Pepsi put the words in copy as spoken by the teens and young adults. Going to any upward mobile college can be a revealing experience as far as the language spoken there. It hardly sounds like English with *slang* and newly coined words like *funda*, being used continuously.

For getting the right creative message, it is best to find out the most important benefit the product will provide to the customers and build the copy around it. An example would help understand how this is done.

1. Maruti esteem cars are being advertised as comfortable family cars.
2. Dove soap as soap for careless people as it takes full care of your skin.
3. Santro cars as ***trouble free, state of the art*** cars.

Once the top benefit is given as headline, other smaller benefits can be put in the body copy along with the distinctive features, which help the product deliver the benefits.

Sale of sewing machine has been dipping as women do not have any time to stitch clothes and ready-made garments are easily available in the market. If the sewing machine sells it is because the sellers are making emotional appeal to the women even with less time, if you can stitch your own designer clothes with embroidery and different types of stitches available in the modern machines they can show off to their friends and relatives their handiwork with pride.

Thinking and idea generation is the basic function of human brain. And yet, copywriters find that getting the right idea is far from easy. Copywriters have to follow some of the ideas given below:

- They must, like all creative people, live a full life, understanding the variety and subtle nuances of living.

Advertising deals with people's logic and emotions. When the carmaker talks about the acceleration, braking torque, seating capacity he is appealing to people's logic or their mind. As the talk transfers to the air-conditioned luxury, magical colours the appeal is to the heart. As can be seen from most advertisements the appeal is for the heart and the mind in practically all the advertisements.

Both the human heart and mind are used in the decision making process. The areas in which the appeals are made are the following:

- *Value for Money:* This appeal gives the customer the satisfaction of being a careful clever buyer.
- Quality appeal transfer is for the Ego boosting. *I buy only the top stuff.*
- Indirect appeals are made by using sponsors and celebrities to endorse the product. Celebrities attract the viewers attention as also provide help in decision masking. Shah Rukh Mayur

Khan suiting gives the viewers a chance of personality transfer. *If I wear Mayur suiting I will look like Shah Rukh Khan.*

- **Who says so** becomes important in high value products. Top star Tabu endorses Samsung products giving the impression that not only she uses them, but finds them good to her liking.
- Most people believe that they are the best in looks, intellect, appearance, and sense of humor. The top model and ex. Miss India says that she uses L'Oreal products, " **because I am worth it"**. Ego satisfaction and personality mindset helps in extending the user acceptance from the endorser to the customer.
- An appetizing dish does more to hunger feelings then any amount of verbose writing. When people see the dish they want to eat it even on full stomach. A well-tailored suit on a Model has bigger appeal than sketches of the suit and description of the cloth. Human have five basic senses, sense of touch, taste, hearing seeing and smelling. Advertisers use all these senses to focus customers mind on their products.
- Social cause advertising uses ***fear and anger*** appeals to draw the attention of the target audience. Aids prevention through safe sex, small family for family health and welfare, drug- de-addiction for life, are some of the areas where fear and anger appeal is used to concentrate on Safety and Security aspect of Maslow's hierarchy of needs.
- People making cosmetic products among others use love appeal. ***Use AXE deodorant and see the effect on the opposite sex.***
- Appeal to the sub-conscious mind is done subtly, in Movie halls when some advertisements are flashed on the screen for a fraction of a second barely visible to the theatregoers. Even then, the effects of such advertisements have been good. Showing a slide for Coke increased its sale in the intermission considerably.
- Anything done in a highly creative manner will have a positive impact on the customers. Sometimes advertisements with negativity like the **Demon advertisement** of Onida TV did wonders for the product.

Creativity can be organized and planned by gathering information about the product, market, competition and the laws.

Art Direction—Elements of Design

Art makes the entire advertising eye-catching, full of life.

Advertising is made catchy by having a strong and dynamic Copy. At other times it is done by making attractive art, graphics. Most times it is a combination of the two, which helps the advertisement become eye catching. Breath-taking advertisement, attention getting campaign, top of the mind recall, all these come with imaginative art and copy, total visuals.

How to have good art:

- *Size:* It plays a vital role in attracting attention. Depending on the product, headlines can be of strong thick lines to draw people in to reading it. Medium size lettering can make the advertisement look like news item with its own impact. The idea is to highlight in bigger fonts. However, in case of a solitary advertisement on a page perhaps small print could be more useful.
- *Colour:* It sets the entire tone of the campaign, creating or generally going with the mood needed for the acceptance of the product. Persistence of a colour scheme helps in faster and easier brand recognition. Colour advertisements are twenty times more eye catching and hence tend to pay for the extra costs involved. In international advertising, care should be taken to ensure that the colour scheme matches with the sensibilities of the country for which the AD Campaign is meant. In China, for instance yellow/gold is associated with purity and religion. In Mexico, yellow is the colour of death.
- *Line:* Straight lines curves and scratchy lines all have their individual effect. Curves look graceful, while vertical lines provide standard of decorum, horizontal lines provide peace and dignity. Diagonal lines show strength in the Ads.
- *Shape:* Can be used effectively to cover the space of the AD. Rectangle, squire's oblongs and circles all have their value in eye catching. Product cutouts mainly used in POP Danglers can also be used to focus attention of the viewers.

Advertising designs are planned on the basis of proportion, lucidity and balance. The idea is to have eye-catching visuals to attract the viewer's attention. These can be shown graphically as follows:

Balance in press ads:

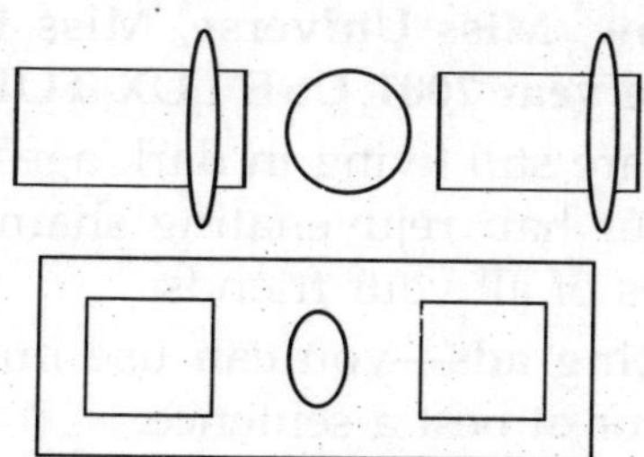

Fig. 11.6. Press Advertising Balance

Proportion in press ads:

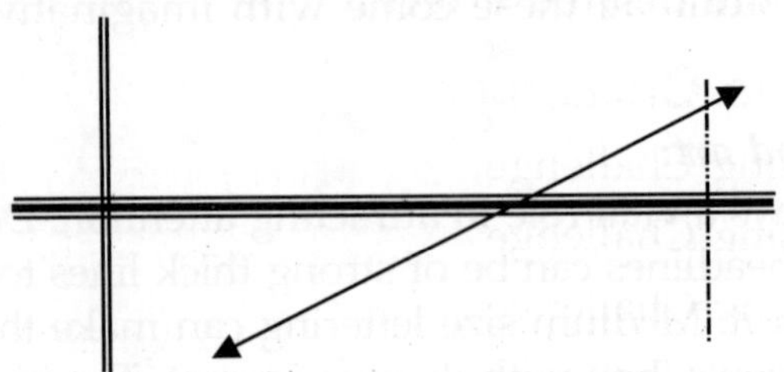

Fig. 11.7. Press Advertising Proportion

Sequencing in press ads:

Balance in ads comes from imagining an axis around which the ad has to be made, or around which it should look like moving.

Balance gives grace to the ad and helps in effecting the viewers through their psyche.

Proportion takes into account the objects shown and their physical shapes and dimensions to make the right impact.

Lucidity or flow comes from the order in which the key elements are put in the ad. The ad story should come out without any jarring notes to be effective.

The AD should look complete in every way, and art and copy should complement each other. For improved recognition the ad should lay emphasis on the main points of the ad, which is to highlight the benefit story.

Before finalizing the ad it is necessary to know " is it exciting enough?" does it arouse the curiosity of the readers, does carry enough punch?

Print ads are designed in a number of ways:

- **Carry a tale, action** and its reaction—used the shampoo, and you all can see the results. Pre-use and after use photos, still or in action have dramatic effect on viewers.
- Use **the latest news, Be like the Indian beauty queens, all three in a row, Miss Universe, Miss World and Miss Asia Pacific in the year 2001 USE LUX TOILET SOAP**
- **Teach**—you are still living in dark ages using **besan** for your hair when our hair rejuvenating shampoo is changing lives and hairstyles of all your friends.
- **Art dominating ads**—you can use minimum copy, may be just a word, or at best a sentence.
- **Copy dominating ads**—these ads have lot of information to give, like in industrial, product ads.

- **In copy different font types and sizes can be used for creating the desired effect.**

THE ADVERTISING CHALLENGE

The Advertising Challenge

The Advertising Challenge

The Advertising Challenge

The Advertising Challenge

The page layout in print ads is important. The agencies start by cutting and pasting to create the press ad.

International Advertising

With globalization Indian firms are trying to succeed in the International Markets. For most firms it has become imperative to go overseas to do business as they are finding International players, MNCs who have come to India are taking away their market share. It may be a good idea to hit them in their own markets for which Indian firms need to know how to cultivate international markets. Partial convertibility of Rupee helps firms earn and keep part of the foreign exchange to be used for importing raw materials and components. Hence for most firms foreign markets are crucial for continued growth and profitability.

To market Indian products to foreign buyers you require an understanding of how Advertising works in other countries. You need the knowledge of communicating with customers/consumers in the international markets.

Following table gives the percentage of Gross National Product spent on advertising to give you an idea of its importance in a nations economy:

Table 11.4. GNP of Countries

Country	*% of GNP*
USA	2.02
SWEDEN	1.88
NETHERLANDS	1.77
UK	1.74
SWITZERLAND	1.59
AUSTRALIA	1.37

India spends about 0.3% of its GNP.

Russia—with disappearance of USSR, Russia has opened up its

economy. Now it has two classes, the rich and the poor. The rich class demands quality consumer goods in large numbers. It would be worthwhile to learn the Russian language its slang, idioms to communicate in the language best understood by the customers.

International players have opened their offices in Russia. They advertise in local press, TV, and at the point of Purchase (POP). RUSSIA is looking for perishable goods, and even old technology products. There is a demand even for second hand goods.

How to advertise in Russia-

- Advertising must provide exact information about the products.
- Explain in detail the uses of the products
- New kinds of products are needed.
- Advertising should create, tastes and develop needs. A lot of concept selling is required.
- Products, which show lifestyles, achievements, are a must.

China: South of China has been as advanced as Hong Kong for sometime now in major cities of China outdoor advertising is fully used. Reach of TV is increasing and would be a major source of communication.

Demonstration of products, how effective they are in reality is what the Chinese customer wants to see before spending money. TV would therefore be the most appropriate media where live demo can be given. Testimonials by experts are favoured and can reap rich harvest for the advertisers.

International Advertising can also be when national companies go global and advertise worldwide. There are two approaches to global advertising as follows:

1. Global—where one set of advertisements are used the world over.
2. Multi-domestic—where advertising campaigns are modified to suit the national sentiments of the countries you are communicating with.

National economies are interdependent and international trade has doubled in each decade. USA imports the following each year:

- Watches 70%
- Cameras 60%
- TVs 45%

You can name several MNC Brands available in India today.

Following is the method of starting international advertising:

1. Selecting an Ad Agency—you have the choice of Indian agency, Indian agency with foreign collaboration, foreign agency with office in India.
2. Many countries go by nationalistic approach and in such countries it may be good idea to appoint a local agency, such as in Canada. Local agencies provide the goodwill of the target market.
3. If there is no binding then select the best agency.

The following are some of the International agencies in India:

- J WALTER THOMSON
- DENTSU JAPAN
- MACCAN ERICCSON
- YOUNG AND RUBICON
- OGLIVY MATHER
- TED BATES
- SSC&B
- BBDO
- LEO BURNETT & FOOTE
- CONE AND BELDING

What message should be used in international advertising?

1. Indian message.
2. Ethnic with local colour, with words phrases used in particular culture.
3. In large multi-cultural countries a common message appealing to the masses to be used.
4. Language barrier can be overcome by using local agency.
5. Standard appeals like for COKE, Mercedes car, Levi jeans offer recognition anywhere in the world. These have advantages of cost, repeat value. At best you can change the models and use local faces. International ads help people associate themselves with lifestyles of the rich and progressive persons. Such ads have easier coordination, campaign preparation is simpler, international travellers recognize the product anywhere in the world.

Marketing Game Part 11

1. How the industrial marketing differs from consumer marketing. Discuss giving examples?
2. What role negotiations play in industrial marketing?
3. How does vertical integration affect industrial business?

CHAPTER 12

Strategies for B-B Management

Aims and Outcomes of The Chapter

With the changes taking place in the market place, the marketers have two choices with them, either they can be reacting to the situations or they can become proactive, on which count they have to take the initiative of planning and **action-ing** their plans for maintaining their market share and brand equity. Today's markets are cruel and they do not forgive delays in decision-making. The students will learn to remain proactive in the market place.

Strategic marketing is the key to present day market planning for the following reasons:

- Firms have to make their selections on the various strategic options.
- Business environment is constantly changing, calling for timely decisions.
- Long range view is required instead of fire fighting plans.
- Strategic analysis is needed to grasp the real issues facing the markets.
- Resource allocation needs to be planned to ensure that the unfruitful tasks are eliminated from the allocations.
- Both horizontal and vertical communication and control systems should be in place.
- Strategic Marketing should help in keeping business ahead of competition during the market change phases.
- To examine the above from the Indian point of view.

Firms keep introducing new products, product variants and timing of the introduction is of strategic importance as wrong timing could meet with disastrous product launch. Wrong selection of market segment, distribution channels, pricing could lead to launch failures.

Manufacturing in India can be categorized as follows:

- Large scale
- Medium scale
- Small scale
- Cottage industry
- Cooperative sector

Besides, the differentiation can also be made as per the nature of competition as follows:

- Monopoly—where there is only one manufacturer of the product.
- Oligopoly—where there are only a limited number of manufacturers say, four to six.
- Fragmented market—in which case there are a large number of manufacturers.
- Section fragmented—in several products like computers, ACs there are two category of manufacturers, the branded ones and unbranded in the unrecognized or small-scale sector, with several players in each group.

Marketing strategy should be made taking the actual ground situation considering the types of manufacturing units are there in competition and how many of them exist.

Business environment can be categorized as (a) General environment. (b) Competitive environment. It is necessary to understand the business environment and the competitive situations for developing right strategies.

The next step is to analyze the situation before planning the marketing strategies. The analyses is done for two areas—

External analysis—most of the things, which the firm needs to know, are outside of it like,

1. The market, its relevant segment.
2. The customer.
3. The competitor. Environment is also outside of the firm.

Internal analysis:

1. Firms performance,
2. Its policy and plans,
3. Objectives and deviations between objectives and performance.
4. Resource allocation for achieving the objectives in future needs to be analyzed before planning marketing strategies.

Products and markets correlate as per the following matrix:

Table 12.1. Markets

Markets	Existing Products	New Products
Present market	Market penetration	Product expansion
New market	Market expansion	Diversification of product

Similarly another matrix gives the correlation between competition and markets:

Table 12.2. Competition

	Existing competition	New competition
Present market	Penetration	Prices wars
Market extension	Promotion plus	Price and promotion

Strategic Marketing is all about gaining Competitive Advantage on a continuous basis and finding out the strategies, which will give you such a competitive advantage. Let us call it **Strategic Competitive Advantage.** Planning strategic competitive advantage the following method is used:

- Plan business scenario, the shape and size of the market after three and five years.
- Plan your market share on the basis of feasibility.
- Resources including cash flow need to be utilized for maximizing the chances of achieving the objectives.
- Focus on core competencies of the firm and synergize efforts for fully exploiting them.

Core competencies of a firm are given below:

- Technology—does it give the firm its cutting edge?
- Marketing— is the firm proactive in the market place and can it take full advantage of the business potential available in the market?
- Finance—is the firm able to generate sufficient funds for growth and expansion?
- Production—can the firms cost to manufacture, including its time dimension be compared to that of competition and is the firm finding ways of reducing cost of manufacture by going in for economies of scale and experience curve?
- Human Resource—is the firms personnel geared to think and plan their each move for the benefit of the customer?
- Government relations—does the firm maintain good and healthy relation with the government and does it avoid being

on loggerheads with the government all the time? Can the firm get the government approvals at short notice?

Once the firm gets the answers to these questions it is ready to take the following strategic decisions:

1. Who should be considered as firm's main competitors?
2. Where should the firm compete? In which markets, geographic areas, niche markets?
3. How should the firm compete? On the basis of price? On quality? Superior service, availability of genuine spare parts?
4. What are the areas in which information is lacking and is needed? One off marketing research is required or should there be a continuous flow of information?
5. Product multiple uses should be exploited. Bundling of products can help in selling slow moving products at least to a degree.
6. Firms should plan business scenario for the next three to five years taking in to consideration competitors plans, possible likely changes in business environment.

Strategic marketing decisions, which need to be taken, are listed below:

- With international players coming to India, technology is going to be rapidly changing. Indian firms would do well to either invest in R&D or purchase the **Latest State Of The Art** technology to keep abreast of the competition or even forge ahead of them.
- If the product is in the maturity stage of its life cycle and demand growth has stagnated, it may be necessary to go for penetrating pricing to maintain its market share or build its brand equity to the extent that it can ask for and get a higher price than competition. Price sensitivity of the market needs to be understood and decision on pricing taken accordingly.
- If new entrants are likely to enter the market with better product, technology and brand image it is required to invest in the product and the market by extra discounts, increased coverage and if possible, joining hands with a technology leader of the product.
- The **Customers of Tomorrow** are looking for (i) product performance improvement, (ii) product technical superiority (iii) easy availability of the product (iv) financial assistance like leasing
- Firms should have correct idea about of the benefits the customers are seeking from the product, as it should be

understood that no one buys a product, the customers buy only the benefits, which they get from the product.

Product Related Analysis

It is important to know the product on offer fully, its detailed specifications—both static and dynamic as also the following:

- Who are the users of the product, how do they buy it, where from do they buy it, how do they buy it and for how much?
- How the customers use the product? Does it have a single use or multiple usages? How often they use it?
- What are the benefits the customers are looking for in the product? Manufacturers may have a view of these benefits while the customers may have an entirely different notion of what they want. The sellers of washing powder are all talking of the whiteness of the wash, where the customers never talk about the whiteness as the reason for their buying a particular detergent powder. The best way to find out about the benefits the customers are wanting in the product is to arrange a market research in the desired market segment.
- Product pricing is an important aspect of marketing strategy. When a new product is launched and there is no competition, sellers go for skimming price, in other words they keep the price high to get the maximum profits before competition starts and they are forced by it to reduce the prices. If the sellers are looking for increasing market share they put penetrating prices, low prices to attract large customer groups. It is important to know if the products sales are affected by changes in price, i.e., price sensitivity of the product must be known by research.
- Knowledge about competition is needed on a continuous basis as regularly new competition keeps increasing and the existing competition keeps changing their plans and policies. It is necessary to know competitors 4 Ps with the knowledge updated regularly.
- Brand loyalty/equity of products, the firms and those of competitors should be well, assessed, as it is this single most important factor, responsible for market share.
- Market survey is required to find out the rate of product need in different market segments. Which segment has highest percent demand of the product and which segments follow the demand pattern. Sub-segments, niche segments and crossover segment demand musty be assessed. Only after this knowledge can the seller decide about the segment/s he should enter or should he plan for sale in niche market.

The airline industry has found that they have basically two types of customers as given below-

1. Business-customers of this class want an air service which is, reliable, on schedule, with wide body aircrafts, easy to use airports with comfortable lounges, frequent flier programs, telephone check-ins, variety of connections and in-flight entertainment. Possible upgrades from business class to first class
2. Tourists—look for low price travel, required schedules and several stopovers. For the sake of low price they do not mind night travels also. They look for package deals in which air tickets and hotel accommodations are all included.

Such details can only be found out by getting proper market research done.

Competitive Analysis

Next let us look at the analysis to be done for the competitors. The firm must know, who are its competitors. There are direct and indirect competitors for most of the firms. The study of competitors is most useful if it is done with the customer-based approach. Once the firm has identified its direct competitors in the first instant, it is useful to evaluate **each of the competitors** on the following parameters-

- What are their business goals and objectives?
- What is the commitment level of the managers and stakeholders of the firms in competition?
- How do the managers of the firm view its growth prospects? Have they at any time considered its closure? What are the barriers to its exiting from the business?
- What is its cost structure, financial structure, cash flow position, assets and liabilities.
- How its suppliers, financiers and distribution system view the firm?
- What is its track record of meeting its financial commitments and other obligations?
- Are their product specifications in line with Indian standards? Can they meet world standards or not?
- How are their international business dealings? Are they importing and exporting or are they having only one of the two?
- Where have they positioned their product, is it up-market or for the masses? Is the product pricing in line with their product positioning?

- Are their advertising and promotional efforts congruent with their product positioning?
- How is the firm's Public Relations effort rated?
- How is the firm's Brand Equity rated?
- What are the firm's core competencies?
- What are the firm's strengths and weaknesses?
- What are the firms unmet needs as far as the customers are concerned? Unmet needs are because of, (a) customers dissatisfaction of the product, (b) customers problems. There are unmet needs of which the customer is aware and there are some of which the customers may not be even aware. Competitors take advantage by advertising their own met needs and firms unmet needs of the customers.

It is useful to do a SWOT Analysis at this stage for each of the competitors.

To sum up the following is the table for different types of analysis:

Table 12.3. Types of Analysis

Market Analysis	*Firm's Analysis*	*Competitive Analysis*	*Competitive Analysis*
1. Size of the market	1. Level of customer satisfaction	1. Sales performance	9. Capacity /its utilization
2. Growth prospects	2. Brand loyalty	2. Market share	10. Product-wise market share
3 Profitability	3. Product quality	3. Brand equity status	11. Segment-wise sales
4. Cost structure	4. Service quality	4. Objectives/ goals	12. Channels/ sales force
5. Channels	5. Brand association	5. Marketing strategies	13. Advertising/ promotion
6. Trends	6. Relative costs	6. Organizational culture	14. Reaction time
7. Key Success Factors	7. New product activities	7. Cost structure	15. Experience curve/exit barriers
	8. Manager's capabilities and performance	8. Strengths and weaknesses	16. Value chain

Once the systems are put in place these activities mentioned in the table become automatic and they do not take much time, while they do provide the vital information for making strategic marketing decisions.

For example, the capabilities of a firm could include its financial strength; marketing base and its constraints could be lack of motivation in the personnel. The analysis should take the Core Competencies in to account.

Strategic Marketing Planning Process

Let us understand the formal process needed for planning marketing strategies in today's competitive age. Plans made should be (a) short term (b) long term. Most firms make annual plans, which are divided into quarterly plans. To be entirely market proactive the plans should be kept flexible to enable firms to alter them to dovetail the changing market environment. The following steps are needed for making the plans:

- Analysis Of External Environment
- Study Of The Firms Internal Strengths And Weaknesses
- Idea Generation For Planning
- Brainstorming For Prioritizing The Ideas Generated
- Customer Behaviour Analysis
- Competitors Analysis
- Market Analysis
- Draft Annual And Short Term Plan
- Final Plans With Forecasting Of Sales And Cash Flow

Customer's Analysis

We have discussed earlier why, how, where, when and how much the customers buy, which can be ascertained with a degree of accuracy through market research. Let us take a simple **Customer Behaviour** pattern. It includes the following elements of internal information processing, guided by external information and stimuli:

- *Belief:* It is the customer's conviction and firm opinion of a product/brand
- Perception—it comes from a customer's product recognition as a desirable product based on his intuition and information gathered on sensory plane.
- *Attitude:* It is the customer's way of thinking about the product, his firm opinion about it.

- *Preference:* Out of his belief, perception and attitude the customer makes his preference of one product over other products, and tries to buy it.

Thus we can define the Multi-attribute Decision Making Process as, "based on concepts of BELIEFS, ATTITUDES, PERCEPTIONS and PREFERENCES" which is the notion that objects in a choice set can lad to external behaviour. Each object in the set has a value on each attribute used to define the choice set.

Let us take an example to illustrate the point. The purchase of a car in a family is a major event and decision-making process is multi-dimensional one. While film stars buy the car as a status symbol, middle class persons buy it as a means of transport only. Let us take four cars in the economy segment and plot their benefits to the customer. (The figures given in the table are only arbitrary and not conclusive).

Table 12.4. Product Benefits

Benefits	*Zen*	*Santro*	*Matiz*
Comfort	7.5	8	8.5
Economy	4	5	6
Safety	3.8	4.5	5
Brand equity	4	7	6
Service facilities	9	6	5

The figures are based on a scale from 0-10

On a different plane another matrix can be made with benefits on one axis and decision making concepts for each car separately, before the final decision is taken as follows:

Table 12.5. Benefit Comparison

Decision Concepts/Benefits	*Comfort*	*Economy*	*Safety*	*Brand Equity*
Beliefs				
Attitudes				
Perceptions				
Preferences				

It therefore calls for a three-dimension matrix, which would help the decision makers. This is done in steps as given below:

1. Which attributes are used to define the product? (For example, for a car it could be its brand name, comfort or economy. For a house it could be it's location, its construction and area.)
2. What is the possession level of the attributes in the product?

(Is the car running very economical as compared to another car in the same category) This is really the value of the attribute, its perception in the customer's mind. Another example could be of an airline, where the passenger safety is of prime concern. However, the airlines never talk about the safety aspect as all airlines are supposed to be safe. They prefer to talk about (a) ease of getting their tickets, (b) food, (c) in-flight service and entertainment, (d) easy check-ins. And the customers form attitudes on the basis of these attributes.

3. What is the relative importance of each attribute in the overall product performance? In airline business is in-flight service more important than easy of getting tickets?
4. Do the customers weigh each of the attributes to reinforce their perceptions of overall product performance? How much weight age is given to each of the attributes and does it differ from customer to customer, or is product specific?

Note:- At this stage the students should do an Attributes-Perception study for different products to find out how the customer's perceptions and preferences are formed.

It will be found that different customers have separate yardsticks for looking at the attributes. They trade off one against the other while making the purchase decisions as can be seen from the following example:

Some people buy car only for its brand name, e.g. Mercedes

Some buy car for its speed and power.

Yet others buy the car for its mileage only.

Some look for several of the attributes in some descending order of their importance. This is called the **Dictionary Rule.**

Dictionary Rule: If a customer finds two products having the first or the most important attribute to be equally present in both the products, and then they look for disparity in the next level attribute. They keep doing so till they arrive at the attribute where there is a difference in the two products. (In dictionary when you look for a word you go with its first alphabet and then to the next, so on, till you find the exact word).

Buying a car, would the customer prefer lower price or better mileage? Can the seller charge one hundred thousand rupees more if the car gives 8 km per liter more?

Multi-Attribute Analysis helps sellers understand customers who represent identifiable segments in terms of their perceptions and preferences.

Let us consider the levels of competition, or competitor's hierarchy. A competitor can be defines as the seller who compete for the same customer rupee as the widest competition level.

Narrowing it down the competitors are those who sell same products from the same industry.

Further narrow definition of competitors would be the market segment competitors.

To clarify the above let us take the Banking business.

First level would be the banking system, which would include Banks, Financial institutions, Non-banking financial institutions, merchant bankers and moneylenders.

Second level would be a bank who cater to the customers with a few of the banking products.

Third level is the bank in the same town or the same street.

Competition is becoming diversified as can be seen from the following:

1. Banking services have competition from software companies now, as a lot of on line Internet banking is being done with the help of relevant software.
2. Used cars compete with the new cars.

It is therefore possible to define competition by analyzing customer's data. It can be tried as given below:

- Define a product.
- Let the prospective customers decide the possible uses and benefits, as many as they can imagine the product is possessing. Can they think of other ways of getting the same benefits? This way the firms can get Differential Competitive Analysis From The Customer's Viewpoint.
- The customers should determine the products, which satisfy with their usage, and the benefits, which accrue to the customers from their use.
- The data thus obtained can be listed with priority as given by the customers.

The data thus obtained will provide the firm the information on the **Competitors For Each Product In Their Range.**

Summarizing it can be said that,

"Competitors analysis requires the prudent use of secondary and primary information to determine current and likely strategies.

Customers can be employed to classify uses and benefits of products and to rank the competitors".

Let us see the **Assets And Skills** grid for competitors. These can be divided in to two parts as follows:

1. *Primary:* Product development, product quality, product manufacturing cost, product differentiation, customer satisfaction and market share.
2. *Secondary:* Flexi-production, financial muscle, sales force, distribution network, brand image/equity, advertising and promotion, quality of service and growth of the market for the product.

Student's Discussion Points-

- Explain the principle of multi-attribute analysis.
- Broad and narrow definition of competition.
- How can a customer help in competitor's analysis?
- Define unmet needs of the customers with examples.

Market Analysis

The following needs to be understood while analyzing the market:

- Market size, actual and potential
- Market growth prospects
- Market, product-wise profitability
- Cost structure
- Distribution pattern
- Success parameters

Market size and its growth can be assessed by knowing the demographic changes taking place in the market, income and salary growth of people in the market and changes in government policies relating to business of the products.

In the maturity and decline stage of PLC, the firm has to identify the following points:

- Price wars start if there is no product differentiation and there is over-capacity I production.
- Level of buyer's sophistication.
- Availability of substitution products.
- Why no growth, is there a new competitive product in the market?

To analyze the profit picture of a market the following points need to be seen:

- The types of competition in the market, is it a monopoly situation, oligopoly or fragmented market with a vast number of sellers. Market share of competitors and how are they safe guarding it, is it through price-cutting or brand management.
- How many new players are likely to join the competition? How serious are they and their potential threat as a competitor.
- How strong are the substitute products which vie for the customer's money?
- Bargaining power of suppliers.
- Bargaining power of buyers.
- For competitors the firm should know their number, size, and similarity of product, level of fixed costs and their exit barriers. For new entrants the firm should know the requirement of capital, economies of scale of the production, availability of distribution channels, raw materials and product differentiations.

High growth markets can suffer from over crowding of players, penetrating prices, and technology changes and resources crunch.

Environment analysis makes the firm understand the effect of changes in technology, macroeconomics, government policies, culture, demography and global.

Segmentation and Positioning

Segmentation allows the firms to focus on specified market sets through positioning, to enable the firm to launch a unique market program to stand out among competitors. Segmentation is essential as the customers have diverse needs and behavior related to market stimuli. It also helps the firms as follows:

- Planning focused marketing programs.
- New product launches.
- Creating competitive advantage.

How to segment the customers? Following are the ways of market segmentation:

1. Benefit—to the customers, like better service needs, convenient pricing.
2. Product usage by the customers—like heavy usage, light usage.
3. Brand loyalty.

4. Product becomes a status symbol like Mercedes car.
5. Geographic—like the north, south, east and west of the country.
6. Demographic—based on age, income, place of residence, sex, religion.
7. Life style, psychographics divide.

Customer is known a king. Let us examine the statement. A guest stays in a hotel once in a year and another one stays six times in a year. It is the usage, which makes the customer the king or the commoner. The following matrix explains the point clearly with the help of customer of a five star hotel:

Table 12.6. Customer's Analysis

Yearly expense in rupees	10,000	25,000	100,000	500,000	1000,000
Tourists in %	55	20	15	9	1
Business traveler in %	1	9	55	20	15

It is easy to describe the business traveler spending rupees 500,000 and above in a year as the king. (Of course, the hotels cannot ignore the small customers for; it is possible that today's common man may be the future king. Facilities like room upgrades, free use of gym are meant to have the king keep coming to the hotel.)

Social class too defines a business market segment, as people belonging to the same class tend to spend their money in buying the same things.

Business-to-Business or Industrial Segmentation

Industries buy raw materials and components from suppliers. The suppliers segment their customers as follows:

- Company size—the larger the company the more product it is likely to buy, be better paymaster (as it has to keep its name as a good company). Sometimes medium size companies prove to be good as they are trying to grow and their reputation is vital for them.
- Innovative companies—they have the lead user concept,: want to be the first users of the product. Small companies have the advantage of being flexible in their production and other plans

The following make a good market segment:

1. The segment should be of adequate size. There should be manageable number of segments.
2. The segments should be concrete with justified measurable base for each segment.

While practically implementing the segment schemes, it is necessary to combine the descriptive variables like age, income for which data is available, with behavior and attitude variables.

At times, sufficient data is not available for making a proper market segment, which is feasible too. There are product specific variables like, light users and heavy users and then there are general descriptive variables like demographic, geographic variables.

The focus should not however shift on just creation of a segment and segmentation should remain a tool of gaining COMPETITIVE ADVANTAGE.

Summarizing it can be said that, " Markets are segmented to satisfy different customer needs to leverage as firm's advantage in size, location to serve identifiable groups of customers, profitably. From segmentation, the firm can target the segment or segments by steering its marketing efforts towards them."

PRODUCT POSITIONING

It involves focusing on a marketing program that one-segment customers will perceive as desirable and which will give the firm a differential advantage over competition.

Usually, there are a number of competitors for the same segment. Positioning gives the firm Sustainable Competitive Advantage because of its customer specific approach. The steps needed are:

1. To identify relevant competition.
2. To draw the differential benefits and attributes significant to the segment where the firm scores better than competition.
3. Delineate firms and competitors current position.
4. Set out segments preferred attribute combinations.
5. Select positioning strategy.
6. Communicate the position.

Discussion Points—

a. Steps I the Positioning Process.
b. Importance of communicating the difference between the firms and competitors product benefits and attributes. Does the firm have a position if the customer does not know about it?

In a nutshell, it can be said that—

- Segmentation allows firms identify potential profitable group of customers.

- Positioning requires firms to identify the right competitors and differentiate their products and other Ps and then effectively communicate the unique benefits of these products to target customers.

Managing Across The Product Life Cycle (PLC)

With a lot of effort going into New Product development, firms have the benefit of introducing new products at some point of time. It is important that care is taken in managing the new introduction to ensure profits and volume business. Later on during the growth, maturity and decline stages of product life cycle proper management is required. The following figure gives the Product Life Cycle's different stages:

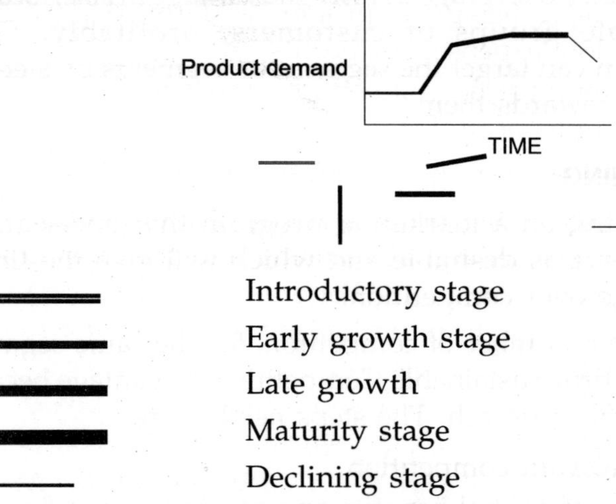

Fig. 12.1. Product Life Cycle

Introductory Stage

It is gaining importance by the day as, due to faster rate of obsolescence in most products the PLC is shrinking. New technologies are emerging in several products to make earlier product obsolete. Firms need to capture maximum market in this stage and as mostly there is little competition they can charge skimming prices to get the maximum revenue. Main conditions in the introductory stage are as follows:

1. Growth is slow as the customers are not aware of the product and its concept. A lot of concept selling is required before actual volume business starts, (a) Product itself is not well defined (b) Channels of distribution are also new, but since they have the customers coming to them for other products, they hold the key to business and have the power over the manufacturers,

(c) Price-the rule of the game have not yet been finalized,
(d) Advertising gives most of the information to competitors about the products, price, channels of distribution and its market segment a thought out by the firm.

2. Only first introduction Firms have some advantage and other leaders and followers are not significant at this stage.
3. Penetrating prices are charged for gaining and maintaining the market share. With low prices, the firms spend good money on advertising and promotion. They depend on volume business and economies of scale in manufacturing for profits.
4. Skimming price is used when competition is yet far away. Customer base is narrow and the firms prefer not to spend a lot of money on advertising and promotion. Firms depend on high prices and low expenses for profits.
5. In case of skimming prices, competition comes in fast as they see the large margins of profits.
6. Penetrating prices keep competition away for quite sometime.

As can be seen the pioneering firms have the task of developing the market through concept selling, advertising and the later firms who follow get the benefit of their efforts. For example, suppose a firm introduces computers in a virgin underdeveloped market it will be doing concept selling telling advantages of using a computer to the customers. They will not be able to talk about their brand say, IBM. Later sellers like Compaq will be able to build on the concept acceptance of the customers and they can advertise their brands and generate brand awareness and brand loyalty, brand equity.

Summarizing, market pioneers managing the introductory stage of PLC, can pursue strategy to capture a narrow customer base with skimming prices for extra profits or they can plan on a broad market base with penetrating pricing.

Students' Discussion Points—

1. What are the benefits and negative points of penetrating and skimming pricing policies?
2. What are some of the characteristics of the introductory stage of PLC?

In early growth stage market growth increases and the distinction between leaders and followers also grows. Product quality stabilizes and firm's dependence on channels reduces hence the power of channels also reduces giving way to advertising and promotions besides personal selling by the firm's salespersons.

Hence it can be concluded that PLCs are identifiable and they require distinct marketing skills at each stage, especially at the introductory stage, when the failure risk and product costs are both high, quality often uneven and market acceptance is not fully assured.

Secondly, marketers have a choice of pricing the product in the introductory stage. They can either have widespread business with penetrating prices and market share, or to gain high unit profits with skimming prices.

Costs, Volumes and Experience Curve

Let us discuss how important are **Costs, Volumes and Experience Curve** in our strategies for marketing.

Marketing strategies are needed to balance core competencies of firms with business environment changes constantly taking place and are essential for the long term well being and growth of the firm. The basics of marketing are good strategies. Strategy needs an analysis of the firm, competition and customers in a dynamically changing business environment.

Let us discuss the market leadership position a firm can enjoy. For getting volumes needed for leadership, the firm has to have penetrating prices. Hence, there is a cost of leadership, by way of reduced profit on unit product basis. In order to reduce the loss in profit the following is required to be done:

- Integrating marketing and production plans.
- Making an objective of High Volume and low cost production as a result.
- Focus on market share.
- Gain cost leadership

Cost leadership is gained through the following methods:

1. Technological advancements.
2. Inputs from suppliers and customers for streamlining cost elements in manufacture.
3. Economies of scale, which help in reducing the Fixed Costs, as for larger production rentals, supervisor's salary and other overheads do not change and hence, unit fixed cost gets reduced.
4. Experience Curve which helps in reducing Variable Costs, as with passage of time, workers get to know the working better and wastage gets reduced, besides production time also

shortens. With increase in cumulative workers experience in production, workers do better. This is most valid in (a) High labour cost industries (b) Complex assembly line operations (c) production of high numbers of standard products, which helps workers in repetitive work.

Experience curve cost reduction comes from the following areas:

- Labour efficiency
- Work specialization and methods improvements
- New production process

It has been observed that experience improves performance from production equipment, changes in resource mix, material substitution. It helps in product standardization and redesign. **Experience effect results from the firm's attempt to achieve lower relative costs than the competition. Low cost production gives highest profit margins.**

Market Share Strategy

Firms are constantly striving to improve their market share. For this purpose the following strategies are planned:

- Plan large capacity production, which will help in achieving Economies of scale of production to reduce the fixed costs.
- Penetrating or aggressive pricing policy helps in getting larger market share as more customers, who are price conscious buy the product. Initially, to gain a foothold in the market sellers resort to selling on marginal costs only where they put the price equal to the fixed cost plus a little element of variable cost. Once the market share is reached as planned, and brand loyalty gained from some customers, the price is increased to include both fixed and variable cost and some profit margin is also added to it. This is especially true for price sensitive segments of the market. The idea is to lower the price and in a way invest in future growth of the market. It can rebound if the market does not grow at all.

Let us discuss some successful cases of experience curve effect below:

- Manufacture of semiconductor devices, including ICs—initially the rejection rate used to be high, up to 50%. As the firms got experience in manufacturing, the workers could reduce the rejections and today the rejections are less than 1%. It has resulted in price reductions of not only these components, but also of the final electronic equipments.
- Honda motorcycles reduced prices substantially (in seven years reduction in price was US$ 100 due to experience effect).

The risks involved with gaining cost reduction through experience curve are given below:

- Manufacturers base their production plan as per the market forecasts. In case the demand projections prove to be wrong and demand fails to come to the anticipated levels, the cost reductions become void as then the production is tailored to the real demand only.
- Customer's tastes keep changing, more especially in fashion garments where the rate of obsolescence is high.
- Induction of new technology in manufacturing also reduces the effect of experience curve.
- Ego or other fixation on the old manufacturing process. The firms can argue that they had spent a lot of money in the old technology and they cannot abandon it so soon. Such mindsets are harming the growth of the firm as also reducing the benefits of experience as with the new technology the firm could achieve even better cost of manufacture.

Tasks for the Students—

1. What are the factors responsible for reduction in costs once the sales volumes increase?
2. Can the managers price products in anticipation of increases in volume sales?

Summarizing, it can be said that—

- Cost leadership is a powerful strategic tool where learning curve and economies of scale provide higher profits and better market share than that of the competitors.
- Economies of scale and learning curve effects must fulfill market needs. The firm must have the resources to finance the more effective operations.

Product Life Cycle—Growth Stage Strategy

Marketing strategies are needed at every stage of the life cycle to combat the market realities and the options available, as the firm and competitors relationships keep changing with the customers all the time.

Early growth involves large increases in volumes, and an increasing number of competitors as market players use advertising to build brand equity to elevate their market share and position. The following changes take place:

1. Sales volumes increase rapidly.
2. Competition rises.
3. Product design and specifications get standardized.
4. Firms plan their advertising and sales efforts to gain brand superiority.
5. Prices may start their downward slide.
6. Distribution network gets in to place and power over customers begins to move towards manufacturers from the channel members.
7. Demand shifts from primary one, say for a PC or CAR to secondary demand as, for Wipro PC or Honda City car, as people/customers become brand conscious.
8. At times the Pioneer, who started the sale of the product and did the initial concept selling, loses his superiority in growth stage to other players. **(Philips pioneered the audio cassettes, did the concept selling in competition with records, LPs EPs and 8 Tracks- they gave their technology to Sony who did well, better than Philips, during the growth stage).**

Growth stage means increase in demand and the manufacturers have to meet the demand. Their strategic options depend on the position they enjoy in the market as can be seen from below:

Let us take the firm's position as that of the **Market Leader** or that of **Market Follower.**

POSITION AS MARKET LEADER

Options—

- Fight————Maintain ————or Enhance
- Flight ————Exit————————or Fortify

For maintaining the market share the firm should increase its business as per the market growth and invest in advertising and selling on that basis.

For enhancing the market share firm should increase its market share at a faster or bigger than the market growth.

In real life situation if the firm plans only to maintain it may end up losing its market share and if it plans to enhance it may just be able to maintain its market share as competitors are also in with their plans.

The next option for some firms could be that of flight, giving up their leadership position. They can either exit or fortify i.e., get in to some niche market. At times the expenditure in maintaining the leadership position through is high and it eats away all the profits. Firms do plan to leave the leadership on such occasions.

HP Calculators gave their leadership to Texas Instruments and went in to niche market. HP had started in narrow market with low level of advertising efforts and they could raise the prices after leaving the market leadership.

Position as a Follower in the Market

Let us examine the options followers have in the market. They can either take up the leadership position or remain as a follower. For each the choices can be as given below:

- Assume leadership ——— by copying the leader —— or by leapfrogging by using latest techniques

In case of copying the follower can do one better by learning from the mistakes committed by the leader. The follower thus challenges the leader. Follower also tracks the mistakes of the leader and turns them in to opportunities.

If the leader is not making a mistake then the follower has to overtake the leader by using new technology, new plans and policies and he can leapfrog in to leadership position.

A good example of leapfrogging is the leadership position now being enjoyed by the Japanese firms in the area of cars, which were the virtual monopoly of the Americans. In the area Consumer electronics also, Japanese firms have leapfrogged to leadership position. Japanese have taken recourse to improvements in process technology and not just planned better products. Re-engineering in production technology and innovative distribution has helped them do the leapfrogging. Hence Japanese firms have gone for high volumes and economies of scale of manufacture. The customers do not see the new process, they see only better and economically priced products.

- The next option for the follower is to settle for being number two. There is only one number one possible and the second place helps in remaining focused (one firm advertises that we try harder to please the customer because we are number two). they can cater to the customers who are not with the leader. The leader could be in the mass market spending large sums of money in advertising and promotion to stay number one. The second number could get in to a niche market. Or, follower could target all customer except those with number one, like the customer with the followers number three four etc. if the follower wants the third position then he can target the customers from the followers numbering four, five etc.

Strategies for Late Growth Stage in PLC

Late growth stage in the life cycle is where segmentation is a useful strategy to satisfy knowledgeable customers. Strategically, the firms need to either defend their position or find out unexplored niche markets.

The salient features of late growth stage are as follows:

- Sales volumes grows slowly.
- Many competitors.
- Price competition starts.
- Excess capacity is likely to occur.
- Channel members play one against the other to gain extra advantage.

Computer industry has suffered the world over as the growth in the last ten years reduced from a healthy 50% to only 25%. This has resulted in excess capacity and the sellers are resorting to promotional plans, they bundle a lot of software with the hardware as sales promotion. With lower demand and reduced production, the fixed costs per unit go up.

- Customers are very intelligent and demand a lot as specific benefits.
- Marketing efforts focus on specified segments.

In late growth stage customer's demands are more specific and market segmentation becomes critical. The strategies, which leaders and followers can pursue, are given below:

Leaders—target many segments.

Followers—target a few segments only.

Each segment needs a different type of at least one of the 4ps.

With the excess production capacity and price pressures the firms could decide to exit from the business altogether. The firm could need money for some other business and it plans to exit. Sometimes the follower has leapfrogged to leadership and the leader may decide to exit.

Summarizing it can be concluded as follows:

2. Early and late growth stages of the product life cycle, are having different increases in sales volumes which require different strategic initiatives.

3. Leaders and followers have separate strategic requirements in all stages of life cycle.

Tasks for the Students—

1. What is the difference between early and late growth stage?
2. What are the factors, which could be responsible for a firm leaving the market even in growth stage?

Strategies for the Maturity Stage of Product Life Cycle

When the products reach the maturity stage, their demand growth stops, it reaches a plateau. Firms need to manage the sales in this stage either for cash or they should plan product differentiation or geographic extension of the markets, in the country or through exports. However, if opportunity costs exceed present value benefits, it is better to exit from the product sales.

Mature markets are known for sophisticated buyers, well-organized segments, reduced differences in products from competition and stable sales volumes.

Maturity stage has the following main characteristics:

1. Constant sales volumes year to year.
2. Product differentiation vanishes as competition also makes "ME TOO" products.

It is however, not necessary that in a product range all the models may be in the same stage of life cycle e.g. in cars one model may have reached maturity and other may be in introductory stage.

Sustainable Competitive Advantage (SCA)—SCA can be achieved by differentiating one or more of the following, in maturity stage:

- Service.
- Distribution.
- Advertising of intangible benefits like brand equity, service.
- Product differentiation does not make much of an impact in maturity stage.
- Pricing takes a toll and it has to be competitive—in India, with new models coming Maruti had to reduce its price.
- Buyers are knowledgeable, know about firms and competitive products are discerning and have bargaining power.
- There are relatively few new buyers. Firms, when they want to increase sales, either take customers from the competition

or they fight for the small number of new buyers. In most cases some old buyers quit the field and the new ones replace them.

Let it be understood that for most products, except for FMCGs taking customers from competition is a difficult task as any action, like price reduction can lead to price war and the lower price can in any case be met by conpetition leaving the market share on status-quo.

In maturity stage, leaders and followers have different strategic options available to them. Leaders may mature products as cash cows or the may harvest for profits. Followers may try to keep the market share at the existing level, grow or even exit as per the following plan:

Leaders—(a) manage for cash —————— or, (b) harvest i.e., reduce market share by going for niche market.

Followers—maintain the market share ——— grow ——— exit

Maintaining or increasing market share needs investments and therefore reduces profits. Market share ceases to be of any importance in maturity stage. Followers can take the leadership position if the leaders are quitting it or taking followers' position. However, the followers must find out the reasons why the leaders are leaving the top spot; is there a new technology available now? Market segmentation is the key to success in this stage. It is necessary to offer Specific benefits to a group of customers or to the segment. It is of importance if the switching costs of customers for changing products are low.

Tasks for the Students—

1. What are the strategic implications in maturity stage with highly sophisticated buyers?
2. How can firms keep gross margins high in the maturity stage?

Let us see how the firm's can keep prices high in the maturity stage. They can have distinct product differentiation to keep the switching costs high. They can build their brand equity high and have superior service. These intangible benefits will place the product in the customers mind set; keep competition away and the firms can still manage high profit margins.

Summarizing—the mature markets are stable with few major players and reduced product differences among competitors. These markets also provide cash for invigorating newer product concepts.

Ford car was down in dumps in 1980. then the new President Don Peterson told his management team ,"Get the best features of the cars worldwide, without omitting any feature, including door handles and glove compartments size," Ford was back on its feet in less time than was envisaged.

Market Strategies in Decline Stage of Product Life Cycle

Decline stage in life cycle is characterized by decrease in Sales Volume as a result of product demand, demographic changes, and technological changes over a period of time. Cheaper substitute products and changes customers taste also account for the decline stage.

Key factors which are present in the decline stage given below:

- Over capacity in production
- Severe price competition
- Several competitors exit.

For at least getting the fixed cost, sales are made with low profit margins, as it is not easy to reduce production. However, if fixed costs are low then the firm can plan to downsize the production. If variable costs are high, exiting is easy otherwise on high variable cost it is not so. Success in maturity stage through fixed costs help the firms survive in decline stage as well. With high fixed costs it is easy to get in to penetrating prices.

The marketing strategies for **Decline Stage** are as given below:

Table 12.7. Decline Stage Strategy

	Hospitable market	Inhospitable market
Leaders	Maintain lead	Harvest
Followers	Harvest	Divest

Hospitable market in decline stage, is when the rate of decline is slow, otherwise it becomes inhospitable. For leaders in hospitable market, they can keep their market going down at the rate the market is declining. For harvesting the firms bring down their market share and try to get in to a niche market. In inhospitable market the follower's best strategy is to exit from the market. Marketing mix wars begin in decline stage starting from price war. It should however be understood that the players are all fighting over a shrinking pie. Penetrating prices, higher investments in advertising and promotion mark the decline stage. It becomes a vicious circle like the arms race of the twentieth century between the USA and erstwhile USSR and hence should be avoided by the firms. Several firms decide to get out of the market. However, the firm which decides to stay, gets in to monopoly situation and can reap the skimming price benefits till the market remains.

One firm in India was making Radio Valves and as most radio manufacturers changed to using semiconductor devices, other valve manufacturers in the world stopped making them resulting in monopoly for the firm. As there was some market in Africa the firm could charge better than Indian market price, skimming price for a few years before the demand dwindled to zero.

In case of some product being reintroduced in the market, the last survivor gets the benefit.

Summarizing, "A life cycle audit helps the firms in determining where their products are placed in the life cycle so that their marketing can be strategically planned".

Hence the firms need to do a **Life Cycle Audit** as follows:

Table 12.8. Life Cycle Audit

Competitive position leaders /followers	*Introductory stage*	*Growth stage*	*Maturity stage*	*Decline stage*
Objectives				
Target customers				
Product				
Price				
Distribution				
Advertising				
Promotion				

The audit summarizes the entire life cycle. It is possible to plan strategies for the entire life cycle with built-in contingency.

PORTFOLIO MANAGEMENT ANALYSIS

Portfolio analysis takes in to account that large multi-product firms have synergies within and they need to provide resources for growing their attractive businesses, divesting poor performers with unattractive profits/or losses. They need to divert resources from mature and stable businesses in to attractive promising businesses.

Portfolio analysis empowers managers to balance future and current opportunities by assessing business attractiveness and competitive position in a two dimensional matrix.

Firms have a life of their own, as a single product firm will die if that product fails. Managers want multi-product firm to ensure that some product would be in growth stage always. Portfolio analysis is managed as follows:

- Focus on two major dimensions of marketing strategy.
- Look for business attractiveness to assess how good is the business opportunity and relative competitive position to understand if the firm can be a winner.
- Understanding of different resource needs—some business need resources and others have excess resources.

BOSTON CONSULTANCY GROUP

Resources can be defined as finance, human, technology, and information and managerial. So far the discussion has been on getting the competitive advantage for individual product. However, in case of a multi-product firm, emphasis should be on managing the products together and not separately. For making an analysis of firm's strength the **Boston Consultancy Group, BCG**, have developed a matrix as given below:

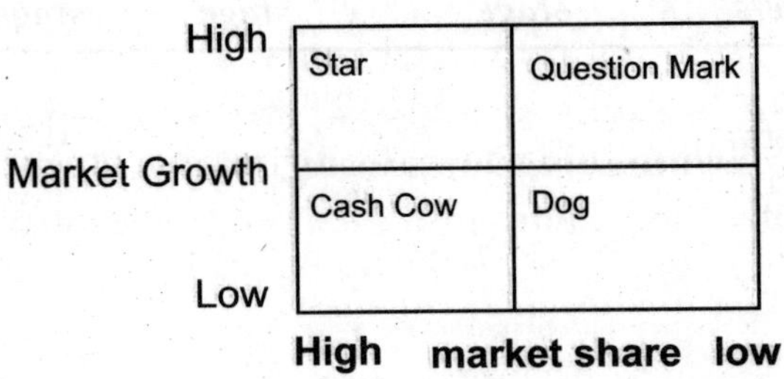

Fig. 12.2. BCG Matrix

In BCG Matrix, the horizontal axis shows the market share of the product and the vertical axis shows the market growth.

Let us see the position of products in different quadrants—

Quadrant Star—in this quadrant the market growth of the product is high and the firm's product enjoys high market share. It is characterized by the following:

- The firm's product enjoys a strong market position that of the leader.
- The market growth of the product is high and attractive.
- Competitor's better technology and superior market acceptance can make the firm's business risky, even if enjoys leadership position.
- Low profits, as the leader has to spend large amount on marketing advertising to maintain the leadership.
- High expenditure required for marketing mix factors.

Strategic options in Star Quadrant are as follows:

1. Increase share—invest in anticipation of higher market growth. Put entry barriers for newcomers through pricing, innovative distribution and advertising.
2. Maintain share—have good market intelligence to be able to counter their actions. Invest in marketing mix selectively.

Quadrant Question mark-in this quadrant, the market share is low although the growth of the market is high. The position of the product is as follows:

- The product is in growth stage while the firm's product is having low market share.
- The firm has the opportunity to increase its market share by investing in advertising and promotion.
- It is often a new entrant. It could be that all players are new or one could have assumed leadership in the market.
- Risks are high, technology and basic product acceptance in the market is not fully established.
- Negative profits and huge expenses in marketing for either concept selling or for increasing market share.
- Needs long-term and strong commitment of the management for the product's growth to attain Star position.
- The firm must decide as to how many of its products are in this quadrant and how many of them can it support on long-range basis.
- The firm could get in to some niche market segment.
- If the firm has several products in this quadrant, and you keep all you in a strategic trap, because it cannot place proper resources for them and is in danger of losing all.

Quadrant—Cash Cow is where the firm has high market share but the market growth is low. The firm can reduce its marketing expenses as it is already in dominant marketing position and can become low cost supplier. The firm can be in the following market situation:

- Dominant market position
- Slow market growth
- Low cost supplier
- Good profit and cash generation
- Low market risk

Strategies for Cash Cow Quadrant are as given below:

1. Manage for cash, maintain market share.

2. Requires cautious investment in market as growth is low.
3. Cash generation can be used for products in question mark quadrant.
4. Harvest—go for niche market if future prospects are low.
5. Divest if product demand is going down at a rapid pace, because of new technology products have come in to the market, or because the customer's tastes have been changing.

Quadrant Dog- in this quadrant, the market growth is weak and the firm has low market share. The market situation can be described as given below:

- Weak market position.
- Slow market growth.
- High cost supplier.
- Poor or no profit and cash generation. However by managing it carefully, using the niche market route it can be profitable too.
- Several times the product could be based on management ego as once it was a star product.
- High management turnover, as the product is not doing well, "customers know us because of this product."
- The product takes a lot of management time in planning its strategies for hardly any gain.

Strategies for Dog Quadrant are given below:

1. Maintain market share for whatever cash the product generates.
2. Plan for changing or adding some market segments.
3. Stop all new investment in the product.
4. Divest—sell and use the funds for other products in question mark stage.
5. Keep the product for any goodwill it may have or there are strong exit barriers.
6. Turn around—by innovating, product differentiation, down sizing
7. Get into niche market.

Investment Cycle for the BCG Matrix, therefore is as given below:

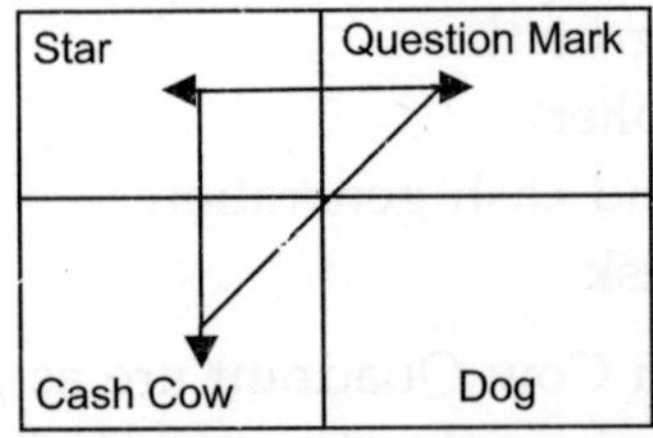

Fig. 12.3. BCG Investment Cycle

The extra cash generated in cash cow stage is invested in the question mark stage to bring the product in to star stage. Over time the market growth of star product goes down when it reaches the maturity stage of its life cycle, and it starts having extra cash, which is invested in question mark stage to complete the cycle.

GE Model

Matrix has been fine tuned by the GE Model, which can be used to define markets and products position as follows:

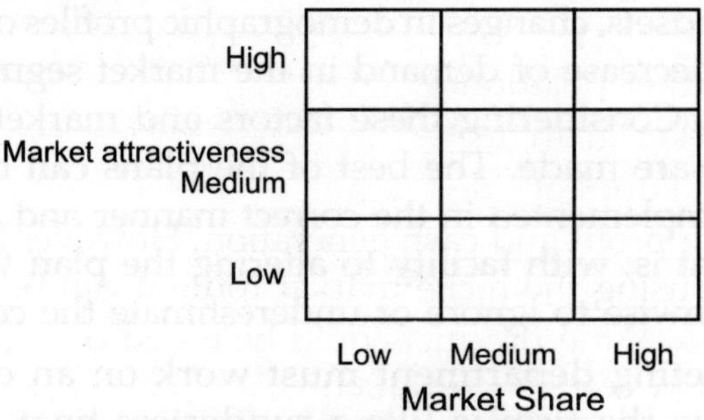

Fig. 12.4. GE Model

In the GE Matrix the market attractiveness and firm's market share for a product can be platted as high, medium and low, thus enabling the firm to understand the position more accurately and plan its strategies accordingly.

Market attractiveness can be measured as given below:

- Market size and growth
- Degree of market concentration, is it localized or is it spread out
- Industry profitability
- Price sensitivity of demand
- Exit and entry barriers
- Strength of channel members
- Rate of obsolescence or technology change

Firms market share and its competitive position can be seen from the following:

- Market share
- Profit margins
- Brand loyalty
- Degree of product differentiation
- Proprietary technology
- Financial position
- Personnel

Summarizing, market share and market potential are mapped in a *portfolio* analysis to provide a visual understanding of the industry players and the attractiveness and competitive positions of the firm's products.

Portfolio analysis can be used to find out where resources should be deployed and to determine the relationship among and competitors.

Customer, Competition and the Firm

In the competitive field firms have to keep looking at the customers to know their mindsets, changes in demographic profiles of the customers and increase or decrease of demand in the market segment, which the firm is targeting. Considering these factors and market dynamics the marketing plans are made. The best of the plans can become useless unless they are implemented in the correct manner and are kept on the rolling mode; that is, with facility to altering the plan with speed and efficiency. It is unwise to ignore or underestimate the competition.

Firm's marketing department must work on an objective basis; without objective the firm is like a rudderless boat, which has no direction in which it wants to go. These objectives of the marketing are finalized after discussions between the CEO, the marketing manager, production head and the finance manager, as the marketing or its main function, selling brings profits to the firm, the importance of marketing objectives can never be overrated. The objectives should be made keeping the opportunities available in the business environment and the resources with the firm. If a firm can produce only 3000 scooters in a month it would be unwise to set the objective of selling 10,000 scooters per month, unless the firm is planning partial out sourcing of scooter production. In case the marketing department is given multiple objectives like selling of number of units of the product, improvement in brand equity by a certain percentage, there would be possibility of direct assistance between the objectives or there could also be conflict when it comes to resource allocation, the salesmen may want bigger allocation of funds for traveling and increase in dealer commission and advertising manager may ask for more funds for advertising. Objectives must be acceptable and the team member of marketing departments must be committed to the achievement of the objectives; besides the objectives must be challenging, achievable but with a stretch only.

Firms need to implement their marketing plans in the following manner:

- Convert marketing plans in to action tasks and procedures.

- Convey the firm's objective, which drives the plan to the marketing team and obtain full commitment of all the members on the objectives.
- Give sufficient authority for taking action on the plan.
- Assign marketing team members with the tasks, both individually and as a team.
- Monitor the progress of the implementation through unobtrusive check points.
- Get the team's commitment on the time needed for the implementation.

The firms need to quickly evaluate the causes of losing the grip on the market as seen by loss in sales, to assess the reason for failure. Is it the plan's failure or that of people implementing the plan? Have the people assigning the implementation to the team gone wrong or is the fault of set objectives or the team has faltered? The other causes of failure could be incorrect budget allocations for the implementation, ineffective training given to the team members or limitations of coordination between the team members, which could be due to ignorance or ego of some of the members. The firm's management must be aware of the process of evaluating the effectiveness of the plan implementation.

Most of the implementation problems arise because of lack of clarity in setting up the marketing goals and objectives and the provision of tools for evaluating the success of the plan. Product Portfolio management is possible only if the firm knows the profit picture of each product it sells. Besides, it is important to understand the marketing and support expenses needed or made for each product. Several firms found to their dismay that they were spending far too much on the products in maturity or decline stage of Product Life Cycle. Firms are known to have kept the loss making products in their range either due to lack of knowledge about its profitability or due to ego problems; "this was our first product launched ten years ago and it gave us lot of profits earlier".

The firms need to look at some of the other areas as well as given below:

- Keep their current assets under control by tracking the inventory levels, using push sales technique by passing on the inventories to the distribution channel members.
- Keep track of competitive pricing. Does the firm want to be price leader or merely price follower? At times firms' increase their prices and they find that the competition was just waiting to follow suit.

- Keep a track on customer complaints, their redress.
- Keep a track on customer complaints, their redress period and improvement or deterioration in customer satisfaction level for the product.
- Keep a technical audit of all technology level complaints and keep the production, quality and R&D people aware of the same, with a time bound correction of the faults levels.
- If the product has really failed then, no amount of marketing effort, advertising can help it and the management must decide quickly to withdraw it from the market soonest as possible.
- An audit on the advertising efforts, promotions must be made periodically to ensure that these expensive efforts do not go in vain. The single variable technique, where the firm imposes a ban on other promotional activities for a period can give most precise results in this complicated issue.
- How good are the salesmen, are they properly trained, totally motivated and committed to their firm and their tasks, is the rivalry among them healthy or destructive can be assessed by obtaining, understanding the daily or weekly reports sent in by the salesmen. These control points and their implementation plans must be made well in advance and told to the concerned people with total transparency to get the best out of the team members.

The firms should keep a good grip on things all the time because it would be futile to cry over the spilt milk. Timely corrective actions, like counseling of erring person, change in plan, altering time schedules can become the guiding factors in the success of the firm.

Is the firm exploiting the marketing opportunities fully, product wise, marketwise or distribution wise? The management team comprising the CEO, Marketing Director, Finance Director should jointly be involved in understanding the market position of the firm, its ethical approach, and societal responsibilities. Marketing Director should use sales analysis, product wise, area wise, salesman wise, and distribution wise, to know the growth of the market, the firms market share, percentage of market expense to each areas sales and compare the same with the objectives. Financial market analyst should look at the profit or loss situation for each product, area salesman, and distributor and compare the same with the objectives. Marketing Manager should evaluate the efficacy of advertising, promotion, distribution channels and the salesmen to help in modifying the plans to make them more effective as follows:

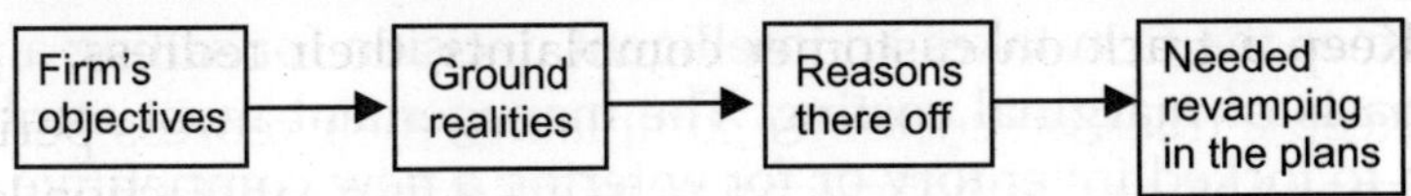

Fig. 12.5. Plan Modification

The decline in sales revenue and profits could be attributed to decline in the total market, decline in the firm's market share, decline due to reduced prices or increase in selling expenses.

A firm selling motorcycles had planned to sell 100,000 bikes in the year at a price of rupees 30,000 each, with the total revenue being rupees 300 crores. It was targeting a total of 25% of the country's market. However, it could sell only 80,000 bikes at a net price of rupees 25,000 each totaling revenue of only rupees 200 crores. The market leaders in the bike business apparently got the balance of the sale. The price revision had to be done to reduce the onslaught of competitive forces. The market in fact increased by ten percent in the year.

By the virtue of market growth the firm should have sold 110,00 bikes. The firm therefore lost total sales of 30,000 bikes. The loss of revenue due to loss in sales is as follows:

30,000 bikes @ rupees 30,000 is rupees 90 crores which is the loss due to decrease in the sales.

80,000 bikes @ rupees 5000 the lowering in price is rupees 40 crores loss.

Audit of various branches can be quite an eye opener as at times when the firm is making profits a few loss-making branches can be carried as extra baggage. The moment the tide turns against the firm, these loss-making branches become the first victims of the axe. Profit picture should be analyzed for each branch, profit center, SBU, market segment, discounts on bulk buying. There are situations when each sale is loss making and increase in sales only adds to the losses. These could be for products in the Dog Quadrant of the BCG Matrix. Firms must decide proper strategy to get out of the loss situation soonest. In case of channels making profits also, is the firm spending too much on helping them make profits, giving high commissions. It is worthwhile to understand the brand equity versus the dealers' reputation to accurately determine the level of dealer commission to be paid. For new products in the market, the dealers do have the power as they have been in touch with the customers selling them other products. Later on the firm develops product brand equity, which helps in selling the product to a large extent, reducing the stranglehold of the dealers. The commission can then be downsized; in a manner the channel members remain loyal, like asking them to participate in promotional plans, joint advertising efforts.

At times the firm takes an intelligent decision for selling a product on the basis of marginal costing. The management must attribute the decision to locked inventory or for entering a new competitive market. Whatever be the reason the loss in profit must be self-evident and should not be made a burden on the sales team that they should bring back the profits in the rest of the sales. Attempts at doing so should be made and are praiseworthy.

Similarly there is an age-old rivalry between product unit and the sales force. When the orders are not received in time and there is an inventory built up, the production team starts blaming the sales force. Conversely when orders exist and there are delays in dispatches the blame is borne by the production. The situations like these can not be totally eliminated, but can be reduced in intensity by establishing coordination teams between the two departments and enforcing transparency in operations of the two departments.

It is therefore important to know if the firm's increase or decrease in market share is in consonance with increase or decrease of the total market demand or not, else the firm can become complacent about its achievements.

Market share therefore assumes great importance in firms marketing plans. Most CEOs consider market share and brand equity as two of the firm's most important assets. While the growth of the market of different is dependence on factors out side of the firm, it affects the firm totally. The firms should therefore realize the area which are responsible for increase or decline of market at any point of time.

The general business environment factors like legal issues affect the business. It is however quite likely that they do not have the same effect on all the competitive firms. The 11th September 2000 assault on the USA did shrink the tourism business but the affect was different on different firms.

Firms should normally benchmark its operating results with the best in the industry. However if the firm is the market leader then it should compare only with it's own past results or with the nearest competitor only.

Market share loss could be due to leaving unprofitable customers and areas and may lead to better bottom line. Entry of new firms in competition would lead to loss of share; but again the percentage loss may not be the same for all the competitors.

Market share depends on the number of customers with the firm, their buying patterns and buying quantities, the ratio of the firms buyers in the market and the purchase averages of the firms customers vis-a-vis competitive customers and it also depends on the price differential between firms. To some extent, especially for products for the low and middle income groups where price sensitivity is a major issue.

The effect of marketing expenses needs to be monitored and it should be a major criteria for the way marketing plans are developed.

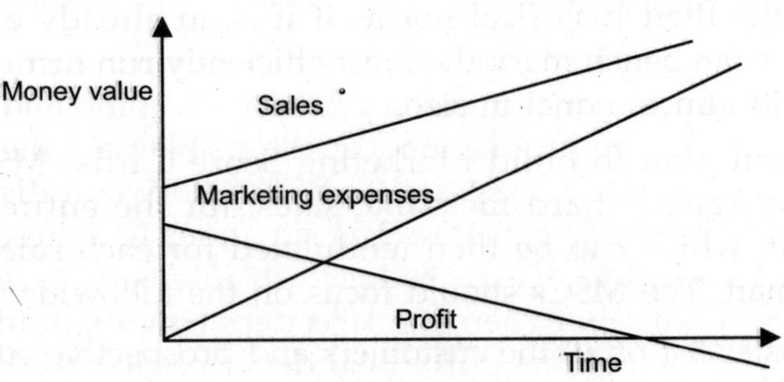

Fig. 12.6. Market Plan

As can be seen from the graph given above, in case the marketing expenses go up, the profit may decline and there may even be a loss. Marketing expenses can be divided as follows:

- Salaries and travel of salesmen
- Advertising
- Sales promotion
- Distribution channel commission (unless of course the channel members are allowed to have a markup on prices)
- Sales overheads like administrative expenses rentals, telephones and other correspondence.
- Marketing research

Depending on firms these could vary a lot. Cola companies spend 25 to 30 percent of their sales revenue on advertising and promotion, while some industrial goods firm may not spend more than 5 percent of the sales revenue. Firm need to bench mark these expenses and keep a check lest at the end of the year it is found that the expenses have gone haywire without resultant increase in sales and profits. There of course cân be regional and seasonal fluctuations in these expenses, but the firms would do well to provide guidelines to the sales teams about the possible upper limits on each of the expenses. Following gives an idea of prevalent expense as percent of sales turn over norms in most industries (it would be better to go by the industry norms in most cases, unless the situation is unusual like a product launch.)—

- Sales team salaries and travel 10–15%
- Advertising 5–25%
- Promotion 3–10%

- Distribution channel commission 7–15%
- Sales overheads 2–5%
- Marketing Research 0.5–1%

The variation seen above takes in to consideration the product types, consumer durables, FMCG, industrial and services. Individual industry needs to take their historical norms if it is an already existing one. Otherwise it can bench mark the most efficiently run firm, in the same business and almost equal in size.

Firms can plan to build Marketing Score Cards- MSCs for soft numbers as against hard facts like sales, for the entire marketing department, which can be then modulated for each sales team and each salesman. The MSCs should focus on the following:

- Master list of all the customers and prospective customers for industrial products.
- Master list of the distribution channel members and their major clients for FMCG and consumer durables.
- Master Cards of all new customers giving their full particulars.
- List of customer complaints and the delay in their redress, and similar study of competition.
- Rating points on customer service as compared to competition.
- Current market segment being catered to and new segments, which can be targeted in the future.
- Product awareness levels in the target market segment.
- Product acceptance level in the target segment.

The two hidden costs of the marketing team must be unearthed so that they could be reduced if not completely eliminated. They are, (a) cost of inefficiency (b) cost of unethical practices.

Cost of inefficiency—it can be seen from low number of sales calls by the salesmen, low call effectiveness, increase in cost per call, increase in entertainment expense without relative increase in sales, increase or decrease in orders received with the money value of increase or decrease, customers lost or gained.

Cost of unethical practices can be seen in undue lowering of rates for low volumes of orders, unmatched inventories of accessories, unauthorized commitment by salesmen to customers causing losses to the firm.

In a nutshell, marketing team should be given freedom of action within the framework of authority but must also be accountable to achieve the firm's marketing objectives. Controls in the area of

achieve the firm's marketing objectives. Controls in the area of marketing should be instituted more as a help to the sales team until they prove to be going totally of the track.

Tasks before the students— discuss the need for control points for marketing teams, how they can be formalized for different type of products, channels.

Tasks for the Students—

1. Discuss the strengths and weaknesses of portfolio analysis.

The study of strategic marketing should make the student aware of the necessity of the study as in today's market business environment keeps changing rapidly and unless fast decisions are taken the firms are going to be left behind in the competitive race. It helps the firm to make long range plans to remain proactive and avoid firefighting measures which firms keep taking today. It also helps in taking short-term actions to beat the competition in instable conditions.

Marketing 21st Century Style

Before planning marketing strategies, we need to have the following information. Database—

- Country's business environment—both General and Competitive
- Target market segment
- Marketing objectives

As the business is managed within it's environment, the Block diagram can be shown as follows:

Table 12.9. Strategic Objectives

Marketing Mix Factors	*Strategies for Marketing*	*Marketing Objectives*
Product	Add promotion plans	Inc.share by 2% pa
Price	Inc. advertising efforts	Inc. brand recall by 10% pa
Placement	Appoint dealers in uncovered areas	Inc geographic coverage by 20% pa
Promotion	Build dealer relations, higher margins, better care, quick response to complaints	Imp. Dealer relationship
People	Training of marketing personnel	

The business is surrounded by

1. General Environment Factors—Demographic, Socio-Cultural, Political-Legal, Macro-Economics, Technology, Global
2. Competitive Environment Factors—Michael Porter's Five Force Model

Customer vs Client

Service providers like the doctors, lawyers have clients because they give individual attention to each of their clients, while mass sellers/ manufacturers have customers, who are nameless entities in a crowd. In order to provide personalized service even to the customers firms are going in for relationship marketing. Car makers like Maruti are offering personalized cars as per their customers wishes, where they can supply custom built seats, music systems, open rooftops. Even FMCG sellers are offering trinket jewelry, which could be found in a pack of wafers. These promotional plans try to bind the customers to a particular brand.

Who is a customer?

Who is a client?

From customer to client transformation- personalization of product, service, ideas, communication.

What is new?

- Customer satisfaction to customer value to customer delight
- Information about customer-database, buyers, non buyers, competitive buyers
- Partnership marketing with distributors
- Communication strategies
- Supply chain management
- Market segmentation

Relationship Marketing

Maruti cars try to ensure that their clients graduate from Maruti 800, to Zen or Alto and from then on to Esteem through the following measures:

- Newsletters
- Clubs and Programs
- Free Gifts
- Personal calls and Follow ups
- What else?—Social activities, being a good corporate citizen.

What is happening in the market place today?

- Downsizing- cutting down excess activities to reduce costs.
- Outsourcing of products or subassemblies for cost reduction.
- Supply chain management for optimizing resources; planning for Just In Time supplies for keeping currents assets as low as possible.
- Logistics optimization for cost reduction.
- Flatter organizations.
- Mergers and acquisitions.
- Impact of globalization.

Product idea and market research should take care of the following:

- Price sensitivity.
- Service orientation of products.
- Sales-feedback-service plans.
- Customer/client education.

Markets Of The Twenty-first Century

When a firm enters the market, it has some commitments to its customers, and those are based on the utility need and performance of its product. With shrinking business world, even political distances can be shortened as no nation can remain as an island. Therefore in order to not just survive, but also to thrive in the market placed, the firms have to have a global vision of the market, even if it selling only locally, as otherwise foreign firms are going to cut in to their business sharply. Hence the nature of commitment of the firms has to widen to not just cope with international competition but also in order to beat them in their own countries as well. The steps required are the following:

- In-depth or intensive marketing within the country
- Extension of geographic boundaries of the markets
- Penetrating pricing strategy
- Strong merchandizing effort
- Advertising, promotion strategy
- New product plans
- New products to be sold in new markets
- Vertical integration of manufacturing base

Intensive marketing—Depending of product surpluses firms have to take a view, which would encourage them in to going in for aggressive selling to their present customers. Gillette is a case in point. When they started with their use and throw Presto razors, they were giving individual razors. Later on they came out with a pack of five razors, taking away the customers choice of product—switch midstream. Built-in gifts schemes, leasing options, deferred payment plans all tend to intensify the thrust of marketing on the customer.

Geographic extensions—customers in India are now much more discerning about the quality of product they purchase and hence products from India are matching international standards. It is therefore in fitness of business that if Indian firms face competition from foreign firms they must find countries where they have a competitive advantage because of low cost manpower, latest technology products.

Penetrating pricing—our products have a built in cost advantage over their foreign counterparts. Yet in export markets the competition could be from other developing countries. Products can be sold on marginal costing, provided there is a good base of sales in India.

Merchandizing is the icing in the cake, the showmanship of products. In order to cater to the sophisticated customers the firms must pay great attention on merchandizing aspect of retailing.

Advertising and promotion are the buzzwords in today's business and need special thrust on a continuous basis.

New products come from either customer needs or new product development, technology innovation.

Marketing research is essential for scanning world markets for new products and these researches pay dividends by optimizing marketing efforts in the right countries and through right channels of distribution.

Vertical diversification helps in reducing transfer costs as then the firm gets its raw materials, from it's own source.

Well-established firms find themselves becoming top heavy over a period of time, especially in the growth stages of life cycle. Downsizing or right sizing as it is spelt today is the order of the day for such firms. The steps required for right sizing are given below:

- A quick audit of the firm's activities to segregate the superfluous ones. Fixing an objective of right sizing exercise.
- Closure of all superfluous activities (those activities, which do not generate any value for the customers.)
- Outsourcing activities, which can be given to outside persons/firms.
- Reducing manpower across the board, in every department at all levels.
- Giving more important assignments and better pay to remaining people.

- Consolidating the gains of reduced activities.
- Bench marking results with the objective with which the firm had started the task.
- If the right sizing does not succeed, it may be a good idea to divest from the product areas completely.

Firms have realized that they cannot operate in isolation. Coordination between two firms can help both in some even when they may be competing with each other as can be seen from the following examples:

- A cash rich firm joins hands with a technology rich firm. Both gain in terms of market share and profits.
- Promotion plans can be jointly worked out. The industry bodies do it regularly when they fight against any government legislation.
- Logistics support can be provided, which will reduce the costs substantially for both the firms. If two neighboring firm can use one common road, power and telephone line it could mean a lot of saving.
- Price collaborations are popular in hospitality industry like hotels, airlines who all provide similar benefits to customers, like upgrades, free tickets for mileage used or free stay for nights used and paid for.

Because of the fast changing market scenario, and business environment, it is best to take the following steps for creating strategies for markets:

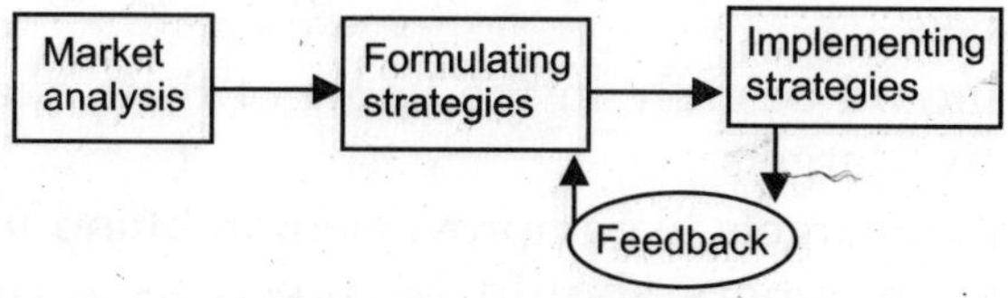

Fig. 12.7. Market Process

As the firm goes in to implementation stage, it should not forget that even than changes are taking place in the market environments. Feedback therefore becomes a powerful tool of ensuring satisfactory management of marketing strategies.

Market Analysis: It starts with Michael Porter's Five Force model and goes on to understand the general environment factors described in the book at several places. However, continuous monitoring of the environment is essential as the competition keeps growing each day.

Planning the Strategy: Starts with allocation of resources, money, human, information and infrastructure in the right area of marketing. It must be budgeted as to how much will be spent on advertising, after sales service, marketing research, developing the new areas, traveling, dealer commission, promotional plans in view of the sales targets finalized by the marketing department. Each sales team needs certain inputs like traveling, communications, live demonstrations (if required by the product), to meet its commitment on sales objectives and these must be provided. New business horizons, like new geographic coverage, new product launches call for separate budgets. Care needs to be taken in manpower planning and deployment to ensure that the people working together work as a team, are congruent in operations, complement each other and are well balanced both in numbers and in experience. Market Information System, MIS, should be kept updated with inputs from the market, sales invoices, and dispatches. Authority to take decisions, along with accountability must be expressed perhaps in writing so that each member of the team knows his tasks, what he can do and what he cannot. Importance of scientific planning for the market has been brought to focus by the myriads of non-achievers who start with a bang and end with a whimper in no time.

Since competing firms have similar goals and objectives the firm, which implements the strategy wins with better profits and improved brand equity.

Implementation of the strategy requires the following steps to be taken by the firm:

- Team members to remain totally motivated, committed to their tasks.
- Team should be fully in the know of their quantitative and qualitative targets.
- Qualitative targets like improvement in brand image, training of team members should be taken as seriously as the quantitative targets.
- Individual members of the team perform their tasks as also assist other members whenever necessary.
- Team leader should act more as a coordinator than a monitor. His actions should inspire the team.
- Assessment of achievement must be made first by each member and then for the team jointly by the team at regular intervals without waiting for the year to end.
- Success story of any member must be circulated within the team to inspire others and also to learn from the methods used

to achieve the success. Failure should also be discussed, not to push people down but to learn from any mistakes the losing team may have made.

Feedback: The last mentioned point goes as feedback to the management for use in other areas the firm may be operating. The feedback helps in reframing the strategies and therefore timely feedback is extremely important for the continued success of the firm.

Controls: Management must have inbuilt control systems to ensure that one unscrupulous person cannot hijack the entire organization by deviating from the targets of the firm to promote his own targets. At times even sincere persons lose track in the rut of day-to-day operations. Punishment or correction needs to be introduced at some stage before things go really wrong. The results should be compared with the targets already accepted by the team, in the following manner:

- With the targets.
- If the team has exceeded the targets then with industry growth.
- With historical figures.
- With new targets if new competitor/s have emerged during the period under review.
- With customer feedback about quality of goods and services offered by the team.
- With the R&D group if improvements have been called for in the product.

New challenges in the twenty first century for the marketers:

Global politics and economics are the most pronounced factors affecting today's business. Open markets one the one hand and economic zones on the other, anti dumping laws and quota systems for imports by some nations, hostilities in many parts of the world, war like situations and the faster communication, faster movements, have thrown the challenges. For marketers these have opened several new routes as also closed some old ones as given below:

- Quality standards at par internationally, ISO 9000 Series
- Low labor costs
- A large technical workforce
- English as a known language
- IT, software expertise
- Presence of several multinational companies already in the country.
- Spread of Internet in the country
- Emergence of e-signatures leading to e-commerce

The firms which can gear themselves up to the challenges have a bright future both nationally and in the international markets.

The Virtual Marts

Internet or Web has the potential of becoming a force to reckon with as a marketing tool. As the PC population increases both in homes and in the offices surfing the net will become more popular. Bazee.com in India has started its business where sellers, both individual and firms can place their products for sale. Websites auctioning products, including airline tickets have emerged. These are only tips of the proverbial iceberg and much more can be expected in the area of web marketing.

These virtual shops with little overheads can give the well established super markets, the only negatives at present are their credibility among the Indian buyers as also the real life buying experience where the Indian housewife excels, doing window shopping bargaining and generally having a great time out of the house. Unless the lady feels the silk of the sari, she is not confident of buying it. It is perhaps time or some innovative, ingenious technique which could help the lady in overcoming these fears.

Hence, the marketer's route to success is as follows:

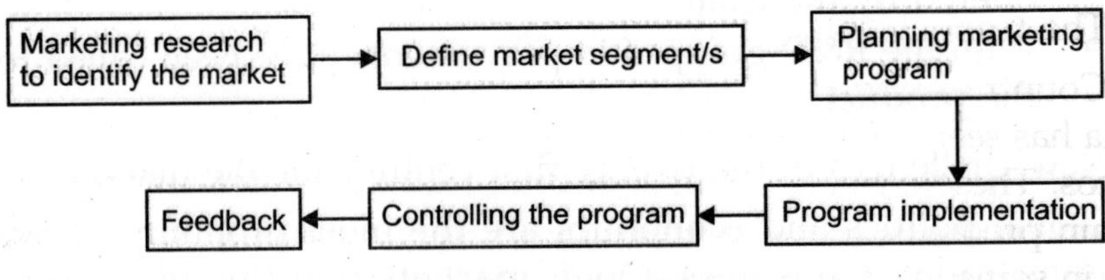

Fig. 12.8. Market Plan

Firms need to make a rolling marketing plan, which may be made for a year, but is reviewed every month and corrected if deviations are found in the business environment factors, both general and competitive.

The Marketing Plan

It should contain the following:

- Executive summary giving the highlights of the plans, especially the control points.
- General and competitive environment factors, new products from competition, market growth forecasts and summary of the findings of marketing research.
- Comparative statement of strengths and weaknesses of the firm *vis-à-vis* competitors, with emphasis on the customer

benefits derived from the usage of products from the firms, both its own and competitors.

- Profitable sales plan for the entire product available for sale, either by manufacture or by purchase, taking the 4 ps and the people into account.
- Fixing individual quantitative and qualitative targets, qualitative targets could be in the nature of continuous training programs, market feedbacks.
- Profit picture derived out of sales revenue and marketing expense budgets.

The word strategy is more commonly used in planning by the defence forces. In the same parlance, marketing in severe competitive markets is like facing a war like situation where the competitor is ready to gobble up firms not ready to face them. It becomes a do or die situation and hence all the possible loopholes need to be plugged, which becomes easy by using a systematic planning and control approach.

Question for discussion: locate the changes taking place in the business environment and discuss how firms can take full advantage of the same, despite severe competition in the market place.

Marketing Game

The teams to understand the Cultural Revolution of the country.

Countries undergo Cultural Revolution, which affect the business. India has seen the teen revolution, the emergence of POP Music; DVDs, Discos. These changes bring about major shifts in demand patterns of certain products. In many areas meat eating and cooking is prohibited and in some, beef eating is taboo. Health awareness in urban areas has brought about huge business potential for health foods, gyms, exercising equipment and dieticians. The increase in the population of teenagers and of senior citizens (those above sixty-five years of age) provides unique opportunities to marketers while the disco culture is emerging with the youth of the country, the return to the roots with yoga, meditation is also happening. The Indian science and art of living that is, yoga, meditation is finding favour in many parts of the world and these with their literature are big export business from India. However, one can argue whether the philosophy and culture of a country can be bought and sold. Swami Vivekananda had spearheaded the religious-cultural spread from India in the west in the nineteenth century.

While the marketers may not be involved in bringing about the cultural changes, they can certainly take advantage of the changes.

Plethora of goods to meet the demand comes to the market. As the customer is fickle, he keeps looking for new brands. The result is that the old brands are being refurbished with cosmetic changes. The desire for possessing something unique also spurs innovators, R&D engineers, designers, and artists to bring newness to the products.

India has the distinction of having twenty-one official languages, cultural diversities, climatic differences, area specialty in foods, which is at once an opportunity and a challenge to the marketing fraternity of the country and the foreign firms.

Strategic Group

Analysis of competition should be undertaken only in the closed area in which the firm is fighting competition, its strategic group. For example, if the firm makes pickles, it should not be looking at the entire packaged food industry; it should confine to pickles group only. Stainless steel utensils can be considered one strategic group and not the steel industry. Deviating from this could land the firm in a quagmire from where it would be difficult to come out.

Cooperation in Competitive Environment

As the country's economics is evolving all the time, firms can decide to pursue cooperation or pure competition. Cooperation in foreign business, R&D, Production technology, can lead to benefits for the competing players. It could lead to market growth, better position in the international market, better standard of living for the members of the firms.

Information on Competition

Competitive information can be gathered through newspapers, magazines, and government agencies, databases, Internet, customers, suppliers and competitors. Gathering competitive information can seldom be considered as espionage.m

Scenario Planning

Firms can plan the shape, size and the business it would be engaged in, in the future, say, five, years down the line. It is necessary to think strategically for future on specific issues, instead of looking at general future trends.

Scenario should include the following areas:

- Uncontrollable areas
- Contrary views

- Relevant issues
- Manageable areas

Scenario planning is a learning process, which can give directions for the future and steer the firm to a bright future.

CHAPTER 13

International Marketing

AIMS AND OUTCOMES OF THE CHAPTER

"Vasudhaiv Kutumbhkam" the two words aptly describe the business world of the twenty-first century. It means that the world is one family. With faster supersonic jets, travel time has been drastically reduced. Internet, Fax, and Cell phones have made communications as fast as any body can want. Flow of technology, finance and market information has become rapid, making it easier to plan global business. It however has opened the doors to wide range of countries creating severe international, competition in practically all areas of business. There have been international or multinational firms for a long time now, like the Lever Brothers, Shell, Exxon, Ford, Nestle'. Today, a much larger contingent of firms are either already in the market or are entering it to vie for the customers globally. There is hardly a nation left which is not a player in the international arena. It depends on the **Supply – Demand** paradigm, which decides the supply point while the economic levels of the countries support the products sales in different countries. The students will learn the methods they can adopt for going international with assured success.

The importance of international marketing has never been felt in India with such intensity as today. With increasing international competition on our shores Indian firms have to compete with them and find other markets as well. With partial **convertibility of rupee,** export earnings become a major source of foreign exchange, which helps in firm's imports of raw materials and components. Now even completely built units are allowed for imports, and many firms are using the benefits to import samples for user trials and sales. Firms have to find markets overseas to survive in the Indian market. It is also true that first the product must be proven in the Indian market before the firm ventures out for its export, unless of course, the product has been manufactured with foreign customers specifications and requirements in mind.

Our manufacturers have been by and large handicapped in the world market, with a few exceptions, because of the following reasons:

1. Indian products have a low brand equity, foreigners consider them as of low quality.
2. Our advertising in the world market is below the mark.
3. Our embassies need to do much more to promote Indian products.
4. India has been considered as a country with snake charmers and elephant rides, the land of Maharajas. This needs to be changed.
5. Our knowledge about the world market is restricted to traditional products and traditional markets. We need to widen our product range as also our geographic world coverage.
6. Till the eighties of the last century, the firms in India found that the home market was more attractive and they had no reason to go overseas.
7. Surprisingly, perhaps, it was some small firms, which had ventured in to exports and built a name for them.
8. With rupee value in favour of exports, now is the time to take full advantage of the situation.
9. Besides, till now, India has low cost of labour, which can make our top quality products competitive.
10. To a new exporter, international business remains a mystery until he ventures out and finds out the benefits and methods of going overseas.

The easy and most suitable way of doing international business is to look at the market as it is done for the local market as follows:

Understand the following **General Business Environment** factors:

- Demographic—which gives a population profile in terms of; income, age, sex, languages spoken, religions followed, urban, semi-urban, rural population. Besides migration of population, seasonal or permanent helps in product demand patterns.
- Socio-cultura—gives information on areas like, health awareness, educational standards, population of working women, family sizes
- Political-legal—the political system of the country, number of political parties, form of the government; monarchy, democracy, legal restrictions and aids to the business, especially foreign firms. Business law as related to the specific country.

- Technology—level of technology available in the firm's area of interest. Speed of technology up gradation. R&D Efforts going on in the country.
- Macro-economics—deals with levies and taxes, balance of payment between the countries, interest rates for borrowing
- Global—it gives information about the business globalization process going on in the country
- Governmental view—how the country's government views foreign investments and entry of foreign goods in to their country. Do they have a long-range perspective on foreign firms?

The firms should understand the competitive environment factors also, in order to plan pro-active activities to nip competition in the bud or put it in its place. **Michael Porter's Five Force Model** should be used to gain knowledge on competition in the country, which is giving below:

Table 13.1. Five Force Model

	Threat of new entrants	
Bargaining power of suppliers	**Rivalry amongst existing players**	**Bargaining power of buyers**
	Threat of substitute products	

A detailed discussion on the subject can be found in the chapter on competitive forces.

Next, the firm wanting to do overseas business should understand the **Competitor's 4 Ps, Product, Price, Placement and Promotion. This is to ensure that apples are compared with apples only and not with oranges.** The firm must know who are the competitors, what are their products in competition to their own products.

After doing the analysis, the firm should take a look at their own strengths and weaknesses *vis-à-vis*, competition and that take the following decisions:

1. To go overseas or not
2. If yes, which market or markets to enter and the priority of markets selected.
3. The methods of entering the market; direct sales to customers, through channels, having own outlets, franchisee operations or even having own production overseas. Production could be from component stage, semi-knocked down product assemblies or import of completely built units.

4. Having own offices and sales
5. Technology transfers to local business/industry.
6. Deciding on marketing program, including market share to be captured, marketing expense to be incurred.
7. Deciding on marketing organization

Managers must be aware of international complexities in business. The following needs to be considered:

- Global perspectives, is their product acceptable in the global market or does it need any modifications to ensure it's acceptance?
- Options available
- Possible strategies
- International marketing and government relations
- Advantages of international marketing to the firm

International marketing helps tide over problems, which may arise while doing business in one market only. It becomes an insurance against political risks as well. However, the firms should well understand the cultural diversities of different countries. Cultural differences can be converted in to firm's advantage by positioning products as attractive ethnic ones.

The three strategies possible in international marketing are as given below:

1. Global
2. Multi-domestic
3. Hybrid

In global strategy, the firms adapt their International Planning on the lines of their single global strategy. Mercedes car remains the same all over the world. There is no change in its marketing plans as well. Lever Brothers however, have different products, brands and other marketing features for each country. This is called multi-domestic strategy. A combination of the two is the hybrid strategy.

Firms which have a universally accepted product, like Coke, Mercedes, Toyota, the keep the global marketing policy, as the product remains the same the world over.

However, firms with products where the tastes of countries differ use the Multi-domestic policy. In this case, they change the product specifications, pricing policy, advertising according to local conditions and tastes. FMCG Firms like Unilever, Proctor &Gamble follow this strategy.

The most popular strategy is the hybrid one, where the firms use the global product, but change its advertising and promotion to suit the local conditions. Even Coke changes their advertising and promotion to suit the country, while keeping the product same universally.

Levi jeans are the dress of the workers in the USA, while in France, Italy and India it is a fashion statement. Mercedes car is mostly used as taxi in Germany, while it is considered a status symbol in the rest of the world.

Bar codes have made a global presence, as Levis link system helps their retailers the world over, to transfer, sale and control their inventories with the help of these codes.

If value is added in upstream activities like commercial aircrafts it is global strategy. If the value is added in downstream like house or prepared food it is multi-domestic strategy.

In most countries, the foreign firms can get competitive advantage by having quality **relations with the government.**

Advantages of global or international marketing for India are as follows:

- Can leverage our low labor cost as a cost leadership advantage *vis-à-vis* competition.
- Get foreign exchange as per partial convertibility of rupee.

Disadvantages for international marketing are given below:

- Currency changes, (exchange rate fluctuations)
- Country's strategies for foreign firm
- Lack of international, experience

Firms take the following route to international business:

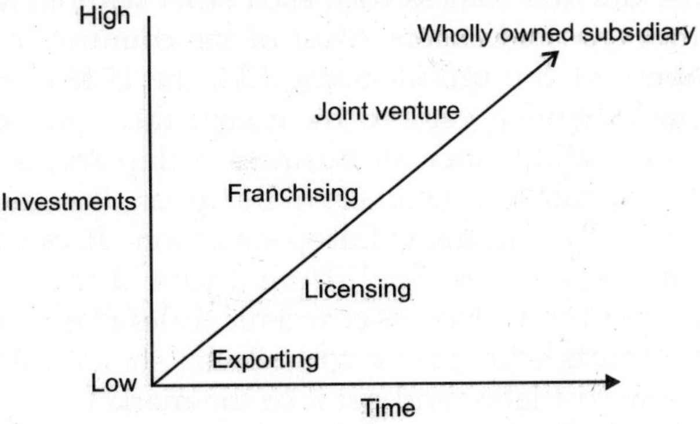

Fig. 13.1. Route to International Business

As can be seen, the firms normally start by exporting; which is followed by licensing the manufacture of the product or the sale. Next comes franchise operation where the local businessman franchisee can use the brand name of the firm get managerial support. On being successful, the firm can start a joint venture manufacturing unit and finally, the firm can have their own organization to manufacture and market products in that and in other countries as well. With firms in international market, firms can enter new international market from any place depending on their own plans and the host government's rules and regulations.

The firms have to decide the markets they want to enter internationally. The Three markets, which cater to the major part of international business, are, the European market, the USA and the Far East markets. The decision should be taken depending on the host country's policy on foreign firms, besides its economic standards. Distances become important, as freight of goods to be exported is dependent on it. India as a market has looked attractive to the western nations due to its large population, which consists of nearly 200 million people belonging to the consumer group.

Seeing the importance of inter-country trade, several geographic economic blocks or zones have been formed to not only do easy and free business with one another, but also to put barriers for outsiders from doing business with them.

Free Trade Zones

Some of the free trade zones are listed below:

- *European Union:* They have recently introduced a common currency the Euro, with the help of which the countries of Europe can do business with each other without any tax levies or other type of barriers. Most of the countries of Europe are members of the union. Some like the U.K. have not fully accepted the idea yet and have kept their own currency the Pound as valid tender for business within and overseas. With nearly 400 million consumers in the union, thy amount to more than 20% of world trade. European union offers a large market to other countries, including India due to its volume requirements however; its economic scales of manufacture shall create threats with power costs. India should take advantage of its low cost labor and get it to the market.
- *NAFTA:* North American Free Trade Agreement, is a free trade zone for the USA, Canada and Mexico, with 365 million people

as consumers. Trading with the USA has its limitations due to their quota system in their import of textiles. Inter-country trade has no barriers, which creates barriers for outsiders.

- *Mercosul:* Mercosul is a free trade zone joining Brazil, Columbia, and Mexico. Venezuela, Columbia, and Mexico the group three, are forming a free trade zone and these could all join NAFTA.
- ASEAN and SAARC are other attempts at forming free trade zones and only time will tell about their success.

Market evaluation is done on the basis of proximity also as the USA sells maximum to CANADA its immediate neighbor.

International Marketing is started as **Exports** to other countries. In India in the 1960s firms found that their local market is not expanding to the expected level and they have surplus product. It was enough to spur the firm to try and enter the export trade. However, once the Indian market came up, these firms diverted export goods in the then more lucrative local market. This inconsistency of supplies, sporadic at times did no good to the firms or country's export effort. Firms had to build export production capacities like the Bajaj Motors did and they reaped the harvest in terms of export earnings and long range benefits. Some exporting organizations after their initial success, started exporting products of several manufacturers to different countries. The small-scale industry was the first to take up the challenge of exporting from India. Exports help in gaining economies of scale, improving quality to international levels, and Cross Parry.

Cross Parry is defined as a method of fighting competition in India from the foreign firms by hitting them in their own country.

Some took up direct exports like, Bajaj, and they could select from one of the following routes:

- Exports through local export department of the firm
- Overseas branches
- Export travelling sales persons
- Foreign distribution networks
- Overseas liaison offices
- Indian embassies

The normal methods of going international are given below:

Licensing

The next level of international marketing is through Licensing. In licensing the firm gets in to overseas business by giving technology, trade name, brand and process of manufacturing against a fee or/ and royalty to the a local firm, of the country the firm wants to do business with. The firm gains entry in the foreign market without much investment. The firm taking the license gets the technology of manufacturing a well-known brand in the world, a proven technology. India has had a number of such arrangements so far, including Maruti-Suzuki, Alcatel-Modi. Some survived the open market economy of the country; others were bought out by the licensors.

The failure in it can be attributed to the following:

- Low control of the licensor over the local operations
- Sale of some vital components by the licensor to the firm at high prices to make extra profits reducing margins for the firm.
- Licensing can be done without looking at the firm's synergy
- Distrust between the two partners

Franchising

It is more detailed and complete form of licensing. The franchiser provides entire product marketing concepts, branding building plans and processes. The firm pays the franchiser a fee and invests in the venture, like the **MacDonald** franchise arrangements.

Joint Ventures

Two firms, one local and the other foreign join hands and they form a third company to exploit the strengths of the respective firms. It became expedient for entering some countries as the governments of those countries were opposed to foreign firms equity beyond a certain level. Joint ventures suffer because of (a) cultural differences between the two partners, (b) level of expertise required being absent for even absorbing the technology of the foreign firm, (c) difference of opinion in running the firm, (d) financial disagreements.

Fully Owned Foreign Subsidiary

It is usually the last step and is taken after the firm has been in the foreign market for a time and established it there. It is dependent on the local government's policy with respect to investments by foreign firms in the country. Countries like India and china have been the focus of western world as these countries are welcoming **Direct Foreign Investments** in their countries.

Overview of International Marketing

Firms which do not take full advantage of the global opportunities well in time lose their home base as well, as, they will suffer loses by their business being taken over by strong foreign players.

Hence, International Marketing is the process for focussing the firm's resources and its objectives on international opportunities. Each firm has some driving and stimulating forces in this regard as also some restraining forces, like laidback ideas, rigidity of views, fear of the unknown. The fact however, remains that international market provides enormous potential of business. Overall it is the place of perfect competition, lots of sellers and lots of buyers too.

Products sold can be undifferentiated products like, ores and raw materials (sold on the basis of price only.) With differentiated or branded product firms charge higher prices and they sell on their brand equity the world over.

Countries differ from each other in their wealth, GNP, Per Capita Income, Education, religious beliefs, size and their ethnicity. Firms planning global marketing must understand other country's human resources, economics, politics and social situations.

Major assumptions in the international trade are given below:

1. Environment is a determinant in International Marketing. Geography, distances and climatic conditions have an impact on business.
2. Scientific and industrial revolution helps the firm's/business to make things happen even when the environment says no it cannot be done. Technology helps in doing more with less effort.
3. Ways in which the firms do business and produce goods are different in different parts of the world.
4. The statement that, "Firm's country is the best for business" may not remain true with international competition with better products.

We can thus conclude that, **the trend in growth in the world business is a result of the interaction of specific driving and restraining forces. The driving forces must overcome the restraining forces.**

Let us discuss the driving force in the world business. Mainly we can see the supply and demand situation and the gap there in new products, newer needs of old products and world wide communication links like television and the Internet have fuelled the world of business as follows:

- Worldwide TV network and worldwide web have driven the markets. Product information, its usage and advantages from its use are now known the world over through these media.
- Technology helps in reducing human drudgery. Products like washing machines, vacuum cleaners, and microwave ovens are ample proof in this regard.
- Costs—the cost of the product to the customer is usually of vital interest to him. Low cost manufacture with the help of economies of scale, experience curve or better technology all helps the firm in becoming more competitive.
- Quality of the products should meet or exceed the customer requirements. With global sales, firms achieve economies of scale and with large production costs come down with quality remaining the same. Small manufacturers have to compromise on quality to reduce the price, a trade off.
- Communication and transportation technology have broadened the market place as products get known, are demanded and can be transported speedily with modern fast aircrafts.
- Leverage—firm's/country's expertise like for India in the software technology, gets the right leverage for the firm in the international markets.

Given below are the restraining forces in the world market:

- Historical demand of the product in the local market.
- Competition from the countries own business enterprises.
- Management myopia-firms may have shortsighted managers who consider that the profit from the country's market should be enough impetus and going global would be a waste of time and money.
- Organizational culture—at times restrict operations overseas.
- International barriers—some countries do not encourage outsiders to come to their country and do business there.

Today the international markets have progressed because the driving forces are more dominant than the restraining forces. Even then there are two different of firms as given below:

1. In this firm the Marketing Manager decides the firm to be domestic in focus, vision and orientation while he keeps looking for opportunities.
2. In this firm the Marketing Manager focusses the firm for serving the international markets and in developing international strategies to compete with other international firms.

Let us discuss the Economic, Social and Cultúral environment of countries where the firms want to do business and see how they have an impact on the business.

The task of International Marketing Manager is to recognize both the similarities and differences that characterize the economic, social and cultural ethos of the countries of the world and incorporate the perception in to the marketing planning process.

The firm must have a focus on its country's orientation. How is the country better than other countries? The firm may have an egocentric view to focus the areas where it is better than other firms of the world. It can also have similar polycentric view of its country, to focus on the areas where the country is better than other countries of the world. The best is, of course to have a geocentric view, with the dual focus, regarding the firms and country's superiority.

Expanding the theme further we see the following paradigm-

Ethno-centric focus of the home country ⟶ Similarities in foreign countries/dissimilarities in foreign countries to show case the similarities and differences as Competitive Advantage.

Polycentric focus ⟶ home country is unique, locate the differences in foreign countries and either modifies the product as per requirements or use the difference as a competitive advantage.

Region-centric focus ⟶ locates similarity in a world region and plan sales accordingly.

Geo-centric focus ⟶ locates similarities and differences in home and host country.

Let us analyze the strengths of some of the countries:

USA- buys superior products may be with high prices and top quality technology

Latin America buys only from the people with whom they have solid relationships, best rapport. Quality becomes secondary consideration. Contacts are built by the behavior of the firm's people, gestures, words and posture.

In some countries, price and benefits of the product assume great importance. In fact the firm needs to know, who are the customers in a country, what they want and what is important to them.

The economic environment of a country is a major determinant of market potential and opportunity. It is possible to identify distinct stages and formulate estimates about the type of demand that will be found in a country or market of a particular stage of economic development.

The vast difference comes when you notice the under-developed countries, the developing countries and the developed countries. Then there is agrarian society, and highly developed one. In each case the GDP, per capita income differs a great deal as follows:

- High-income countries with per capita income > $12,000. There are 27 countries with population of 818 million.
- Upper middle-income countries with per capita income between $2000 and $12,000. There are 35 countries with population of 912 million.
- Lower middle income countries with per capita income between $400 and $2000. There are 65 countries with population of 1.775 billion.
- Lower income countries with per capita income < $400. There are 42 countries with population of 1.725 billion.

These figures are given only as guidelines and should not be taken as sacrosanct.

In the eighteenth century, most countries of the world were having agrarian economy. It was only after the industrial revolution of the eighteenth century in Europe, which gave the world industrial economy, with assembly line mass production techniques and material wealth. Rich countries today have high productivity per worker, in as much that their labor costs are high too. Poor countries have low labor cost and lower productivity per worker. The following need to be addressed in selecting the markets:

- Population and income
- Number of households
- Climatic conditions
- Price negotiating culture
- Languages spoken

India with large population has good market potential. USA is a bigger market than Brazil. China has come up as a big market with its vast population. Russia as an emerging market provides opportunity to sell high tech. Products.

Cold countries have huge need of heating equipment while warm countries need air conditioners and coolers.

Price has been an important factor in purchase decisions. In several countries the method of price negotiations differ. Small to large gifts (read bribe) are norms in some countries. Inviting the customers of large potential purchase for cocktail parties is prevalent in some countries. However, the firms must know if it is good manner to invite ladies to such parties or not. In most countries, it is advisable to hire a local guide who can tell about the customs of the country and translate the language with all its nuances so that no slip up takes place. Forcing your own will does not necessarily success in business.

The task of the International Marketing Manager is to identify similarities and differences that characterize individuals and cultures of the countries of the world, so that strategies, products and marketing plans are efficiently adapted to global markets.

The plans for expansion by firms should start by comparing, contrasting and analyzing the economic environment of different countries. Marketers should recognize that the economic environment is but one of the several influential factors for analyzing the global market. The culture and social environment need to be considered as well.

Product

The first method used in the international market is selling the same product as sold in the local market. Managers have to find customers for **the product**. Mercedes is one example where the product sold the world over is the same, but in this case also, depending on the country left hand drive or right hand drive cars are sold.

Most products in Japan have to take in to account the fact that Japanese population height is averagely less than that at other places. The following matrix shows how it works:

Table 13.2. International Marketing Plan

Promotion	Do not change product	Adapt product	Develop new product
Do not change promotion	Same product as local market product	Product adaptation	New product invention
Change promotion	Modify communication/ advertisements	Dual adaptation	New product invention

Super markets have been opened in India with some variations. Going to even less developed countries like some African countries some more innovation may be required. In some countries nudity could be permitted in advertising but in most it will not be allowed. Some countries prefer some specific colors , like the Muslim green and the firms must keep it in mind. Advertising mostly need local color and touch, use of local models and festivals for timing the advertising efforts.

Products for the international market—if a product has succeeded in the home country, it cannot be assumed it will do well internationally too. Products are meant to satisfy human needs as per Maslow's hierarchy of needs., physiological, safety, social acceptance, esteem and self actualization. A car is just not a car, it is besides being a means of transportation, is also a reflection of a person's life style.

Local products are meant just for one country, it could be because there is a big demand for it in the home country. AT&T the American telecom giant stayed inside their own country till the last quarter of twentieth century, as there was a large enough market for its products in the USA. Sometimes product specifications differ like voltage requirements in some countries may be different than home country. The following are the reasons for going overseas:

- The firm can utilize its local expertise in the global context and thus improve it.
- Use of experience of one market to further the efforts in other markets.
- Managerial expertise can be better exploited.

International Products: They have the potential of being sold in a number of markets. Industrial products are less dependent on environment and can be exported with greater ease than consumer products. For consumer products product modifications may be needed and the modifications should be cost effective. Large milk bottles were not successful in Japan where in small homes people have small refrigerators, which could not accommodate the large bottle.

Global Products: These are made with global market in mind. Mercedes car sells the same everywhere. Sony's Walkman is another example. The high cost of product development needs to be amortized over a large volume as the global market can provide.

Global brands stick with a common market positioning. Mercedes is in the top bracket of cars everywhere. Heineken beer is positioned worldwide as a premium beverage.

Market Approach: While global products are marketed the same way in the world, some of the Ps like promotion or placement may need to be changed. Advertising campaign must be translated in the local language and at times this is difficult as the subtle nuances of any language are not so easily translatable. The global product/brand must be guided by the same strategic plans and principles. Coke and Pepsi are two examples of global brands. Even then, their tastes differ, as in the east sweeter colas are preferred than in the west.

Price in the Global Market: Following are the pricing considerations for export markets:

- Price—quality parity
- Price competitiveness
- Penetrating or skimming pricing or any other consideration
- Trade discounts, cash discounts and volume discounts needed to be offered in any overseas market
- Segment price differntial required or not
- Price elasticity of demand in the overseas market
- Overseas governments pricing regulations if any
- Any anti-dumping law
- International transportation costs
- International currency fluctuations
- Government tax laws.

International pricing strategy takes costs and competitive pricing in to account. In case the demand of the product is not price elastic, it may be worthwhile to keep high prices.

The total of Fixed and variable costs tend to go up with addition of product adoption costs. Marketing costs could well be much higher as compared to domestic marketing costs. It is best to select a price with highest margins after taking the expenses on channel members and marketing has been accounted for.

Introductory pricing is done on the Cost-plus basis or taking only variable cost in to consideration with only an element of fixed cost. However, if the market is in the growth stage of PLC a higher price can be fixed.

Price

Firms have to be careful in pricing the product in different countries. Import levies, currency rate fluctuations, grey markets and price escalations are areas, which need careful consideration of the firm. Some of the methods used for price fixation are given below:

- Worldwide same price—not really practical if the firm is marketing in both rich and poor countries.
- Prevailing market price—adapt the price at which local vendors are selling the product.
- Modified prevailing price—if the export firm can charge higher price due to its better brand equity it should sell at a higher price as, price get equated with the product quality. Hence if

the firm charges low price or the same as the local vendors price and its product is superior the customers will put it in the same league as the local product.

- Cost plus pricing—it is adapted when the product is far superior and there is no competition worth the name. As there is no basis of competitive pricing the firm can charge higher price on the basis of its cost to make and sell by adding extra amount by way of price of quality and brand equity.

In case of a country going through inflationary phase price increase can be resorted to at regular intervals.

Distribution Channels

When the product is manufactured in one country and sold in another country, the firm selling it has to consider internationalization of channels. The firm may have its marketing center for both local and export sales in its own country. Later on it may start its export marketing office in either of the country to which export is being made or in some third centrally located country. The distance and freight need to be taken into account. The marketing set up would take shape as given below:

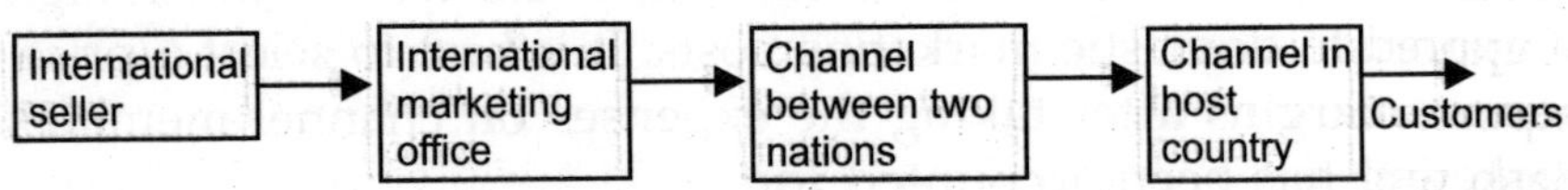

Fig. 13.2. International Channel

For finding the best channel within the host country it is best to have a market survey done, because for different products it could be quite different.

Exceptions can be, if the firm has world monopoly of the product. In the seventies of the twentieth century one firm in the area of electronic components had such a monopoly and the customers were coming to India to buy the product, as the firms dictated prices and distribution in their country on their own.

The first step taken by firms normally is starting exports to designated countries. For the purpose they need to have an export Sales Department with one Export/International Marketing Manager. As the business increases the firm starts offices in host countries as well. Experts who arrange for market surveys, appointment of distribution channel members, market information system, man these offices.

Advertising and Promotion

For international marketing the firm has to decide to have one of the following plans for advertising and promotion:

i. Global strategy where the same advertising and promotion works for the entire world market. Pepsi circle of blue and red is recognized all over the world.

ii. Multi-domestic strategy where the firm allows each country's local management to plan their own advertising and promotion most suited to local conditions, like what Lever Brothers do.

iii. Hybrid strategy where the firm keeps the global perspective and yet alters the advertising and promotion to a limited degree. Most firms change the models in their advertisements. Japanese advertisements are better appreciated with Japanese models.

Market Globalization

Firms usually start marketing their products in their own country, the domestic market. Once established as a known brand and accepted supplier of goods they need to diversify their markets and the first step in that direction is exports to another country. Excess production, which cannot find market in the country of origin, is the starting point of exports. Later on firms do take up special production of goods for exports. Some others build an export bank (inventory) to avoid any clash with the demands of domestic market. Firms have to realize that the product, which is considered as giving value for money and fulfilling customer's needs must do the same in overseas market.

Once the firm wants to get established in the export market, it has to understand the business environment of the foreign country. The four Ps of host country Product, Price, Placement and Promotion may not have the same relevance outside.

In prehistoric times, the city-states traded through barter system. One state had one product while the other had some other product and they both needed the product, which the other had. The same type of advantage in tradable product in one country over the other works well even today, except the scene is much more complex with several countries, myriads of products having global access.

In India exports are firm's imperatives due to following reasons:

- Partial convertibility of rupee, which gives foreign exchanging to exporters they need for their imports for production
- Need to achieve economies of scale of production for lowering costs and making prices competitive for exports too.

- With MNCs getting a foothold in India, firms need to have greater markets, which India cannot provide.
- Intangible benefits are, bettering of product quality, improvements in communication systems.
- Upgradation of technology.
- Cost reduction due to large scale manufacture.
- Utilization of human resources like in IT sector where India has a large workforce.
- Internationalization of Indian brands.

Let us discuss the negative factors of going for exports, which are as follows:

- Low image of the country as a supplier of quality goods. This is gradually changing.
- Firm's culture, which does not give the required fillip to exports.
- Inexperience of international business and the fear of the unknown
- Cultural differences in nations.
- Entry barriers in some countries, their governmental controls and in some cases like the USA, quota system for exporting to that country (e.g. textiles imports in to the USA).

There are some common factors as given below:

- Balance of payment between trading nations
- Stability of their currency
- Transportation costs
- Infrastructure status
- Quality control plans in each country and how these manifest in international trade
- Trading blocks like Euro, NAFTA, ASEAN
- WTO the world body that regulates international trade and settles trade disputes.
- Political instability in some regions
- Economic upheavals of the far east, Japan

Cultural Aspects of Global Business

It is widely believed that culture is not inherent but is learnt. Different areas of culture are interrelated and the areas population shares culture and it differentiates the area from other areas. Culture guides people to respond to situations and since it has been learnt, it is difficult to change. Marketers need to find some common reference point between cultures of different countries, because it is the culture of the country, which defines behavior norms and reactions to out side stimuli given to its people.

The home country objectives of business are dependent on its cultural ethos and transposing them on other country would need defining the cultural ethos of that country. If the marketers try to impose their country's culture on the other country, it may complicate the issue and hence own country's cultural bias must be taken out while formulating objectives of business for other countries. There may be however products which have universal appeal and they would not need any such action.

Product Innovation: In one country the product could be introduced as an innovative product while it may be already in maturity stage in some other country. Product acceptance in new countries takes the following steps:

- Product knowledge or awareness which comes from advertising.
- Interest in the product makes prospective customers to obtain more information about the product.
- Judgment to the value of the product is made at this stage.
- Next step is the trial stage when the customer tries out the product before adopting it.

The rate of adoption of product depends on the following considerations:

- Competitive advantage of the product and also the country from which it is coming like low cost labor, balance of payment situation, currency rates.
- Acceptance of change—some countries like the USA need to change their product all the time while countries like Japan and India prefer to stay with the old products unless some thing of great interest comes along.
- Ease of usage of the product and its compatibility with other products in use.
- Ease of trial helps in making sure of the product usage.
- Availability of information when needed is vital for customer trying to make a change.

Major difference in culture can be seen in the culture of the USA and Japan. While the USA has individualistic management style, Japan's management is based on group decisions.

The following table shows the differences in the two cultures:

Table 13.3. Cultural Differences

Japan	*USA*
Formal indirect business	Direct informal business
Prolonged bargaining	Hard bargaining
More stability in jobs	Top management shifts
Bargain is a long drawn out process	Persistent bargaining

International marketers must take the cultural factors in to account to succeed in their business.

International Market Research

The secondary data available for different countries are not compatible and its comparison can pose problems. Consumer expenditure in Germany is taken from turnover receipts and in the USA, household surveys and production sources also add to the information base. International, market research has to take multiple countries in to account and consider each country's unique market situations. In low profit markets a major research could prove expensive. In many underdeveloped countries, data availability is scarce and not reliable.

International research needs the following rules:

- Ask yourself, what information do I need?
- Where can I get it- files, library or database?
- Why do I need the information?
- When do I need it?
- What is the money value of the information to me?
- What would be the cost of ignorance?

Start with secondary research by using libraries, online database, trade associations and government publications. Find out from foreign embassies about the information available from their countries. Crosscheck piece of information from several sources.

Survey research—it is conducted by using a questionnaire and asking questions from potential customers. The questionnaires should be simple, easy to be answered and recorded. Questions should be clear and to the point.

The research should give the following information:

- Demand analysis is dependent on country's gross national product, per capita income. Low-income countries are more on core products like food, clothing's. With high-income countries heavy industries start emerging.

- Income elasticity of demand can be found out both for consumer and industrial products. Basic necessities do not have much of income elasticity, while luxuries demand change with income changes.

Country's entry barriers are listed below and these will confirm whether or not market is conducive for entry.

- Government regulations regarding foreign firms
- Low infrastructure like telephones, power, roads railways and ports
- Poor availability of raw materials
- High cost of money, borrowing rates
- High rate of import duties

International Monetary Fund was created under the auspices of the United Nations Organization. It is the body, which regulates smooth to compensate for balance of payment deficits. SDRs are assets allotted by the IMF on the basis of country's GDP and share of world trade.

Foreign exchange is the currency sold or bought in the foreign exchange market. The transaction takes place as given below:

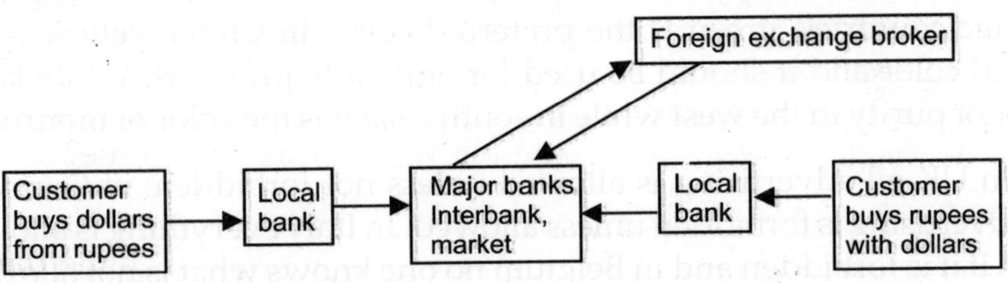

Fig. 13.3. International Finance Dealings

Local banks major tasks in the international business are handling money. The most common form of money transactions is the Letter of Credit LC. LC can be of the following types:

- Revocable LC with recourse
- Revocable LC without recourse
- Irrevocable LC with recourse
- Irrevocable LC without recourses
- Part shipment allowed or not

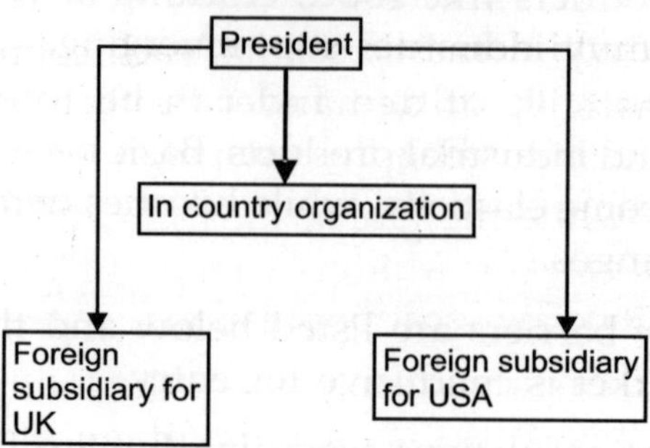

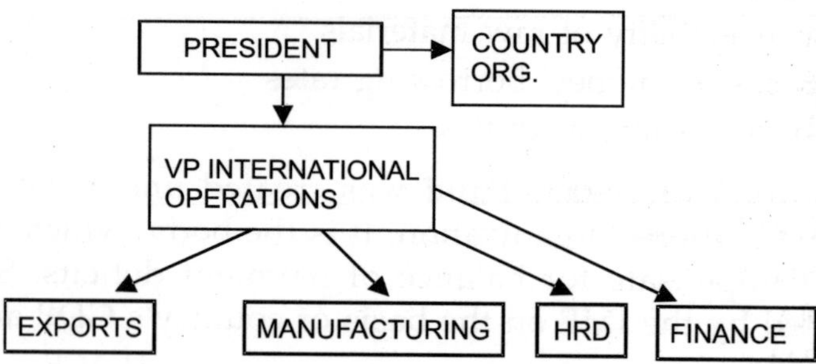

Fig. 13.4. Exports Organizations

Global Communications- advertising in the international market must take the country's cultural ethos in to account. For example, in Islamic countries, green is the preferred color. In China, yellow is the sacred color and it should be used for only holy products. White is the color of purity in the west while in south Asia it is the color of mourning.

In UK all advertising is allowed unless not forbidden; in Germany all advertising is forbidden unless allowed. In Italy everything is allowed even if it is forbidden and in Belgium no one knows what is not allowed.

Advertising takes three forms in the international market as given below:

1. Global
2. Multi-domestic
3. Hybrid

In global advertising one campaign is planned and used globally whereeever the firm is selling the product. Mercedes car is a typical example as the same car sells without any modification and same advertising goes with it.

In contrast, in multi-domestic selling, each country plans its own campaign according to its culture. Lever Brothers give total freedom to local management regarding the campaign.

In hybrid plan while the global idea remains each country can change to suit its market. Models can be of local ethnicity and metaphors, understood by local population.

Countries spend on advertising as per the following table giving the advertising expenditure as a percentage of country's Gross National Product:

Table. 13.4. International GNP & Advertising

USA	2.02
SWEDEN	1.88
NETHERLANDS	1.77
UK	1.74
SWITZERLAND	1.59
AUSTRALIA	1.37
INDIA	0.3
NEPAL	TRACE

Russia has become a nation of rich and the poor. The rich Russians are looking for new products. They see a lot of TV and are happy even with second hand goods. The best way to advertising in Russia is as follows:

- Provide exact information
- Give usage detail
- New kinds of products
- Concept selling
- Life style products

In China outdoor advertising is used. For product demonstrations Chinese want to see the TV ads. Testimonials by experts are favored too.

While selecting an Advertising Agency, following needs to be considered:

- Indian agency with foreign collaboration or foreign agency with office in India
- Some countries go by nationalistic approach like in Canada it is a good idea to appoint a local agency. Local agencies provide the subtle nuances of local culture and language as also goodwill of the target market.

Marketing Channels

In order to decide the most effective channel the firm must consider the market segment it wants to cater to end the product positioning in the market. Channel selection should reflect firm's strengths and competitive advantages. In the beginning it is correct to use similar channels as already in use by the competition. Distributors should be selected on the basis of their experience with similar products, commitment to the firm's objectives and financial and human resources for the task. Trainability of their staff in selling the product is useful. If they can provide after sales service it would be an added advantage.

The distributors normally appoint retailers, but initially it is a good idea to approve their appointment to ensure long-term profitable association with them.

For industrial products firm should look for technically oriented distributors. They will then be able to supplement firm's salespersons efforts in a positive way.

Following graph gives the relative importance of advertising and personal selling, either by firm's salesperson or distributor's:

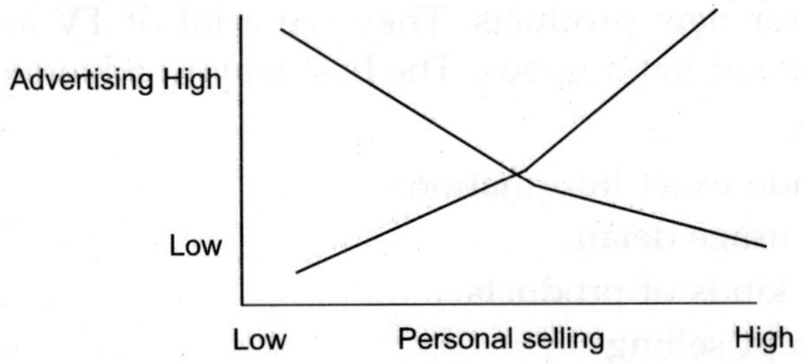

Fig. 13.5. Personal Selling *vs* Advertising

Consumer products ————

Industrial products ————

In most developing countries, the age-old distribution systems are valid as given below:

- Sole distributors
- Area distributors
- Dealers
- Agents
- Stockists

- C&F Agents
- Retailers
- Firm's own shops
- Franchise outlets
- Super stores

In developed nations distribution through new channels like the Internet, tele-shoping, personal door to door selling are gaining popularity.

Question for discussion—Time is the essence of success in business. What needs to be done must be done with a sense of urgency and therefore, it is imperative for the firm to keep a continuous scan of the environment factors, both general and competitive, and take proactive decisions for continued success. Otherwise, the firms will remain in the fire-fighting mode all the time trying to cope up with the immediate and current problems and will not be able to take advantage of the opportunities the business environment keeps generating all the time. Discuss the statement.

Marketing Game

The teams should discuss with some personnels of the company under review to find out the qualitative strengths of their workers and their learning standards. Organizations must be in learning stage if it wants to maintain and increase its market share and brand equity. Hence organizational analysis is the most important area, which should be analyzed with care. Viewing the behaviour pattern of its people can help assess the organizational culture; do they look up and about moving with a purpose, or are they having a laidback attitude towards the firm and its results. Are all they members of the firm committed to the vision, mission, goals and objectives of the firm? These soft areas of a firm are candid reflections of the direction the firm is going to take.

The better-managed firms permeate a positive sense of urgency in the managers. They keep comparing their own results with the results of their competitors. They keep raising the bar of excellence to push themselves to better performance, even if they are the best in the business. Innovation, creativity form the bedrock of their enthusiastic working energy, which separates the winners from non-winners.

CHAPTER 14

Strategic Audit

AIMS AND OUTCOMES OF THE CHAPTER

There are four main components of strategic audit as given below, and are discussed in some detail for ease of reader's understanding:

1. Marketing Concepts
2. Behaviour Concepts
3. Financial Analysis
4. Balance Sheet

The chapter deals with the concepts to provide an in depth knowledge on the subject through practical experience to the students.

MARKETING

The marketing strengths of a firm are the most important single factor for its success. Firms selling the entire produce at a reasonable profit, increasing sales of the same product portfolio, selling at a higher price or successfully developing new products and selling them too profitably would not face serious problems. Evaluating the marketing strengths of the firm the following areas are examined:

- Marketing environment—markets, customers, brand equity, competition levels, economic trends, money supply position in the market, legal issues, and social developments, causes and problems besetting the market.
- Marketing action—products, pricing, distribution channels, advertising and promotion, and personal selling, publicity.

The real questions to be asked during audit are sunmarized below:

- Customers primary and secondary levels of satisfaction derived from the product; the idea of PRODUCT as sold by the firm and the customers viewpoint about what PRODUCT he is purchasing.

- Environmental issues shaping the markets, competition and the customers.
- Firms special skills as compared to competition in marketing.
- Marketing problems and opportunities the firm is facing today and may have to face in the future.

Environmental Threats and Opportunities

In the dynamics of country's economics, firms must understand that the changing conditions will make some markets more amenable than the others. Firms need to have constant vigil in the following areas:

- *Law and Politics:* Government regulations can change product emphasis in the market; a recent example being the stopping of sales of cars not conforming to the Euro emission norms. Other examples are, Government of India disinvestments in some prominent firms, their Volunteer Retirement Scheme, the famous VRS, price regulation of some commodities and at times deregulation of prices. These effect the business of some firm or the other.
- *Competition:* Competitive action needs continuous attention, especially if the market is an oligopoly one. Remaining proactive on competitive product launches, new pricing, advertising and promotion would help the firm in retaining their market share and in even increasing it.
- *Suppliers:* Oligopoly supply firms tend to have the edge and they keep changing the prices (always to the higher side), and other terms of business to their advantage. Firms, which have diversified vertically, are at a distinct advantage over others. It is therefore necessary for firms to keep a constant vigil on supply scene and always keep more than one supplier for vital raw materials.
- *Demographics:* Population composition is changing; there is a large teenage group, a large population of senior citizens and migration of workers from villages to towns is a continuous phenomenon. These all, present business opportunities.
- Alternate products are available with better technology (electric shavers became popular for a while in the 1970–1980 period); lower air fare prompt train travelers to go by air.
- Understanding the product location in it's life cycle is important to understand the behavior of competitors who could be market leaders or market laggards. The firms have

their own priorities with regard to placing the product in a particular segment. Competitive information can lead the firm to a vigilant proactive decision in terms of its own products business plan.

- *Understanding the Consumer:* Consumer needs, their buying patterns and habits, purchase decision triggers, and the answers to the five W and one H questions is required—what they buy, why they buy, where they buy it from, when they buy, which price they buy at, and finally how they buy. In the normal circumstances, when the firm is making a profit and selling its entire produce these questions become irrelevant. It is only when new technology competitive product swamps the market, the firm does not know what hit it. Maslow's hierarchy of needs and the Freudian theory of desires must be addressed to plan market policies. A car is just not a means of transportation alone; it could reflect the owner's status. Mercedes is bought more as a status symbol than for any other purpose. Firms do better if they understand consumer behavior in their selected market segments for the product.

Market Segmentation

In the first half of the twentieth century the firms stress used to be on production and what ever was produced was sold, competition was either not there or it was just not enough, with market for all the players in the field. With severe competition from international players, each selling multiple brands and models, it would be futile for firms to sell in the mass market. The segment variety needs different selling techniques, advertising messages and what works for one segment may not work for the other. Product, price promotion and placement all need different strategies for different segments. Segmentation is done on the following lines:

Table 14.1. Market Segments

Demographic Variables	*Geographic Variables*
• Age	• Country
• Sex	• Climate
• Family size	• City size
• Children's ages	• State
• Occupation	• Population density
• Income	• Country's main religions
• Education	
• Religion	
• Social status	

Psychographics Variables	*Product Usage Variables*
• Life Style	• Heavy users
• Personality	• Light users
• Product loyalty	
• Product awareness	

Strategic audit should trace the firm's growth and standing in the market place, which can be done on the following parameters:

- *Market Growth:* (i) same product increased sales through penetrating prices and increased efforts of the marketing team, (ii) Same product sales increase in extension of geographic areas, (iii) New or improved product in the same geographic area.
- *Acquisitions:* Involves investments of available funds of cash rich firms in product or business diversification by acquiring other firms, business. Diversifications can be vertical or horizontal depending on whether the firm has bought into its supplier or a product with which it has some synergy.
- Distribution channels—ability of selection of the type of distribution network as also the actual dealers of the product to cover the geographic segments is of vital importance for the success of the firm, especially for consumer goods. It is the last link in the chain connecting the manufacturer to the consumer and the only one which gets the buyer money in exchange of goods supplied.
- Pricing policy are governed by the following considerations:
  a. Elasticity of demand—does the price change affect the product demand or not; the firm if they are marketing in multiple segments must be fully aware of the demand changes in each segment on variation of price.
  b. Government price regulations—in some products the government has its own price mechanism, especially in the food and drugs, and the firms must take this into consideration while fixing the price
  c. Competitors—price becomes a function of competitive pricing, unless the firm can claim a higher price based on their better brand equity.
  d. Pricing and promotions—short term extra benefits are given to customers, which reduce the profits for the firm, but gain additional market share. Such increases are mostly short lived as they invite competitive reaction nullifying the increase in

the market share. At times the commission given to the channel members change as the firm expects the channel members to pass on the benefits to the customers, putting a smoke screen before competitors, giving the impression that they are not involved in any price war on their own.

e. Price and quality—for premium quality goods high prices can be kept with high brand equity, for low quality goods keeping high prices could be the means of getting quick profits before competition catches on. Keeping low prices of high quality products would mean generic product, high growth market and firms wanting to improve its market share. Low quality low price would be for bargains and discounts often times to unload extra inventory.

f. Product strategy—it should take the product's brand equity, stage of its life cycle, competitive products, production capacity or product availability (heavy advertising and promotion will fall flat if the product is not available, unless the firm is trying to create artificial scarcity to increase demand.

g. Advertising and promotion—creating product awareness, leading to interest in owning it can be generated through intelligent use of advertising, which does not over sell the product and remains in the realm of plausibility. Besides, personal selling, publicity and promotion have definite roles to play in market communications. The audit judges the efficacy of these communications with the market segment.

Organizational Behaviour

In a firm people work, individually, in teams and there is interaction between people, which is both sideways and two ways vertical. Instructions from one side, reports from the other and overlap of authority and work jurisdiction create conflicts, which if not nipped in the bud become gigantic problems for the management of the firm. Hence the importance of organizational behaviour has assumed great importance in the success of the firm and it needs separate study, which is undertaken in the following manner:

- Manager, supervisor and worker—individual behavior depends on the persons education, knowledge base, skills, experience relevant to his present situation in the firm, family back ground, family life, any negative history (say, of violence).
- Energy and motivation levels—extra money, perquisites, promotions, better working conditions, good health, growth

prospects are the motivating factors, while the opposites are factors that sap the energy. To understand the trigger points of what really motivates an employee helps in proper alignment of these factors. For example, a supervisor may be better motivated if instead of Rs. 2000 extra pay, he is given a company run motorcycle. The strategic audit should look from the Maslow's hierarchy of human needs point of view and the correct motivation points will emerge on their own.

- Attitudes towards the firm and each other—people perceive events, actions and even ideas differently, depending their own mindset of the moment. Employees' biases can be the eye openers for the management, which can help in team formations, identifying the lead players, motivators and de-motivators.
- Team work—as teams are formed, they go through the storming process where individual expectations, frustrations, strong beliefs are brought out in the open. Later on norming process takes place when the team starts performing. Firstly the team is like a group of people; what gels them into a team is the common goal, the unitary direction they all need to take, even while performing multifarious tasks connected with their goal. The problems in group work arise due to the following reasons, which must be considered during the audit.
  a. In teams even intelligent people, experts, tend to take the easy way out to remain non controversial as they believe that accolades or blame would all be shared by the team.
  b. At times individuals by habit or because they have an axe to grind dominate the team and get the decisions based on their plans.
  c. Team members tend to shy away from voicing opinion to show solidarity with what the management has created as an elite team.

Team controls—there are power groups within the teams, which dominate it; in order to resolve this issue the firm has to consider the following:

- The team leader may plan reward and punishment system for its members.
- Team can be controlled by the leader's charisma, his work style, his sense of fairness, his farsightedness and his tolerance level for mediocrity.

- Teams can be controlled by thorough planning where each task is well defined and assigned to the person capable of performing it even with a stretch.

Financial Analysis

The audit must take into account of the fact that financial analysis is the starting point of the audit, as also of management decision-making process. Considering the entire picture is a massive tasks; the audit should take only the most relevant figures, accept the limitations of the study and then only give the recommendations.

Income and Balance Sheet

The balance sheet is the mirror image of the firm as it reflects its strengths and weaknesses, at a given point of time, usually at the end of the financial year of the firm, which is 31st March for most Indian firms. From the audit view point monthly trial balance, which may even be un audited by the firm's statutory auditors, would suffice. The balance sheet gives the firms resources, its debt and equity base, its assets and liabilities. It tells about the financial health of the firm. The audit could define and also design the resource needs of the firm and its justifiable allocation.

Business Audit Check List

The checklist covers the essential points of any business plan or strategic audit. All the points are not relevant for every firm. Certain points are for start up firms, others for on going firms. Certain points are for service industries as compared to product firms. There is a separate list for firms offering equity to the market.

The check would be found useful in the following areas:

- Preparing a comprehensive business plan by presenting the required relevant information on the format as per the check list.
- As a questionnaire while interviewing firms employees to gather information to prepare documents needed for strategic audit.
- For evaluating the business plan or the firm's strategies as it provides specific points for evaluation. It is not required that the check list format is adhered to completely but the evaluators would find it appropriate to stick to the check list to the extent possible.

Summary Check List

1. Brief statements on the firm
2. Activities

3. Management
4. Performance
5. Special features of products or service
6. Market growth
7. Financial projections
8. Amount of money needed now
9. Form in which the money is needed, equity debt or both
10. Purpose of the funds needed
11. Is the proposal made by the firm so far understood by the evaluator?
12. Is it interesting enough?
13. Will it stimulate investments?
14. Background of the firm in the business
15. Business intending to enter
16. Products/services
17. Prospective customers
18. Physical area of operations
19. History of the firm; when was it formed?
20. Product selection methods
21. Business development process and roles played by the CEO and other top managers in it.
22. Present plans of business expansion—sales
23. Profits
24. Return on investments
25. Information on setbacks and losses
26. Type and extent of losses and plans for avoiding recurrences
27. Information missed out in the questions so far
28. Current status and prospects of the industry
29. Main competitors
30. Competitors performance
31. Competitors profit and loss
32. Competitors forecast for the year regarding sales and planned profits
33. New entrants and exiting firms with reasons for both
34. Major trends affecting business
35. Economic trends
36. Social trends
37. Technological trends
38. Regulatory trends

39. Features and Advantages of Products and Services, what is sold, customer benefits, drawbacks and business opportunities
40. Description of products in demand, what needs they will satisfy
41. Diagrams, pictures, sketches
42. Distinctive features as compared to competition
43. Advantages feature wise
44. Disadvantages feature wise
45. Proprietary position
46. Patents
47. Trade secrets
48. Other proprietary features
49. Product early launch and its advantages
50. Potential
51. Extension of product line
52. Development of related products and services
53. Market Research & Analysis-will market support the sales target?
54. Customers
55. Who are the buyers?
56. Wherefrom they buy the products
57. Why do they buy the products
58. When do they buy the products
59. Is there seasonality in business
60. Rank by customer value
61. Price
62. Quality
63. Service
64. Personal contacts
65. Political pressure
66. Master list of customers and prospective customers
67. Reason of the firms customers interest in the product
68. Customers dropped or having no interest now.
69. And reasons thereof (of no interest)
70. Plans for overcoming the negative reactions
71. Market size and trends
72. Size of the market segment
73. Numbers of product on demand
74. Demand in rupees
75. Source of information

76. Is the information from the dealers, sales team, customers
77. Next three years demand projection, factors affecting the demand
78. Industry trends
79. Technological developments
80. New or changing customer needs
81. Review the previous trends
82. Differences between past and present trends
83. If there is no change in trends identify the reasons thereof
84. Competition
85. Competitive products and services
86. Strengths
87. Weaknesses
88. Data for competitive analysis
89. Product comparison with the competitors
90. Price
91. Performance
92. Service
93. Warranties
94. Other features
95. Table used or not
96. Competitors management strengths
97. Marketing strengths
98. Operational strengths
99. Finance strengths
100. Recent trends in market share
101. Sales
102. Profitability
103. If competition has failed why the firm can succeed
104. Why customers buy from more than 2 or 3 competitors
105. Strategy for taking customers from competitors
106. Estimated market share and sales
107. Major customers ready to buy from the firm
108. Extent of commitment in numbers and rupees
109. Estimated market share in numbers and rupees
110. Market share in the next two years and by quarter
111. Last two years sales
112. Correlation with assessment of customers

Marketing Plan Check List

1. How the firm plans to achieve the sales target
   a. Sales and service policies
   b. Pricing policy
   c. Distribution plan
   d. Advertising and promotion plan
   e. What is to be done, when and by whom
   f. Public relations plans

Design and Development Check List

a. Feedback from market research on product specifications and demand
b. Time and costs involved
c. Engineering, industrial and aesthetic design plan
d. Special tooling
e. Manpower and equipment needed
f. Software and hardware required
g. New skills needed

Costs Planning

a. Labor
b. Materials
c. Consultants fees
d. Contingency plan on expenses

Operations Plan

a. Plant location
b. Location of major businesses
c. Availability of labor, wage structure, unions
d. Taxation
e. Transport
f. Communication links
g. Power and water availability
h. Raw materials and components
i. Land and construction costs

Capital and Working Capital

a. Debt equity ratio
b. Capital base

c. Promoters capital
d. Detailed project report
e. Overheads
f. Profit planning
g. Profit and loss forecast for the next 3 years
h. Three years cash flow projections
i. ROI, Profit on sales percentage
j. Cash flow with price increase and decrease
k. Ability to attract finance from the market and financial institutions

MANAGEMENT TEAM

a. Key personnel education experience and training
b. Staff in different departments
c. Organization structure
d. Duties, authorities and responsibilities of key people
e. Role of consultants
f. Profit, productivity, reduction in operating costs; living within the budget benchmarking the performance of key people
g. Plans for training
h. Persons showing leadership qualities
i. Management compensation packets, stock options
j. Employee turnover,
k. Board of Directors, their background
l. Management check points, controls, PERT, BAR CHARTS

MARKETING GAME

Quantitative Analysis

It is done to understand the viability of the firm and its intrinsic strengths and weaknesses. A close look at the P&L Statement and the firm's balance sheet for the past few years gives a clear picture. The following ratios need to be seen:

- Liquidity ratios—
    i. Current ratio = current assets/current liabilities (availability of current assets to pay current liability)
    ii. Quick ratio = current assets—inventory/current liabilities (ability to pay current liabilities and inventories through current assets)
    iii. Cash ratio = cash and cash equivalents/current liabilities (availability of cash to pay current liabilities)

iv. Inventory to net working capital = inventory/current assets—current liabilities (affect of changes in inventories on playability from current assets)

- Profitability ratios—
  i. Net profit margin = net profit after tax/net sales
  ii. Gross profit margin = sales—cost of goods/net sales
  iii. Return on investment = net profit after taxes/total assets (rate of return, management efficiency indicator)
  iv. Return on equity = net profit after taxes/shareholders equity
- Activity ratios—
  i. Inventory turnover = net sales/inventory
  ii. Assets turnover = sales/total assets
  iii. Account receivable turnover = annual credit sales/account receivable
  iv. Fixed asset turnover = sales/fixed assets
- Leverage ratio—
  i. Debt equity ratio = total debts/shareholders equity
  ii. Current liability to equity ratio = current liability/shareholders equity
  iii. Earnings per share = total dividend declared/number of shares in the market with shareholders

Besides it is important to know the following:

1. Firm's ability to raise additional capital
2. Cost of the capital
3. Relationship with creditors and stockholders
4. Dividend policy
5. Match between resources and usage of funds

These analyses would certainly throw up improvement opportunities in the firm. Financial comparisons should be made with the following:

- Firm's own historical figures,
- Industry norms
- Besting the line, the benchmarks.

CHAPTER 15

Case Studies

Understanding Case Studies

Case studies help the students and the readers of the book to relate to the practical aspects of the theories given in the book. In fact the students can analyze the information given, find alternative solutions, assess the best option and then give their recommendations on the case. It would be the task for the teacher or the guide, to steer the students on the right path enabling them to arrive at the best recommendations. The following method is suggested for arriving at the recommendation stage:

- Read the case cursorily in the first stage
- Study any figures or tables provided in the case
- Analyze the figures
- Study the case in detail again
- Use the tools available for analyzing the case
- Write down rough report
- Discuss the rough report with your guide
- Make final report on the basis of the discussions.

Final report should have the following elements in it:

- Title page
- Acknowledgements page where you express your gratitude to those who helped you in the case analysis
- Table of contents with page numbers
- Executive summary of the recommendations on the case
- Brief information on the case
- Tools you are planning to use in the case study
- Case analysis
- Recommendations (with possible expected results, if possible) and conclusions

- Glossary of important words used
- Bibliography of written matter used in the case study

The students must understand that while solving case studies there is no absolutely right or wrong answer. The areas to look for are the following:

- The student has understood the case, its problem areas well
- The student is using the right tools in solving the case
- The student has analyzed the figures and tables given in the case (if any)
- The student has presented his recommendations in a forthright unambiguous manner.
- The recommendations need not be many, but they should be hard hitting and direct
- The recommendations must arise out of the case analysis, the tools used. Any major deviation, which is not explicitly mentioned in the case, must be stated clearly with reasons for the same.

Case Study No.1: Faith Tyre Company

Relationship Marketing

Ram had just joined the Faith Tyre Company as the head of marketing. He had to make friends with the automobile manufacturers purchase managers. His major customer was the large vehicle maker Zed Cars. Zed cars purchase manager Madan was a tough customer, very upright and a hard taskmaster. He wanted every thing as per his own ideas and any change or delay could result in Faith losing the business. Ram had been advised by his MD, that he should handle Madan carefully else there will be major problems for the firm as also for Ram. He decided to make a personal visit to know Madan better and took an appointment with him. The following conversation took place after the initial pleasantries.

Madan, "So you are the new salesman at Faith. Frankly I have been losing faith in the Faith Company. The deliveries are delayed, billings are wrong. In fact the list of my complaints is virtually endless. Anyway, since you are new I cannot possibly put the blame on you. I will give you just two months to amend the situation. Otherwise you know there are other better tyre people in the market."

Ram, "Perhaps you are right. Anyone who gets such treatment as you have described to me would feel let down. Let me just reassure you that while I am not a wonder worker, you will, in the next three months, get the best service any tyre company can provide in the country."

Madan, "What about the defective tyres we have returned to you? In the first place why should you be sending such tyres to us? Secondly, what about replacements, or at least a credit note to cover the cost of the tyres?"

Ram, "Sir, permit me to put some facts before you. When we explained the latest development in tyre technology to your Quality engineers, they have not only accepted all the tyres, but given us a green signal for using the same technology for future dispatches too. I am sure you too must have read about the bubble barrier technology prevalent in the west."

Madan, "Good. Now I would like to discuss new prices for our next order for the next year supplies. Are you ready for the same? Incidentally, tomorrow, the salesman from Keats tyres your main competitor is coming to see me."

Notes for the Students—

1. Where do you think the tyre sales people have been missing out on the customer to make him almost inimical towards the firm?

2. When there is a change in marketing personnel, what sort of guidance, introduction, orientation should be given to the new sales person?
3. In B-to-B business what are the options available to the sellers for building relationships with their customers?

Guide for the Students—

- Marketing person should take prior appointment for meetings with the customers irrespective of the level of person they have to meet. This gives the person importance, a little ego boosting, while it helps, in most cases the marketing person getting undivided time and attention of the customer.
- Marketing person should ALWAYS be on time or a few minutes early for the meeting. This spare time lets the person become composed, collect his wits and arrange his talk properly.
- Marketing person should be wearing clean dress, not flashy but sober business suit, should be well- groomed and impeccable in manners.
- He should be good listener to become a good conversationalist.
- He should carry the required documents, testimonials, and sales records and not leave anything for the next call. Most of all he should be carrying his visiting cards.
- If the buyer has become friendly it may be a good idea to invite him for a dinner or luncheon meeting. Take him away from his office in a neutral more friendly, peaceful place and it would add to building the relationship. If the marketing person is meeting the customer for the first time, it is a good idea to do some background research on the customer, his habits, likes and dislikes. Genuine praise helps while flattery may create a barrier between the two.
- There is a thin line between bribery and gift, and the customer's perception of the difference between the two. Marketing person should know it and use to his advantage.
- Newsletters, yearly calendars, dairies are worth considering. At festival time gifts are exchanged between friends and relatives. These opportunities can be exploited as in many cases the customers are even expecting the gifts.
- Trying to be a genuine friend, who helps when help is required can make a big difference between being one of the sellers and being the friend and a seller.

Let us categories the customers as follows:

- Users of FMCG Products
- Dealers in FMCG Products
- Buyers of consumer durables
- Dealers in consumer durables
- Industrial buyers
- Industrial distributors
- Services buyers

Customer and Client: The difference between a customer and a client can be defined as follows:

When there is only one to one relationship between the user and the supplier, the user is the client and not a customer. On the contrary, if there are large numbers of users or buyers, they are the customers. In relationship marketing the idea is to try and convert as many of the customers in to clients as possible, as then individual attention can be provided and the buyers become more loyal, as a spin off.

Now let us demonstrate the methods by which firms can conduct relationship marketing for the customer groups—

FMCG Users-since these are in large numbers, it is most difficult task to build relationships with them. However, in these days of cut throat competition, firms have devised ways of doing just that. Product promotion like, "open the package and you may be the lucky winner of a gold ear ring." Those who get the earring become loyal customers and others remain loyal in the hope of getting the earring. Hence, relationship, although a loose one is developed between the seller and the buyer. For heavy users, "buy two and get one free" becomes the binding force.

Dealers in FMCG Products-Relationship between the seller and the channel member for FMCG Products are based on the profit the dealer / retailer can make by selling the product. Sales depend on utility value, quality and availability of the product. Hence, if the seller can provide a product, much in demand of good quality and having VALUE FOR MONEY, it would surely build good custom as also a good relationship between the channel and the seller. Better discounts, handling of complaints, effective advertisement in the right media help build business for the channel member. Next, the seller can train the sales persons of the retailers to build the **RELATIONSHIP.**

Buyers of consumer durables- as consumer durables are not purchased often; it is of great importance that the buyers keep a good healthy attitude towards the product. This is possible by using the following plan:

- Supplying quality product
- Offering speedy after sales service to the satisfaction of the customer.
- Making accessories and spare parts available when and where needed
- Publishing and distributing free newsletters to the customers giving them new product information, new researches in the area
- Organizing special events like cultural programs where the buyers are invited
- Making them special offers, promotional program offers before offering them to the public.

Dealers in consumer durables—profit and profit potential are the two motivating factors for the dealers in consumer durable goods. Turnover discounts, target based incentives can play a vital role in building relationship with these dealers. Firms are known to give interesting and expensive gifts to the dealers. Dealers could be multi-brand sellers and the firm offering greater incentive will get better business from them. Paid foreign holidays, luxury cars or equivalent cash are some of the methods used by the sellers to keep the dealers loyal to them.

Industrial buyers-industrial purchase decisions are often taken by a team consisting of, the purchase manager, technical manager, R&D Manager, finance manager, the ultimate user of the product and the CEO of the firm. A good brand image/equity of the firm helps in building relations. Frequency of visits, timely redress of complaints, JIT supplies, help a lot in building the relationship. Additionally, dinners with the families, outings, picnics, and gifts on birthdays of the spouse and children, assistance in any official or personal problem go a long way in that direction.

CASE STUDY NO.2: ARYAN LUBRICANTS

Rattan was the smart sales person for Aryan Lubricants. He was popular with his customers as also with his own team. His greatest challenge was that next to his housing complex lived the owner of the biggest industrial giant of the north India and the entire business of that group was with the major competitor of Aryan. Incessant attempts to gain even an appointment with the Purchase Manager had been futile.

One day, as Rattan was returning home after a day's hard work, near the crossing a large car came from the right and before he could swerve his Maruti it hit his car. Rattan had lost a big sale and was in a bad mood. He got out of his car and went to the driver of the big car hoping to get him to pay for the damage. He saw the owner of the industrial group Shiva come out of the car, Shiva gave him his card and said, "I am sorry for the accident. Please get the car repaired and send the bill to me. I will have it paid".

Rattan replied, composing himself, "sir, it does not matter at all. My insurance will cover for the repair expense. I am happy to have met you."

Shiva, "In that case be my guest. Come over to my house. Better still come to my industrial complex and we will chat some more."

Rattan thanked him and sure enough in the earliest opportunity went to Shiva's office. He was called to his chambers instantly. The two discussed the state of country's policy and Rattan came out after thanking him for his time and accepting his invitation to come again with his family.

Such visits continued for nearly two months and Rattan never even mentioned about his business or his interest in getting business from Shiva. Rattan had given his visiting card to Shiva during first meeting itself and was hoping for an opening from Shiva's side. He had taken his wife to meet the family in Shiva's bungalow who had promised to reciprocate soon. After a week a call came from Shiva that he planned to bring his wife to Rattan's house that evening.

That day as Shiva was entering Rattan's house he saw the nameplate announcing that Rattan was the Marketing Manager of Aryan Lubricants.

Sipping coffee, Shiva said, "Rattan you are from Aryan and yet you never once mentioned the fact to me. How come? Don't you want our business at all?"

Rattan replied, "I definitely wanted the business and made several efforts in the direction. However, after becoming your friend I thought you might not want to mix business with friendship, and I certainly would not like to lose your friendship".

Shiva, "That is really admirable. And yet, now let me do my bit for you. Please go and meet my Purchase Manager at 10 AM tomorrow".

Next day a trial order for about ten percent demand was waiting Rattan when he reached the Purchase Manager's office. How Rattan converted the ten percent order in to hundred percent is another story of salesmanship.

Questions—

1. Was Rattan right in not asking for business immediately on becoming Shiva's friend?
2. What actions would need to be taken for converting ten percent in to hundred percent, considering a strong reaction from the competitor who had lost the order? Is relationship enough for this increase and for sustaining the business in future? Don't forget that earlier also; the competitor must have built some good relationship with the customer.
3. Does relationship always get the firm business?

CASE STUDY NO. 3: JAGS ELECTRONICS

Jags Electronics is a large manufacturer of electronic and telecom products. They have a workforce of three thousand and yearly turnover of Rupees thousand crore. Besides three factories, they also have a major research facility. Jags have a rule that any new vender or a new product must be approved by the research engineers, before can be inducted in the products.

Megaton is a producer of components and other products like test instruments needed by Jags. Megaton was having a difficult time in getting any approvals even though their products were not only acceptable but also just right for Jags. Marketing Manager Ramesh was in real dilemma as to what should be his next action.

One morning after taking an appointment with Dr. Kaushal, Ramesh had reached the R&D Labs well in time. There was no sign of Dr. Kaushal. After waiting for nearly half an hour he was about to leave when he found Kaushal, red in the face with two-day beard, running towards his chamber.

Ramesh said, "There seems to be some problem. Can I be of some help?"

Dr. Kaushal, "Oh, so you have come. See, I am in great hurry. I came here only to take some cash lying in my office and may borrow some from my friends. My son is seriously sick in the hospital and of all days only today my car had to conk out. Anyway, please allow me to proceed and we shall meet again."

Ramesh, "please stop. I think I have the answer to all your problems. See I am free today and my car is in your car park. I am carrying extra cash of about forty thousand which I can loan to you without hesitation or problem."

Dr. Kaushal, "are you sure? Then what are we waiting for? Let us get out of here and head for the hospital."

For the next three weeks Ramesh attended the hospital daily till Kaushal's son became all right. On the day he was being discharged Ramesh brought flowers, pen set, chocolates school bag as gifts for the son which were not be refused by Kaushal.

Need it be said that in all future cases Ramesh's products were taken up for quick approval and seldom rejected. Even when they were rejected it was only for a temporary period for minor changes.

Questions—

1. Was Ramesh right in neglecting his other assignments for being with Kaushal and his son?
2. Was it ethical to loan his company's money to Kaushal?
3. Was it ethical for Kaushal to take Ramesh's help and later on gifts for his son?

Case Study No. 4: Pawan Sugar Mills

Pawan Sugar Mills was situated on the outskirts of Rampur town in U.P. The entire supplies of the mill were coming from Delhi, which is about three hundred kilometers from Rampur. The main supplier was Grants Ltd. and Mohan who worked for its closest rival Bentleys had joined the firm about three months back. He was operating from Delhi only. Mohan used to start from Delhi early morning but would inevitably reach Rampur by the noontime. He would send his visiting card to Chander Pawan's purchase boss. Every time he would be told that Chander is busy and he will have to come again to meet him. Mohan sensed that the Grants salespersons are well entrenched in the mill and it would be extremely difficult to dislodge them. He was a born optimist and believed that if he remains patient he can find the chink in the armor of his competitor.

He started planning his strategy. He made an appointment with Chander for Monday but when he reached Rampur at noon, he got the same answer. He found from the visitor's book that Grants people had met Chander only two days back. His belief started becoming more positive about some kind of relationship between Chander and Grants.

Mohan started doing his homework of finding out what clicked with Chander. He came to know that while he is giving business to Grants he is not entirely happy with them. He could not decipher the reason thereof. He became adamant in his quest for the truth about the relationship between Grants and the customer.

Next time when he reached Rampur, he sent his card to Chander with a note asking him to arrange for a room for his overnight stay in the mill guesthouse. He got the permission at once. From the guesthouse register he found that the Grants people usually stay there for two to three days at a time. He became friendly with the caretaker of the guesthouse, who organized a good lunch for Mohan. He started reading the customers file and drew a blank as far as getting business was concerned. None of his predecessors had got any business too. At six in the evening the caretaker told him that Chander had come to meet him. Business was different but surely Mohan cannot take Chander as a bad host.

Chander said, "Look here, the food at our guesthouse is no great shakes. I would request you to join me at my house for dinner. If you are interested in badminton then you can come with me now and we will play a few games, work up, an appetite before we sit down for dinner."

Mohan happily agreed to the proposal. They played badminton and in the first game Mohan was on the verge of winning when he lost concentration and the game. In the next two games Chander played well to defeat Mohan convincingly. (As can perhaps be imagined Mohan the better player purposely lost but without making it obvious, to put Chander in a happy frame of mind). At this point Mohan invited Chander to Delhi to be his guest in the near future, to which Chander gave his assent. After dinner, Chander suggested that Mohan meet him first thing in the morning at nine, before the rush of work starts.

Promptly at nine Mohan was at Chander's office discussing the terms of business, product delivery and special testing on products for the mill. He walked away with twenty percent of business on this visit much to the delight and amazement of his colleagues.

Questions—

1. Was the visit timing of fruitless calls the factor of the results?
2. Is it fair to play game badly to win in business?
3. Do you agree with the tactics used by Mohan? If yes give your reasons. Could he have done in any other way? Please discuss?
4. Can Mohan convert the twenty percent to hundred percent? If yes then how can he achieve it?

Case Study No. 5: Computers Ltd. (CL)

Pricing in An Explosive Market

In November 1976, HCL announced a dramatic reduction in prices of their Personal Computers (PCs) the prices came down from Rs.60,000 to Rs.30, 000 per PC. At that time CL wanted to introduce their PCs in the Indian market. Other players, like Wipro, DCM Data. PCL, were trying to match the HCL prices. The market had just about started picking up and the growth rate was six percent per annum likely to go up to twenty percent as per marketing gurus who had been watching the international market of PCs for a while.

Background—CL is a wholly owned subsidiary of Telecom and Electronics Ltd. (TEL) TEL is a major firm dealing in electrical and electronic goods since 1960. They have been dealing in motors, generators, process control instruments, tape recorders and domestic appliances.

TEL exports motors to Australia, Asia and Africa markets, besides having fifteen percent share in the domestic market. They have built brand equity in India and hope to make full use of it in the area of computers as a spin off.

Competitive Environment

Threat of new entrants is quite real as the world players including IBM, Compaq are eyeing the Indian market as it gives the impression of almost a virgin market. With government of India's support the MNCs will have easy entry and with their brand name alone take over a big chunk of the market.

Bargaining power of buyers is increasing with new players and local assemblers offering their product with marginal cost only. Local assemblers have low overheads and compete on price and personalized service. Buyers are at an advantage as they get the best deals at low prices.

Bargaining power of suppliers is weak, as they want to sell in large volumes, which is possible only if they can cut down their prices of chips, motherboards connectors and other components.

Rivalry amongst existing players is increasing by the day as the business growth has yet to reach the expected levels and the players have already set up manufacturing facilities. The known brands get an advantage with large firms, but the smaller buyers and individual buyers look for the latest product at downsized prices, which the assemblers are able to provide. They also resort to bundling the PC with software of the customers' choice, mostly pirated versions and offer site maintenance for the product.

Price behaviour—as the average price of a branded product was Rs.30,000/, local, brands and assemblers were selling the product about 15–20% cheaper. With the local brand the customer was usually in danger of loss of technical support, as many player would close shop after they have made a profit and start again, perhaps at a new location with a new name to avoid problems with the pirated software. The assemblers could further reduce the price as they were getting components from overseas through dubious means.

CL wants to market their branded product at Rs.26,000 and keep dealer margin at Rs.3000. They are able to get a gross margin of Rs.4000. However should the necessity arise they can sell it even at Rs.23,000.

CL believes that's since HCL has just reduced the prices drastically no further price cut would be possible by branded products.

CL has to decide on its pricing strategy. It can go for penetrating prices at Rs.18,000 also if they want to capture a large share of the market, or keep to skimming price at Rs. 26,000. They can follow the medium pricing at Rs.22,000. Depending on the market growth the **profit** situation for CL will be as follows:

Table 15.1. CL Prices

Pricing/Market growth	*Low*	*Medium*	*High*
Penetrating /low	–150,000	100,000	550,000
Medium	100,000	300,000	250,000
Skimming/high	50,000	200,000	400,000

The firm has to decide about the strategy taking the optimum scenario or most likely future demand seeing the environment factors of today. In case of skimming prices the firm can keep the option of heavy investment in brand building and other marketing inputs and still get a good market share.

Tasks for the students—to use the decision tree, or Delphi technique to find out the best possible price for the CL Computers. Will bundling with software help? Discuss the pros and cons of each type of pricing formulae. Also, looking at the Indian market work out a promotional strategy for CL.

Case Study No. 6: Price Waterhouse-PW

Traditionally an accountancy firm, it was started by Samuel Price and Edwin Waterhouse in 1849 in London UK. 1930, the partners fanned out across the world, establishing semi autonomous practice for accountancy investigations, liquidation and other financial services.

It was only from 1980 PW started Management consultancy in a big way as several firms started accepting consultancy as a useful profession. PW has added technical research to their portfolio, an advance technology center in Artificial Intelligence in the US with a $410 million Development Center in London for IT Skills.

PW's USP comes from combining the roles of a consultant and an implementer.

PW's Vision reads as follows:

The firm is committed to turning strategic insight into tactical action (Strategic Implementation), for our clients. In doing so we provide them with high quality, leading edge, industry focused services and solutions, wherever they do business.

Their mission statement reads as follows—to be the global consultants to TOP–LAYER firms by solving their complex business problems.

The international growth phase of PW began the two world wars, where partnerships were set up in different parts of the world. These were mainly offices to serve audit clients in the first instance. Tax consultancy services were added in the large offices. Today. PW has 434 offices in 119 countries.

The highly regarded Emerson Research firm rates PW as simply one of the best in its 1998 clients satisfaction survey of high technology firms PW ranked first, in eleven of thirteen client satisfaction categories among 293 audit clients of the big six firms. PW earned five star status in four categories and it bagged more number one rankings than any other big six firms.

Category	*PW's Ranking*
Overall client satisfaction	1*
Responsiveness of the partners	1* five star
Understanding clients needs / expectations	1
Audit and accounting services	1 five star

Contd.....

Category	*PW's Ranking*
Information technology services	1*
Corporate finance	1*five star
Tax services	1*
Contribution to success of the client's business	1*
Staff responsiveness	1*five star
Proactive contribution	1* five star
Consultancy services	1

Clients have singled out PW among the big six in serving high technology firms as can be seen from below-

"They have a high degree of responsiveness and professionalism"

"Overall they are exceptional"

"I think they do mergers and acquisitions very well. It is a specialty of PW".

Auditing is a competitive area and therefore the firm has diversified its management consultancy to cover such industries as entertainment, media and high tech. To keep abreast of industry trends PW has formed a new consulting group on of electronics and on-line financial services.

PW is restructuring itself along product lines, as opposed to territorial divisions to serve the full range of its multinational clients. The purpose of the renewal efforts is helping firms in implementing strategies to improve business performance and Shareholder values. Affecting organizational and strategic change using IT for competitive advantage and meeting audit and tax requirements with greater speeds with improved software packages.

Price Waterhouse, the Indian profile

PW was established in India in 1880 as a part of the worldwide network of Price Waterhouse. PW has access to worldwide resources in terms of experience and expertise. If has the largest professional resource based in India enabling it to have a greater subject and sector specialization with 41 partners, around 1500 professional staff and supported by a panel external technical or professional experts.

Various disciplines include the following:

- Audit and business advisory services ABS
- Tax
- Management consultancy services MCS
- Corporate finance recovery and disputes CFRD

Clientele includes large and prestigious organizations in the following areas:

- MNCs
- Indian private sector
- Public sector or government
- Bilateral donor agencies/foreign embassies
- Multilateral funding/development agencies.

PW is registered with WORLD bank, ADB, UNDP, UNESCO, IDBI, and FIEO. Besides, it has regular working and consultative relationship with various Indian ministries.

PW has over the years acquired specialization in the following industrial sectors:

- Agro based industry, including food processing
- Banking, finance and insurance services
- Engineering and electronics
- Finance and insurance
- Hotel and leisure
- Informatics including software
- International funding/development agencies
- Mining
- Manufacturing and allied industries
- Retail trade-consumer goods
- Transportation
- Telecom
- Petroleum utilities including power and water

PW has other divisions operating in India as follows:

- Price Waterhouse Associates
- Price Waterhouse & Co
- Choksey & Co
- IPAN

Price Waterhouse India is a separate PROFIT CENTER for the parent firm; it is their SBU-Strategic Business Unit. Partners of Indian operations have stock options in the parent firm. The parent firm does regular internal audit in order to ensure that they conform to their strict guidelines.

In order to scan the competitive environment Porters Five Force Model is used as given below:

Bargaining power of the customers—it is moderate as the customers have choice to select from the consultants, but it is not high as most of them are providing certain specific and specialized services.

Bargaining power of the suppliers—they include the business schools and the Institute of Chartered Accountants of India. Their bargaining power is moderate as consultancy is a refined form of business dealings – an aspect highly appealing to intelligent experts. The managerial talent of business schools prefers to join the consultants.

Threat of new entrants—the threat of new firms entering the area is high as it is growing and profitable business.

Threat of substitute products would come from internal experts of the clients. The threat from them is low as the internal experts may not have the vat resources, which are with the consultants. Firms generally prefer to go the consultants.

Competition among rival firms is high. The major players include the following:

- Anderson Worldwide
- Vooz Allen
- PA Consulting Group
- PE Consultants
- Mackenzie
- Boston Consulting Group
- KPMG

Critical Success Factors for the consultancy firms like PW are as follows:

- Consultants form the backbone of the firm/two basic characteristics of consultants are high intelligence and expertise in different areas as needed. John Foden CEO of PA Consulting group identifies three characteristics of an ideal consultant, which are (a) ability to listen, (b) capacity for analyzing the situation and capacity to come up with creative knowledge base solutions.
- HR Planning a recruitment they employ meticulous care in recruiting management trainees from the best of the schools.
- Career development opportunities—the promotions are performance related
- Pay package
- Continuous training and skill up gradation
- Establishment of relationship with clients

- Uniqueness of ideas
- Development of new ideas
- Experience
- Latest management ideas
- Efficient management information systems

The dictum is that the firm is as good as its clients.

Task for the students—do a SWOT Analysis of the firm and recommend strategies for marketing to combat the competitive forces.

Case Study No. 7: B to B Giant—Hindustan Graphite Electrodes

The Indian graphite industry is a 700 crores industry, which has garnered around 10 percent of the world trade of the product. It is also an industry that has continued to grow even when the entire industry and business both worldwide and in India, has been shrinking for the last decade. The graphite electrode industry has its fortunes linked to that of secondary steel production through the electric arc furnace EAF, technology and other factors like the structure of domestic industry, electrode production technology and costs, exports, accessibility to raw materials and customers. India beats the developed countries of the world in terms of cost of production because of its lower fixed costs, labour and overheads.

The Indian graphite electrode industry is having only three major domestic players. HEG Ltd. is a leading graphite electrode maker and also operates the single largest graphite electrode plant in South Asia. Supporting a global perceptive the firm has decided not to restrict itself to the domestic market and it aims at achieving a respectable market share worldwide.

HEG's strength include possession of sophisticated electrode manufacturing technology, ISO 9002 certification, competent workforce and management. Reduced risks of business cycle because of horizontal diversifications deep financial resources and related backward diversifications.

HEG's weaknesses include dependence on imported raw materials, high levels of inventory, poor cash flow, stiff and bureaucratic organization structure and a weak RD.

Intense competition, exchange rate fluctuations, changing technology, high bargaining powers of customers and suppliers are some of the threats facing HEG.

Growing demand for graphite electrodes in fast developing countries HEGs global experiences and image, installed production base are some of the plus points.

The Indian Graphite Electrode (GE), industry is concentrated as there are three major players in India. Between them they share Rs.700 crore market, the Jhunjhunwalas and the Bangurs share the battleground.

The Jhunjhunwala's own the country's largest GE factory HEG. The Bangur group through its own firms Carbon Everflow Ltd. (CEL), and GIL are the biggest in the GE industry in India. The total installed capacity of the industry HEG, GIL AND CEL is 54,000 tons, with HEG having 40% share and the other two of Bangur group having the balance.

The biggest threat today is the imports, which are eating in to the market of the domestic players, as imported GEs are available at much lower cost. This has happened after the rationalization of duty structure, which went against the domestic industry.

Imports and exports of GE is given below:

Table 15.2. HEG Impex

Year	*Imports in tons*	*Exports in tons*
1993	475	11,148
1994	500	15,003
1995	3080	17,001
1996	5500	18,291
1997	4000	21,000

The dramatic increase in imports since 1994 was primarily because Chinese producers were dumping their products in India at low prices $1100 per ton, while the average price in the international market was $2600 per ton. In 1997, dumping duty was imposed on China and there was a drop in the total GE imported in the country in 1997.

At present the scenario can be described as being between the devil and the deep sea. At a time when domestic players were fighting to create a strong base, infiltration started. These foes are none other than the mighty international players, while Indians are fighting for survival. The present sentiment is down as players are crying hoarse about the international players are resorting to dumping practices and the industry is feeling ignored by the government. Duties on imported Electrodes have been reduced.

The fact that the user industry, the steel making is doing reasonably well, does not ensure good days for the GE industry. The size of GE is the main cause for its sufferings. For a government with an agenda the state of steel industry and the GE industry, the formers gets the concessions and not the GE industry.

HEG Ltd. is the leading GE maker as it also operates the single largest GE plant in South Asia. HEG Ltd. an ISO 9002,firm has its GE plant at Bhopal. HEG has facilities for GE production and specialties, set up in technical collaboration with Societe Des Electrodes ET Refractaries Savoie (SERS), A subsidiary of Pechiney of France. HEG is India's largest exporter with 55% of its produce being exported to more than 40 countries of the world.

HEGs vision statement is powerful as given below:

Vision—to have a global perspective

Mission—never restrict to the domestic market and aim at achieving respectable world market share.

Goals—investments to be made for new facilities for growth in market share. Product mix to be expanded with quality improvement

Objectives—the major thrust is on producing GE at low cost and focus on higher segment of the users ready to pay the price or better quality product.

HEGs market segments are as given below:

- High efficiency product segment of Essar Steels Tisco in India and Sigri of Germany and Ucar Carbon of the USA.
- The middle segment wants value for money product
- The lower end segment is the one competing with the Chinese players.

HEG has defined its marketing policy in the following words-

- Ensure full customer satisfaction with prompt service courteous behavior and motivate the employees for such efficient service.
- Locate customer complaints and nip them in the bud only.
- Build relationship with the customers.
- Work at the relationship all the time.
- Keep generating enthusiasm in the customers with special attention, gifts.
- Approach new customers and provide them with prompt courteous service.

HEG Is Focussed On Providing Value To The Customers And Not Just Satisfaction. Customers Are Retained Through Superior Service And Products. New Customers Come Through Heg's Efforts And The WORD OF MOUTH PUBLICITY PROVIDED BY ITS CUSTOMERS.

HEG has selected the following foreign markets where they have got a good market share:

- North America
- South America
- Europe
- South East Asia
- Middle East

The countries where HEG does business are 40, some of them are the following:

USA, Canada, Italy, France, Australia, Taiwan, Singapore, South Korea.

SWOT Analysis of HEG—

- Strengths—leading GE maker in India with 45% market share, exports 55% produce exported to 40 countries in the world. Has ISO 9002 certification, well up in finance and management areas.
- Weaknesses—dependence on imported raw materials, heavy inventory of finished goods due to recession, poor R&D.
- Opportunities—growing demand of the product in developing nations, it has global marketing experience.
- Threats—severe international competition, including the one from China. GEs demand is a derived demand and it depends on the demand of steel, which fluctuates with the country's GNP.

Michael Porter's Five Force Model Analysis

- Threat of new entrants is less as the industry requires huge capital; existing players have achieved Economies of Scale.
- Supplier's bargaining power—they have great bargaining power as they are well organized and a few in number.
- Customer's bargaining power is high as the product is undifferentiated, has large production base and imports are available at competitive prices.
- Threat of substitute products is not there, but the steel making technology is undergoing changes, which threatens to do away with GEs.
- Existing firms rivalry is intense as the product made is same, in large quantities by all the players.

Improvement Opportunities/Problems of the Industry

- Middle segment has Chinese products where HEG had a stronghold earlier.
- Changes in steel making technology.
- Challenges of possible price wars.
- Political instabilities in the world.
- Success or failure of quality program of HEG.

Marketing Solutions

1. To fight the price competition from China HEG should start building relationships with the customers, to enlighten them on the hidden extra expenses they have to undergo when they use inferior Chinese products.
2. HEG should plan down sizing its operations to become cost effective.
3. Eliminate non-value adding tasks.
4. Arrange order based production and inventories.
5. Organize cross-functional teams for greater coordination.
6. Along with international sales agents, HEG should start their own marketing operations in the countries they have a strong footing.

Task for the students—Define the goals, which HEG should set for itself and the methods it should use for achieving the same.

Case Study No. 8: International B-to-B Giant – Microsoft Inc. USA

Start any computer around the world and more than ninety percent you will find it running on Microsoft windows operating system. The firm is as controversial as it is successful and influential. It touches the lives of billions of people and it has changed the way people manage and work in offices, homes, factories and how they correspond with others.

It is a firm, which evokes intense feelings of love or hatred it is Microsoft! Its founder Bill Gates is already a cult figure, worshipped and idolized by millions of young and old in the world. From a middle class family he inherited his acumen from his mother and shrewdness from his father. In just twenty years he is the richest man on the planet.

Where Do They Go from Here?

Microsoft strives to produce innovative products to meet the evolving needs of the knowledgeable customers.

Mission: Microsoft started in 1975, with a **mission** to create software for the personal computer that empowers and enriches people at home and at their workplace, at schools and in the laboratories.

Vision: Its early **Vision** was to see a computer on every desk, every home and it is now coupled with a strong commitment to Internet technologies expanding the reach and power of PC users.

Values: Microsoft's values are enshrined in the following tenets:

- Customers—helping them achieve their goals by listening to them and quickly delivering new innovative products; building relationships based on trust, respect and understanding and seivice support.
- Innovation—moving with the speed of light for bringing new products in the market to remain competitive with reduced costs as well.
- Partners—helping them grow in their business.
- Integrity—acting with utmost integrity Microsoft's team is guided by what is right for their customers.
- People—the team must have an exciting challenging career with growth opportunity and well balanced home and work life.
- Entrepreneurial culture—the team must remain passionate about the work, contributing to evolution of technology to remain competitive.
- Diversity—the team is encouraged for diverse activities, with equal chance of promotion and increments for the members.

- Community—Microsoft feels responsible to the community in which they operate and wants to make a meaningful difference in its life.

Finance as on June 1999

Net revenue $ 19.75 billion

Net income $ 7.79 billion

Microsoft headcount and revenue growth is given below:

Table 15.3. Microsoft Growth

Year	*Head count*	*Revenue $B*	*%Growth*	*Income $M*	*%Growth*
1990	5635	1.18	47	279	63
1991	8226	1.85	56	463	66
1992	11,542	2.78	50	708	53
1993	14,430	3.79	36	953	35
1994	15,017	4.71	25	1150	20
1995	17,801	6.08	29	1450	27
1996	20,561	9.05	49	2200	51
1997	22,232	11.94	32	3450	57
1998	27,055	15.26	28	4490	30
1999	31,575	19.75	29	7790	79

The head count is in the vicinity of 40,000.

Microsoft has been living in the shadow of its illustrious founder. While Bill Gates has many friends his opponents believe he is shrewd and manipulative and wants to dominate the world. Microsoft needs to improve its image to come out of the predicament it faces today.

In 1995, the firm almost lost the battle of Internet to Netscape and Sun Microsystems and Microsoft was caught napping. Microsoft needs feedback from marketing to their R&D to get the latest customers needs. MICROSOFT MUST MAKE MORE FRIENDS THAN FOES. It should not consider that it is a **Know All** firm. It could consider splitting in to several small firms with independent decision making under one over all umbrella.

IBM is reeling under competitive pressure and does not know what hit them. Microsoft must not fall in the same trap. If they do not learn from history than history is likely to repeat itself.

Task for the students—discuss the strengths and weaknesses of Microsoft and recommend a marketing strategy which would help them in retaining their leadership position.

Case Study No. 9: Infosys Technologies Ltd.

ITL is a leading Indian firm in software services and packages for exports and the domestic market. Its clients include several fortune 500 companies. Indian software industry is fragmented with several players in the field. India's USP in the global market is that there is a large English speaking trained workforce, which is still relatively available at low cost.

IL has grown in strength with special products developments like, In 2000 for Y2K solutions, IntERPryz for ERP, and InEuro for Euro banking services. It is the first Indian firm to be listed on the US Stock Exchange NASDAQ after its successful issue of ADR in 1999.

Management of ITL is totally inspired by its CMD Mr. Narayan Murthy and it is characterized by the following qualities:

- Technically qualified professional management
- Having rich experience of large export orders
- Stakeholder friendly approach
- Positioning in high growth areas
- HR Policies for merit recognition
- Focus on core areas

India's Position

Till 2000, Indian industry had a boom time in software. Only the events of 11th September 2001 have brought the industry down at least temporarily. India's competitive advantage lies in the following areas:

- Cost effective software
- World class quality
- High reliability

Rapid delivery. India's position can be seen from the following matrix:

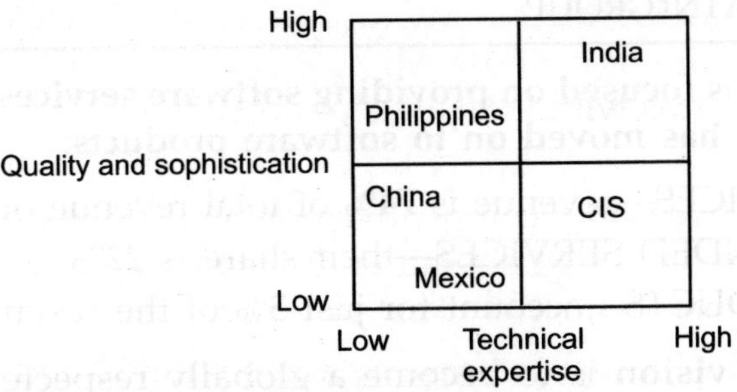

Fig. 15.1. India's Position

Software industry in India is given in the following table

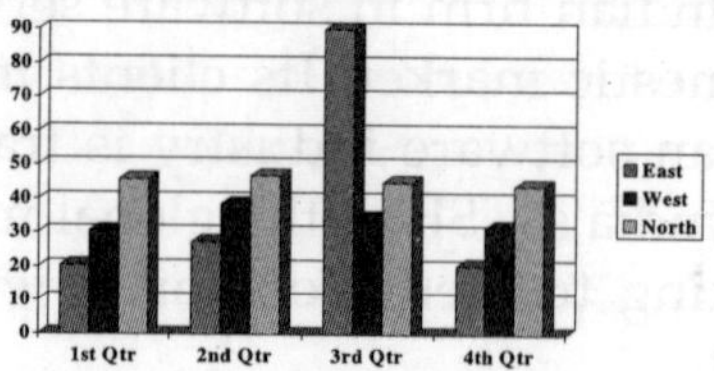

Fig. 15.2. Software Industries

Table 15.4. Exports

Year	1997	1998	1999	2000
Exports US M $	1755	2700	3900	5700
Domestic M Rs.	63,100	100,400	158,600	245,000

In 1999 the growth of the industry was 46% and it was expected to grow at 50%, but the USA catastrophe of 11 September 2001 derailed the momentum of growth.

Top ten firms of India had the following turnover in million rupees in 1998:

Table 15.5. India's Top 10

1	TCS	10,836
2	WIPRO	4816
3	HCL	3455
4	NIIT	3254
5	PENTAFOUR	2845
6	INFOSYS	2576
7	IBM GLOBAL	2428
8	TATA INFOTECH	2117
9	SATYAM	1784
10	PATNI GROUP	1375

Infosys has focused on providing software services with branded products and has moved on to software products:

- SERVICES—revenue is 74% of total revenue of Infosys
- BRANDED SERVICES—their share is 22%
- PRODUCTS—account for just 3% of the revenue

Infosys's vision is to become a globally respected firm, which provides best of the software solutions by the best in class people.

Its mission is to grow with protected margins by focusing on horizontal applications and vertical industries.

Infosys goals are to have development centers for software in different parts of the world to provide quality speedy solutions at affordable prices

Its objective is to restrict revenue generation of any division to less than 25%.

Infosys competitive position is given below:

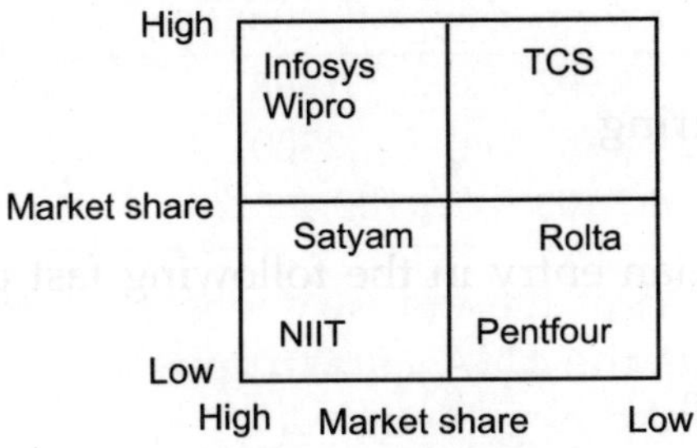

Fig. 15.3. BCG Matrix

Infosys is in the Star position of the BCG Matrix

Infosys track record is envious, with its shares surpassing the industry norms, including the ADR, which is also performing well in the market. Infosys could be planning on the following lines to keep its growth rate:

- Geographic expansion—Infosys gets the major share of business from the north American market as can be seen from the table given below:

Table 15.6. Business Expansion

Revenue Area	*1999 in lakh Rs.*	*%*	*1998 in lakh Rs.*	*%*
North America	41,739.11	82	21,224.46	81
Europe	4753.03	9	2317.20	9
Rest of the world	3533.27	7	1552.10	6
India	1248.43	2	942.81	4
Total	51,273.83	100	26,036.57	100

Europe and Japan are almost not there, which came in focus after 11th September 2001. Infosys would do well to open its markets in untapped areas so far.

- As a cash rich firm Infosys could be planning joint ventures in India and overseas to utilize its cash profits and zero debt status.
- Infosys could extend the services offered. Its present portfolio includes the following services.

  i. Apparels
  ii. Commodity trading
  iii. Customer management
  iv. e-business
  v. Financial services
  vi. Insurance
  vii. Logistics
  viii. Manufacturing
  ix. Retailing

  Infosys could plan entry in the following fast pace areas as well:

  a. Aviation
  b. Health care
  c. Tourism
  d. Transport
  e. Security industry
  f. Telecom
  g. Training in software development
  h. Retailing in the country

Tasks for the student—please do the SWOT Analysis of the firm and plan out the best marketing strategy for Infosys.

CASE STUDY NO. 10: EXHIBITIONS INDIA P. LTD.

Exhibitions India (EI)has an outstanding reputation for organizing international and national exhibitions and conferences. Under the EI umbrella it has the following other firms:

- Comnet Exhibitions P. Ltd
- Comnet Advertising P.Ltd.
- Comnet Travels P. Ltd.
- Comnet Publishing P. Ltd.

EI's genesis starts from the idea of providing a forum for Business-to-Business interaction. From small beginning of being an agency of international organizers now it has become one itself.

EI's present portfolio includes the following:

1. Convergence India—International exhibition and conference of broadcast, cable and satellite equipment.
2. Commsindia—is comprehensive event for the telecom sector.
3. Bank net—it is for banking sector.
4. Space'99 an exhibition on the Space technology.
5. Captech 2000 for the Capacitor industry.
6. Build India/Environment India/Water India.
7. Pride of India an exhibition held in Vietnam.

Vision: EIs vision is to be leader in B-to-B interaction with total transparency, honesty and ethical behavior.

Mission: Statement is crisp and to the point, "Committed To Excellence".

Goals: To increase trade between different areas through B-to-B interactions.

Objectives: To maintain high level of excellence for providing neutral platform for business, industry, government interactions through exhibitions and seminars.

EI manages its value chain efficiently, which involves the following activities:

- Government approvals and support of the ministries
- Support of industry associations
- Corporate world for participating in the events
- Bringing out brochures and pamphlets
- Setting up of stalls
- Opening day inaugural functions

Marketing at EI—as per the norms of service industry they have nothing tangible to offer, other than space in the exhibition. The marketing tasks includes communicating the benefits the exhibitor will obtain from taking part in the exhibition.

Among its clients are public sector, government bodies and the private firms. Private firms take much less time in deciding to participate. The governmental bodies take much longer to decide necessitating the need of differential time approach by the EI.

EI uses telemarketing as one of the initial tools to familiarize the clients with the event, which is going to take place. They have generated a database of over 5000 firms as prospective clients for their events. The phone calls gives an idea of interest generated in the clients mind regarding the event. Personal meetings to solicit participation follow the calls. These visits are carried forward by mails, phone calls, e-mails with the details of the event and participation entry forms with rate card.

EI believes that Direct Mail is a good beginning of sales campaign. This is carried out through teaser mail, brochures, pamphlets, and reports of previous exhibitions with their results.

EI believes that after the event management of the clients is as important as managing the client for getting his consent for participation in the event. This is one through post exhibition reports, which gives the order bookings, effective business dialogues and some photographs of the dignitaries from the business world, the government and the media coverage of the event.

EI has competition; major one's being the following:

- CII—Confederation of Indian Industries.
- ITPO—Indian Trade Promotion Organization.

EI is comparatively small and enjoys the benefits of a flat structured firm with fast decision making. It is also competing as a cost effective firm as it can offer competing rates for stalls in the exhibitions.

EIs shortcomings are the following:

- Services provide are common to other competitors with no differentiation.
- Low manpower affects the performance at times.
- No venue of their own for exhibitions.
- Low brand equity, which is surely but slowly improving in the area, which matter to them.

In order to overcome the shortcomings EI could arrange the following:

- Buyer Seller meets both national and international.
- Organize general purpose fairs for both, the public and business.
- Try to get better rates from the exhibition ground owners.
- Arrange exhaustive market survey in different areas of current business interest.
- Communicate with major clients through focussed information, which would be of interest to them rather than sending the general brochure.
- Increase worldwide geographic coverage.

Task for the students—do a SWOT Analysis of the firm and give detailed recommendations for improving its marketing efforts.

Index

7s Model 286

A

Advertiser and the Agency Selection 424
Advertising 73
Advertising Agency 406
Advertising Agency & Its Working 420
Advertising Agency Selection Process 424
Advertising and Creativity 447
Advertising Budget 441
Advertising Defined 403
Advertising Mix Factors 405
Advertising Research 379, 427
Advertising Research and Dagmar 379, 427
Advertising Standards Council of India 60
Advertising—A Mass Communication System 352
Agency Operation 274
Analysing a Talk for its Movers 197
Analysing Product for Sale Movers 198
Ancillary Services 410
Appeal to Pride on Favourable Conditions 222
Approach 174
Art Direction—Elements of Design 452
Assets and Skills 305

B

Backward Vertical Integration 11
Balance Score Card 356
BCG Matrix 283, 488
Behaviour—Positivism and Interpretivism 123
Boston Consultancy Group 486
Branded and Generic Products 67
Brands 68, 312
B-to-B Advertising 295
B-to-B Marketing Advantage 291
B-to-B Payment Terms 296
B-to-B Pricing 295
Build, Operate and Transfer 8
Business Audit Check List 541
Business General Environment 55
Business Myopia 60
Buyer's Loyalty 319
Buyers Purchase Viewpoint 298
Buying Situations 120

C

Call Closing 233
Call Objectives 170
Call Plan Verification 177
Call Planner 174
Catalogue Sales 273
Competition 84
Competitive Action 135
Competitive Advantage 94, 282
Competitive Analysis 304, 464
Competitive Business Environment 57
Competitor's Strengths 131
Competitors Plan for Markets 136
Complaint Cell 92
Completely Creative Call 218
Consignment Agents 274
Continuous Market Information 133
Cooperation in Competitive Environment 506
Core Competencies 461
Core Process Based Organization 105
Core Processes 45
Corporate Vision 99
Cost Center or Profit Center 100
Cost Differential 130
Cost Leadership 69
Costs, Volumes and Experience Curve 476
Countering the Obstacles 191
Countries Classifications 268
Countries with Economies in Transition 269
Creative Strategy—Art and Copy 447
Credit and its Control 74
Credit as a Sales Tool 156
Crises Management 339
Critical Success Factors 148, 255
Cross Functional Structure 88, 106
Cross Parry 93, 134, 139, 515
Cultural Aspects of Global Business 526
Customer Orientation 291
Customer Promotion 318
Customer Reach 275
Customer Relationship Management 317
Customer Targets 142
Customer Value 241
Customer Vs Client 498
Customer, Competition and the Firm 490
Customer's Analysis 466
Customers' Assessment of Competitors 133
Customising Or Individualising the Benefits 182

D

Data Processing and Analysis 378
DAVP Publications 288
Decline Stage ofproduct Life Cycle 484
Defining Sales Obstacles 189
Demand Management Process 45
Demonstration 184
Designing Persuasive Communication 126
Detailed Call Planning 170
Dictionary Rule 468
Differentiated Competition 129
Differentiation 69, 129
Direct Demanding Office 6
Director General of Supply and Disposals 6
Distribution Channels 284
Distribution Patterns—Industrial Goods 272

E

Economic Business Environment 262
Economic Growth 271
Economic Outlook 121
Economies of Scale 19
Environment Factors 121
Environmental Threats and Opportunities 536
Essential Information 171
Ethics in Business 60
Ethno-centric Focus 519
Examples of Contact Mover in Action 215
Examples of Obstacles 230
External Stakeholders 93

F

Feature-benefit Worksheet 179
Feeling and Emotions 125
Financial Analysis 541
Firms and Society 337
Fixed Cost 70
Flatter Organisations Structures 109
Follower Competitor 132
force Majeure 252
forward Vertical Integration 11
Fragmented Market 129
Franchise Outlets 273
Franchising 516
Free Trade Zones 514
Fully Owned foreign Subsidiary 516

G

Gaining and Retaining Customers 97
Ge Model 489
General Business Environment Factors 510
Geo-centric Focus 519
Getting the Sales Talks Started 216
Global 77
Global Factors 57
Goal 100
Gross Domestic Product 268
Gross National Product 268
Growth Stage Strategy 478
Guarantees 156
Guaranty 252
Guidelines for Making A Questionnaire 386

H

Hand Crafted 67
Handling Objections 185
Handling Objections Details 187
Handling of Complaints 147

I

Imf 307
Implementation of the Strategy 502
Improving Market Share 133
Income and Balance Sheet 541
Indirect Financial Support 90
Industrial Products Advertising 419
Industrial Segmentation 306, 472
Industry Situation 136
Inflation 271
Information On Competition 506
Information Outsourcing 258
Innovation Decisions 111
Internal Stakeholders 93
International Advertising 455
International Environment for Business 261
International Market Research 528

International Markets of the Twenty-first Century 275
International Monetary Fund 529
International Products 522
Interpretivism 123
Investment Cycle 488
Iso 9000 Series 280
Iso 9000 Standards 69

J

Joint Ventures 516
Just in Time 9
Just in Time 90
Just in Time Orders 7

K

Knowledge Is Business 313

L

Late Growth Stage 481
Legal 77
Letter of Credit 317, 529
Licensing 515
Life Cycle Audit 485
Life Insurance Corporation of India 19
Locating New Customers 166
Loyalty Indicators 93

M

Mackenzie's 7s Model 285
Macro-economic Factors 7
Macroeconomics 77
Macroeconomics Factors 270
Mail Order 273
Market Analysis 278
Market Analysis 470, 501
Market Based Marketing Organization 105
Market Economy of the World 264
Market Environment 52
Market Environment 84
Market Focus 130
Market Follower 479
Market Globalization 525
Market Globalization 53
Market Information—As Competitive Advantage 282
Market Leader 131
Market Leader 479
Market Recession 53
Market Segment 101
Market Segmentation 81
Market Share 69
Market Share Strategy 477
Market Situation Analysis 101
Marketing 21st Century Style 497
Marketing Mix 70
Marketing Mix Factors 70
Marketing Mix Factors 85
Marketing Myopia 141
Marketing Organization 74
Marketing Organization Structure 102
Marketing Strategy 145
Markets of the Twenty-first Century 499
Markets—the Customers 90
Maslow's Hierarchy of Needs 179
Maslows Hierarchy of Needs 44
Mass Production Techniques 67
Maturity Stage of Product Life Cycle 482
Mean Time Between Failures 316
Mean Time Between Purchase 77
Media Planning 339, 433

Media Planning and Product Positioning 433
Media Research 428
Media Status 340
Meeting the Obstacles 231
Methodology 382
Michael Porter 394
Michael Porter's Five force Model 278
Michael Porter's Five force Model 98, 498, 511
Misuse of Compliments 213
Mixed Economies 265
Modes of Payment 317
Monopoly: 129
Motivating Factors 422
Motivating the Salesmen 154
Multi National Companies 36
Multi-attribute Decision Making Process 467
Multiple Analysis of A Sitution 202
Mystery Competitor 132

N

Networking Teams 108
New Product Development 113

Objectives 100
Objectives of Advertising 412
Observation Method 364
Obstacle Descriptors 228
Oligopoly: 129
Opportunity to See 17
Order Fulfillment Process 45
Organizational Behavior 539
Organizational Culture 88
Organizational Policy Changes 122
Original Equipment Manufacturers 298
Over Selling 292

P

Partial Convertibility of Rupee 509
Partly Created Sales 218
Patents and Patent Laws 67, 312
Payment Terms 250
Per Capita Income 268
Personal Prestige Can Be Built By Action 212
Personal Selling 405
Personal Selling and Salesmanship 73
Personal Traits and Characteristics 314
Philip Kotler 374
Planning for Success 93
Planning Presentations for Specific Calls 185
Planning Sales Calls 163
Planning the Strategy 502
Plans and Policies 143
Point of Purchase 20, 26, 342
Polycentric Focus 519
Portfolio Management Analysis 485
Positivism 123
Post Call Analysis 237
Power Brokers 52
PR and the Government 338
PR Consultants 410
PR too Depends On Endorcements 336
Presentation Ready 175
Press Conferences 338
Press Releases 338
Price Objection 189
Price-quality Strategy 146

Problems in the Use of the Prestige Mover 220
Product Development Process 45
Product Innovation 527
Product Life Cycle 416, 474
Product Or Brand Managers 103
Product Positioning 102, 441, 473
Product Related Analysis 463
Product Supply Chain 39
Profit and Profiteering 86
Profit Centres 142
Profit Impact of Market Strategy 139
Progress Signals and the Progress Test Questions 226
Prospect Identification 167
Prospecting 167
Prospects Basic Needs and Desires 204
Public Relations 330
Public Sector Undertakings 262
Puffery 17
Purchase Committee 4, 299
Purchase Decision 127
Purchase Decisions Plan 127
Purchase Order the Final Destination 247
Purchasing Power 269

Q

Qualifying the Customer 168
Qualitative Research 359
Quality Standards 69, 313

R

Region-centric Focus 519
Relationship Marketing 83, 498
Reporting and Control System 239
Response to Market 130
Responsibilities and Objectives of the Prospects Job 204
Retail Sales and Merchandizing 73
Retail Store Chains 13
Rolling Plan 143
Rural Marketing 76
Rural Products 77

S

Sales Contract 42
Sales Cost Control 239
Sales Expense Budget 238
Sales Presentation 178
Sales Promotion 73, 318
Sales Targets 158
Sales Territory Allocation 157
Salesperson—the Strategist 243
Sample Selection 372
Sample Size 372
Satisfaction Value 43
Scenario Planning 506
Segmentation and Positioning 471
Selling After Sales 96
Selling Strategy 146
Service 130
Strategic Audit 538
Strategic Competitive Advantage 461
Strategic Group 506
Strategic Marketing Planning Process 466
Strategic Mission 100
Strategies and Tactics 173
Structural Support to the Customers 90
Summary Check List 541
Supply Chain Management 9, 89
Sustainable Competitive Advantage 29, 143, 482
System for Buying 120

T

Targeting Markets 81
Team Controls 540
Technology 77
Technology and Innovation—Competitive Advantage 110
Technology Factors 57
Technology Plans 113
The 4 Column Situation and Correction Analysis 199
The Advertising Challenge 455
The Appeal To Pride Mover 213
The Bridge of Understanding 207
The Complete Marketing Plan 140
The Contact Mover 215
The Design Theory 449
The Explanation Mover 225
The Good Turn Mover 214
The Investing Public 338
The Marketing Plan 504
The Media 407
The Personal Prestige Mover 212
The Pr Base 332
The Proposition Mover 224
The Question Mover 210
The Sales Policy 152
The Spar 230
The Twenty-first Century Challenge 193
The Virtual Marts 280, 504
Top of the Mind Recall 13, 14
Top of theMind Recall 71
Total Customer Management 243
Total Quality Management 97, 242
Trade Promotion 319
Training of Sales Persons 74
Training of Salesmen 153
Turnkey Solutions 6
Types of Calls and Objectives of the Calls 217

U

Umbrella Buying 6
Understanding People and Dealing with Them Effectively 194

Value for Money Product 164
Variable Cost 70
Vertical Integration 130
Virtual Organizations 108

Web Marketing 274
What is Our Business? 60, 309
Women Managers 53
Word of Mouth Publicity 92
World Bank 307